In-line/On-line: Fundamentals of the

Internet

and the World Wide Web

Second Edition

Raymond Greenlaw
Armstrong Atlantic State University

Ellen Hepp
The University of New Hampshire

Mc
Graw
Hill

Boston   Burr Ridge, IL   Dubuque, IA   Madison, WI   New York   San Francisco   St. Louis
Bangkok   Bogotá   Caracas   Kuala Lumpur   Lisbon   London   Madrid   Mexico City
Milan   Montreal   New Delhi   Santiago   Seoul   Singapore   Sydney   Taipei   Toronto

McGraw-Hill Higher Education

A Division of The **McGraw-Hill** *Companies*

IN-LINE/ON-LINE: FUNDAMENTALS OF THE INTERNET AND THE WORLD WIDE WEB
SECOND EDITION

Published by McGraw-Hill, a business unit of The McGraw-Hill Companies, Inc., 1221 Avenue of
the Americas, New York, NY 10020. Copyright © 2002, 1999 by The McGraw-Hill Companies, Inc.
All rights reserved. No part of this publication may be reproduced or distributed in any form or by
any means, or stored in a database or retrieval system, without the prior written consent of The
McGraw-Hill Companies, Inc., including, but not limited to, in any network or other electronic
storage or transmission, or broadcast for distance learning.

Some ancillaries, including electronic and print components, may not be available to customers
outside the United States.

This book is printed on acid-free paper.

1 2 3 4 5 6 7 8 9 0 DOC/DOC 0 9 8 7 6 5 4 3 2 1

ISBN 0-07-236755-5
ISBN 0-07-112200-1 (ISE)

General manager: *Thomas E. Casson*
Publisher: *Elizabeth A. Jones*
Developmental editor: *Melinda Dougharty*
Executive marketing manager: *John Wannemacher*
Senior project manager: *Marilyn Rothenberger*
Production supervisor: *Sherry L. Kane*
Coordinator of freelance design: *Michelle M. Meerdink*
Freelance cover/interior designer: *Rokusek Design*
Cover image: *PhotoDisc and Rokusek Design*
Senior supplement producer: *David A. Welsh*
Media technology senior producer: *Phillip Meek*
Compositor: *Techsetters, Inc.*
Typeface: *11/14 Times Roman*
Printer: *R. R. Donnelley & Sons Company/Crawfordsville, IN*

The credits section for this book begins on page 679 and is considered an extension of the copyright
page.

Library of Congress Cataloging-in-Publication Data

Greenlaw, Raymond.
     In-line/On-line: fundamentals of the Internet and the World Wide Web/Raymond Greenlaw,
Ellen Hepp.—2nd ed.
        p.   cm.
     Includes index.
     ISBN 0-07-236755-5
     1. Internet. 2. World Wide Web. I. Hepp, Ellen. II. Title.

TK5105.875.I57 G743   2002
004.67′8—dc21   2001018727
                                                                                         CIP

INTERNATIONAL EDITION ISBN 0-07-112200-1
Copyright © 2002. Exclusive rights by The McGraw-Hill Companies, Inc., for manufacture and
export. This book cannot be re-exported from the country to which it is sold by McGraw-Hill. The
International Edition is not available in North America.

www.mhhe.com

To Laurel and Celest.

To Mark, Andrew, Elisa, and Crissy.

Contents in Brief

Preface   xvii

1   Fundamentals of Electronic Mail   1
2   Jump Start: Browsing and Publishing   43
3   The Internet   97
4   The World Wide Web   141
5   Searching the World Wide Web   187
6   Telnet and FTP   233
7   Basic HTML   265
8   Web Graphics   323
9   Advanced HTML   367
10   Newsgroups, Mailing Lists, Chat Rooms, and MUDs   431
11   Electronic Publishing   469
12   Web Programming Material   485
13   Multimedia   529
14   Privacy and Security Topics   547

A   Internet Service Providers   567
B   Text Editing   573
C   Pine Mail Program   579
D   Basic UNIX   591
E   HTML Tags   601
F   Acronyms   609
G   My URLs   615

Glossary   631
Bibliography   653
Credits   679
Index   683

Contents

Preface   xvii

1 Fundamentals of Electronic Mail   1

1.1   Introduction   2
1.2   Email: Advantages and Disadvantages   3
   1.2.1   Advantages   4
   1.2.2   Disadvantages   5
1.3   Userids, Passwords, and Email Addresses   6
   1.3.1   Userids   7
   1.3.2   Passwords   8
   1.3.3   Email Addresses   8
   1.3.4   Domain Names   10
   1.3.5   Email Address Determinations   12
   1.3.6   Local and Systemwide Aliases   13
1.4   Message Components   16
1.5   Message Composition   19
   1.5.1   Structure   19
   1.5.2   Netiquette   22
   1.5.3   Composition   23
1.6   Mailer Features   25
   1.6.1   Compose, File, and Reply   26
   1.6.2   Bracketed Text and Include   27
   1.6.3   Forwarding   29
1.7   Email Inner Workings   30
   1.7.1   Mailer, Mail Server, and Mailbox   30
   1.7.2   Store and Forward Features   31
   1.7.3   Central Mail Spool and IMAP   33
   1.7.4   Bounce Feature   35
1.8   Email Management   36
   1.8.1   Action Options   37
   1.8.2   Vacation Programs   39
   1.8.3   Email and Businesses   39
1.9   MIME Types   40

2 Jump Start: Browsing and Publishing   43

2.1   Introduction   44
2.2   Browser Bare Bones   44
   2.2.1   Browser Window Terminology   45

	2.2.2	Menu Bar	46
	2.2.3	Toolbar	48
	2.2.4	Hot Buttons	49
	2.2.5	Hyperlinks	50
2.3		Coast-to-Coast Surfing	51
	2.3.1	Web Terminology	52
	2.3.2	Uniform Resource Locator (URL)	53
2.4		HyperText Markup Language: Introduction	56
	2.4.1	HTML Tag Syntax	57
	2.4.2	HTML Document Creation	58
2.5		Web Page Installation	61
	2.5.1	Basic Principles	62
	2.5.2	A Specific Example	63
2.6		Web Page Setup	66
	2.6.1	Head Tag	66
	2.6.2	HTML and Colors	72
	2.6.3	Body Tag	75
	2.6.4	HTML Font Colors	79
	2.6.5	Font Size	79
	2.6.6	Font Face	80
	2.6.7	HTML Comments	80
2.7		HTML Formatting and Hyperlink Creation	84
	2.7.1	Paragraph Tag	85
	2.7.2	Heading Tags	86
	2.7.3	Anchor Tag	87
	2.7.4	Image Tag	93

3	**The Internet**		**97**
3.1		Introduction	98
3.2		The Internet Defined	98
	3.2.1	The Information Superhighway	99
	3.2.2	Interesting Internet Facts	100
3.3		Internet History	101
	3.3.1	1960s Telecommunications	101
	3.3.2	1970s Telecommunications	102
	3.3.3	1980s Telecommunications	103
	3.3.4	1990s Telecommunications	104
	3.3.5	Internet Growth	106
3.4		The Way the Internet Works	108
	3.4.1	Network Benefits	108
	3.4.2	Interconnected Networks and Communication	109
	3.4.3	Physical Components	111
	3.4.4	Network Connections	111
	3.4.5	Client-Server Model	113
	3.4.6	IP Addresses	114
	3.4.7	Internet Protocol Version 6 (IPv6)	116
	3.4.8	Web Page Retrieval	116

3.5   Internet Congestion   118
       3.5.1   World Wide Wait Problem   119
       3.5.2   Technical Solutions   119
       3.5.3   Issues and Predictions   120
3.6   Internet Culture   122
       3.6.1   Critical Evaluation of Information   122
       3.6.2   Freedom of Expression   123
       3.6.3   Communication Mechanisms   125
       3.6.4   Advertising   127
       3.6.5   Societal Impact   127
3.7   Business Culture and the Internet   128
       3.7.1   On-line Businesses   129
       3.7.2   Three Sample Companies   131
       3.7.3   On-line Business Hurdles   132
       3.7.4   Cookies   133
       3.7.5   Business and Safety/Security on the Web   134
       3.7.6   Legal Environment   134
       3.7.7   U.S. Government's Commitment to Electronic
                Commerce   135
3.8   Collaborative Computing and the Internet   136
       3.8.1   Collaborative Computing Defined   136
       3.8.2   Applications   137
       3.8.3   Impact   139
       3.8.4   Future Prospects   139

4   The World Wide Web   141

4.1   Introduction   142
4.2   The Web Defined   142
4.3   Miscellaneous Web Browser Details   144
       4.3.1   Personal Preferences   144
       4.3.2   Bookmarks   145
       4.3.3   Plug-ins and Helper Applications   148
       4.3.4   Web Browsers Comparison: Netscape
                and Microsoft   150
4.4   Web Writing Styles   152
       4.4.1   The Biography   153
       4.4.2   The Business Exposition   155
       4.4.3   The Guide   157
       4.4.4   The Tutorial   158
       4.4.5   Writing Genres Summary   160
4.5   Web Presentation Outline, Design, and Management   161
       4.5.1   Goal Setting   163
       4.5.2   Outlining   164
       4.5.3   Navigating   168
       4.5.4   Designing and Coding   173
       4.5.5   Revising   174

4.6   Registering Web Pages   176
4.7   Lynx: Text-Based Web Browser   178
       4.7.1   Starting Lynx   180
       4.7.2   Basic Navigation   181
       4.7.3   Features   181
       4.7.4   Bookmarks   182
       4.7.5   Printing   182
       4.7.6   Images   182
       4.7.7   Lynx Commands Summary   184

5   Searching the World Wide Web   187

5.1   Introduction   188
       5.1.1   Useful Resources About Search Tools   189
5.2   Directories, Search Engines,
       and Metasearch Engines   190
       5.2.1   Directories   191
       5.2.2   Popular General Directories   199
       5.2.3   Some Subject Guides   200
       5.2.4   Search Engines   200
       5.2.5   Popular Search Engines   202
       5.2.6   Specialty Search Engines   202
       5.2.7   Popular Specialty Search Engines   204
       5.2.8   Metasearch Engines   204
               Ellen and Ray's Choices   206
       5.2.9   Popular Metasearch Engines   206
       5.2.10 White Pages   206
       5.2.11 Popular White Pages   207
5.3   Search Fundamentals   208
       5.3.1   Search Terminology   212
       5.3.2   Pattern Matching Queries   212
       5.3.3   Boolean Queries   214
       5.3.4   Search Domain   216
       5.3.5   Search Subjects   216
5.4   Search Strategies   219
       5.4.1   Too Few Hits: Search Generalization   220
       5.4.2   Too Many Hits: Search Specialization   220
       5.4.3   Sample Searches   221
5.5   How Does a Search Engine Work?   224
       5.5.1   Search Engine Components   224
       5.5.2   User Interface   225
       5.5.3   Searcher   225
       5.5.4   Evaluator   225
       5.5.5   Gatherer   227
       5.5.6   Indexer   230
       5.5.7   Summary   231

6   Telnet and FTP   233

6.1   Introduction   234
6.2   Telnet and Remote Login   234
        6.2.1   Telnet   234
        6.2.2   Remote Login   241
6.3   File Transfer   243
        6.3.1   Graphical File Transfer Clients   245
        6.3.2   Text-Based File Transfer Clients   252
        6.3.3   File Compression   258
        6.3.4   Anonymous File Transfer   258
        6.3.5   Archie   260
6.4   Computer Viruses   261
        6.4.1   Definitions   262
        6.4.2   Virus Avoidance and Precautions   262

7   Basic HTML   265

7.1   Introduction   266
7.2   Semantic- Versus Syntactic-Based Style Types   266
        7.2.1   Semantic-Based Style Types   266
        7.2.2   Syntactic-Based Style Types   273
        7.2.3   Style Type Usage   276
7.3   Headers and Footers   278
        7.3.1   Headers   278
        7.3.2   Horizontal Rule Tag   279
        7.3.3   Footers   281
7.4   Lists   284
        7.4.1   Ordered Lists   284
        7.4.2   Unordered Lists   287
        7.4.3   Definition Lists   288
        7.4.4   Nested Lists   291
7.5   Tables   296
        7.5.1   Table Usage   296
        7.5.2   HTML Table Tags   298
        7.5.3   Frequently Asked Questions   311
7.6   Debugging   317

8   Web Graphics   323

8.1   Introduction   324
8.2   Popular Image Formats   324
        8.2.1   Image Compression   325
        8.2.2   Image Acquisition and Display   325
        8.2.3   Graphics Interchange Format (GIF)   328

	8.2.4	Joint Photographic Experts Group (JPG)	330
	8.2.5	Portable Network Graphics (PNG)	331
8.3	**GIF Features**		**333**
	8.3.1	Animated GIFs	333
	8.3.2	Interlaced GIFs	334
	8.3.3	Transparent Images	336
8.4	**Image Tag Revisited**		**337**
	8.4.1	Image and Text Alignment	337
	8.4.2	Additional `ALIGN` Attribute Values	340
	8.4.3	Summary: `ALIGN` Attribute Values	340
	8.4.4	Horizontal Image Alignment	341
	8.4.5	Wrapped Text	341
	8.4.6	Text Wrap Prevention	343
	8.4.7	Spacing Control	343
	8.4.8	Centered Images	344
	8.4.9	Image Borders	345
	8.4.10	Low Source (`LOWSRC`) Images	346
8.5	**Image Maps**		**347**
	8.5.1	Server-Side Image Maps	347
	8.5.2	Client-Side Image Maps	349
	8.5.3	Summary: Image Maps	354
8.6	**Scanners**		**355**
	8.6.1	Scanner Types	356
	8.6.2	Scanner Selection	357
8.7	**Miscellaneous Graphics Topics**		**359**
	8.7.1	Thumbnail Sketches	359
	8.7.2	Image Height and Width	360
	8.7.3	Image Load Time	363

9   Advanced HTML   367

9.1	**Introduction**		**368**
9.2	**Frames**		**368**
	9.2.1	Frame Usage	369
	9.2.2	Frame Tags	370
	9.2.3	Frequently Asked Questions	373
	9.2.4	Additional Frame Tag Attributes	376
	9.2.5	Targeted Hyperlinks	376
	9.2.6	Nested Frames	379
	9.2.7	Frameset Design Algorithm	380
	9.2.8	Frames Reality Check	384
9.3	**HTML Forms**		**386**
	9.3.1	Form Tags	388
	9.3.2	Form Methods	389
	9.3.3	Mailto URLs	391
	9.3.4	Form Input Tags	391
	9.3.5	Frequently Asked Questions	399

9.4	CGI Scripts	401
	9.4.1 Scripts and Forms	402
	9.4.2 Security	402
9.5	Dynamic Documents	403
	9.5.1 Client Pull	403
	9.5.2 Server Push	405
	9.5.3 New-Address Notification	405
9.6	HTML Tools	407
	9.6.1 Editors	407
	9.6.2 Syntax Checkers	412
	9.6.3 Converters	415
9.7	Next-Generation HTML	417
9.8	Cascading Style Sheets	418
	9.8.1 Introduction	418
	9.8.2 In-line Styles	419
	9.8.3 Internal Styles	421
	9.8.4 External Styles	426
	9.8.5 Advantages and Disadvantages of CSS	429

10 Newsgroups, Mailing Lists, Chat Rooms, and MUDs   431

10.1	Introduction	432
10.2	Newsgroups and Mailing Lists History	432
10.3	Newsgroup Fundamentals	434
	10.3.1 Newsgroup Terminology	435
	10.3.2 Newsreaders	438
	10.3.3 Newsgroups Model	441
	10.3.4 Newsgroup Hierarchies	444
	10.3.5 Controversy	447
	Ellen and Ray's Choices	448
10.4	Mailing List Fundamentals	448
	10.4.1 Mailing List Terminology	449
	10.4.2 Mailing List Subscriptions and Posts	450
	10.4.3 Helpful Hints	454
	10.4.4 Mailing Lists and Web Pages	455
	10.4.5 Mailing Lists Versus Newsgroups	455
	Ellen and Ray's Choices	457
10.5	Newsgroups and Mailing Lists Availability	458
10.6	Chat Rooms	459
	10.6.1 Chat Room Entrance	459
	10.6.2 Chat Room Culture	461
	10.6.3 Chat Rooms and Education	462
10.7	MUDs	462
	10.7.1 MUD Connections	463
	10.7.2 MUDding	464

	10.7.3	MUD Etiquette	466
	10.7.4	Additional MUD Uses	466
	10.7.5	MUD Creation	467

11 Electronic Publishing — 469

11.1	Introduction	470
11.2	Electronic Publishing Advantages and Disadvantages	470
	11.2.1 Advantages	470
	11.2.2 Disadvantages	472
11.3	Copyright Issues	473
	11.3.1 Definition	473
	11.3.2 Credit Issues	475
11.4	Project Gutenberg and On-line Books	477
	11.4.1 Project Gutenberg	477
	11.4.2 Other On-line Books	478
11.5	Electronic Journals, Magazines, and Newspapers	479
	11.5.1 E-zines	479
	11.5.2 Journals	480
	Ellen and Ray's Choices	481
	11.5.3 Magazines and Newspapers	481
11.6	Miscellaneous Publishing Issues	482
	11.6.1 Plagiarism	482
	11.6.2 Electronic Publishing Do's and Don'ts	483

12 Web Programming Material — 485

12.1	Introduction	486
12.2	The JavaScript Programming Language	486
	12.2.1 JavaScript and HTML	487
	12.2.2 JavaScript Basics	489
	12.2.3 Objects, Properties, and Methods	491
	12.2.4 Event and Event Handlers	492
	12.2.5 Dialog Boxes	494
	12.2.6 More Event Handlers	500
	12.2.7 Sample JavaScript Temperature Conversion Code	503
12.3	Applets	506
	12.3.1 HTML Applet Tags	507
	12.3.2 Java-Enabled Browsers	508
	12.3.3 Sample Applets	509
12.4	The Java Programming Language	511
	12.4.1 Sample Java Source Code	512
	12.4.2 Java and Object-Oriented Programming	514
12.5	Guest Books	515
	12.5.1 Standard Input Fields of a Guest Book	517
	12.5.2 Guest Book Dynamics	518
	12.5.3 Mailto Guest Books	520

12.6 Web Page Counters 523
   12.6.1 HTML Code for a Counter 524
   12.6.2 Counter Usefulness 525
   12.6.3 Counter Display Decision 526
12.7 Server-Side Includes 526
   12.7.1 Common Inclusions 526
   12.7.2 Utilization 527

13 Multimedia 529

13.1 Introduction 530
13.2 Important Multimedia Issues 531
   13.2.1 Multimedia Displays 531
   13.2.2 Current Multimedia Concerns 532
13.3 Audio 534
   13.3.1 Audio Installation 535
   13.3.2 Audio and Web Pages 535
   13.3.3 Audio Repositories 536
13.4 Movies and Video 537
   13.4.1 Formats 538
   13.4.2 Video and Web Pages 538
13.5 Virtual Reality and 3D Modeling 540
   13.5.1 Virtual Reality Modeling Language (VRML) 541
   13.5.2 QuickTime Virtual Reality (QTVR) 543
   13.5.3 Virtual Reality Summary 543
13.6 Multimedia and HTML Documents 544
   13.6.1 Object Tag 544
   13.6.2 Embed Tag 545

14 Privacy and Security Topics 547

14.1 Introduction 548
14.2 Known Information 548
   14.2.1 Volunteered Information 549
   14.2.2 Information Collection 550
14.3 Software Complexity 551
   14.3.1 Contributing Factors 551
   14.3.2 Browsers, Networks, Operating Systems,
          and Servers 552
14.4 Encryption Schemes 553
   14.4.1 Basic Concepts 553
   14.4.2 Prime Numbers 555
   14.4.3 Private Key Cryptography 556
   14.4.4 Public Key Cryptography 557
   14.4.5 Hashing Algorithms 558

14.5	Secure Web Documents	560
14.6	Digital Signatures	561
	14.6.1 Digital Signature Example	562
	14.6.2 Pretty Good Privacy	564
14.7	Firewalls	565

A	Internet Service Providers	567
B	Text Editing	573
C	Pine Mail Program	579
D	Basic UNIX	591
E	HTML Tags	601
F	Acronyms	609
G	My URLs	615

Glossary	631
Bibliography	653
Credits	679
Index	683

Preface

The Internet has experienced spectacular growth over the last few years. A wide range of knowledge is needed by anyone interested in publishing on and participating in the *World Wide Web*. Many would argue that everyone should have a basic understanding of computing principles and the ability to track down information on the Web. In other words, everyone should be *Internet literate*. The amount of information available on-line is so vast that anyone interested in obtaining timely news, stock updates, a hard-to-find product, or basic research information cannot overlook the Web.

The level of sophistication for which we are aiming in this book is not the "point and click" level, nor the "hacker" end of the spectrum. We are interested in helping you learn enough that you are comfortable performing the following functions (among others):

- Sending and receiving electronic mail (email).

- Browsing the World Wide Web.

- Publishing on the Web.

- Coding in HyperText Markup Language (HTML).

- Using search engines.

- Processing on-line information in a critical fashion.

- Using such Internet applications as Telnet and FTP.

- Submitting forms on-line.

- Conducting research on-line.

- Developing a good grasp of computer terminology and acronyms.

- Reading and posting to newsgroups and mailing lists.

- Understanding chat rooms and MUDs.

- Downloading and installing plug-ins to view multimedia.

- Understanding basic security and copyright issues involving computers.

Who Should Read This Book

Anyone interested in learning about the Internet and the World Wide Web will benefit from this book. You will learn about concepts, rather than specific details about short-lived pieces of software. Our goal is to help you develop the confidence and skills to create a lifelong interest in computers, the Internet, and the Web. Computers already play a significant role in the lives of nearly everyone. So, even if the Web is not around in its current form in five years, a technology based on similar principles involving computers no doubt will be.

More specifically, this book is a good starting point:

1. For the student with an interest in becoming computer literate.

2. For the professional who needs to ramp up quickly before getting left behind in the technological world.

3. For all those seeking a career in a computer-related field.

4. For retired people who want to add another dimension to their[1] lives.

Organization of the Text

The material in this text is organized for a one-semester college course. The subject matter is presented in an order acceptable to an inexperienced computer user. Those with more experience may decide to skim over some of the early sections. The book also contains many exercises at the end of each section. It can also be used as a self-study guide for anyone interested in recent computing developments revolving around the Internet.

The book chapters deal with the following topics: email, Web browsing, Web page installation, the Internet, the World Wide Web, search tools, Telnet and FTP, HTML, Web graphics, HTML tools, newsgroups and mailing lists, chat rooms and MUDs, electronic publishing, Web programming, multimedia, and privacy and security issues.

The appendices deal with more specialized issues, such as Internet service providers, text editors, mailers, and operating systems. In addition, we provide a bibliography, a list of on-line references, a list of all HTML tags presented in the book, a glossary, a list of all acronyms used in the book, a place for you to record your own URLs, and an index.

---

1   In this book, we use the pronouns "their," "them," and "they," even where the correct usage is singular. This seems to be a better solution than: (1) using he/she, (2) alternating the gender of pronouns throughout the book, or (3) using "she" to compensate for years of overuse of masculine pronouns.

Icons are used in the margins of the text to highlight important or interesting points and to suggest activities to the reader.

Useful Item

Denotes an interesting tidbit of information, a factoid, or a recent news item.

Go On-Line

Indicates to go on-line and experiment with the topic or the commands described in the text.

Hot Topic

Marks extensive or important information or a hint.

Second Edition

The second edition has involved a comprehensive update of the first edition: New material on search engines, Cascading Style Sheets, and JavaScript has been added. The discussion of FTP and Telnet has been expanded. Many of the exercises in the book have been revised, and many new problems have been included. Suggestions from many reviewers have been incorporated to further improve the book. Many new figures have also been included. The supplemental materials that accompany the book, described in more detail later in the preface, have all been updated and expanded. In addition, quizzes, more on-line content, and PowerPoint lecture notes have been created.

As is traditional in computer science books, our book now has a theme, namely the **Appalachian Trail,** one of the largest continuous footpaths in the world. When Ray visited McGraw-Hill in May 2000, the lunchtime discussion turned to his thru-hike. John Wannemacher of McGraw-Hill had the idea of connecting the theme of the Appalachian Trail to *In-line/On-line*. For anyone hiking the entire Appalachian Trail, the trail represents a journey of a lifetime, a beautiful struggle to reach a worthy goal. Similarly, learning about the Internet and World Wide Web for the first time can initially be overwhelming and stimulating. The possibilities for learning and achievement are essentially endless. Thus, as you delve into this book chapter-by-chapter to achieve the goal of having learned its contents, think of your authors as guides on a long journey. You will progress through the book chapter-by-chapter as a hiker progresses state-by-state along the

Appalachian Trail. When you complete the final chapter, you will have accomplished something significant and your eyes may just be opened to an extent that you view the world differently. To keep you on the path, this edition includes vignettes about episodes along the trail. We wish you well on your journey.

Accompanying Web Presentations

Two Web presentations are associated with this book: one called "class" and the other called "book." The class presentation can be customized by an instructor and includes the following material: assignments, frequently asked questions, grading information, a hall of fame, information for parents, a project outline, a student directory, a syllabus, and a "welcome" message.

The book presentation contains the following items: a set of lecture summaries, a collection of useful links for each chapter, additional examples (not contained in the book) that utilize many HTML tags, HTML code for all of the "screen shots" contained in the book, search engine links, sample quizzes, updates of recent material/new developments, and corrections.

The on-line presentations can be accessed through McGraw-Hill's Web presentation:

www.mhhe.com

or by visiting one of our Web pages.

Online Learning Center

Together with the authors, McGraw-Hill has developed an on-line learning center to accompany this text. The learning center contains supplemental materials, including interactive quizzes, one per chapter. This material will give students a hands-on opportunity to practice many of the concepts they learn about in the text.

Legal and Ethical Guidelines

You will want to read on-line information, review paper handouts, and discuss local policies with your system administrator. The standard rules follow common sense. Let us express the guidelines in the form of a "do not" list:

- Copy, borrow, or steal another person's work.

- Try to break into another person's account.

- Forge email.

- Steal passwords.

- Make selfish use of system resources.

- Produce offensive material.

- Violate computer policies.

In summary, exercise good judgment and remember that using computer facilities is considered a privilege, not a right.

Bibliography

This book contains a bibliography plus a list of supplemental hyperlinks for each chapter. The 10 to 20 hyperlinks provided per chapter are also accessible through the book's accompanying on-line material. Both instructors and students are encouraged to explore these hyperlinks. We have gone through each Web page linked into the site and selected well-known and key sites for each additional topic. Some of these Web pages will have moved or will no longer exist by the time you try to access them. We would appreciate a quick email letting us know which hyperlinks are out of date.

HTML Source Code

We should point out that the source code **for all** HTML examples contained in this book is available in the book's accompanying on-line supplements. For each figure in the book involving HTML, the reader can load the figure on-line through a Web browser and then view the corresponding HTML. Due to the vast number of examples contained in the text, it is not feasible to include all of the HTML in the text itself. However, both students and instructors should keep in mind that full HTML source code for all HTML examples presented in the text is available on-line. Furthermore, additional examples not mentioned in the text are also available on-line.

Instructors

We have developed a set of PowerPoint lecture notes for each chapter of the book. These notes should provide an excellent starting point for developing a customized set of lecture notes.

We have developed a Quiz Book that consists of 350 multiple choice quiz questions.

The Instructor's Resource Guide that accompanies the text contains the solutions to all exercises presented in the book. It also contains sample exams and an exam question bank.

The Web sites that accompany the text may be customized by instructors to suit the needs of their class. Grading hints and sample projects are available in the on-line material as well.

Source code for all HTML examples used in the text is available on-line. References are available in the back of the text as well as conveniently located on-line.

Supplements

The following supplementary materials are available:

- *Student Solutions Manual*—contains the solutions to all odd-numbered problems in the book.

- *Instructor's Resource Guide*—contains the solutions to all exercises in the book, sample exams, and an exam question bank.

- *Quiz Book*—consists of fourteen 25-question multiple choice quizzes.

- *PowerPoint Lecture Notes*—consists of a total of almost 600 PowerPoint slides. Each chapter is outlined in an easy-to-customize manner.

- *Accompanying Web Presentations*—a class and a book Web presentation with lots of information for students and instructors. The class Web presentation is designed so instructors can easily customize it for their classes. The book Web presentation contains lots of additional HTML examples, useful hyperlinks, and all of the screen shots from the text, including their source code.

- *McGraw-Hill's Online Learning Center*—an on-line repository for all sorts of supplemental book material.

Suggestions and Corrections

The text may contain some errors, and certain topics that readers feel are especially relevant may have been omitted. In anticipation of possible future printings, we would like to correct our mistakes and incorporate as many suggestions as possible. Please send comments to us via email at:

emhepp@cs.unh.edu   or   greenlaw@armstrong.edu

Corrigenda and additions to this work can be found at:

Go On-Line

`www.mhhe.com/greenlaw`

We especially welcome input from students.

Acknowledgements

A very special thanks to Jim Cerny for providing expert advice on a large number of topics described in this book and for braving the original Internet course waters with Ray. Jim greatly influenced the way the course and book developed; both are much better because of his early involvement. Jim provided us with hundreds of wonderful suggestions.

A very special thanks to Jim Wogulis, also known as "Javaman," who co-authored the first edition of Chapter 12 with us.

A very special thanks to Laurel for a careful and timely reading. Her comments greatly helped to improve this work.

Thanks to Chris McCarthy for working with us on developing Power-Point lecture notes. Thanks to Carolyn Smith for her input on the lecture notes.

A very special thanks to Christine Ransom for a careful reading and for her expert help in developing the Web presentations for the book.

A special thanks to Greg Geller for assisting with screen captures for the second edition.

A very special thanks to Andy Evans for quick, concise, and knowledgeable answers to numerous technical questions. Thanks to Gina Ross and Andy Evans for excellent technical support.

A special thanks to Mark Bochert who taught from an early version of the book.

Thanks to Linda Spring-Andrews for her support during this project. Thanks to Linda and Dana Pavel Hulubei for assistance with the cover design of the first edition.

Thanks to Dan Bergeron for his timely answers to a number of questions relating to the graphics material.

Thanks to the reviewers: Dennis Foreman, of Binghamton University; Sherry Clark, of Oregon State University; Hugo Moortgat, of San Francisco State University; Tom Costello, of the University of Massachusetts, Lowell; Floyd Lecureux, of California State University, Sacramento; and Hilbert Levitz, of Florida State University. We appreciate your interest in this book and your valuable suggestions.

A very special thanks to the students at the University of New Hampshire who enrolled in Computer Science 403 during the academic years

1996–97 and 1997–98.   Their comments and suggestions have helped to make this a better book.   Many students in these classes deserve a special mention and thanks: Nathaniel Burnham, Carolyn Coe, Jeremy Collins, Christine Connelly, Rebecca Cook, Damon Gabrielle, Matthew Goddard, James Sabol, Meghan Simone, Natalia Starosselskaia, Heather Tatham, Katharine Tristaino, Jonathan Whorf, and Jeremy Willis. An extra special thanks to Monalisa Agrawal, Michael Klein, Dan Lipsa, and Tyrone Lochmandy.

Thanks to the students at the University of New Hampshire who used our book from 1998 to 2001 and to those at Armstrong Atlantic State University who used our book from 2000 to 2001.

A warm thanks to the staff at McGraw-Hill for their hard work on this project. In particular, a special thanks to Betsy Jones, Melinda Dougharty, and Marilyn Rothenberger. Thanks to John Wannemacher for suggesting the connection of In-line/On-line to the Appalachian Trail.

Finally, thanks to the late Killface the cat, who sat on Ray's lap for hundreds of hours while this book was being written. Her company is sorely missed.

Ray Greenlaw
Ellen Hepp

Fundamentals of Electronic Mail

Each thru-hiker of the Appalachian Trail assumes a trail name, and my friend's name was "Fish-out-of-Water" or "Fish" for short; he is a former world-class swimmer. Fish's and my long-term dream was beginning. The months of planning were done; we had reached the approach to the Appalachian Trail (AT) with all of our backpacking gear. Our spirits were high and we were extremely excited to begin our great adventure. We were about to try to walk 2,170 miles in less than 100 days carrying our fully loaded packs. There was some self-doubt as to whether or not we could make it. (Trail angel: a person who goes out of their way to do something special for thru-hikers.) Our first trail angel, "Dave," drove us to Amicalola Falls State Park in northern Georgia. We were happy to take our first steps on the eight-mile approach trail to the AT's southern terminus— the summit of Springer Mountain. "Appalachian anticipation" was over, and we were hiking. Almost immediately, we found ourselves going up an incredibly steep trail that was barely even cleared. We were both thinking, but did not let on, that "if it is like this all the way to Maine, I don't know if I can make it." Of course, it turned out we had made our first of many wrong turns. We continued toward North Carolina one step at a time.

Georgia
76 miles

Chapter 1

1.1 INTRODUCTION

Electronic mail, or *email* as it is most commonly referred to, is the subject of this chapter. Our goals are to acquaint new users with the fundamental principles of email, to reinforce these basics for intermediate users who have been working with email for a few years, and to point out a few subtleties to more experienced users. The following topics, among others, are discussed in this chapter:

Objectives

- Basic email facts

- Email advantages and disadvantages

- Email addresses, passwords, and userids

- Message components

- Message composition

- Mailer features

- Email inner workings

- Email management

- Multipurpose Internet Mail Extensions (*MIME*)

Email infiltrates many areas of the Internet, which is one of the primary motivations for including this topic at the beginning of this text. For example, in Chapter 10, you will learn about *newsgroups* and *mailing lists*, for which the vehicle for communication is email. You will find uses of email throughout the book.

Since there are so many different *email programs* (synonyms being *mailers*, *mail clients*, and *mail applications*), we will stick to a generic description of email. (The Pine mail program is covered in detail in Appendix C.) The basic concepts carry over directly to most mailers. It is important to grasp the fundamentals of email, since new and improved email programs are continually introduced. Additionally, if you switch employers at some point in your career, there is a good chance your new employer will use a different email system than the one you are currently using.

Mail clients are programs that are used to manage, read, and compose email. These programs have become very sophisticated in the last few years. This has made using email much easier and more efficient. A few popular mail clients are: Elm, Eudora, mail-tool, mailx, Microsoft Exchange, and Pine. Most *Web browsers* come with a built-in mail application although at present these are not as sophisticated as some stand-alone mail clients. Many *Internet Service Providers* (ISPs) provide their own mail client. (Appendix A discusses how to select an ISP.)

Email is one of the most popular services available through the Internet. In the early days of the Internet,[1] email emerged as an inexpensive and efficient means of communication between researchers, scientists, people in high-tech jobs, and those in academia. The words *inexpensive* and *efficient* are used here in relation to a telephone call; email is a lot less expensive than a phone call and nearly as fast. And, like postal mail (*snail mail* or *s-mail* as it is sometimes called now), a message can easily be printed to provide concrete documentation of the correspondence. Furthermore, from the user's point of view, sending a 100-page document requires no more effort or cost than sending a one-page document: both documents will typically have the same delivery time. However some email systems cannot handle very large messages, so the user might have to find an alternative way of getting the information to the intended recipient.

1.2   Email: Advantages and Disadvantages

Today, many people all over the world have been exposed to email—they have either heard of it, used it occasionally, or felt they could not function without it. Email began as a system in which an individual user could send a plain-text message via the Internet to another user. Email has grown in ways that no one predicted. In contrast to the simplicity of email functions a short while ago, people can now receive and send email to:

---

1   Prior to 1990.

Useful Item

- Nearly any country in the world.

- One of millions of computer users.

- Many users at once.

- Computer programs.

This last point is worth elaborating. Examples in which sending a message directly to a computer program proves useful include subscribing to a mailing list, submitting a paper or form electronically, and accessing remote Internet services such as *file transfer* and *gopher*.

1.2.1   Advantages

As in the early days of the telephone, the original users of email only had a limited number of people with whom they could communicate. Now that email is more prevalent, some of the advantages of using it are clear.

Convenience—There are no trips to the post office and no need to search for stationery and stamps. Sending a memo or short note is easy. A message can be informal or formal. Email makes publishing and discussing very easy, for example, in the forms of mailing lists and newsgroups.

Speed—Email is fast, based on the speed of the underlying communication network.

Inexpensive—Once you are on-line, the cost of sending a message is small.

Printable—A hard copy is easy to obtain. However, since a great deal of correspondence does not need to be printed, using email saves on natural resources. You can keep an electronic copy of a message for your own records.

Reliable—Although messages are occasionally lost, this is rare. Many mail systems will notify the sender if an email message was undeliverable.

Global—Increasingly, people and businesses all over the world are using email.

Generality—Email is not limited to text; it allows the transfer of graphics, programs, and even sounds.

1.2.2   Disadvantages

Despite all of the advantages, we should bear in mind that not everyone everywhere has access to email. Although the telephone is not truly universal either, it still far outdistances email in terms of its worldwide availability.

Misdirection—With email, you are your own worst enemy. It is far more likely that you will accidentally send email to an unintended recipient than it is for someone actually to intercept your email.

Interception—It is possible, although unlikely, that eavesdroppers are "listening in" on email correspondence. As a rule of thumb, never send an email message that you would not want the whole world to see. It is simple for someone to pass on your message, called email *forwarding*, to another party.

Forgery—Email does not preclude forgeries, that is, someone impersonating the sender, since the sender is usually not authenticated in any way.

Overload—Email can also be too convenient and result in a flood of mail.

Junk—Another more recent negative development involves "junk email," or unsolicited commercial email. This flooding of undesirable or inappropriate email is sometimes referred to as *spam*[2] and is becoming a serious problem. Some on-line services provide help in dealing with this unwanted email, and there are Web sites that suggest strategies for coping with spam. The process of sending junk email to lots of sites simultaneously is known as *spamming*. Please avoid this type of abuse of the email system. Spam is an intrusion on a user's privacy.

No response—A mild frustration sometimes associated with using email is dealing with recipients who do not read and respond to their email on a regular basis. However, this occurs using regular

---

2   As an historical note, we point out that Spam was a meat product originally fed to soldiers in World War II. Spam is commercially available and celebrated its 50th birthday in 1997. Spam has a cult-like following. The use of *spam* for email was made famous by the Monty Python skit in which John Cleese (customer) asks Eric Idle (waitress) what they have on the menu for breakfast. "She" then rattles off endless combinations of "eggs and Spam," "Spam, eggs, and Spam," and so on to the point that everyone is finally ready to scream if they hear the word again.

Useful Item

postal mail as well. There are programs that can be used on some systems to check when a person last received an email message. Although email is highly reliable, do not immediately assume that a lack of a response from someone indicates a negative reaction. They may not have received your message, or they may not have read their mail.

Despite the disadvantages, which are for the most part the same as those associated with any communication mechanism, many people prefer using email to either using the telephone or writing a letter. Email is less formal than a letter and not as intrusive as a phone call. An email response can be pondered and formulated, if necessary, or sent back right away. On the whole, the advantages of email are great, and the disadvantages, although real, are acceptable when compared with alternatives.

EXERCISES 1.2

Email: Advantages and Disadvantages

1. Write a paragraph or two aimed at someone who was around before the advent of computers. Describe your idea about email for the future, including how and why you see it becoming popular and universal.

2. Is it possible to receive email while out hiking in the woods? Would you want to receive email while out hiking?

3. Write a paragraph explaining your vision of the future of email.

4. Describe one good and one bad experience that you or someone you know has had with email.

5. What is an *email bomb*?

6. Have you ever received spam? If so, what was the nature of the message?

1.3   Userids, Passwords, and Email Addresses

Before continuing with our email discussion, it is worth devoting one section to *userids*, *password* selection, and *email addresses*. This section should be particularly useful for new computer users.

The paramount issue for you is to get access to a computer system. You may already have an Internet Service Provider and use email, or perhaps you are a student who has an account on a campus computer. The important items you must know to access a computer system are your *userid* or *login name* and your *password*.

1.3.1   Userids

Synonyms for userid are *user name* and *account name*. Userid is merely the concatenation of the word "user" and the abbreviation "id," standing for identification. Your userid identifies you to the computer.

In most settings, userids have some mnemonic meaning. For example, Ponette Beth Lucas' userid might be her first two initials joined by her last name, `pblucas`, while Nick Michael Walters' userid might be his last name, `walters`. Such userids are much easier to remember than something like `P13245`. Very few people will be able to put a name together with `P13245`. If you have a choice, pick as descriptive a name as possible, but one that is also easy to type and associate with you. In some cases, these goals are mutually exclusive, but keep them in mind.

If your name were Mary H. Lamb, sensible login names would be `mhlamb`, `MaryLamb`, `mlamb`, or `lamb`. Note that uppercase or lowercase is normally not significant in email names. That is, `MaryLamb` and `marylamb` are treated the same. However, one is easier to read and maybe shows a bit more respect for the account owner. If your name is Steve Village, do not pick a user name of `Steve`, since there are several million Steves in the world, and such a userid by itself would not uniquely identify you.

Internet Service Providers sometimes perform the unfortunate practice of handing users their next available letter or number combination as a userid. Their behavior is akin to that of a division of motor vehicles. When you obtain a license plate for your car, the sequence of symbols you get for your plate depends only upon when you arrive at the counter and sign your check. What we recommend is that, if possible, you get a "vanity plate" for your userid. Also, many users keep the same userid for years, so it is worthwhile selecting a good one the first time around.

If you have a common name or are part of a large organization, your first name and last name combined will probably not uniquely identify you. In such cases, it may be necessary to append a number to your name. For example, `SusanSmith14` identifies the fifteenth Susan Smith on a system (assuming `SusanSmith` or `SusanSmith0` identifies the first).

1.3.2   Passwords

Your *password* is a secret code that *authenticates* you to the computer. This is done simply to check that you are who you say you are. In theory, you are the only one who knows the password to your computer account, and no one except you should be able to log in to your account. Without having passwords to authenticate users as a security measure, others could gain access to your account and perform unwanted operations.

On most computer systems, your password will have to meet basic criteria in order to be allowed. That is, the computer system requires these conditions to be met as a security measure. After all, if your password is a word in the dictionary, a programmer might be able to write a program that tries to break into your account by simply testing every word in the dictionary as a password. Since dictionaries are easily accessible on-line, this is not as hard as it might sound.

A good password should:

- Be at least five characters long.

- Contain a nonalphabetical symbol such as &, %, or !.

- Contain a number.

- Possess uppercase and lowercase letters.

Case is significant in passwords. Hard-to-guess passwords are `v1p!J!`, `OG&$jaNp`, and `MuL()a#`. The drawback to these examples is that they are also hard to remember. One school of thought is if you are going to be logging into a multiuser system, pick fairly easy-to-remember passwords and change them regularly. Another alternative is to set a good password and stick with it.

You should change your password immediately if you think it has been compromised. On most systems, changing a password involves running a program, typing in the old password, typing in the new password, and finally typing in the new password a second time for verification. When you type a password, it is not echoed on screen. Modern systems usually keep an individual history file on passwords, so that you cannot quickly reuse or switch back to a previous password if the system forces you to change passwords. Avoid writing down passwords, especially in on-line files.

1.3.3   Email Addresses

The basic form of an email address is

```
username@hostname.subdomain.domain
```

There are some exceptions, but this format covers most common addresses. The text before the @ (pronounced "at") sign[3] specifies the `username` of the individual, while the text after the @ sign indicates how the computer system can locate that individual's *mailbox*. We have already covered userids, so let us focus on the suffix following @.

Consider a few sample email addresses before we make any general statements. For example:

```
maria@cs.colorado.edu
```

The first important point to be aware of is that the suffix following the @ sign gets more general from left to right. That is, `cs` is a subdomain of `colorado`, `colorado` is a subdomain of `edu`, and `edu` specifies a (*generic*) *top-level domain name*. In this case, Maria is a computer science major at the University of Colorado. If `maria` had her own computer called `tennis`, the email address

```
maria@tennis.cs.colorado.edu
```

would also work.

The number of periods (a period is pronounced "dot") varies from one email address to another. Most addresses have either one or two dots. For example, consider the following email address:

```
mark@wheelabrator.com
```

This address has a top-level domain of `com`. The `com` stands for commercial. The subdomain `wheelabrator` is a commercial entity, and `mark` is a computer user who works at Wheelabrator.

A given field in an email address, that is, a part separated by dots, can be no more than 63 characters long. All fields combined must total less than 256 characters.

How are email addresses read out loud? This is important to know so that you can communicate your email address and can record someone else's. The first address example is read as "maria at c s dot colorado dot e d u," and the second one is read as "mark at wheelabrator dot com."

---

3   The @ was selected in July 1972 by Ray Tomlinson at Bolt, Beranek, and Newman, Inc. According to *Where Wizards Stay Up Late*, Hafner and Lyon, page 192: "I got there first, so I got to choose any punctuation I wanted," Tomlinson said. "I chose the @ sign." The character also had the advantage of meaning "at" the designated institution. He had no idea he was creating an icon for the wired world.

Useful Item

1.3.4   Domain Names

Currently only a small number of top-level domain names exist in the United States, and they are listed in Table 1.1. The big seven generic top-level domain names in the United States are com, edu, gov, int, mil, net, and org. In addition, every country has its own top-level domain name. In the United States, these are called *country codes*, a sampling of which are shown in Table 1.2. It is easy to track down a listing of all country codes on-line.

Useful Item

There have been many proposals to expand the number of top-level domain names. The decision involves economics and politics as much as technology. In November 2000, the International Corporation for Assigned Names and Numbers (ICANN) approved the creation of seven new top-level domain names in an effort to relieve the overloaded .com domain names. The new generic top-level domain names are areo (for the aviation industry), biz (for businesses), coop (for cooperatives), info (for general use), museum (for museums), name (for individuals), and pro (for professionals). Despite ICANN's approval, several hurdles must be overcome before registration can begin. Because the names are not official as of this writing, we have not included them in Table 1.1. In total, including all country codes, there are more than 250 top-level domain names.

Figure 1.1 provides a convenient way of viewing the organization of the domain names. In the figure, we show a very small fragment of the *domain name space* (DNS). It is important to realize that this is a *distributed naming scheme* that follows the boundaries of countries and organizations, rather than those of networks. The DNS represents a key feature of the success

TABLE 1.1

The Generic Top-Level Domain Names Used in the United States.

Domain Name	Meaning
com	commercial business
edu	education
gov	U. S. government agency
int	international entity
mil	U. S. military
net	networking organization
org	nonprofit organization

■ **TABLE 1.2**

■ A Small Sampling of Country Top-Level Domain Names.

Domain Name	Meaning
au	Australia
ca	Canada
cl	Chile
de	Germany
ee	Estonia
es	Spain (España)
fr	France
hk	Hong Kong
jp	Japan
nl	The Netherlands
uk	United Kingdom
us	United States
za	South Africa

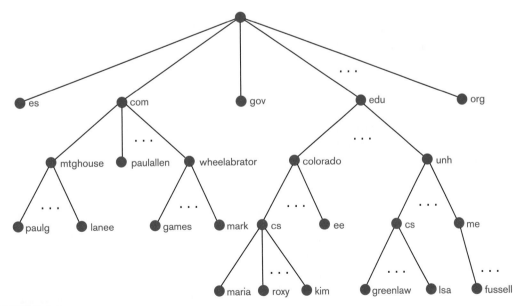

FIGURE 1.1

A small fragment of the domain name space.

of the Internet—distributed assignment and recordkeeping of a database, so that a local authority (and its backup) is responsible for local information. This means that administrators do not face the impossible task of trying to maintain one enormous central database that would be a choke point and would strangle Internet use.

Imagine Figure 1.1 as an inverted *tree*, with the top circle being the root. Traversing a path from the root to a leaf corresponds to going from right to left in an email address. For example, the user `kim` would have an email address of

`kim@cs.colorado.edu`

1.3.5   Email Address Determinations

Once you know the basic principles behind email addresses and you have the picture of Figure 1.1 in mind, it should be fairly easy for you to guess someone's email address. For example, suppose you know that Frank Denellio has his own company called Hoopsters. An educated guess as to his email address would be

`denellio@hoopsters.com`

Since you know his company is not a nonprofit, you guess `com` instead of `org`. Similar principles and a speckle of logic can be used to make informed guesses about anyone's email address. For those times when you cannot locate someone, a number of different methods are available for determining someone's email address.

- Ask the person directly.

- Use a program specially designed for locating people. This usually works best for finding network or site support staff.

- Go through your browser. For example, Netscape Navigator includes a "People" button that provides access to a group of *white page directories*. White pages are like on-line phone books.

- Use a program such as *finger* to verify a guessed address. But be aware that as a security measure, many sites disallow external fingering.

- Use a *search engine*, such as *Yahoo!*, and submit a query on that person's name.

- Use a search engine to determine the primary *Web server* for the site or organization where the person is located. Then look for directory information on the site's Web pages by using a search option at that site.

1.3.6   Local and Systemwide Aliases

Having determined an individual's email address, you may find that the email address is too cumbersome to remember. In that case, an *alias* for the address can be set up within your own email system. An alias is an easy-to-remember name that you create. The mail client associates the alias with a particular email address. Each mailer has its own procedure for setting up aliases, but they are similar and are typically called something like "address book" or "nickname feature" by the mailer. For example, if your mother has an email address

```
LoisLane@aol.com
```

and you frequently send her email, you may want to set up an alias, such as MOM. Then, every time you want to send email to your mother, you would select the address MOM and the mailer would insert your mother's email address (or make it available for you to insert). If you have to type in the address, typing MOM clearly is much faster. Conceptually,

MOM gets replaced by LoisLane@aol.com

An email alias can also be established for a whole group of people to whom you need to send the same message. For example, you may want to send a message to members of a class or a special interest group. To send a message to everyone in your bowling club, you might select an alias of club and list all your club members' email addresses. Then simply addressing your email to club will result in everyone receiving a copy of the message. Obviously, this is very convenient, because you do not have to look up the email addresses of everyone who is in the club. This type of alias is sometimes referred to as a *distribution list* or *private distribution list*. The aliases we have been discussing only affect the email that you send; such aliases are known as *local* or *private aliases*. Someone else's alias of club might include the members of their softball team.

In addition to setting up a local alias, a systemwide or *public alias* can also be established. These are aliases that are usable by everyone on any system that can send email. The primary use of a public alias is to buffer the owners and their correspondents against change. The public alias should be selected to be as stable as possible and to point to the real delivery address, which can be expected to change over time. A secondary use of a public alias is to make it easy or convenient to locate someone. For example, the system administrator might decide that it would be helpful to use an alias, such as `bill`, for himself, so that anyone on the system can easily mail him questions and comments. Even though you personally do not have `bill` designated as an alias, the mailer will determine that a message sent to `bill` is a public alias and will direct your message to the correct address.

One question is, What happens if you have already designated a particular alias as one of your local aliases? Assume that you have established `bill` as a local alias for your college roommate Bill Patterson. The client will check your list of nicknames and make an appropriate substitution if one exists. Otherwise, the client will take the name at face value and send the message on its way, leaving it to other parts of the mail system to discover if the address is valid and where to deliver the message. Since, in this case, `bill` is defined locally, your email to `bill` will wind up being sent to `bill@biology.ucla.edu` and not to the system administrator.

Sometimes, it is useful for the system administrator to set up public aliases for you. This way, if someone is taking an educated guess at your email address, chances are that it will match one of your system aliases. For example, Bill Patterson might be assigned email aliases of `billp`, `billpatterson`, `bp`, and `patterson`.

When a system administrator establishes a global alias for a list of addresses, the result is a private distribution list that allows a user to send a message to a whole group of people. To send messages to each person on the list, the sender addresses the email to the name of the list. Instead of the message being received by an individual, who would then forward the message, the mailing software automatically distributes the message to each name on the list.

EXERCISES 1.3

Userids, Passwords, and Email Addresses

7. What user names would you suggest for the following famous Appalachian Trail hikers:

    Warren Doyle, David Horton, Peter Palmer, Sheila Kennon, Peter Solomon, Dan Bruce, Susan Jones, Mark Holmes?

8. (This problem requires discrete mathematics.) If you are allowed to have passwords consisting of only five lowercase letters, how

many possible passwords are there? What if we also allow uppercase letters in combination with lowercase letters? Now, suppose we allow digits (0–9), as well as uppercase and lowercase
letters. How many different passwords are possible of lengths
five, six, and seven characters? (Factoid: Some operating systems allow passwords of up to 31 characters long.)

9. Would "hiker" be a good password for a well-known backpacker?
Explain.

10. A computer *algorithm* (which is really just a set of specific rules)
for automatic userid generation follows these sequential rules:
   (a) Last name, or
   (b) First initial, last name, or
   (c) First, middle (if there is one), and last initial, or
   (d) First, middle (if there is one), and last initial, followed by a
       counter that starts at 2.

   Note that all account names are lowercase. If the following users
   were the first people added to the system in sequence, what
   userids would they have: John Allen, Eleanor Allen, Kendra
   Allen, Shirley Allen, John Allen, John K. Allen, Johnny Allen,
   Joseph Allen, Joseph Mike Allen, Mark Allen, Marcus Allen,
   Robert John Allen, Jill Kendra Allen? Do you see any problems with the automatic userid generating algorithm? Why do
   you suppose computer operators use such algorithms?

11. On your computer system, what is the *default password* a new
user is assigned? How long do you have before it must be
changed? How frequently must the password be changed? Are
there any rules you must follow in choosing a password?

12. This exercise should make you aware of the number of countries
currently using email. Put together a list of *all* top-level country
code domain names, not just those listed in the text. Are they all
two letters long? How many different countries could you locate?

13. Suppose you met a hiker on the Appalachian Trail and exchanged
email addresses, but you lose the address. The text describes
several ways to track down an email address. List three additional methods (not given in the text) of tracking down the hiker's
email address.

14. A mechanical engineering professor named Barry Mark Messer
works at the University of Arizona. What are two informed
guesses as to what his email address might be?

15. Test out any programs available to you for tracking down an email
address. Use them to locate an old acquaintance. Report your
findings.

1.4   Message Components

You may have already been using email for a while and have a pretty good handle on the basics. Nevertheless, it is worth considering what comprises an email message. Hopefully, a few items we touch on will be new to you. Let us begin by looking at a sample email message. Of course, in most email clients, before you see the message, you see a list of the messages showing

- Date.

- Sender name.

- Size (*bytes*).

- Subject line (usually truncated).

Sometimes, additional symbols are used to flag whether or not you have already viewed the message (see Figure 1.4). Our goal here is to explain a message's different components. Figure 1.2 depicts a sample email message.

The first five lines of the message are referred to as the *email header*. Each mail client will display slightly different header information. Often, header information is part of the email message, but the mail client may not be set to display that information. Sometimes you can see these extra lines if you save the message in a mail client folder and then look at the file with an ordinary text editor or just print the message out. The header we have shown is actually an abbreviated email header. The *full header* includes some additional information, such as parts of the route the message took to reach your computer and the unique *message id* associated with this particular message.

While most parts of the message are self-explanatory, we will mention them briefly to familiarize you with the terminology.

The *From* field indicates who sent the message and when. In this case Alex Diaz, whose address is `alex@eng.ephs.edu`, sent the message on Wednesday, June 18, 1997, at 11 A.M. Eastern Daylight Time (EDT). Time is represented using a 24-hour clock.

The *Date* field repeats the date and includes an interesting feature: the −0400. This tells us that EDT is four hours behind Greenwich Mean Time (*GMT*). Greenwich, England, is the location where standard time is kept. Since email is sent throughout the world, a reference by the mailer to GMT lets us deduce when the user sent the message in relation to our local time.

```
        ┌ From: Alex Diaz <alex@eng.ephs.edu> Wed Jun 18 11:00 EDT 1997
        │ Date: Wed, 18 Jun 1997 11:00:46 -0400 (EDT)
Header ⟨ To: shiller@aol.com
        │ Subject: bean dip
        └ Cc: wong@sport.middlebury.edu
```

Greeting ⟨ Hi Guys,
```

        ┌   Someone accidentally finished off the black bean dip last
        │ night. Can one of you pick up another case of it on your
 Text  ⟨ way home? I think Luke is on his bike today so you might
        │ have to, Tak.
        └


        ┌                      -- Alex                                    ⟩ Body


          ****************************************************************
Signature ⟨  Alex T. Diaz              |   office:     (401) 437-2134
          │  332 Toast Lane            |   messages:   (401) 437-0012
          │  East Providence,          |   fax:        (401) 437-2137
          │  Rhode Island 02915        |   alex@eng.ephs.edu
          └  ****************************************************************
```

FIGURE 1.2
A sample email message.

In this example, the message was sent at 3 P.M. GMT. If the message had been sent from Claremont, California, instead of East Providence, Rhode Island, we would see a reference to Pacific Daylight Time (PDT) rather than EDT. In general, the date field will include a reference to the time zone the sender is in.

The *To* field specifies to whom the message was sent. In this case, the recipient is shiller@aol.com.

The *Subject* field provides a hint as to what the message is about. Here, after only seeing the Subject field, we can assume the message will have something to do with "bean dip."

The *Cc* field tells us that the message was "carbon copied" to another user. Long ago when a duplicate message needed to be sent, carbon paper was used to generate the extra copy, hence the term carbon copy for a duplicate message. Those familiar with business letters will often see a "cc:" at the bottom, followed by the names of other recipients of the letter. In our example, the message was also delivered to the email address

wong@sport.middlebury.edu

One field that does not appear that is worth mentioning is *Bcc*, which stands for *blind carbon copy*. Additional copies of the message may have been sent out. If the Bcc feature was used, we would not see it in the heading. *Bcc* is used when you do not want one or more of the recipients to know that someone else was copied on the message. If several recipients are blind carbon copied on a message, no one will know about the others.

The opening

```
Hi Guys,
```

is called the *greeting* of the message. More formal messages are addressed like off-line letters and usually begin with Dear.

The main content is called the *text* of the message.

```
Someone accidentally finished off the black bean dip last
night.  Can one of you pick up another case of it on your
way home?  I think Luke is on his bike today so you might
have to, Tak.
```

The final part of the message is known as the *signature*.

```
                     --Alex
```

```
****************************************************************
   Alex T. Diaz            |  office:    (401) 437-2134
   332 Toast Lane          |  messages: (401) 437-0012
   East Providence,        |  fax:       (401) 437-2137
   Rhode Island 02915      |  alex@eng.ephs.edu
****************************************************************
```

In many business situations involving frequent message exchanges, it is standard to omit the greeting and signature altogether.

The greeting, text, and signature form the *body* of the message. Most email clients recognize the header and body divisions of email messages. A third part of some messages is a *MIME attachment*. MIME is described in Section 1.9.

EXERCISES 1.4

Message Components

16. Print out the full header of an email message that you composed and sent to yourself.

17. Set up an email alias for yourself using your mail client. Send a test message to yourself using the alias. What name appears in the *From* field? How about the *To* field? Is the alias automatically expanded by the mailer?

18. Print out an email message you received and label the different parts.

19. Write a sample email message to Grandma Gatewood, who thru-hiked the Appalachian Trail three times. Ask her what she enjoyed most about the trail. Print out your message.

20. Does your mail client support the *Bcc* feature?

21. If you *Cc* yourself on a message twice, do you get two copies or only one?

22. Print out the most interesting and the "ugliest" signatures you have ever encountered in an email message. Compare and contrast them.

23. Will your email program allow "random" signatures? Explain what a random signature is.

1.5   Message Composition

The manner in which you compose an email message may vary from one mail program to another. However, the basic elements remain the same, even if you are composing your email outside the mailer, using a simple *text editor*.

1.5.1   Structure

If you are composing an email message within a mailer, it will "prompt" you for certain information. Let us begin our discussion from the point at which you have selected the "compose" button or command. Figure 1.3 shows a typical template that a mailer might provide.

The mailer's first field is generally the *To* field. Here you should enter the email address of the person to whom you are sending the message. Rather than going to the *Cc* field to enter other email addresses, many mailers allow you to enter a list of names, separated by commas, on this line. This is one way to make everyone feel equally important. For example,

```
To: Joe@waterworks.com, Martha@glasses.com,
    Sally@pistols.firearms.com
```

FIGURE 1.3
Typical email
template for
message
composition.

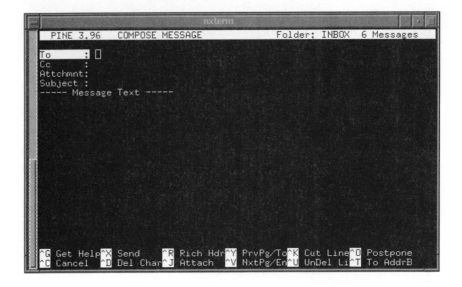

After entering to whom you want to send an email message (either in the form of an alias or an email address), you can specify a file to be attached to this message in the optional *Attachment* field. Then you will be prompted to enter a short description of your message, called the *Subject*. This is your opportunity to grab the attention of your recipient; it is especially critical if the person receiving your message gets a lot of email. If the Subject line is empty, uninteresting, or cryptic, the addressee may not bother reading your email right away, or even at all. On the other hand, a Subject line that is too long may be truncated, or may have its own *scroll bar*. Including a Subject line that is concise and descriptive is a good idea, since this introduction, along with your email address, is usually the only information displayed when the recipient checks their mailbox and decides what to look at. For example, a mailer might display the information shown in Figure 1.4 when you open your mailbox.

The first message contains no subject. If you did not recognize the sender of this message, you might delete it without reading further. The subjects of the remaining messages are:

```
heads up
R: your mail
back in the good ole USA
office hours
Re: copy edits
```

You can surmise that the message from "plum" is a warning about something. Usually, it is a good idea to read such a message right away.

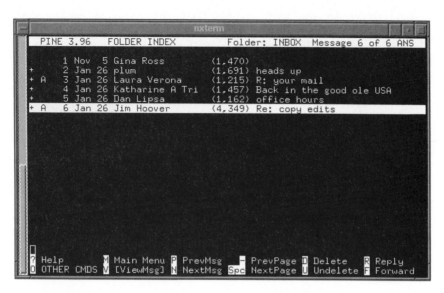

FIGURE 1.4
Sample of a
mailer display for
multiple email
messages.

The message from Katharine indicates a return to the United States from a recent trip. This is an example of a good choice of subject. The third and sixth messages are *replies* to messages the owner of this account sent. In one case, this is indicated with R:, and in the other case by Re:.

Do not get into the habit of just hitting the Reply button to answer a message. After several iterations, the subject deteriorates to the point where it has absolutely nothing to do with the contents of the message. Also some mailers have two reply buttons, one that lets you reply just to the sender of the message and the other that lets you reply to everyone who received the first message. Be careful, as people have embarrassed themselves and irritated other users by accidentally replying to everyone. (Most computer users hate this worse than tailgating!)

The date and time that the email is sent, as well as your email address, will automatically be filled in by the mailer when you send your message. You will be given the option of sending copies of the message to others when the mailer prompts you with Cc and perhaps with Bcc. Simply enter the other email addresses or aliases, as desired. For important correspondence that you want to maintain a record of, it is a good idea either to Cc or Bcc yourself, unless your mailer automatically keeps sent messages.

Most mailers let you specify your favorite text editor for message composition. That is, if you are composing your message in a separate window, you can usually select the editor you would like to use. If not, you will be provided with a default editor. The text editor acts as a word processor; it allows you to type and modify your message. Also, most mailers provide on-line documentation about how to use their editor. For example, the Pine mailer uses the *Pico* (*Pine composer*) *text editor* by default, and documentation is available on-line to learn about both the mailer and the editor. In fact, most mail clients have an associated on-line *help* that is worth perusing. This is particularly important if you want to customize your mail client.

1.5.2   Netiquette

For the most part, when writing your email message, you should follow the rules of informal letter composition. The greeting you select will often set the tone for the message. For example,

```
Dear Professor Jones,
```

is clearly very different than

```
Hey Jonesy,
```

If the person you are writing to is a close friend, you would naturally be less formal than if you are mailing your résumé to a prospective employer.

The overall tone of the message body is also very important. Email messages seem to be inherently direct, so it can be easy to misinterpret, or to phrase a message incorrectly. When we communicate in person (or, to a certain extent, even via the telephone), facial expressions, volume and tone of voice, and hand gestures all provide clues as to how you and the other person are reacting to the conversation. With written words, all these indicators are absent.

Hot Topic

Informal rules of network etiquette, or *netiquette*, suggest practicing restraint when using email to express opinions or ideas, especially when the message will be read by people who do not know you well. When the message is informal, a common practice is to use a *smiley* :-) or a *wink* ;-) to indicate something said in jest. These little symbols and others like them are called *emoticons* and resemble little sideways faces.

Typing a message in capital letters is considered "shouting," and doing so signals that the sender is either an email novice, very angry, excited, or ignorant of the rules of netiquette. Not following the rules of netiquette (or sometimes just message content) may result in a *flaming* by someone who took offense to what you said. A flame is a nasty response from the offended party. Flaming often happens on mailing lists when one user does not show consideration for others on the list.

Figure 1.5 shows a screen shot of a graphical mail client. You should have little trouble interpreting the interface.

1.5.3   Composition

For sending email to friends or people you know, simply type in a message as you would say it. For people you do not know, or with whom you have had little conversation, be slightly more formal and proofread your message. When applying for jobs or communicating with people for the first time, proofread and spell check your message. Many mail applications have a built-in spell checker. A message littered with typos may offend and will certainly distract.

When sending to a large group of people, do all of the above and then reread the message one or two more times, making sure that you have phrased things in an appropriate way. Most people find that it takes much more concentration to do a thorough job of proofreading on a screen than on a printed page.

You should always "sign" your name (that is, identify yourself with your actual name or nickname, not just your email address or userid) or end the message with your *signature file*. If you opt to use a signature file, many mailers will automatically append it to all messages you send. The file should contain standard contact information. For example, it might consist of your nickname, name, phone number, fax number, email address (even though it's already included by the mailer), favorite quote, favorite

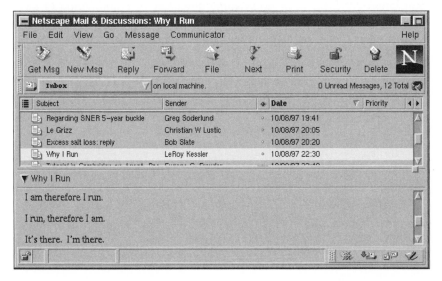

FIGURE 1.5
Graphical mail client.

ASCII graphic,[4] and World Wide Web address. For example, we showed the following signature in Figure 1.2:

```
                           --Alex


*************************************************************
    Alex T. Diaz            |  office:     (401) 437-2134
    332 Toast Lane          |  messages:  (401) 437-0012
    East Providence,        |  fax:        (401) 437-2137
    Rhode Island 02915      |  alex@eng.ephs.edu
*************************************************************
```

Try to limit the size of your signature file—too much can be annoying. Also, if you have frequent correspondence with a person, do not bother to include your signature file with every message. With 50,000,000 users sending 10 email messages per day, each having a signature file of 200 bytes, this results in an "extra" terabyte (10^{12} bytes) of information being sent over the network every 10 days! Unless you are specifically sending someone your address or sending email to someone for the first time, simply sign your name.

After composing your message using the text editor and signing it, you are ready to send. Again, for important correspondence or correspondence you would like to keep a record of, it is a good idea to Cc yourself on the message. Depending on the mailer, you may have to click on a Send icon, press CONTROL-D, or press some other key or combination of keys to indicate that you want the email sent. Before sending the mail, you sometimes have the opportunity (again, depending on the mailer) to *attach files* that you would like to append to the message. Some mailers also let you *insert a file* or a graphic at any point in the message body. Up until the time you actually send the mail, you can make changes and even decide not to send. Once the message is sent, you cannot get it back. It is like dropping a letter in a mailbox.

---

4   ASCII stands for American Standard Code for Information Interchange. Think of it as representing standard keyboard characters. Some people consider sending an ASCII graphic poor netiquette.

EXERCISES 1.5

Message Composition

24. Can your mailer handle a subject line of 500 characters? If not, what is the limit your mailer can handle? Write down the name of your mailer, this value, and a description of the experiments you ran.

25. Can you set the editor for message composition, or are you stuck with the default editor with your mailer?

26. Read the on-line documentation about your mail client. Report two interesting facts that you learned.

27. Compose a sample cover letter for a campground job to which you are applying, email it to yourself, and print out the message.

28. Compile a list of your ten favorite emoticons.

29. Compose a personal signature file, send yourself a message with it appended, and print the message.

30. Print out your favorite two pieces of *ASCII art* (i.e., graphics created using just the symbols appearing on a standard keyboard) that were found in signature files.

31. Can you invoke a spell checker from inside your mailer? Write a paragraph describing how you go about doing this. Does your spell checker think the words *thru-hiker* and *Appalachian* are misspelled?

1.6   Mailer Features

The best way to learn how to use a mailer effectively is to experiment with it. This usually means sending lots of test messages to yourself. You should also read the on-line documentation, as you will usually be able to glean some knowledge about one or two lesser-known features. In this section, we mention a few features that are common to most mailers.

Most mailers provide functionality for manipulating your mailbox contents, composing messages, and saving messages to disk. For example, many mail applications allow easy access to directories or folders to organize your email according to sender, subject, and so on. We will describe a generic mailer that has a *graphical user interface* (*GUI*). For those using a keyboard interface, the principles are similar.

A typical mailer opened in a window will contain a series of buttons (or menu items) with names such as **Compose**, **Copy**, **Delete**, **Edit**, **File**, **Forward**, **Move**, **Next**, **Reply**, **View**, and so on. We will examine a few of these options in more detail.

1.6.1   Compose, File, and Reply

A **Compose** button typically provides the following features:

- *New*—Compose a message from scratch.

- *Reply*—Reply to the current message.

- *Forward*—Pass the message on.

- *Vacation*—You are going away and want automatic responses to be generated, and have email saved.

A **File** button often has the following functionality:

- *Save*—Save the current message into a file on disk.

- *Insert*—Include a file in the body of the message being composed.

- *Exit*—Leave the mailer.

- *Open*—Open a file from disk.

- *Attach*—Append a file to a message.

A **Reply** button usually consists of the following items:

- To sender.

- To all.

- Forward (the functionality of this option is the same as that of the **Compose** button).

- Include.

- Include bracketed.

Figure 1.6 depicts the Netscape Messenger email client.

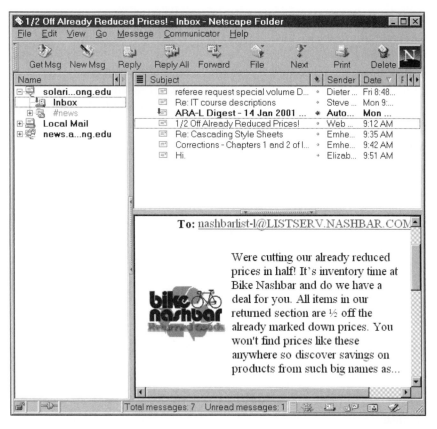

FIGURE 1.6
Netscape
messenger
mailer.

1.6.2   Bracketed Text and Include

When replying to a message, keep in mind that a period of time may have elapsed since you received the message. Thus, a reply of Yes to a message may have no meaning to the recipient. They may not recall whether you are answering the question "What is your favorite rock group?" "Do you know the French word for love?" or "Did you ace the test?"

Generally, it is a good idea to include the context of the original question along with your reply. Most mailers allow you to do this, and the format may look something like this:

    (original text from sender)

if you select the include option, or

    > (original text from sender)

if you select the bracketed option. "Greater than" signs (>) are usually

Hot Topic

inserted at the beginning of each line. If possible (and it generally is, since you can edit the message body), only include the original text that is pertinent to your response; do not include the whole message, unless it is brief. For example, suppose you received the message body shown in Figure 1.7. You might use the reply with the bracketed include option, as shown in Figure 1.8. If the include option is not available, be sure to give some background about the message you are responding to when replying.

```
Hi,

  I was wrong.  I really would like to go to dinner next
Friday.

  Oh, and by the way I got the flat tire on my bike fixed.
It was glass, ugh.

  Hope you're having a great day!

  Hasta la vista.

                        --Carme
```

FIGURE 1.7
Sample email message body.

```
Dear Carme,

   >  I was wrong.  I really would like to go to dinner
      next Friday.

      Sorry.  I have made other plans.  Maybe the
      following Friday?

   >  Hope you're having a great day!

      I'm stuck at the office.  :-(

      *Tuesday*
```

FIGURE 1.8
Sample email reply using a bracketed include.

We emphasize that the key to becoming competent with your mailer is to explore different options and read the help file. New mailers frequently appear, or at least new versions of old mailers. The features we have described may not all be present in your mailer; perhaps yours has many more capabilities. The point here is to understand the basic functionality of most mailers so you know what is out there, how to use it, and whether or not you should switch mailers.

1.6.3   Forwarding

At some point, you may have more than one email address. For example, you might have several different computer accounts. Instead of reading mail from two different accounts, it is often more convenient to have all email directed to only one account. This is usually possible by forwarding all your email from one account to the other, or, in general, directing a number of email addresses to one. On some systems, there is a special hidden file called something like `.forward`, where you can specify the email address to which you would like the mail from that account to be forwarded.

Care must be taken to avoid infinite email loops. For example, do not forward email from account A to account B and also forward email from account B to account A.

If you are going to be working at a different location for an extended period of time, it can be very useful to set up mail forwarding. This way your correspondents can continue to send you email as before, even if they are not aware you are working at a new location.

EXERCISES 1.6

Mailer Features

32. What are the primary features of your mailer?

33. Explain the difference between attaching a file and inserting a file in relation to an email message.

34. Create a sample email message, describing the food you have packed for an upcoming backpacking trip. Illustrate how the bracketed include feature can be used effectively to provide content for a reply.

35. How does your mailer distinguish between replying only to the sender versus replying to all parties receiving the message?

36. Can you "retrieve" a sent message (before it arrives at its destination) using your mailer?

37. Once you have deleted an email message, does your mailer let you undelete? At what point is the message really lost?

38. Does your mailer allow you to cut and paste between different windows? That is, can you grab on-screen text and then insert it into an email message you are composing?

39. Describe the process of saving an email message to disk using your mailer. Does your mailer automatically save sent messages? If so, how often do you need to delete them so your disk quota is not approached?

1.7   Email Inner Workings

Here we provide a simplified description of how email actually works. Our goal is not to describe the low-level implementation details of a program, such as *sendmail*, but simply to acquaint you with some of the issues involved with the workings of email. We will allude to postal mail for comparison purposes. In fact, we begin by considering the process you go through in mailing a piece of s-mail.

If we split the mailing of a letter into three phases, in phase one, the steps you need to perform are compose, address, package, stamp, and deposit the letter in a suitable place for pickup. In phase two, a mail person, on a fixed pickup schedule, retrieves the letter from its place of deposit. Then the letter, if correctly addressed and with the proper postage, is routed to its final destination mailbox. In phase three, the recipient checks for mail, retrieves the letter from the mailbox, opens the envelope, reads the mail, and perhaps files it away. Similar phases need to be carried out in the electronic setting.

1.7.1   Mailer, Mail Server, and Mailbox

Although the phases in the on-line world are not identical, it is helpful to use the familiar physical setting for analogies. Three main components (*mailer*, *mail server*, and *mailbox*) are necessary for the email system to work. In reality, the system is much more complex.

- **Mailers**   We introduced you to mailers in Sections 1.1 and 1.5. A mailer is also called a *mail program*, *mail application*, or *mail client*. A mailer is the software that allows you to manage, read, and compose email. Think of the mailer as the function or system that allows you to perform the tasks corresponding to phase one in the s-mail analogy.

- **Mail servers**   The *mail server* is a computer whose function[5] is to receive, store, and deliver email. Conceptually, the mail server is always "listening" for the arrival of new email. If new email has arrived for you, the server keeps track of it. The mailer may be on the same computer that acts as a mail server.

- **Mailboxes**   An electronic *mailbox* is a disk file specifically formatted to hold email messages and information about them. Your mailbox is generally created for you by a systems administrator when you first establish your account. It is a good idea not to delete your mailbox. On some systems, even if you do remove your mailbox, it will automatically be regenerated for you when new email arrives. Properly managed, the mailbox is private and only the "owner" can read from it, while everyone else can only send email to it. Your mailbox is uniquely identified by your account name. Think of an electronic mailbox as the system that serves the same purpose as a mailbox in the physical setting.

There are several different ways in which users typically obtain their email. We will examine two that are widely used.

1.7.2   Store and Forward Features

A mail server needs to be running nearly all the time, waiting for email messages and routing them appropriately. If a mail server crashes or is down for an extended period (3–4 days), email can be lost. Since a PC with an Internet connection is generally not turned on all the time, many PC users do not run mail servers locally on their computers. Email is very important to people, and it is unacceptable for messages to be delayed or discarded. Thus, the mail server must be a *7 by 24 machine*, that is, a machine running 7 days a week, 24 hours a day.

It is common for PC users to have their *inboxes* on a very reliable computer on which the mail server is always running. Here, we use the term *inbox* to indicate where new email is stored. For some users, the

---

5   The mail server computer may have many other functions as well. It does not have to be, and usually is not, a "dedicated" mail server.

inbox is the same as the mailbox. For others, the mailbox really consists of a disjointed set of file folders.

When email arrives, it is saved for the addressee in the inbox until they "pick it up" by downloading the messages. The save and pick-up processes comprise the store-and-forward function.

Note that there may be a space limitation on the size of your mailbox. Generally, once this limit is reached, new incoming messages are refused until you free up space by deleting some messages. Check with your systems administrator or service provider to obtain that limit.

How do users obtain their email? They rely on *Post Office Protocol* (*POP*) to retrieve their email from a remote location. A *protocol* is a set of rules that computers use for communicating with one another. Figure 1.9 shows how the store-and-forward email process works. The incoming and outgoing labels in the figure are with respect to the mail server.

Let us suppose that Ricardo is sending Jane an email message. Ricardo composes the message on his mail client and then selects the Send option. The message is routed via the *Simple Mail Transfer Protocol* (*SMTP*) to

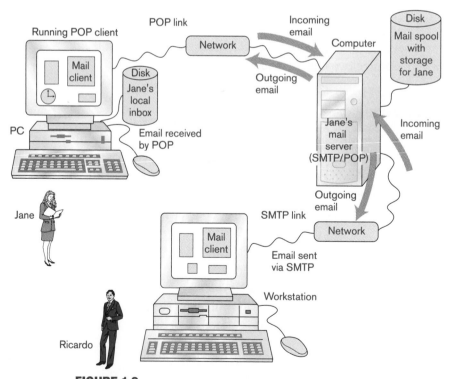

FIGURE 1.9

Example of how users communicate via email in a store and forward email system.

Jane's mail server. We have labeled the network connection between Ricardo's workstation and Jane's mail server as an SMTP link because SMTP is used to transport Ricardo's message to the mail server. Once the message arrives, the mail server stores it on disk in an area designated for Jane. The disk storage area on a mail server is often called the *mail spool*, which is the "store" part of "store and forward."

For the sake of discussion, let us suppose that

- Jane was already logged into her PC when Ricardo sent his message.

- Jane is running a POP client.

- Jane is running her mailer.

Jane's POP client knows how to communicate with Jane's mail server. Periodically, it *polls* the POP server to check if any new email has arrived for Jane. In this case, there is a new message from Ricardo. His email is forwarded over the network to Jane's PC and stored on her local disk. This is the "forward" in "store and forward."

We have labeled the network connection between Jane's PC and her mail server as a POP link, since POP was used to bring Ricardo's message over. The message is stored on Jane's local disk in her inbox. Jane's mailer will notify her that she has new email. For example, the notification may be done via sound (with a beep) or via an icon (where a mailbox flag pops up). At this point, Jane can read and process the message. Note that if Jane were not on a PC, but were instead logged directly into her account on the mail server, there would be no POP client and dialog.

1.7.3   Central Mail Spool and IMAP

Another popular method by which users obtain their email is called a *central mail spool* system as shown in Figure 1.10. Again, the incoming and outgoing labels in the figure are with respect to the mail server. This type of setup is particularly useful if someone is going to be accessing email from multiple computers. In the figure, we see that Ricardo has a workstation at his office, as well as a PC at home. His inbox is maintained on a central mail server. Also, Ricardo shares his email account with his son Joaquim.

Imagine what could happen if Ricardo were reading email at work while his son Joaquim was simultaneously trying to read the same inbox from home. Suppose Joaquim deleted an email message from his teacher addressed to his father. Would Ricardo still have access to it? If Ricardo

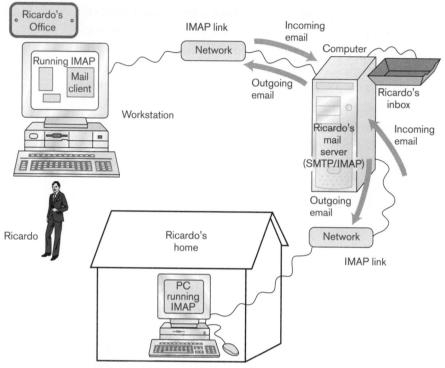

FIGURE 1.10
Example of how a central mail spool system works.

read a message, would it be marked as "read" for Joaquim too? Lots of complications can arise in this scenario, and a protocol has been designed to handle many of the relevant issues. It is called *Interactive Mail Access Protocol* or *IMAP*.[6]

In Figure 1.10 we labeled the network connection between Ricardo's workstation and his mail server as an "IMAP link," since IMAP is used to transport messages over this connection. The network connection between Ricardo's PC and his mail server has been similarly labeled. Ricardo's email remains on his mail server. The email is not brought over to the computer from which he is working. Leaving the email in a central location allows Ricardo to access it from several places. If the email were forwarded to his workstation, there would be no way to read it from his PC, and vice versa. Various commands are available to Ricardo for manipulating his email at the central site.

---

6   We have also seen IMAP expanded as Internet Message Access Protocol.

One advantage of IMAP over some other protocols is that it "encrypts" passwords. For example, when Ricardo is on his workstation and he wants to read his email, he must send a password to the mail server; that is, he needs to authenticate himself to the mail server. Otherwise, someone else could request to read his email. IMAP encodes the password so someone *sniffing* the network cannot directly obtain his password. This provides higher security than some systems that transmit the password as plaintext, which means that the password is not encoded. A disadvantage of IMAP or any other system is that if you spend a lot of time on-line connected to the server while reading and composing messages, this time counts against your monthly quota (if any) of connect hours. In such a situation, it may be important to learn techniques for off-line mail manipulation.

A *kilobyte* consists of 1,000 bytes and is denoted by the letter K. A *megabyte* consists of 1,000,000 bytes and is usually shortened to M. So, 1,000K is 1M. Since most servers will restrict you to 2–5M of disk space for your email, and since it is common for some people to get 200K of email per day, with IMAP and other similar systems, you have to be very attentive to your quota.

Other methods by which email is obtained are not explored here. In addition, hybrid systems are evolving that include the best features of the currently existing systems. Depending on the application, one setup may be preferable to another. It is clear that email is still rapidly changing.

Useful Item

1.7.4   Bounce Feature

When you send an email message, the mailer software sends a copy of it over the Internet. The message has to be split up into small pieces called *packets* containing appropriate header information and *sequence numbers*. The sequence numbers are needed so the message can be reassembled in the correct order. The mailer uses the destination email address to identify the computer to which the message should be routed. Eventually, the message arrives at the recipient's inbox. Some *handshaking* is needed to make sure the delivery process works smoothly. The details of this handshaking are technical, but we provide an intuitive description of the process. The receiving end must notify the server that all went according to plan and that the email was delivered properly. This is necessary because email sometimes *bounces*; that is, it is undeliverable. The major reasons for a bounce are:

1. *Bad user account name*—The email bounces after it gets to the target system and that system discovers the address does not exist.

2. *Bad domain name*—This causes an immediate bounce.

3. *Domain name server (DNS) is down for a number of days*—If a mail server is not working, the mail system will keep trying to send the message for a period of time. Eventually, the mail system will time out on retries, and the email will bounce back. You will sometimes see the message "DNS not responding." This means the server is not working properly.

4. *Some other malfunction*—For example, if the message being mailed is too big, a warning may be sent to notify you of this. Sometimes it is okay to ignore the warning, but other times problems might occur. For example, the message might be divided up into many small pieces that the recipient needs to assemble.

The receiving end might also need to ask the server to resend some packets, if there was a problem. If everything went well (as it usually does), your email message will be waiting in your friend's mailbox when it is next checked.

Go On-Line

Email capability is a feature supplied by most commercial on-line service providers, such as *America Online*. Other companies also provide email-only accounts, sometimes for as little as a couple of dollars per month. Naturally, the best way to locate such companies is on-line.

EXERCISES 1.7

Email Inner Workings

40. Look into the *traceroute* program. What is the purpose of the program? If possible, print out a session in which you demonstrate this program.

41. Do some in-depth research about mail servers and write a short report summarizing them.

42. Which companies in your area are reputable ISPs? Can you obtain an email-only account? For how much per month?

43. Describe how your email account works. Is it store and forward, a central spool system, or some other type?

1.8   Email Management

You have already seen that email is a complex communication mechanism with many uses. Here we share a few tips that may be helpful to you.

Clearly, you will develop your own email style, but you should not just let it evolve without thought. It is worth spending some time evaluating how you use email and how effective your responses are. Here are some questions to think about.

- Does email help you at work?

- Is email a waste of your time?

- Are you flooded with email from mailing lists?

- Is email a distraction?

- Are you constantly reading forwarded jokes?

- How can email make your life more enjoyable?

- How can email make you more productive instead of less efficient?

- Do you receive a lot of useless gossip?

A new email arrival is usually signaled to you by your mailer. If you are already logged on, there may be a beep, which can usually be suppressed if you find it annoying, or perhaps something like an icon of a mailbox with a flag up. If you are just logging on, a note may be printed on the screen that says you have new mail.

When you decide to view your email, your mailer will provide some sort of index of messages, with the subject line displayed (as in Figure 1.4). Usually, the messages are numbered in sequence. They might be displayed in either chronological or reverse chronological order. The mailer typically displays the first or current message.

1.8.1   Action Options

At this point, you have a number of options for dealing with the message. A few are listed here:

1. You might decide, based on the subject line and the address of the sender, that you want to delete the message without reading it. This is one way to deal with junk email and one reason to make sure that your subject line makes sense when sending mail.

2. You may decide that you do not have time to read the message right now and that you will get back to it later. In this case, you could simply skip over it or save it to a file.

3.   You may decide to read the current message now. After reading the message, you have the option(s) of deleting the message, replying to it, forwarding the message to someone else, saving the message in a file, or saving the message in the mailbox. Note that it is sometimes worth scanning your entire mailbox before replying to a message, since another later message may supersede the contents of the earlier one.

If you do not receive a lot of email (say, less than twenty messages per day), it may be tempting to let them "lie around" in your mailbox. However, if the volume of email you receive picks up, either because you find that you really like this method of communicating or because you subscribe to one or more mailing lists, you will need another strategy for dealing with your email.

One recommended strategy is called *triage* and can be summed up as follows:

1.   Skim for the most important messages (from your best friend, boss, and so on).

2.   Skim for what you can delete unread.

3.   Then work through the remainder.

Another possible strategy, called *skim and delete*, works as follows:

1.   Skim through your mailbox, reading only those messages that are important to you while deleting the rest.

2.   If possible, deal with each message immediately and generate a response, if necessary.

3.   If the message requires more than a couple of minutes to address, save it for later, if time does not permit handling it now.

If a message is very important, you should save it. Messages can be stored in folders organized by subject, date, and so on, or they can be saved in your inbox.

Naturally, the mileage you get from such strategies will vary. However, it is critical to develop some sort of protocol for dealing with email, especially if you find it becoming a burden.

1.8.2   Vacation Programs

If you receive a lot of email, you may consider the possibility of configuring a *vacation program* when you go away for an extended period of time. A vacation program is one that automatically replies to your email. Usually, the program sends a brief reply back to each message you receive. For business purposes, it is customary to include the name and telephone number or email address of someone to contact in your absence. You should be aware that a large number of users despise vacation programs. Consider the following points before routinely setting up such a program.

1.   Do most of your friends know you are going away?

2.   Do most of your business associates realize you are on vacation?

3.   Are you subscribed to any mailing lists where 1,000 or so innocent users could be bombarded by your vacation program?

4.   If someone knows you are away for a week, will it make a big difference to them?

5.   Do you want people to know you are away, especially strangers? What if they use the Internet to figure out where you live? Or, what if they decide that while you are away, it would be a good time to attempt to break into your account, since it will probably go unnoticed for a while.

6.   Do you want to generate lots of additional and perhaps unnecessary email?

7.   Does your "vacation" message tell recipients who to contact in your absence?

Not all vacation programs are created equal. With a good one and the right mailing list server software, things can work very well. Nevertheless, at least think about the points mentioned here before installing such a program.

1.8.3   Email and Businesses

When working in a business environment that uses email, you should be aware that it is currently legal for an employer to read all company email. Very few companies actually do read employees' email, but you should be aware that they can. A company could maintain backups of all email for a long period of time. If necessary they could go back and review the email messages of an employee. Such backups can also be subpoenaed.

Hot Topic

Businesses sometimes use *email filters*. The filters can work in both directions, to limit either incoming or outgoing email. The filtering mechanism examines each message's email address before deciding whether or not to send the mail on. Businesses use email filters to restrict with whom their employees can communicate.

EXERCISES 1.8

Email Management

44. For a one-week period, chart the number of messages you receive per day, how many you read, and how many to which you actually reply. What percentage of the messages is useful?

45. Write a short summary describing your most embarrassing or frustrating email experience.

46. What have you found to be the most helpful strategy for managing your email?

47. Suppose you were planning to section hike the state of Maine along the Appalachian Trail. How would you set up a vacation program for email on your computer system during your four-week absence?

48. Estimate how much money you save per month by using email instead of the telephone.

1.9   MIME Types

As previously stated, MIME is an acronym for *Multipurpose Internet Mail Extensions*. Originally, only plain ASCII text files could be sent via email. Today, an email message may contain an attachment that consists of virtually any type of file. Usually, people refer to ASCII files as text or *plaintext* files and to all other types of files as *binary files*. For example, in addition to text, another form of media such as graphics, *HTML* code (see Chapter 2), a spreadsheet document, video, voice, and/or a word processor document could also be attached to a message. All that is necessary is that your mailer and the recipient's mailer be MIME compliant.

For example, suppose you want to send a word processor document that has a group of tabular columns with complex formatting. If you try to transfer the file as text, all the formatting may be lost and the message will likely appear jumbled, if at all. However, having MIME-compliant mailers at both ends takes care of the messy details and the message arrives intact, as desired. If the recipient has the corresponding application, they will then be able to view the document.

Suppose someone sends you a message that contains an attachment consisting of an HTML document. If your mailer has a graphical user interface and is MIME compliant, it may display an icon indicating that the file attachment is an HTML document. In some mailers, if you select the attachment for viewing, an HTML previewer is automatically launched that renders the HTML document for you. You do not have to save the document and then run a program to preview the document; the mailer takes care of everything for you. This is very convenient.

We should point out that some security problems exist with MIME. For example, suppose you receive an email message that has an attached Microsoft Word file. Assuming you have configured your mailer accordingly, when you select the attachment to view, your mailer will open up the Word document for you. If a clever, malicious user sent you the message, they may have included one of the many *Microsoft Word macro viruses*. At this point, it is possible that the intruding program can *infect* your files. Because of this and other similar security problems, some locations are reluctant to support MIME. To avoid this problem, you can have your mailer save attachments to disk and then run a *virus check* on them before opening the files. We should mention that, to date, there is no way for your computer to be infected with a virus by the simple act of reading a non-MIME message.

A number of MIME types are important and will play a significant role in later parts of this book. In Table 1.3 we summarize a few of them.

EXERCISES 1.9

MIME Types

49. What happens if your mailer supports MIME, but the recipient's mailer does not?

50. Investigate how MIME works and write a summary of your findings. Try to track down a *Request for Comments* (*RFCs*) about MIME.

Go On-Line

51. Does your email client provide you with any security mechanisms, that is, can you encrypt a message? Explain.

TABLE 1.3

Common MIME Types.

Type	Subtype	Description of Content Type	File Extension(s)
Application	postscript	printable postscript document	.eps, .ps
	tex	TEX document	.tex
	troff	printable troff document	.t, .tr, .roff
Audio	aiff	Apple sound	.aif, .aiff, .aifc
	au	Sun Microsystems sound	.au, .snd
	midi	*Musical Instrument Digital Interface*	.midi, .mid
	realaudio	Progressive Networks sound	.ra, .ram
	wav	Microsoft sound	.wav
Image	gif	*Graphics Interchange Format*	.gif
	jpeg	*Joint Photographic Experts Group*	.jpeg, .jpg, .jpe
	png	*Portable Network Graphics*	.png
	tiff	*Tagged Image File Format*	.tiff, .tif
Model	vrml	*Virtual Reality Modeling Language*	.wrl
Text	html	*HyperText Markup Language*	.html, .htm
	plain	unformatted text	.txt
	sgml	*Standard Generalized Markup Language*	.sgml
Video	avi	Microsoft *Audio Video Interleaved*	.avi
	mpeg	*Moving Picture Experts Group*	.mpeg, .mpg
	quicktime	Apple QuickTime movie	.qt, .mov
	sgi-movie	Silicon Graphics movie	.movie

Jump Start: Browsing and Publishing

Leaving Georgia's beautiful azaleas and red clay behind, it was a thrill to get into our second state. We had already given away a substantial amount of our gear to reduce our pack weights—most of it to a hiker who was out soul searching as to whether or not to go through with his upcoming marriage. I had gotten rid of a couple of cooking pans, silverware, a book, a trail seat pad, and some food. I was to soon regret off-loading the food. We totally ran out of food just before Rainbow Springs, North Carolina, our next resupply stop. In fact, we had been out of food for a while and were feeling so desperate that we had already licked out the inside of a couple of plastic bags that had contained powdered gatorade. This hardly provided sufficient calories to keep hiking. We were sitting exhausted at roadside a mere five miles from our resupply point when trail angel "Ron" appeared and offered us each an apple. We quickly ate them. We exchanged looks that said "If you are not going to eat the core of that apple, give it to me and I will. I don't want to have to pick it out of the dirt and dust it off if you discard it." We both ate everything except the stem. Ron gave us each another apple (same result) and two sodas apiece. We thanked him heartily. We pushed on having learned several valuable lessons during this stretch.

North Carolina
193 miles

Chapter 2

2.1 INTRODUCTION

This chapter provides the background necessary to start using the World Wide Web and to create Web pages. We will introduce the following topics:

Objectives

- Web browsers

- Web surfing

- *HyperText Markup Language* (HTML)

- Web page installation

- Web page setup

- HTML formatting and hyperlink creation

2.2 Browser Bare Bones

We begin with browser essentials to get you up and surfing the Web. Even if you have already been browsing the Web, please read on; a few pointers may be useful.

Very few agreed-upon precise definitions have been given for new terms involving the Internet, such as *Web browser*. A Web browser is one of many software applications that function as the interface between a user and the Internet. The browser not only sends messages to Web servers to retrieve your page requests, but also *parses* and *renders* the HTML code once it arrives. That is, the browser interprets the code and displays the results on the screen. Many browsers have built-in mail clients and/or newsreaders. Additionally, auxiliary programs such as *helper applications* and *plug-ins* can be configured into the browser. (We will describe these features in more detail later.) It is safe to assume that browsers will continue to grow in complexity and functionality in the foreseeable future.

Popular browsers include Netscape Navigator, Microsoft's Internet Explorer, Mosaic, and Lynx. The first few are *graphical-based Web browsers*, whereas Lynx is a *text-only browser*. This makes Lynx (see Section 4.7) very fast, since graphics often cause Web pages to load more slowly. For our presentation, we will describe the Netscape Navigator, although most browsers have similar features (the exception being Lynx).

2.2.1   Browser Window Terminology

Figure 2.1 illustrates a sample browser window. The different components of the window are numbered. We will provide a name and a short explanation of each part and will then discuss the parts in more detail.

1. *Title bar*—The location where the document's title is displayed.
2. *Menu bar*—The place showing the headings of the main pull-down command menus.
3. *Toolbar*—The area providing access to a number of single-mouse-click commands.
4. *Location*—The area where the *Uniform Resource Locator* (URL) (discussed in Section 2.3.2) of the document is displayed. The item in the location field usually begins with `http://`, although you may also see `file://`, `https://`, `ftp://`, `gopher://`, `javascript:`, `mailto:`, `news:`, or `telnet://`.
5. *Hot buttons*—Single-click buttons that provide a number of convenient features.
6. *Netscape icon*—An image that shows movement to indicate when a document is being downloaded from the Internet.
7. *Scroll bar*—Arrows that allow the user to display a different part of a "large" document.
8. *Document area*—The part of the window that is used for displaying the currently loaded document.
9. *Status bar*—A field used to convey helpful (and current) information to the user, such as a URL or a programmer-specified message.
10. *In-line image*—An image appearing within a document.
11. *Hyperlink*—A highlighted (usually underlined) part of a document that, when selected, causes the browser to retrieve and display a (new) document.

Title bar (1) ———→

Tool bar (3) ———→

Hot
buttons (5) ———→

In-line
image (10) ———→

Hyperlink (11) ———→

←——— Menu bar (2)

←——— Netscape
icon (6)

←——— Location (4)

←——— Scroll bar (7)

←——— Document
area (8)

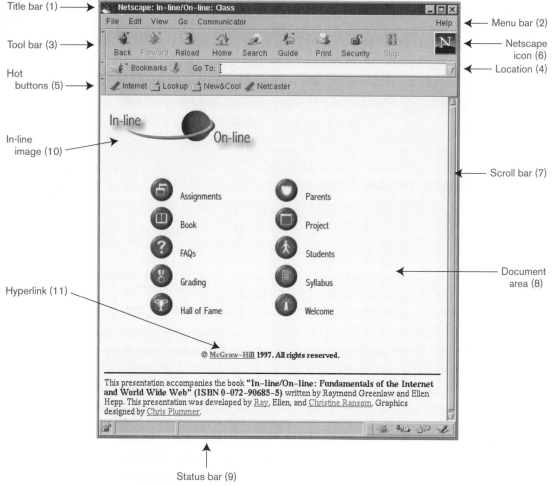

Status bar (9)

FIGURE 2.1
Sample screen illustrating the terminology associated with a browser window.

2.2.2   Menu Bar

Useful Item

Looking at the Netscape[1] window in Figure 2.1, you will notice the items **File**, **Edit**, **View**, **Go**, **Communicator**, and **Help** in the menu bar. (You will see different items, such as **Bookmarks**, **Options**, **Directory**, and **Window**, in earlier versions of Netscape.) As is customary when using

---

1   It is common to refer to the Netscape Navigator by the name of the company, Netscape, that developed it. Netscape's terminology is very confusing. With version 4.x of their browser, it is still the Navigator, part of a suite called *Communicator*, but many people now call the browser Communicator.

menus, menu items that are not available to the current configuration of the browser are shown in a lighter color gray ("grayed out").

- The **File** menu item will allow you to launch a new browser, utilize the Netscape mailer, open a new URL, open a local file, save a file, print a screen, or exit the browser. The **Send Link** option provides a convenient way to email the URL of the page you are currently visiting to someone else. If you are surfing the Web from someone else's account, this is a good way to send yourself a URL so you can bookmark it later.

Hot Topic

- The **Edit** button provides basic text editing capabilities.

- The **View** menu item is especially useful because it allows you to view the HTML source code of the document being displayed. This is a great way to learn how someone else achieved a certain layout on their Web page. Other functions allow you to reload a page, load images, refresh a page, obtain document information, view *frame* source code, and view frame information.

- The **Go** menu item displays a list of Web pages that you have visited and allows you to select any one to return to. It also provides **Back**, **Forward**, **Home**, and **Stop** loading options.

- In Netscape 4.x, the **Communicator** menu contains the items **Collabra Discussions** (Netscape's *collaborative computing* software), **Page Composer** (Netscape's *HTML editor*), **Message Center**, **Bookmarks**, and **History**, among others.

- The **Bookmarks** menu item lets you add a bookmark or directly select a (previously saved) bookmark. A *bookmark* is simply a saved Web location (i.e., URL). URLs are often cumbersome to type. For Web pages you visit often or just want to remember, the bookmark mechanism is a handy tool.

- The **Help** menu item provides Netscape help and information.

- (Netscape 3.x) The **Options** menu item has a number of features that allow you to customize your browser. For example, you can toggle the images setting (see page 49), specify *cache* size, and allow or disallow *cookies* to be written.

- (Netscape 3.x) The **Directory** menu item provides a vertical list of the hot buttons.

- (Netscape 3.x) The **Window** menu item provides access to news, mail, your address book, bookmarks, and a history mechanism.

2.2.3   Toolbar

Go On-Line

The toolbar is located under the title bar and contains buttons for **Back**, **Forward**, **Reload**, **Home**, **Search**, **Guide**, **Print**, **Security**, and **Stop**. (You will see different items, such as **Images**, **Open**, and **Find**, in Netscape 3.x.)

Hot Topic

- **Back**   A browser normally saves copies of the pages you have viewed in a *cache*. Think of a cache as local computer disk space from which the browser can quickly retrieve a document. For example, suppose you load a Web page with lots of graphics from a Web site located across the country. If this document is cached locally, then the next time you request it, the browser can load the copy stored in cache. The document can thus be loaded much faster. How much disk space should be allocated to cache? This is an option that the user can set. What if a document is updated but you keep retrieving the old cached version? You can try to reload the document and, if necessary, clear the cache. Many other interesting issues involving caches are dealt with in introductory computer science courses.

  Suppose you just visited Web pages A, B, C, D, and E, in that order. At this point, hitting the **Back** button would take you from E to D. Clicking on **Back** again takes you to C, and so on. The **Back** button allows you to access the most recently visited page without typing in its URL. The page is usually loaded quickly, since it is available from cache.

- **Forward**   The **Forward** button allows you to page forward in much the same way that the **Back** button operates.

- **Reload**   The most current version of a Web page can be loaded by clicking on the **Reload** button. This is particularly useful if you have just modified the source code for a page and want to view and check the changes.

- **Home**   The user can specify what Web page to load when the browser is first activated. This page is often called the *homepage*. The **Home** button will load the homepage that has been designated. The default page is often set to the Web page of the company that developed the browser.

- **Search**   Clicking on the **Search** button brings up one of the many useful search tools that Netscape "knows" about. Once the search tool is loaded, you can use it to search the Internet.

- **Guide**   The **Guide** button leads you to a mini information center (provided by Netscape) from which you can locate all kinds of useful items. The information displayed is updated frequently.

- **Print**   You can obtain a hardcopy of the currently displayed Web page by clicking the **Print** button.

- **Security**   The **Security** button allows you to examine and specify security options.

- **Stop**   The **Stop** button is used to stop the transfer of a Web page. This can be handy if you realize that you have selected the wrong link, or if the page you selected is going to take too much time to load. This button also allows you to stop endlessly looping animated GIFs.

  Hot Topic

- **Images**   (Netscape 3.x) The **Images** button lets you "toggle" the state of image downloading; that is, if the browser is currently downloading images, selecting the **Images** button tells the browser not to download images. If the browser is not downloading images, then selecting the **Images** button tells the browser to download images. Since images require a lot of storage and therefore a lot of time to download, this button comes in handy when you do not need or wish to download images.

  Hot Topic

- **Open**   (Netscape 3.x) The **Open** button provides you with a dialog box in which to type a URL. When you hit the return, the browser requests and then renders the Web page you specified.

- **Find**   (Netscape 3.x) The **Find** button initiates a search within the current Web page for a word or phrase that you specify. If the pattern of the word or phrase occurs in the document, the browser scrolls the page to the first occurrence of that pattern and then highlights it. If the pattern is not found, the browser will usually ask if you want to search in the reverse direction. (This function is now located in the Menu bar under the **Edit** entry in Netscape 4.x.)

2.2.4   Hot Buttons

Beneath the location area are the hot buttons (also called *directory buttons*) that Netscape provides. Other browsers provide their own versions of these buttons. These buttons include:

Go On-Line

- **Internet**   This button has the same effect as the **Guide** button of the tool bar.

- **Lookup**   This button contains two options: **People** and **Yellow Pages**.

    - **People**   Various search programs that are available to locate an individual.
    - **Yellow Pages**   Various search programs that are available to locate a business.

- **New&Cool**   This button contains two options: **What's New** and **What's Cool**.

    - **What's New**   A list of new, interesting Web pages.
    - **What's Cool**   A selected list of "cool" Web pages.

- **Netcaster**   This button takes you to information about Netscape's Netcaster product, which allows you to open a "channel" to receive a continuous flow of information to your computer.

The following buttons appeared in earlier versions of Netscape.

- **Destinations**   This allowed access to a list of "cool" hyperlinks.

- **Net Search**   This provided a quick way to access a variety of search programs.

- **Software**   This button accessed information about Netscape software that was currently available for downloading.

2.2.5   Hyperlinks

Let us elaborate on the important concept of a *hyperlink*. Hyperlinks are clickable text and/or images that generally cause the downloading and rendering of a new HTML document. Hyperlinks are often displayed in a different text color than the remainder of the document, and they are usually underlined to make them stand out. An image serving as a link may have a border around it that is the same color as other hyperlinks on the page. In either case, moving the mouse over a hyperlink (termed *mousing over a hyperlink*) will cause the mouse cursor to change appearance, perhaps from an arrow to a hand.

Useful Item

The location (URL) of the link being moused over will be displayed in the status line. It is very helpful if you understand URLs. An experienced user, upon seeing a URL, will know where the document is stored and approximately how long it should take to download (assuming an educated guess can be made as to the size of the document).

EXERCISES 2.2

Browser Bare Bones

1. Print the source code for a Web page related to the Appalachian Trail. Print the browser screen of the same Web page and label the different components of the page on the hardcopy.

2. Explain the types of facts that are available when viewing document information. For example, for an HTML document, can you tell how many bytes long it is or when it was created? What about the size of an image?

3. Is there a difference between typing in a URL in the location area versus selecting the **Open Page** option of the **File** button?

4. Experiment with the history mechanism of the browser. Write a paragraph explaining how it works.

5. What options are available for customizing your browser? Describe them in a few paragraphs.

6. Skim through the on-line help for your browser. Summarize in two paragraphs what type of information is available.

7. Using the hot buttons, try to track down Grandma Gatewood or Earl Schaffer on the Web. Describe how you proceeded and whether or not you were successful.

2.3 Coast-to-Coast Surfing

We are now ready to start using the browser to discover information on the World Wide Web. As is customary, we have been shortening the phrase World Wide Web to "Web." Other common short forms are WWW, W3, and W^3.

The Web provides a means of accessing an enormous collection of information, including text, graphics, audio, video, movies, and so on. One of the most exciting aspects of the Web is that information can be accessed in a nonlinear and experimental fashion. Unlike reading a book by flipping to the next page in sequential order, you can "jump" from topic to topic via hyperlinks. This nonlinear approach to information gathering, or browsing, is sometimes referred to as "surfing the Web." As a reader, you have the option to select what to explore next. Different readers will proceed through the same Web presentations in totally different ways, depending on their backgrounds, needs, and personalities.

2.3.1   Web Terminology

Go On-Line

Web surfing is a great way to become familiar with the Web. To begin our discussion of Web surfing, we first introduce and review some common Web terminology[2]:

Hot Topic

- **Page** or **Web page**   A file that can be read over the World Wide Web.

- **Pages** or **Web pages**   The global collection of documents associated with and accessible via the World Wide Web.

- **Hyperlink**   A string of clickable text or a clickable graphic that points to another Web page or document. When the hyperlink is selected, another Web page is requested, retrieved, and rendered by the browser.

- **Hypertext**   Web pages that have hyperlinks to other pages. More generally, any text having nonlinear links to other text.

- **Browser**   A software tool used to view Web pages, read email, and read newsgroups, among other things. Browsers are also called *Web clients*.

- **Multimedia**   Information in the form of graphics, audio, video, or movies. A multimedia document contains a media element other than just plaintext.

- **Hypermedia**   Media with links and navigational tools.

- **Uniform Resource Locator**   A string of characters that specify the address of a Web page.

- **Surfer**   A person who spends time exploring the World Wide Web.

---

2   In a number of sections in this book, we introduce special terminology. The terms are presented in a logical order, rather than an alphabetical order. The terms may be found in alphabetical order in the glossary and index.

- **Web presentation** A collection of associated and hyperlinked Web pages. Usually, there is an underlying theme to the pages. For example, a Web presentation for a company may describe facts about the company, its employees, its products, and the method for ordering the products on-line.

- **Webmaster** A person who maintains, creates, and manages a Web presentation, often for a business, organization, or university. This person usually "signs" Web pages, so that questions and comments can be sent to them.

- **Web manager** Synonym for Webmaster.

- **Web site** An entity on the Internet that publishes Web pages. A Web site typically has a computer serving Web pages, whereas a Web presentation is the actual Web pages themselves. For example, `www.lsu.edu` is the name of a Web site, whereas

$$\texttt{www.lsu.edu/}{\sim}\texttt{holmes/index.html}$$

is the name of a Web presentation.

- **Web server** A computer that satisfies user requests for Web pages.

- **Mirror site** A site that contains a duplicate copy of a Web presentation from another site. If a Web presentation is extremely popular, other sites may be used to mirror the original presentation; that is, they contain the same information as the original site. This allows the load on the Web server and the network to be distributed. If one server is down, a mirror site can be tried. If several mirror sites exist, it is a good idea to try the one closest to you first.

Hot Topic

2.3.2 Uniform Resource Locator (URL)

In Section 2.2, we mentioned that the address of the Web page being displayed is shown under the toolbar in the location area of the browser window. This Web page address is a URL (pronounced "you-are-ell" or sometimes "earl"). Typing a URL in the location area and hitting the return key will cause the browser to attempt to retrieve that page. If the browser is successful in finding the page, the browser will display it. This high-level explanation does not, however, convey any of the details of what is happening. To go from a URL to having the Web page displayed, the browser needs to be able to answer such questions as:

Useful Item

1.   How can the page be accessed?

2.   Where can the page be found?

3.   What is the file name corresponding to the page?

The URL is designed to incorporate enough information to answer these questions. Quite naturally, then, the URL has three parts. We can view the format of a URL as follows:

<code>how://where/what</code>

At this point, it is helpful to consider a sample URL to illustrate the three parts:

<code>http://pubpages.uminn.edu/index.html</code>

Let us break this example down into its components.

1.   `http`—Defines the *protocol* or *scheme* by which to access the page. In this case, the protocol is *HyperText Transfer Protocol*. This protocol is the set of rules by which an HTML document is transferred over the Web (see further comments about `index.html`).

2.   `pubpages.uminn.edu`—Identifies the domain name of the computer where the page resides. The computer is a Web server capable of satisfying page requests. Just as a waiter serves food, a Web server "serves" Web pages. The name `pubpages.uminn.edu` tells the browser on which computer to find the Web page. In this case, the computer is located at the University of Minnesota.

3.   `index.html`—Provides the local name (usually a file name) uniquely identifying the specific page. If no name is specified, the Web server where the page is located may supply a default file. On many systems, the default file is named `index.html` or `index.htm`.

This example demonstrates that the URL consists of a protocol, a Web server's domain name, and a file name.

Like a social security number (SSN), which uniquely identifies a person, URLs uniquely identify Web pages. An SSN is an identifier; it indicates where someone lived regionally when their SSN was issued, and the year of issue. For example, 001 through 003 are for New Hampshire. The middle two digits are an indirect code for the year of issue. However, based on a person's social security number you cannot tell whether they currently live in Alaska or Rhode Island; you also cannot tell what type

■ TABLE 2.1
■ Protocols that May Occur in URLs.

Protocol Name	Use	Example
ftp	File transfer	`ftp://ftp.bio.umaine.edu`
gopher	Gopher	`gopher://gopher.tc.umn.edu/11/Libraries`
http	Hypertext	`http://www.chem.uab.edu/~pauling/argon.html`
https	Hypertext secure	`https://www.bankvault.com/`
mailto	Sending email	`mailto:kim-lee@mycompany.com`
news	Requesting news	`news:soc.penpals`
telnet	Remote login	`telnet://www.amnesty.org/`

of job they have. In comparison, the URL provides all the information a browser needs to locate and access a Web page anywhere in the world. The URL format is somewhat flexible so that the system can be adapted when necessary.

Entering a URL in the Location field of the browser will bring up the designated Web page, barring any problems. For example, if the Web page has moved to another machine or has been removed, or if you type an invalid URL, or if the server you are trying to access is unavailable, an error message will be displayed. Another way to retrieve a Web page is to mouse over and click on a hyperlink in the Web page that is currently being displayed. Recall that a hyperlink is a string of text or a graphic that points to other pages.

In the URL example presented earlier, the protocol to access the page was http. This is used for transferring an HTML document. Much of the power of browsers is that they are *multiprotocol*. That is, they can retrieve and render information from a variety of servers and sources. Table 2.1 provides a summary of other common protocols.

Useful Item

┃ EXERCISES 2.3

Coast-to-Coast Surfing

8. Surf the Web and locate three Web pages that contain glossaries of computer jargon. List three terms you were previously unaware of and their definitions.

9. Compare and contrast an email address and a URL.

10. Give legal URLs for seven different top-level domains. Give legal URLs for three backpacking-related Web sites.

11. When a Web page is requested, a number of different error messages are possible. List their numerical codes and describe what each one means.

12. Can you locate any information about the `file` protocol? Describe your findings.

2.4 HyperText Markup Language: Introduction

Here we describe some basic HTML *tags* to get you started publishing a Web page, and we introduce the most useful *attributes* of each tag. Since HTML is not completely standardized yet, and since there is room for differences in interpreting and implementing a standard, it is possible that not all versions of all browsers will support all attributes.

A Web page is created when an ordinary ASCII text file is "marked up" using HTML tags and is then displayed using a browser. The tags are predefined combinations of characters enclosed between < and > characters. These symbols are called "less than" and "greater than," respectively. Sample tags are <HTML>, <CODE>, and <TITLE>. The tags are embedded within the text of a file, and they indicate how the text is to be interpreted and displayed by the browser. The word "markup" is used because copy editors use similar notations for editing printed matter.

How a Web page looks when displayed depends on (at least) three things:

Useful Item

1. The HTML tags used.

2. The specific browser rendering the page.

3. The user's system and monitor.

HTML tags do not define exactly how the Web page is supposed to look; rather, the tags describe how the elements of the page, such as headings, lists, paragraphs, and so on, are to be used. For example, many people think of a heading as being numbered, appearing in boldface, and being displayed in a larger font. The Web browser actually formats the HTML document, and different browsers may display the (same) HTML code differently. This is a point worth repeating. What you see using your browser may be

Useful Item

different than what someone else sees when viewing the same Web page. Since not all monitors support the same set of colors, the quality of the user's monitor affects the appearance of the colors in a document.[3] That is, your cranberry color may be very different than somebody else's.

HTML is not case sensitive. That is, the tag `<HTML>` means the same as `<html>`, which means the same as `<Html>`. However, you should be consistent with your tags, since it will make them easier to locate when you are editing files or debugging your code. Some Web authors prefer to use all capitals or a particular color for their tags, as these make the tags stand out from the remainder of the document. We follow both of these conventions throughout the book.

2.4.1   HTML Tag Syntax

Fortunately, learning HTML tag syntax is easy. The basic form for all HTML tags can be written abstractly as

```
<TAG ATTRI1 = "V1" ATTRI2 = "V2">item to be formatted</TAG>
```

where `ATTRI` means *attribute*. `TAG` means any HTML tag.

Many HTML tags have attributes. In the general form presented here, we have listed two attributes, called `ATTRI1` and `ATTRI2`. The number of attributes varies from tag to tag. Attributes typically have a choice of several values. In the expression we gave, the values are denoted `V1` and `V2`, respectively. Note the equals (=) sign; this is programming syntax for assigning `ATTRI1` the value `V1`. Also notice that we put quotes around `V1` and `V2`. For all HTML attributes, it is safe to quote their values. However, if the value is a number, it is sometimes not necessary to quote it. Nevertheless, we prefer to quote all values. Also observe that we have not left any white space between the item to be formatted and the surrounding tags. This is a good habit to get into, as otherwise the hyperlinks you format will not appear as you might want.

Hot Topic

`TAG` has a corresponding *ending tag* (also referred to as a *closing tag*), namely `</TAG>`. The ending tag is the same as the starting tag except for the "/" character. Not every tag has an ending tag, but most do. Also, some ending tags are commonly omitted. We will mention these where appropriate. Ending tags can always be identified by the forward slash preceding

---

3   Actually, it is more than just the monitor. Even if you come down to the basic 256 colors, Windows PCs and Macs, for example, use inherently different color palettes, with only 216 colors in common. Also, the brightness setting on the two kinds of systems is different.

the tag name. If you keep these basic rules of syntax in mind while learning new HTML tags, you will have an easier time coding properly.

Many new users of HTML begin learning to program by cutting and pasting code from existing Web pages. Although it is often helpful to look at someone else's HTML code, we recommend against copying it, for the following reasons:

Hot Topic

1. Copyright issues must often be considered.

2. A great deal of HTML code is poorly written.

3. A lot of HTML code contains bugs.

4. It is easy to fool yourself into believing you have learned the basic elements of HTML.

5. A significant fraction of HTML documents have inconsistent styles within them, since they have been cut and pasted together many times over.

Occasionally, you may find that someone else did something so well you want to "borrow" it. In such cases, it is a good idea to ask the person for permission to use the code or to credit the person's work, as appropriate.

2.4.2   HTML Document Creation

To produce an HTML document, you need to use a text editor (Appendix B contains a discussion on text editing and file creation) to create an ASCII file with an extension of .html or .htm.[4] Remember the MIME type file extensions for HTML given in Table 1.3? The file you produce must contain correct HTML code so the browser can render it. Once you have constructed and saved the file, you need to set the file *permissions* accordingly so that other people on the Web can access the document. In Section 2.5, we describe the basics of installing a Web page, and we address such issues as file protections. Here we focus on creating a simple HTML document.

Every HTML document has two parts: a *head* and a *body*.[5] The associated HTML tags for these parts are <HEAD> with closing tag </HEAD>, and <BODY> with closing tag </BODY>. Surrounding all the text in the entire file are the beginning and ending HTML tags—<HTML> and </HTML>.

---

4   You could create the file using an HTML editor, which we discuss in Section 9.6. In this text we focus on learning to use HTML tags and attributes as a way of introducing the reader to computer programming.

5   There are a few exceptions, such as frameset pages.

These tags let the browser know that the file is indeed an HTML file. If the browser tried to render a Visual Basic program or a Word file as an HTML document, there would be lots of problems. Thus, the opening `<HTML>` tag and the closing `</HTML>` tag give the browser the go-ahead to render the file as an HTML document.

A title tag, `<TITLE>`, is contained within the head of the document to provide a title for the document. Its corresponding ending tag is `</TITLE>`. Do not include any HTML formatting within the title tag. The title should provide a concise description of the page, since the title is prominently displayed in the browser window's Title bar when the page is being viewed. Perhaps even more important is the fact that the title is also used as the default *bookmark description* when a Web page is bookmarked. A title such as "My Homepage" is a poor choice, whereas "Sung Lee's Homepage" is much more descriptive. Finally, an HTML document's title can affect how the document is indexed by some *search engines*.

Hot Topic

Useful Item

To demonstrate the basic elements of an HTML document, we will create a simple one and place it in a file called `cone.html`, standing for "creation one." In our example, "In-line/On-line: Creation Number One" is an appropriate title. As described so far, we have the following HTML code in `cone.html`:

```
<HTML>

<HEAD>
<TITLE>In-line/On-line: Creation Number One</TITLE>
</HEAD>

<BODY>
</BODY>
</HTML>
```

Notice that the spacing (i.e., putting each item on a separate line) makes the code easy to read. Compare this with the following:

```
<HTML> <HEAD> <TITLE>In-line/On-line: Creation Number
    One</TITLE> </HEAD> <BODY> </BODY> </HTML>
```

We suggest you take the time to make your code readable. In the long run, you will save time editing and debugging. Some authors also use indentation to *pretty print* their code. For example:

```
<HTML>
    <HEAD>
        <TITLE>In-line/On-line: Creation Number One</TITLE>
    </HEAD>
    <BODY>
    </BODY>
</HTML>
```

FIGURE 2.2
The file
`cone.html` as
rendered by a
browser.

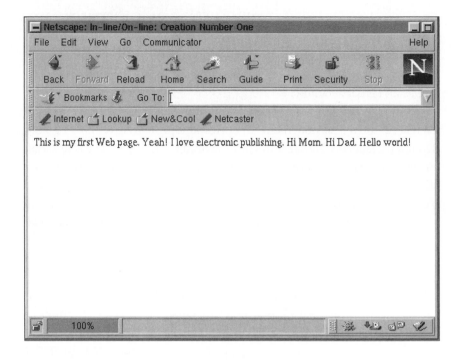

Looking at `cone.html` using your browser will not be very exciting at this point since the document area of the browser window has nothing to display. The only thing you will see is the title, "In-line/On-line: Creation Number One," in the Title bar. To display some words in the document area, add text between the `<BODY>` and `</BODY>` tags, as follows:

```
<BODY>
This is my first Web page.  Yeah!  I love
electronic publishing.  Hi Mom.  Hi Dad.  Hello world!
</BODY>
```

In Figure 2.2, we show the results of viewing `cone.html` with a browser. Notice the text in the document area of the browser window. Closely observe how the text is positioned in the browser window here and in succeeding examples. Browsers incorporate a simple *line breaking algorithm* to wrap the text if it would be too wide for the window's document area. If a window of another width is used, the text will wrap differently.

In the next section we cover how to actually set up Web pages so you can make your Web material available to everyone on the Internet.

HyperText Markup Language: Introduction

13.   Create a file called `index.html` having the basic set of tags that any HTML document should contain.

14.   A field hockey player's coach asks her to design a Web page for the university's team. What are two possible titles for it? Create the code for a simple version of the page using one of your titles.

15.   Create an HTML file that contains all the basic tags you have learned so far. Include a title for the page that would be a sensible title for your *personal page*. A personal page, also called a *homepage* by some people, is an individual's top-level HTML document. A personal page typically contains data about the individual, contact information, a table of contents to the Web presentation, and so on.

Useful Item

16.   Write two paragraphs explaining to a friend, who has a limited knowledge of computers, how to prepare a basic HTML document.

17.   Does your browser hyphenate words when it wraps the end of lines? Is hyphenation a choice that you can toggle on or off?

18.   Create a Web page that lists the lengths of the Appalachian Trail, Continental Divide Trail, and the Pacific Crest Trail.

2.5   Web Page Installation

In order to view your pages on the Web, you will need to install them on a *Web server*. A Web server is a program, located on a computer with Internet access, that responds to a browser's request for a URL. That is, a Web server meets the demands of users by supplying or serving them the Web pages requested. Ideally, the server should have an uninterrupted Internet connection, so that the pages it handles are always available.

A Web server is accessible to many of us through work or school, and many ISPs include space on their computer that runs the Web server as part of the basic set of services covered in their monthly fee. The systems administrator responsible for the server can usually fill you in about the site-specific details for publishing your Web pages. In this section, we describe, at a high level, the basic steps necessary for installing your Web presentation. We then take a more detailed look at how Web pages can be set up on a UNIX-based Web server. UNIX is a type of computer operating system. Appendix D contains an introduction to UNIX. Other Web servers, such as those that are Windows based, will require a different installation procedure for Web pages.

Why are we discussing the UNIX platform?

- The basic principles we describe for UNIX can be applied to several other systems.

- The first Web servers developed were built on the UNIX platform.

- A huge number of sites are currently running UNIX-based Web servers. In July 1997, there were about 550,000 UNIX Web servers running *Apache* (the most popular Web server on the Internet).

- UNIX is prevalent in academic settings.

- Many new Web server features appear first on UNIX-based servers.

- The source code is often free for programs developed under UNIX, or at least some version of the software is often available for public use.

We should note that desktop operating systems are increasingly shipped with a simple Web server that can optionally be set up and used. This will eliminate one more distinction between server and client. The last big remaining distinction will be accessibility, that is, whether the server is normally on-line.

2.5.1   Basic Principles

What items are necessary for someone in, say, another country to view your Web pages? Here are a few of the requirements.

1. You need to have Web pages to publish.

2. A Web server where the files can be placed must be available to you, and you need to learn the steps to put the files in place, either to create them in place or (more often) copy them into place after you develop and test them.

3. The permissions on the files need to be set so that any user anywhere can read them. Such file permissions are often referred to as *world readable*.

4. When someone requests your Web page, the server has to deliver it.

The details of exactly how these steps are performed vary from platform to platform. Under normal circumstances, you will only have to go through this entire setup process once. Thus, even though the procedure may be a bit technical, it is worth performing, as the rewards are great.

2.5.2   A Specific Example

In a UNIX environment, setting up a Web page usually involves creating a special directory in your home directory that contains all of your files to be published on the Web. This directory may contain subdirectories as well. Usually, the name of this special directory is fixed. Your systems administrator can tell you what the name of the directory should be on your system.

Suppose the name of the directory is `public_html`. You will need to use the `mkdir` UNIX command, which stands for "make directory," from within your home directory to create the `public_html` directory.

Since this directory must be accessible by others in order to permit them to read your Web pages, you will need to change the permissions on `public_html` to be world readable and world executable. You will also have to change permissions on your home directory so that it is world readable and world executable. This will allow others to access your `public_html` directory.

Be careful not to give anyone extra permissions on your home directory; do not make it world writable. Additionally, you should set permissions on private files sitting in your home directory so that only you can read them. Once the `public_html` directory is in place and the permissions on it and your home directory are set correctly, all your HTML files should be located there, or in subdirectories of the `public_html` directory.

When a Web page request is received for a URL that ends in a directory name, the Web server usually tries to load a default file. Again, the name of this default file can be determined by asking your systems administrator. Many installations use a file called `index.html`, which becomes your top-level Web page. Of course, you need to make this file world readable. If you use the default file name, users who know only your account name can access your Web page. How is this possible? Suppose you know that Sarah Conners' account name is `sarahc` and that her Web pages are served from a UNIX-based Web server called `pubpages.yikes.gov`. To access her pages, you could try the following URL:[6]

```
http://pubpages.yikes.gov/~sarahc
```

---

6   The ~ and an account name combined are used to refer to the account owner's home
    directory. For example, ~`sarahc` refers to Sarah Conners' home directory.

With a server default top-level page name of `index.html`, this is an abbreviation for the following URL:

> `http://pubpages.yikes.gov/~sarahc/index.html`

In other words, the server automatically looks in the `public_html` directory and appends the default file name to a URL that does not contain a file name. Notice that the directory `public_html` is not included in the URL for Sarah's personal page even though `public_html` is part of the path for the file `index.html`. By convention the server always completes this portion of the URL and so it does not need to be specified by the user.

As you create new directories and Web pages, you will need to set the permissions on them so that others can access the directories and files. If you are creating a Web presentation with many HTML files (those with `.html` or `.htm` extensions) and graphics files (for example, those files ending in `.gif` or `.jpeg` extensions), you may be wise to organize your files into subdirectories of the `public_html` directory. For starters, you may want to create `HTML`, `GIF`, and `JPEG` subdirectories.

Hot Topic

Summary: UNIX Web Page Setup

We will describe a typical scenario you might go through in setting up your Web page on a UNIX-based Web server. Suppose the directory where Web pages are placed is called `public_html` and the default file the server returns is called `index.html`. The following steps illustrate how to install this page. These steps assume you have read Appendix D or that you are familiar with the UNIX operating system. The commands must be executed in the order shown.[7] We preface each command with the UNIX prompt % and then give a brief explanation of what the command accomplishes.

1. `%cd`—Change to your home directory.

2. `%chmod og+x ~`—Set the permissions on your home directory to be world executable.

3. `%mkdir public_html`—Create the directory `public_html`.

4. `%chmod og+x public_html`—Set the permissions on the directory `public_html` to be world executable.

5. `%cd public_html`—Change directories from the current directory to the `public_html` subdirectory.

---

7   Technically, different sequences would work, but some steps depend on others.

6.   %edit index.html—Here, edit stands for your favorite text editor. The idea is to create a file called index.html and include the appropriate HTML code in it.

7.   %chmod og+r index.html—Set the permissions on index.html to be world readable.

Go On-Line

Once this sequence of steps, or a similar one depending on your local site, has been carried out, your index.html file should be ready to be viewed on the Web. Enter the URL for your page in the location area of the browser. For example, if your Web server is www.chem.unlv.edu and your account name is shannon, your URL would be something like

www.chem.unlv.edu/~shannon/index.html

If the page loads, congratulations, as you have just published your first Web page. If your page does not load, you may get an error indicating that the file protections are not set properly. Review the steps again and use the command ls -l to check that the protections on the necessary directories and the file index.html are set properly. Remember, as you install new files and subdirectories, you will need to set the permissions on these as you did on index.html and public_html, respectively.

EXERCISES 2.5

Web Page Installation

19.   Create the necessary directories and files to install your Web page. For starting out, create a simple HTML document with a title of your name. Check to see that your page is accessible on the Web. Document any problems you have during the installation process.

20.   What is the URL of your Web page? Does your server supply a default file name? If so, what is it? Can you use an abbreviated URL to access your Web page? If so, what is it? (When providing someone else with the URL of your personal page, it is often best to give them the shortest possible URL and thus minimize the chances for typing mistakes.)

Hot Topic

21.   Create new folders or directories to hold GIF and JPEG images. Set the protections on them so that images stored within them will be accessible.

2.6   Web Page Setup

Earlier you saw that each HTML document contains a head and a body. You will learn about the <HEAD> and <BODY> tags in detail here. In addition, we will examine colors, the <FONT> tag, the inclusion of hidden comments in an HTML document, and the methods for producing interesting backgrounds. Using the techniques described in the last section, you should be able to implement and test all of the HTML features discussed in this section. Keep in mind that many of our examples are HTML code fragments and not complete documents.

2.6.1   Head Tag

The head tag, <HEAD>, has no attributes. However, several tags can be included inside it. The most important of these is the title tag described earlier. A couple of others that you may find useful are described in the following paragraphs.

Basefont Tag

The basefont tag, <BASEFONT>, defines the font size to be used in the HTML document and may be included in the head of the document. It is also possible to use the basefont tag in other locations of an HTML document. Most browsers permit a range of font sizes. Seven different sizes are commonly available, with the sizes ranging from 1, which is the smallest, to 7, which is the largest. Figure 2.3 displays the seven different text sizes. Each browser renders an HTML document using a default font size, which is usually 3. To set the font size slightly larger for the overall document, you can use the SIZE attribute of the basefont tag, as follows:

```
<HEAD>
<BASEFONT SIZE = "4">
</HEAD>
```

You can also use a setting stated as

```
<BASEFONT SIZE = "+1">
```

Notice the plus sign. This sets the font one size larger than the default. In typing this tag, it is common practice to omit the double quotes. The ending tag </BASEFONT> returns the font size to its default value. Note: when <BASEFONT> is used in the head of a document, the ending tag is usually omitted.

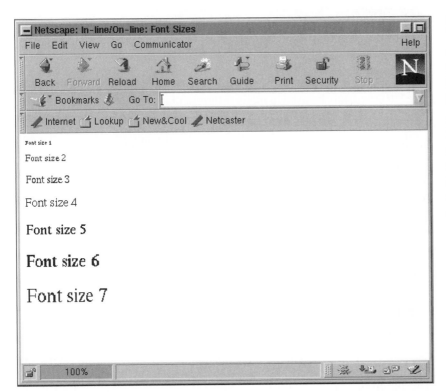

Base Tag

The base tag, <BASE>, is useful for setting some *global parameters* of an HTML document and may be included in the head of the document. A global parameter is an attribute that has an effect on the entire document. Before explaining how the base tag is used, you need to understand *absolute* versus *relative* URLs. An absolute URL is complete in that it contains all the components of a URL: the how, where, and what. For example, the following:

```
http://www.hospital.arizona.com/library/books/main.html
```

is an absolute URL. The how is

```
http
```

the where is

```
www.hospital.arizona.com
```

and the what is

`library/books/main.html`

By comparison, a relative URL, as the name implies, relates to some base URL and may be used in many different places in an HTML document. The default base URL of an HTML document is the URL of the document itself. However, the base URL can be changed using the <BASE> tag and its attribute HREF. For example, suppose we have the following code:[8]

```
<HEAD>
<TITLE>Water Sports to Die For</TITLE>
<BASE HREF =
  "http://www.fishing.com/BOATS/outboard.html">
</HEAD>
```

in the HTML document whose URL is

`http://www.paloalto.gov/entertainment/water.html`

Then all references to URLs in the file `water.html` would be relative to the base URL,

`http://www.fishing.com/BOATS/outboard.html`

instead of the default URL,

`http://www.paloalto.gov/entertainment/water.html`

More concretely, suppose a hyperlink in the file `water.html` referenced the URL

`http://www.fishing.com/BOATS/inboard.html`

Having set the base URL to

`http://www.fishing.com/BOATS/outboard.html`

---

8   Notice that we have split the HREF over two lines. This is not significant. We have only done this so the reference did not extend into the margin of the book. In your files, you may include the expression on a single line. To minimize ambiguity, we normally break a line at a delimiter, such as a comma or an equals sign, or between attributes.

the referenced URL could be specified simply as `inboard.html`, since the prefix of the URL can be determined from the base URL. Why is this useful? If, for example, there are many references to URLs in the document collection found on the `www.fishing.com` server, their names can all be shortened.

Web addresses change frequently, and as explained here, the base tag can be used to simplify the updating of hyperlinks inside a file. If absolute URLs are hard-coded into HTML documents, then if a collection of documents moves to a new server, it may be necessary to edit all the files in the collection to update the URLs. This can result in a tremendous amount of editing. However, if relative URLs are used, it would probably only be necessary to update the base tag's `HREF` at the beginning of each document. We recommend using relative URLs where possible. An example should make this point clear.

Suppose a student at Winthrop University has the following absolute URL for her personal Web page:

Hot Topic

```
http://www.winthrop.edu/~JenniferJones/index.html
```

Figure 2.4 illustrates Jennifer's file structure, viewed as a tree. In her account, she has two top-level directories (or folders) called `private` and `public_html`. In her `public_html` directory, which contains her WWW material, she has four subdirectories and a file called `index.html`. The four subdirectories of `public_html` are `books`, `family`, `gif`, and `jpg`. The directories `gif` and `jpg` contain some of her graphics. The absolute URL for her Web page about her mother is

```
http://www.winthrop.edu/~JenniferJones/family/mom.html
```

Suppose Jennifer's brother Jeff, who attends Tennessee Technical University, wants to include a picture of South Carolina in his HTML document called `sister.html`. Jeff could do this using an absolute URL of

```
http://www.winthrop.edu/~JenniferJones/jpg/sc.jpg
```

He would have to type equally cumbersome URLs to include the picture of Rock Hill and also the picture of Jenny's favorite lake. In the interest of future portability, Jeff decides instead to use a base tag by including the

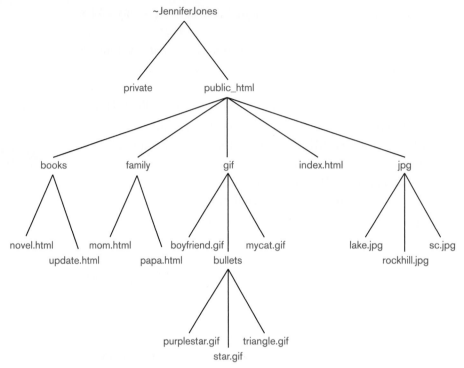

FIGURE 2.4
File structure of Jennifer Jones' computer account.

following code in his file called `sister.html`.

```
<HEAD>
<TITLE>Jenny Jones: My Cool Sister</TITLE>
<BASE HREF = "http://www.winthrop.edu/~JenniferJones ←
    /jpg/sc.jpg">
</HEAD>
```

(We use the symbol ← to denote that the line continues without any spaces.)
The reference

     `http://www.winthrop.edu/~JenniferJones/jpg/sc.jpg`

can now be replaced by just `sc.jpg`. Similarly, a reference to

     `http://www.winthrop.edu/~JenniferJones/jpg/lake.jpg`

can be specified simply as `lake.jpg`. When Jenny graduates and moves
her document collection to a new Web server, Jeff only has to update the

HREF in his base tag, as opposed to changing all references to Jenny's files individually.

Jenny can also refer to her own document collection using relative URLs. Suppose, for the sake of discussion, that www.winthrop.edu is a UNIX-based Web server. Also assume that Jenny has not set the base tag in her papa.html file. If Jenny wants to include a picture of Rock Hill in her papa.html file, she could use an absolute URL of

http://www.winthrop.edu/~JenniferJones/jpg/rockhill.jpg

or she could use a relative URL of

../jpg/rockhill.jpg

(Note: the symbol .. is a way of moving up the directory structure one level.) This URL is relative to the default URL for the file papa.html, which is

http://www.winthrop.edu/~JenniferJones/family/papa.html

In other words, the default URL for a file is just the URL of the file itself.

The expression ../jpg/rockhill.jpg can be best understood if partitioned in the following way:

- ".." says go up one directory, which places us in the directory /public_html.

- /jpg says go into the directory /jpg.

- rockhill.jpg tells us the file name to include.

An expression such as

../gif/bullets/triangle.gif

in the file update.html could be used to refer to the triangle icon called triangle.gif. To refer to the purple star bullet from within the file index.html, Jenny could use the expression

gif/bullets/purplestar.gif

We will have more to say about the base tag, and in particular its TARGET attribute, when we discuss the concept of frames.

If possible, try to use all lowercase or all uppercase in your own URLs, since this may help people avoid typing errors. Also, try not to use "underscore" (_) and "dash" (-), and try never to use both of these in the same URL (or email address). These symbols may be hard to distinguish on some monitors.

Meta Tag

The least well understood and second most widely used (and occasionally abused) tag inside the head tag is the meta tag, <META>. This tag is used to include additional information about a document and can be used to pass additional information to a browser. There is no ending tag for <META>, and a document can have multiple <META> tags.

Useful Item

The attributes of the meta tag are NAME, CONTENT, and HTTP-EQUIV. You should include a modest list of keywords, say three to five, as the value of the CONTENT attribute. If someone is searching for a particular topic, your page may be returned if one or more of your keywords match their search request. Do not abuse the meta tag by expanding the number of items in the CONTENT attribute to ridiculous lengths. People who abuse the meta tag in this fashion are known as *spamdexers*, and there are many classic cases of this behavior.

For example, someone who has a Web page about woodworking might include the following:

```
<HEAD>
<META NAME = "keywords"
      CONTENT = "woodworking, cabinetmaking,
                 handmade furniture">
</HEAD>
```

2.6.2   HTML and Colors

Go On-Line

Colors can help or hinder readers of your Web pages. There are two ways of defining colors in HTML documents. One involves straightforward color names, such as blue, cranberry, green, orange, red, and yellow. Many browsers have a list of predefined color names. Such lists are usually easy to find on-line. However, since different browsers have different lists and since the definitions of individual colors may vary from browser to browser, we recommend using the color numbering scheme. Although somewhat more complex, this scheme is better supported across different platforms.

A little computer numbering terminology is necessary first. A *bit* is either 0 or 1. The term bit stands for *bi*nary digi*t*. Bits are useful for counting in base two. Table 2.2 shows some binary numbers and their

■ **TABLE 2.2**

■ Sample Decimal Numbers and Their Corresponding Binary Values.

Decimal	Binary
0	0
1	1
2	10
4	100
5	101
29	11101
255	11111111

corresponding decimal values. In this text, we use the phrase "decimal number" to represent a base ten number from the set of natural numbers, 0, 1, 2, ... For example, 11101 in binary represents 29 in decimal, as follows:

$$(1 \times 2^4) + (1 \times 2^3) + (1 \times 2^2) + (0 \times 2^1) + (1 \times 2^0)$$

equals

$$16 + 8 + 4 + 0 + 1 = 29$$

(Remember that any natural number raised to the zero power equals one.)

This explanation of binary numbers is really just a useful warmup. Colors in HTML documents are represented as *hexadecimal* numbers, which are numbers in base sixteen. Hexadecimal can also be considered a shorthand for representing four bits, since only four bits are needed to represent the numbers 0 through 15. Since there are only 10 base ten digits (0–9), we need six additional symbols in the hexa decimal number system: A, B, C, D, E, and F. Table 2.3 provides the values of these and some other hexadecimal numbers, with their corresponding decimal values. For example, 752 in hexadecimal represents the number 1874 in decimal, as follows:

$$(7 \times 16^2) + (5 \times 16^1) + (2 \times 16^0) = 1792 + 80 + 2 = 1874$$

You will be most concerned with hexadecimal numbers having two digits, because colors in HTML documents are represented by three two-digit hexadecimal numbers. Each of the two digits signifies the amount of one of three primary colors. In other words, a color is formed by mixing different amounts of red, green, and blue. The first two digits represent the

◼ TABLE 2.3

◼ Sample Decimal Numbers and Their Corresponding Binary and Hexadecimal Values, with Each Hexadecimal Number Written as Four Binary Digits.

Decimal	Binary	Hexadecimal
0	0000	0
1	0001	1
10	1010	A
11	1011	B
12	1100	C
13	1101	D
14	1110	E
15	1111	F
17	0001 0001	11
35	0010 0011	23
255	1111 1111	FF
1874	0111 0101 0010	752

red component, the next two the green portion, and the last two the amount of blue. This method of representing colors is called the *RGB color model.* We can view this as follows:

$$\underbrace{\text{digit1 digit2}}_{\text{red}} \quad \underbrace{\text{digit3 digit4}}_{\text{green}} \quad \underbrace{\text{digit5 digit6}}_{\text{blue}}$$

The first two digits, designated digit1 and digit2, represent the red component. For example, if digit1 = 0 and digit2 = 0, there is no red component. However, if digit1 = F and digit2 = F, the maximum possible red component is used. Since FF is the largest two-digit hexadecimal number (it represents 255 in decimal), this is the maximum red we can specify using two hexadecimal digits. The green component is specified by digit3 and digit4, whereas the blue portion is given by digit5 and digit6.

As an example, 000000 means 00 or no red, 00 of green, and 00 of blue. This total absence of color is the color black. So, 000000 represents black.

It is common practice to preface these six-digit combinations by a # sign to denote that they represent a color. You can imagine the possible ambiguity arising from a six-letter color name consisting only of the letters A–F. Did the user want a color name, or a hexadecimal number to be interpreted as a color?

■ TABLE 2.4
■ Some Colors and Their Corresponding Hexadecimal Representations.

Color	Hexadecimal Value	Color	Hexadecimal Value
black	#000000	orange	#FFA500
blue	#0000FF	plum	#DDA0DD
chocolate	#D2691E	purple	#800080
crimson	#DC143C	red	#FF0000
gold	#FFD700	salmon	#FA8072
green	#00FF00	silver	#C0C0C0
gray	#808080	violet	#EE82EE
maroon	#800000	white	#FFFFFF
navy	#000080	yellow	#FFFF00

The color #FFFFFF represents bright red, bright green, and bright blue. This complete mix of these three colors yields white. Table 2.4 lists several color names and their corresponding hexadecimal values.

Desktop window systems allow the opportunity to download and install a *freeware* or *shareware* utility with a "color picker" to determine the hexadecimal value of any color you click on.

Hot Topic

2.6.3 Body Tag

The body is the second and main part of every HTML document. The text and HTML code that goes between the body beginning and ending tags is rendered and displayed in the document area of the browser's window. The body tag, `<BODY>`, has a number of useful attributes that let you set some global parameters. The most interesting attributes deal with the document's text color and background color, and the properties of hyperlinks.

Text Color

The TEXT attribute is used to change the default text color for an entire document. (We will see how to override this setting in the next section on fonts.) Suppose you have a document and would like to use a maroon-colored text. The following HTML code shows how:

```
<BODY TEXT = "#800000">
```

A common mistake for beginners is the use of a text color that clashes with the background color. This makes your document hard to read and

Hot Topic

less desirable to visit. Make sure to select a background that goes well with your choice of text color. If possible, view the color combination on several different platforms.

Background Color and Tilings

Hot Topic

Including effective colors (legible text and coordinated colors) in your Web pages can really improve appearance and navigability. Not only that, if you have a consistent color scheme running throughout your presentation, visitors will know they are still at your presentation as they select new hyperlinks. Conversely, if someone is surfing your Web pages and they click on a hyperlink taking them to a new page having a completely different color scheme, they will assume that they have left your pages. A carefully chosen color scheme can unite your pages and give them your own "look."

Two attributes to the body tag that let you add color to a Web page background are BGCOLOR and BACKGROUND. (The default is typically either a gray or white background.) The BGCOLOR attribute is used to set the background of an HTML document to a single color. For example, the following HTML code sets the document background area to blue:

```
<BODY BGCOLOR = "#0000FF">
```

You can also use color names:

```
<BODY BGCOLOR = "blue">
```

As we explained earlier, we recommend you stick with hexadecimal numbers, since there are many shades of blue, and the one you see on your screen may not match the one another viewer might see on their system.

Hot Topic

Choosing a good background color is not easy and may require some experimentation. Just because your favorite color is aqua does not mean that it is the best choice for your Web pages. Select a color that is easy on the eyes and makes the text easy to read. White is usually safe. Black is difficult to use effectively. If you use a black background with white text, many users will have a problem printing your Web page. The black background color will not be printed, and the white text will not show up on white paper.

Useful Item

As for the BACKGROUND attribute, imagine holding up a postage-stamp-sized tile in front of your face. When you see an interesting tiled pattern on a Web page, it is usually created by taking postage-stamp-sized images and repeating them as necessary to fill in the document area in the browser's window. If you widen the document window, the pattern "expands" to fill it. Shrink the window and the pattern "contracts" to fill it.

The concept we are describing is called *tiling*. You may take any image and include it in your HTML document so that it tiles the background. The tiling is performed by the browser using a *tiling algorithm.* Abstractly, the tiler starts in one corner of the screen and horizontally lays tiles, which are copies of the image, until the right edge of the browser window is reached. If necessary, a tile is "cut." The tiler then moves down to the next horizontal row. The entire process is repeated, with the possibility that all tiles in the last row need to be cut.[9] Since computer scientists have figured out very efficient tiling algorithms, you do not notice any delay caused by the tiling procedure.

When using an image to tile a background, choose something that will not interfere with the legibility of your text. Common choices involve patterns of paper, clouds, and water. Marble textures are also popular. If you have an image called `marble.jpg`, the following HTML code would include it as a tiled background for you:

```
<BODY BACKGROUND = "marble.jpg">
```

As we said, be careful to choose a background pattern that makes your text easy to read. For example, a complex psychedelic image may be awesome, but it may not be suitable as a background. If no text color is clearly readable against that background, do not use it.

Hot Topic

Some Web authors like to create *splash screen* effects by first loading in a color and then tiling a pattern over it. The following HTML code first loads in a color and then a background pattern:

```
<BODY BGCOLOR = "#008888" BACKGROUND = "dotblue.jpg">
```

Notice that when two attributes are used within the same tag, by convention a single blank space is used between the value of the first attribute and the name of the second attribute.

One reason for including the `BGCOLOR` attribute, even if you plan to use the `BACKGROUND` attribute, is that if someone has the automatic display of images turned off in their browser, the background image will not tile, but they will still get the background color. As a routine, the `BGCOLOR` attribute should be specified before the `BACKGROUND` attribute.[10]

Hot Topic

Hyperlink Colors

Three attributes are used for changing the color of a hyperlink, where the color depends on the current *state of the hyperlink.* The three possible

Go On-Line

---

9   There are many presentations on the Web where good background graphics are available for free. This book's on-line Web presentation provides the URLs of several.

10   In theory, the order should not matter, but it seems to on some systems.

states are: unvisited, visited, and currently thinking of visiting. These are defined as follows:

> LINK   Unvisited hyperlinks. The color value assigned to LINK sets the color for all unvisited hyperlinks in the HTML document.

> VLINK   Visited hyperlinks. The color value assigned to VLINK sets the color for all visited hyperlinks, that is, hyperlinks the user has already explored.[11]

> ALINK   A hyperlink the user is thinking of visiting. The *A* stands for *active hyperlink.* The color value assigned to ALINK sets the color of a hyperlink that the user has moused over and depressed the mouse button on. (This option is not supported by all browsers.)

Hot Topic

Most browsers provide default colors for the three types of hyperlinks, and text-based browsers usually use underlining or reverse video to make hyperlinks more prominent on screen. However, many HTML documents specify all three attributes in the body tag. We encourage you to think carefully before you select colors that change the browser defaults people are used to seeing. Also, try to select colors that go well with your background and document text. Make sure your hyperlinks stand out; that is, do not set both the background color and LINK to red.

Suppose you have an HTML document that has a white background. The following code specifies unvisited links as red, visited links as gray, and the active link as yellow:

```
<BODY BGCOLOR = "#FFFFFF"
      LINK = "#FF0000"
      VLINK = "#808080"
      ALINK = "#FFFF00">
```

Body Attributes Combined

Conceptually, it is straightforward to use all of the body attributes in combination. To do this effectively often requires some trial and error. When you see particularly effective colors used on someone's Web page, look at the document source and note the colors used. To create a white-colored

Useful Item

---

11   Your browser keeps a history file of where you have been, in addition to the cache and bookmarks, so it can determine which hyperlinks are to be treated as VLINKs.

document area with red text, along with green unvisited hyperlinks, orange visited hyperlinks, and purple active hyperlinks, use the following HTML code:

```
<BODY BGCOLOR = "#FFFFFF"
      TEXT = "#FF0000"
      LINK = "#00FF00"
      VLINK = "#FFA500"
      ALINK = "#800080">
```

2.6.4   HTML Font Colors

In the previous section, we saw how to set the text color of an entire document to any (single) color. In this section, we examine the font tag, `<FONT>`, which allows us to change the color of any portion of text. Modifying the color of a segment of text is easy using the `COLOR` attribute of the font tag. For example,

```
<FONT COLOR = "#0000FF">
I am going swimming today
</FONT>
```

changes the text "I am going swimming today" to blue. The preceding and succeeding text is unaffected. Only the text between the font beginning and ending tags is changed. When altering the color of small segments of text, check to make sure that the text is still readable when rendered. In general, do not use a large number of text color changes in a single HTML document.

Hot Topic

2.6.5   Font Size

As previously stated, the basefont tag is commonly used in the head of a document to alter the font size for the entire document. The `SIZE` attribute of the font tag is typically used to change the font size of an individual part of a document.

One option, for example, makes the first letter of the first paragraph slightly larger than the rest of the text. This can be accomplished with the following code:

```
<FONT SIZE = "+3">W</FONT>elcome my friend.
```

Figure 2.5 illustrates the effect of this sample code. The remarks pertaining to the `SIZE` attribute of the basefont tag are also relevant here. For example, the `SIZE` attribute can have an absolute value of between 1 and 7.

FIGURE 2.5
Illustration of
enlarging the first
character in the
beginning
paragraph of an
HTML document.

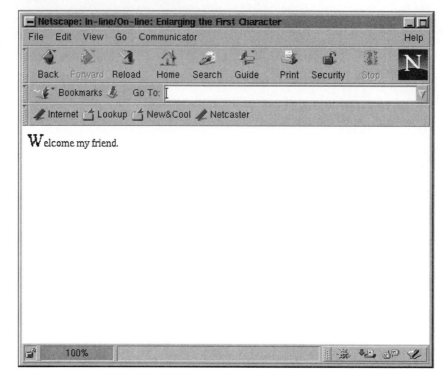

2.6.6   Font Face

Most browsers also support a FACE attribute for the <FONT> tag, allowing
you to specify a particular font type. For example,

```
<FONT FACE = "avantgarde">New font type</FONT>
```

Hot Topic

specifies that the phrase "New font type" should be displayed in the Avant-
garde font. However, not all browsers support the same font families, and
various fonts are rendered in different sizes. We therefore recommend using only a limited number of different font types. Otherwise, the spacing
and font type you see may be completely different than what someone else
sees when viewing your Web page.

2.6.7   HTML Comments

The comment feature provides you with a way to document your HTML
files and make notes to yourself. Those who have written program code
realize the importance of documenting the process concurrently with program construction. The same can be said for Web page design. Without
such notes, it is unlikely you will be able to remember all the important
details that went into a Web page's design.

The comment tag is not `<COMMENT>`; it is the set of symbols `<!--` for the beginning tag and `-->` for the ending tag. A comment, properly included, does not change the appearance of your Web page.

To use the comment tag, place the comment text between the pairs of dashes in the tag. For example,

```
<!-- This is a comment. -->
```

The browser will not interpret (i.e., display) the text between the pairs of dashes.

Do not include any embedded HTML code in commented text, since the results are unpredictable. Making a solid line of dashes may also cause unpredictable results in some browsers. Use periods or asterisks instead to get a similar effect. In the exercises, we ask you to experiment with how your browser handles HTML embedded within a comment declaration.

Here is an example of how the comment tag might be used.

Hot Topic

```
<!-- How to paint a house in seven easy steps. -->
<!-- Written in July of 1999.  Gretchen von Gelder -->
<!-- Most of the description is from my file Home-notes. -->

Hi.  Welcome to the house painting scrap book.  A gallon
of paint covers about 400 square feet.  So, if you live
in a box that is 10 yards on a side, you would need
<!-- (4 x (10 x 3) ∧ 2)/400 = 9 -->
9 gallons of paint to cover it.
```

(We have formatted the text inside the comment so that it looks good on the printed book page.) Including a comment like the last one helps you recall the actual calculation that you made. If some user sends you email in January of 2002 asking how you figured on 9 gallons of paint, you can simply consult your comment to review the math. The notes at the top of the document remind you what the HTML code is about, who wrote it, and when. It is generally a good idea to include this information in an HTML file, or any on-line file for that matter. The output resulting from this HTML code is shown in Figure 2.6.

You could also embed a copyright notice at the top of a document. For example,

Hot Topic

```
<!-- copyright (c) 2002, Mark Jackson -->
```

With the basic principles and HTML tags described thus far, you should be able to create some interesting Web pages. Remember to comment them so you can easily recall what you did, why, and when.

FIGURE 2.6

Display of a web page that includes comments.

Note that the comments are not rendered by the browser.

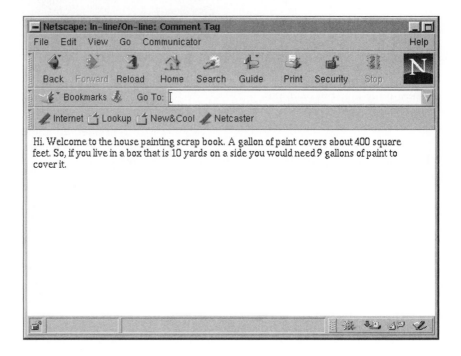

Hi. Welcome to the house painting scrap book. A gallon of paint covers about 400 square feet. So, if you live in a box that is 10 yards on a side you would need 9 gallons of paint to cover it.

EXERCISES 2.6

Web Page Setup

22. Provide the head specification for an HTML document in which the entire document's font size is set to a value two less than the default size.

23. Provide an absolute URL that Jennifer Jones could use to include her South Carolina image in her `novel.html` file. What is a relative URL she could use to do the same thing?

24. Document two widely published cases involving spamdexers. (Hint: Use a search engine such as Yahoo!)

25. What are the decimal equivalents of the following hexadecimal numbers: 16, 22, AD, CB, FG, 79, and FF?

26. What are the probable hexadecimal values for the following colors: black, cranberry, lime, orange, paleblue, royalblue, and white?

27. If you were designing a Web page about the mountains and wanted to create a "wilderness feel" for the page, what colors might you decide to use in your presentation? What are their corresponding hexadecimal values?

28.   Andrew "Thumbs" Michaels is typing in a color specification, intending to use a color name, not a hexadecimal number. He "accidentally" hits the Shift key while bumping the 3 key, so the code starts out with a # sign. He then keys in his desired color name, making at most four typos. Are there any color names he could have botched that would result in a valid hexadecimal number? As an example, if he meant to key in "beige" but made three typos i ↦ a, g ↦ a, and accidentally appended an a, the result in capitals would be BEAAEA, a valid hexadecimal number.

29.   Report the URLs for three different Web pages that have cross references providing hexadecimal values for color names.

30.   Can you locate a Web page that allows you to enter a color name and then have it return the corresponding hexadecimal representation? How about vice versa?

31.   Are color names case sensitive? How about letters in hexadecimal color representations? (Notice that we have always used lowercase letters for color names and capital letters in hexadecimal numbers.)

32.   Write a body tag specification to produce a salmon-colored background. Do this once using the color name "salmon" and once using the hexadecimal representation for salmon.

33.   Suppose you did not have (and could not find) a table to look up hexadecimal values for a given color. Describe how you could obtain an approximate value just using HTML code and your browser.

34.   What colors do the following hexadecimal patterns probably represent: #00FF00, #FF0000, #FFFF00, #FA5723, and #00BC51?

35.   Write a <BODY> tag specification to generate a background that is tiled using the pattern

   `http://www.herewego.com/backgrounds/droplets.gif`

   If you use an absolute URL, then every time your page loads, this background pattern would need to be loaded from another server. This is considered bad practice and is certainly time consuming.[12] Suppose instead that you copy the image to your disk area. Now write a specification using a relative URL to generate the same background.

---

12   We know the Jennifer Jones example contained some code like this. For illustration purposes of URLs and since we did not expect to get caught by readers too often, we decided to leave it.

36. Write HTML code for a body tag in which you have gold unvisited hyperlinks, silver visited hyperlinks, and bronze active hyperlinks. Do you think this is a good combination to use? Why or why not?

37. Design a single-screen Web page about your favorite animal, using the tags described so far. That is, only use tags presented thus far in the book and do not omit any tags. Use a sensible set of colors. For example, if you love turtles, use a green background with a variation on yellow as a text color, or whatever else makes sense to you. Carefully think about your design and style when you code the page. Make sure to comment the code, explaining why you chose the colors you did.

38. Design a single-screen Web page about your favorite trail mix, using the tags described so far. (See previous exercise for further details.)

39. Describe three scenarios indicating when it would be a good idea to include a comment in an HTML file.

40. How does your browser handle embedded HTML tags within a comment? Does it try to render them?

2.7   HTML Formatting and Hyperlink Creation

At this point you should be creating and viewing simple HTML documents. This section introduces you to four more HTML tags. They are `<P>` for paragraph, `<Hi>` for heading i, `<A>` for anchor, and `<IMG>` for image. By using these tags, you can make your pages more readable, interesting, and polished. The most interesting of these tags is the anchor tag; it allows you to create hyperlinks to other Web pages.

HTML tags describe the desired structure of a Web page, rather than exactly how it should look. For example, HTML tags identify emphasized text, headings, lists, and so on, not items like 11-point font and 0.75-inch margin. Because various browsers will render the same HTML code differently, it is important not to try to force a very specific layout on a Web page. Doing so may cause the page to look fabulous using one browser and awful using another. Keep this point in mind as you increase your repertoire of HTML tags.

Hot Topic

2.7.1   Paragraph Tag

The paragraph tag is used to break the text into paragraphs. Most browsers place an empty vertical space between paragraphs so they stand apart from each other. To designate a block of text as a paragraph, enclose it within the paragraph beginning and ending tags: <P> and </P>. The ending tag is considered optional since (most) browsers assume that the current paragraph ends when the browser encounters the next <P>. Nevertheless, we recommend treating <P> as a paired tag, even though it is not mandatory. The following HTML code illustrates the use of the paragraph tag:

Hot Topic

```
<P>
This is the title sentence for the first paragraph.
You will notice that after learning a lot of HTML tags,
they are a little hard to keep straight.
This concludes paragraph one.
</P>
<P>
This is the start of paragraph two.
One good way to learn HTML tags is to practice using
them by creating Web pages.  In this way, they are
easier to remember.
This concludes paragraph two.
</P>
<P>
</P>
Yoga is an ancient art form.
```

The last paragraph tag leaves a blank vertical space between the sample text and the succeeding HTML elements. One rendering of the HTML code for the paragraph example is depicted in Figure 2.7.

Some Web authors will put a series of paragraph tags adjacent to one another to skip some vertical space. For example,

```
<P> <P> <P> <P>
```

will cause most browsers to leave approximately 1 inch of vertical space. This is the type of HTML programming we generally recommend against. Do not try to force a precise spacing, because it may look exactly as intended on your desktop, but it could look quite different to someone else using a different window size and/or browser.

FIGURE 2.7
Sample rendering of the paragraph tag example.

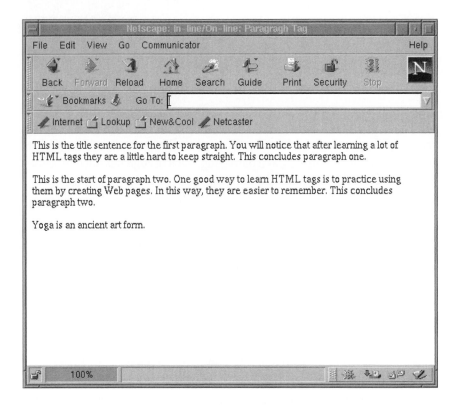

> This is the title sentence for the first paragraph. You will notice that after learning a lot of HTML tags they are a little hard to keep straight. This concludes paragraph one.
>
> This is the start of paragraph two. One good way to learn HTML tags is to practice using them by creating Web pages. In this way, they are easier to remember. This concludes paragraph two.
>
> Yoga is an ancient art form.

2.7.2   Heading Tags

In many forms of writing, it is common to include section headings to provide the reader with a sense of the document's structure. When viewing any page of text, not just material on the Web, the first things most readers notice are headings and subheadings. As an example, glance at any page of this book containing a heading and observe that it stands out from the surrounding text.

Hot Topic

Most browsers support a hierarchy of six levels of HTML headings. The beginning tag for heading i is <Hi>, where i can be any value from 1 to 6. The corresponding ending tag, as expected, is </Hi>. The largest heading is <H1> and the smallest is <H6>. Note that this is the reverse of the way sizes are specified in the font and basefont tags.

The heading tags are very useful for dividing a document into sections: the more important the section, the larger the heading tag. Subsections are usually less important and so receive smaller headings. Here is sample HTML code that illustrates the use of the heading tag.

```
<H1>Complete Sentences</H1>

Most of us would agree that well-written English ...

<H2>Fragments and Run-on Sentences</H2>

Keep in mind that rambling endlessly can lead to ...

<H3>The Phrase Fragment</H3>

Phrase fragment description goes here.

<H3>The Appositive Fragment</H3>

Appositive fragment description goes here.

<H4>Examples</H4>

There are two types of examples: sentence fragment and
sentence complete.

<H5>Sentence Fragment</H5>

<H5>Sentence Complete</H5>

<H6>Copyright, English Grammar for the Rest of Us</H6>
```

Figure 2.8 illustrates how one browser renders the example heading code. The browser determines the exact style of the headings; that is, the font size for each heading, whether the heading is boldface, whether the heading gets numbered, and so on. Notice that as the topics become more specialized, the heading sizes become smaller. Three or fewer levels of headings will suffice for most writing.

It is a fairly common practice to use level 5 or 6 headings for copyright notices and disclaimers, as Figure 2.8 shows. These headings are usually too small for anything else.

Useful Item

One important attribute of the heading tag is `ALIGN`, which can have values of `left`, `center`, or `right`. For headings that are not as long as the width of the document area, the `ALIGN` attribute has the expected effect. Caution should be exercised here. If the document is viewed in a small window, the `ALIGN` attribute may produce an undesirable appearance.

2.7.3   Anchor Tag

The anchor tag, `<A>` and `</A>`, is the mechanism by which hyperlinks are placed in hypertext documents. Its syntax is more complicated than that of most other tags. The term *anchor* is used because it indicates the static positioning of a hyperlink. In this section, we explain how to create clickable text hyperlinks, clickable images, `mailto` hyperlinks, and

FIGURE 2.8
Sample
rendering of the
heading tag
example.

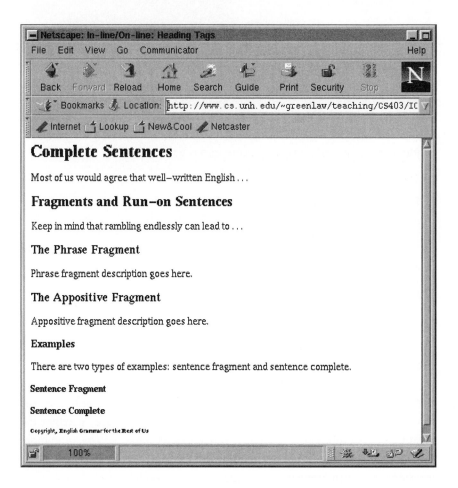

hyperlinks that point inside a document. We also provide some guidelines on hyperlink construction.

The three basic parts of a hyperlink are:

- The beginning and ending tag pair <A> ⋯ </A>.

- The HREF attribute that specifies the URL of the page to be loaded when the hyperlink is selected.

- The text (or graphic) that appears on-screen as the active link.

Clickable Text Hyperlinks
Consider the following example:

```
<A HREF = "http://www.usa.gov/documents/ ↩
        whitehouse.html">White House</A>
```

We have used the HREF attribute of the anchor tag to create a hyperlink labeled "White House." Several items about this hyperlink are worth pointing out. First, most graphical browsers will change the text color and underline the "name" of the hyperlink, which in this case is White House. When someone clicks on this phrase, the file /documents/whitehouse.html is requested from the server www.usa.gov. Second, notice that we did not leave any blank spaces before or after the text "White House." If you leave blank spaces, the hyperlink underline is drawn too wide. For example, the hyperlink,

```
<A HREF = "http://www.usa.gov/documents/ ←
        whitehouse.html">   White House  </A>
```

Useful Item

results in the following underlining:

<u> White House </u>

Third, the phrase "White House" is short and descriptive. Most users would be able to guess quickly what type of information they would be retrieving by selecting this hyperlink. In your Web pages, use short, informative hyperlink names. Finally, notice that in our example, we used an absolute URL. It is possible to use relative URLs, as well.

Clickable Image Hyperlinks

The principles behind creating a clickable image are the same as for creating a clickable text hyperlink. The type of hyperlink we describe here consists of a single image, for which one mouse click returns an HTML document. (In Section 8.5, we discuss how to define images that can have a number of mouse-sensitive areas, each with the potential to return a different Web page.) The idea is simply to replace the clickable text with an image. As an example, consider using the file wheelbarrow.gif, which contains a 50-by-50 *pixel* image called "Under Construction."

```
<A HREF = "http://www.usa.gov/wogulis/notready.html">
   <IMG SRC =  "wheelbarrow.gif"
        ALT = "Under Construction"
        HEIGHT = "50"
        WIDTH = "50">
</A>
```

If a user clicks on the wheelbarrow image, the document named notready.html will be loaded. Browsers will typically draw a highlighted border two pixels wide around the image. It is not always completely obvious that an image is a hyperlink, so it is sometimes worthwhile to add

Hot Topic

text to alert the reader to this fact. This requires some thought in order not to defeat the purpose of using the image.

Mailto Hyperlinks

It is common practice to add a `mailto` hyperlink to a Web page. This provides a convenient method for someone viewing your page to send you email. Suppose Pascal Leno has an email address of

<code>leno@oli.rustica.it</code>

and wants to include a `mailto` hyperlink labeled "Contact Pascal" on his Web page. The following code does it:

```
<A HREF = "mailto:leno@oli.rustica.it">Contact Pascal</A>
```

Note that the syntax for the `mailto:` URL is different from the `http://` URL because the double slashes are not allowed.

When the user clicks on the hyperlink "Contact Pascal," a mail dialog box (this is not your usual mail client bundled with the browser) will be launched, with the *To* field filled in with `leno@oli.rustica.it`. All the user has to do is complete the remainder of the message and send it. This presupposes that you filled in your name and email address under options or preferences for your browser, or in a public room situation, that you have verified the settings and updated them to point to you.

Intradocument Linking

Another important attribute of the anchor tag is `NAME`. The `NAME` attribute lets you create a hyperlink to any part of your document, rather than just the beginning. That is, any portion of the document can automatically be displayed at the top of the browser's document area. This is particularly useful if you have a long Web page and would like users to be able to jump to various sections of it without scrolling. Many Web authors provide an index at the top of a page, with hyperlinks that jump to other parts of the document. Using `NAME` hyperlinks means you do not have to break the document down into pieces to allow the reader easy and rapid navigation.

How are `NAME` hyperlinks created? The following HTML code demonstrates the process:

```
Welcome to the Lemonade Parade.  We serve the best
lemonade anywhere.  Each flavor has a history of its
own.  We offer
<A HREF = "#blueberry">Beautiful Blueberry</A>,
<A HREF = "#cherry">Cherry Delight</A>, and
<A HREF = "#lemon">Luscious Lemon</A>.
  . . .
```

Hot Topic

```
<A NAME = "blueberry">
<H3>Beautiful Blueberry</H3>
</A>
...

<A NAME = "cherry">
<H3>Cherry Delight</H3>
</A>
...

<A NAME = "lemon">
<H3>Luscious Lemon</H3>
</A>
...
```

A rendering of this code is shown in Figure 2.9. Note that if the hyperlink is in the same file, as in our case, the URL does not need to be specified. You can begin the HREF value with the # symbol, as shown here.

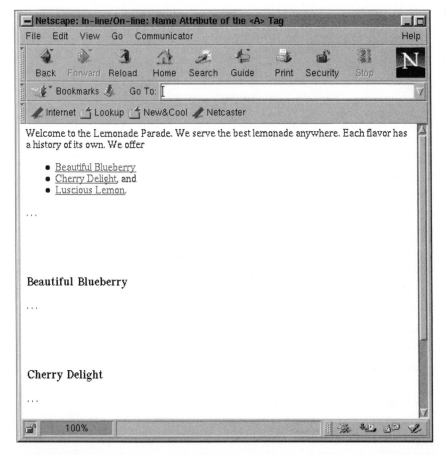

FIGURE 2.9
Sample rendering of the code used to illustrate the NAME attribute of the anchor tag.

Hot Topic

The NAME attribute is used to label three separate sections of the document. Notice that between the beginning <A> and ending </A>, we have included the section heading (in this case, for the particular flavor of beverage described). You should always include at least one line of text between the anchor tags.

You can create a hyperlink to a label by using the URL for the file in which it is contained, followed by the # symbol and then the label name, as follows:

```
HREF = "http://systemname/docpath#labelname"
```

where systemname/docpath is the URL, and labelname is the actual label used.

What is the effect of selecting one of these hyperlinks? If a user clicks on the Luscious Lemon hyperlink, for example, the cursor immediately moves down to the section labeled Luscious Lemon. Here, this section is contained in the next screen. This feature obviates the need for scrolling and provides the user with a more convenient method of accessing different parts of a long document.

Hot Topic

Hyperlink Creation Guidelines
Do:

- Carefully choose the text that goes into a hyperlink.

- Create hyperlinks that are interesting.

- Keep the hyperlink text short and descriptive.

- Create hyperlinks that read well together, even without any intervening text.

Don't:

- Use hyperlinks that may split over two or more lines.

- Use additional underlining near hyperlinks.

- Put two or more hyperlinks side by side.

- Use full-line-length hyperlinks.

- Use such phrases as "click me," "click here," or "click now."

Figure 2.10 illustrates the Don't list.

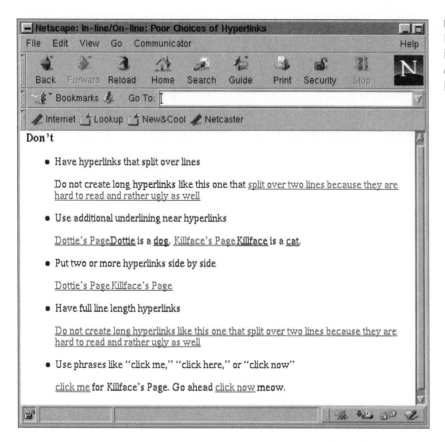

FIGURE 2.10
Examples
illustrating poor
choices of
hyperlinks.

2.7.4   Image Tag

The image tag, `<IMG>`, is used for including in-line images in HTML documents. An example of the use of the tag is:

```
<IMG SRC = "wheelbarrow.gif"
     ALT = "Under Construction"
     HEIGHT = "50"
     WIDTH = "50">
```

We will explain the meaning of this code, a number of attributes of the image tag, and several style issues. Chapter 8 contains a more comprehensive treatment of images and graphics.

The most important attribute of the image tag is SRC, which is used to specify the image to be displayed. Any type of image can be specified, using either a relative or an absolute URL, where the relative URL would relate to the document in which the image appears. The most common image types on the Web are gif, jpg, and png where png is a distant third. To include the image friend.gif in a file located in the same directory, you could use the following HTML code:

```
<IMG SRC = "friend.gif">
```

This is the minimum amount of code you can use to include an image.

When a browser retrieves a Web page, it does not automatically get the images that go along with that page. Each image must be retrieved separately. To render the document on-screen, the browser must know the sizes of the images. The browser can obtain these sizes either from code entered by the image's developer (as we recommend), or by reading the sizes as the images are brought over. The latter case takes longer, because the browser has to do the interpreting. So, a Web page will render more quickly if you include the size, using the HEIGHT and WIDTH attributes of the image tag, for each image.

Image dimensions nearly always are expressed in *pixels*. Suppose the picture friend.gif is 60 pixels wide and 90 pixels high. The following code would include the image in the Web page and would specify its dimensions to the browser:

```
<IMG SRC = "friend.gif"
     HEIGHT = "90"
     WIDTH = "60">
```

While the order in which you specify the HEIGHT and WIDTH attributes is not significant, we usually specify them in the order shown. On the other hand, a browser will list image dimensions as $x \times y$, where x is the WIDTH of the image and y is the HEIGHT.

When a browser parses this HTML code, it can determine how much space to leave for the image. Thus, the surrounding text can be rendered immediately. The browser does not have to wait until the image itself arrives. This is why you often see all of the text in a page long before all of the images are rendered.

How can you determine the size of an image? Most browsers have a "document info" menu item where you can find the dimensions of an image (in pixels). Of course, if you create an image yourself, you can record its size at that time.

The HEIGHT and WIDTH attributes can also have percentages as values, allowing them to be used to scale an image relative to the size of the browser's window. For example, the following code produces a version of friend.gif that occupies 50 percent of the browser's window in each dimension.

```
<IMG SRC = "friend.gif"
     HEIGHT = "50%"
     WIDTH = "50%">
```

You can create some interesting scaling effects by using percentages. However, when you scale an image downward, you do not reduce the amount of disk space required to store the image. Thus, it is not possible to create a reduced-size *thumbnail sketch* by using percentage values for the HEIGHT and WIDTH attributes.

Useful Item

The image tag has another interesting attribute known as ALT, which is short for "alternative." The value of ALT is a text string that usually describes the image in words. In our wheelbarrow.gif example, we used the words "Under Construction" as a value of the ALT attribute, because wheelbarrow.gif contains the picture of a wheelbarrow at a construction site. You have probably seen many Web pages that have "Under Construction" images. If a browser has images turned off, or is text-only, the words in the ALT attribute will be displayed on-screen where the image would have been. Obviously, the size of the image will not exactly match the text replacing it. Most Web authors do not worry about this detail, as most of their effort goes into making the pages look good with the images displayed.

Go On-Line

In the latest versions of some browsers, when the user mouses over an image, the text in an ALT attribute is displayed in the form of a *tooltip*. This is usually a light-colored dialog box that is just large enough for the text. For pages that contain a lot of images, the tooltips can become a distraction. This has prompted some users to stop including ALTs. Remember, however, that the purpose of ALTs is to serve those users who are unable to display images, or who are using text-based browsers. In such cases, the text of an ALT can provide the reader with some continuity.

Occasionally, square brackets have been used around the ALT attribute value. This mimics the convention adopted by some text-based browsers. However, on some browsers on some systems, this can create a problem, so we recommend against this practice. For example, do not use:

Hot Topic

```
ALT = "[Under Construction]"
```

Instead use:

```
ALT = "Under Construction"
```

As another attempt at presenting an image in a text-based browser, some extremely clever Web authors place an ASCII graphic of the original image in the ALT tag. This is interesting, but very time consuming unless you can locate a free copy of the ASCII graphic you want to include.

Useful Item

With the material we have covered so far, you should be able to include images on your Web pages. Remember to set protections on your image files, similar to what you did for your index.html file.

EXERCISES 2.7

HTML Formatting and Hyperlink Creation

41. Create an HTML document that contains the paragraph tag. What happens if you include five paragraph tags in a row, with no intermediate text? Does the paragraph tag have any attributes? If so, explain and provide examples.

42. Create an HTML document that uses heading tags. As an example, the document could outline a recent or planned backpacking trip. Focus on the outline and on the use of the heading tags, rather than on the details of the trip.

43. Does your browser support six different-sized headings, or are some of them the same size? What happens if you try to close an `<H1>` tag with `</H2>` instead of `</H1>`? Report the URL of a Web page that makes effective use of headings.

44. Explain what happens if you use an `ALIGN` value of center in an `<H4>` tag that surrounds text that is wider than the browser's document area.

45. Create an HTML document containing hyperlinks to three Web pages about the Appalachian Trail.

46. Create a Web page containing a hyperlink to itself. What happens when you click on the hyperlink? Explain.

47. Produce a Web page that has hyperlinks to three of your friends' Web pages.

48. Design a Web page that contains a `mailto` hyperlink to you. Test it. Were you able to send yourself email?

49. Create a Web page that can be used to link in the assignments for this course.

50. Code an HTML document that contains a clickable image.

51. Locate an "Under Construction" image and include it on a Web page. In addition to `SRC`, be sure to use the `ALT`, `HEIGHT`, and `WIDTH` attributes of the image tag.

52. Experiment with scaling an image. How small can you scale an image before it becomes "fuzzy"? Does this depend on the image quality with which you started? How large can you expand an image? What happens to the quality of the image as it gets larger?

The Internet

3

The Great Smoky Mountains are a wonderful place to hike, and many of our memories of Tennessee are of the Smokies. One night we camped at an altitude of 5,800 feet. We had just hiked more than 20 miles and were very tired. I only had a 40°F sleeping bag—meaning it could only keep you warm down to a 40°F outside temperature. Well, it got down to about 30°F that night. I wore all of my clothes in the sleeping bag and spent a shivering night on the mountaintop. We also encountered our first black bear in Tennessee in the Smokies. Two rangers came and drugged the bear with a special tranquilizer gun. Then they loaded him up and relocated him. We were getting in trail shape, and our boots were finally breaking our feet in (not the other way around).

Tennessee
183 miles

Chapter 3

3.1 INTRODUCTION

Even though you may have been using the Internet for a while, you may not know very much about how it works, its culture and history, and some of its uses. The goals of this chapter are therefore to:

Objectives

- Present a "definition" of the Internet and a variety of interesting facts about it.

- Discuss the history of the Internet (in the form of a timeline classifying some of the important events in the development of the Internet).

- Provide an intuitive idea of how the Internet works.

- Discuss Internet congestion and what, if anything, can be done to address it.

- Teach you about the Internet's rich culture.

- Talk about the importance of business in the Internet setting.

- Define some of the issues pertaining to *collaborative computing* and its relationship to the Internet.

3.2 The Internet Defined

Many people, including the president and vice president of the United States, refer to the Internet as the *Information Superhighway*. The extended metaphor with cars and freeways is a useful one.

The following definition of the Internet was formulated by the *Federal Networking Council (FNC)*, which passed a resolution on October 24, 1995, defining the term. The resolution states:

> The Federal Networking Council (FNC) agrees that the following language reflects our definition of the term "Internet."

"Internet" refers to the global information system that—

1. is logically linked together by a globally unique address space based on the Internet Protocol (IP) or its subsequent extensions/follow-ons;

2. is able to support communications using the Transmission Control Protocol/Internet Protocol (TCP/IP) suite or its subsequent extensions/ follow-ons, and/or other IP-compatible protocols; and

3. provides, uses or makes accessible, either publicly or privately, high level services layered on the communications and related infrastructure described herein.

This definition of the Internet can be simplified to:

The Internet is a global system of networked computers together with their users and data.

To explain, the system is global in the sense that people from all over the world can connect to it. Also, since the users of the Internet have developed their own culture, they are a defining factor of the Internet. Finally, without the possibility of accessing data or personal information, no one would be excited about connecting to the Internet.

The concept of being able to access information quickly and easily and to communicate more easily and quickly led to the vision of the Internet. Thirty years ago, information exchange and communication took place via the "backroads"—regular postal mail, a telephone call, a personal meeting, and so on. Today, they take place almost instantaneously over the Internet. The history section of this chapter describes the evolution of the Internet into today's Information Superhighway.

3.2.1 The Information Superhighway

Expanding on the freeway metaphor: with cars, there are various levels of knowledge; learning to drive is easy, and it is all you really need to know about cars. This is like learning to surf the Internet. In the course of driving, you learn about highways, shortcuts, and so on, and using the Web is very similar; that is, with practice, you will learn where and how to find things.

Also, in driving, you can go another step and learn how an engine works and how to do routine maintenance and repairs, such as oil changes and tune-ups. On the Web, the equivalent is to learn how Web pages are put together, which you have already started to do.

A still deeper level of involvement with cars is learning how to do complex repairs, or to design and build them. Not many people pursue cars to this stage. On the Web, a similar level of involvement is writing software, either building *applets* in a language such as Java, or developing more general-purpose tools for others to use in navigating the Web. Again, only a limited number of people aspire to this level.

Today, the Information Superhighway is in place, but for many people, the mysteries surrounding it involve where to go and how to travel. Like traveling a highway in a foreign country and being unable to read the road signs, navigating the Information Superhighway can be frustrating and time-consuming without the right knowledge and tools.

Consider that there are many ways to travel sidewalks, roads, and freeways to get to where we want to go. We can take a bicycle, a bus, a car, or a pair of in-line skates. Similarly, there are many ways to use the Internet to send and retrieve information. These include, but are not limited to: email, *file transfer*, *remote login*, and the Web. New methods of using the Internet will probably be conceived and developed in the near future, and existing methods will be improved.

3.2.2   Interesting Internet Facts

Another way to gain insight about the Internet is to examine a few statistics about it.

- Each day, approximately 25,000 new users go on-line.

- In early September 2000, there were 377,650,000 users worldwide. Extrapolating growth to October 2002, yields an estimate of over 400,000,000 users.

- As of July 2000, about 51 percent of Internet users in the United States were female. In other countries men still outnumber women in Internet use.

- In October 2000, the number of Internet hosts exceeded 73,000,000.

- Internet connections are available in over 200 countries.

- Every two months, the number of World Wide Web sites approximately doubles.

- It is estimated that there will be 1 billion email accounts by the year 2002, with 569 million email accounts existing at the end of 1999 (from Messaging Online).

EXERCISES 3.2

The Internet Defined

1. Update the statistics presented in this section to be as current as possible. Provide URLs for your sources.

2. Present four more interesting facts about the Internet. Explain why each is interesting to you. Provide references for your sources.

3. What conclusions can you draw from the Internet growth statistics presented in Section 3.2.2?

4. It has been said that the number of Internet users doubles every year. How long can this process go on, assuming the earth's population is six billion? Explain why the growth will slow down at some point.

3.3   Internet History

The history of the Internet is best explained with a timeline, as shown in Figure 3.1. We have included events that were important and required innovation, as well as other interesting and related items. For each item mentioned on the timeline, we provide a brief synopsis. While the timeline begins in 1969, we present some general comments on the 1960s, for background. The history of the Internet is fascinating both for itself and as a case study of technological innovation.

3.3.1   1960s Telecommunications

Essential to the early Internet concept was *packet switching*, in which data to be transmitted is divided into small packets of information and labeled to identify the sender and recipient. The packets were sent over a network and then reassembled at their destination. If any packet did not arrive or was not intact, the original sender was asked to resend the packet. Prior to packet switching, the less efficient *circuit switching* method of data transmission was used. In the early 1960s, several papers on packet switching theory were written, laying the groundwork for computer networking as it exists today.

FIGURE 3.1
Timeline
illustrating
important dates
in Internet
history.

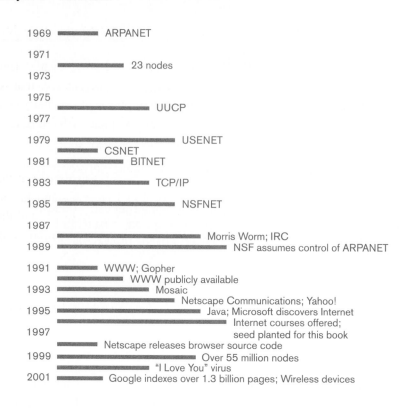

ARPANET, 1969

In 1969, Bolt, Beranek, and Newman, Inc., (*BBN*) designed a network called the *Advanced Research Projects Agency Network* (*ARPANET*) for the United States Department of Defense. The military created ARPA[1] to enable researchers to share "super-computing" power. It was rumored that the military developed the ARPANET in response to the threat of a nuclear attack that might destroy the country's communication system.

Hot Topic

Initially, only four nodes (or *hosts*) comprised the ARPANET. They were located at the University of California at Los Angeles, the University of California at Santa Barbara, the University of Utah, and the Stanford Research Institute. The ARPANET later became known as the Internet.

3.3.2   1970s Telecommunications

In this decade, the ARPANET was used primarily by the military, some of the larger companies, such as IBM, and universities (for email). The

---

1   Over the next several decades, ARPA flip-flopped between being called ARPA and *DARPA* (*Defense Advanced Research Projects Agency*). As of 1998, the name is DARPA.

general population was not yet connected to the system, and very few people were on-line at work.

The use of *local area networks* (*LANs*) became more prevalent during the 1970s. Also, the idea of an *open architecture* was promoted; that is, networks making up the ARPANET could have any design. In later years, this concept had a tremendous impact on the growth of the ARPANET.

Twenty-Three Nodes, 1972

By 1972, the ARPANET was international, with nodes in Europe at the University College in London, England, and the Royal Radar Establishment in Norway. The number of nodes on the network was up to 23, and the trend would be for that number to double every year from then on. Ray Tomlinson, who worked at BBN, invented email.

Hot Topic

UUCP, 1976

AT&T Bell Labs developed *UNIX to UNIX CoPy* (*UUCP*). In 1977, UUCP was distributed with UNIX.

USENET, 1979

User Network (*USENET*) was started by using UUCP to connect Duke University and the University of North Carolina at Chapel Hill. Newsgroups emerged from this early development.

3.3.3   1980s Telecommunications

In this decade, *Transmission Control Protocol/Internet Protocol* (*TCP/IP*), a set of rules governing how networks making up the ARPANET communicate, was established. For the first time, the term *Internet* was being used to describe the ARPANET. Security became a concern, as viruses appeared and electronic break-ins occurred.

Hot Topic

The 1980s saw the Internet grow beyond a research orientation to include business applications and a wide range of users. As the Internet grew, the *Domain Name System* (*DNS*) was developed, to allow the network to expand more easily by assigning names to host computers in a distributed fashion.

CSNET, 1980

The *Computer Science Network* (*CSNET*) connected all university computer science departments in the United States. Computer science departments were relatively new, and only a limited number existed in 1980. CSNET joined the ARPANET in 1981.

BITNET, 1981

The *Because It's Time Network* (*BITNET*) formed at the City University of New York and connected to Yale University. Many *mailing lists* originated with BITNET.

TCP/IP, 1983

The United States Defense Communications Agency required that TCP/IP be used for all ARPANET hosts. Since TCP/IP was distributed at no charge, the Internet became what is called an *open system*. This allowed the Internet to grow quickly, as all connected computers were now "speaking the same language." Central administration was no longer necessary to run the network.

NSFNET, 1985

The *National Science Foundation Network* (*NSFNET*) was formed to connect the *National Science Foundation's* (*NSF's*) five supercomputing centers. This allowed researchers to access the most powerful computers in the world, at a time when large, powerful, and expensive computers were a rarity and generally inaccessible.

The Internet Worm and IRC, 1988

The virus called *Internet Worm* (created by Robert Morris while he was a computer science graduate student at Cornell University) was released. It infected 10 percent of all Internet hosts. Also in this year, *Internet Relay Chat* (*IRC*) was written by Jarkko Oikarinen.

NSF Assumes Control of the ARPANET, 1989

NSF took over control of the ARPANET in 1989. This changeover went unnoticed by nearly all users. Also, the number of hosts on the Internet exceeded the 100,000 mark.

3.3.4   1990s Telecommunications

During the 1990s, lots of commercial organizations started getting on-line. This stimulated the growth of the Internet like never before. URLs appeared in television advertisements and, for the first time, young children went on-line in significant numbers.

Graphical browsing tools were developed, and the programming language HTML allowed users all over the world to publish on what was called the World Wide Web. Millions of people went on-line to work, shop, bank, and be entertained. The Internet played a much more significant role in society, as many nontechnical users from all walks of life got involved with computers. Computer-literacy and Internet courses sprang up all over the country.

Gopher, 1991

Gopher was developed at the University of Minnesota, whose sports teams' mascot is the the Golden Gopher. Gopher allowed you to "go for" or fetch files on the Internet using a menu-based system. Many gophers sprang up all over the country, and all types of information could be located on gopher servers. Gopher is still available and accessible through Web browsers, but its popularity has faded; for the most part, it is only of historical interest.

World Wide Web, 1991

The *World Wide Web* (*WWW*) was created by Tim Berners-Lee at CERN (a French acronym for the European Laboratory for Particle Physics) as a simple way to publish information and make it available on the Internet.

Hot Topic

WWW Publicly Available, 1992

The interesting nature of the Web caused it to spread, and it became available to the public in 1992. Those who first used the system were immediately impressed.

Mosaic, 1993

Mosaic, a graphical browser for the Web, was released by Marc Andreessen and several other graduate students at the University of Illinois, the location of one of NSF's supercomputing centers. Sometimes you will see Mosaic referred to as *NCSA Mosaic*, where NCSA stands for the *National Center for Supercomputing Applications*. Mosaic was first released under X Windows and graphical UNIX. To paraphrase a common idiom, each person who used the system loved it and "told five friends," and Mosaic's use spread rapidly.

Hot Topic

Netscape Communications, 1994

The company called *Netscape Communications*, formed by Marc Andreessen and Jim Clark, released *Netscape Navigator*, a Web browser that captured the imagination of everyone who used it. The number of users of this software grew at a phenomenal rate. Netscape made (and still makes) its money largely through advertising on its Web pages.

Yahoo!, 1994

Stanford graduate students David Filo and Jerry Yang developed their Internet search engine and directory called *Yahoo!*, which is now world-famous.

Java, 1995

The Internet programming environment, *Java*, was released by *Sun Microsystems, Inc.* This language, originally called *Oak*, allowed programmers to develop Web pages that were more interactive.

Microsoft Discovers the Internet, 1995

The software giant committed many of its resources to developing its browser, *Microsoft Internet Explorer*, and Internet applications.

Internet Courses Offered in Colleges, 1995

Some of the first courses about the Internet were given in 1995. Course development has been difficult, because of the rapidly changing software.

Netscape Releases Source Code, 1998

Netscape Communications released the source code for its Web browser.

Over 55 Million Nodes, 1999

The number of Internet hosts grew to over 55,000,000.

"I Love You" Virus, 2000

The "I Love You" virus spread from the Philippines and infected millions of computers worldwide.

Google Indexes Over 1.3 Billion Web Pages, 2001

The search engine *Google* has a huge index of more than 1.3 billion Web pages.

Wireless Devices, 2001

Many people now browse the Web and send email over the Internet using wireless computer technology.

3.3.5   Internet Growth

Hot Topic

The Internet is still growing at a rate of 100 percent each year; as of 2001, the number of computers linked to the Internet was over 100 million and increasing. What permitted the technology to be adaptable enough to handle this amazing growth? Over the past three decades, the Internet has proven to be extremely flexible. Even though there were no personal computers, workstations, or LANs when the early Internet came into being, the emerging Internet was versatile enough to be able to incorporate these new technologies. The early researchers working on Internet technology may have had no inkling that what they were designing would one day accommodate such a thing as the World Wide Web and other applications for hundreds of millions of users. The built-in flexibility has been a key to this continuing growth.

In retrospect, there were a number of key reasons for the Internet's great success:

1.   Decisions were made on a technical rather than political basis, especially without the need for international political groups.

2.   The Internet did not require a centralized structure that would not scale up; it was and is a distributed operation.

3.   Due to the homogeneity of language and outlook, a sharp focus on the Internet itself could be maintained.

4.   The Internet allowed people to do things of inherent interest, such as sending and receiving email.

5.   The software involved was free or very low cost.

Based on past history, we can assume that the Internet will continue to grow, change, and support new applications. Now, however, instead of only researchers initiating change and implementing new ideas, we also see entrepreneurs and politicians getting involved. Both small and large businesses will play an important role in setting new trends, and we can anticipate a dynamic and exciting future for the Internet.

EXERCISES 3.3

Internet History

5.   Fill in five more important events in the timeline during the years 1994–97. List your sources.

6.   Research one item from the Internet timeline in more detail, and prepare a one-page Web document about it. Include the sources you referenced in the document, and use as many HTML tags as appropriate.

7.   Plot the number of users of the Internet on a yearly basis since 1980. Label the x-axis with the years 1980, 1981, ..., through the present, and the y-axis with the number of users. Using your plot, extrapolate to predict how many users there will be one year, two years, five years, and ten years from now. What assumptions did you make in performing your extrapolation?

8. According to our timeline, in 1983 TCP/IP was mandated for all ARPANET hosts. Why was this significant in promoting the growth of the Internet?

9. Suppose you bought 100 shares of stock in each of the following: Microsoft in 1986, CISCO Systems in 1990, and Netscape Communications in 1995. Assuming you did not reinvest the dividends, how many shares of each stock would you have today? What was the original stock in each company worth and what is their stock worth today? That is, what was your original total investment in each company, and what is your current total investment in each?

10. Look into the history of non-English Web pages. What foreign languages are supported? When did support for them originate? How widely are they supported? Can you locate any foreign language Web pages about the Appalachian Trail? What do you see for the future of non-English languages on the Web?

3.4   The Way the Internet Works

Here we present an intuitive look at how the Internet works, again using the analogy of a highway system. Keep in mind that this is a simplified description. Additional technical details can be found in the references.

3.4.1   Network Benefits

To begin our discussion of the Internet, we first identify some of the benefits of networks in general.

- *Provide convenience*—Computers on a network can back up their files over the network.

- *Allow sharing*—Networked computers can share resources, such as disks and printers.

- *Facilitate communications*—Sending and receiving email, transferring files, and videoconferencing are examples of how networks promote communication.

- *Generate savings*—Networked computers can provide more computing power for less money. Several small computers connected on a network can provide as much as or more computing power than a single, large computer and will cost much less. Also, since resources can be shared, not everyone needs their own peripherals, which can result in a substantial cost savings.

- *Provide reliability*—If one part of a network is down, useful work may still be possible using a different network path.

- *Simplify scalability*—It is relatively easy to add more computers to an existing network.

3.4.2   Interconnected Networks and Communication

The Internet is essentially a network of networks, and its success depends upon "cooperation." Since no one person, organization, or government is responsible for the Internet, cooperation among the networks and computers that compose the Internet is paramount. This cooperation is accomplished by a common set of protocols. The protocol that determines how computers connect, send, and receive information on the Internet is Transmission Control Protocol/Internet Protocol (TCP/IP). In fact, TCP/IP consists of about 100 different protocols, and new ones are developed and added regularly. Drawing on the freeway analogy, think of these protocols as forming the rules of the road, ranging from who has the right of way to how you register your vehicle and get a driver's license.

TCP/IP has been described as the "language of the Internet." In the same way that a common language allows people of diverse backgrounds to communicate, TCP/IP allows many different kinds of computers, from personal computers to mainframes, to exchange information. The two main protocols in the TCP/IP suite are TCP and IP. TCP permits communication between the various computers on the Internet, while IP specifies how data is routed from computer to computer.

To illustrate how TCP/IP works, consider either sending an email message or requesting a Web page. In either case, the information is "formatted" according to its specific application protocol: Simple Mail Transfer Protocol (SMTP) is used for your email message, and HyperText Transfer Protocol (HTTP) is used for your Web page request. Assuming that TCP/IP software is installed on your computer, the information to be sent is split into *IP packets*, called *packets* for short, and transmitted over the Internet. The advantages of packets are as follows:

- *Error recovery*—If a packet gets corrupted, only that (small) packet needs to be resent, not the entire message.

- *Load distribution*—If one area of the network is congested, packets can be rerouted to less busy areas.

- *Flexibility*—If the network experiences a failure or disruption in one locale, packets can be rerouted.

Figure 3.2 depicts the process of splitting a message into packets.

In addition to the message pieces, each packet of data also contains information about the computer that sent it, the computer it is being sent to, a *sequence number* indicating where the packet fits in the overall message, and error checking information to ensure that the packet is not corrupted while in transit. The packets are reassembled after being received at the destination computer. A message is sent from the destination computer to the sending computer to resend any missing or corrupted packets. Using this method, called packet switching, it is not necessary to send the data packets in sequential order, or even over the same network route. If packets arrive out of order, the sequence numbers can be used to reconstruct the original message. Figure 3.2 shows how this is done, with packets 8 and 5 still incoming. After receiving the message, the destination computer

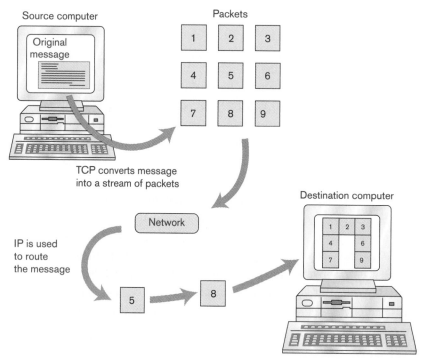

FIGURE 3.2
Schematic of message split into packets and sent over the Internet.

responds, either by delivering the email message to the recipient's mailbox or by servicing the request for a Web page, as required.

In the scenario we have described, suppose that a packet does get corrupted. The destination computer must send a message requesting that the packet be resent. You may wonder what happens if the "resend" message gets corrupted or lost. While we cannot get into such details here, we can say that the protocols must be complex enough to recover from all types of worst-case error situations. Protocol design is a complicated process.

3.4.3 Physical Components

In addition to the various software protocols, the Internet includes a host of physical components as well. These components include servers, routers, and the networks themselves. *Servers* are computers that answer requests for services, such as list servers, mail servers, and news servers.

A *router* is a special-purpose computer that directs data packets along the network. Routers can detect whether part of the network is down or congested and can then reroute traffic. Think of a router as a highly efficient and well-functioning traffic cop.

Networks provide the physical means to transport packets of information. The following mediums are used:

- Copper wires, which transmit messages as electrical impulses.

- Fiber-optic cables, which use light waves to transmit messages.

- Radio waves, microwaves, infrared light, and visible light, which all carry messages through air.

3.4.4 Network Connections

Someone connecting to the Internet from home generally uses a *modem* and a regular telephone line (copper wire) to connect to an *Internet Service Provider* (*ISP*). A second modem at the ISP's end completes the connection, and the slower of the two modem speeds determines the maximum connection speed, usually 56 *kilobits* per second (Kbps). A kilobit is 1,000 bits. Many people use the term *bit rate* and *baud rate* interchangeably.[2] It is worth noting that some important parts of the network are still

---

2 Technically, there are differences between the two.

audio-based, such as the part of the phone system in your home or office. The modem is needed to convert from *analog* to digital and back again.

A business, organization, or school network typically uses *network interface cards* instead of modems to connect the personal computers that are part of their LANs. These systems often have a higher-speed connection, usually 56 Kbps or better, to their ISPs. Such connections are usually leased from the telephone company.

Another option is an *Integrated Services Digital Network* (*ISDN*), which is slightly more expensive[3] but uses regular telephone lines and replaces modems with special adaptors up to five times faster than a traditional modem. Another possibility, not yet widely available but definitely on the horizon, is a cable television connection. Bill Gates and Craig MacCaw's new company, *Teledesic*, is going to put 288 low-earth-orbit satellites in the sky and offer data service everywhere. The company has awarded Boeing a contract to begin the project. Teledesic is expected to be operational in 2003.

If the connection to the ISP is a "driveway" in our highway analogy, then the backbones of the Internet are the "freeways." These freeways are run by *Network Service Providers* (*NSPs*). Local ISPs connect to NSP networks like IBM's Advantis or networks provided by AT&T, MCI, or Sprint. The connection between the ISPs and NSPs is over leased lines from local telephone companies. These phone lines typically transmit data at a rate of 1.54 *megabits* per second (Mbps). A megabit is 1,000,000 bits.

The NSPs lease or buy lines consisting of copper wire, fiber-optic cable, or satellite communications from large telecommunications companies. The NSP networks, like a freeway, can operate at very high speeds and can transmit a lot of data over long distances.

In summary, to access the Internet, a user connects to a local ISP through a modem or ISDN adapter (or possibly some other method). The ISPs connect to the larger NSP networks through leased lines from the local telephone companies. To transmit a message over the Internet, TCP/IP divides the message into packets that are sent over the lines and directed by routers to their destination. When the packets arrive at their destination computer, they are reassembled and the destination computer responds to any request. Figure 3.3 illustrates the entire process.

---

3   Costs vary widely across the telephone systems and are often tariffed to be a lot more than a modem. Installation may be hundreds of dollars and rates can be $100 to $150 per month.

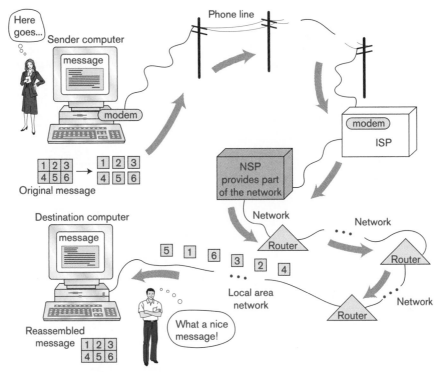

FIGURE 3.3
Illustration of a message split into packets, routed to destination through an ISP and an NSP, and reassembled.

3.4.5   Client-Server Model

In Figure 1.8, we showed how mail clients and servers interact. Browsers, also called Web clients, and Web servers were described in Chapter 2. The interaction between clients and servers can be generalized to other applications. Figure 3.4 depicts the general arrangement known as the *client-server model*. In the picture, only one client is shown, although a large number of clients typically use a small number of servers. A client makes a request to the server and the server responds by satisfying the client's request.

The client-server model provides many of the network benefits described in Section 3.4.1. For example, the client-server model is easily extendable and therefore scales well; that is, new clients and servers can be added incrementally as more users come on-line and the demand for services increases. Many clients can share the resources provided by a single server. This eliminates the need for each client to have their own "copy" of those resources.

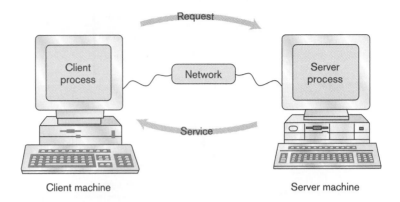

Each Internet service has its own associated set of clients and servers. We have already seen examples in the email and Web domains, and later we will see others.

3.4.6   IP Addresses

Each computer and router on the Internet must have a name so that it can be uniquely identified. After all, how can an email message be delivered if there is an ambiguity in its destination? While the *domain name* provides a convenient people-oriented computer naming framework that uses symbolic names, computers are better suited to manipulating numbers. *IP addresses* are numerical names that uniquely identify each computer on the Internet.

An IP address consists of 32 bits, or four *bytes*. (A byte consists of eight bits.) In Table 2.2, we saw that the largest possible eight-bit number was 255. Thus, one byte can represent a number from 0 (00000000) to 255 (11111111). Oversimplifying, each IP address consists of a *network component* and a *host component*. Figure 3.5a illustrates the concept. Each of the four bytes of an IP address can represent a natural number from 0–255. It is common to express IP addresses as four natural numbers separated by dots. Figure 3.5b shows an example, and part (c) shows the corresponding binary numbers.

IP addresses play a vital role in the routing of packets over the Internet. Source and destination IP addresses are included in each packet. In essence, the addresses provide directions on where the packet should go. How are IP addresses assigned? A central authority manages IP addresses; otherwise, conflicts might arise. The *Network Information Center* (*NIC*) is in charge of assigning IP addresses. (However, there is a plan to expand to multiple registries. It is not yet clear how they will coordinate.)

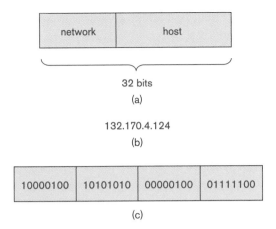

FIGURE 3.5
(a) Schematic of
an IP address;
(b) the customary
way of writing an
IP address;
(c) the binary
equivalent of the
IP address
from (b).

What is the relationship between IP addresses and domain names? IP addresses are 32-bit numbers, whereas domain names are easy-to-remember symbolic strings. When you type in an email address, you always enter a symbolic string such as

```
rudolph@northpole.org
```

How does a computer use this, since it needs to work with IP addresses? A program called a *resolver* takes care of the translation; that is, the program converts a symbolic name into its corresponding IP address. Think of the resolver as functioning in a manner similar to telephone directory assistance. On some systems, there is a program that allows you to enter an IP address and obtain its symbolic name back, or vice versa. An example on UNIX-based systems is the program *nslookup*. It is important to realize that for each symbolic name, there is a unique IP address.

On occasion, you may come across an IP address. For example, while surfing the Web you might see a message such as "invalid IP address." When this happens, there is usually a problem with the computer name you specified. Either you typed the name wrong, or the server was not responding for some reason. Other times, you may see a message like "host name could not be resolved." Again, the first thing to do is check your spelling. If you configure TCP/IP or *Point-to-Point Protocol* (*PPP*) for your computer, you may have to enter an IP address for your domain name server. If you use an ISP, you may need to obtain this address from them. (See Appendix A for more about ISPs.)

A permanently assigned IP address, one that is given to a computer or router connected to the Internet, is called a *static IP address*. If you connect to the Internet through an ISP, then typically each time you connect, you

Useful Item

will be assigned a different IP address, called a *dynamic IP address*, from the ISP's pool of IP addresses.

3.4.7   Internet Protocol Version 6 (IPv6)

Hot Topic

IPv6 is the latest version of the IP routing protocol. It was originally called IPng (*next generation*) and is still under development. The new protocol is necessary to accommodate the greater demands being placed on the Internet. The major changes in the new version will be:

- *More addresses*—This will be done by increasing the IP address size from 32 to 128 bits.

- *Simplified IP headers*—The number of header fields needed in an IP packet will be reduced.

- *Added security features*—The new protocol will provide greater support for privacy and security.

Go On-Line

In other words, IPv6 is being designed with many efficiency considerations in mind. You can find additional details about IPv6 on the Web.

3.4.8   Web Page Retrieval

Suppose you select the following URL:

`http://pubpages.oklahoma.edu/~bosworth/food/menu.html`

either by clicking on a hyperlink or by entering this URL in the location field of your browser and hitting the return key. How is this Web page retrieved? Having discussed browsers, DNS, IP, IP addresses, TCP, URLs, and Web servers, we are now in a position to answer this question. The following steps occur, in the order listed:

1. Based on your actions, the browser determines that the URL you selected was

   `http://pubpages.oklahoma.edu/~bosworth/food/menu.html`

   The how part of the URL is `http`.

2. Using the where part of the URL, the browser queries the DNS for the IP address `pubpages.oklahoma.edu`.

3. In this case, suppose the DNS responds with the IP address

   172.177.173.2.

4. The browser next establishes a TCP connection to 172.177.173.2. The default *port* for Web servers is port 80. Think of the browser as letting pubpages know it wants to talk on a reserved category called "80."

5. The browser then sends a message asking for the what part of the URL,

   ~bosworth/food/menu.html

6. The server, pubpages.oklahoma.edu, services this request and sends back the file menu.html.

7. The TCP connection is closed. This ends the "conversation" between the client and the server.

8. The browser renders the text portion of the HTML code contained in the file menu.html.

9. The browser repeats these steps to obtain any in-line images contained in the file menu.html.

10. The browser displays the images as they are retrieved.

This procedure can easily be generalized to illustrate how any Web page is retrieved. Notice that a separate TCP connection is required to bring over each in-line image. This fact explains why images load last when a new Web page is brought over, and why a Web page containing a lot of images takes a long time to load.

EXERCISES 3.4

The Way the Internet Works

11. Find out what ISPs are available in your area and what connection options they offer. Can you directly connect to an NSP? What is the highest (fastest) connection rate available to you?

12. Determine how your school, organization, or company is actually connected to the Internet. Draw a small map to illustrate your connection.

13. Write a short Web page about the current state of cable television connections. List your sources.

14. Define and explain two additional positive benefits of networks.

15. To help you appreciate the complexity of protocols, describe in detail the "protocol" for waterproofing hiking boots. For example you first take them off your feet, . . .

16. Write a short Web page where you compare the network of hiking trails making up the Appalachian Trail and its connecting trails to a physical computer network. What role do hikers play on the Appalachian Trail? Are they analogous to packets? What about IP addresses?

17. To help you appreciate the complexity of protocols, describe in detail the "protocol" for making a telephone call. For example, you lift the receiver off the hook, . . .

18. In Section 3.4.5, we explained how the client-server model supports the network benefits of scalability and sharing. How does the client-server model relate to the other network benefits described in Section 3.4.1?

19. There is a movement to change the addressing scheme of the Internet. Conduct a search on-line for proposals about new addressing schemes and summarize your findings.

20. Experiment with your browser to try and find the answer to the following question: If an HTML document contains a number of identical copies of the same image, does the browser bring over multiple copies of the image, or is it "smart" enough to reuse the first copy it brings over?

3.5   Internet Congestion

The Internet works amazingly well for such a heavily used system. However, the number of users and their demands continue to grow almost without bound. In this section, you will learn what researchers are trying to do to reduce congestion on the Internet. First, we consider some of the limiting factors, from a user's point of view.

Once you get a network connection (assuming you have a modem with a speed of 28.8 Kbps or higher), the factor limiting how quickly you can view Web pages often becomes the speed with which your computer renders the pages. The computer speed depends on a complex balance of CPU speed, bus speed, memory quantity, disk speed, and so on. In addition, there is a hierarchy of link speeds, with major backbones aiming for OC12 (622.1 Mbps),[4] more and more regional and site-direct T3 (44.7 Mbps) links, and T1 (1.5 Mbps) links to institutions. The slowest link speed involved in a connection determines the overall level of performance. The rate of growth of the Internet is so rapid that it is hard for technological improvements to keep up.

3.5.1 World Wide Wait Problem

The phrase *World Wide Wait* has been around awhile, especially overseas, where connections are notoriously slow. For example, in Spain, Internet users say,

```
Espera en la Red Mundial
```

The literal translation of this phrase is "Wait in the World Network." It refers to the ever-increasing delays experienced when trying to access information on the Internet.

With the advent of the World Wide Web and the development of graphical browsers came a surge of interest in the Internet. This increase in the number of Internet users, coupled with the accompanying requests for Web pages containing elaborate in-line images, sound, and video clips, has degraded the speed of the Internet to the point where the Information Superhighway sometimes appears to have a traffic jam. Although new technologies are being employed to remedy the situation, the problem persists and is getting worse. We will discuss what is currently being done to address the problem and what we can expect in the future.

3.5.2 Technical Solutions

Researchers working in conjunction with the *World Wide Web Consortium*[5] (*W3C*) are addressing the issue of network congestion. One of their stated goals is to "save the Internet from the Web" by developing new technologies to help relieve the slowdown that has resulted from retrieving and displaying Web pages.

Hot Topic

Hot Topic

---

4   OC stands for *optical carrier*.
5   The W3C provides an open forum to facilitate communication between people dealing with matters related to the World Wide Web. The *Internet Engineering Task Force* (*IETF*) plays a similar role regarding the Internet. The official documents developed by the IETF are called *Requests for Comments* (*RFCs*).

Some of the solutions offered involve HTTP itself, as well as improvements in the way HTTP and TCP/IP interact. In particular, the researchers have focused on the following issues:

- Improving the process of connecting to a Web server.

- Introducing new techniques to expedite Web page requests.

- Refining how a URL is resolved, using "persistent connections" that make it more efficient to retrieve pages from the same Web server.

W3C researchers have also put forth some suggestions for Web page design. Since Web page content (that is, the graphics, sound, text, and/or video that make up the page) dictates download time, one recommendation is to avoid unnecessary graphics. *Cascading Style Sheets* (*CSS*), a Web page design tool, also has the potential to improve download time. Finally, the researchers recommend using the *Portable Network Graphics* (*PNG*) format over the *Graphics Interchange Format* (*GIF*) for images on Web pages, since PNG images are generally smaller than GIF images and they render more quickly.

Another active step being taken is a reduction in the size of router tables by rearranging how blocks of addresses are identified. Routers face a formidable task when data flows at 44.7 Mbps or faster. They must examine each packet to see where it is going, look up that destination, and then send the packet on its way. They cannot fall behind, because they would never catch up. Packets that cannot be resolved in the *threshold time* are thrown away and must be retransmitted.

By developing these and other technological improvements, researchers and the W3C are trying to ease the Internet congestion created by the World Wide Web. It is believed that these new technologies can reduce Internet traffic due to the Web by up to 50 percent. However, network traffic is increasing in many dimensions. New users are being added, and experienced users are requesting more information and spending more time on the Web. Thus, although suggestions like those given here are worthwhile if many users treat them seriously, they are actually expected to provide very little noticeable relief.

3.5.3   Issues and Predictions

While recent technological advances have been significant, they have not yet managed to alleviate the World Wide Wait problem. Some users try to deal with the slowdown by using the Internet during less busy periods. Still others, frustrated by the delays and failures in transmitting and receiving information, may severely limit their use of the Internet. Plans have moved forward to create the "Internet II" to be used exclusively by academia and researchers, with no commercial traffic permitted, and with operation at much higher speeds. A number of businesses are already bypassing the Internet and are creating isolated *intranets* for their companies. An intranet is a private network. Such networks can have their own internal Web.

Hot Topic

One reason why the Internet has become so popular, especially in the United States, is that it is very inexpensive. Most ISPs offer a flat-rate plan that allows for unlimited usage for a single, low monthly fee. Some economists feel it may be time to charge more for the use of the Internet in order to limit demand.

Originally, the government financed the Internet. Now, users pay ISPs to connect them, ISPs pay NSPs, and NSPs pay the long-haul carrier. The payments are not based on hours of use, but on how much capacity is provided. This contrasts with the telephone billing system, in which there is a unit charge based on how far the call travels and/or how long it lasts. If the telephone system were run like the Internet (and were just as cheap), the demand for phone service would greatly increase, as would delays and busy signals. However, since the telephone system is comparatively expensive, people have figured out ways of having "phone" conversations over the Internet.

To reflect the true costs involved in using the Internet, some economists have suggested prioritizing information and then charging more for high-priority transmissions. Another idea is to charge (more) for transmissions that occur when Internet traffic is heavy. How to meter usage once a billing method is selected is currently being investigated.

It seems clear that unless technology offers a viable solution to the World Wide Wait problem, our days of surfing the Web for "free" could be numbered.

EXERCISES 3.5

Internet Congestion

21. How long have you been using the Internet? Do you notice a more significant delay in retrieving documents now than you used to? Do you try to restrict your access to the Internet to certain times of the day? Have you ever surfed the Web from a foreign country? Describe your experience.

22. How many times a week do you get a "busy signal" when you try to connect to a site? That is, the server refuses your connection. Do you use your browser's **Stop** button more often than before to cancel a Web page request that seems to be taking forever to load?

23. A lot of people in Europe and Japan are heavy users of the Internet. Based on the different time zones and the fact that the majority of Internet users are located in the United States, when would you expect the World Wide Wait problem to be the worst? Explain your answer.

24. Write a short Web page describing the current state of the art for placing a "phone" call over the Web. Describe the hardware necessary and its cost. Do you believe this technology will take a significant amount of business away from the telephone companies at some time in the future?

25. What methods are being suggested to meter network usage? Describe them. In a Web page, summarize your thoughts about metering network usage.

3.6   Internet Culture

An entire culture has sprung up around the Internet. What began as an exclusive club for researchers and academics is now open to the masses. Some of the original club members are not happy about this transition. The Internet has emerged from being a research medium to one that includes advertising, commerce, and forums for exchanging ideas on a nearly infinite set of subjects. Here we describe the philosophy of this unique culture and some important issues to bear in mind while browsing.

3.6.1   Critical Evaluation of Information

Hot Topic

Since the Internet is not regulated for content (and there are no immediate plans to regulate it), anything and everything can be found on the Web. The editorial control that is applied to traditional print media is missing. Being able to distinguish between inaccurate and accurate information is a necessary part of the Internet culture. Experienced Internet users know that not everything published on the Web is sound. They are cautious about believing anything they read, looking at information with a critical eye.

To find valuable information, you need to be able to sift through Web pages and separate the useful from the useless, the valid from the invalid.

Suspect information can appear on the Internet in any form: email messages, mailing lists, newsgroups, or Web pages. For example, in the 1996 U. S. presidential campaign, bogus presidential Web pages were published.

What are some reliable forms of information? Web presentations that contain refereed and reviewed information, or are monitored for accuracy, could be considered reliable. An example would be electronic journals whose contents are refereed. Commercial presentations also try to provide accurate and up-to-date information, since their reputations depend on presenting valid information. Some authors, by the very nature of who they are, can be trusted to display only accurate information. For example, if Miguel Indurain, five-time winner of the Tour de France, had a Web presentation about cycling, you could assume that the information about the Tour de France would be accurate.

How can you critically evaluate information? You might start by asking the following questions:

Useful Item

- *Who wrote the information?*—Was the person who wrote the material knowledgeable and careful? Was the author aware of what others have written? Does the author have a reputation to uphold? Can the author be trusted? What is the author's professional background?

- *Is the writing quality high?*—A document riddled with typos is more likely to have inaccurate content than a carefully crafted Web page.

- *Is the document up to date?*—Try to determine whether the information is current. When was it last updated? Does the document deal with up-to-date information?

- *Are there obvious errors in the content?*—For example, if you know that the game of baseball requires 9 players on a team and the document you are reading says it only requires 6, be wary.

3.6.2 Freedom of Expression

The lack of regulation that permits the proliferation of information on the Internet also facilitates the interchange of ideas. Anyone with an Internet connection can express their views globally. This also allows small groups of people with something in common to find each other. For example, there are people with very rare medical problems who can offer each other support and can exchange experiences in coping. Many believe that this freedom of expression is the best, and most defining, feature of the Internet. A large number of Web authors exhibit this fact by displaying a small blue-ribbon graphic at the bottom of their pages in support of on-line freedom of speech.

Hot Topic

Related to the idea of personal expression is another aspect of Internet culture—not everyone agrees that everything and anything should be publishable. For example, some people find the availability of obscene or offensive material on the Internet unacceptable. Other people worry that small children may stumble across something they should not see or read. These concerns are definitely valid, and several camps are busy discussing them.

What constitutes obscene material? What is pornographic material? Certainly, not everyone is in agreement on the answers to these questions. However, there are legal definitions of *obscenity* and *pornography*, and corresponding bodies of case law. Problems arise when there is an attempt to legislate restrictions without a careful definition of what is covered. For example, child pornography is subject to proscription by special laws, and that might seem clear, but questions are now arising as to whether they apply to computer animations or simulations in which no real children are involved.

In the early days of the Internet, many users were young, technically oriented males from universities and research laboratories who were, relatively speaking, like-minded. Today, people from all walks of life are getting information from and publishing on the Internet—children as well as adults. For some people, the accessibility of offensive material has created a negative image of the Internet. Unfortunately, some people lose sight of all of the great benefits that the Internet provides:

- More educational opportunities for both children and adults.

- The ability to communicate more readily with others all over the world.

- The sharing of research ideas and information.

- The convenience of performing many functions, such as banking and shopping, on-line.

- Opportunities for entertainment.

- Rapid and global dissemination of important information.

- Worldwide discussion forums to promote solutions to global problems.

Prohibiting material on a specific topic from being published on-line diminishes freedom of expression. On the other hand, parents, for example, may feel their freedoms are being violated if they cannot have the Internet and its benefits without risking unintended exposure of their children to "unacceptable" information. The issue of *censorship* is a volatile one that has both supporters and opponents in the Internet community, and the issues involved in worldwide censorship are very complex.

One possible compromise being tried is the use of labels to identify the content of Web pages. Authors can thus steer viewers away who might be offended by the material or for whom the material might be inappropriate. The *Platform for Internet Content Selection (PICS)* provides a set of technical specifications for designating such labels. (PICS was initially designed to aid parents and teachers in limiting what children could access on the Internet.) The PICS specifications work with vendor-supplied filtering software (some of which is already built into browsers) and rating services. Some currently available PICS-based software systems and their distributors are: *Net Shepherd* (Net Shepherd), *Cyber Patrol* and *Cyber Sentry* (Microsystems Software), *Surfwatch* (Spyglass), and *Internet Explorer 3.0* (Microsoft). In addition, some ISPs offer PICS-based filtering.

The Internet leaps borders and boundaries, so that content that is legal in the jurisdiction where it is created could be illegal in some other part of the world. Does this mean that the creator should be subject to the lowest common denominator of "acceptable" conduct? Experience with book publishing shows that there are few, if any, books that would not be subject to banning by some group, if they could. This suggests that the proper place for content control is with the content viewer, not the creator. PICS is one approach to this solution.

Although PICS provides an alternative to government control of Internet content, many are still concerned about promoting any censorship technology. The case concerning filters and PICS is not clear-cut. The issues involved are similar to those concerning media, such as cassette tapes and compact disks. However, although you can buy a CD without buying an offensive one, you cannot get only partial Internet access without using filters. There are many overlapping and conflicting interests in the way *cyberspace* develops, and we all need to be active, informed participants.

3.6.3   Communication Mechanisms

Another aspect of Internet culture is created by the communication channels that the Internet has spawned. People from all over the world can exchange ideas via email, *Internet Relay Chat (IRC)*, instant messaging, mailing lists, newsgroups, and so on. Since there are no facial expressions, voice inflections, or body language to convey or interpret these communications, users must avoid ambiguity or misunderstanding by either spelling things out completely or using *emoticons*. Table 3.1 depicts a number of common

■ TABLE 3.1
■ Emoticons.

Emoticon	Meaning
O:-)	angel
>:-)	devil
:-(	frown
:-[	grim
:-D	laugh
:-)	smile
:-o	surprise
;-)	wink

emoticons. While *videoconferencing* is a way to include the otherwise missing audio and video, this technology is still in its infancy.

To save time when typing messages, users sometimes employ a (friendly) shorthand for commonly used phrases:

- AFAIK—As Far As I Know.

- BRB—Be Right Back.

- BTW—By The Way.

- FOAF—Friend Of A Friend.

- FWIW—For What It's Worth.

- IMHO—In My Humble Opinion (usually not so humble, of course).

- LOL—Laughing Out Loud.

- ROTFL—Rolling On The Floor Laughing.

- RTFM—Read The Fine Manual (you might see this if you ask for something that is explained in a manual).

- TY—Thank You.

- TTYL—Talk To You Later.

- YMMV—Your Mileage May Vary.

Even when you are trying to be very clear (or perhaps because of it), people may sometimes misinterpret or take offense at a message. Being rude or overly confrontational is called *flaming*, and such messages are called *flames*. Some people find it easy to be rude when they do not have to confront a person face to face, while others are just plain unaware of how their messages come across. Flaming is not considered appropriate on the Internet; it violates the commonly accepted guidelines of netiquette.

3.6.4   Advertising

Prior to 1995, there was very little advertising on the Internet. Along with the Web has come an avalanche of advertisements. Users who began surfing the Web in 1996 or later are accustomed to ads, but those who started earlier remember the days of very limited advertising.

Ads generate huge incomes for such companies as Netscape Communications, Infoseek, and Yahoo!. The Web pages of these companies get millions of hits per day, so an ad placed on one of their Web pages has a tremendous audience. Naturally, marketing experts take advantage of this potential consumer base.

Most of the ads shown on Web pages are clickable images. They are typically about one inch high and three to four inches wide. Many of the most popular Web pages have *revolving advertisements*; that is, each time you revisit the page, or while you are visiting the page, you get a different ad. The ads usually consist of a carefully designed graphic with a catchy phrase superimposed over it. When you click on the graphic, the advertiser's Web page loads.

Many users manage to browse the Web without paying too much attention to the advertisements, other than noticing that the ads slow down the loading process. Obviously, the ads influence some people, because companies continue to invest huge amounts of money in them.

The marketing techniques for advertising on the Web are also becoming more sophisticated. An industry is developing to monitor who visits what sites, so that ads can be targeted more specifically to certain users.

The style, form, and content of ads is a rapidly emerging part of the Internet culture.

3.6.5   Societal Impact

The Internet has had an enormous impact on society, and its influence will no doubt continue. Nearly all facets of life have been affected. Many people now work in Internet-related jobs, either building computer network components, writing software, creating Web pages, performing marketing research, designing graphics, or conducting business on the Web. Unless you are hiking the Pacific Crest Trail, you will probably run across at least a few URLs every day (yet even on the trail, people are carrying laptop computers). Many people obtain all their information and perform most of their communication using the Internet. Such things as weather, news, stock prices, and travel information are accessed by millions of users every day. It is difficult to think of any areas of society that have not been strongly affected by the Internet.

EXERCISES 3.6

Internet Culture

26. In a single Web page, summarize your thoughts about whether or not the Internet will ever be regulated; that is, will the contents placed on the Web ever truly be limited and controlled?

27. Locate two pages on the Web with the following properties: one of the pages should contain what you believe to be inaccurate information, and the other should contain what you perceive as accurate information. Compare and contrast their differences in a Web page you develop.

28. What is your personal opinion about the issue of censorship on the Internet? Do you think filters are a viable solution?

29. Decipher the following shorthand expressions: BTW, FYI, KSA, and WRT. List five other common abbreviations you have encountered, along with their meanings.

30. How much money does a company pay to place an ad on Netscape's Web pages? List your source(s).

31. Describe how ads affect you during Web browsing. What do you think is the future of Web advertising?

32. Report the URLs of three Web pages containing the phrase "Appalachian Trail" that also contain advertisements.

33. What role do you see the Internet playing in the future of society? Describe the facet of society on which you feel the Internet has had the greatest impact. How about the least impact?

3.7   Business Culture and the Internet

Many businesses are recognizing opportunities in on-line activities. In newspapers and magazines, we constantly see URLs listed. For example, the following URLs may look familiar:

`www.mastercard.com`	Mastercard International	Go On-Line
`www.msdw.com`	Morgan Stanley Dean Witter	
`www.toyota.com`	Toyota USA	

Even on television,[6] we are flooded with URLs, such as:

`www.sixflags.com`	Six Flags Theme Parks
`www.edf.org`	Environmental Defense Fund
`www.dell.com`	Dell Computer Corporation

Not too long ago, there was a big debate among advertisers about whether or not to include the `"http://"` part of a URL in a televised ad. On the radio, you will hear announcers giving out URLs almost constantly. Some radio announcers still do not know how to read a URL; nevertheless, they continue to try, and most are getting the hang of it.

Another question that many users and companies pose is, "Is it safe to do business on the Internet?" Several large computer companies have television ads trying to convince you that it is safe. Consumers are worried that businesses are going to "find out everything about them." Businesses are concerned, because they are not knowledgeable enough about the Internet.

Because business on the Web is still in its infancy, many questions remain unanswered. Here, we explore business issues and look at several businesses that are successfully using the Internet to increase their markets.

Hot Topic

3.7.1 On-line Businesses

The Internet functions nicely as a way to facilitate communications both within and between companies. The Internet is also an excellent venue for advertising and conducting trade with consumers. It is currently possible to shop for goods and services through on-line catalogs; subscribe to on-line versions of magazines and newspapers; and purchase software. These are just a few types of business transactions taking place on the on-line marketplace.

In addition to lowering transaction costs, the Internet is transforming the marketplace into a global environment in which businesses and

---

6   Compare the attention span of someone channel surfing versus surfing the Web. The main difference is that instead of using your remote to view 57 channels, you use a mouse and have millions of channels from which to choose.

consumers are no longer restricted by their geographical locations. For companies, this means more potential customers; for consumers, this means a greater selection of services and products. This revolution is literally changing the way a lot of companies do business. Here are a few of the new and interesting business models on the Internet.

- Advertising

  - Example: *AltaVista*.
  - AltaVista is a *search engine*.
  - Advertisers pay for the search service, and consumers can be targeted for specific types of ads on the basis of their search requests. This specialized type of advertising is very effective at reaching target markets.

- Marketing

  - Example: *AmericaNet*.
  - This service helps businesses get started on the Web and also has a section for classified ads.
  - Businesses can either purchase Web presentations or advertise through AmericaNet.

- Partnership

  - Example: *FedEx eBusiness Tools*.
  - FedEx offers eBusiness Tools as a way to partner with businesses who want an on-line presence. The tools provide ways to build and manage on-line stores and catalogs, process orders and payments, and ship and track orders.

- Retail

  - Example: *L. L. Bean*.
  - L. L. Bean sells outdoor gear and clothing.
  - Consumers can view, select, order, and pay for their merchandise on-line.

- Service

  - Example: *Travelocity.com*
  - This is a full-service travel agency (great for comparing airline fares).

- • Travelers can examine, reserve, and pay for tickets on-line as well as book hotel rooms, reserve rental cars, and book vacations and cruises.

- • Software

  - • Example: *Netscape*.

  - • Buyers are able to download software, use it, and pay for it on-line. One of the key features here is that potential buyers can try a product out for a month or so before purchasing it.

- • Subscription

  - • Example: *The Wall Street Journal Interactive Edition*.

  - • This is an electronic newspaper. Some features are available to non-subscribers.

  - • Subscribers can view a continuously updated version of the newspaper on-line 24 hours a day. This is the fastest method for getting the most current news. Since many business investments are time-critical, having the latest available information can be paramount.

Notice that in each situation, business costs are reduced by using the Internet, and the convenience afforded the customer over the traditional method of conducting business is significant. This combination will lead to many more successful businesses and satisfied customers.

3.7.2   Three Sample Companies

FedEx eBusiness Tools

FedEx provides eBusiness Tools as a way to create a sort of partnership between FedEx and businesses seeking to tap the on-line market. FedEx provides the means to create an on-line presence so that it is possible for a small company, located anywhere in the world, to expand its market without a lot of overhead and without a lot of risk. The eBusiness Tools permit companies to easily create and maintain an on-line store, e-catalog, or Web site. They also provide order management capabilities to process orders and credit cards, business analysis to monitor site activity, and integration with their other systems to ship and track orders and process returns.

Go On-Line

NetGrocer

An interesting on-line business is grocery shopping. Shoppers visit a grocery store Web presentation and select items to purchase, filling their virtual

Go On-Line

shopping carts. One company providing on-line grocery shopping is Net-Grocer.

Using point-and-click tools, shoppers can select items (and put them back), view pictures of them, read label information, determine the sizes available, view specials and check the prices of the items—in short, everything but actually handle the goods. At the "check-out," the order is totaled, and customers are prompted to enter billing and shipping information. Products are shipped from a warehouse using FedEx Express Saver, which permits tracking the orders.

The benefits of selling grocery items on the Web are great for both the grocer and the customer. The grocer can update prices in real time, use a warehouse-based operation, and easily keep track of inventory. Besides saving the customer a trip to the grocery store, the on-line grocery store offers convenience to its customers by remembering their food preferences—it saves their grocery lists. The customer can also specify a recurring order that will be sent at regular intervals.

ONSALE, Inc.

Go On-Line

Another unusual on-line business application that has proven highly successful is ONSALE, Inc. (ONSALE, for short). This is an on-line interactive real-time *auction* that markets refurbished and closed-out electronic equipment. There are many other forms of on-line auctions as well. With ONSALE, auctions are held on-line on Mondays, Wednesdays, and Fridays. Participants browse through available items, bidding and rebidding, until the bidding concludes. If you are outbid, you will receive an email message so indicating. Winning bidders are notified by email, and ONSALE transmits the orders to the participating merchants, who fill the orders and collect the payments. ONSALE has been rated as a top shopping business, because it not only provides some real bargains, it is also extremely entertaining.

3.7.3   On-line Business Hurdles

Thus far, we have mentioned only three of the many companies conducting business on-line. The concept sounds great, and many businesses are turning a handsome profit. However, some hurdles must be overcome. Here we discuss some of the problems and concerns of on-line buyers and sellers.

Probably the most significant consumer concerns about doing business on-line are *privacy* and *security*. While we devote Chapter 14 to these subjects, it is appropriate to include some remarks here. When disclosing personal information and revealing spending habits on-line, consumers want assurance that the information will go no further. It may be a bit unsettling to revisit a Web page and have them ask if you would like to pick up where you left off. Some users could also get nervous if their favorite on-line catalog remembers their hat sizes, shoe sizes, and credit card numbers. What is to prevent this information from falling into the wrong hands? These data are actually stored on your hard disk in a file usually called `cookies`. They may also be stored in a `cookie` directory. For our discussion, we assume that the personal data is stored in a file called `cookies`, and we refer to each entry in the file as a *cookie*.

3.7.4   Cookies

Sometimes when you visit a Web page, information about you is collected. It might be your name, password (if you are registering for that page), preferences, your computer's name, flags that keep track of what you looked at, credit card number, phone number, address, etc. We often volunteer this information by filling out a *form* on the Web page. Or the information exchange may be inherent in the transaction process, such as supplying a mailing address when ordering. Parts of this information may even be *encrypted*.

Hot Topic

A Web server sends this information to your browser, and the data is written to the `cookies` file stored on your disk. This process is known as *setting a cookie*. Some browsers allow you to select an option that notifies you when a cookie is to be written; you have the option of not allowing the cookie to be written. Using the `cookies` file, a Web server can keep track of the Web pages you visit. The next time you visit a particular Web page, the server will search the `cookies` file, retrieve the information stored there, and use that information to customize its Web page to accommodate you.

In actuality, the amount of data that can be stored in a cookie is very limited. The most likely scenario is that the server stores an `id` for you, fetches that `id` from the cookie, and then looks you up in the server database for your more detailed profile and history.

The purpose of putting information in the `cookies` file on your disk is to reduce the server's search time in locating a specific cookie, namely yours. Since the `cookies` file is limited in size (it typically contains only about 300 cookies), locating a specific cookie can be fast. However, the size limitation also means that after a period of time, some cookies must be removed. The least recently used entries are deleted when space is needed. Cookies also specify an expiration date after which time they may be removed from the file. The term *persistent cookie* derives from the sometimes long periods of time that elapse before entries are deleted from the `cookies` file.

One concern about the `cookies` file is that information may be retrieved and used to determine one's personal habits. Aside from credit card account numbers, it is generally felt that the recorded information is fairly harmless. Credit card security is a valid concern, but such numbers are encrypted. Many feel that the pluses of cookies outweigh the potential negatives. For instance, cookies are used to keep track of items on your shopping list as you go through an on-line catalog. When using the Netscape browser's preference options, your preference selections are saved as cookies on your disk, so your preferences do not have to be set every time you start the browser. These are examples of two interesting and harmless uses of cookies.

Consumers will have to decide on the cookie controversy on their own. The general feeling is that their benefits and functionality are sufficient to justify their use. And, as with the use of credit card transactions, there is a tendency for journalists to stress the possibility of risk.

3.7.5   Business and Safety/Security on the Web

Hot Topic

Probably the biggest concern of consumers conducting business on-line is the issue of secure payment: Is it safe to use your credit card on-line? The more relevant question may be whether it is as safe to do business on-line as it is to conduct business in other ways. If conducting business on-line is no more vulnerable than conducting business over the telephone, then many users will feel comfortable about on-line purchasing.

While a concern for and understanding of the transaction process is healthy, the news media tend to exaggerate the risks. In reality, even the normal use of credit cards is not without similar risks. When ordering by credit card over the telephone, we trust the retailer to handle our information with care and confidentiality. In a restaurant, if we pay with a credit card, we assume the establishment will not use our card for any other purpose.

Mechanisms for ensuring secure payments are currently being developed in the private sector. *Secure Electronic Transactions* (*SET*) is a new technical standard to be implemented by Visa and MasterCard to make credit card payments over the Internet more secure. Other payment options being developed include *electronic money*. Business transactions over the Internet are becoming more widespread and also more secure. It is only a matter of time before the relative level of security matches that of other transaction mechanisms.

3.7.6   Legal Environment

While concerns about secure payments may scare some potential on-line consumers, issues concerning the legal implications of doing business on-line have discouraged some companies from taking their businesses on-line. Consumers and businesses recognize that electronic commerce is new and uncharted territory. Without a predictable legal structure and without a guarantee that governments will not suddenly impose taxes and tariffs on trade conducted over the Internet, a number of companies find the risk too overwhelming. However, this number is probably small compared to the pragmatic and legitimate concerns that Web page visits will not translate into sales.

3.7.7 U. S. Government's Commitment to Electronic Commerce

In July 1997, President Bill Clinton made a strong commitment to promote global electronic commerce with the release of the report "A Framework for Global Electronic Commerce," or *Framework* for short. The Framework defines how policy on the *Global Information Infrastructure (GII)* should be developed to promote "the development of a free and open global electronic marketplace." The report is significant both for what it plans to do and for what it will not do. The underlying principles, summarized from the Framework, are as follows:

1. Governments should encourage self-regulation of the Internet and encourage the private sector to take the lead in organizing standards when needed.

2. Because technology is changing so quickly, governments should not try to regulate or restrict electronic commerce on the Internet, since such policies may be obsolete before they are even enacted.[7]

3. Governments should provide a legal environment to support electronic commerce and to protect consumers when necessary.

4. Governments should acknowledge the uniqueness of the Internet by not trying to impose other regulatory structures on it, such as those applying to the telecommunications industry, radio, and television.

5. Electronic commerce on the Internet should be promoted globally in a consistent manner, regardless of where the buyer and seller reside.

The report addresses financial, legal, and market-access issues and advocates a "hands off" policy whenever possible. The recommendations

---

7 Except for the U. S. policy on the export of encryption technology.

made cover the government actions that may be necessary to ensure secure electronic payment systems and to safeguard personal privacy.

Currently, the Internet and electronic commerce seem poised for a free-for-all without any clearly defined boundaries. As governments around the world formulate their policies on electronic commerce, and the legal environment becomes better defined, we anticipate that both consumers and businesses will grow to feel even more comfortable conducting business on-line.

EXERCISES 3.7

Business Culture and the Internet

34. Record five URLs that you encountered either in off-line magazines, newspapers, radio, or television. Note the media form in which the URL was found.

35. Research an on-line business that sells hiking gear. Write a short summary of how the company functions.

36. Do you feel cookies are an invasion of a user's privacy?

37. Copy an entry from your `cookies` file and label what each part represents.

38. Has anyone you know purchased something on-line using a credit card? Were there any problems? Have you done so? If so, describe your experience.

39. What are your thoughts about the role the U. S. government is taking toward commerce on the Internet?

3.8   Collaborative Computing and the Internet

Collaborative computing is currently generating great interest in many different areas of computing. Here, we will describe what collaborative computing means, explore several examples, and consider its impact. We will also examine where collaborative computing is going.

3.8.1   Collaborative Computing Defined

Collaborative computing is defined as applications that allow the sharing of information and resources between two or more people. It is also referred to as *teamware* or *groupware*. The World Wide Web, with its panoply of

Web pages, is a collaborative computing platform that employs HTML and Web browsers. *Lotus Notes*, Novell's *Groupwise*, and *Microsoft Exchange* are other examples of software supporting collaborative computing.

The need for collaborative computing is clear, as businesses and individuals must cope with more and more information and the cost of travel for face-to-face meetings continues to escalate. Employees spend too much time sorting through data in email, faxes, mail, memos, reports, and voice messages. This problem is compounded by downsizing and restructuring in many companies, which translates to fewer people doing more work. Organizing the information and correctly forwarding it is also time-consuming. To stay competitive, businesses and organizations are turning to collaborative computing to share knowledge and resources and to move information efficiently.

A networked computer system provides the basis for a collaborative computing infrastructure. The software that makes up the collaborative computing platform (sometimes referred to as *groupware*) allows users to schedule meetings, coordinate calendars, send email, work jointly on a document, or confer without physically being in the same geographic location.

3.8.2   Applications

From customer and account service to research and product development, collaborative computing can enhance many aspects of business. The most basic collaborative computing application, email, has been around the longest. Email has replaced the written memo in many organizations, saving both time[8] (distributing the memo) and money (paper costs).

Collaborative computing can also simplify the process of filling out an expense report. Using an *intelligent form*, an employee need only enter expense amounts; the expense figures are then automatically calculated and the report is electronically submitted. After the form is automatically routed to the appropriate supervisor for review, it is electronically directed to the accounting department, which disburses payment. At any point in the process, the employee can track the report to determine its status. Similarly, purchase orders can be filled in and dispatched. This model permits fast and easy distribution, as well as convenient tracking.

Version control is another use of collaborative computing, in which the software makes it possible for more than one person to work on a

---

8   Some would argue that email only results in a shifting of time spent. Email speeds communication, but it can also increase the time spent in reading and writing messages.

document at the same time. The software keeps track of the latest version of the document, and updates all other copies as needed. Since hard copies of the document need not be sent back and forth, a large time savings is realized. If the system works properly, there is little chance that users will be out of synchronization while working on a document.

One of the most exciting applications of collaborative computing involves real-time interaction through *video teleconferencing* or simply *videoconferencing (VC)*. Traditionally, business communication has involved the exchange of data and voice information; however, VC enables the real-time exchange of colorful video images and audio. While the potential uses for VC seem almost limitless, the most universal example involves the business meeting.

Businesses were the first to embrace VC technology, despite its high initial cost; they could justify their investment in terms of travel costs and time savings. Often, different groups of people in a single location need to communicate with other groups somewhere else. Thus, multiple VC equipment sets are necessary. Since the cost of good VC equipment is still fairly high, its use is not yet standard practice.

A less expensive technology for remote conferencing is *Desktop Video-conferencing (DTVC)*. DTVC uses regular personal computers and provides interaction between individuals situated at their own PCs, rather than between groups of people. Schools could benefit from DTVC by connecting teachers and home-bound students. A simple DTVC setup might consist of a PC connected to a miniature video camera through a video card. A microphone either could be connected through a sound card to the PC or might be part of the camera itself. More sophisticated DTVC systems contain the camera and microphone inside the monitor. Either way, a high-speed ISDN line, rather than a regular telephone or slower line, should be used to connect to the Internet, since transferring audio and video data requires much more *bandwidth* than transferring just data. (Bandwidth refers to the transmission capacity and is usually measured in bits per second.)

CUSeeMe is a free videoconferencing software tool that was developed at Cornell University in 1992. It is low bandwidth, so the quality is limited. CUSeeMe is available for both Macs and Windows systems. You can put together a very low-cost (under $200), nonproduction videoconferencing system using CUSeeMe. To receive, you only need a monitor that can display 16-level grayscale and an Internet connection; to send, you only need a (cheap) camera and a *digitizer*. You can find out more about CUSeeMe in the references.

Go On-Line

It is worth emphasizing that a videoconferencing system may include any or all of the following aspects in order of increasing bandwidth requirements with varying technological costs.

1.   Real-time talk or chat.

2.   Whiteboard graphics.

3.   Audio.

4.   Black and white video.

5.   Color video.

The costs of these technologies vary widely.

3.8.3   Impact

The major benefits of collaborative computing are convenience and time savings; these amount to money. Employees can examine, organize, and route data efficiently, while managers can have easy access to data and can find information in a timely manner. Electronically forwarding and accessing information saves time, since paper does not have to be physically distributed. The use of audio, graphics, and video plus text in a collaborative computing environment provides the means for clearer communications. This can result in fewer errors and misunderstandings. In addition, travel time and expenses can be significantly reduced by collaborative computing, since being in the same location is no longer a prerequisite for the exchange of ideas.

3.8.4   Future Prospects

Collaborative computing may soon become a necessity for businesses that want to remain competitive. Unfortunately, a number of the commercial groupware products are quite expensive. However, some applications make use of Web technology and provide a cheaper alternative. For software that costs only a fraction of the well-known groupware products, some companies are utilizing a Web-based platform as their collaborative computing environment. In addition to being cheaper, the Web technology may be easier to use. Both Microsoft and Netscape include groupware in their version 4.x browser suites.

Hot Topic

 The infrastructure for a Web-based collaborative computing platform is an intranet. Access within an intranet is limited to employees and business contacts only, by a security measure known as a *firewall*. Web software developers are busy developing more sophisticated security measures and are quickly producing workable solutions. Intranet-to-intranet communication across the Internet is possible, if you use a technology that does not require dedicated bandwidth.

In response, groupware providers are trying not to compete directly with the Web technology. Instead, they are trying to make their products compatible with the Web by allowing various browsers to access their databases. The ease and effectiveness with which groupware can meld with the Internet may determine its success. In the meantime, some companies are using a combination of Web technology and groupware. For example, an internal Web page may serve as a bulletin board or a means of displaying company manuals, while a product like Lotus Notes may be used for applications that require security.

Many businesses are already improving worker productivity through the use of collaborative computing. It seems clear that as developers overcome some of the current hurdles, collaborative computing will become even more prevalent.

EXERCISES 3.8

Collaborative Computing and the Internet

40.   Describe three additional applications for collaborative computing beyond what was discussed in Section 3.8.2.

41.   Research and report on the top three platforms for collaborative computing. Describe the major features of these platforms, including whether or not they are Web-based. Report on the prices of each. List your sources.

42.   Suppose that you were in charge of researching and selecting the groupware for your company, Antique T-Bird Car Parts, Inc., a mail order company that supplies genuine and replica car parts for antique Thunderbirds. Select a platform to use and describe how you arrived at this decision. Describe the features of the platform that you think would enhance the productivity at your company.

43.   Would you want someone to see your calendar so they could schedule you into meetings? How would you feel about most of your office's communication taking place electronically?

44.   If you were to go long distance hiking, would you bring a computer with you so you could send and receive email along the trail? Why or why not?

The World Wide Web 4

I had an ankle injury in Virginia and almost had to quit the trail. Fish was forced to push on without me while I iced my ankle. It was very hard for him to go on without me; it was very hard for me to remain behind without him. We had been through hundreds of miles of hiking together and our friendship went back 30 years. After three days at a tiny hole in the wall in Virginia, I felt ready to push north. My ankle was not ready, however. I decided I would walk on the ankle as long as I could, and if the pain was too much, I would take a bus home. (We had burned our return airline tickets a couple of weeks earlier in a joyous, we-are-going-to-make-it ceremony.) Surprisingly, after five back-to-back 25-mile days, my ankle was pain-free. I ramped up to 30 miles per day, hoping to catch Fish-out-of-Water. I did catch him in Virginia, but he was in a town when I passed him. For a while, neither one of us knew where on the trail the other was. We were both hiking alone now. It rained nonstop for one entire week in Virginia. I was actually struck by lightning on "Thunder Ridge." Upon my arrival at a shelter on that memorable night, five hikers looked up at me and said, "You look like you just got hit by lightning!" I replied, "I did" and went to bed completely soaked, skipping dinner. I got up the next morning and was happy to be alive and still hiking. When the rain finally subsided, the trail was glorious.

Virginia
551 miles

Chapter 4

4.1 INTRODUCTION

In this chapter, we examine the following:

Objectives

- The World Wide Web

- Miscellaneous Web browser features, including a comparison of Netscape's and Microsoft's Web browsers

- HTML writing styles

- The outline, design, and management of a Web presentation

- The *registration* of Web pages

- *Lynx*, a text-based Web browser

Much of what you will eventually learn about the Web and browsers will be self-taught. Our goal here is to help speed up this process by presenting key ideas. While the construction of quality Web pages is not easy, this chapter will give you enough background to put together a thoughtful Web presentation.

4.2 The Web Defined

The *World Wide Web* (WWW), or *Web* for short, is a software application that makes it easy and possible for nearly anyone to publish and browse hypertext documents on the Internet. You can think of the Web as encompassing all of the information available through Web browsers. The Web has developed a huge following because of its ease of use and visual appeal. It is called a "web" because the interconnections between documents resemble a spider's web.

How does the Internet differ from the WWW? The Internet can be thought of as a very large group of networked computers. The information on the Web is transported over the Internet. The Web therefore uses the

Internet. In fact, the Web is now the driving force behind the Internet. The Web generates the greatest traffic demands on the Internet, and new Internet technology is being developed to meet the needs and wishes of Web users.

Figure 4.1 shows the relationship between the Web, the Internet, and a number of other applications. Each application uses the Internet as a transport mechanism. The Web runs on the HTTP protocol. Browsers are *multiprotocol*, which means they can talk to many different kinds of resources that make up the Internet, and the number of protocols being included in browsers is steadily increasing. This illustrates an important distinction between the browser and the Web.

A central idea in the development of the Web was the *Uniform Resource Locator (URL)*, described in Section 2.3.2. A URL is a Web address that uniquely identifies a document on the Web. Such a document can be an image, an HTML file, a program, or another type of file. Unique addresses make linking to anyone's Web documents possible.[1] The nonlinear

Hot Topic

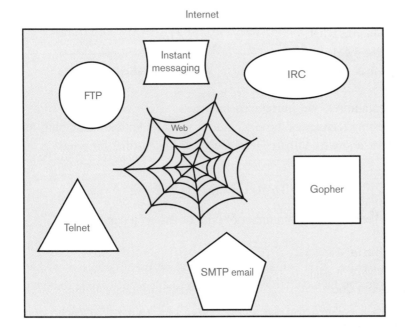

FIGURE 4.1
The relationship between the Web, the Internet, and a number of common applications.
(The particular geometric shapes are arbitrary.)

---

1   This is what a mathematician would call a *many-to-one mapping*. Each URL points unambiguously to a particular document, but multiple different URLs may resolve to that particular document, due to the use of aliases and shortcuts in the way names are assigned and used.

nature of the Web is one of its main attractions. Since people all over the world are participating in and publishing on the Web, the entire system has evolved into something far greater than any individual contribution. The sheer amount of information available on the Web makes it the greatest collaborative nongovernmental effort in the history of humankind.

EXERCISES 4.2

The Web Defined

1. Many people find surfing the Web fun and entertaining. In your own words, try to explain why people find the Web so fascinating.

2. Assuming a 50 percent increase in the number of Web users per year, how many years will it take before you have more experience than all but 10 percent of Web users?

3. Write an HTML document summarizing your interest in the Web.

4.3   Miscellaneous Web Browser Details

In Section 2.2, we introduced browsers. Here we describe some other interesting features of these programs, including bookmarks, plug-ins, and helpers, and we compare Netscape's and Microsoft's browsers.

4.3.1   Personal Preferences

Most browsers have a number of options that you can set.

*   **Cookies** You can ask to be notified before a cookie is written, and you can then decide whether or not to allow the cookie to be written.

*   **Disk cache** You can set the size of your cache. The cache stores the HTML source code and images of Web presentations you have visited. Then, if you reload one of these pages, the browser can load the cached copy and the page will appear very quickly.

*   **Fonts** You can select a font specification and also set a default font size.

- **Helper applications**   You may configure *helper applications* to handle certain types of data that the browser is unable to process, for example, Word or PostScript files.

- **Home page location**   You can specify the page that gets loaded when the browser is first launched.

- **Images**   You may specify whether or not images are loaded. Options for color selection are also available.

- **JavaScript and Java**   You can enable or disable these types of programs from running within your browser.

- **Messages**   You may specify a default signature file or a default carbon copy address for outgoing messages. This can be set for regular email or for posts to newsgroups.

4.3.2   Bookmarks

A convenient feature of browsers allows you to save the URL of any Web page you display. The saved URL is called a *bookmark* (or *favorite*). If you save the URL of a Web page, you have *bookmarked* the page. The bookmark is a pointer (URL) to a location on the Web, just as a physical bookmark inserted in a book is a pointer to a specific page. A collection of bookmarks is sometimes referred to as a *hotlist*, *list of favorites*, or simply a *bookmark list*. Since bookmark interfaces are usually mouse driven, selecting a bookmark from the list merely involves a point, select, and click process. Since URLs are generally cumbersome and difficult to type accurately, the mouse-driven interface is very convenient. For example, typing

Useful Item

```
rw.warnerbros.com/ns1_indx.html
```

to send a Warner Brothers greeting card is a lot more time-consuming than simply selecting this URL from a bookmark list.

Many new users begin bookmarking a wide range of URLs when they find new and interesting Web pages that they would like to be able to return to later. New users sometimes fear that they may not be able to relocate a cool page, so they tend to bookmark more Web pages than they will actually return to.

When you bookmark a Web page, the title of the page (as specified in the title tag), by default, is what goes into your bookmark list. Fortunately, browsers allow you to change this entry. Thus, for Web pages with non-descriptive titles, such as "My Cool Page," you can specify an entry that will remind you what the page was about. For example, "My Cool Page" might become "Luca Tomba's Home."

The bookmark pull-down menu, where your list of bookmarks can be viewed, usually appears in the browser's menu bar. As you accumulate more bookmarks, which are displayed vertically, the list may require more than one screen to display. As a result, you will not be able to view all your bookmarks at once. Many browsers let you sort[2] your bookmarks. Given the wide range of titles people use on their Web pages, sorting by title is typically not very helpful. An appropriate way to manage bookmarks so that you can locate the Web page you want with the least amount of effort is to create folders representing various categories in which you have saved multiple bookmarks (and then sort the bookmarks within these folders).

Useful Item

Bookmark folders are created using the browser's bookmark editor. The editor is usually mouse driven and user-friendly. Probably the most important feature of such editors allows you to create a new folder and specify its name. As you accumulate bookmarks, you can organize them into categories and then move the relevant bookmarks into their appropriate folders. The move is done by "dragging and dropping." Although this organization process is initially time-consuming, it can save you lots of time in the long run, if you use your bookmarks often. Also, the newer browsers allow you to file a bookmark as you save it. This is a very useful feature.

The two main, and very different, reasons for saving a bookmark are:

1.   It is a page you expect to visit often.

2.   It is a page you may never find again, so you bookmark it on the chance you will want to go back.

For illustration purposes, consider how a fictitious computer user, Björn, might manage his bookmarks. (You can apply a similar approach, or a different strategy that works well for you. The goal is to arrange things so that you can access your bookmark list easily.)

Initially, Björn had between 10 and 15 bookmarks; even without much organization, they were easy to use. As this number grew to 30 and then 40, it became apparent that it would be more efficient to group related URLs

---

2   That is, place the bookmarks in alphabetical order according to their titles. Most browsers let you sort all bookmarks within the same folder.

into separate folders. By the time Björn could actually spend the time to
create the folders and organize his bookmarks, he was up to 80 bookmarks.
He created the following folders:

Abba	Architecture	Badminton
Cycling	Food	Friends
Hiking	Hobbies	Jobs
Miscellaneous	Parallel Computers	Project
Swedes	Travel	Universities
Work	Yes	Zoo

For the most part, each folder contained four or five bookmarks. For
example, under "Food," Björn had bookmarked Web pages about beverages, dessert recipes, junk food, and Swedish dishes. Under "Friends," he
had bookmarked the page of his old college roommate, Roxette, and the
pages of two friends from graduate school. His "Miscellaneous" category
took care of items that did not fit into any other folder. If enough related
items ended up in Miscellaneous, he planned to create a new folder and
migrate those bookmarks into it. Figure 4.2 illustrates his organization.

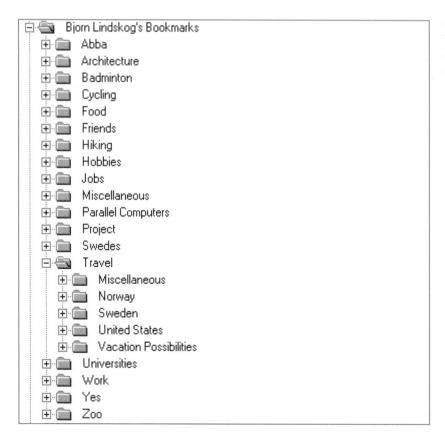

FIGURE 4.2
The arrangement
of Björn's
bookmarks.

Many of Björn's bookmarks fell under the "Travel" umbrella. He had lots of URLs about the United States, a number of URLs about Sweden, several about Norway, and a whole group about vacation destinations. Within the Travel folder, Björn decided to add five new folders:

Miscellaneous	Norway
Sweden	United States
Vacation Possibilities	

Over time, Björn's bookmark collection has grown. He now has about 350 bookmarks spread over 30 folders, with each folder containing up to 10 subfolders. When Björn views his bookmarks, all 30 of his main folders fit easily on one screen. He then picks a category and either selects a bookmark from there or enters a subfolder. Most of his folders contain 10 subfolders at most, and each folder rarely contains more than five bookmarks. This makes selection easy. Periodically, he finds it useful to delete or update bookmarks that have moved, and to migrate bookmarks from his various Miscellaneous folders, which appear in some subfolders as well, into specific categories. When adding new bookmarks, Björn usually waits until he has a batch of five to ten before he places them into appropriate folders.

This example illustrates how organizing bookmarks periodically can cut down on maintenance time and improve efficiency. Although you may not want to be as methodical as our fictitious user, a half-hour here or there is time well spent in the long run.

Useful Item

Many browsers contain a feature called "What's New" that automatically tests your bookmarks and reports back which pages can no longer be found on the Internet. This is a great way to eliminate outdated URLs, or to prompt you to track down the URL of a page that has moved. Since URLs change so often, it is a good idea to use the "What's New" function. On average, every few months, when updating our bookmarks, we find that about 10 percent of our bookmarks have moved and another 5 percent are invalid. The entire checking process (for 300 bookmarks) takes anywhere from 10 to 30 minutes, depending on network traffic and the specific sites we currently have bookmarked.

4.3.3   Plug-ins and Helper Applications

Hot Topic

Newly released browsers are equipped with even more features. New Web products and file formats are constantly being developed. When a browser is designed, it cannot handle every product and file format that currently exists or may exist in the future. Furthermore, browsers are not built to handle all existing data formats. Browsers are already huge programs, and bundling in more features makes them even larger. Yet, there are times when your browser is unable to handle a file that you would like it to be able to process, so you examine the possibility of extending the browser's capabilities.

For example, suppose you went to load a page and received a message such as:

```
no audio player installed
```

This message means that the Web page you loaded contains an audio component that your browser does not know how to play. You can fix the situation using one of two closely related mechanisms: *plug-ins* and *helper applications*.

Plug-ins and helper applications do the same thing; they extend the power of the browser. Plug-ins are more tightly integrated with the browser, so there is less work for you to do. All you have to do is put (drag) plug-ins into the browser's `plug-ins` folder so that it will find them and load them at start-up. Be aware, however, that there is a memory cost to using plug-ins, especially memory-hungry ones such as *Macromedia's Shockwave*.

There are plug-ins that are capable of playing audio, showing movies, running animations, and working with calendars, among other things. Some plug-ins do no more than ease the running of a separate application, instead of being self-contained. The *Adobe Acrobat* plug-in is an example of such a program. Normally, plug-ins run in the browser window, but there are exceptions.

Netscape established and made public the programming interface for plug-ins, so anyone with the requisite programming skills and a C++ compiler can create one. More importantly, Microsoft now supports this plug-in standard, and Netscape plug-ins can normally be used with Internet Explorer and vice versa.

Helper applications, or *helpers*, are stand-alone programs that are used to process or display data that is not directly integrated into a Web page. Helpers do not display their information inside the browser's window; instead, they are launched in their own window. The browser activates the appropriate helper application when the browser encounters a file type that it does not know how to handle. Helper applications are usually configured in a list of preferences. You associate a file extension and MIME type with a particular software program. The helper application must be downloaded and placed in the appropriate directory.

Table 4.1 summarizes the features of plug-ins and helper applications. The choice of which ones to use will depend mainly on product functionality, product availability for your specific platform, and the memory

TABLE 4.1

A Comparison of the Features of Plug-ins and Helper Applications.

Plug-ins	Helper Applications
Closely tied to browser.	Program stands alone.
Displays inside browser window.	Displays in separate window.
Installation involves downloading the plug-in and running a procedure.	Configuring involves downloading the helper application and editing your preferences.
Broad selection available.	Broad selection available.
Launches quickly.	May launch more slowly than plug-in.

requirements. You will need enough memory for your operating system plus your browser plus the plug-in or helper, all running at the same time.

A word of caution is in order regarding plug-ins and helper applications. Since new formats are constantly being introduced one often finds that the plug-ins and helper applications are in *beta test* form. Software that is in beta test form is still being debugged, so you may experience some unexpected behavior. This is as opposed to *production software,* which is at a more advanced stage of development than beta software. Production software should be completely debugged and highly reliable.

4.3.4   Web Browsers Comparison: Netscape and Microsoft

Hot Topic

Go On-Line

The two most popular graphical Web browsers are *Navigator* from Netscape and *Internet Explorer* from Microsoft. The Netscape release includes the browser, as well as many other features; the entire suite is referred to as *Netscape Communicator*.

Our goal in this section is briefly to compare and contrast these two applications. The best way to evaluate these two products is to try each one out for yourself.

The two browsers are actually quite similar, and they include many of the same features. Both browsers are large programs and are approximately the same size, depending on the exact versions. The number of HTML tags they support is large; however, you cannot assume that because your Web presentation looks great under Navigator, it will look equally impressive using Internet Explorer, or vice versa. Until now, neither company has truly embraced standards. Both companies have always incorporated some of their own features. For example, Netscape introduced tables and frames, whereas Microsoft supports marquees and a wide range of font faces. Such discrepancies have created challenges for Web designers who would like their pages to look equally good across all platforms.

Currently, for every person using Netscape, about two people use Internet Explorer. Netscape's market share used to be much greater than Internet Explorer's but it has decreased in recent years. While both browsers are excellent products, the shift in market share has resulted from how the products have been distributed. Netscape is usually downloaded off the Web or bought from a software vendor as a stand-alone product. However, Internet Explorer is packaged and distributed with a variety of other Microsoft products.

EXERCISES 4.3

Miscellaneous Web Browser Details

4.   What are some personal preferences and corresponding values you like to set in your browser?

5.   Some browsers have a bookmark feature called "Import." Describe what it does.

6.   Describe your strategy for organizing bookmarks. Is it effective? How could you improve it?

7.   What is the maximum number of bookmark folders your browser allows? How many bookmarks are allowed per folder?

8.   Provide the names of three plug-ins and describe the purpose of each. Give the names of three helper applications and explain their use.

9.   What platform seems to have the most plug-ins and helpers available? How many are there compared to other platforms? Does this give one platform an advantage over another?

10.   Have you ever received a message like "plug-in not found," or something similar? What options did you have at that point?

11.   Download a plug-in and test it. Describe the process.

12.   Download a helper application and configure your browser to handle it. Test it and describe the process.

13.   Describe two more differences between plug-ins and helpers.

14.   Compare and contrast the Netscape and Microsoft browsers. Summarize your findings in a Web page. List your sources.

15.   Research the antitrust suits against Microsoft's Internet Explorer.

16.   Have you used both Netscape's and Microsoft's browsers? If so, explain which you prefer and why.

17.   (The purpose of this exercise is to have you conduct on-line research, alert you to the startling number of different versions of these products, make you aware of why the appearance of Web pages varies so greatly, and help you gain some insight into why it is so difficult to keep these products bug free.) How many different versions of Navigator are there? How many different versions of Internet Explorer are there?

18.   Prepare a table that compares the sizes of Netscape's and Microsoft's browsers over a variety of different platforms. Does one product have an advantage over the other?

19.   Prepare a table that compares at least five features of Navigator and Internet Explorer. Which product do you prefer?

20.   As of today, how many people use Navigator as compared to Internet Explorer? Cite your source.

4.4   Web Writing Styles

The writing style required for a typical Web page is different than the writing style for the average printed page, because:

- Readers usually spend less time looking at a Web page than they do reading an off-line magazine or newspaper article.

- Web pages are typically very short, only one or two screens in length.

- Off-line material has greater longevity than on-line material.

- Web designers usually try to grab the reader's attention. If a presentation is not cleverly designed, a reader can easily move on.

- Web pages are hyperlinked documents, so readers typically do not go through them in sequential order.

- Published off-line material is generally written and edited by professionals, whereas Web pages may be published by anyone, sometimes with little or no writing and editing skills.

- Web pages are dynamic, and they often involve *multimedia*.

- With off-line material, the quality of the writing holds the reader's attention. The appearance and form of the writing are secondary. However, appearance and form are critical components of a Web page.

We can easily distinguish between publications designed primarily for on-line presentation (and secondarily for print) and those designed primarily for print (and require conversion for on-line display). It is possible, however, to design for an intermediate or meta format that is then converted or filtered to both on-line and print versions.

Because of the inherent differences in writing styles for on-line and off-line material, some practice is needed to write specifically for the Web. We will consider a number of different genres that have become popular on the Web. The goal is to learn how to evaluate and become more aware of different Web writing styles, what works and why, and how on-line and off-line writing differ.

4.4.1   The Biography

Figure 4.3 depicts Paul Allen's biography from the Web. The page has a black background and is covered with information. If not properly laid out, a page as information packed as this one risks being too cluttered. The organization of this page, however, is excellent. The page has an image of Paul and numerous hyperlinks. The hyperlinks are displayed as a group of images as well as clickable text. Each image incorporates a short, descriptive phrase explaining where the hyperlink leads. The page makes heavy use of multimedia (it provides an excellent demonstration of the *Shockwave* plug-in), and it offers the user a choice of pages, depending on the capacity of their connection.

What else can we learn about writing styles by looking at this page?

Go On-Line

- This on-line biography contains up-to-the-minute information and is continually being revised. Off-line biographies are quickly out of date, and it is impossible for them to remain as current as this presentation. This biography allows you to skip around, selecting what is most interesting to you. The material is written so that each hyperlink is more or less self-contained. Since the different subpages are not dependent, they can be read in any order. This is very different from a typical off-line biography, which is usually chronologically ordered.

FIGURE 4.3
A sample Web biography page (`www.paulallen.com`).

- You can select any aspect of Paul Allen's background in which you are interested. The exploratory nature of the page greatly contributes to its effectiveness.

- The in-line images and animations help make the presentation fun to explore.

- The hyperlinks actually are the writing; very little writing is not contained in a hyperlink. In most other cases, you will find more text outside the hyperlinks. The writing here is short and descriptive, but in most cases, even shorter hyperlinks are advisable.

The page is creatively done and contains a lot of information. The presentation meets its goal of providing readers with biographical information about Paul Allen.

4.4.2   The Business Exposition

Figure 4.4 depicts RubberChicken's business Web page. The page is brightly colored, and the text is very easy to read. Along the left margin is a narrow, colorful strip that includes a number of hyperlinks. This style is found on many Web pages. In this case, the hyperlinks are small, in-line images. The right-hand side of the page consists of a yellow background. The material in this portion of the page is formatted into a number of short paragraphs.

Go On-Line

The descriptive title of the page is "FakeMail, pranks & gags: Rubber-Chicken.com." The header of the page consists of a graphic of the company name, RubberChicken.com, plus a quote from Victor Borge and an image of a rubber chicken. A menu that consists of a number of hyperlinks follows the header. Each hyperlink has a short, descriptive name. The menu is followed by information about the awards won by the company. At the bottom of the page, which is just over one screen long, is a footer that consists of an email address for questions and also a copyright notice.

A careful examination of successful Web pages will help you to gain new insights into effective on-line writing. Things to note in Rubber-Chicken's page include:

- The images catch your attention. The menu is located in an easy-to-use spot, and very little must be read before a hyperlink can be selected. The images allow you to position your mouse quickly on information of interest to you. The narrow strip on the left has easy-to-use hyperlinks and interesting-looking images.

- The page is compact, colorful, and easy to explore.

- The writing style is simple and direct. In our example, a number of facts about the awards are presented, but there is very little additional writing. Short, descriptive, and consistent-looking hyperlinks are included in the menu. The majority of people are skimming and scanning on most Web pages, not reading every word.

FIGURE 4.4
A sample Web business page (`www.rubberchicken.com`).

- The page has a descriptive title, an effective header, a short footer, and a centrally placed, well-designed menu. Such ingredients create a high-quality Web page. The page is just over one screen long and therefore does not require much scrolling.

As evidenced by the large number of awards[3] this presentation has won, the writing style it uses is very effective. The presentation designers met their goal of having a lot of visitors enjoy their pages.

4.4.3   The Guide

Figure 4.5 depicts a page called the Ultimate Band List guide. The page starts with a descriptive title, "Welcome to the Ultimate Band List." The header is an image map that appears at the very top of the page. The image map provides hyperlinks for easy navigation. The descriptions on the hyperlinks are all short, informative, and consistent. A number of brief paragraphs then describe activities in which you can participate. These are offset from each other by horizontal image bars. The footer consists of a number of clickable graphics, one of which is set to an email address where you can pose questions about the information.

Go On-Line

By incorporating the best features you see into your Web pages, you will be able to produce a more effective and informed presentation. For our example:

- The page provides convenient information about bands. The search mechanism in the header allows you to look for the band of interest immediately. In addition, the page has a huge "database" of bands, so there is a good chance you will turn up the group in which you are interested. By being easy to use and comprehensive, the page delivers on the promise in its name.

- The graphics are well done, the page is easy to read, and the hyperlinks are easy to follow. You can make the guide work for you without effort. The page is even easier to use than a dictionary.

- The image map at the top of the screen and the search mechanism allow you to locate the information you are after quickly. Other hyperlinks are effectively blended into the writing. At the bottom of most screens, there is a hyperlink to return you to the presentation's main page.

- The color scheme is appealing, and the text is very easy to read on the white background. The choice of colors and the preparation of graphics were carefully done. Notice the alternating-color horizontal bars that separate the different sections.

---

3   Awards, while seemingly impressive, should be examined as to their criteria and the people applying these criteria.

FIGURE 4.5
A sample Web
guide (`ubl.com`).

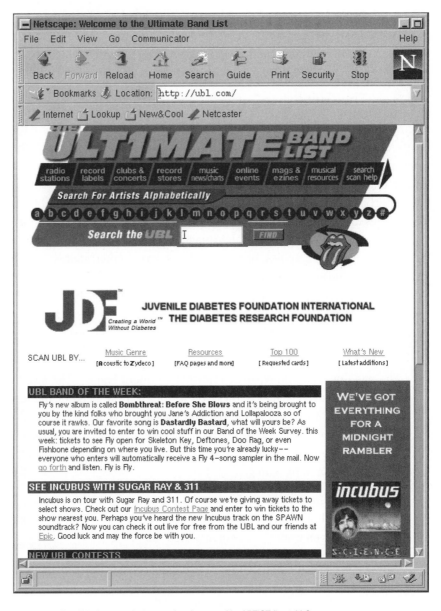

The Ultimate Band List Internet site is owned and operated by ARTISTdirect, LLC.

The presentation is coherent, informative, and easy to use. It creates an uncluttered, user-friendly environment.

Go On-Line

4.4.4   The Tutorial

Figure 4.6 depicts the Cookie Central tutorial page that explains everything you ever wanted to know about cookies. The Cookie Central presentation

FIGURE 4.6

A sample Web tutorial (`www.cookiecentral.com`).

is visually appealing; its color scheme works well. The title of the presentation is a simple and descriptive "Cookie Central." The header consists of a graphic that repeats the title of the presentation. This is useful in that if someone makes a hardcopy of the page, the title will be included.

The left-hand side of the page consists of a separate-colored, narrow strip. The strip contains a *select menu*, from which you can choose a topic to follow. The right-hand side of the page is formatted with an HTML table. The first column of the table contains clever phrases, with associated small icons. A hyperlink is included as the "heading" of the corresponding phrase. The right-hand column of the table consists of a list of hyperlinks. The hyperlinks are short, descriptive, clickable text.

The page is about two screens long, and it concludes with a footer that has a hyperlinked copyright notice. This hyperlink takes you to information about the presentation and provides `mailto` links for sending in comments or questions about the material.

- The presentation, although packed with information, is not intimidating. The text phrases are easy to read. The select menu allows you to decide what topic to pursue next. All of these features combine to create a very user-friendly presentation.

- The writing is short, descriptive, and light but informative. The graphics are visually appealing. It is easy for you to explore the presentation in a nonlinear fashion.

- This presentation is far less intimidating than most computer manuals. The information is clear, concise, and easy to understand. Information in the tutorial is much easier to find than it would be in most other forms of computer documentation.

- The graphics spruce up the appearance of the page. In addition, the images suggest what pages they lead to, as the in-line images themselves are hyperlinks. The graphics are lighthearted, yet they lead to serious information.

The goals of this tutorial are met because the presentation is fun, and learning from it is easy. Contrast this with your typical computer manual. The consistency of the presentation adds to its overall design.

4.4.5   Writing Genres Summary

In the last few sections, you have explored four different writing genres: the biography, the business exposition, the guide, and the tutorial. Some key points that made these presentations effective are:

- A theme and clear goals for the presentation.

- The ability to permit exploration, while providing sufficient navigation so that you can easily avoid getting lost.

- Good choice of colors, with the text easy to read.

- Consistent and careful page design, with hyperlinks normally situated near the top of the page.

- User-friendly navigation.

- Short, descriptive writing.

Other genres will also contain many of these key ingredients. It is a good idea to include most of these items in your own presentations.

EXERCISES 4.4

Web Writing Styles

21. List three important similarities between off-line and on-line writing styles.

22. Describe two other writing genres that are popular on the Web. Identify URLs to presentations that exemplify those genres.

23. List two URLs for each of the following writing categories:
    (a) Biography
    (b) Business
    (c) Guide
    (d) Tutorial

24. Can you locate any on-line writing guides for Web page development? List their URLs. Report two interesting facts you learned.

25. Locate a Web presentation that interests you, and critically evaluate how well it accomplishes its goals, by posing and then answering a number of questions about it. Carefully assess how well the Web author attended to details.

4.5   Web Presentation Outline, Design, and Management

A *Web presentation* is a collection of associated, hyperlinked Web pages that usually have some underlying theme. Scan a number of presentations on the Web and you will see a radical difference in the quality of those presentations. Most users have an innate ability to distinguish between an effective presentation and one that is poorly done. Why is it so easy to get an accurate first impression of a Web presentation? Because Web presentations are so visually oriented, you can often get an idea of the author's capabilities just by glancing at a few pages.

Some of the key elements in an effective Web presentation are:

Useful Item

- **Details** A presentation that includes well-thought-out touches can make a positive impression on the reader. Good choices of background color, headers, footers, and appropriate font size are all important. Typos, poorly aligned images, and a clashing color scheme create a negative image. Carefully prepared pages help to enhance the credibility and readability of the presentation.

- **Coding** A competent HTML programmer uses the appropriate elements of style, not to show off, but to contribute to the overall quality of the presentation. Overly simplistic pages could indicate a lack of knowledge by the designer, and cluttered pages indicate poor design.

- **Features** A few "bells and whistles" can improve the feel of a set of pages. For example, *splash screens*, *applets*, or some *JavaScript* can spruce things up. However, it is better to include too few fancy items than to go overboard. Remember that each "cool" feature takes extra time to download and display.

- **Graphics** A modest use of in-line images is probably one of the most significant ways to enhance your design. Many free images can be found on the Web. It is important to integrate the images effectively into the presentation. Randomly positioning images usually does not enhance the design.

- **Layout** If the pages are visually appealing and if they provide convenient navigation, they are likely to be visited by more users. A poor layout will discourage people from spending too much time on the presentation.

- **Writing quality** Good writing and an interesting style are also necessary for a solid presentation.

- **Load time** Since some users have dial-up connections, care should be taken not to include too many graphics or any large (in bytes) graphics. Also, users should be given the option of downloading large images separately. If users get frustrated during the loading process, they are likely either to stop loading the page altogether or be more critical of the page when it finally arrives. Single pages should be limited to about one or two screens in length.

- **Hyperlinks**   Navigation is a key element to any good Web presentation. If readers can move around the pages easily, they will be more impressed. If they can easily get lost and are not able to find the desired information, they may become frustrated. However, it is also possible to include too much navigation. For example, some presentations include an icon of a house, an image of an index finger, and the phrase "Return Home" to indicate how to go back to the topmost page. Any one of these items would suffice.

The sample writing genres covered in the last section all receive high marks for each of these criteria.

4.5.1   Goal Setting

The important steps in producing a high-caliber presentation are goal setting, outlining, navigating, designing, coding, and revising.

The object of goal setting is to decide on specific parameters for your Web presentation, to aid you in focusing your project. Most people find it helpful to write down their goals. The written record allows you to go back and see how successful you were at accomplishing your goals. A number of issues for you to consider before creating your Web presentation are discussed here. Each project will merit its own additional questions.

Useful Item

- *Audience*—Ask yourself who the intended audience is. Are you writing for children, single moms, business executives, retired persons, or a general audience? Are your intended visitors scattered throughout the world, or are they all on the same LAN? Is your goal to have a certain number of hits per month? Knowing who you are targeting will greatly influence your design.

- *Date*—What is your time frame? Many things published on the Web need to be displayed in a timely manner. Is your goal to finish your presentation by the end of a school semester? Time constraints will affect the depth and extensiveness of your project.

- *Graphics*—How many graphics do you intend to include? Do you want to impress your audience? Are you going for a conservative approach? Remember, graphics take a long time to download. If your audience is local, you can use more graphics than if you are targeting a global group. Also, custom graphics take a long time to design, so your schedule will affect the number of graphics you can create.

- *Length*—How much material is going to be included in your presentation? Is your goal to produce a comprehensive presentation? In contrast, do you want just to touch on a few key ideas and provide references to other, more in-depth presentations? Your time constraints will also affect how much material you can develop.

- *Maintenance*—Is your goal to design a presentation that does not need any maintenance, or is the nature of the material such that items will need to be modified from time to time? How thoroughly you comment your code may depend on who will be maintaining the presentation. Do you need to build in flexibility to accommodate future changes?

- *Money*—Are you trying to earn money from your presentation? Is your goal to impress people to obtain other jobs? Are you building an on-line gallery? Such factors will influence your design.

- *Objective*—What is your main objective? Are you designing your presentation for personal satisfaction, for a class, for a friend, or for a business? Write a couple of sentences that summarize the most important points about your presentation.

- *Research*—Does your project require a lot of research? Can the necessary research be accomplished on-line? How many sources do you want to include? Are you going to incorporate a history of what other people have done? Alternatively, does your presentation not need any in-depth research? Again, your time frame will influence the level of research you can conduct.

- *Writing*—Is your goal to have accurate and error-free writing? Do you want high-quality prose? Do you want visitors to read everything you write? Are you trying to teach your readers about a certain subject? Set goals for what you would like your writing to accomplish.

Before designing a Web presentation, run through this checklist; it will help you get started and focus more clearly. As you develop more and more presentations, modify this list to suit your needs better.

4.5.2   Outlining

Once you have set goals for your Web presentation, it is a good idea to produce an outline. The subject matter, combined with your goals, will dictate the way the material is most naturally partitioned. Most students work best if they design their outline in HTML, rather than just handwriting it on paper. Creativity seems to be enhanced when working on-line.

Actually seeing the outline on-line seems to help students decide what is missing, what needs to be deleted, and what needs to be moved.

There are different schools of thought on the Web page development process. Ours is to produce the HTML code concurrently with the actual writing. Others believe in a two-step process:

1. Develop the writing for the presentation.

2. Then code it in HTML.

These two steps can be completely independent, but our experience shows that writing and coding together (not independently) leads to an incremental development process, and typically a better design. When writers experience a "mental block," they can focus on coding. Seeing the presentation take shape on-line can also stimulate more thoughts about what to write. Similarly, writing something and seeing it on-line can generate ideas on layout. Also, observing the incremental progress is rewarding; it shows that the effort is paying off. This can be much more satisfying than producing a few paragraphs on a sheet of paper. Staring at a piece of paper with a lot of cross-outs does not give you the same sense of achievement and satisfaction that a couple of paragraphs coded in HTML and viewed on-screen does. For these reasons, we recommend coding and writing simultaneously.

The best way to describe how an outline is made is to make one. For our sample outline, we used the process that describes how to clean a typical dorm room. The goal is to provide a set of instructions about cleaning. Suppose, for this example, that the dorm room consists of a bedroom, a bathroom with shower, and a small kitchen. Figure 4.7 illustrates the features of the room.

We begin by listing the main items and creating a title for the page.

```
<HTML>

<HEAD>
<TITLE>How to Clean a Dorm Room</TITLE>
</HEAD>

<BODY>
<H1>How to Clean a Dorm Room</H1>

<H3>Bathroom</H3>
<H3>Bedroom</H3>

<H3>Kitchen</H3>

</BODY>

</HTML>
```

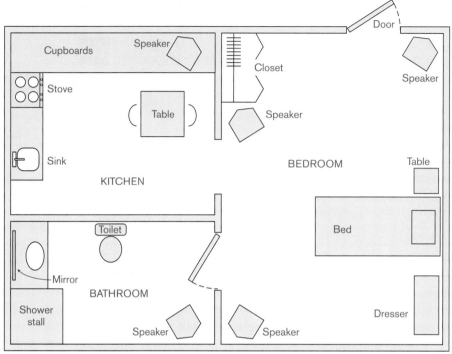

FIGURE 4.7
The dorm room used to illustrate the outlining process.

Useful Item

Notice in the code that we simply listed the names of the different rooms, and we chose to put them in alphabetical order. We also chose to capitalize the words in the title, using the rules of grammar. Observe that we listed the title of the document twice, once in the title tag and again as part of the body of the document. In the latter case, we used an <H1> level heading. The primary reason for repeating the title is so that it will be included on a hardcopy. We chose a modest size, <H3>, for our section headings. Figure 4.8 shows how the HTML code is rendered at this point.

Thus far, we have created a simple HTML document and a subheading for each of the three "rooms." Next, we expand the outline by inserting the subtasks into each room heading. This really amounts just to listing the items in the room. For example, for the bathroom, we need to include the floor, mirror, sink, shower stall, and toilet. For the bedroom, we have to deal with the bed, closet, dresser, floor, and table. For the kitchen, we list the countertops, cupboards, dishes, floor, sink, stovetop, and table. When we add these items into our outline, we will include some descriptive language to indicate exactly what needs to be done.

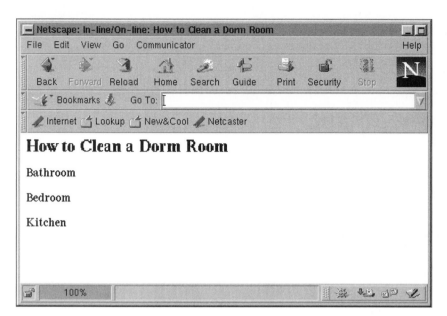

Here is a second cut at the outline. Observe how we have written the code to suggest further the structure of the outline.

```
<HTML>
<HEAD>
<TITLE>How to Clean a Dorm Room</TITLE>
</HEAD>
<BODY>
<H1>How to Clean a Dorm Room</H1>
<H3>Bathroom</H3>
<H5>Mop Floor</H5>
<H5>Wash Mirror</H5>
<H5>Clean Sink</H5>

<H5>Scrub Shower Stall</H5>
<H5>Scour Toilet</H5>
<H3>Bedroom</H3>
<H5>Change Sheets and Make Bed</H5>
<H5>Hang up Clothes in Closet</H5>
<H5>Straighten up and Close Dresser Drawers</H5>
<H5>Vacuum Floor</H5>
```

```
<H3>Kitchen</H3>

<H5>Wipe Down Countertops</H5>
<H5>Wipe Down Cupboards</H5>
<H5>Wash, Dry, and Put Away Dishes</H5>
<H5>Mop Floor</H5>
<H5>Clean Sink</H5>
<H5>Wipe Down Stovetop</H5>
<H5>Wipe Down Table</H5>

</BODY>

</HTML>
```

Note that for the subtopics related to each room, we have used <H5> headings. Figure 4.9 depicts our second pass at the outline.

At this point, the outline is pretty solid and will suffice for our purposes. Of course, items like "put away cleaning supplies, deodorize the rooms, and take out the garbage" could also be added. The key to becoming good at outline design is practice. The outlining process is partially dependent on the navigation process explored in Section 4.5.3.

Useful Item

We have skipped over one detail, debugging. Our code "came out correctly." While you are coding, however, it is a good idea to enter only a small amount of new code and then view it using your browser, to ensure that everything works correctly. Check to make sure you ended all tags appropriately, correctly spelled all tag names, used valid tags, and so on. The debugging process can be simplified by this approach, since errors are much more localized if only a few changes are implemented at a time. In Netscape 3.x or higher, if you have a syntax error and use the View Source option, the browser will flag the error with a special color and blink.

When you create your first Web pages, you might consider them to be expendable. Their purpose is to practice HTML and prototype. We should also note that you do not need a Web server to view your pages during development. They can be viewed from your own computer using your browser and can then be installed when they are ready.

4.5.3   Navigating

Useful Item

The *navigational tools* you provide are hyperlinks that allow your readers to move more smoothly through your pages. Readers should be able to jump over material that is uninteresting to them or move directly to any of the main sections. It should be convenient for them to return to either the main page or an index, which can easily be crafted from your outline.

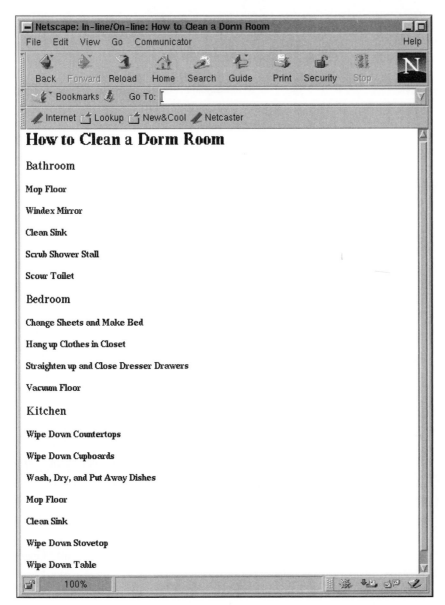

The organization of a Web presentation will dictate the nature of its accompanying navigational aids. Several general organizational arrangements have become popular.

- *Circular*—The circular arrangement of Web pages supports forward and backward movement through the pages. This format is especially good for describing step-by-step procedures or instructions or for

Useful Item

FIGURE 4.10
A four-page
circular Web
presentation.

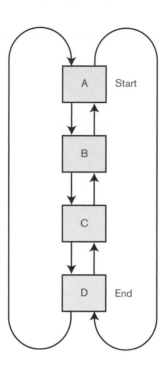

dividing up text that should be read sequentially. Figure 4.10 illustrates a four-page circular organization.

In Figure 4.10, the four pages are labeled A, B, C, and D, where A is the starting page and D is the ending page of the presentation. The hyperlinks are shown as arrows pointing to other pages. From the entry page A, a user can move to B, C, and then D. From D, they can return to the beginning by using the hyperlink to A. Notice that the hyperlinks from A to D can be followed in reverse order, to go from D to A.

Conceptually, the pure circular organization is very clean. Users have little trouble following the hyperlinks, and they always know where they are in the presentation. One drawback to this approach is that there is no way to jump to the middle of the presentation. However, since circular organizational structures are usually reserved for sequential presentations, this is not a serious hindrance. Furthermore, at the risk of introducing a bit more complexity to the navigation, hyperlinks to the middle of the presentation could be added when many pages are involved.

Useful Item

•   *Exploratory*—The *exploratory arrangement* allows jumping from nearly every page to nearly every other page, in an order determined by the user. This form is similar in structure to a spider web, and it works best for describing things like geographical areas or maps. Figure 4.11 depicts a nine-page exploratory arrangement.

The first thing you notice about the exploratory arrangement shown in Figure 4.11 is that there are a lot of hyperlinks. This gives the reader the freedom to move about as desired, but it also provides many opportunities for becoming lost. The weblike structure has no real beginning or ending, so it may be difficult to determine where you are in the presentation. Yet, for an on-line tourist map of a city, this type of navigation works best. However, for presentations of a more sequential nature, the exploratory arrangement may confuse the reader.

Another issue in the exploratory model is the effective display of the hyperlinks. For example, notice that page A has six outgoing hyperlinks. For a map, such names as N, NE, E, S, SW, and W might be effective for these links. In any case, the hyperlinks should be kept short and descriptive; otherwise, they may overwhelm the reader. *Image maps* work well in the exploratory type of organization.

- *Hierarchical*—The *hierarchical arrangement* permits a more limited number of hyperlinks from the introductory page, and each succeeding page leads to additional hyperlinks. This arrangement yields a treelike or directory structure. The *fanout*, defined as the maximum

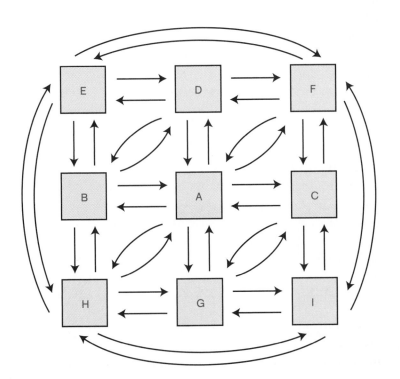

FIGURE 4.11
A nine-page exploratory Web presentation.

number of hyperlinks available from any page, should be kept small. In general, fanout should be no more than ten hyperlinks. The *depth* of the presentation, defined as the number of levels of the tree, should be restricted to five at most.

Useful Item

The hierarchical model is well suited for describing companies, institutions, and organizations, that is, entities that have an inherent hierarchy. For a typical presentation, values of three for fanout and three for depth should suffice. Figure 4.12 illustrates a 13-page hierarchical layout.

The arrangement shown in Figure 4.12 is very regular; that is, from each page on the second level, there are three subpages; each page on the third level has just one upward hyperlink; and so on. Obviously, such a regular structure makes it easy for the user to anticipate the navigational options that will be available on each page. Many organizational structures are not quite so regular. However, it is easy to modify a regular hierarchical arrangement to meet the organizational needs of most presentations, without giving up navigational ease.

Go On-Line

As you navigate different Web presentations, pay attention to the type of organization and navigation that you feel works best. Try to incorporate these designs into your Web presentations. Before embarking on the development of your own presentation, plan a global navigational scheme.

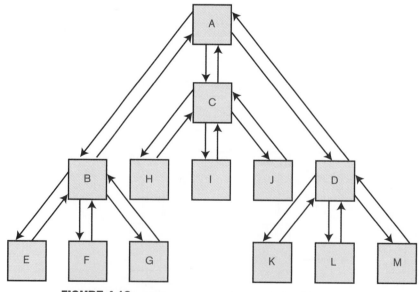

FIGURE 4.12
A thirteen-page hierarchical Web presentation.

In addition to the structure the user sees in your pages, you must decide on the physical organization of your files into directories and subdirectories. Suppose you were developing a page for your organization and you wanted to include a list of members. You might put all the biographies in one directory. If you had pictures of members, you might put those in yet another directory. The rule is to divide the material into as many different directories as makes sense.

Another practical issue is the way you name your files. Aim for consistency, and try to avoid simple but insidious coding errors. For example, on most modern operating systems, case is significant in file names. We recommend that you always use either upper or lowercase, but not a mixture, with some files uppercase and others lowercase. People sometimes capitalize the first letter of directory names and treat regular files as all lowercase. Even though the file system may allow blanks in file names, do not use blanks in Web file names—they get rendered as "%20" in URLs. If you use hyphens or underscores, use one or the other, but not both.

Useful Item

4.5.4   Designing and Coding

To write an effective Web presentation, set your goals and develop an outline and a global navigational design. Producing an HTML document from a design involves coding as well as writing. Therefore, you must be competent with HTML before trying to develop a serious Web presentation. You need to know what HTML provides in order to take full advantage of it.

The HTML tags presented in this book will enable you to produce a quality Web presentation. Some might argue that a decent writer could develop a reasonable Web presentation; others might suggest that a good HTML programmer could generate an effective Web presentation. We believe that neither of these skills is sufficient by itself. The writing and coding are both essential, and they should take place in parallel. This is true whether the presentation is being developed by an individual or a group.

Many good Webmasters acquired some of their skills by studying other Web presentations. Although useful, this strategy can only take you so far. Our goal is to provide you with the means to design, develop, and code your own presentations. The design and coding process that we have found works best is as follows:

1. *Navigating*—Use your list of goals and your outline to design a navigational strategy based on one of those presented in Section 4.5.3, or modify one of those to suit your needs better, or formulate a new navigational scheme. Once the strategy is designed, add the HTML

code. Set up the appropriate number of pages and the hyperlinks between them. Migrate the relevant parts of the outline into each page, but keep a copy of the original outline. Use section headings from the outline as titles for the pages, or assign new titles. Design, code, and insert *headers and footers* into each page, as discussed in Section 7.3. You should now have a shell for the entire presentation. You should also be able to navigate through the presentation and get a good feel for what the final result will look and feel like.

Useful Item

2. *Coding and writing*—With the outlining and coding you have done so far, you have created places for the writing. Our experience shows that writing flows more readily when writers have a good sense of what and how much they need to write. The shell you have developed should provide a reasonable direction for the text.

    If you hit a writing block, continue coding. When you are not sure how to code something, do more writing. Periodically view what you have created. This will help with the debugging.

3. *Revising*—After you have completed the first draft of the presentation, if you let it sit for a while, you will probably come back to the project with a new perspective. It is then time to begin the revising process.

4.5.5   Revising

Having completed the first draft of your Web presentation, you have decided on a topic, set goals, outlined the project, developed the navigation, done some designing, and then written, coded, and debugged the material. Fine-tuning is the crucial step for converting an average presentation into an excellent one. The goal at this point is to move forward with the remaining work of perfecting your presentation.

Useful Item

Prototyping, which has played an important role in computer science, involves designing a system to work out the kinks and learn how the system should really be built. Sometimes the prototype is discarded and a completely new system is built. The main idea is to keep revising until you are satisfied with the final product.

If you decide to solicit feedback from others, explain your goals and ask for critical evaluations of your presentation. Other viewpoints can provide constructive ideas that can help you to improve your presentation. As you become more accomplished at Web design, the revision process will require fewer iterations.

Some of the issues to consider when revising a Web presentation are:

Useful Item

- *Check navigation*—Test all hyperlinks. Make sure the overall navigation is appropriate and easy to use. Critically evaluate the descriptions of the hyperlinks themselves, using the criteria established in Section 2.7.3.

- *Comment code*—Thoroughly comment your code so that on a later revision, you can recall what you did and why.

- *Final evaluation*—Did you meet your goals? Did you complete all of the tasks from the outline? If not, address the issues that are still outstanding.

- *Graphics*—Are the graphics you used necessary, are there enough graphics, and do they enhance the presentation? Do the graphics load fast enough? Are the graphics properly positioned? Would they look better elsewhere?

- *Headers and footers*—Make sure all headers and footers are consistent.

- *Reread*—Critically evaluate your writing. Check that everything makes sense. Pay attention to the little details, such as consistent spacing after punctuation, consistent capitalization, and so on.

- *Spell check*—At a minimum, run the pages through a spell-checking program.

- *View pages with another browser*—This will confirm that your pages will look good using various browsers and not just the one you used to develop the pages. Recall that different browsers can render certain HTML tags differently (or not support certain HTML tags at all). Also, some browsers are more "forgiving" and will allow HTML syntax errors to render correctly, while other browsers may not even display the page or may display it in an unexpected fashion.

The better the overall design, the less time will be needed to manage the completed presentation. The management of a well-designed presentation should only involve updating. As you gain more experience, you may want to modify this revision checklist to suit your personal needs better. Learn your own strengths and weaknesses, so that you can better focus your attention.

EXERCISES 4.5

Web Presentation Outline, Design, and Management

26. Construct a humorous Web page containing an exaggerated use of images and phrases indicating how to return home.

27. Create a Web page outlining the rules of your favorite board game. Among other things, use various heading tags.

28. Outline the process of obtaining a college degree in your major. Put your description into a Web page that uses a number of heading tags for various section levels.

29. In HTML, outline the process of buying new hiking boots.

30. Produce an HTML outline describing the process of eating around a campfire.

31. Describe two other possible organizational models for a Web presentation. (The text describes circular, exploratory, and hierarchical.) When might they prove useful?

32. Draw a circular organizational scheme with three pages. In a circular organization consisting of n pages, what is the maximum number of hyperlinks you would need to follow to reach any other single page?

33. Draw a five-page exploratory organization of pages in which it is possible to go directly from each page to every other page. How many hyperlinks are involved? Can you devise a formula, as a function of the number of pages, for the number of hyperlinks involved in such a "complete" scheme?

34. How many pages would a fanout four and depth five hierarchical scheme be able to accommodate? How many hyperlinks are involved?

35. List three management tasks that an ongoing Web presentation might require. Elaborate on each one.

4.6   Registering Web Pages

Registering a Web page means having the page *indexed* by a search engine or having other prominent pages display hyperlinks to the page. The goal is to have the page viewed by more users. If a search engine indexes a page, then the search engine can return the page to users' queries. The more search engines that know about the page, the more likely the page will be accessed. Similarly, having several other pages add hyperlinks to a page increases the likelihood that the page will be visited.

How do you register your Web page? Many search engines allow you to fill out and submit an on-line form telling the search engine about your page. Search engine designers want their programs to know about more Web pages than any other search engine. Program performance is judged by the speed of the search and the number of *hits* a search engine finds. A hit means the search engine found a page that matched a query. By registering your Web page, you are helping a search engine to expand its knowledge base. Most users register their pages with many different search engines.

Search engines may index your page automatically, since they have techniques for "going out and seeing" what is currently available on the Web. This begs the question of whether search engine registration is necessary, in the sense of proactively seeking registration, rather than waiting to be found eventually. Adequate publicity may occur in a group newsletter or a posting on an email list.

There are some businesses on the Web whose pages get visited often. Usually, a business will add a hyperlink to a specific page, for a fee. This service is most commonly used by people with commercial pages. Several nonbusiness-related pages also receive a tremendous number of hits, and under the appropriate circumstances, you can ask them to include a hyperlink to your page. For example, they might find your page interesting and complementary to their pages. There are also noncommercial, nonsearch engine sites that are interested in having hyperlinks to pages on a specific topic. For example, someone may have the definitive "Theta Gamma Pi" page and be interested in a hyperlink to your Greek chapter.

Useful Item

There are also directory services that you can notify about your page. Such services are generally subject-specific or may pertain only to a certain group. For example, there is a Web page where Appalachian Trail thru-hikers can register their Web pages. Other groups have indexes where a member can add a hyperlink to their page. Once listed in the directory, a page is more likely to be visited.

Another consideration to registration and publicity is *traffic*. The person responsible for the server on which your pages reside may not be prepared to handle an enormous bulge in traffic. Consult with your server manager if you have a Web page that you feel could become very popular.

The challenge is knowing where to register your page to obtain a larger audience. If your goal is to maximize the number of hits to your pages, register the pages in as many places as possible.

EXERCISES 4.6

Registering Web Pages

36.   Does your school or organization have a listing of Web pages where you can register yours? If so, describe the registration procedure. If you would like, register your page with them.

37.   Provide the URLs of three businesses that will add a hyperlink to your Web page from their presentation. What are the costs of doing this, and how many hits do the businesses claim to receive per week?

38.   (This exercise illustrates the unlikelihood of someone randomly coming across your page.) Suppose Tammy Howard is able to visit one Web page every 15 seconds, and there are a total of 1,000,000,000 Web pages. Using a random search strategy, how long will it take before Tammy has at least a 50 percent chance of visiting the Appalachian Trail Place Web page?

4.7   Lynx: Text-Based Web Browser

The most widely used text-based Web browser is called *Lynx*. Its name is a pun on the word "links," short for hyperlinks. Lynx is available on a number of platforms. It can be used through a shell account. Unlike graphical-based browsers, such as Netscape and Internet Explorer, Lynx cannot display graphics or other forms of multimedia. However, Lynx is fast and easy to use.

Useful Item

An important advantage of viewing an HTML document with a text-based browser is that it will load more quickly, since the browser does not have to handle images. A distinct disadvantage is that you cannot view the images that often add to the effectiveness of the page. Most Web authors use graphics liberally in their pages, including for navigation; for the most part, they assume that readers use graphical browsers. Therefore, some content and context may be lost without the accompanying images, and navigation through such a Web presentation might be less straightforward. Nevertheless, a well-thought-out and carefully planned Web presentation designed with all users in mind can be understandable and easy to navigate, regardless of the browser used.

The best way to explore the differences between Lynx and a graphical-based Web browser is to see how the two render the same HTML document. Figure 4.13 depicts a Web page rendered by Lynx, and Figure 4.14 shows

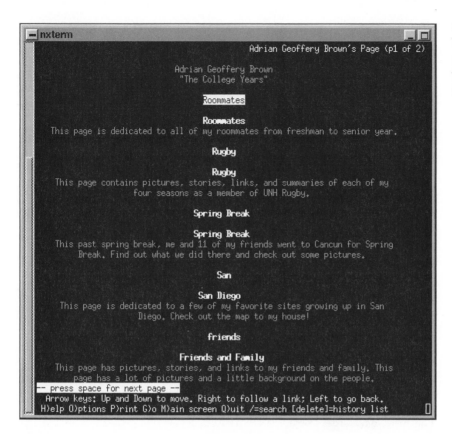

FIGURE 4.13
Web page rendered with a text-based browser.

how a graphical-based browser renders the same page. In Figure 4.13, notice that the page is just as readable as the page in Figure 4.14. The ALT attribute of the image tag provides the reader with a description of the image. If the ALT attribute is not used, Lynx displays [INLINE] where the in-line image was supposed to go.[4]

If you include the ALT attribute on all of your in-line images, your Web pages will be readable using Lynx, even though some other HTML elements will not come through. Designing a page specifically for Lynx is not the same as designing a page for a graphical client. For example, colors, font faces, syntactic- and semantic-based style types, and so on will usually not show up. Lynx may also have trouble with more complex

Useful Item

---

4   [INLINE] is displayed as long as the *pseudo_inlines mode* is on. If the mode is off, in-line images without an ALT attribute will be ignored; there will be no indication that an image was supposed to be on the page. Always use the ALT attribute on images, so that Lynx users will be able to follow your pages.

FIGURE 4.14
Web page
rendered with a
graphical-based
browser.

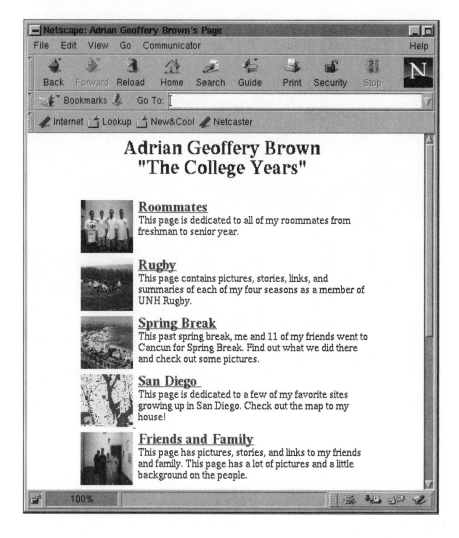

HTML elements, such as forms, frames, and tables, depending on how they are used. However, simple HTML documents created for graphical-based browsers generally render well with Lynx.

4.7.1   Starting Lynx

Go On-Line

Lynx is run by typing `lynx` at the operating system prompt (or by launching a Lynx application from a menu). This brings up the default home page or "main screen." Typing `lynx` followed by a specific URL will cause that document to be loaded initially. For example, entering

```
%lynx www.mhhe.com
```

will start you off with McGraw-Hill's Web page.

To exit Lynx, type q. Lynx will ask if you really want to quit. If you respond by entering y, you will exit Lynx; entering n will return you to Lynx. To exit Lynx without being asked for verification, enter Q or CONTROL-D. This is sometimes called "quick quit."

Pressing ? or h will provide on-line documentation about Lynx. You can also set the program to display some of the basic commands at the bottom of each screen, as shown in Figure 4.13. This is a configurable option.

4.7.2   Basic Navigation

Hyperlinks in a document viewed with a graphical browser are usually underlined and highlighted in color. Hyperlinks usually do not stand out as well in Lynx as they do on graphical browsers. Viewed with Lynx, hyperlinks normally appear in a darker text when the cursor is over them. Sometimes, they appear in reverse video, and on some systems, they may appear in color.

You can use the up (↑) and down (↓) arrow keys to move from hyperlink to hyperlink. To position the cursor at the next hyperlink, use the down arrow. To move the cursor back to the previous hyperlink, use the up arrow. To follow a hyperlink, press the enter key, the right arrow (→), or the right parenthesis ()) while the cursor is positioned over the link. This will load the selected Web page. To return to the previously loaded page, use the left arrow (←).

If an HTML document does not fit on one screen, you will have to scroll. With graphical browsers, this can be accomplished by using the mouse to click on the scroll bar beside the window. In Lynx, you must use the plus (+) key or press the space bar to scroll down to the next page; use minus (−) or b to scroll up to the previous page.

4.7.3   Features

Lynx maintains a history list in which each entry is a document that you previously visited. To display the history list, use the backspace key or the delete key. A document can also be revisited by selecting it (that is, moving the cursor to it and pressing the return key). Return to the main screen by pressing m. The equivalent of typing a URL in the location area of a graphical browser window and pressing the return key is to enter g, type in a URL, and then press the return key.

A useful browser feature is the ability to view HTML source code for a document. With graphical browsers, you click on View Source. The backslash (\) command in Lynx toggles between the rendered version of the document and the HTML source code. To display information about the document (or the currently selected link), such as the URL, title, number of lines in the document, and so on, use the equal (=) key.

To stop the transmission of a document once you have requested it, use the z command. This is the same as clicking on the Stop button on a graphical browser. To reload the document you are viewing, press CONTROL-R.

The Options Menu allows you to view and change a number of configurable options. To look at the Options Menu, press o. One option is Bookfile, which specifies the filename and location of your bookmark file. Another option is User Mode, which determines the help information to be displayed at the bottom of your screen (the help information uses space allotted to the document display area). If "novice" is the mode specified, several lines of help information will be displayed. The "intermediate" user mode displays nothing at the bottom of the screen. The "advanced" user mode displays the URL of the currently selected hyperlink in much the same way that a graphical browser displays the URL of a highlighted hyperlink.

Useful Item

4.7.4   Bookmarks

In Lynx, a bookmark filename must be specified in the Options Menu, under the Bookmark file (on your system, this may have a default value). While viewing a document, press a to create a bookmark. You will be asked if you want to save the document's URL (option d), save the URL of the hyperlink that is currently selected on the page (option l), or cancel without saving any bookmark (option c). To view your list of bookmarks, use the v command. The bookmarks list will be displayed as hyperlinks.

4.7.5   Printing

The p command is used to print a document. A document cannot be printed directly from Lynx; therefore, the p command will present you with several choices. One option allows you to mail the document to yourself. Figure 4.15 demonstrates using the p command to mail a document to emhepp@aol.com. Another option is to "Save to a local file" and then print from there. Other print options may be available, depending on what the system administrator has set up at your installation.

4.7.6   Images

Images cannot be viewed with Lynx. However, images can be downloaded and then viewed using a graphics viewer, such as LViewPro. In-line images

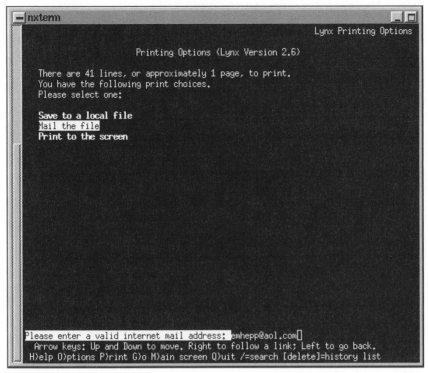

FIGURE 4.15
The process of mailing a Lynx-rendered document to emhepp@aol.com.

will (usually) be depicted as either [INLINE] or an ALT string. Comparing Figures 4.13 and 4.14, you will see that San and friends are ALT strings representing the image of San Diego and the image of Adrian's friends and family, respectively. To download an image, view the source code by using the backslash command and note the URL

```
<IMG SRC = "...">
```

used in the specification. If the URL is absolute, use the g command and enter the URL. If the URL is relative, you must find the complete path name, which you can do by using the equal (=) command. Next, use the g command and enter the absolute URL. You will then be prompted either to Download (d) or Cancel (c). Select d and then choose "Save to disk." You can then enter a new filename for the file or just press the return key and save it using the original name. A copy of the image file will then be located in your home directory.

If the image you want to view is an *external image* (an image that is loaded when you select its hyperlink), simply select that hyperlink and, when prompted to Download or Cancel, choose d. Then, as with in-line images, select "Save to disk" and either rename the file or save it as is by pressing the return key. After downloading an image, you can return to the Web document you were viewing by pressing the back arrow.

4.7.7   Lynx Commands Summary

Go On-Line

Other Lynx commands and topics not mentioned here can be explored either on-line via the h command or through a Lynx tutorial, a number of which are available on the Web. Additional topics worth exploring include the Lynx Forms Interface, USENET News Posting with Lynx, and Directory Editing of Local Files.

- a—Add to bookmarks.

- – or b—Scroll up to previous page.

- g or)—Go to a specific URL.

- h or ?—Help.

- m—Return to main screen.

- o—Show Options Menu.

- p—Display print options.

- q—Quit Lynx.

- Q or CONTROL-D—"Quick quit" Lynx.

- v—View bookmarks.

- z—Stop the transmission of a document.

- ↓—Move the cursor to the next hyperlink.

- ←—Return to the previous HTML document.

- →—Follow a hyperlink.

- ↑—Move the cursor to the preceding hyperlink.

- + or space bar—Scroll down to the next page.

- =—Show document information.

- \—Toggle between rendered code and source code.

- CONTROL-R—Reload the document.

- backspace or delete key—Show the history list.

EXERCISES 4.7

Lynx: Text-Based Web Browser

39. Find two Web pages:
    (a) One that uses images but displays effectively using either a graphical browser or a text-based browser. Provide the URL of the Web page and discuss why the page works.
    (b) One that does not display well using Lynx. Provide its URL and describe how the page could be modified to make it suitable for viewing with a text-based browser.

40. Find out if there is a way to search for a text string in a document using the Lynx browser. If so, what is the command or procedure and how is it applied?

41. Save an image of mountains through Lynx. Were you able to use the steps from Section 4.7.6, or did you need to do something different on your computer?

42. Design an HTML document, specifically for viewing with Lynx, that describes your favorite hiking trail.

43. Run some experiments loading a number of Web pages through Lynx and then through a graphical browser. How much time savings did you notice in downloading the pages using Lynx? If you turn off images on the graphical browser, do you still notice Lynx loading faster? Explain. Do you feel that the time savings provided by Lynx justifies its use, or is too much content and context lost?

Searching the World Wide Web

I was getting close to the halfway point of my journey, but I had not been averaging the number of miles needed to finish the trail in under 100 days. I started hiking longer days and from this point on did not take any more rest days—days when I did not hike. Harper's Ferry, West Virginia is where AT headquarters is located. Each thru-hiker who stops here poses for a picture, and photo albums categorized by year house all their images. In the trail registers, I had been reading about a lot of the hikers I was now seeing for the first time. It was great to identify real people with the adventures I had been reading about, and it was exciting to think I would be meeting many of these folks just a little further up the trail. I left civilization once more and was happy to head back out into the woods with the anticipation of making many new friends.

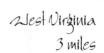

West Virginia
3 miles

Chapter 5

5.1 INTRODUCTION

With the advent of the World Wide Web came the widespread availability of on-line information. It is no longer necessary to travel to the library to find the answer to a question or engage in research on a specialized topic. Much of what you might want to know is available through the Web. Since anyone can publish on the Web, the range of topics that can be found is nearly all-encompassing. However, while a lot of information is available on-line, not all of it is accurate. In Section 3.6.1, you learned that it is necessary to evaluate information on the Web very critically.

In all likelihood, the answers to your questions are somewhere on the Web, but how do you locate them? In the early days of the Web, unless you knew exactly where to look, you had trouble finding what you wanted. Unlike a library, the pages on the Web are not as neatly organized as books on shelves, nor are Web pages completely cataloged in one central location. Even knowing where to look for information (that is, knowing a URL) is not a guarantee that you will find it, since Web page addresses are constantly changing. Usually, a forwarding address is provided for a page that has moved, but it may only be available for a short time.

Imagine walking into a library where books are piled up and strewn about without any order. Finding what you are looking for would be next to impossible. As the World Wide Web rapidly grew, so did the need to keep track of "what's what" and "what's where." In the initial stages of the Web, it was hard to locate useful information.

In the early days of the World Wide Web, two graduate students at Stanford University, Jerry Yang and David Filo, came up with a way to organize hyperlinks by category in a way that they found useful. In late 1993 this collection was known as "Jerry Yang's Guide to the WWW." The name was soon changed to Yahoo! and the first search tool was born.

Today there is quite a collection of search tools available that allows us to find information on the Web quickly and easily. The collection of search tools is constantly evolving, with new ones coming on the scene and others disappearing. Rather than report on how each of the popular search tools works, we will explain a few of them and suggest some Web presentations that provide reviews of all of the current search tools available. Figure 5.1 shows the Search Engine Watch Web page. In addition to providing a very good comparison and analysis of the search tools available, Search Engine Watch is also an excellent source for current news about search engines and

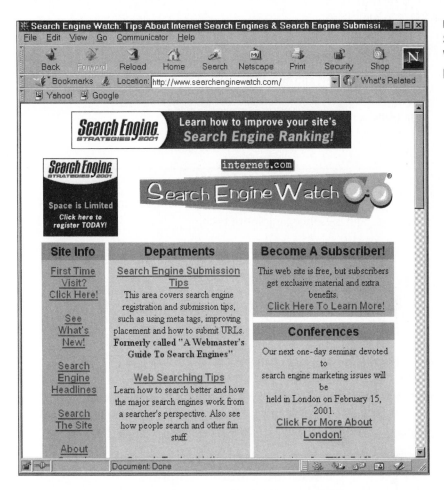

FIGURE 5.1
Search Engine
Watch main
page.

directories. A list of useful resources about search tools (including Search
Engine Watch) is provided in what follows:

5.1.1   Useful Resources About Search Tools

Finding Information On the Internet: A Tutorial—
   `www.lib.berkeley.edu/TeachingLib/Guides/Internet/`
   `FindInfo.html`

Guide to Effective Internet Searching—
   `www.thewebtools.com/tutorial/tutorial.htm`

Search Engine Guide—`www.searchengineguide.com`

Search Engine Watch—`www.searchenginewatch.com`

Spider's Apprentice—`www.monash.com/spidap.html`

Go On-Line

You have probably already been using some of the search tools, but perhaps not as effectively as possible. Other tools may be new to you. In this chapter, you will learn what types of search tools are available, how to use them efficiently, and how they work. The references accompanying this book provide many additional avenues in which to explore search engines. Our goals here are:

Objectives

- To describe directories, search engines, metasearch engines, and white pages and present examples of each.

- To define the "invisible Web."

- To discuss search fundamentals, such as query types.

- To describe search strategies using a number of sample searches.

- To explore several search tools in depth.

- To examine how search engines work.

5.2 Directories, Search Engines, and Metasearch Engines

Two basic approaches have evolved in response to the need to organize and locate information on the World Wide Web: directories and search engines. (As we will see, many directories also offer a search feature that allows you to locate information in the directory easily.) In both approaches, information about Web pages is contained in some database that has already been created, either manually or using special programs that search the Web for pages. Your request for information is answered by the search tool retrieving the information from its already-constructed database of indexed Web pages.

Various factors will determine how well a search tool will work for you: how large its database of information is, how up-to-date the database is (no "dead" or expired hyperlinks), Web pages with current information, whether the Web pages that are cataloged are quality pages and nonredundant, how well the search tool organizes and catalogs the information to be accessed in the database, and finally, how proficient you are at using the tool.

In creating the database for a search tool, it is obvious that a human editor will be better than a computer program at interpreting Web pages to decide what categories to place a page in and what logical relationships exist between topics on a page (for example, distinguishing between Java, the programming language and java, the coffee). However, even though the special programs that search the Web for pages to add to the database lack the analytical skills of a human being, they work tirelessly, adding new information and keeping a database current. Indexing Web pages is a huge job—as of this writing, it is estimated that Google, one of the larger search engines, has over 1.35 billion Web pages cataloged.

5.2.1   Directories

The first method of finding and organizing Web information is the directory approach. A directory offers a hierarchical representation of hyperlinks to Web pages and presentations broken down into topics and subtopics. The hierarchy can descend many levels. The specific number of levels is determined by the taxonomy of the topic. Human editors (either a paid staff or volunteers) usually review and classify the Web pages and presentations that are added to a directory.

Directories can be classified as either *general* or *specialized*. A general directory is also called a *Web directory,* a *subject directory,* or sometimes a *Web guide*. The top level of a general directory provides a wide range of very broad topics such as arts, automobiles, education, news, science, sports, and so on. Figure 5.2 illustrates the top level of Yahoo!, a popular Web directory. Yahoo! offers 14 top level categories on its main page but only four are visible in Figure 5.2: Arts & Humanities, Business & Economy, News & Media, and Recreation & Sports. Not shown in Figure 5.2 are Computers & Internet, Education, Entertainment, Government, Health, Reference, Regional, Science, Social Science, and Society & Culture. Figure 5.3 displays the main page of another Web directory, Look-Smart. LookSmart has 10 top-level categories on its main page, so browsing through categories in each of the two Web directories will be different.

In addition to being very easy to use, another benefit of a directory structure is that you need not know exactly what you are looking for in order to find something worthwhile. You select (click on) the category for the topic in which you are interested. You continue to move down through the hierarchy, selecting subcategories and narrowing the search at each level, until you are presented with a list of hyperlinks that pertain to your topic.

Useful Item

FIGURE 5.2

Yahoo! main
page.

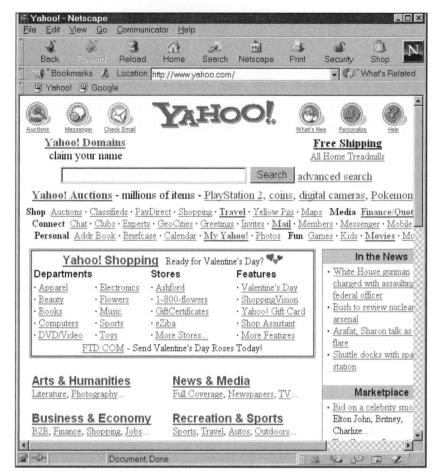

Reproduced with permission of Yahoo! Inc. © 2000 by Yahoo! Inc. Yahoo! and the YAHOO! Logo are trademarks
of Yahoo! Inc.

As you begin to zero in on your topic, you may find other interesting
items of which you were previously unaware. On the other hand, you may
reach the bottom of the directory without finding the information you were
after. In such cases, you may need to backtrack, going up several levels
and then proceeding down again. Of course, it is possible that the directory
you are searching does not contain the information you want, in which case
you may decide to try either a different directory or a search engine.

When traversing a directory downward, you are moving toward more
specific topics. When going upward, you are heading back to more general
topics. Directories are useful if you want to explore a topic and its related
areas, or if you want to research a subject, but not at a very detailed level.

If you are interested in a very specific topic, you may want to start
off by using a search engine or a metasearch engine. Arriving at a very
specific topic in a directory structure involves traversing between five and
ten hyperlink levels.

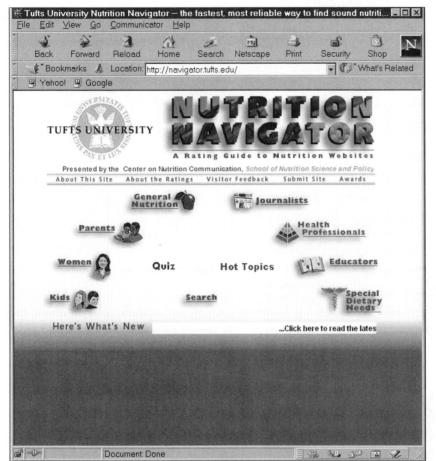

FIGURE 5.4
Tufts University
Nutrition
Navigator main
page.

Infomine—Scholarly Internet Resource Collections—
   `infomine.ucr.edu/Main.html`

Pinakes: A Subject Launchpad—
   `www.hw.ac.uk/libWWW/irn/pinakes/pinakes.html`

WWW Virtual Library—`conbio.rice.edu/vl/database`

Yahoo! Reference > Web Directories—
   `dir.yahoo.com/Reference/web_directories`

In addition to providing a shortcut to finding obscure information on
the World Wide Web, some subject guides also provide access to what
as become known as the *invisible Web*—information that is not available
to general search engines accessing the Web. The invisible Web is also

Hot Topic

FIGURE 5.5
Tufts University
Nutrition
Navigator
General Nutrition
page.

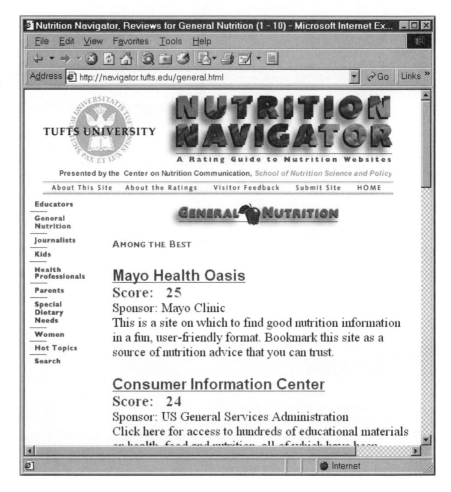

referred to as the *hidden* or *deep* Web, while the other part of the Web that can be cataloged by search engines has been dubbed the *surface Web* or *visible Web*. The invisible Web includes information in databases and other searchable resources like archives that search engines such as Google cannot access. Other documents on the Web might be overlooked by the search engines because they contain data types that cannot be cataloged, such as multimedia files and *PDF* files (*PDF* stands for Adobe's *Portable Document Format*). The company BrightPlanet.com estimates that the invisible Web is 500 times larger than what search engines can cover.

The information available through the invisible Web is very specific. For instance, to find real-time information about airline flights in the United States, you can check the FAA database that is considered to be part of the invisible Web. Figure 5.7 depicts a Web page from TRIP.com that displays real-time flight information about in-flight planes. The Web page

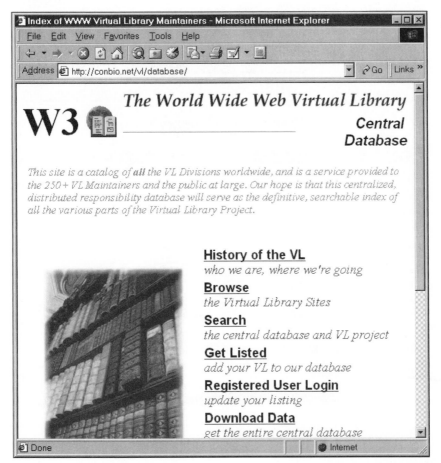

FIGURE 5.6
WWW Virtual
Library main
page.

contains the departure time and expected arrival time of a particular flight; it is updated each minute with new information from the flight database concerning the speed of the plane as well as its altitude and heading.

One of the problems with tapping the invisible Web is knowing what databases and archives are available. Some Web presentations, such as Direct Search, whose main page is shown in Figure 5.8, offer a gateway to the invisible Web. By using a gateway to the invisible Web, you can find relevant databases and then use the database-specific search tool to retrieve the information you want efficiently.

Some interesting gateways to the invisible Web are:

Complete Planet—www.completeplanet.com

Direct Search—gwis2.circ.gwu.edu/~gprice/direct.htm

Go On-Line

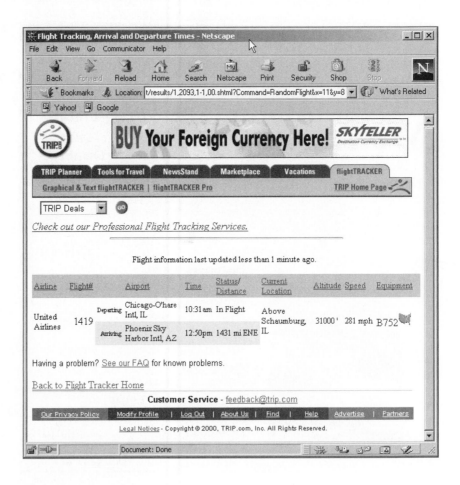

Infomine—infomine.ucr.edu/search.phtml

Invisibleweb.com—www.invisibleweb.com

Invisible Web Catalog—
    dir.lycos.com/Reference/Searchable_Databases

Useful Item

Some tools are also being developed to search the World Wide Web, including IntelliSeek's BullsEye and BrightPlanet's LexiBot are downloadable software that sit on your desktop and allow you to search multiple Web presentations and databases for information. For example, LexiBot gathers information from 600 sources (you can specify which of them you want searched) and then saves the information for you to review off-line in a desktop database.

FIGURE 5.8
Direct Search
main page.

5.2.2 Popular General Directories

Go On-Line

Here is a list of some of the popular general directories.

LookSmart—`www.looksmart.com`

Lycos—`www.lycos.com`

Open Directory Project (ODP)—`www.dmoz.com` or `www.dmoz.org`

Yahoo!—`www.yahoo.com`

These Web directories can be considered general directories in that they provide links to pages on a wide range of topics.

Notice that the URLs for many of the directories have the following form[1]:

`http://www.directoryname.com`

Useful Item

URLs for search engines, metasearch engines, and white pages often have this form as well. Some browsers allow you to type just the name of the search tool into the location area. For example, if you enter `yahoo` into the location area in the Netscape browser window and press the Return key, the browser expands `yahoo` into

`http://www.yahoo.com`

and takes you to the Yahoo! directory.

5.2.3   Some Subject Guides

Go On-Line

The following are examples of specific directories. They provide hyper-links to Web pages or presentations pertaining only to a particular field or topic.

The Alternative Medicine Home Page—
   `www.pitt.edu/~cbw/altm.html`

Copyright Resources on the Internet—
   `groton.k12.ct.us/mts/pt2a.htm`

Financial Aid Resource Center—`www.theoldschool.org`

Tufts University Nutrition Navigator—`navigator.tufts.edu`

5.2.4   Search Engines

The second approach to organizing information and locating information on the Web is a search engine, which is a computer program that does the following:

1.   Allows you to submit a form containing a *query* that consists of a word or phrase describing the specific information you are trying to locate on the Web.

---

1   Recall that we omit the leading `http://` and the trailing `/` on URLs, unless discussing a specific point about naming.

2.   Searches its database to try to match your query.

3.   Collates and returns a list of clickable URLs containing presentations that *match* your query; the list is usually ordered, with the better matches appearing at the top.

4.   Permits you to revise and resubmit a query.

A number of search engines also provide URLs for related or suggested topics.

Like directories, search engines can be classified as either *general* or *specialty search engines.* A general search engine retrieves information from a database that contains information on a wide variety of topics. A specialty search engine is also called a *vertical search engine* or a *topic search engine,* and its database contains information on a specific topic. Because its focus is narrow, a specialty search engine can usually provide in-depth information on specific topics that may be more valuable for a particular application.

Many people find that search engines are not as easy to use as directories. To use a search engine, you supply a query by entering information into a field on the screen. To be effective—that is, to have the search engine return a small list of URLs on your topic of interest—you often need to be very specific. To pose such queries, you must learn the *query syntax* of the search engine with which you are working. Learning the syntax so that you can phrase effective and legal queries often requires that you read and understand the documentation accompanying the search engine. A hyperlink to the documentation is usually provided next to the query field, and example queries are often given.

Once you learn to use a specific search engine's query language effectively, you can quickly zoom in on very narrow topics. This is the advantage of a search engine. The disadvantages are that you have to learn the query language and you have to learn a search strategy.

The user-friendliness and power of query languages vary from search engine to search engine. We recommend you try several of them and then learn the syntax of one search engine's query language. Since each search engine searches a different database, you would be best off learning about a search engine that has indexed an extensive amount of material of interest to you. You may be able to gauge this by posing similar queries to a number of search engines and seeing which one finds the best matches.

Some versions of Netscape 4.x allow you to enter a search query directly into the browser's location area. The query must contain a space; otherwise, the browser will try to interpret it as a URL. One of the search

Useful Item

engines that Netscape knows about will be used to process the query. For example, typing

```
Killface cat
```

into the browser's location area will result in the query `"Killface cat"` being posed to a search engine. This saves you a step, because you do not have to bring up a search engine separately before posing a query.

Go On-Line

5.2.5   Popular Search Engines

Here is a list of some popular search engines.

> *AltaVista*—`www.altavista.com`
>
> *AskJeeves*—`www.ask.com`
>
> *Excite*—`www.excite.com`
>
> *FAST Search*—`www.alltheweb.com`
>
> *Google*—`www.google.com`
>
> *NorthernLight*—`www.northernlight.com`

By visiting the sites listed in Sections 5.2.2 and 5.2.5, you can see that a number of sites provide directory, as well as search engine, capabilities. This is not surprising, since a large database can support either mechanism if the appropriate interface is in place.

The distinction between directories and search engines may become blurred over time, and a new hybrid category called "direct search" or something similar may be necessary to classify the new search tools.

5.2.6   Specialty Search Engines

Specialty search engines exist for a multitude of topics, including MP3s, shopping, news, travel, and medical information. Many Web presentations exist that provide search tools to find specialty search engines (often these will provide links to subject guides as well). In addition to finding information on a narrow topic, specialty search engines are another way that we have to tap the invisible Web.

Moreover.com is a specialty search engine for news; it searches 1,800 on-line news sources for up-to-date news items and stories. This search engine can categorize and retrieve content by using *XML (eXtensible Markup Language)* database technology. Because it is not trying to catalog the entire Web, Moreover.com can visit its sources as often as every 15 minutes. This allows it to maintain a news database that is relevant and current. Moreover.com provides access to on-line news items that would take weeks to appear in a general search engine that tries to catalog the entire Web.

Another specialty search engine is the comparison shopping search engine, mySimon, shown in Figure 5.9. mySimon maintains a database of on-line shopping information that allows consumers to easily compare millions of products at thousands of on-line stores. Figure 5.9 shows the result page of searching for "Aeron chair" at mySimon.

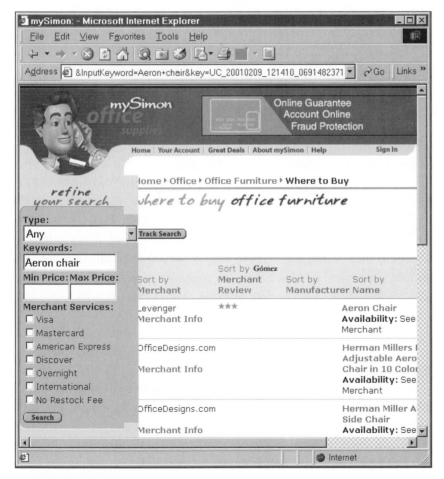

FIGURE 5.9
mySimon with a query of "Aeron chair."

5.2.7   Popular Specialty Search Engines

Go On-Line

Here is a list of a few specialized search engines:

Moreover—`www.moreover.com`

MP3 Search—`www.mp3search.nu`

MySimon—`www.mysimon.com`

Travelocity.com—`www.travelocity.com`

To locate specialized search engines, refer to the InvisibleWeb Catalog:

The Search Engine of Search Engines—`www.invisibleweb.com`

5.2.8   Metasearch Engines

A *metasearch engine* or *all-in-one search engine* performs a search by calling on more than one other search engine to do the actual work. A metasearch engine does not maintain its own database of information; by submitting searches to other search engines, it queries the databases of the other search engines. The particular set of search engines that each metasearch engine will send a query to varies. For instance, as of this writing, the metasearch engine Dogpile submits its search queries to LookSmart, GoTo, FindWhat, Open Directory, and Google (as well as others). As of this writing, metasearch engine MetaCrawler submits its search queries to AltaVista, DirectHit, Excite, FindWhat, and Google (and others as well).

Many metasearch engines will collate the search results into one list, remove duplicates, and then rank the pages according to how well they match your query. Others, like Dogpile, will provide results from each search engine separately. Figure 5.10 shows the results from a query of Appalachian Trail submitted to Dogpile. On the results page displayed in Figure 5.10, the LookSmart directory located one Web page about the Appalachian Trail, while GoTo.com found 10 pages. (The GoTo.com results are not visible in the figure.) Some metasearch engines allow you to customize how your results are displayed and which search engines your query will be sent to.

Along these lines are Copernic (`www.copernic.com`) and WebFerret (`www.ferretsoft.com/netferret`), two examples of metasearch tools

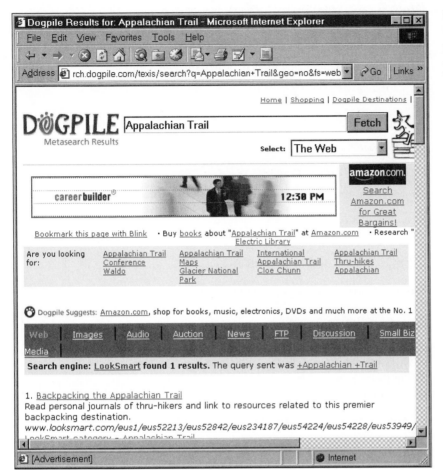

FIGURE 5.10
Dogpile results page for a query of "Appalachian Trail."

that are downloaded and installed on your desktop. Although they involve a learning curve, they enable you to customize your metasearching.

The advantage of a metasearch engine is that you can access a number of different search engines with a single query. The disadvantage is that you will often have a high noise-to-signal ratio; that is, a lot of the "matches" will not be of interest to you. This means you will need to spend more time evaluating the results and deciding which hyperlinks to follow.

For very specific, hard-to-locate topics, metasearch engines can often be a good starting point. For example, if you try to locate a topic using your favorite search engine, but fail to turn up anything useful, you may want to query a metasearch engine.

Useful Item

Go On-Line

ELLEN AND RAY'S CHOICES

We have found the following tools to be extremely helpful:

- Directory: *Yahoo!*—www.yahoo.com

- Search engines: *Google*—www.google.com

- Metasearch engine: *Metacrawler*—www.metacrawler.com

- White pages: *Bigfoot*—www.bigfoot.com

Go On-Line

5.2.9   Popular Metasearch Engines

Here is a list of some popular metasearch engines:

DogPile—www.dogpile.com

InFind—www.infind.com

Mamma—www.mamma.com

MetaCrawler—www.metacrawler.com

Metasearch—www.metasearch.com

5.2.10   White Pages

White pages provide you with an on-line mechanism for looking up information about individuals. They can be used to track down telephone numbers, s-mail addresses, and email addresses. Users can request that information about them be put into a database for a given set of white pages. Some white pages also permit you to submit requests to delete your listing from their information. Many of the white pages are very comprehensive, listing information about people who are not even listed in the telephone book (including their telephone numbers).

Hot Topic

When you submit a request for information about a person, some of the white page services may make a record of your request. In addition, many of the white pages have a hyperlink describing their acceptable use policy. In practice, such policies are impossible to enforce. Obviously, people can abuse white pages, and some people feel that white pages are an invasion of their privacy.

5.2.11   Popular White Pages

Go On-Line

Here is a list of some popular white pages.

- *Bigfoot*—www.bigfoot.com

- *Four11*—www.four11.com

- *WhoWhere*—www.whowhere.com

Yellow pages contain information about businesses.

EXERCISES 5.2

Directories, Search Engines, and Metasearch Engines

1. Pick two directories from Section 5.2.2. How many hyperlinks must you go through to obtain information about the following items: lobster, Toyota Rav4's, and movie reviews? Based on this limited test, how do the two directories compare?

2. Develop a set of five criteria to compare the directories listed in Section 5.2.2. Try to suggest comparisons that distinguish between each pair of directories.

3. (This exercise is designed to illustrate the differences between search engines' databases.) Search for the word "flamenco" using three search engines mentioned in Section 5.2.5. How many matches did each search return? Did any of the searches retrieve any of the same hyperlinks?

4. Develop a set of five criteria to compare the search engines listed in Section 5.2.5. Try to suggest comparisons that distinguish between each pair of search engines.

5. Design an experiment to compare the speeds of the metasearch engines mentioned in Section 5.2.9. Explain your methodology and findings.

6. How many different search engines does each metasearch engine in Section 5.2.9 call on? Explain why a metasearch engine needs to obtain a balance between too few and too many search engines.

7. Which metasearch engine would you rate as having the most user-friendly interface, and why? Is there anything you would do differently?

8.   Search for your own name in the white pages listed in Section 5.2.11. What were the results? How many people can you locate in the U. S. with the same name as you?

9.   Give the URLs of two yellow page services. Search for a company at which a friend works. Were you successful?

10.   Using the yellow pages, can you locate the business, Meeting House Data Communications? Using other Web search mechanisms, can you locate this company? Report your findings.

11.   Read the documentation supplied on the help pages of two general directories. Name three things that differentiate the two Web directories.

12.   Read the search tips offered on the help page of your favorite search engine and explain how to pose an effective query to find out who won last year's Boston Marathon.

13.   Would a Web directory or a search engine be better suited to find information about the Seven Cities of Cibola? Explain your answer.

14.   To find information about Cujo, a well-known Appalachian Trail hiker, what search tool would you use and why?

15.   Suppose you wanted to buy a digital camera on-line and had $300 to spend. What search tool(s) would you use to find information about digital cameras in general and then to find a camera to purchase?

5.3   Search Fundamentals

Go On-Line

Figure 5.11 shows the Google search engine user interface, which we will use to explain search fundamentals and to fill in a few details about what directories and search engines typically display on their Web pages. Although not all search tools have the same features as Google, you should be able to use this discussion as a basis for many of them.

First, notice that the Google interface is very straightforward. Since it is a search engine, there is a form in the center of the page directly under the Google logo. The form box is where you type in a query to submit to the Google search engine. Above the form is the text "Search 1,326,920,000

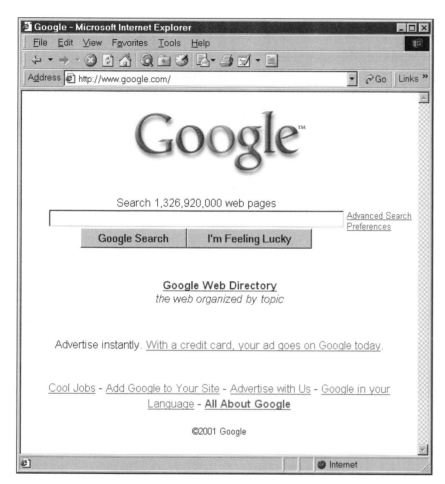

FIGURE 5.11
Google main page.

web pages." This statistic is constantly being updated to reflect how many Web pages the Google search engine has cataloged. After entering your search query, clicking on the `Google Search` button or hitting the Enter key will submit the query. Next to the `Google Search` button is a button that says "I'm Feeling Lucky." Selecting the `I'em Feeling Lucky` button will submit your query and then take you directly to the first page in the result set without showing you all of the other results.

The hyperlinks to the right of the form allow you to customize your search. The Advanced Search hyperlink links to a page that lets you refine your search. The Preferences hyperlink links to a page that lets you specify certain preferences, such as filtering (to block potentially offensive pages from displaying in the result set), the number of hits to be displayed on each result page, and the interface language to be used.

There is a hyperlink to the Google directory below the Submit buttons. Google uses information in the Open Directory but uses its own formula to rank the sites. Web pages and presentations contained in the directory have all been reviewed by one of more than 30,000 volunteer Open Directory editors so the information may be more on topic. Queries that are submitted to the Google search engine are also searched for within the Open Directory automatically. You may want to browse Google's directory when you are not sure how to narrow down a topic or how to phrase your query. Figure 5.12 shows the Google Web Directory interface.

Beneath the hyperlink to the Web directory on the Google main page is a link that provides some information about how to advertise on the Google pages. The footer of the Google search interface provides links to job opportunities with Google, how to include Google's search technology on your site, more information about how to advertise on the Google pages,

FIGURE 5.12
Google directory page.

a shortcut to changing the interface language, and a link to a help page about using the Google search engine.

When learning how to use a new search tool, the help page is probably the most important documentation to read. Figure 5.13 displays the page loaded when the All About Google hyperlink is followed. This page provides everything you need to know about how to become an effective Google search engine user. One reason we like Google is that its on-line documentation is complete, user-friendly, and contains good examples as well as a page of Frequently Asked Questions. You will learn more about Google's search query syntax later, when we discuss various types of search queries.

On the bottom of the help page displayed in Figure 5.13 is a footer (not visible in the figure) containing copyright information and links to Google's privacy policy, as well as terms of service. The terms of service

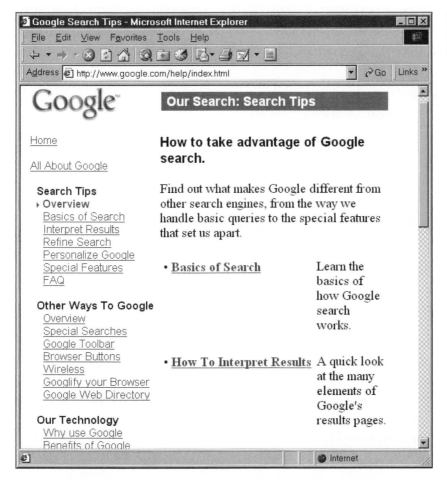

FIGURE 5.13
Google help page.

page contains a disclaimer that states that Google does not guarantee the accuracy of any information returned by its search tools and that some search results and links may contain obscene or objectionable material. As you will see, all search tools display similar disclaimers.

5.3.1   Search Terminology

Here are a few common search-related terms you should know about.

Useful Item

- **Search tool** Any mechanism for locating information on the Web; usually refers to a search or metasearch engine, or a directory.

- **Query** Information entered into a form on a search engine's Web page that describes the information being sought. Note that a query is not usually phrased as a question.

- **Query syntax** A set of rules describing what constitutes a legal query. On some search engines, special symbols may be used in a query.

- **Query semantics** A set of rules that defines the meaning of a query.

- **Hit** A URL that a search engine returns in response to a query.

- **Match** A synonym for hit.

- **Relevancy score** A value that indicates how close a match a URL was to a query; usually expressed as a value from 1 to 100, with the higher score meaning more relevant.

5.3.2   Pattern Matching Queries

The most basic type of query is a *pattern matching query*. You formulate a pattern matching query using a keyword or a group of keywords. The search engine returns the URL of any page that contains these keywords. What we really mean by the phrase "contains these keywords" varies between search engines. For example, some search engines return the URL of any Web page they know about in which the keywords occur. Others return the URL of any page in which the keywords appear within the first 100 words of the page. Still others return only the URLs of those pages in which the keywords appear in the title. Is it necessary that all the keywords appear? Usually, you have the option of specifying whether you want all keywords to be found or whether just one will suffice. The exact details of how pattern matching queries are resolved is search-engine specific.

Suppose you want to find Web presentations with information about the men's University of New Hampshire ice hockey team. A pattern matching query of `ice hockey` submitted to Google turned up 812,000 hits.[2] This means that Google located 812,000 pages that contained both of the words—`ice` and `hockey`. To ensure that the words `ice` and `hockey` are next to each other, we enclose the phrase in quotes. Now a search on `"ice hockey"` turns up 591,000 hits—still too many to consider, but we have eliminated those that do not contain the phrase `"ice hockey."` Some search engines use quotes to specify that keywords must appear next to each other on the Web page. Others will expect a hyphen between the keywords, as in `ice-hockey`. Notice that without the quotes, Google looked for pages that contained both words, though not necessarily next to each other. Many search engines will look for either word—`ice` or `hockey`—when searching for `ice hockey`. This has the potential to return even more pages.

To narrow our search even further, we want to include the term `men` in our keywords. A query of `men "ice hockey"` returns 243,000 hits. These Web pages contain the phrase `ice hockey` and the word `men`, although the word `men` does not need to appear anywhere near the phrase `ice hockey`. To fine-tune this, we submit a query of `"men's ice hockey"` to Google. Now the result set contains 8,280 pages—still too many hits. To restrict the search to include only Web pages containing references to the University of New Hampshire's men's ice hockey team, we need to add the words `University of New Hampshire` to the list of keywords. A query of `"men's ice hockey" University of New Hampshire` submitted to Google turned up 323 hits. These Web pages contain the phrase `"men's ice hockey"`, `University`, `New`, and `Hampshire`. Notice that these pages may or may not contain the actual phrase "University of New Hampshire." To ensure that it does, we need to enclose University of New Hampshire in quotes. We should also point out that Google ignores the word "of" because it considers it a *stop word*. Any single letter, number, or article such as *the, of,* or *a* is ignored. To force Google to include a stop word in its list of keywords, you place a + before it. In a query where you are searching for information about Division I ice hockey, for instance, your keywords should include a + sign before the I: `"Division +I ice hockey."`

---

2 Your search results may vary from ours, since the Web and search engines change so quickly. All of the search statistics reported in this section were compiled from searches conducted within a half-hour time period.

To continue our search for information about the University of New Hampshire's hockey team, we want to include the phrase `"University +of New Hampshire"` along with `"men's ice hockey."` Now our result set contains 117 matches. To experiment, we also submitted our search using only lowercase letters, that is, our search query was `"men's ice hockey" "university +of new hampshire."` The result set contained the same number of matches, so we know that Google does not differentiate between upper- and lowercase when searching.

To refine our search even more, we decide to add one more keyword to the list. A query of `scores "men's ice hockey" "University +of New Hampshire"` returned 30 matches. Changing `scores` to `score` resulted in 34 matches. Some search engines perform a process known as *stemming*, which means that they use variations on the endings of words in your query. For example, the search engine may try the plural form of words, as well as the singular, or vice versa. Google does not use stemming. Other search engines use the asterisk wildcard to pick up variations on a word. For example, `theat*` would look for theater, theaters, theatre, and theatres.

Table 5.1 summarizes the search results presented here, as well as some other searches. It is important to note that keywords in a query must be spelled correctly. Misspelling a keyword might result in zero hits, hits that are unrelated to your topic, or hits that link to pages containing errors (or at the very least, misspelled words!). When we submitted a search query to Google of `"ice hocky"` we received a result set with 263 hits.

5.3.3   Boolean Queries

George Boole was a famous mathematician who worked on algebra; *Boolean algebra* was named after him. *Boolean queries* involve the Boolean operations AND,[3] OR, and NOT. Most search engines allow you to enter Boolean queries.

Let us consider some examples of Boolean queries (posed to a generic search engine[4]) to illustrate how they work. A query such as

    paint AND house

will turn up all Web pages that contain both `paint` and `house`.

---

3   We use the small capital font to denote Boolean operations. Some search engines require Boolean operators to be in capital letters while others do not.

4   Our discussion here assumes that the generic search engine *indexes* the full text of a Web page, which is now very common.

TABLE 5.1

Google Search Results.

Google Query	Number of Hits
`ice hockey`	812,000
`"ice hockey"`	591,000
`men "ice hockey"`	243,000
`"men's ice hockey"`	8,280
`"men's ice hockey" University of New Hampshire`	323
`"men's ice hockey" "University +of New Hampshire"`	117
`"men's ice hockey" "university +of new hampshire"`	117
`scores "men's ice hockey" "University +of New Hampshire"`	30
`score "men's ice hockey" "University +of New Hampshire"`	34
`Division I "men's ice hockey"`	1,920
`Division +I "men's ice hockey"`	1,370
`"Division +I" "men's ice hockey"`	1,080
`"Division +I men's ice hockey"`	180
`"ice hocky"`	263

Some search engines permit using multiple ANDs. For example,

`Janet AND Tito AND Michael AND LaToya`

would turn up any Web page containing all four of these names. Notice that we have capitalized the names. When posing queries, it is a good idea to capitalize proper nouns and names.

In contrast, the query

`Husky OR Akita`

will find all Web pages that contain at least one of the words `Husky` or `Akita`; that is, they must contain either `Husky`, `Akita`, or both. Analogous to the use of AND, some search engines also permit using more than one OR. In a pattern matching query, the default of some search engines is to OR the words together (meaning find pages containing at least one of the words); for other search engines, the default is to AND the words together (meaning find pages containing all of the words).

To exclude an item from a search, you can use the Boolean NOT operation. For example, to find all Web pages containing information about John Lennon but not the Beatles, a query such as

`John Lennon NOT The Beatles`

could be used. To find information that also does not include Yoko, you could try a query such as

```
John Lennon NOT The Beatles NOT Yoko Ono
```

In many search engines, using quotes around a phrase means the words must appear together, in the order you typed them. So, the previous query might be entered as

```
"John Lennon" NOT "The Beatles" NOT "Yoko Ono"
```

The exact syntax of a query will vary from search engine to search engine. For example, some use AND, OR, and NOT, while others use + for AND, nothing for OR (that is, just list the words, which are OR'd by default), and – for NOT.

5.3.4   Search Domain

Useful Item

Most search tools provide some flexibility in the choice of domains to search. For example, you can search the Web, newsgroups, specialized databases, or the Internet. Depending on the item for which you are looking, you may decide to try either a more specific domain first, in hopes of a more efficient search, or a comprehensive and more time-consuming search.

5.3.5   Search Subjects

Go On-Line

Several search and metasearch engines provide a way for you to view the search queries of anonymous users in real time. You will see either a ticker tape of search queries or a list of queries that are currently being processed by that search engine. Since users are submitting the queries in real time, your display of queries may be refreshed every 15 seconds or so. Figure 5.14 shows the main Web page for Metaspy, the spy page for MetaCrawler, a popular metasearch engine. Metaspy offers a filtered and nonfiltered version, acknowledging that some queries are obscene and/or offensive. The page displayed in Figure 5.15 is the filtered version of MetaSpy showing the actual queries that are being submitted in real time. The spy page may also allow you to view the search results for a particular query, as Metaspy does, by selecting its hyperlink. Viewing spy pages is interesting for several reasons:

1.   You can see how busy the search tools are.

2.   You can "spy" on other anonymous users.

FIGURE 5.14
Metaspy main
page.

3.   You can sometimes "see" the same user modifying the search. For example, you may see a typo corrected in a subsequent query.

4.   You can see the variety of people's interests.

5.   You may turn up a page of personal interest that you otherwise might not have come across.

Some Web pages that allow you to view real-time searches are:

Go On-Line

Ask Jeeves Peek Through the Keyhole—
    www.askjeeves.com/docs/peek

*Excite Search Voyeur—*www.excite.com/voyeur_xt

*MetaSpy—*www.metaspy.com

FIGURE 5.15
Metaspy filtered
spy page.

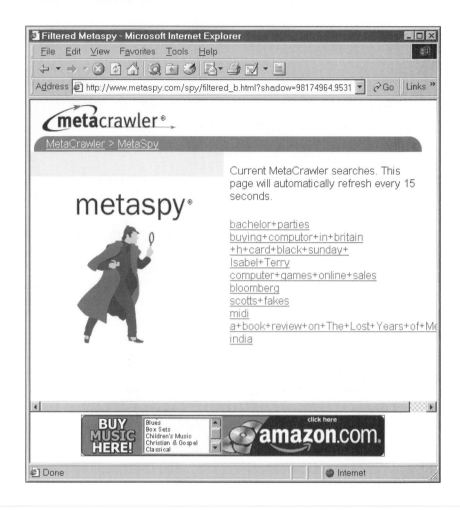

WebCrawler Search Voyeur—
    www.webcrawler.com/SearchTicker.html

*Yahoo! Buzz Index—*buzz.yahoo.com

EXERCISES 5.3

Search Fundamentals

16.   Repeat the following queries three times, using three different
       search engines (nine queries in total):
       (a) World's Highest Mountain
       (b) Mount Everest
       (c) Everest
       What were your results? Explain.

17.   Execute a Boolean query on your favorite search engine to locate information about Lewis and Clark.

18.   On your favorite search engine, what query would you use first to find information about appetizers and desserts? Experiment with other types of queries. Which query yielded the best results?

19.   Phrase a query to locate information about Janet Evans and swimming that does not include any reference to Stanford. What were your results?

20.   Phrase a query about cycling that does not retrieve any information about mountain biking. Experiment and explain the results. What was your most productive query?

21.   (The purpose of this exercise is to help you determine how many pages a given search engine has indexed.) Try to maximize the number of hits you are able to get in a single query to a search engine. What was the most hits you were able to get, what was the query, and what search engine did you use? Repeat this problem using a metasearch engine.

22.   Perform the following pattern matching queries, using a single search engine: `waffle`, `Waffle`, `Belgian Waffle`, `waffles`, `Waffles`, and `Belgian Waffles`. What were the resulting numbers of hits? Were they as expected? Explain.

5.4   Search Strategies

Determining which search engine to use can be challenging. You can begin by testing a number of different search engines, trying to find one that you believe meets the following conditions:

Useful Item

- Possesses a user-friendly interface.

- Has easy-to-understand, comprehensive documentation.

- Is convenient to access; that is, you do not have to wait several minutes before being able to submit a query.

- Contains a large database, so that it knows a lot about the information for which you are searching.

- Does a good job in assigning relevancy scores.

If you can find a search engine that meets most of these criteria, you should concentrate on learning it well, rather than learning a little bit about several different search engines.

Once you have learned the query syntax of that search engine, you can begin to formulate your search strategy. When you post queries to the search engine, two common situations can occur: either your query does not turn up a sufficient number of hits, or your query turns up too many hits. In the next two sections, you will learn strategies for dealing with these situations.

5.4.1   Too Few Hits: Search Generalization

Go On-Line

Suppose your query returns no hits or only a couple of hits, neither of which is very useful to you. In this case, you need to generalize your search. The ways to do this include:

- If you used a pattern matching query, eliminate one of the more specific keywords from your query.

- If you used a Boolean query, remove one of the keywords or phrases with which you used AND, or delete a NOT item you specified.

- If you restricted your search domain, enlarge it.

- If you are still having no luck, try keywords that are more general, or exchange a couple of the keywords with synonyms.

- If this fails, you may decide to use a directory and work your way down to the topic of interest. Another alternative would be to use a metasearch engine.

5.4.2   Too Many Hits: Search Specialization

Go On-Line

Suppose your query returns more URLs than you could possibly look through. In this case, you need to specialize your search.

- If you started with a pattern matching query, you may want to add more keywords.

- If you began with a Boolean query, you might want to AND another keyword, or use the NOT operator to exclude some pages. When you phrase a new query, many search engines let you search just the results of your original search or refine your search. This restricts the domain of your search. What you are essentially doing in this case is a search within a search.

- If you are still retrieving too many hits, try capitalizing proper nouns or names.

- If nothing seems to work, try reviewing the first 20 or so URLs, since search engines list the best matches near the top. If they do not contain what you are looking for, the information they do contain may help you refine your search.

- If this fails, you could resort to a directory and work your way down to the topic of interest.

5.4.3   Sample Searches

Go On-Line

Suppose you are interested in hiking the Appalachian Trail through New Hampshire. At the very least, you want to know how long the trail is through New Hampshire. What is a good search strategy for locating information about this on the Web? We will explore several search queries, using Google, to illustrate how this might be done. The process carries over to other searches.

One of the keys to an effective search strategy is to examine the results you obtain and then revise your search accordingly. Initially, we perform a very general search using the keywords `appalachian trail`. This turns up 99,100 hits. We know that Google is not case sensitive, so `appalachian trail` is considered the same as `Appalachian Trail`. It is obvious that the search is too general, so we decide to enter the query

```
"appalachian trail"
```

Recall that the quotes around `appalachian trail` indicate a phrase so that the words `appalachian` and `trail` must appear next to one another. This results in 66,700—still too many. Since we are looking for information about the length of the trail, we decide to add miles to the search query

```
miles "appalachian trail"
```

This search query returns 26,300 matches. On the results page returned by Google for this query we notice that for each match, Google returns the title of the page (or URL if there was no title or if Google has not indexed the Web page's content yet). Below the title is an excerpt from the Web page that displays the search keywords you entered in the query; they are shown in boldface. (The Google results page for a related query can be viewed in Figure 5.16.) By examining some of these excerpts we determine that perhaps we should use `mileage` instead of `miles`, so we resubmit our query using

```
mileage "appalachian trail"
```

We decided to try using `mileage` instead of `miles` since we know that Google does not use stemming. The result set now contains 1,570 hits. To further narrow our search, we add `New Hampshire` to the query

```
mileage "appalachian trail" "new hampshire"
```

FIGURE 5.16
Google search
result page.

■ TABLE 5.2

■ Google Query Results for Appalachian Trail Mileage.

Google Query	Number of Hits
appalachian trail	99,100
"appalachian trail"	66,700
miles "appalachian trail"	26,300
mileage "appalachian trail"	1,570
mileage "appalachian trail" "new hampshire"	228

We have included quotes around new hampshire so that it will be considered as a phrase. This search nets 228 matches, and the results page is shown in Figure 5.16. We decide to examine the first page of results, knowing that better matches appear in the beginning of the result set. Reading the text below the title of the first entry in the result set reveals that this Web presentation contains a table of mileage along the Appalachian Trail. This is exactly the information we sought. An experienced user might have attempted a query similar to our final query to start. Table 5.2 summarizes the queries. Once you learn to use a search engine well, most of the queries you pose will get you close to your goal. Very few of the queries will be wasted or will cause you to lose ground.

EXERCISES 5.4

Search Strategies

23. A friend of yours is new to the Web and search engines. Write one paragraph that explains how to generalize a search and another that explains how to specialize a search.

24. In traversing through a directory to locate information about kayaking in Prince William Sound, how may different URLs did you have to follow? What were the corresponding categories you went through?

25. Your parents are interested in buying a VCR from Sony. Can you locate any information on the Web from *Consumer Reports* about Sony VCRs? Describe your search strategy.

26. Try to locate ticket information for the next Olympic Games. Were you able to find out what ticket prices are going to be? What queries did you perform, and what were the results of those queries?

27. Using your favorite general search engine, perform a search to determine who holds the record for hiking the Appalachian Trail in the shortest amount of time and what that record is. Indicate the search engine and query you used and the total number of hits returned in the result set.

5.5   How Does a Search Engine Work?

5.5.1   Search Engine Components

If you understand how a search tool works, there is a good chance you will be able to use it more effectively. In this section, we describe how a search engine works. For the most part, these same ideas apply to directories; the main difference is that the hierarchical organizational structure and categorizations for directories need to be in place and displayed. The bibliography includes additional information about how directories are put together.

To describe how a search engine works, we split up its functions into a number of components: user interface, searcher, and evaluator.

User interface   The screen in which you type a query and which displays the search results.

Searcher   The part that searches a database for information to match your query.

Evaluator   The function that assigns relevancy scores to the information retrieved.

In addition, a search engine's database is created using the following:

Gatherer   The component that traverses the Web, collecting information about pages.

Indexer   The function that categorizes the data obtained by the gatherer and creates the index.

For comparison, think of the different facets of a typical library, such as acquisitions, cataloging, indexing, and on-line searching.

5.5.2   User Interface

Figure 5.2 depicted the Yahoo! user interface, which is typical for a search engine. The user interface must provide a mechanism by which a user can submit queries to the search engine. This is universally done using forms. In addition, the user interface should be friendly and visually appealing. Hyperlinks to `help` files should be displayed prominently, and advertisements should not hinder a reader's use of the search engine. Finally, the user interface needs to display the results of the search in a convenient way. The user should be presented with a list of hits from the search, a *relevancy score* for each hit, and a "summary" of each page that was matched. This way, the user can make an informed choice as to which hyperlinks to follow.

5.5.3   Searcher

The *searcher* is a program that uses the search engine's index and database to see if any matches can be found for the query. Your query must first be transformed into a syntax that the searcher can process. Since the databases associated with search engines are extremely large (with perhaps 50,000,000 to 1,350,000,000 indexed pages), a highly efficient search strategy must be applied. Computer scientists have spent years developing efficient search and sorting strategies; some of these sophisticated algorithms are implemented in the searcher. More details about the basic principles behind these strategies can be found in any introductory computer science algorithms textbook.

5.5.4   Evaluator

The searcher locates any URLs that match your query. The hits retrieved by your query are called the *result set* of the search. Not all of the hits will match your query equally well. For example, a query about "Honey Bees," might be matched by a page containing the phrase "Honey Bees" in the following sentence:

```
Ants, honey bees, and crickets are all insects.
```

or by the page titled

```
Everything You Ever Wanted to Know About Honey Bees
```

Clearly, in most cases, it would be better to rank this second page much higher, as it probably contains many more references to Honey Bees. The ranking process is carried out by the evaluator, a program that assigns a relevancy score to each page in the result set. The relevancy score is an indication of how well a given page matched your query.

How is the relevancy score computed by the evaluator? This varies from search engine to search engine. A number of different factors are involved, and each one contributes a different percentage (according to a weighting scheme) toward the overall ranking of a page. Some of the factors typically considered are:

Hot Topic

- How many times the words in the query appear in the page.

- Whether or not the query words appear in the title.

- The proximity of the query words to the beginning of the page.

- Whether the query words appear in the CONTENT attribute of the META tag.

- How many of the query words appear in the document.

Another factor some search engines consider in computing relevancy scores is the popularity of a Web page or presentation. The idea is that a "popular" page might be more relevant, since other users have found it useful. DirectHit keeps track of which matches in the result set are selected more often and then ranks those pages higher. Google keeps track of how many other pages link to a particular page and then uses "link popularity" as a factor in computing its relevancy score. Still other search engines like GoTo sell listings that allow companies to pay to be ranked higher in the result set.

Search engines are always coming up with new ways to compute relevancy scores and new factors to consider. Each factor is weighted, and a value is computed that rates the page. The values are usually normalized and are assigned numbers between 1 and 100, with 100 representing the best possible match. As part of the user interface, the result set and relevancy scores computed by the evaluator are displayed for the user, with the best matches appearing first. Hyperlinks to each hit are provided, and a short description (two lines or so) of the page is usually given.

Useful Item

With many search engines, you can set the maximum number of hits that you want returned. This can make your search more efficient, since fewer hits need to be found and ranked. Once the actual number of hits is displayed and you page through them based on their relevancy scores, you can decide whether to enlarge your search.

The algorithms used by evaluators are imperfect, but they are getting better. Also, in addition to direct hits, a search engine will sometimes display the hyperlinks of pages that contain information about related topics.

5.5.5   Gatherer

A search engine obtains its information by using a *gatherer*, a program that traverses the Web and collects information about Web documents. The gatherer does not collect the information every time a query is made. Rather, the gatherer is run at regular (short) intervals, and it returns information that is incorporated into the search engine's database and is indexed. Alternate names for gatherer are *bot*, *crawler*, *robot*, *spider*, and *worm*.

A gatherer may employ essentially two different methods to search the Web for new pages. (In practice, hybrids of these procedures are often used.) Both techniques are well-known search strategies in computer science; they are called *breadth-first search* and *depth-first search*. We will describe both methods on a basic level. The interested reader may consult any introductory computer science algorithms textbook for a more detailed explanation.

Breadth-First Search

A breadth-first search proceeds in levels "across" the pages. The gatherer begins at a particular Web page and then explores all pages that it can reach by using only one hyperlink from the original page. Once it has exhausted all Web pages at that one level, it explores all of the Web pages that can be reached by following only one hyperlink from any page that was discovered at level one. In this way, a second level, which usually contains many more Web pages than the first level, is explored. This process is repeated level by level until no new Web pages are found. When no more pages can be located, the search may need to jump to a new starting point.

Figure 5.17 illustrates the process. In the figure, we have greatly simplified things by representing a very small corner of the Web as two discrete collections of documents. Each Web page is represented by a circle, and hyperlinks are represented by lines connecting the circles. We assume that hyperlinks go in both directions (another simplification). The search begins from point A. We have numbered the Web pages in the order that they are visited by our hypothetical gatherer.

The initial Web page where the search begins is labeled 1_0. The subscript shows the level in which the page appears. The gatherer will normally

FIGURE 5.17

An illustration of the order in which a gatherer visits Web pages using a breadth-first search strategy.

The primary number indicates the order in which the page was visited, and the subscript indicates the level in which the page was found. The document collection used here is a simplified one.

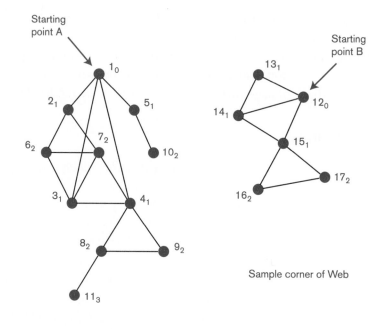

Sample corner of Web

choose a random hyperlink to follow from its current level. For illustration purposes, we have always chosen to follow the leftmost link first. So, for example, the first page explored from page 1_0 is its leftmost hyperlinked page, which is labeled 2_1. This is the second page visited, and it appears at level one. The three other pages discovered at level one are 3, 4, and 5. Pages 6, 7, 8, 9, and 10 are found at level two, and page 11 is found at level three.

Having found page 11, the gatherer has exhausted the entire collection of Web pages hyperlinked to the starting point A. The gatherer then chooses a new starting point B and continues from there. As before, we begin with level zero. Details such as how new starting points are chosen, how the gatherer knows it has been somewhere already and so does not go into an infinite search loop, how the gatherer reports its findings, and so on, are not important for our discussion. The curious reader should consult the bibliography for further information about these issues.

Depth-First Search

A depth-first search proceeds by following a chain of hyperlinks "down" as far as possible. The gatherer begins at a particular Web page and explores one of its hyperlinks. At the new page, the gatherer follows another hyperlink. At the next page, one of its hyperlinks is followed, and so on. In contrast to the breadth-first search, hyperlinks on a given page are not fully exhausted before the gatherer goes to the next-level page. When the

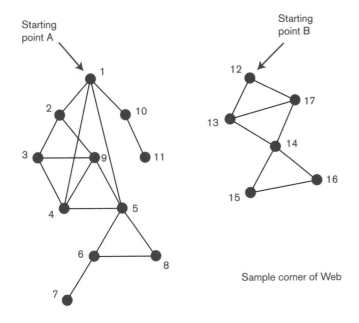

Starting point A

Starting point B

Sample corner of Web

FIGURE 5.18
An illustration of the order in which a gatherer visits Web pages using a depth-first search strategy.
Each number indicates the order in which the page was visited. The document collection used here is the same as that used in Figure 5.17.

gatherer reaches a page from which no new pages can be discovered, the search backtracks until it can go forward again and discover new pages. The search goes as deep into the document collection as possible before backtracking. As with a breadth-first search, when no more pages can be located, even with full backtracking, the search jumps to a new starting point.

Figure 5.18 depicts the depth-first search process. For illustration purposes, we use the same document collection as we did for the breadth-first search example. The search begins at point A. We have labeled the Web pages in the order they are visited by our hypothetical gatherer. The initial Web page where the search begins is labeled 1. The gatherer will normally choose a random hyperlink to follow from its current location. However, as we did in the breadth-first case, we have always chosen to follow the leftmost link first. So, for example, the first page explored from page 1 is its leftmost hyperlinked page, which is labeled 2 as the second page visited. With a depth-first search, the levels on which the different pages are found are not as important as in breadth-first search.

Notice that a deep chain is followed from page 1, reaching pages 2, 3, 4, 5, 6, and 7 before the search needs to backtrack. The search backtracks and discovers page 8 from page 6. Again, the search must backtrack and page 9 is discovered from page 5. After backtracking once more, the gatherer located page 10 from page 1 and page 11 from page 10. Having found page 11, the gatherer has exhausted the entire collection of Web pages hyperlinked to the starting point A. This is not discovered until we have backtracked to page 1. A new starting point B is chosen and the gathering continues from there. For illustration purposes, we continue the numbering from where we left off. Pages 13, 14, 15, and 16 are found by following a single chain from page 12. Backtracking to page 14, we find page 17. Once the search backtracks to page 12, we determine that the entire document collection reachable from starting point B has been exhausted.

Precise details of how a depth-first search is carried out are not important for our discussion. Curious readers should consult the bibliography.

Miscellaneous Facts about Gatherers

Useful Item

- Gatherers place a very heavy load on Web servers.

- The depth of searches that gatherers perform is restricted.

- Gatherers have trouble dealing with documents that are created using frames.

- The best gathering strategy depends on the underlying collection of documents.

- Some gatherers may only retrieve the head of a document, while others retrieve the entire content of the page. *Full text indexing*, which allows you to search for any word in the entire text of a document, requires that the entire document be retrieved. Full text indexing requires a tremendous amount of storage space.

5.5.6   Indexer

Once the gatherer retrieves information about Web pages, the information is placed into a database and *indexed*. The *indexer* function creates a set of keys (an index) that organizes the data, so that high-speed electronic searches can be conducted and the desired information can be located and retrieved quickly.

Libraries have card (or computerized) catalogs that index books by author name(s), by title, and by subject. Each book has a unique ISBN. The equivalent elements that should go into a Web page's bibliographic record include the URL, document title, and descriptive keywords. What else should be included? This question is still being debated. Because resources on the Web vary so widely and because they change so rapidly, indexing is more difficult, and indexes need to be rebuilt frequently. There was a time when about one in three URLs that a search engine returned was out of date. Now that indexes are being rebuilt more frequently and more pages have stabilized, the ratio is not quite as high.

Hot Topic

5.5.7   Summary

A search engine's functionality depends on a number of different components: user interface, searcher, evaluator, gatherer, and indexer. The software involved in any single item is very complex, and tying all of the different modules together so that they interface properly is also a complex task.

You may be wondering how your search query gets handed over to the search engine. This process is described in Sections 9.3 and 9.4, which cover HTML forms and *CGI scripts*, respectively.

EXERCISES 5.5

How Does a Search Engine Work?

28.   Is there any search engine for which you can locate information that describes how its search strategy works? Does having this information help you in posing more intelligent queries?

29.   Define the phrase *Uniform Resource Characteristic* (*URC*) and describe the role it is designed to play in the indexing of Web pages.

30.   Can you locate any information describing how Web pages are indexed by any specific search engine? If so, describe the process in the particular case you found and list your reference(s).

31.   How does Infoseek compute its relevancy score?

32.   How does NorthernLight compute its relevancy score?

33.   Do you use the max hits option when searching? Explain.

34.   Write a paragraph summarizing the items that you feel are the most important in computing a relevancy score.

35.   Have you found that the evaluator for a particular search engine is better than that of other search engines? Explain.

36.   Do some search engines compute result sets for common queries in advance? That is, are there search engines that compute the answer to an expected query themselves, before the query is asked by any user? If so, what are the trade-offs in doing this?

37.   How does a metasearch engine work?

Telnet and FTP

6

Many thru-hikers pride themselves on walking through Maryland in a single day. My mother had spent a lot of time in Maryland so it was nice to walk through this state. I remember hitch-hiking a ride to a McDonald's in Maryland. When I arrived at McDonald's, I was extremely hungry. Everything I saw on the menu sounded wonderful and so I ordered it all, "Give me a big mac, two cheeseburgers, a filet-o-fish, quarter pounder, apple pie, cookies, chocolate shake, fries, salad, two cokes, and super-size the whole thing!" I ran up a very large bill for McDonald's. I ate the entire order and suffered greatly during the next three hours of hiking. However, after that, the calories became energy and I felt great for the remainder of the day.

Maryland
40 miles

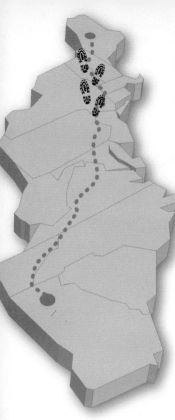

Chapter 6

6.1 INTRODUCTION

The goals of this chapter are to acquaint you with the following topics:

Objectives

- Telnet and remote login
- Graphical-based file transfer clients
- Text-based file transfer clients
- Computer viruses

6.2 Telnet and Remote Login

Telnet and *remote login* are two programs that allow you to log in to another computer from an account into which you are already logged. They let you use and interact with software on the remote machine. To do this, you will need a second computer account that is accessible to you. The second computer is usually at a different physical location; hence the phrase "remote login." Figure 6.1 illustrates the basic idea. Rita is logged in to computer A. Using Telnet or remote login, she logs in to computer B. It is almost as though she were physically at computer B entering commands.

6.2.1 Telnet

The `telnet` command uses the *Telnet protocol* to log in to a remote computer on the Internet. The command is often called `telnet`, but different programs may use other names, such as *tn3270*, *WinQVT*, and *QWS3270*.

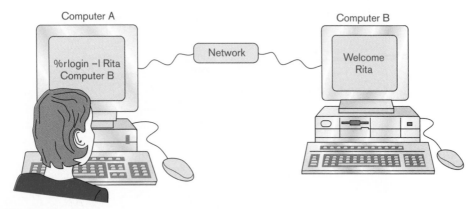

FIGURE 6.1

Rita was logged in to computer A, and from there, she remote logged in to computer B.

She is executing commands on computer B via computer A.

There are a wide range of Telnet clients, and many of them have a user-friendly interface. Most Telnet clients function in a similar manner. Here, we describe several different ways of invoking Telnet. On a desktop system, a Telnet client can usually be launched from one of the system's menus simply by selecting the Telnet option. On many such systems, a Telnet icon can be found on the desktop. A typical Telnet icon is shown in Figure 6.2 in the third row, fourth column. Telnet can be invoked by double-clicking on the Telnet icon.

If Telnet is not located on your desktop, and you are on a Windows operating system, there is still a good chance that there is a Telnet client on your system. To determine whether you have a Telnet client, go to the Start menu and select **Find.** Under **Find,** select the "Files or Folders" option. Now simply enter the word "telnet" in the search area. The result of performing this command on our PC is shown in Figure 6.3. The `telnet.exe` files are the executable Telnet programs. You can run these in the standard way you run a program on your PC.

In a Windows environment, the Telnet interface may appear as shown in Figure 6.4. Selecting the `RemoteSystem` option from the **Connect** pull-down menu causes the `Connect` window to display within the Telnet window. The form in the `Connect` window (which is visible in Figure 6.4) lets you specify the hostname, port, and terminal type of the computer to which you are connecting. Generally, all you need to do is type in a hostname and push the `Connect` button. For example, to connect to the host `pirates.armstrong.edu`, you would type in this machine name or its IP address in the "Host Name" field. The result of this is shown in Figure 6.5.

FIGURE 6.2
Telnet icon
displayed in third
row, fourth
column.

FIGURE 6.3
Result of search
for Telnet using
the find
command on a
Windows PC.

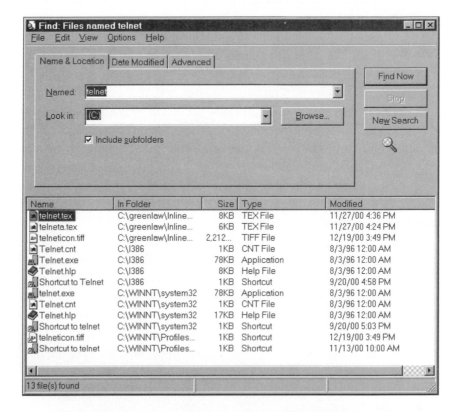

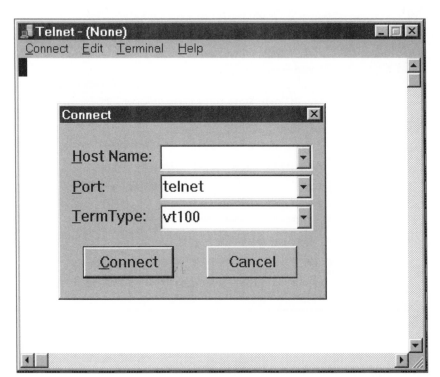

FIGURE 6.4
A Windows
Telnet screen.

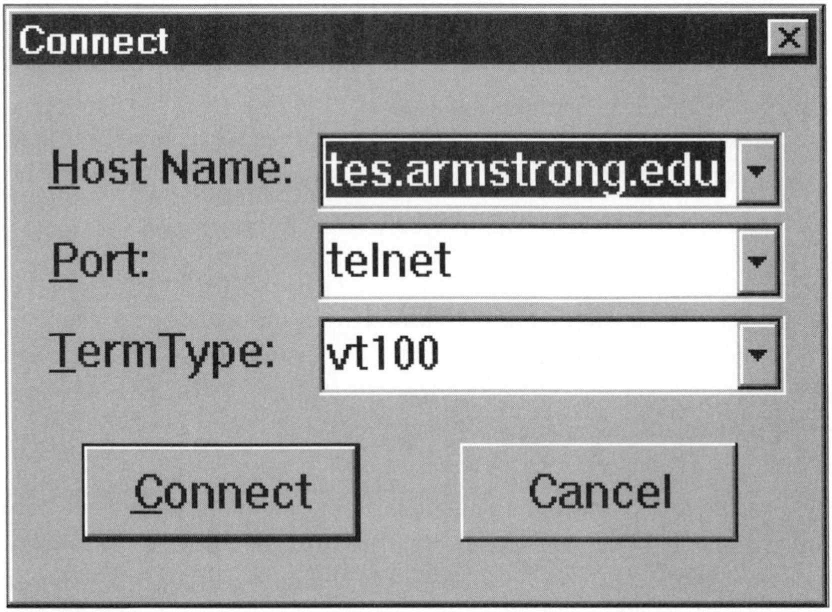

FIGURE 6.5
Result of typing in `pirates.armstrong.edu` into the hostname field.

FIGURE 6.6
Connecting to a
remote computer
using Telnet.

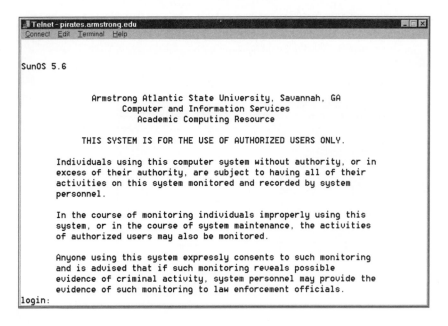

```
Telnet - pirates.armstrong.edu                                    _ □ ✕
Connect  Edit  Terminal  Help

SunOS 5.6


              Armstrong Atlantic State University, Savannah, GA
                   Computer and Information Services
                      Academic Computing Resource

           THIS SYSTEM IS FOR THE USE OF AUTHORIZED USERS ONLY.

         Individuals using this computer system without authority, or in
         excess of their authority, are subject to having all of their
         activities on this system monitored and recorded by system
         personnel.

         In the course of monitoring individuals improperly using this
         system, or in the course of system maintenance, the activities
         of authorized users may also be monitored.

         Anyone using this system expressly consents to such monitoring
         and is advised that if such monitoring reveals possible
         evidence of criminal activity, system personnel may provide the
         evidence of such monitoring to law enforcement officials.
login:
```

Note that only the tes in pirates is displayed. This is because the field
for entering the hostname is not large enough to display the entire machine
name. In Figure 6.6 we show the result of clicking on the Connect button.
In this case we are greeted by the login prompt of the machine pirates.
We can now log in in the usual fashion. Convenient on-line documentation
is available with most Telnet clients, and Figure 6.7 illustrates the help
screen available for "Connecting to a Remote Computer." Documentation
for other topics is also available in a similar format.

On some systems, such as UNIX, you can type the command telnet
at the operating system prompt. When you receive the Telnet prompt,

```
telnet>
```

you can type the open command, followed by the hostname of the computer
you would like to connect to:

```
telnet>open hostname
```

The hostname is the machine domain name (for example, hopper.unh.edu)
or the numerical Internet address of the machine. In some cases, you may
have to specify a port number, as well. Typing help or ? at the Telnet
prompt will usually result in the Telnet documentation being displayed.
The on-line help displayed on our machine as a result of typing ? is
shown in Figure 6.8. When your Telnet session is completed, you can type

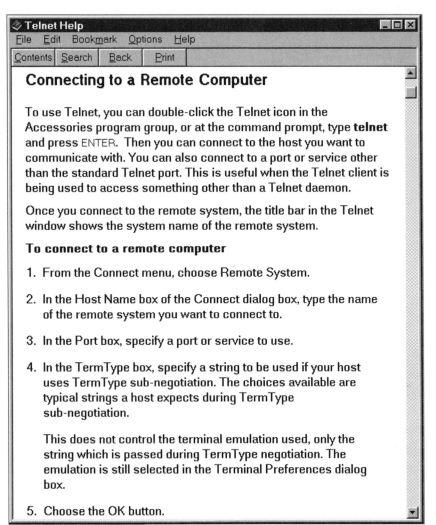

FIGURE 6.7
Windows Telnet
help screen.

`close` or `quit` to end it. Of course, you will first have to log out of the remote machine if you did, in fact, log in somewhere else.

If you invoke Telnet on a Mac, the Telnet commands will become part of the Mac's menu bar (as is customary of applications on a Mac). From these menus, you can select the `Open Connection` option. This will provide a field in which you can enter the name of the remote system.

From within your browser, if you have a Telnet application configured, you can enter a URL such as

```
telnet://hostname
```

and you will be provided with a Telnet window. Figure 6.9 depicts a window

FIGURE 6.8
Telnet help on a
UNIX system.

```
┌─────────────────────────────────────────────────────────────────────┐
│  ▽           shelltool – /bin/csh                                     │
├─────────────────────────────────────────────────────────────────────┤
│cervino% telnet                                                        │
│telnet> ?                                                              │
│Commands may be abbreviated.   Commands are:                           │
│                                                                       │
│close           close current connection                              │
│logout          forcibly logout remote user and close the connection  │
│display         display operating parameters                          │
│mode            try to enter line or character mode ('mode ?' for more)│
│open            connect to a site                                      │
│quit            exit telnet                                            │
│send            transmit special characters ('send ?' for more)       │
│set             set operating parameters ('set ?' for more)           │
│unset           unset operating parameters ('unset ?' for more)        │
│status          print status information                              │
│toggle          toggle operating parameters ('toggle ?' for more)     │
│slc             change state of special charaters ('slc ?' for more)  │
│z               suspend telnet                                        │
│!               invoke a subshell                                     │
│environ         change environment variables ('environ ?' for more)   │
│?               print help information                                │
│<return>        leave command mode                                    │
│telnet> []                                                            │
└─────────────────────────────────────────────────────────────────────┘
```

that was produced in this manner. In this case, the URL we specified was

telnet://hopper.unh.edu

Once you have specified the hostname of the computer and established a connection using Telnet, you can log in as you normally would (assuming you have an account) and begin executing commands on the remote machine.

One important thing to notice when you first bring up Telnet is the *escape sequence* that is displayed on the screen. It can be used to disconnect from the remote machine in case there is a problem. On most systems, the escape sequence is CONTROL-]; that is, by typing CONTROL-] you can disconnect from the remote machine. The CONTROL key must be used because keys typed without CONTROL are interpreted as inputs to the remote machine. Figure 6.9 shows the escape sequence message. In the Windows Telnet interface (Figure 6.4), you can also terminate Telnet by selecting Disconnect or Exit from the **Connect** pull-down menu.

As we mentioned before, it is usually necessary to have an account on the remote system in order to Telnet to it. However, there are some systems, including libraries, that allow "guests" to access their databases (though registration may be necessary). In the on-line portion of this book, we provide information about some of the sites that offer "guest" or free login.

Go On-Line

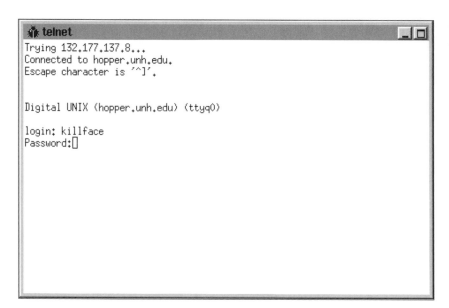

FIGURE 6.9
A Telnet window.

One of the most common uses of Telnet is to log in to your personal machine to retrieve email when you are traveling. Be warned that the process of reading email in this fashion can be very tedious from many countries. The connections are often so slow that it is impossible to retrieve, read, and compose messages. If you are going to travel and if you plan to read email while away, you should probably unsubscribe from all mailing lists you are on.

6.2.2   Remote Login

The `rlogin` command is similar to the `telnet` command, except that it provides the remote computer with information about where you are logging in from. If the machine that you are performing the remote login from is listed in the remote machine's file of hostnames, you may not have to enter a password. On UNIX systems, the list of hostnames is given in a hidden file called `.rhosts`. From a UNIX prompt, the syntax for the `rlogin` command is

```
%rlogin hostname
```

where `hostname` is the name of the machine from which you want to establish a remote login connection.

As with Telnet, once you are logged in to a remote machine, you will not be able to execute commands using your local login session. All the

FIGURE 6.10
Man page for
`rlogin`.

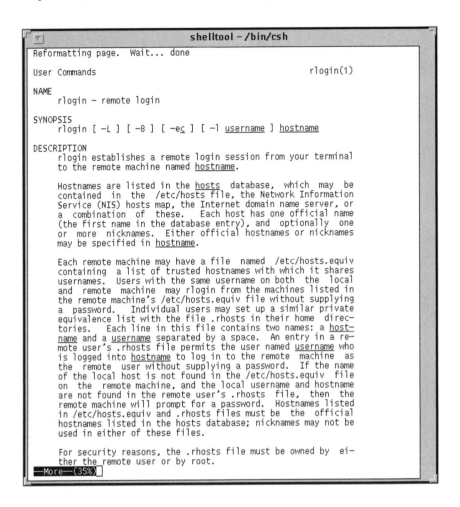

```
┌─────────────────────────────────────────────────────────────────┐
│  ▽                    shelltool - /bin/csh                       │
│ ┌─────────────────────────────────────────────────────────────┐ │
│ │Reformatting page.  Wait... done                             │ │
│ │                                                             │ │
│ │User Commands                                     rlogin(1)  │ │
│ │                                                             │ │
│ │NAME                                                         │ │
│ │     rlogin - remote login                                   │ │
│ │                                                             │ │
│ │SYNOPSIS                                                     │ │
│ │     rlogin [ -L ] [ -8 ] [ -ec ] [ -l username ] hostname   │ │
│ │                                                             │ │
│ │DESCRIPTION                                                  │ │
│ │     rlogin establishes a remote login session from your terminal │
│ │     to the remote machine named hostname.                   │ │
│ │                                                             │ │
│ │     Hostnames are listed in the hosts  database,  which  may be │
│ │     contained  in  the  /etc/hosts file, the Network Information │
│ │     Service (NIS) hosts map, the Internet domain name server, or │
│ │     a  combination  of  these.   Each host has one official name │
│ │     (the first name in the database entry), and  optionally  one │
│ │     or  more  nicknames.  Either official hostnames or nicknames │
│ │     may be specified in hostname.                           │ │
│ │                                                             │ │
│ │     Each remote machine may have a file  named  /etc/hosts.equiv │
│ │     containing  a list of trusted hostnames with which it shares │
│ │     usernames.  Users with the same username on both  the  local │
│ │     and  remote  machine  may rlogin from the machines listed in │
│ │     the remote machine's /etc/hosts.equiv file without supplying │
│ │     a  password.   Individual users may set up a similar private │
│ │     equivalence list with the file .rhosts in their home  direc- │
│ │     tories.   Each line in this file contains two names: a host- │
│ │     name and a username separated by a space.  An entry in a re- │
│ │     mote user's .rhosts file permits the user named username who │
│ │     is logged into hostname to log in to the remote  machine  as │
│ │     the  remote  user without supplying a password.  If the name │
│ │     of the local host is not found in the /etc/hosts.equiv  file │
│ │     on  the  remote machine, and the local username and hostname │
│ │     are not found in the remote user's .rhosts  file,  then  the │
│ │     remote machine will prompt for a password.  Hostnames listed │
│ │     in /etc/hosts.equiv and .rhosts files must be  the  official │
│ │     hostnames listed in the hosts database; nicknames may not be │
│ │     used in either of these files.                          │ │
│ │                                                             │ │
│ │     For security reasons, the .rhosts file must be owned by  ei- │
│ │     ther the remote user or by root.                        │ │
│ │ ─More──(35%)                                                │ │
│ └─────────────────────────────────────────────────────────────┘ │
└─────────────────────────────────────────────────────────────────┘
```

commands entered will run on the remote machine until the remote session is terminated by using an exit command.

A number of flags can be specified to the UNIX `rlogin` command. Executing the

```
%man rlogin
```

command will return help about `rlogin`. The documentation returned by executing this command on our system is shown in Figure 6.10. The 35% shown at the bottom of this screen capture denotes that we are viewing 35 percent of the documentation. There are approximately two more screenfuls of material about `rlogin`. By using the -l option, you can start a session on the remote machine with an account name that is different from the one you are currently using on your local machine. For example, suppose Martin McGrath (account name mmg) enters the command

```
%rlogin -l oreilly hal9000
```

He is going to log in to the remote machine hal9000 using the account of his girlfriend, Mary O'Reilly. Of course, to be successful, Martin must know Mary's password.

As a final note, Telnet is a more secure remote login mechanism than rlogin.

EXERCISES 6.2

Telnet and Remote Login

1. Can you Telnet to the machine you regularly use? Can you rlogin to this same machine? If so, is there a reason why you would want to do this?

2. Invoke your Telnet client. What is the escape sequence used on your system?

3. Configure your browser so that you can enter Telnet URLs to launch Telnet. Describe what you needed to do to accomplish this.

4. Research Telnet and remote login using the Web. Write a paragraph comparing and contrasting the security risks of each.

6.3 File Transfer

There are times when you may need to transfer a file from one computer to another. For example,

Useful Item

- You scan in images on one system, and you need to move them to another for permanent display.

- You work on a computer at home, and you need to transfer a file to a machine at your office.

- You and a collaborator need to exchange files.

- You want to download a helper, plug-in, or freeware application from another computer.

- You develop software on one machine and need to move it to another.

Useful Item

File Transfer[1] is an application that allows you to transfer files between two computers on the Internet or on the same network. The two most important file transfer functions are:

1. Copying a file from another computer to your computer.

2. Sending a file from your computer to another computer.

Figure 6.11 diagrams the process. In the figure, fileA resides on computer A. A file transfer connection to computer B is opened. Next, fileA is sent over the network to computer B, using file transfer. The figure shows that fileA has arrived at computer B. This process is called *uploading*. We say fileA has been uploaded from computer A to computer B, or the file has been uploaded to computer B, for short. When you copy a file from another computer to your machine, we say you *download* the file. The process of bringing copies of files over to your computer from another location is known as downloading. When copying files, you should first run virus detection software (see next section) on them before using them on your computer. This helps safeguard against your computer getting infected, but it is not a guarantee.

Although file transfer is the fastest and most convenient method, there are other ways of copying a file from one computer to another. For example, if the file to be transferred is not too large, you may be able to email the file to an account on the second machine. In some circumstances, emailing a file is not practical, especially when it may be requested many times, as is often the case with freeware. Another option is to copy a file onto a diskette and then use the diskette to install the file on a different machine. However, for computers separated by hundreds or thousands of miles, "walknet" (or "sneakernet") is not a satisfactory solution.

In Section 6.3.1 we explore graphical FTP clients, and in Section 6.3.2 we explore text-based FTP clients.

---

1   We use this as a generic name here. Your file transfer client may have a different name. The process of transferring files this way is often called FTP, after the UNIX client *File Transfer Protocol* (*FTP*).

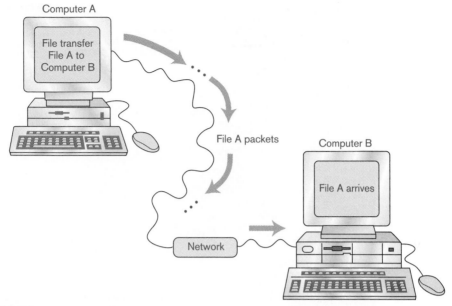

FIGURE 6.11
Schematic of how file transfer can be used to copy a file from computer A
to computer B.

6.3.1   Graphical File Transfer Clients

Graphical file transfer clients are the easiest to use. These applications
display the sending computer's file system in one window and the receiving
computer's file system in a second window. Note that requiring you to
log in to each computer prevents unauthorized users from connecting to a
machine and transferring files.

Many PCs are equipped with an FTP client. Often, a shortcut to the
FTP client is displayed on the user's desktop. An example of this is shown
in Figure 6.12. In the first column, the sixth icon down represents the
WS_FTP Pro client available from Ipswitch. Such FTP clients can be
invoked by double-clicking on them. Figure 6.13 illustrates the result of
double-clicking on this icon on our system. You may notice a different setup
on your computer. Notice that the right half of the figure, representing the
remote site, is empty. This is because we have not yet logged into a remote
site.

In order to connect to a remote site using a graphical FTP client such
as the one shown in Figure 6.13, you first click on the Connect button.
This will cause a pop-up dialog box such as that shown in Figure 6.14 to
appear. In the first line you simply type in the hostname or the IP address
of the remote system you are connecting to; in the third line you enter your

Useful Item

FIGURE 6.12
FTP icon
depicted in first
column, sixth
row.

FIGURE 6.13
Initial FTP screen
of a graphical
FTP client.

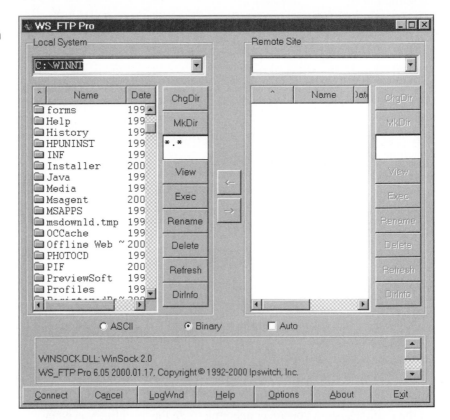

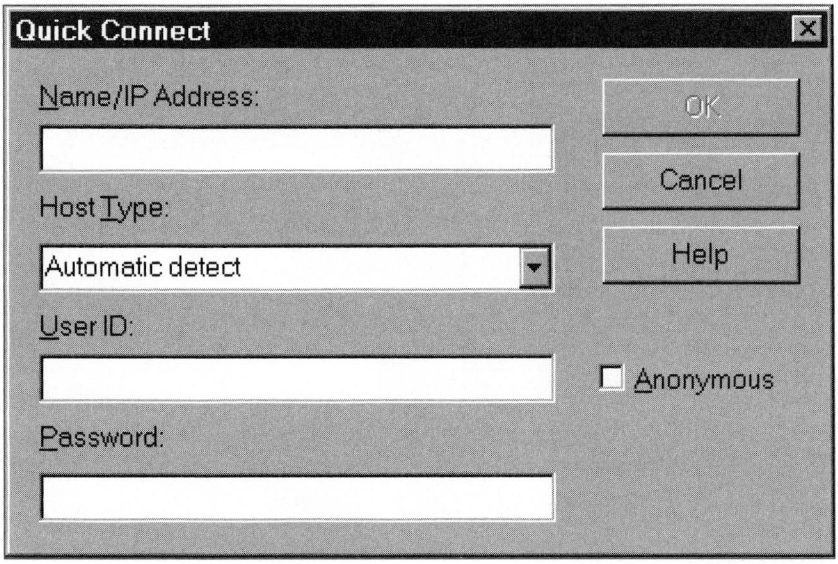

FIGURE 6.14
Connecting to a
remote site using
FTP.

account name; in the fourth line you type in your password. For security
reasons the password is not echoed on the screen. Once you type all of
this information into the dialog box, you can press the OK button. This will
connect you to the remote system.

Figure 6.15 shows a typical user interface once a user has logged into a
remote site. Notice now that the right part of the window contains information. In this case the local system is a Windows PC running a graphical FTP
client, and the remote system is a workstation running Unix. Notice that
the slashes in the current directory names displayed in Figure 6.15 go in
opposite directions. To change directories on either side, you simply click
on the up arrow to move to a parent directory and click on the directory
itself to move down the directory structure.

Many features of a graphical FTP client are self-explanatory. For example, to transfer a file from one system to another, you can "drag" it using
the mouse and "drop" it on the other system. Files can thus be exchanged
in either direction. You can also highlight a file to transfer by clicking on
it once. Pressing the middle arrow with its tail pointed to the side that a
highlighted file is on will cause the file to be transferred to the opposite side.
Double-clicking on a file will usually cause it to be automatically tranferred
to the other side. If a copy of the file already exists on the other side, care
should be used. Usually, you will be asked whether or not you want to
overwrite the existing copy. To send a group of consecutively appearing
files across to the other computer, you can highlight them by holding down

FIGURE 6.15
Windows FTP
client user
interface.

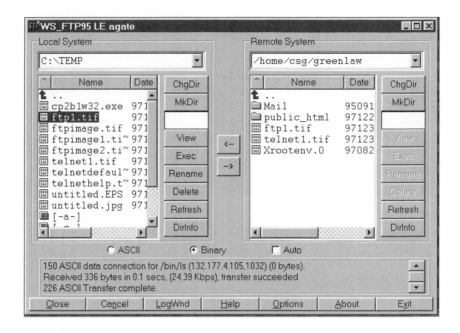

the Shift key while selecting them using the mouse. Depressing the appropriate middle arrow will cause the files to be transferred to the other side.

A few general remarks about graphical FTP clients are in order. One important point is the *transfer setting mode*. This can usually be specified by clicking on a button. Most clients have a *text transfer mode* (ASCII) and a *binary transfer mode*. Note in Figure 6.15 that there are three modes: ASCII, Binary, and Auto. The binary transfer mode is selected in the figure. All file types can be transferred correctly using binary mode, but not all file types can be transferred using text mode. Therefore, the mode should be set to binary when transferring images, files containing special characters, or executable files. When in doubt, transfer a file using the binary mode setting.

After completing an FTP session, it is a good practice to close the session by clicking on the Close button and then exit the FTP client by clicking on the Exit button. At the bottom of Figure 6.15, notice that FTP prints out some log information about what you have been doing. Oftentimes a log file is written to the system, and you can keep track of what transfers were made by reading this log file.

We have provided a general overview of graphical FTP clients. Now let us restrict our attention to a specific example using FTP to transfer a file over to a UNIX account from a Windows account so that the file may be displayed on a Web page. We provide a step-by-step procedure for doing this, but note that there are several other ways to accomplish this goal. For example, one could copy the image to a floppy disk or send the image as an email attachment. Nevertheless, FTP is an excellent method for the fast transfer of files between computers.

To make our discussion more concrete, suppose you have a file on your PC called `atsummit.jpg` that you would like to move to a machine with hostname `cervino.armstrong.edu`. Furthermore, suppose `atsummit.jpg` is residing on the C drive in the directory `greenlaw\←↩ InlineOnline` and that you would like to deposit the file into the directory `public_html/JPG` on the UNIX system `cervino.armstrong.edu`. Figure 6.16 shows where the file `atsummit.jpg` is located. You will spot it two-thirds of the way down the first column. So, step 1 of our procedure is really to locate the file to be transferred.

The second step is to start up the FTP client on the PC. Note that you could also obtain the image by using the FTP client on the UNIX system, but since we have not covered text-based FTP clients yet we outline the steps using a graphical FTP client. After reading about text-based FTP clients, you will see how the process can be done using a UNIX FTP client. As discussed earlier in this section, if your FTP client is located on the desktop, you simply double-click it to start it up; otherwise, you can run FTP from the command line.

The third step is simply to connect and log in to the remote UNIX system using the same procedures as already described in this section. For our scenario at this point, Figure 6.17 shows the state of things. We have

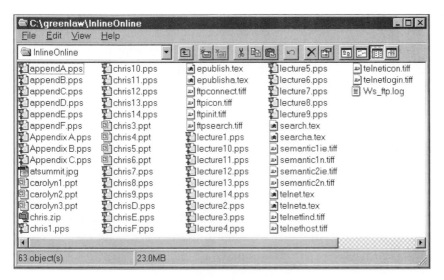

FIGURE 6.16
Directory listing on a PC showing the location of the file `atsummit.jpg` to be FTP'd to a UNIX system.

FIGURE 6.17
Initial directories
displayed after
connecting to the
remote UNIX
system cervino.

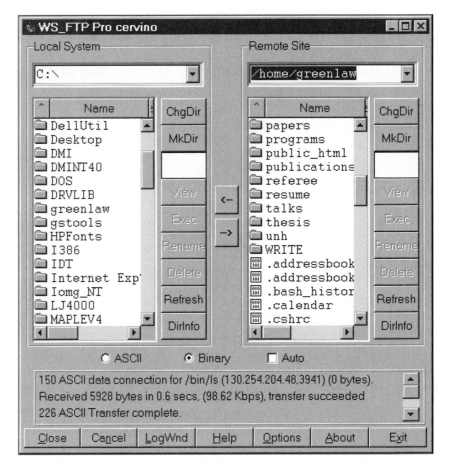

scrolled down on both the local system and the remote system so that the directories in question are displayed. This is done using the vertical scroll bars as one would guess. Note that on the left is the local machine, in this case the PC running Windows, and on the right is the remote machine, in this case a workstation running UNIX.

The fourth step is to change to the appropriate directories on both systems. For the local system, we can do this by double-clicking on greenlaw and then double-clicking on InlineOnline. For the remote system, this is accomplished by double-clicking on public_html and then JPG. The result of these operations is shown in Figure 6.18. The width of the screen prevents the complete directory names from fitting in the picture. Notice the file atsummit.jpg that we want to transfer to the remote system is displayed five files up from the bottom on the local system.

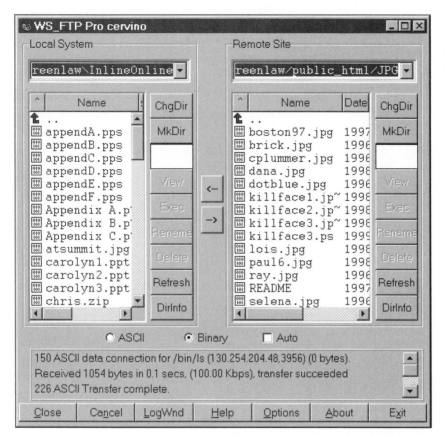

FIGURE 6.18
Switched to appropriate directories to execute the upload of `atsummit.jpg` to `cervino` the remote UNIX system.

In step 5 you select the appropriate file transfer mode. In this case we are transferring a binary (JPG) file. Notice that the transfer mode shown in Figure 6.18 is set to binary.

In step 6 the file to transfer, `atsummit.jpg`, can be highlighted by single-clicking on it. The file can be transferred to the right in step 7 simply by clicking on the lower of the two arrow buttons. Notice the direction of the arrow ($\rightarrow$) implies movement to the right. The file will be transferred to `cervino` and a log of the transfer will be displayed as shown at the bottom of Figure 6.18.

In step 8 you can exit from FTP if you are done transferring files for now. This is done by clicking `Close` followed by clicking `Exit`. The file is now residing on the UNIX system and ready for you to `telnet` or `rlogin` to the system and set the permissions on it to world readable so that it can be displayed on the Web. (Some FTP clients will set the permissions to world readable automatically.)

The steps for the entire FTP procedure we just described are outlined here. Note that there are other orders to these steps that could be used to carry out the same function. We have simply specified one possible order. Finally, we should note that it generally takes an experienced user about twenty seconds to perform this procedure. Thus, once you get the hang of it, you will see that transferring files in this manner is straightforward.

Useful Item

Summary of Steps for Moving an Image From a PC so that It Can Be Displayed on a UNIX Web Server

1. Locate the file to transfer.

2. Launch your FTP client on the PC.

3. Connect and log in to the remote UNIX system.

4. Change to the appropriate directories on both the local and remote systems.

5. Select the appropriate transfer mode.

6. Select the file to transfer.

7. Transfer the file.

8. Close and exit FTP.

9. Telnet or rlogin into your UNIX account and set the permissions on the file to be displayed on the Web (if necessary).

Useful Item

As a final note about graphical FTP clients, notice in Figure 6.18 that the last file on the local system is called `chris.zip`. Such a file is a compressed file or a group of compressed files. (See Section 6.3.3.) Compressed files should be transferred using binary transfer mode. Such files can be uncompressed using the appropriate decompression routine. On a Windows system, this usually involves simply double-clicking on the file, whereas on a UNIX system, it may involve running a program like `gunzip` or `uncompress` on the file.

6.3.2   Text-Based File Transfer Clients

Useful Item

There are text-based file transfer clients, as well as graphical systems. For example, you can launch the UNIX file transfer client called *File Transfer Protocol (FTP)* by entering the command

```
%ftp hostname
```

Here `hostname` is the name of the computer with which you want to exchange files. Once you have successfully initiated an FTP session by supplying a userid and password, you will usually be greeted by the prompt `ftp>` or something similar.

At this point, you can enter a variety of commands. Some may look and function like UNIX commands, but others will vary depending on the file transfer program being used. The most important commands allow you to `get` a file (obtain a copy) and `put` a file (deposit a copy). The following list summarizes typical commands for a text-based file transfer client. (The list is not intended to be exhaustive.)

- `bye`   Terminate the session and exit the file transfer program.

- `cd`   Change directory.

- `get`   Copy a file.

- `help`   View a list of commands or help on a specific command.

- `ls`   List the files in the current (or working) directory.

- `put`   Send a copy of a file.

- `pwd`   Print the name of the current directory.

Entering `help` will display a list of commands available at the site, and `help` followed by a command name will provide a description of how that particular command is used. Figure 6.19 provides a list of the FTP commands available on our system. If you are on a UNIX system, entering `man ftp` will provide documentation about FTP. Figure 6.20 shows a small portion of the on-line FTP documentation available on our system.

The first command you will use when transferring files is the `open` command. This will allow you to open a connection to another machine. Typing

```
ftp>help open
```

results in the following display

```
open connect to remote tftp
```

As you can see, `ftp`'s help facility is a bit cryptic. The idea is to open a connection to the machine you want to exchange files with. For example,

FIGURE 6.19
List of commands
available with the
UNIX `ftp`
command.

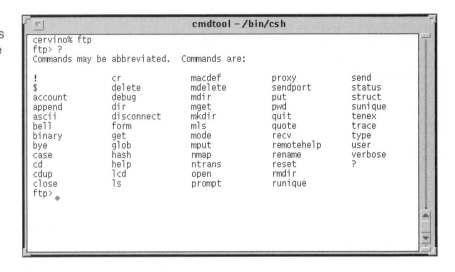

```
                        cmdtool - /bin/csh

cervino% ftp
ftp> ?
Commands may be abbreviated.  Commands are:

!              cr            macdef         proxy          send
$              delete        mdelete        sendport       status
account        debug         mdir           put            struct
append         dir           mget           pwd            sunique
ascii          disconnect    mkdir          quit           tenex
bell           form          mls            quote          trace
binary         get           mode           recv           type
bye            glob          mput           remotehelp     user
case           hash          nmap           rename         verbose
cd             help          ntrans         reset          ?
cdup           lcd           open           rmdir
close          ls            prompt         runique
ftp>
```

FIGURE 6.20
Portion of the
main page for the
UNIX `ftp`
command.

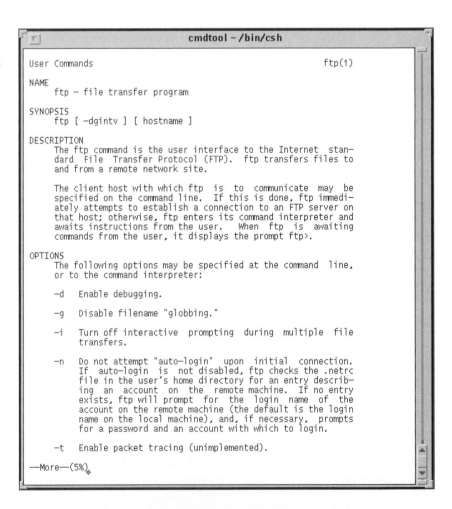

```
                        cmdtool - /bin/csh

User Commands                                              ftp(1)

NAME
     ftp - file transfer program

SYNOPSIS
     ftp [ -dgintv ] [ hostname ]

DESCRIPTION
     The ftp command is the user interface to the Internet  stan-
     dard  File  Transfer Protocol (FTP).  ftp transfers files to
     and from a remote network site.

     The client host with which ftp is  to  communicate  may  be
     specified on the command line.  If this is done, ftp immedi-
     ately attempts to establish a connection to an FTP server on
     that host; otherwise, ftp enters its command interpreter and
     awaits instructions from the user.   When  ftp  is  awaiting
     commands from the user, it displays the prompt ftp>.

OPTIONS
     The following options may be specified at the command  line,
     or to the command interpreter:

     -d   Enable debugging.

     -g   Disable filename "globbing."

     -i   Turn off interactive  prompting  during  multiple  file
          transfers.

     -n   Do not attempt "auto-login" upon  initial  connection.
          If  auto-login  is  not disabled, ftp checks the .netrc
          file in the user's home directory for an entry describ-
          ing  an  account  on  the  remote machine.  If no entry
          exists, ftp will prompt for  the  login  name  of  the
          account on the remote machine (the default is the login
          name on the local machine), and, if necessary,  prompts
          for a password and an account with which to login.

     -t   Enable packet tracing (unimplemented).

—More—(5%)
```

suppose you wanted to obtain a file from the host `cervino.armstrong.edu`. To establish this connection, you would enter

```
ftp>open cervino.armstrong.edu
```

If the connection is opened successfully, you will see a response such as

```
Connected to cervino.armstrong.edu
220 drake FTP server (SunOS 5.6) ready.
Name (mymachine.school.edu:userid):
```

where `mymachine.school.edu:userid` is the name of your machine followed by your userid. This message is a login prompt, and you can now log in to the remote machine as you would normally log in to any machine. You simply enter your userid and password for the remote machine. If there is a problem opening the connection, it is likely that you mistyped the name of the remote host or that perhaps the host is down.

There are two fundamental `ftp` commands: one that allows you to download a file to your computer and the other that allows you to upload a file to a remote computer. We next explain both of these in detail.

The command to bring a file over to your compute is `get`. The command `recv` (an abbreviation for "receive") has the same effect as `get`. Once you open the connection to a remote machine, you can use the `ls` and `cd` commands to list files and change directories, respectively, on the remote machine. To bring over the file `athike.text`, simply `cd` to the directory where the file resides and perform an `ls` to verify that the file is where you thought it was. Then enter the command

```
ftp>get athike.text
```

If the transfer is successful, you will see a message such as

```
200 PORT command successful.
150 ASCII data connection for athike.text
  (130.154.188.11,34200) (376 bytes).
226 ASCII Transfer complete.
local: athike.text remote: athike.text
388 bytes received in 0.024 seconds (16.02 Kbytes/s)
```

Notice the last line of this message includes the size of the file and the rate of transfer of the data. The rate of transfer is expresed in terms of

Kbytes/s. A Kbyte or *kilobyte* is 1,000 bytes. So, in this case the transfer rate was 16,020 bytes per second.

If the transfer is not successful, you will get an error message. This usually means you mistyped the name of the file you were trying to retrieve or the file is not where you thought it was. Note that the local (new) copy of the file was also called `athike.text`. To have the file brought over with the file name `atrail.text`, you can enter the command

```
ftp>get athike.text atrail.text
```

In this case a copy of the remote file `athike.text` will be placed in the current directory on your local machine in a file having the name `atrail.text`. Be careful not to overwrite an existing local file.

The command to upload a copy of a local file onto a remote machine is `put`. The `send` command has the same effect. Initially, it is a good idea to `cd` to the local directory where the file that you want to send resides. As before, you next need to establish a connection with a remote host. Once this is done, you can `cd` to the directory where you would like to place the copy of the file. Suppose you want to deposit a copy of the file `backpack`. Simply enter the command

```
ftp>put backpack
```

If successful, you will see a message such as

```
200 PORT command successful.
150 ASCII data connection
for backpack (130.154.188.11,34206).
226 Transfer complete.
local: backpack remote: backpack
376 bytes sent in 0.0042 seconds (87.03 Kbytes/s)
```

If the transfer is not successful, you will get an error message. This usually means you mistyped the name of the file you were trying to send or the file was not in your current working directory.

Hot Topic

Note that when sending or retrieving files using `ftp` it is important to exercise caution. It is very easy to overwrite an existing file without any warning. For example, getting the remote file `compass` will overwrite an existing local copy of `compass`, and sending the local file `swissarmy` will overwrite the existing remote copy of the file `swissarmy`.

The `mget` and `mput` abbreviations stand for "multiple get" and "multiple put," respectively. These options allow you to retrieve multiple files at once or send multiple files at once. They are very useful when you need to transfer a large number of files. If you do not want to be asked whether to transfer each file, you can turn `prompt` off by entering

```
ftp>prompt
```

When using `mget` and `mput`, be careful not to overwrite existing files having the same names as the files you are transferring.

Several other commands are helpful for you to know while using `ftp`. We now run through several of them. The `lcd` command stands for "local change directory." This command will allow you to change directories on your local machine. Remember, while using `ftp`, the `cd` command is used to change directories on the remote machine. Normally, before launching `ftp` it is a good idea to change to the local directory where you will be transferring from or receiving to. However, if these are two separate directories, the `lcd` command will come in handy.

The `status` command displays current information about your `ftp` session. A sample output from the `status` command follows:

```
Connected to drake.armstrong.edu.
No proxy connection.
Mode: stream; Type: ascii; Form: non-print; Struct: file
Verbose: off; Bell: off; Prompting: on; Globbing: on
Store unique: off; Receive unique: off
Case: off; CR stripping: on
Ntrans: off
Nmap: off
Hash mark printing: off; Use of PORT cmds: on
```

A great deal of the `status` information is self-explanatory, and what is not can easily be checked out through the `ftp help` facility. One general remark is in order, though. Notice that there are lots of `on` and `off` messages. Many of the options to `ftp` function in a toggle manner like switches. That is, they are either `on` or `off`. You can switch between the two options by executing the corresponding command. For example, in the figure we see that "Hash mark printing" has a `status` of `off`. To turn hash mark printing on, you simply enter

```
ftp>hash
```

Thus, the command names act as switches. If the feature was on, typing the corresponding command switches the feature `off`, and vice versa. When transferring large files, you may want to set `hash` to on. The `hash` feature prints a hash mark, #, on the screen after each segment (a buffer full) of the file is transferred. This can serve as a reassurance to you that the file is still being transferred properly. Otherwise, your terminal may sit idle for half an hour while you are wondering if something went wrong.

Another important option of `ftp` that is worth mentioning is the `binary` option. You should turn this option on by entering

```
ftp>binary
```

if you are going to transfer a binary file—for our purposes a file that does not consist of plain text. For example, a compressed data file or an image file should be transferred with the `binary` option on.

Once you have completed your `ftp` session, you can end it by typing

```
ftp>bye
```

The `quit` command can also be used for this purpose. It is a good idea to check the permissions on files that you bring over using `ftp`. Sometimes files are brought over as world readable, whereas you may prefer that they are only user readable.

6.3.3   File Compression

It is common to *compress* files that are to be transferred between two computers. Compressing a file makes it smaller, and the compressed file can be transferred more quickly over a network. A wide variety of compression tools are available, including: *compress*, *gzip*, and *PKZIP*. When you transfer a file, the file extension will usually alert you to whether or not the file is compressed (`.Z` for compress, `.gz` for gzip, and `.zip` for PKZIP). You will need to decompress the file to use it. (On some systems, you can set things up so that files are automatically decompressed for you.) You must use the appropriate decompression tool, which depends on how the file was compressed: *uncompress* for compress, *gunzip* for gzip, and *PKUNZIP* for PKZIP. There are a number of sites from which you can download compression and decompression programs.

Go On-Line

File compression is an extensive field in computer science, and the algorithms used are very interesting. Consult an introductory computer science algorithms textbook to learn more about this subject.

6.3.4   Anonymous File Transfer

On some systems, files are made available to anyone who wants to retrieve them (for example, *freeware*, public documents, and so on). If a file needs to be widely distributed, it may not be feasible to assign accounts and passwords to everyone interested in receiving a copy of the file. *Anonymous file transfer* was established in response to this problem. Users log in with anonymous as their account name and then provide a password. The standard practice is to use your email address as a password, because this helps the administrator at the file transfer site to monitor file transfer usage. On other systems, a password of guest is expected. You should never use your real account password when logging in anonymously, since the information you submit is not secure.

After logging in via anonymous file transfer, you will be restricted to specific directories. Usually, accessible directories are in an area named something like public. Within those directories, you will often be confined to just downloading files. In many cases, such directories contain a help file, called something like README, where additional information can be found. Figure 6.21 illustrates an anonymous file transfer session. In this case, after logging in, we checked to see what files were available and then retrieved one of them, called stamp, using the get command.

Note that file transfer can also be launched from within a browser window by entering the URL

FIGURE 6.21
An illustration of an anonymous file transfer session.

```
ftp://hostname
```

Here, `hostname` specifies the site to which you want to connect.

6.3.5   Archie

Unless you know exactly where a file is located on the Internet, it will be very difficult to find it, since files can be archived at file transfer sites scattered throughout the world. *Archie*, derived from the phrase "file archive," is a service that maintains databases containing listings of files from various file transfer sites. Performing a query to find a specific file involves either sending email to an Archie site or connecting to an Archie server via Telnet. Archie will respond and will indicate the location(s) of the file you want, provided that the file is listed in one of its databases. To locate an Archie server, you can connect to any of the major search engines and enter the query "Archie."

Go On-Line

The Lycos search engine has created something called FTP Search, which has a much friendlier user interface than Archie. Using this facility, you can search an enormous repository of files. The interface to this tool is shown in Figure 6.22. The user simply types in a filename and clicks on the `GoGetIt` button. A list of retrievals, matching filenames, is returned.

FIGURE 6.22
Lycos FTP
search tool.

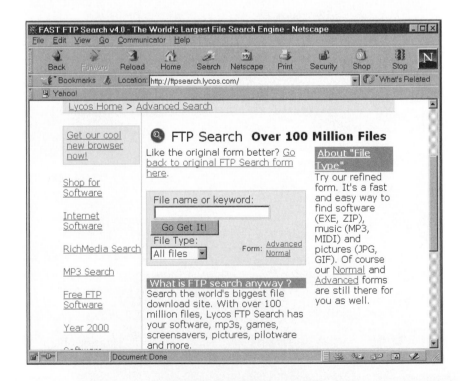

More advanced FTP search tools are continually evolving. The reader should check on-line for the most recent advances.

EXERCISES 6.3

File Transfer

5.   Provide the names of three graphical FTP clients for Windows and URLs containing information about these clients.

6.   Do you have a graphical, textual, or both type(s) of file transfer client(s) available on your system? What are the transfer modes you can use with your client(s)?

7.   What factors determine how quickly a file transfers over the Internet? Describe them.

8.   Print out a sample file transfer session in which you transfer a file to your system.

9.   What file compression programs are available on your system? Can they be configured to decompress compressed files automatically? Explain.

10.   Try to compress several different types of files. What space savings did you obtain? Did the file type make a difference?

11.   Does file compression or file decompression take longer? Experiment. Explain your findings.

12.   Research Archie using the Web. Summarize in a paragraph what you learned.

13.   Provide the addresses of two "nearby" Archie servers. Try to connect to one of them and locate file compression programs. Were you successful?

14.   Bring up the URL `ftpsearch.lycos.com`. Enter a filename of `atrail`. Explain your results.

15.   What is *Veronica*? Conduct research on the Web and describe your findings.

6.4   Computer Viruses

Some of the programs that you download from the Internet or obtain as email attachments may threaten the security of your computer if they contain *viruses*, *Trojan horse programs*, or *worms*. In this section, you will learn different strategies for handling such annoyances.

6.4.1   Definitions

A virus can be thought of as a program that, when run, can "replicate" and then embed itself within another program. Although there are harmless viruses, most are intended to damage the host system. The damage can occur immediately, by filling all available space on your hard drive, for instance, or it may occur at some later time, after the virus has had a chance to be passed along to other programs and computers. The damage to your computer might involve something as innocent as a message being displayed on your desktop, or, more likely, the destruction or modification of data or the deletion of files. Before doing the damage, however, the virus could infect other programs on your computer, as well as other computers if you send program files to anyone else and they run them. A specific event, such as the tenth time that the host program is run, or a particular date on which the host program is run, may *trigger* the virus to become active.

A Trojan horse program (the name comes from Greek mythology) is a legitimate program for carrying out some useful function, but within it is hidden code that is activated by some trigger. When the hidden code is executed, it might release a virus, permit unauthorized access to the computer, or destroy files and data.

A worm is a stand-alone program that tries to gain access to computer systems via networks. For example, a worm might try various password combinations until it is successful. The 1988 *Internet Worm*, created by Robert T. Morris, is a highly successful example. Although not designed to be destructive (the worm was intended to be an experiment), the worm caused major problems when it inadvertently consumed the available memory in the systems it invaded.

6.4.2   Virus Avoidance and Precautions

Relatively speaking, UNIX viruses are rare, because of the strict security measures on UNIX systems. Most viruses are designed to infect either PCs or Macs. A virus is usually targeted at one type or the other of such systems, since nearly all viruses are operating-system specific. To protect yourself from viruses and Trojan horse programs, we recommend the following precautions:

Hot Topic

- Run *antivirus software* (also called *virus detection software*) on any new programs. This software looks for viruses and Trojan horse programs by comparing data patterns found in your programs to characteristic data patterns found in programs infected by known viruses.

- Do not download files from unknown sources. This includes mail attachments from individuals and organizations unknown to you. If you do download something, run antivirus software on it before opening the file or running the program.

- Do not used pirated copies of software.

- Keep your antivirus software up to date, since new releases will contain information necessary to identify the latest viruses and Trojan horse programs.

- Back up your files regularly (after ensuring that they are virus-free by running antivirus software on them). If you do lose files or data because of a virus, you will be able to recover if you have current backup files.

Although viruses, Trojan horse programs, and worms are a very real computer security threat, they also present an opportunity for hoaxes and misinformation. A common misunderstanding is that viruses can somehow be transmitted directly via email. This was the premise of the "Good Times" hoax, a message that stated there was a virus being spread through email. The alleged viral email message contained the expression "Good Times" in the subject, and recipients were warned not to download or even read the message. They were then urged to forward the hoax message to everyone they knew. Of course, a regular email message is a text file, and viruses need to be embedded in programs, so reading an email message is fine; however, downloading and running programs that are attachments to email require caution. An interesting Web page dedicated to Internet hoaxes is the CIAC Internet Hoaxes Page, and a link is provided in this book's accompanying Web presentation.

Go On-Line

EXERCISES 6.4

Computer Viruses

16. Research the Microsoft Word macro viruses. How many different strains are there? Were you surprised by this? Why is it so easy to have viruses in Word? Speculate why these viruses spread so rapidly.

17. Compare and contrast a real live human virus, such as the Hantavirus, with a computer virus.

18. Have you or a friend ever had problems with computer viruses? Describe your experiences. Do you regularly use virus detection software? Did you receive the "Good Times" message? When? Did you forward it?

19. How can you obtain virus detection software? Explain how to get around the danger of obtaining virus detection software that is itself infected.

20. Write a summary describing the "Love Letter Virus" that appeared in the year 2000.

Basic HTML

I remember Caledonia State Park, where a couple invited me to their picnic. They fed me salads and barbecued chicken. When I was leaving, they insisted I take a beer with me. There was no way they were letting me go up the trail without a beer in my pack, oh well. Pennsylvania is known as Rocksylvania because the trail is so rocky. My feet became extremely sore. I was walking a lot of miles per day and enjoying camping out. I met some really nice people in Boiling Springs. One morning when I was sleeping in a state park, a trail angel woke me with a dozen donuts. The people you meet on the trail are wonderful! Another night I was sleeping in an otherwise empty shelter, or so I thought. A snake woke me up by slithering beside me. Since I had no light nor matches, I swept out the entire shelter in total darkness hoping to sweep out the snake. I got back in my sleeping bag and it took a while for me to fall asleep again—the typical snake you see in Pennsylvania is the poisonous copperhead.

Pennsylvania
232 miles

Chapter 7

7.1 INTRODUCTION

In this chapter, we expand our discussion of HTML, covering the following topics:

Objectives

- Semantic and syntactic style types
- Headers and footers
- Lists
- Tables
- Debugging

7.2 Semantic- versus Syntactic-Based Style Types

Many HTML tags are used for specifying different types of text fonts. These tags allow you to enhance the appearance of your Web pages, using bold, italics, and underlining to highlight an item of importance or to illustrate a definition. However, text changes used incorrectly can clutter up a Web page and make it less readable.

7.2.1 Semantic-Based Style Types

There are basically two ways to specify how text should be rendered by a browser. (These may be superseded by Cascading Style Sheets in the future.) The first is the *semantic-based style type* (also called the *content-based style types*), in which HTML tags are used to indicate the content of the text. For example, the text may be an address or a citation, and the browser renders addresses and citations according to built-in settings. You merely tell the browser the category into which the text falls. If you use the address tag, <ADDRESS>, for all addresses on a Web page, they will all be rendered similarly. The form of the writing then suggests a meaning to the reader.

A number of the most important semantic-based style types, and examples of each, are listed here. Figures 7.1 and 7.2 depict how Netscape renders the various examples. Figures 7.3 and 7.4 depict how Internet Explorer renders the various examples. Figures 7.5 and 7.6 depict how Lynx renders the various examples. Compare and contrast the figures carefully. Notice that the items appear different from browser to browser.

Emphasis Tag

The emphasis tag, <EM>, with its corresponding </EM> ending tag is used for highlighting text. An example would be:

```
Meet me tonight.  It is <EM>important</EM>.
```

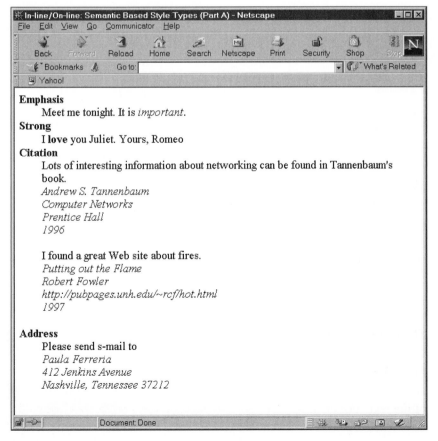

FIGURE 7.1
Netscape's rendering of semantic-based style types (Part A).

FIGURE 7.2
Netscape's
rendering of
semantic-based
style types
(Part B).

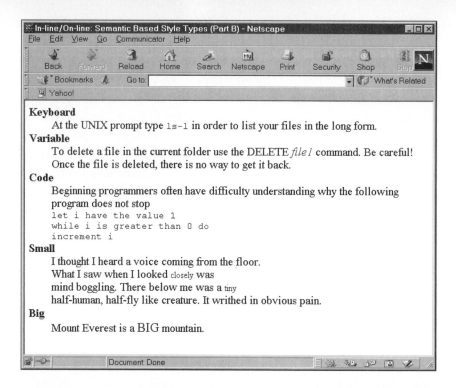

FIGURE 7.3
Internet
Explorer's
rendering of
semantic-based
style types
(Part A).

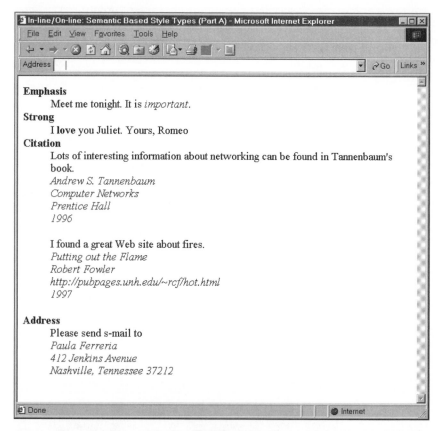

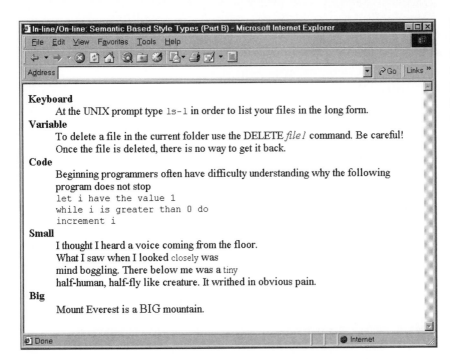

FIGURE 7.4
Internet
Explorer's
rendering of
semantic-based
style types
(Part B).

Strong Tag

The strong tag, <STRONG>, is used to indicate an even higher level of emphasis. An example is:

```
I <STRONG>love</STRONG> you Juliet.  Yours, Romeo
```

Citation Tag

The citation tag, <CITE>, is used to specify a reference. A collection of citations creates a bibliography. Using the citation tag facilitates that collection (possibly automated), since every reference is bracketed between <CITE> and </CITE>. A sample of the citation tag is:

```
Lots of interesting information about networking can
be found in Tannenbaum's book. <BR>
<CITE> Andrew S. Tannenbaum <BR>
Computer Networks <BR>
Prentice Hall <BR>
1996 <BR>
</CITE>
```

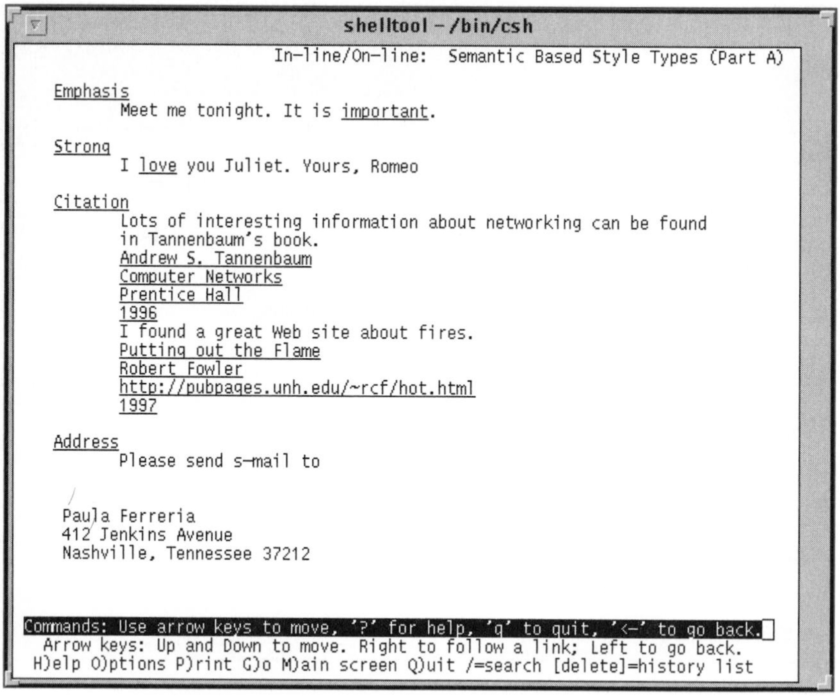

FIGURE 7.5

Lynx's rendering of semantic-based style types (Part A).

```
┌─────────────────────────────────────────────────────────────────┐
│  ▽                       shelltool – /bin/csh                     │
│               In–line/On–line:  Semantic Based Style Types (Part A)│
│                                                                    │
│      Emphasis                                                      │
│            Meet me tonight. It is important.                       │
│                                                                    │
│      Strong                                                        │
│            I love you Juliet. Yours, Romeo                         │
│                                                                    │
│      Citation                                                      │
│            Lots of interesting information about networking can be found│
│            in Tannenbaum's book.                                   │
│            Andrew S. Tannenbaum                                    │
│            Computer Networks                                       │
│            Prentice Hall                                           │
│            1996                                                    │
│            I found a great Web site about fires.                   │
│            Putting out the Flame                                   │
│            Robert Fowler                                           │
│            http://pubpages.unh.edu/~rcf/hot.html                   │
│            1997                                                    │
│                                                                    │
│      Address                                                       │
│            Please send s–mail to                                   │
│                                                                    │
│                                                                    │
│      Paula Ferreria                                                │
│      412 Jenkins Avenue                                            │
│      Nashville, Tennessee 37212                                    │
│                                                                    │
│                                                                    │
│ Commands: Use arrow keys to move, '?' for help, 'q' to quit, '<–' to go back.│
│   Arrow keys: Up and Down to move. Right to follow a link; Left to go back.│
│   H)elp O)ptions P)rint G)o M)ain screen Q)uit /=search [delete]=history list│
└─────────────────────────────────────────────────────────────────┘
```

Notice that we also use the *line break* tag, <BR>, which forces a line break; that is, the text must go to the next line to continue. There is no ending tag for <BR>.

To cite an on-line reference, people generally include the title, the author, the corresponding URL, and a date. The title is usually extracted from the title bar. Since some Web documents may not include all four of these pieces of information, you should try to include as many as possible. Remember that since Web addresses change frequently, URL citations are not as reliable in the long term as printed matter citations. However, a URL can be more convenient for the reader to track down, because they do not have to go to the library.

Here is an example of citing a Web page.

```
I found a great Web site about fires. <BR>
<CITE> Putting out the Flame <BR>
Robert Fowler <BR>
```

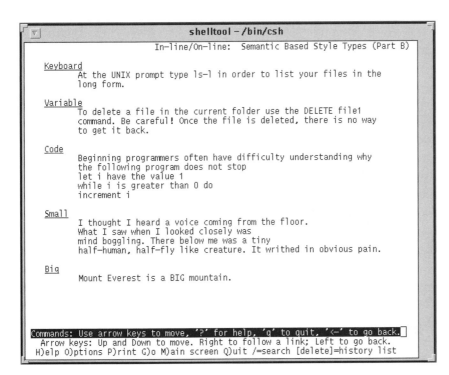

FIGURE 7.6
Lynx's rendering of semantic-based style types (Part B).

```
http://pubpages.unh.edu/~rcf/hot.html <BR>
1997 <BR>
</CITE>
```

A number of documents on the Web suggest citation models. There is no accepted standard, either on-line or in a printed bibliography. The bibliography of this book contains many examples of on-line citations and several more remarks about them.

Hot Topic

Address Tag

The address tag, <ADDRESS>, is used to indicate an address. If it is used throughout a series of Web pages, it is easy to automate the process of developing an address book for the pages. An example of this tag is:

```
Please send s-mail to
<ADDRESS> Paula Ferreria <BR>
412 Jenkins Avenue <BR>
Nashville, Tennessee 37212 <BR>
</ADDRESS>
```

Some authors pretty-print their HTML code by including additional spaces. Although this does not affect how the text is rendered by the browser, it could make the source code easier to read, thereby simplifying debugging. For example, the previous address code might be written as:

```
Please send s-mail to
<ADDRESS> Paula Ferreria              <BR>
          412 Jenkins Avenue          <BR>
          Nashville, Tennessee 37212 <BR>
</ADDRESS>
```

Keyboard Tag

This tag is used to delineate keyboard input. For example,

```
At the UNIX prompt type <KBD>ls −l</KBD> in order to
list your files in the long form.
```

It is good practice to use the keyboard tag, <KBD>, for all typed commands. Among other things, this ensures a consistent style for such inputs. Consider the following scenario: You are setting up a group of Web pages that describe how to learn to type more efficiently. Initially, you decide to use bold text for keyboard input, since you really want the keystrokes to stand out. You begin writing your HTML code. A couple days later, you are interrupted by a coworker, who urgently needs you to complete a different task. When you finally return to your typing page, you have forgotten that you were using bold for keyboard input, and you switch to emphasis. This results in inconsistent styles for keystrokes, which can confuse your readers.

Scenarios such as this are quite common, especially when multiple users are developing a Web presentation together. For this reason, we suggest using the keyboard tag consistently. In general, try to use the semantic-based style type that fits the application.

Variable Tag

Computer scientists developed HTML, and many of them like to talk about programming. To do so on Web pages, they introduced the variable tag, <VAR>, and the code tag, <CODE>, which is discussed in the next section. The variable tag is used to indicate an expression, usually just a sequence of letters, that has a number of different possible values. For example, in the equation

$$x + y = 10$$

x and y are variables that can equal 7 and 3, respectively, or 4 and 6, or 1 and 9, etc.

In some operating systems, the DELETE command is used to delete a file. The "argument" to the command is a file name. For example, let the variable name `file1` represent any file name. In the on-line documentation we are developing about file manipulation, we can specify how to delete a file, using the following HTML code:

```
To delete a file in the current folder use the
DELETE <VAR>file1</VAR>
command.  Be careful!  Once the file is deleted, there
is no way to get it back.
```

Code Tag

The code tag, `<CODE>`, is used for specifying program code. For example,

```
Beginning programmers often have difficulty
understanding why the following program does not stop:
     <CODE> let i have the value 1 <BR>
            while i is greater than 0 do <BR>
                 increment i <BR>
     </CODE>
```

Small Tag

Earlier, we saw how to use the basefont and font tags to either increase or decrease the font size. Another method for reducing the *relative font size* is to use the small tag, `<SMALL>`. Text appearing in this tag is made proportionally smaller than the surrounding text. Here is one possible use:

```
I thought I heard a voice coming from the floor.
What I saw when I looked <SMALL>closely</SMALL> was
mind boggling.  There below me was a <SMALL>tiny</SMALL>
half-human, half-fly like creature.  It writhed in
obvious pain.
```

Do not overuse the small tag, as it can make the text too small to read.

Big Tag

The big tag, `<BIG>`, plays the opposite role of the small tag.

7.2.2   Syntactic-Based Style Types

In contrast to the semantic-based style types, *syntactic-based style types* (also called *physical-based style types*) allow you to tell the browser specifically how you want the text to appear. For example, you may want it to be in bold or italics. When you specify that text is to be in italics, the browser formats that text in italics. Notice the difference between this and an indication that the text should be rendered, say, as an address. How

FIGURE 7.7
Samples of
syntactic-based
style types.

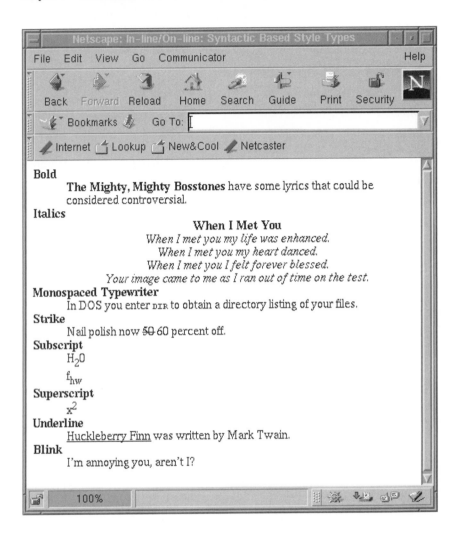

is an address to be formatted? Should it be indented? Bold? Italics? In the semantic-based style, the browser takes care of these details. In the syntactic specification, the HTML programmer must describe all of the formatting details.

Here we present the most important syntactic-based style types and examples of each. Figure 7.7 depicts how one browser renders the different examples. They might look slightly different on another browser.

Bold Tag

The bold tag, <B>, is used to make text in boldface. Most browsers darken the text and widen the letters. A sample use of the tag is as follows:

```
<B>The Mighty, Mighty Bosstones</B> have some lyrics
that could be considered controversial.
```

In this case, the name of the band stands out on the Web page. The strong tag would be a good choice here as well.

Italics Tag

To place a portion of text in italics, use the italics tag, `<I>`. For example, italics might be a good choice for the text of a poem:

```
<CENTER>
<STRONG>When I Met You</STRONG> <BR>

<I>
When I met you my life was enhanced. <BR>
When I met you my heart danced. <BR>
When I met you I felt forever blessed. <BR>
Your image came to me as I ran out of time on the test.
</I>
</CENTER>
```

Notice that we also used the center tag, `<CENTER>`, to center the poem horizontally on the screen.

Monospaced Typewriter Text Tag

The typewriter text tag, `<TT>`, is used for placing text in a monospaced typewriter font. This can be used to indicate that a certain phrase needs to be typed in. For example, suppose you are writing a Web page describing how to list your files in DOS. You could do the following:

```
In DOS you enter <TT>DIR</TT> to obtain a directory
listing of your files.
```

Strike Tag

The strike tag, `<STRIKE>`, may be used for crossing out a word by having a line drawn through it. If you have a business Web page and want to indicate that an item is on sale, you can use the strike tag to show that prices have been slashed. For example,

```
Nail polish now <STRIKE>50</STRIKE> 60 percent off.
```

The strike tag is also useful for depicting information that is no longer valid and has been updated. Except in a business situation, like that noted here, and in some specialized legal documents, this tag is rarely used.

Subscript Tag

The subscript tag, <SUB>, is used to generate a subscript. Suppose you are producing a Web page for your chemistry class and you want chemical formulas on your Web page to look professional. You might specify the formula for water as follows:

```
H<SUB>2</SUB>O
```

You can also include more than a single character as a subscript. For example, suppose you have a function, f, that depends on both height and weight. You might specify it as:

```
f<SUB>hw</SUB>
```

Superscript Tag

The superscript tag, <SUP>, produces on-screen superscripts, working in much the same way as the subscript tag works.

Underline Tag

Useful Item

The underline tag, <U>, is used to underline text. Since hyperlinks are depicted by underlining, the underline tag should be used sparingly and only in situations where no confusion can result as to whether or not the underlined item is a hyperlink. Here is a sample use:

```
<U>Huckleberry Finn</U> was written by Mark Twain.
```

Most users tend to try to click on underlined text, even though the underlining may be done in a different color than that of a hyperlink and even if the underlined text is not highlighted, as are hyperlinks.

Blink Tag

Flashing text is created using the blink tag, <BLINK>. Because most users find flashing text very annoying, it should be used very sparingly. Here is an example:

```
<BLINK>I'm annoying you, aren't I?</BLINK>
```

7.2.3   Style Type Usage

Hot Topic

In theory, you should use semantic-based style types wherever possible, because these codes reflect the meaning of the formatted text. For example, if the citation tag is used, it is usually safe to assume that the enclosed text is a reference. It is easy to imagine a computer program that reads an HTML file and outputs a listing of all the citations, creating a bibliography.

On the other hand, if the citations are formatted with italics, the computer program would not be able to distinguish the citation from other text also in italics. In practice, most users tend to use the syntactic-based style type, to exercise a higher degree of control over the appearance of their pages.

You may notice a difference in the way various browsers render semantic tags. For example, some browsers may render addresses in italics, while others use bold. For the most part, however, the popular browsers are fairly consistent. If a browser renders an address in italics, why not use the italics tag? Again, at some point, a computer program that uses the address tag to extract an address book automatically could be applied to a Web presentation. Also, it is much easier for the reader if each style element, such as an address, hyperlink, reference, and so on, appears in its own consistent format.

Some older tags you may encounter are called *deprecated tags*. This means that the tag is of little value and will eventually disappear from the HTML standard. Examples of such tags are `<LISTING>` and `<XMP>`. Do not use deprecated tags.

Try not to overuse the various style types. Too many changes can make a document harder to read.

Useful Item

EXERCISES 7.2

Semantic- versus Syntactic-Based Style Types

1. Load the Trailplace.com Web page at `www.trailplace.com`. How many semantic-based style tags does it use? List them. How many syntactic-based style tags? List them.

2. Load the Web page of any Appalachian Trail thru-hiker. How many semantic-based style tags does it use? List them. How many syntactic-based style tags does it use? List them.

3. Create HTML fragments in which you make effective use of the following tags:
    (a) Emphasis
    (b) Strong
    (c) Citation
    (d) Address
    (e) Keyboard
    (f) Variable
    (g) Code

4. Locate a Web page that is cluttered with too many style tags. Provide its URL and critique it.

5.   What is the result of nesting small tags? Experiment and find out if you can make text tiny by nesting several of these. At what point does the text stop getting smaller? Repeat the same experiment for the big tag. Are the results the same?

6.   Show how the superscript tag can be used effectively to express numbers in scientific notation.

7.   Format your favorite poem relating to nature using the HTML tags discussed in this section.

8.   Supply the URL of a Web page that makes poor use of underlining in the sense that its hyperlinks are hard to distinguish from simple underlined text.

9.   Is it possible to underline an item twice? That is, can you produce something like <u>twice underlined</u>?

10. Is it possible to make an entire screen blink?

11. Can you find any more semantic- or syntactic-based style tags that are supported by your browser? If so, list them and produce a sample use of each.

12. Can you find any other deprecated tags?

7.3   Headers and Footers

7.3.1   Headers

You have probably noticed that many Web pages contain similar types of information at the top. The beginning part of a rendered Web page is called the *header*. The header is the information contained at the top of a rendered Web page, not at the top of an HTML source file. The header is not an HTML tag. Do not confuse the header with the contents of the head tag. The header is not formatted within the head tag, but in the body of a document. Most headers contain a (nonempty) subset of the following information:

Useful Item

- The title of the page

- Last-update information

- Signature of the page developer

- An icon or logo associated with the page

- A counter of the number of visitors

- An advertisement

The purpose of the header is to convey the most important information about the page, introduce the page, and set the tone for the page. Figure 7.8 shows a screen shot of a sample header. This header consists of a title, an icon, last-update information, and the signature of the page developer, ROXY. In our example, the header information is offset by horizontal lines.

Useful Item

In any collection of related Web pages, it is a good idea to use consistent headers. This helps the reader to determine the boundaries of the presentation. If a hyperlink leads to a different-looking header, readers realize they may have left the original presentation. Consistent headers help tie the presentation together.

7.3.2   Horizontal Rule Tag

Horizontal lines are produced using the horizontal rule tag, <HR>; there is no accompanying ending tag. To draw a horizontal line all the way across

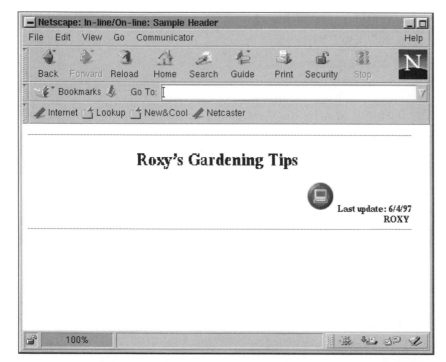

FIGURE 7.8
A sample header.

the browser's window, merely include the following HTML code:

```
<HR>
```

The horizontal rule tag has several attributes that are supported by most browsers. They are WIDTH, SIZE, NOSHADE, and ALIGN. The WIDTH attribute is used to specify how wide the horizontal line should be. The default draws a line that crosses the entire width of the browser window, as shown in Figure 7.8. The WIDTH attribute's value can be specified either as a percentage of the browser window's width, or as a fixed number of pixels.[1] Depending on how you are using the horizontal rule tag, one method may be preferable to the other. To draw a horizontal line across 45 percent of the browser's window, use the following HTML code:

```
<HR WIDTH = "45%">
```

To produce a line 150 pixels wide, use:

```
<HR WIDTH = "150">
```

Useful Item

By default, horizontal lines drawn by the horizontal rule tag are about 3 pixels high. The SIZE attribute allows you to define a taller (thicker) line. For example, to draw a horizontal line across 75 percent of the screen that is 10 pixels high, use the following HTML code:

```
<HR WIDTH = "75%" SIZE = "10">
```

The order in which the WIDTH and SIZE attributes appear is not important.

By default, the horizontal rule tag draws what looks like an engraved line. To produce a darker, flatter-looking horizontal line, use the NOSHADE attribute, which functions like a switch and has no value.

When a horizontal line is less than 100 percent of the width of the screen, it needs to be aligned. The ALIGN tag, which accomplishes this function, may have any of the following values: left, right, and center. It is possible to create a tapered-looking graphic by combining all of the attributes of the horizontal rule tag. Figure 7.9 provides an example.

The HTML code used to produce the horizontal lines in Figure 7.9 is as follows:

```
<HR ALIGN = "center" NOSHADE SIZE = "4" WIDTH = "40%">
<HR ALIGN = "center" NOSHADE SIZE = "4" WIDTH = "30%">
```

---

1   Recall that a pixel stands for "picture element" and is a very small unit of measure.

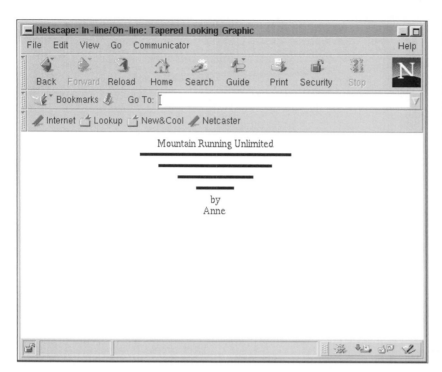

FIGURE 7.9
Illustration of a tapered-looking graphic, created by using all the attributes of the horizontal rule tag.

```
<HR ALIGN = "center" NOSHADE SIZE = "4" WIDTH = "20%">
<HR ALIGN = "center" NOSHADE SIZE = "4" WIDTH = "10%">
```

Useful Item

If you decide to include a tapered set of horizontal lines, be careful. The effect you end up with will depend largely on the width of the browser's window.

7.3.3   Footers

The bottoms of many Web pages contain similar types of information. The ending part of a Web page is called the *footer*. A footer is not an HTML element but rather Web page content appearing at the bottom of a page. Most footers contain a (nonempty) subset of the following information:

Useful Item

- Navigational aids

- Last-update information

- The Webmaster's name

- A `mailto` hyperlink to the Webmaster

- A hyperlink leading to a *frequently asked questions* (*FAQ*) page

- A copyright notice

- A disclaimer

- A README file that usually contains acknowledgements

- A publication date

- Advertisements

The purpose of the footer is to convey additional important information about a page, such as navigational aids, copyright notice, Webmaster, and Webmaster's email address. Figure 7.10 shows a screen shot of a sample footer, which consists of a set of navigational aids, telephone numbers to obtain more information, a couple of hyperlinks for questions, a copyright notice, and a hyperlink providing information about the server used for the presentation. Notice also that the footer is offset by a horizontal line.

Useful Item

Most HTML servers allow the use of keywords to insert a boilerplate in the footer; that is, to insert the date and a hyperlink automatically. However, the conventions for this are server-specific and could affect file portability if someone develops and tests them on one server and then moves them to a different server.

FIGURE 7.10
A sample footer.

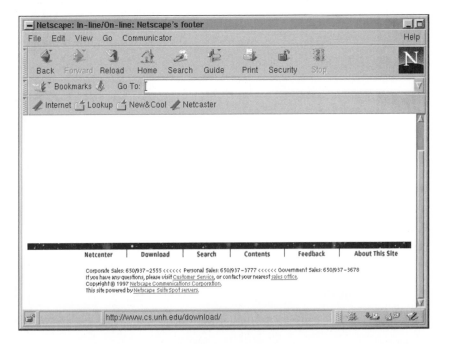

A standard practice for navigation information in a footer is the use of vertical bars or some other symbol to separate the hyperlinks. It is also customary to use a smaller font size. Figure 7.11 shows an example that was rendered from the following HTML code:

```
<H5 ALIGN = "center">
<HR>
<A HREF = "alaska.html">Last Frontier</A> |
<A HREF = "yosemite.html">Yosemite</A> |
<A HREF = "bigsky.html">Glacier Park</A>
</H5>
```

Notice the use of the <H5> heading tag, which produces a small font size. We have also used the ALIGN attribute of the <H5> tag to center the menu items. The center tag would have done equally well. The division tag, <DIV>, with a value of center for its ALIGN attribute, will also center the hyperlinks. You could also use the ALIGN attribute of the paragraph tag with a value of center. This type of navigation is very effective and easy to use.

Useful Item

The remarks pertaining to the desirability of consistent headers also apply to footers. The reader then knows what to expect at the bottom of each page. This makes them feel more comfortable with the presentation.

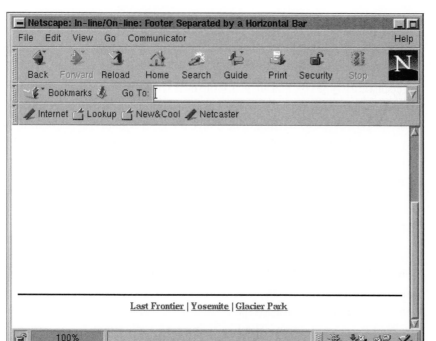

FIGURE 7.11
Hyperlinks separated by vertical bars in a footer.

We should point out that there is a certain amount of overhead that goes into maintaining a consistent set of footers and/or headers in a large collection of pages. One key to maintaining such a set is to exclude any dynamic information in the headers and footers, and to settle on a fixed format early in the design of your presentation. Another strategy for maintaining consistent footers and/or headers would be to use Cascading Style Sheets. These are discussed in Section 9.8.

EXERCISES 7.3

Headers and Footers

13. Design a sample header suitable for your Web pages.

14. Design a tapered-looking set of five horizontal lines to go under the phrase "Appalachian Trail—Georgia to Maine."

15. Can you "black out" an entire screen by drawing a wide enough horizontal line and setting the appropriate attributes?

16. Design a sample footer suitable for your Web pages.

7.4   Lists

Three primary types of lists are available in HTML: *ordered lists*, *unordered lists*, and *definition lists*. Each list environment is well-suited for one or more specific types of writing. The entire list is surrounded by a beginning and an ending list tag, which varies depending on the type of list. In addition, list item tags are used to identify each entry in the list. The list item tag also depends on the type of list you are using.

7.4.1   Ordered Lists

In an *ordered list*, the elements are prefixed by a symbol that denotes their relative order within the list. The most commonly used symbols for marking the elements of an ordered list are Arabic numbers, letters, and Roman numerals. An ordered list is used for a series of sequential steps or specifically ordered items. The beginning and ending tags for an ordered list are <OL> and </OL>, respectively. The beginning tag for each list item

Useful Item

is <LI>. No ending tag is necessary for an item, since the browser can determine the end of a list item by encountering either another list item tag, <LI>, or an ending tag for the list, </OL>. By default, the items in an ordered list are numbered using Arabic numbers. The following HTML code illustrates the use of an ordered list to describe the process of walking a dog.

```
<H3>How to Walk a Dog</H3>
<OL>
    <LI> Call the dog.

    <LI> Call the dog with a dog bone in hand.
    <LI> Feed the dog and attach the leash to the dog's
         collar.
    <LI> Walk, stop, pull, walk, stop, pull.
    <LI> Return home.
    <LI> Remove the leash from the dog's collar.
    <LI> Give the dog a biscuit and pat it on the head.
</OL>
```

Note that the order of the elements in this list is important. Thus, the ordered list environment is necessary. Figure 7.12 shows how this code is rendered by a browser.

What if you want to use characters or Roman numerals instead of Arabic numbers to label the items? This can be done by using the TYPE

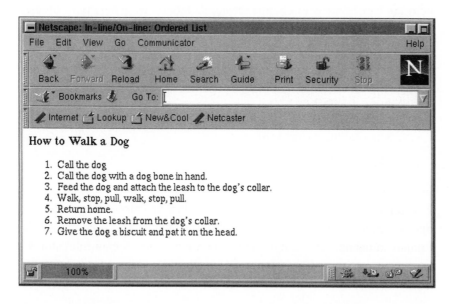

FIGURE 7.12
An example of an ordered list that describes the process of walking a dog.

attribute of the ordered list tag. TYPE can take the values a, A, i, and I. The lowercase a results in labels a, b, c, and so on. Similarly, the uppercase A results in labels A, B, C, and so forth. The i or I TYPE attribute values generate either lowercase or uppercase Roman numerals, respectively. For example, i results in a numbering of i, ii, iii, iv, v, and so on.

It is also possible to begin numbering from a value other than 1. The starting value can be defined with the START attribute of the list item tag. For example, to generate Arabic numbers starting from a value of 4 instead of 1, you would use the following code:

```
<OL START = "4">
    <LI> Step four.
        ...
</OL>
```

Many books use this type of numbering in the exercises. If you want to use lowercase characters starting from e, you would use the following code:

```
<OL TYPE = "a" START = "5">
    <LI> Step e.
        ...
</OL>
```

The starting values for Roman numerals can be similarly adjusted.

The list item tag also has an attribute. The VALUE attribute of the list item tag can be used to change an item's label. To generate an ordered list whose items are numbered 1, 2, 5, and 6, the following code would be used:

```
<OL>
    <LI> Step 1.
    <LI> Step 2.
    <LI VALUE = "5"> Step 5.
    <LI> Step 6.
</OL>
```

Note that once you change an item's value, the succeeding items continue on from that new value. The VALUE attribute may be used in a similar fashion to change the "numbering" when letters or Roman numerals are used.

7.4.2   Unordered Lists

The ordered list is used when the order in which the items appear is significant. If the order is not important, you can use the *unordered list*. Rather than being numbered, the items are usually marked with *bullets*.

The beginning and ending tags for an unordered list are <UL> and </UL>, respectively. Each item in an unordered list is identified by a list item tag, as it was for an ordered list. The following HTML code describes some "House Sitting Chores" using an unordered list:

```
<H3>House Sitting Chores</H3>
<UL>
     <LI> Pick up mail.
     <LI> Walk the dog.
     <LI> Water geraniums.
     <LI> Feed the cat.
</UL>
```

Figure 7.13 shows how a browser renders this code. Notice that the items are not interdependent; that is, they can appear in any order.

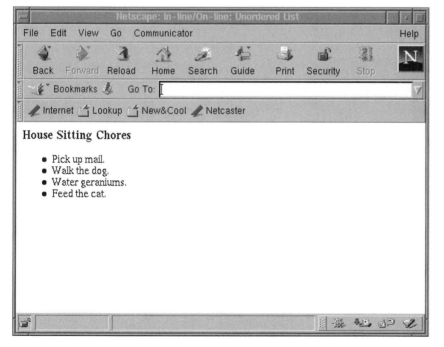

FIGURE 7.13
An example of an unordered list that describes some house sitting chores.

Each item is prefaced by a bullet, and the default bullet is a shaded disk. It is also possible to use other bullets in HTML. You can use the TYPE attribute of the unordered list tag to generate an open circle or an open square. For example, the following HTML code would use open circles as bullets:

```
<H3>House Sitting Chores</H3>
<UL TYPE = "circle">
    <LI> Pick up mail.

    <LI> Walk the dog.
    <LI> Water geraniums.
    <LI> Feed the cat.
</UL>
```

Useful Item

You can also include "custom" bullets, which is best done using *definition lists*, as discussed in Section 7.4.3.

7.4.3   Definition Lists

Definition lists are unordered lists in which each item has two parts: a *term*, and its corresponding definition. The beginning and ending tags for the definition list are <DL> and </DL>, respectively.

Instead of using a list item tag for each item, the term portion requires a definition term tag, <DT>. The definition portion uses a data definition tag, <DD>. The corresponding ending tags for the definition term and data definition tags are </DT> and </DD>, respectively. However, they are rarely used.

The following HTML code provides an example of a definition list used to describe running races:

```
<H3>Common Foot Race Distances</H3>
<DL>
    <DT> <STRONG>5K</STRONG>
    <DD>A sprint.

    <DT> <STRONG>10K</STRONG>
    <DD>A quick, hard run.

    <DT> <STRONG>Marathon</STRONG>
    <DD>A 26.2 mile run (hurts over the last 6 miles).

    <DT> <STRONG>50K</STRONG>
    <DD>A short Ultra of 31 miles.
```

```
<DT> <STRONG>Century</STRONG>
<DD>A 100 mile run.
</DL>
```

Figure 7.14 shows how the code is rendered. Notice that the browser placed each term on its own line, and the definition is on the succeeding line and is slightly indented. Also observe that we used the strong tags for the terms to be defined: 5K, 10K, Marathon, 50K, and Century. This makes them stand out better.

The definition list environment is often used for displaying a glossary, or for defining a group of terms. Another common use of the definition list tag is the presentation of a group of items with custom bullets. Suppose you want to produce a page, located in your `public_html` directory, that contains a list of your textbooks for the semester. You would like to include a custom bullet called `purplepin.gif`, which sits in your `GIF` directory, which in turn is located in your `public_html` directory. The following HTML code does what you want:

Useful Item

```
<H3>My Textbooks This Semester</H3>
<DL>
    <DT> <IMG SRC = "../GIF/purplepin.gif"
             HEIGHT = "21"
             WIDTH = "21"
             ALT = "*">
    <DD>Deutsch Heute

    <DT> <IMG SRC = "../GIF/purplepin.gif"
             HEIGHT = "21"
             WIDTH = "21"
             ALT = "*">
    <DD>In-line/On-line

    <DT> <IMG SRC = "../GIF/purplepin.gif"
             HEIGHT = "21"
             WIDTH = "21"
             ALT = "*">
    <DD>U. S. History

    <DT> <IMG SRC = "../GIF/purplepin.gif"
             HEIGHT = "21"
             WIDTH = "21"
             ALT = "*">
    <DD>The Complete Works of Shakespeare
</DL>
```

Figure 7.15 shows how this code is rendered.

FIGURE 7.14
An example of a
definition list
used to describe
common running
races.

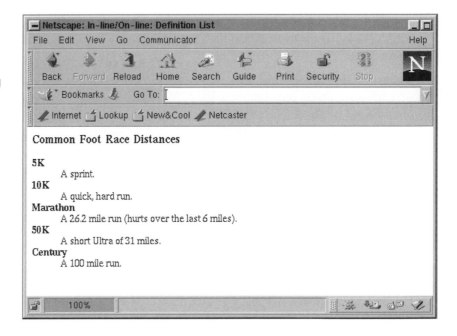

FIGURE 7.15
An example of a
definition list that
uses custom
bullets.

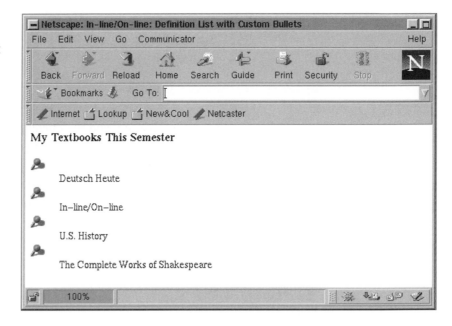

Some Web authors omit the data definition tag and simply place the
definition on the same line as the definition term tag.

7.4.4 Nested Lists

It is possible to *nest* the different types of lists within one another, or to nest multiple lists of the same type. In computer science, the word *nest* is used to indicate layers within layers. Think of an onion; when the outer layer is removed, a new inner layer is exposed. The inner layer is completely nested inside the outer layer. When nesting list environments (or any environments, for that matter), you should not let them overlap. An example of a poorly written nesting sequence is as follows:

Useful Item

```
<H3>How to Make a Tossed Salad</H3>
<OL>
     <LI> Open Martha Stewart book on the subject.
     <LI> Wash veggies.
     <LI> Dry veggies.
     <LI> Slice veggies.
     <UL>
          <LI> Cut tomatoes into wedges.
          <LI> Tear lettuce into small pieces.
          <LI> Thinly slice the radishes.
          <LI> Grate carrots.
          <LI> Slice cucumbers.
     </OL> <!-- This is incorrectly nested. -->
</UL>
```

The inner list environment must be closed before the outer list environment is closed. In our incorrectly coded example, the opening unordered list tag is mismatched with the closing ordered list tag, and the opening ordered list tag is misaligned with the closing unordered list tag. When nesting different types of lists, make sure you close them off properly.

Nested lists are useful when you would like to expand on one or more items. The following code illustrates nested ordered and unordered lists.

```
<H3>UNH Scores Its First Goal at A Hockey Game</H3>
<OL>
     <LI> Puck goes past opposing goalie.
     <LI> Goalie yells #$&*.
     <LI> Sticks are raised.
     <LI> Puck enters net.
     <LI> Red light comes on.
     <LI> Referee heads for net.
     <UL>
```

```
            <LI> Someone grabs for a
                <EM>long, ugly frozen fish</EM>.
            <OL TYPE = "a">
                <LI> Fish is thrown.
                <LI> Fish clears boards.
                <LI> Fish hits ice.
                <LI> Doors at side of rink open.
                <LI> Man with bucket appears.
                <LI> Fish is scooped up into bucket.
                <LI> Man and fish leave.
                <LI> Doors at side of rink close.
                <LI> Goalie watches.
            </OL>
            <LI> Fans go wild.
            <OL TYPE = "a">
                <LI> Students go berserk.
                <LI> "Sieve" (to make the opposing goalie
                    feel at home) is shouted.
                <LI> Fingers are pointed indicating number
                    of goals scored, here "1."
                <LI> Goalie slaps his pads with stick.
                <LI> Goalie pretends to drink water.
            </OL>
            <LI> Referees showboat.
            <OL TYPE = "a">
                <LI> Referees skate wildly around the ice.
                <LI> Referees fix their hair.
            </OL>
        </UL>
        <LI> Announcement of goal scorer's name.
        <LI> Fans remain standing.
        <LI> New face-off.
    </OL>
```

Figure 7.16 shows how this code is rendered.

At most levels, ordered lists are used because the steps actually happen in a certain sequence. We use the TYPE attribute of the ordered list tag to change the inner layers from Arabic numbering to letters. The first nested list is unordered. It indicates that the three items involving fish, fans, and referees all happen in the same time frame. Each of these is further divided into a sequence of steps. Notice how indentation is used to make it easy to line up the beginning and ending list tags.

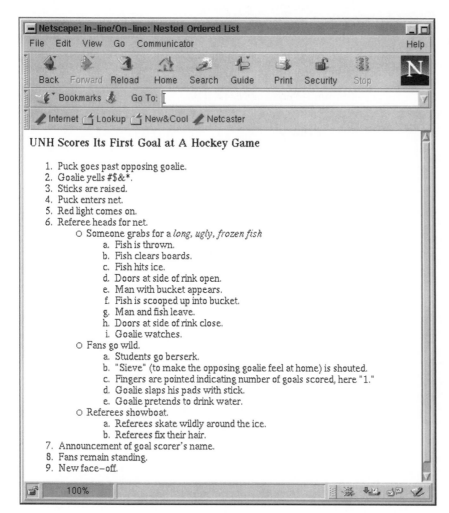

FIGURE 7.16
An example of nested ordered lists.

Not all nested lists are as elaborate as the example shown in Figure 7.16. In fact, it is usually a good idea not to nest lists more than one or two levels deep. Also, it is common practice to use a mix of Arabic numbers and letters. Another popular setup is uppercase letters for the outer level and lowercase letters for the nested items. Alternatively, you could use capital Roman numerals for the outer level and lowercase Roman numerals for the inner level. It is generally not a good idea to blend Arabic numbers, letters, and Roman numerals. The three combined can create an unappealing and hard-to-follow list.

If the items in a group of nested lists do not have any inherent order, there is no reason to assign one artificially. In this situation, you may want

Useful Item

to use unordered lists. The following HTML code is an example:

```
<H3>Critters</H3>
<UL>
    <LI> <STRONG>Mammals</STRONG>
    <UL>
        <LI> Blue whale.
        <LI> Cat.
        <LI> Water buffalo.
    </UL>
    <LI> <STRONG>Reptiles</STRONG>
    <UL>
        <LI> Alligator.
        <LI> Lizard.
        <LI> Snakes.
        <UL>
            <LI> Boa.
            <LI> Cobra.
            <LI> Python.
        </UL>
    </UL>
    <LI> <STRONG>Insects</STRONG>
    <UL>
        <LI> Dobb's Fly.
        <LI> Hornet.
        <LI> Mosquito.
    </UL>
</UL>
```

Figure 7.17 shows how a browser displays this code. Notice that, by default, a shaded disk is used at the outer layer, an open circle is used for the middle items, and an open square is used at the innermost layer. These symbols can be changed using the TYPE attribute of the unordered list tag.

Definition lists, as well as any combination of definition, ordered, and unordered lists, can all be nested. It is uncommon, though, to see all three mixed together, as this can result in a cluttered and "over-organized" look.

EXERCISES 7.4

Lists

17.   When would it be useful to begin an ordered list at a value other than 1? Give an example.

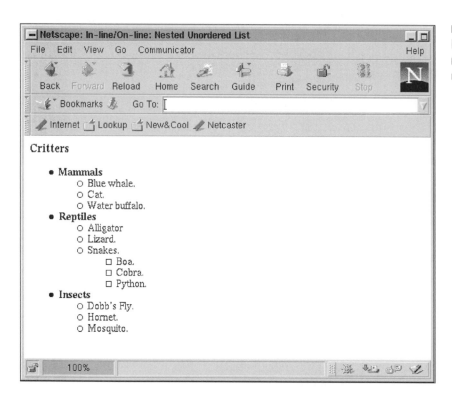

FIGURE 7.17
Example of
nested
unordered lists.

18.   Create an ordered list of the five lightest chemical elements.

19.   Code an ordered list that uses lowercase Roman numerals, starts at a value of 9, and contains four elements.

20.   Create an ordered list of the states along the Appalachian Trail going from south to north.

21.   Create an ordered list of the states along the Appalachian Trail in increasing length of trail miles.

22.   Create an unordered list containing hyperlinks to five "cool" Web pages.

23.   Using custom bullets, code a definition list that describes your favorite four dinner entrées, as well as the best local restaurants where they can be found.

24.   Find five interesting pieces of Internet jargon on the Web. Create a definition list with custom bullets, in which the terms and their definitions are given.

25.   Present an application of nested ordered lists and code it.

26.   What happens if you nest an unordered list more than three levels deep? Are some of the bullet types reused?

27. Present an application of nested unordered lists and code it.

28. Are there applications where it makes sense to use both ordered and unordered lists together? If so, describe and code one.

7.5   Tables

Tables in HTML pages allow you to organize information in a row and column format. For example, you might want to display your courses and their corresponding grades in a tabular form on your resume. Table 7.1 illustrates one possible layout of such information. The horizontal and vertical lines are called (table) *dividers* (see Figure 7.19). Using HTML tables, you could display this information in a similar fashion in your on-line résumé.

In addition to laying out information in a tabular format, HTML tables are used to present any type of information for which you want a lot of control over the positioning of the material. For example, HTML tables could be used to achieve a newspaper-like appearance. We usually do not think of a newspaper as being in a tabular format, but a newspaper format can most easily be produced on a Web page using tables with the dividers suppressed. Tables have many uses, some nonintuitive, for achieving specific layouts.

7.5.1   Table Usage

Useful Item

There are many ways to use tables to format information on the Web. When you see an interesting layout on a Web page, view the source code and see

TABLE 7.1

A Sample Tabular Format Consisting of a Student's Courses and Grades.

Fall Semester		Spring Semester	
Business	B−	Accounting	B−
German 1	C	German 2	C+
Math	A	In-line/On-line	A
Sociology	B+	Philosophy	A−
Tennis	A+		

how the effect was achieved. There is a good chance it was produced using tables. The following are some situations for which you might use tables:

- *Present tabular information*—If you have information or data that is naturally divided into rows and columns, it can probably be easily and effectively formatted using HTML tables.

- *Control layout*—If you want to control the layout of text, position a group of images, or present an extensive menu, you may decide to use tables to achieve the desired appearance.

- *Express relationships*—If you need to display relationships between a group of items, tables are usually a good mechanism to use. For example, in Table 7.2, we show whether a number of people can play the guitar or piano, and whether they have acting experience. Using the table, it is easy to locate someone, namely Jan, who plays both the guitar and the piano, and also has some acting experience. If a table is laid out properly, relationships between elements can be expressed clearly, and "new" relationships can be easily discovered.

(In Figures 7.24 and 7.25, we show how Tables 7.1 and 7.2 appear when formatted in HTML).

TABLE 7.2

A Table Illustrating the Relationships Between People, Musical Instruments, and Acting Experience.

Name	Play Guitar	Play Piano	Acting Experience
Alice	YES	NO	NO
Claude	NO	NO	YES
Heidi	NO	NO	NO
Jan	YES	YES	YES
Jean-Yves	NO	NO	NO
Mara	YES	YES	NO
Nadine	YES	NO	NO
Pearl	NO	YES	YES
Sun-Lee	NO	YES	YES
Woo	NO	NO	YES

7.5.2   HTML Table Tags

Rows and Columns

Tables are created using the table tag, <TABLE>, with the ending tag </TABLE>. The most important tag that goes inside the table tag is the table row tag, <TR>. Its corresponding ending tag, </TR>, is often omitted. Browsers can determine where the next row starts by encountering another beginning table row tag. When the browser sees the </TABLE> tag, the table is ended.

The items in a row are specified using the table data tag, <TD>. Its corresponding ending tag, </TD>, may be omitted, for the same reason that </TR> can. We sometimes refer to the location where the elements in table data tags appear as *table cells* (see Figure 7.22). Nearly any HTML element can appear in a table data tag.

There is no table column or <TC> tag. Instead, the number of columns is determined by the row containing the most items, expressed by table data and table header tags (discussed later in this chapter). If any row has fewer than the maximum number of items, its elements will be positioned starting from the leftmost column and continuing to the right, as necessary.

The final version of Table 7.1 requires some experience to produce in HTML. Therefore, we will generate this table incrementally by adding features to a simple starting version. Our goal is not to produce an exact copy of Table 7.1, but rather incrementally develop a table that contains the same information and looks good on-line.

Figure 7.18 shows a screen shot of a five-row, four-column version of Table 7.1. (We did not count the boldface headings as a row.)

This table was produced by the following HTML code:

```
<CENTER>
<TABLE>
    <TR>
        <TD> Business
        <TD> B-
        <TD> Accounting
        <TD> B-
    <TR>
        <TD> German 1
        <TD> C
        <TD> German 2
        <TD> C+
```

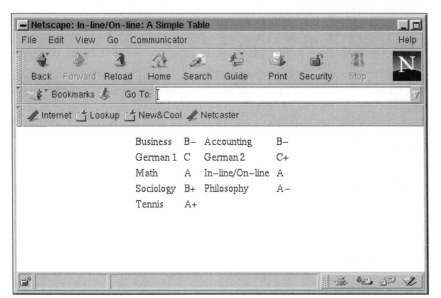

FIGURE 7.18
A simple version
of Table 7.1.

```
        <TR>
            <TD> Math
            <TD> A
            <TD> In-line/On-line
            <TD> A
        <TR>
            <TD> Sociology
            <TD> B+
            <TD> Philosophy
            <TD> A-
        <TR>
            <TD> Tennis
            <TD> A+
    </TABLE>
    </CENTER>
```

Notice that we used the center tag to center the table on the page. You will probably want to center most tables, especially if you decide not to let text flow next to them. Most browsers do not support a value of center for the ALIGN attribute of the table tag. You should therefore use either <CENTER>, <P> with a value of center for the ALIGN attribute, or <DIV> with a value of center for the ALIGN attribute.

The ALIGN attribute of the table tag with a value of left will position the table at the left edge of the page; this is the default positioning. If text appears adjacent to the table declaration, it will flow along the right edge of the table. With a value of right for the ALIGN attribute, the table will be positioned flush right and text will flow along the left side of the table.

In many situations, the text crowds the table, since the browser leaves very little space between the table and the text. It is therefore often desirable to add some space between the text and the table. To add horizontal space, you can use the HSPACE attribute of the table tag, with a pixel value indicating how much space to add. The VSPACE attribute works similarly, controlling the amount of vertical space between the table top and bottom and the adjacent text.

In contrast to Tables 7.1 and 7.2, the table shown in Figure 7.18 does not have a border. You can easily add a border using the BORDER attribute of the table tag. When used without an argument, the BORDER attribute adds a 2-pixel-wide perimeter and 2-pixel-wide row and column dividers. For example, the following code creates a table partitioned by 2-pixel-wide lines:

```
<TABLE BORDER>
```

Including a border makes it easier to see the row and column divisions. The table cells appear as enclosed rectangles. The BORDER attribute can have a pixel value as an argument. The following code adds a border 3 pixels wide around the table:

```
<TABLE BORDER = "3">
```

This is added to the 2-pixel-wide dividers between each consecutive pair of rows and each adjacent pair of columns. The result is shown in Figure 7.19.

Notice how the second half of the fifth row is blank. If you would like to include the partitions here, you can add two *placeholder* table data items. This is usually done as follows:

```
<TR>
    <TD> Tennis
    <TD> A+
    <TD>  
    <TD>  
```

The expression   is the *character entity* for a nonbreaking space.

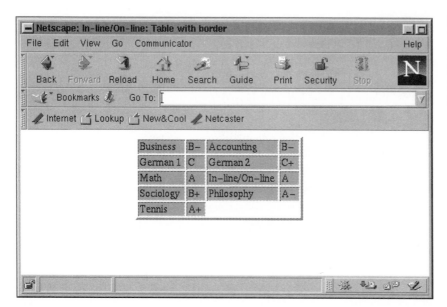

FIGURE 7.19
The table from
Figure 7.18,
shown with a
3-pixel-wide
border.

Element Spacing

The information in the table shown in Figure 7.19 looks crowded. The
CELLSPACING and CELLPADDING attributes of the table tag allow you to
control the width of the dividers between rows and columns and the amount
of space between the information in a cell and the borders of the cell. The
following code has the effect of "spreading out" the information in the
table, because the table dividers are set to be 6 pixels wide:

```
<TABLE BORDER = "3" CELLSPACING = "6">
```

The table's perimeter is also made 6 pixels thick. Figure 7.20 shows the
effects of these changes. The information is more readable, but it is still
not laid out well.

What the table in Figure 7.20 really needs is additional space between
each element in the table and the dividers surrounding it. For example,
the item "Business" is too close to the table dividers. The CELLPADDING
attribute expands the space or "padding" around items in each cell of the
table. The effect of the following code on the table is shown in Figure 7.21:

```
<TABLE BORDER = "3" CELLPADDING = "12">
```

The widest item in a column determines the width of that column. A
CELLPADDING attribute with a value of 12 has the effect of adding 12 pixels

FIGURE 7.20
The table from
Figure 7.18,
shown with a
3-pixel-wide
border and a
CELLSPACING
attribute value
of 6.

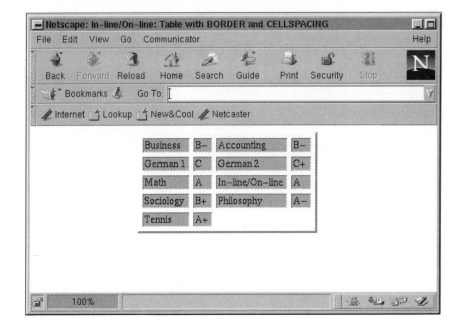

all around the widest element in a column. For example, the course entitled "In-line/On-line" is the widest item in column 3. Twelve pixels of space are added around "In-line/On-line." Figure 7.22 illustrates the effect. The result is that the column appears as though more than 12 pixels have been added around the shorter items.

Figure 7.22 also shows what parts of a table are affected by the CELLSPACING and CELLPADDING attributes. To recap, CELLSPACING affects the table dividers, and CELLPADDING affects the size of the table cells.

The items in the table shown in Figure 7.21 now appear spaced out a bit too far. By combining CELLSPACING and CELLPADDING with the values shown in the following, we obtain a table that is more visually appealing. The declaration

Hot Topic

```
<TABLE BORDER = "3"
       CELLSPACING = "6"
       CELLPADDING = "12">
```

can be used to combine the attributes. The order in which these attributes appear is not significant. However, it is a good idea to use a consistent style. The resulting table is shown in Figure 7.23.

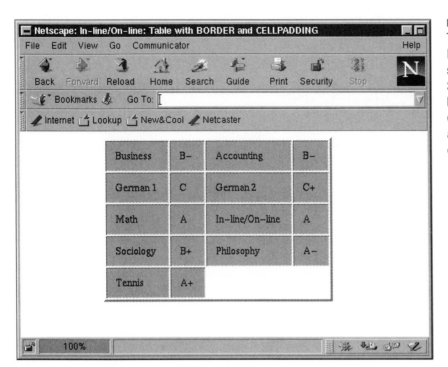

FIGURE 7.21
The table from Figure 7.18, shown with a 3-pixel-wide border and a CELLPADDING attribute value of 12.

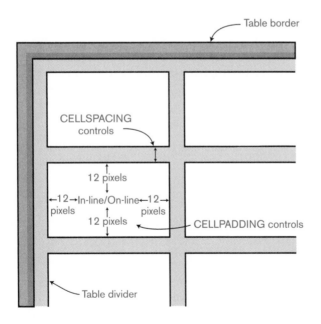

FIGURE 7.22
The effect of a CELLPADDING attribute of 12 on the widest cell of a column.

Table Headers

The columns in Table 7.1 have the headers, **Fall Semester** and **Spring Semester**. Notice that the headers are boldface and centered. It is often

FIGURE 7.23
The table from
Figure 7.18,
shown with a
3-pixel-wide
border, a
CELLSPACING
attribute value of
6, and a
CELLPADDING
attribute value
of 12.

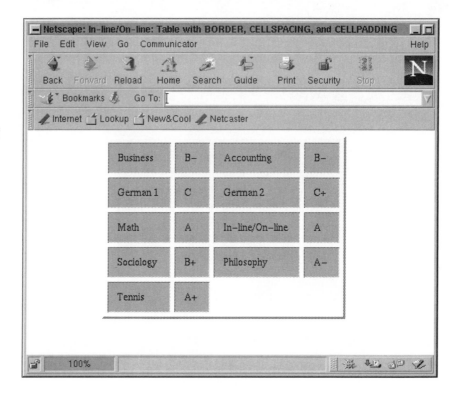

desirable for tables to include headers and to format them this way. The table header tag, <TH>, is useful for this. The following code shows how to add headers to the table we have been constructing:

```
<TABLE BORDER = "3"
       CELLSPACING = "6"
       CELLPADDING = "12">
    <TR>
        <TH COLSPAN = "2"> Fall Semester
        <TH COLSPAN = "2"> Spring Semester
        ...
</TABLE>
```

An inspection of Table 7.1 reveals that the headings each span two columns. To achieve the same effect in HTML, we use the COLSPAN attribute of the table header tag. The value of this attribute is a number indicating how many columns the header is to span. The result of this code, which is our final version of Table 7.1, is rendered in Figure 7.24.

There is also a ROWSPAN attribute to the table header tag, and it behaves as you would expect. In fact, COLSPAN and ROWSPAN can be used in a

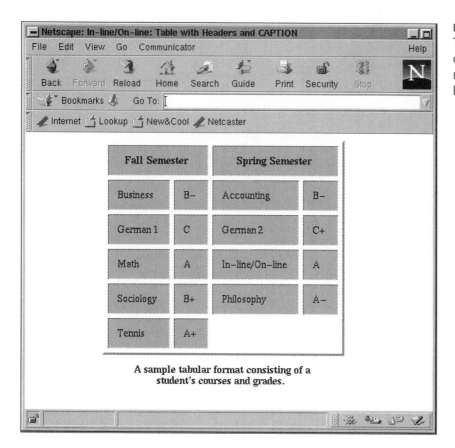

A sample tabular format consisting of a
student's courses and grades.

FIGURE 7.24
The final version
of Table 7.1
rendered in
HTML.

manner similar to attributes of the table data tag. For example,

```
<TD ROWSPAN = "2">
```

specifies that a table item spans two rows. In general, the table data and
table header tags possess the same attributes.

Item Positioning

In Table 7.2, notice that in columns 2 through 4, the information is centered,
but in column 1, the information is flush left. By default, information
included in a table data tag is set flush left, whereas information included
in a table header tag is centered. Both of these tags possess the ALIGN
attribute, which is useful for positioning material in other ways. The values
for ALIGN are left, center, and right. The table row tag also supports
the ALIGN attribute and the same set of values. It can be used to position
all items in a row at one time.

The code that follows shows one way that the first three rows of Table 7.2 could be produced in HTML. There are many other ways of producing them. For illustration purposes, we have coded each row differently, although we would normally never code using such an inconsistent approach.

```
<!-- do not code using an inconsistent style -->
<TABLE BORDER>
    <TR ALIGN = "center">
        <TD> Name
        <TD> Play Guitar
        <TD> Play Piano
        <TD> Acting Experience
    <TR ALIGN = "left">
        <TD> Alice
        <TD ALIGN = "center"> YES
        <TD ALIGN = "center"> NO
        <TD ALIGN = "center"> NO
    <TR ALIGN = "center">
        <TD ALIGN = "left"> Claude
        <TD> NO
        <TD> NO
        <TD> YES

    . . .
</TABLE>
```

To produce headings that are not in boldface, we used the table row tag instead of the table header tag. It is important to note that the ALIGN attributes of the table data and table header tags override the ALIGN attribute of the table row tag.

In the first row, each item is centered, so we used the center value for the ALIGN attribute of the table row tag. This centered all four table data elements in row 1. In the second row, we used left as the value for the ALIGN attribute of the table row tag. However, because the last three columns have centered items, we had to use the ALIGN attribute of the table data tag, with a value of center, to center them. For the third row, we used an ALIGN attribute value of center for the table row tag and therefore only needed to use a single ALIGN attribute to the table data tag. We did this so we could flush left the item in the first column. Rows 1 and 3 are coded cleanly, whereas row 2 is not. Figure 7.25 shows how Table 7.2 appears when rendered.

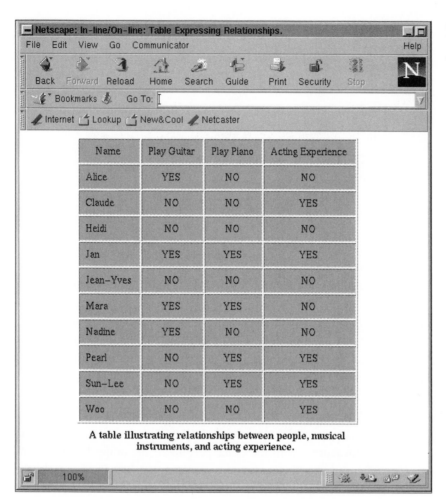

FIGURE 7.25
The final version
of Table 7.2
rendered in
HTML.

Table Captions

It is often important to annotate a table by adding a caption. For example,
all tables shown in this book have captions. You can also create captions
for HTML tables. Captions are produced using the beginning and ending
caption tags, `<CAPTION>` and `</CAPTION>`. The default setting positions
the caption at the top of the table. However, the `ALIGN` attribute of the
caption tag can be used to position the caption at the bottom of the table,
by using a value of `bottom`. Specifying a value of `top` for the `ALIGN`
attribute will result in the default setting.

The caption tag is best placed either immediately after the table tag or
immediately inside the ending table tag. Whichever approach you adopt,
use it consistently. The following code places the caption directly under-
neath the table:

Useful Item

```
<TABLE BORDER = "3"
       CELLSPACING = "6"
       CELLPADDING = "12">

<CAPTION ALIGN = "bottom">
    <STRONG>
        A sample tabular format consisting of
        a student's courses and grades.
    </STRONG>
</CAPTION>

    . . .

</TABLE>
```

Notice that we have formatted the caption using the strong tag in order to make the caption stand out.

Hot Topic

We should mention that most browsers center captions automatically. With a long caption and a narrow table, this usually creates several lines of ragged-left, ragged-right, centered text. If you have a fixed-width table, you may try using the paragraph tag and its ALIGN attribute to reposition the text so that it looks better (i.e., justified on one side). We recommend keeping captions short in on-line tables.

Table Width

The table tag has a WIDTH attribute that allows you to control the width of the table measured from the outer perimeter, including borders. The attribute takes either a pixel value or a percentage value. For example, the following code instructs the browser to produce a table 600 pixels wide:

```
<TABLE WIDTH = "600">
```

If the table is actually more than 600 pixels wide, the browser ignores the setting. If the browser's screen is less than 600 pixels wide, the reader will need to scroll to see the entire table.

The following code instructs the browser to produce a table that takes up 60 percent of the browser's window:

```
<TABLE WIDTH = "60%">
```

If the table is actually larger than 60 percent of the screen, the WIDTH specification has no effect. Using a percentage setting means that the table size will scale according to the browser's window size. A value of 100% means that the table will scale to occupy the entire width of the browser window, unless it is already larger than this.

Many Web designers specify a pixel value for the WIDTH attribute so that they can obtain more control over their table layouts. If a user has a narrow browser window, this can force the reader to have to scroll to see the entire table. However, if a table is rendered too narrow, the material intended to fit in a single row of a table cell may end up taking more than one "row." This can lead to an undesirable overall appearance. When you see a table on a Web page, experiment with different-sized browser windows and observe the effect on the table. The goal is to make the table look good regardless of the screen size.

Table Column Widths

Both the table data and table header tags have a WIDTH attribute. Using this attribute, you can create equal-sized or proportionately sized column widths.

As with the table tag's WIDTH attribute, the WIDTH attribute of the table data and table header tags can take either a pixel value or a percentage value. The WIDTH attribute is used most effectively when the items in the column are not really wide and you would like to scale up the widths of the columns to achieve a more uniform appearance. For example, the following code produces a table in which the first column width is 20 percent of the screen, the second column width is 40 percent of the screen, and the third column width is 20 percent of the screen:

```
<TR>
    <TD WIDTH = "20%"> Butter
    <TD WIDTH = "40%"> English Muffin
    <TD WIDTH = "20%"> Jelly
```

This assumes that:

1. None of the items in the corresponding columns is wider than these percentages.

2. These are the only WIDTH attributes specified for the table data or table header tags.

3. No other row contains more than three items.

Notice in the specification that the value 40 was chosen because

$$40 = 2 \times 20$$

which helps create a more uniform appearance than would a value of, say, 47 for the width of the middle column.

It is good programming practice to include the WIDTH attributes in the table header tags or in the first table data tags, rather than to bury these settings somewhere else in the table. It is also a good idea to specify these values only once for each column. If you do specify more than one setting, or if the items in a column are actually wider than the setting specified, the widest setting or actual size is used, whichever is larger.

Useful Item

If you need to control the exact width of a column, you should use a pixel value, not a percentage. You may want to do this when you are including an image in the table cell or when you want more control of the text layout.

Vertical Alignment

On occasion, you may generate a table with a "tall" row(s). The VALIGN attribute of the table row, table data, and table header tags allows you to position the text vertically within the row. The default positioning centers the material vertically in a row. The most common values for VALIGN are top, center, and bottom. They have the expected positioning effect. The scope of the VALIGN attribute is just the row in which it occurs.

As usual, if a VALIGN attribute is specified for a table row tag <TR> and also for a table data tag <TD> in the same row, the VALIGN attribute of the table data tag will override that of the table row tag.

It is generally a good idea to position all text in a given row at the same level, rather than in a stepwise pattern; even text across a table is easier to read and in most cases is more visually appealing.

Colors

Many browsers support the use of colors in tables. The BGCOLOR attribute of the table, table data, table header, and table row tags can be used to add color to any or all parts of your table. Again, however, settings at the table level can be overridden by those at the table row level, which in turn can be overridden by those at either the table data or table header levels. The allowable values for the BGCOLOR attribute are the same as those for the BGCOLOR attribute of the body tag. For example, the following code produces a white table:

```
<TABLE BGCOLOR = "#FFFFFF">
```

Useful Item

For most tables, it is a good idea to restrict yourself to one or two colors, and those colors should go well with each other and with your page's background pattern or color. In rare situations, more than two colors can be used effectively. For example, in a borderless table, if each entry is colored differently, a patterned effect can be created in which each item stands out.

However, the colors must be carefully chosen. This style can be especially effective when each table data item is a hyperlink.

The on-line presentation accompanying this book compares many effective and ineffective uses of color in tables, as well as a number of more complex table formats.

Go On-Line

HTML Table Evolution

You should be aware that not all browsers support all table features described in this chapter. In addition, some browsers support new features not mentioned here. To be completely current with what is available for tables, look on the Web. The standards change quickly. The on-line Web presentation accompanying this book provides information on where to find the most recent data.

7.5.3   Frequently Asked Questions

• *How can I produce a newspaper-style layout using tables?*

The key idea is to use a single row with very long columns. So, for a three-column newspaper, you would use three table data tags in the first row. The text for the first column follows the first table data tag; the text for the second column follows the second table data tag; and the text for the third column follows the third table data tag. If you want to achieve balanced column lengths, you will need to adjust the amount of text following each table data tag.

Hot Topic

The code described will produce three separate columns. However, you will probably want to include the VALIGN attribute of the table row tag, with a value of top, so that all text starts at the top of each column. In addition, you may want to add a couple of equal-sized placeholder columns for spacers between the text. This can be done using the following code:

```
<TD WIDTH = "5%">
```

Finally, you will want to set the BGCOLOR attribute of the table tag to #FFFFFF (white) and the text color to #000000 (black).

• *One of the items in my column is making the whole column too wide. What can I do to solve this problem?*

You can insert a line break tag somewhere in the long item, which will force the rest of the text in that item to move down to the next line. The text will stay in the same cell; it will not go into the next cell down. In some situations, other options might be to split the item over two columns, or use a shorter phrase.

- *Can I nest tables?*

Yes, and nesting tables is straightforward. In the most common form of nesting, the table tag is included inside a table data item. So, if you want, each table cell can itself be a table. The following HTML code illustrates how to nest tables. The rendered code is shown in Figure 7.26.

```
<HTML>

<HEAD>
<TITLE>In-line/On-line:  Nested Tables</TITLE>
<META NAME = "keywords"
      CONTENT = "Internet, Web, World Wide Web,
                 tutorial, guide, teaching,
                 book, textbook, learning,
                 Java, Javascript, HTML">
<HEAD>

<BODY BGCOLOR = "#FFFFFF">

<CENTER>
<TABLE BORDER = "0"
       CELLPADDING = "20"
       CELLSPACING = "0"
       WIDTH = "75%">
```

FIGURE 7.26
Nested tables.

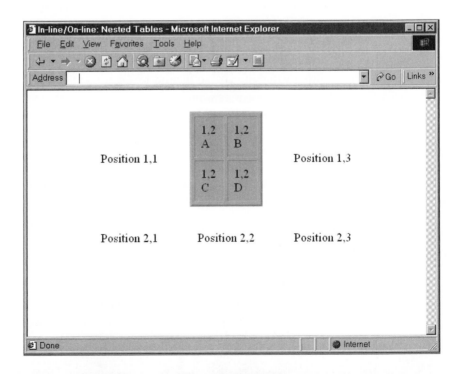

```
<TR ALIGN = "center">
<TD WIDTH = "25%">
Position 1,1

<TD WIDTH = "25%">
   <TABLE BORDER = "3"
          BGCOLOR = "#FFFF11"
          CELLPADDING = "10"
          CELLSPACING = "5">
   <TR>
   <TD> 1, 2 A
   <TD> 1, 2 B

   <TR>
   <TD> 1, 2 C
   <TD> 1, 2 D
   </TABLE>
<TD WIDTH = "25%">
Position 1, 3

<TR ALIGN = "center">
<TD WIDTH = "25%">
Position 2, 1

<TD WIDTH = "25%">
Position 2, 2

<TD WIDTH = "25%">
Position 2, 3

</TABLE>
</CENTER>

<BODY>

</HTML>
```

- *Can I include images and hyperlinks in tables?*

    Yes, you can include them in any table cell, using the tags you would normally use for including these features in an HTML document. The following HTML code illustrates how to include images and hyperlinks in a table. The rendered code is shown in Figure 7.27.

```
<HTML>

<HEAD>

<TITLE>In-line/On-line:    Table Including a
      Hyperlink and an Image</TITLE>
```

FIGURE 7.27
Table including a
hyperlink and an
image.

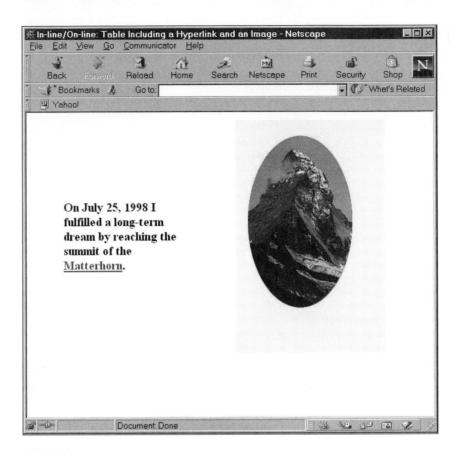

```
<META NAME = "keywords"
      CONTENT = "Internet, Web, World Wide Web,
                 tutorial, guide, teaching,
                 book, textbook, learning,
                 Java, Javascript, HTML">
</HEAD>
<BODY BGCOLOR = "#FFFFFF">
<CENTER>
<TABLE WIDTH = "85%">
<TR>
<TD WIDTH = "40%">
<STRONG>
On July 25, 1998 I fulfilled a long-term dream
by reaching the summit of the
<A HREF =
    "http://www.peakware.com/encyclopedia/peaks/←
        matterhorn.htm">
```

```
Matterhorn</A>
</STRONG>

<TD>
<IMG SRC = "matterhorn.jpg"
     HEIGHT = "368"
     WIDTH = "244"
     ALIGN = "right"
     ALT = "The Matterhorn, Switzerland">

</TABLE>
</CENTER>

</BODY>
</HTML>
```

•   *Are HTML editors useful for producing tables?*

Yes, they can be helpful, particularly if you are producing a very simple and regular table. By this we mean the table has the form of a grid. However, for any irregular or complicated layouts, you will need to hand-tune the basic code an editor produces. You should therefore be familiar with all the tags related to tables, as well as their corresponding attributes and values. An HTML editor is most useful for quickly providing you with the "shell" of a simple table.

•   *What is a good way to control the layout of a form?*

Tables are the best way to exercise control over the exact layout of a form. For example, it is easy to create a columnar layout of radio buttons or checkboxes using a table. Other form elements can also be laid out precisely using tables.

•   *Can I convert tables from other formatters, such as Microsoft Word, into HTML?*

Yes, there are conversion utilities. However, in many cases, you will need to hand-tune the results.

EXERCISES 7.5

Tables

29.   Create a tic-tac-toe game in the form of a table; show a win for X's.

30.   Insert a three-by-three table into a long paragraph of text, position the table flush left, and position the text 10 pixels away from the table in both the vertical and horizontal directions.

31.   Pick your favorite sport at school. Produce a table that lists the opposing team's name, their score, your team's score, and whether it was a W (Win) or L (Loss). The last row should "total" columns. Use results either from last year or the current season.

32.   Generate a four-row, six-column table with the headers "**span 1-3**" and "**span 4-6**." These headers should span columns 1 through 3 and 4 through 6, respectively. The content of the table should be as follows:
  •   The first row has two items called "one-three" and "four-six." (As expected, they span columns 1 through 3 and columns 4 through 6.)
  •   The second row contains the single item "one-six," and it spans all six columns.
  •   The third row has three items: "one-two," "three-four," and "five-six." (As expected, they span columns 1 and 2, 3 and 4, and 5 and 6, respectively.)
  •   The fourth row has six items, each of which is a placeholder.

33.   Produce a three-row, three-column table in which each column takes up 25 percent of a browser's window.

34.   In a three-column table, what is the effect of setting the table WIDTH attribute to 75% and the table data WIDTH attributes all to 33%?

35.   Generate an HTML table that describes your class schedule this semester. Include a caption beneath the table.

36.   Generate an HTML table with days of the week as column headers. In row 1, include the values "15," "20," "15," "20," "15," "20," and "rest." In the remainder of each column list the types and quantities of food a hiker would need to walk these mileages.

37.   Does your favorite browser support the BORDERCOLOR, BORDERCOLORDARK, or BORDERCOLORLIGHT attributes for any of the following tags: table, table data, table header, or table row? Experiment with these attributes and, based on your findings, describe their functions.

38.   Program a table that is borderless and contains the colors of the rainbow as columns.

39.   What is the function of the NOWRAP attribute of the table data and table header tags?

40.   Find an issue of your campus newspaper. Lay out its front page on-line using tables. (Provide descriptions of the graphics.)

41.   Welcome to the halls of industry. Your boss walks in and says to you, "I need an HTML table with the following specifications and

I need it now!" She hands you a sheet of paper and walks out of the room saying, "I'll be back in 10 minutes." The paper says:

> Produce the HTML code for the following table: it is three columns wide and two rows deep. From left to right, top to bottom, the colors should be red, orange, yellow, green, blue, and salmon. The contents of the cells, in the same order, are to be Songs, Books, Recipes, Junk Mail, Autos, and Flowers. The contents are to be centered, and some space, say 20 pixels, should surround the text in each box. The columns should each take up exactly 25 percent of the browser's window. Don't include borders if you'd like to keep your job!

Reading the specification has taken longer than you anticipated. However, you feel inspired. Code the table described in the specification and display it on the Web.

7.6   Debugging

Using examples, we review the most common mistakes made by HTML programmers, as well as how to avoid them. For hard-to-find bugs, you can always use an HTML syntax checker. HTML editors also do syntax checking. HTML syntax checkers and editors are discussed in Section 9.6. Sometimes you will find it helpful to view the page's source code to detect bugs. For example, the Netscape browser displays parts of the source code where bugs are in flashing text. This makes it easy to pinpoint the first coding error in a Web page. As you will see, the key to minimizing the time spent during the debugging phase is to use a consistent programming style.

Two of the most common mistakes in HTML programming are:

Hot Topic

1. Omitting the leading / on an ending tag, thereby not closing its corresponding beginning tag, as intended, but instead opening a new environment.

2. Incorrectly nesting tags.

By using an appropriate programming style, you can avoid both of these problems, or at least make them easier to detect.

To illustrate the first type of error, we present two examples of flawed HTML code that center, emphasize, and increase the font size of the word "Warning."

```
        . . .
    <CENTER>
        <STRONG>
            <FONT SIZE = "+2">
                Warning
            </FONT>
        </STRONG>
    <CENTER>                    <!-- Bug -->
        . . .
```

Because blank lines separate this code from its surrounding code (indicated by the "..." in the example) and because the tags are indented, it is easy to see that the second center tag is missing the leading / symbol. Contrast this code with the following:

```
<TABLE BORDER=2><TR><TD>TR test</TD></TR>
</TABLE><CENTER><STRONG><FONT SIZE=+2>
Warning</FONT></STRONG><CENTER><EM>compressed
code is hard to read</EM>
```

It is much more difficult to detect the problem with the center tag in this case, because the code is jammed together. A case can also be made for not using blank lines while coding HTML, since this will allow a programmer to fit more code on a screen, for example, in a Telnet window.

The next example illustrates nesting errors:

```
        . . .
    <CENTER>
        <STRONG>
            <FONT SIZE = "+2">
                Warning
            </FONT>
        </CENTER>                        <!-- Bug -->
    </STRONG>
        . . .
```

It is easy to see that the beginning strong and ending center tags have been mismatched. Contrast this with the following code:

```
<TABLE BORDER=2><TR><TD>TR test</TD></TR>
</TABLE><CENTER><STRONG><FONT SIZE=+2>
Warning</FONT></CENTER></STRONG><EM>compressed
code is hard to read</EM>
```

It is obviously much more difficult to detect the bug in this case. If you indent your code, use blank lines, and use consistent capitalization in tags, your debugging will be considerably easier.

EXERCISES 7.6

Debugging

For each problem in this set of exercises, indicate the bug(s), if any; otherwise report "no bug."

42. `<PARAGRAPH> AT Headquarters. </PARAGRAPH>`

43. `<h6>Welcome to my Homepage.<h6>`

44. ```
    <UL>
         <DD> Data goes here.
         <DD> More data goes here.
    </UL>
    ```

45. `<EMP> italics </EMP>`

46. `<STRONG>this would probably be boldface<STRONG/>`

47. `<HEADER> Red Hot Dollar </HEADER>`

48. `<H3 ALIGN == "almost-center">Just Off</H3>`

49. `<FONT WIDTH = "10%" COLOR = "red">Sunset</FONT>`

50. `<IMG SOURCE = "bruins.gif" ALGN = "left">`

51. `<HEAD> <TITLE> Welcome Yoda! </HEAD> </TITLE>`

52. ```
    <BODY BACKGROUND = "white">
            Harpers Ferry.
    </BODY>
    ```

53. `<HR COLOR = "blue">`

54. `<h4> Small text. </h4<`

55. `<SMALL <SMALL <SMALL tiny text goes here >>>`

56. ```
    <OL BEGIN = "3">
         <LI> Number 3.
         <LI> Number 4.
    </OL>
    ```

57. `<BODY BGCOLOR = "#FGAA00"></BODY>`

58. `<A HREF =
        "http://~petreschi\myfile.html"> Rossella</A>`
    ```

59. `<ALIGN CENTER>` In the middle of the road. `</CENTER>`

60. `<ITALICS>` in slanted form `</ITALICS>`

61. `<IMAGE = "glass.html">`Soft drink`</IMAGE>`

62. `<BR>` Make a new line here. `</BR>`

63. ```
<IMG SRC = "me.gif"
     WIDTH = "10 pixels"
     HEIGHT = "20 pixels">
```

64. ```
<OL STYLE = "Roman">
     <LI> Florence
     <LI> Naples
     <LI> Venice
     <LI> Verona
</OL>
```

65. ```
<CAPTION = "Data for the Heart">
<TABLE>
        <TH> Time
        <TH> Number of Beats
</TABLE>
```

66. ```
<HTML>
<BODY>
<BODY BGCOLOR = "orange">
<TITLE>
<B>My Orange Tree Page</B>
</TITLE>
You will learn all about citrus fruit
on this page.  In particular, my favorite ---
oranges.
</BODY>
</HTML>
```

67. ```
<P ALIGN = "center">
<TABLE>
        <TR ROWSPAN = "3" COLSPAN = "4">
        <TD> Georgia in March
        <TD> Tennessee in April
        <TR>
        <TD> Maine in October
<TABLE>
</P>
```
```

```
68.   <TABLE BORDERCOLOR = "green">
            BGCOLOR = "red"
            ALIGN = "center">
            <TC>
                    <TD> Column 1
                    <TD> Column 2
                    <TD> Column 3
      <TABLE>
```

Web Graphics

8

Although New Jersey is called the Garden State, people who have never left the interstate do not have a very good impression of it. After all, New Jersey is the most densely populated state and has the highest number of autos per capita. New Jersey surprised me. On entering the state, I nearly stepped on a rattlesnake. Shortly thereafter, I saw a lot of deer and raccoons and some really interesting birds. The scenery was very nice. On one stretch of trail where there was very little water available, a trail angel had left out gallon jugs of water (in the middle of nowhere). I refilled my water bottles and thanked the trail spirits for saving me from yet more dehydration. I was pushing through the smaller states in just a few days.

New Jersey
74 miles

Chapter 8

8.1 INTRODUCTION

Our goal in this chapter is to explore Web graphics. This is a rich, rapidly changing area that many people find very interesting. It is difficult to keep up with all the new developments involving graphics. The most current information can, of course, be found on the Web itself. Here you will learn about the following concepts:

Objectives

- Basic graphics principles

- Popular image formats
    - Graphics Interchange Format (GIF)
    - Joint Photographic Experts Group (JPG)
    - Portable Network Graphics (PNG)

- Features of GIF

- Additional attributes of the image tag

- Methods for creating and using image maps

- Scanners

- Miscellaneous topics, including thumbnail sketches, image height and width, and load time of images

8.2 Popular Image Formats

The two most popular types of graphics on Web pages are *GIF*, which stands for *Graphics Interchange Format*, and *JPG* or *JPEG*, which stands for *Joint Photographic Experts Group*. A relatively new image format that is an alternative to the GIF format is *PNG*, which stands for *Portable Network Graphics*. In some instances, GIF or PNG formats are preferable to JPG; in other situations, JPG is more suitable.

8.2.1   Image Compression

The concept of *image compression* is integral to our discussion of image formats. Similar to general file compression, which was discussed in Section 6.3.3, image compression involves reducing the size of the file containing the image. Compressed images take up less disk space. Complex algorithms, called *compression algorithms*, compact or discard nonessential data in the image file. The compression is handled by the format in which the image is being saved, rather than by explicitly running a program, such as compress, gzip, or PKZIP. GIF, JPG, and PNG all use different compression algorithms.

Smaller image files permit faster transmission over the Internet, so the image-containing Web pages can load more quickly. To view an image, the software displaying the image (such as a Web browser or *image editing program*) must decompress the image. The MIME type specifying the image format is indicated by the file extension: .gif, .jpg,[1] or .png. Some compression methods may work better than others, depending on the content of the image being saved. That is, different compression algorithms will achieve different reductions in any given image's file size, and there is no clear-cut winner for all images.

In addition to the different compression methods, the popular image formats also vary in the number of distinct colors they are able to represent in an individual image. The word *palette* (or *color palette*) refers to a group of distinct colors. Palette is sometimes used in conjunction with an 8-bit color scheme in which 256 (which equals 2^8) distinct colors may be represented. Different image formats support different color palettes.

Useful Item

8.2.2   Image Acquisition and Display

In this chapter, you will learn when to use the various formats. First, we describe how to copy an image off the Web. There are several ways to obtain images for display on your Web pages. For example, you can create your own images, using an image editing program; draw your own on paper and use a *scanner* to enter the drawing into a file; or scan your own photographs. Some image editing programs make it possible to modify scanned photographs and create special effects. Many also have the capability to create *interlaced* and *transparent* GIFs. Besides creating your own images, it is possible to:

---

1   Throughout this chapter, read the extension .jpg as ".jpg or .jpeg," since both file extensions are commonly used to indicate a JPG format.

- Use images from *clip art* libraries that are available at some Web sites.

- Buy clip art packages from software retailers.

- Copy images that you find on other Web pages.

- Scan someone else's photographs or printed matter.

Go On-Line

The term *clip art* encompasses nearly any graphic located on the Web, except for scanned photographs. Usually, clip art refers to a collection of images that were developed using an image editing tool. The word *clip* refers to the fact that it is very easy to cut and paste Web graphics; the word *art* refers to the fact that the graphics are "painted" using image editing programs.

Image Copyright Issues

To use someone else's icons or pictures without their permission is tantamount to stealing their work. This is against copyright law. You should be very careful not to copy images that are copyright protected. Also, images published in books and magazines are copyrighted, so these are off-limits to scanning. Some clip art collections let you know explicitly whether you can publish their images or not (displaying on the Web constitutes publishing). You should always read the fine print associated with a clip art collection you intend to use. Some Web authors may include a statement with their email addresses, inviting you to use their images but requesting that you ask permission first. They might also ask you to cite them in your Web page. As a general rule, if nothing is stated, do not use someone else's images.

Linking directly to someone else's image is not recommended, for the following reasons:

1. If the image file is moved, you will be left with a dead hyperlink and a "hole."

2. You have no control over the image. If you rely on the image in your design and it is deleted, this will present a problem.

3. Your link may put an unexpected strain on their server.

4. They may unexpectedly decide to replace the image with a "crude" one, to get back at people who are "borrowing" the image.

5. Your page may load more slowly.

6. It is considered bad netiquette and generally is not an acceptable practice.

Image Editing Software

Volumes are written about the various image editing programs, and many Web sites are dedicated to making the software publicly available. The software is usually quite intricate and time consuming to master. It is a good idea to read the relevant documentation first. After having tried a *freeware* or *shareware* version of the software, you may want to purchase a commercial version, if possible.

Let us clarify the often confused terms freeware, *public domain software*, and shareware.

Useful Item

- **Freeware** Software you can use at no charge. The author usually retains the copyright on it, but freeware is frequently unregistered. Usually, you are not provided with the source code.

- **Public domain software** Free software for which the source code is often available. There may be guidelines as to how you are allowed to modify the original source code.

- **Shareware** Software you can download and test for a brief trial period. If you decide to use the software, you should pay a small fee; this fee is often collected on an honor system basis.

Copying a Web Graphic

The URLs for some clip art collections are given in the accompanying on-line presentation. Copying an image located on another Web page involves making a copy of the .gif, .jpg, or .png image file and saving it to one of your world-executable directories. Once saved, the image needs to be made world-readable in order to be redisplayed. We will describe the procedure for saving an image file, assuming the use of a Netscape browser.

One way to copy the image file is to use the **View** menu button to look at the HTML source code of the document. In the source code, you will be able to find the URL of the desired image in the image tag. Typing this URL into the location field and hitting enter will display that image by itself in the document area of the browser window. For this to work, the URL needs to be an absolute URL, not a relative URL. If a relative URL is specified in the SRC attribute, you will need to construct the appropriate absolute URL. To do so, you will need to check if the base tag is used in the document heading. Once the image is displayed in the document area, you can use the **File** menu button to select the **Save As** option. Next, fill in a filename in response to the prompt. Once you press the enter key, the image will be saved in your directory under the filename you specified.

A second, simpler way to copy an image is to hold down the mouse button while mousing over an image. A pop-up menu that appears will offer several options: **View Image**, **Save Image As**, and **Copy Image Location**. These options may vary, depending on the version of the browser you are using. If you select **View Image**, the image will be displayed by itself in the browser window and, as before, you can use the **File** button to select the **Save As** option. Selecting the **Save Image As** is the quickest way to save the image, as it eliminates the need to display the image separately. As in the **Save As** case, you will be prompted for a filename for your copy of the image. The **Copy Image Location** option simply copies the URL to a clipboard. You would then need to open the image in the browser window, if you wanted to save it.

Useful Item

In summary, to copy an image using the Netscape browser:

1. Display the Web page containing the desired image.

2. Mouse over the image and hold down the right mouse button.

3. Select the **Save Image As** option from the pop-up menu.

4. When prompted for a filename, enter a name for the file in which the image will be stored.

Other browsers have similar capabilities (except for text-based browsers; see Section 4.7 on Lynx for a description of how to save images using a text-based browser). The pull-down menus may have a slightly different look, and the menu buttons may have other names, but they all offer the same functionality.

If you save or scan in an image at one computer, you can move it to another machine using a file transfer program. Be sure to set the transfer mode to binary when moving images.

8.2.3   Graphics Interchange Format (GIF)

GIF image files are identified by the `.gif` extension. GIF is the format commonly used to save simple images that require only a small number of colors. Such images include buttons, icons, and simple line drawings (cartoons and logos). GIF was developed by *CompuServe*, and it uses a patented form of *lossless compression* called *LZW*.[2]

---

2   LZW stands for the names of its developers, three computer scientists named Lempel, Ziv, and Welch. The LZW compression algorithm can be used to compress any form of data and is not image-specific.

Lossless compression algorithms try to capitalize on color repetitions and patterns in an image. Images that contain large areas of the same color, such as buttons and icons, lend themselves to compression using this technique. Using this method, all information about the image is preserved. Thus, when the image is decompressed, it looks exactly the same as it did originally—hence the name lossless compression. Because the compression is lossless, the image file may not be as small as it might be for some other form of (*lossy*) compression, but the image itself remains intact.

GIF supports up to 256 colors. This is the number of colors that can be represented using 8 bits. We know from the discussion of colors being represented using the RGB color model (see Section 2.6.2) that six hexadecimal numbers (24 bits) are used to represent a color in HTML:

- Two hexadecimal numbers (8 bits) to represent the red component, R.

- Two hexadecimal numbers represent the green component, G.

- Two hexadecimal numbers represent the blue component, B.

In all, it is possible to represent more than 16.7 million different colors using 24 bits.[3] GIF does not care which of the more than 16.7 million colors are selected for an image, as long as no more than 256 distinct colors are chosen. If you are converting an image that contains a large number of colors to GIF using an image editing program such as *LViewPro* or *Paint Shop Pro* (for Microsoft Windows), or *ImageMagick* or *TransGIF* (for UNIX and X Windows System), it may be necessary to reduce the number of colors in the image to 256. The image editing program allows you to select how many colors you would like in the image. The advantage of using fewer than 256 colors is that the resulting compressed file will be smaller. However, the reduced-color version of the image may not appear identical to the original image, although the results are usually quite good.

A process called *dithering* can be used to reduce the number of colors in an image. The basic idea is to approximate the color of each pixel in the image by using a combination of colors in the limited-color palette. (Remember, a pixel is a "picture element" and each pixel is assigned a color.) Many different dithering algorithms are in use. Dithering is used to display images with a large number of colors in limited palettes; the compression obtained by using a smaller color palette is a nice side effect. In a dithered image, a lot of information is lost from the original image, and it cannot be reconstructed from the file containing the dithered image.

---

3   2^{24} equals 16,777,216.

8.2.4   Joint Photographic Experts Group (JPG)

Images saved in the JPG format are identified by the .jpg file extension. JPG is used to store complex images that involve a large number of colors, such as photographs and complex artwork. JPG was developed by the Joint Photographic Experts Group and, in contrast to GIF, it uses a *lossy compression* scheme.

Useful Item

As the name implies, lossy compression involves throwing away some of the information contained in the data. The challenge is determining which information to get rid of without significantly reducing the image quality.[4] The key to the JPG compression algorithm is that subtle differences in color are not perceptible to the human eye. Thus, it is not necessary to maintain the information that keeps track of these subtle differences; people will not be able to detect them anyway. The JPG compression method takes advantage of the number of colors and color variations found in photographs and realistic artwork. Using this strategy saves a great deal of space without too much image quality deterioration. The resulting smaller files are suitable for Web images.

The image quality is reduced when an image created using a lossy compression algorithm is displayed. In fact, many image editing tools allow you to vary the amount of compression, so that you can control the quality and size of the image file, trading one for the other. In an image such as a photograph, the deterioration of image quality due to lossy compression will probably be minor. On the other hand, if the image being compressed

Go On-Line

is a line drawing with only a few colors (an ideal GIF candidate), the resulting decompressed image will appear grainy with blurry lines. The left side of Figure 8.1 illustrates how a browser renders a simple drawing that was saved as a GIF. The right side of the figure shows how the same drawing, saved in JPG, is rendered.[5]

One benefit of JPG is that it can save full-color information about an image. Where GIF is limited to 8 bits of color information per pixel, JPG stores 24 bits per pixel. This translates to over 16.7 million different colors. It is important to note that full-color hardware is necessary in order to view all the colors in such images. Many PC monitors now support 24-bit color.

---

4   Another challenge is how to represent the important information more compactly. For example, the string "000000000000000000000000000000" can be represented by the phrase "30 0's." The latter phrase is much more compact, but it contains essentially the same information.

5   The GIF file size is 1809 bytes, whereas the JPG file size is 6216 bytes.

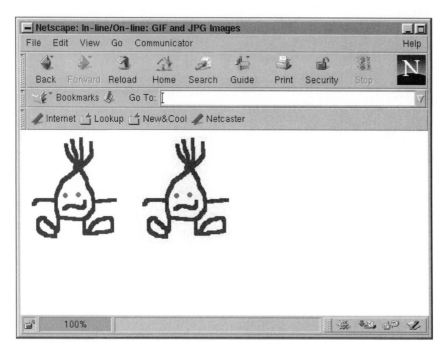

FIGURE 8.1
Simple drawing saved in GIF (left) and JPG (right). Despite being less than one-third the size, the GIF image actually looks better (check on-line).

Image Editing

Because information is lost each time an image is processed by the JPG compression algorithm, repeatedly saving the same image in JPG will result in a gradual loss of detail. If you anticipate having to modify an image, the original image should be saved in a format that preserves all the image information. *TIFF* (*Tagged Image File Format*) and PNG are good formats to use for this purpose. From these formats, a JPG version can be saved for displaying on the Web. In this way, no more detail than necessary is lost.

Image Decompression

Lossy compression schemes will usually result in smaller files; however, these smaller files may take longer to decompress for display, because of the more complex, and therefore more time-consuming, compression scheme. The extra time necessary to display an image saved in JPG is balanced by the time saved in transmitting a smaller file over the network. In contrast, GIF files are generally a bit larger (except for simple images). They take longer to transmit, but they are quickly decompressed.

8.2.5   Portable Network Graphics (PNG)

PNG is a newer image format. Images stored in this format have .png as a file extension. The development of PNG was a response to the controversy surrounding the patent held by Unisys on the LZW compression algorithm. Once Unisys and CompuServe began charging software developers royalties for the use of the LZW compression algorithm, the nonpatented PNG alternative was devised.

Like GIF, PNG uses lossless compression. This means that, when saved in this format, detailed images such as photographs may result in very large files. However, for simple images, PNG advocates claim several advantages over GIF:

- PNG compresses images slightly more than GIF—a savings of about 20 percent is usually obtained.

- PNG supports full-color representations of images, as well as reduced color, whereas GIF only supports 8-bit color. Since it uses lossless compression, PNG also provides a way to save images without losing any of the image information, as you would with JPG.

- Of course, the major advantage (and a big reason you will probably be seeing more of PNG) is that it is patent-free. This makes the format very attractive to software developers who currently pay royalties for using GIF.

However, one interesting feature of GIF that is not replicated by PNG is *animation* support.

EXERCISES 8.2

Popular Image Formats

1. Using one of the procedures outlined in this section, copy a GIF image and a JPG image from a clip art collection. Redisplay these two images on a Web page you create, include an appropriate page title, and state where the images came from.

2. Explain why repeated editing and saving of a JPG image leads to a degradation of the image quality.

3. If you have an image editing program available, experiment with saving images of various sizes using GIF and JPG formats. What differences in resulting file size did you observe? What conclusions can you draw from the experiment?

4. Does your browser support PNG format?

8.3   GIF Features

8.3.1   Animated GIFs

While surfing the Web, you may have come across eye-catching Web graphics that appear to move. An easy way to achieve this effect is to use *animated GIFs*. An animated GIF is actually a series of images displayed in rapid succession, thereby creating the illusion of continuous motion. GIF animation is a feature of GIF89a, the newer version of the GIF file format. GIF89a was released in 1989 and is an extension of the earlier version, GIF87a. Most browsers now support the GIF89a animation format, and those that do not will typically only display either the first or last GIF image in the series.

To create an animated GIF, you need a series of at least two GIF images that will serve as *frames*. These can be created using any image editing program. You will also need a GIF animation program (or an image editing program that allows saving GIF animations) to assemble the frames. GIF animation works along the same lines as a cartoon flip book. Each frame in the series has a slight variation. When the frames are displayed quickly in succession, the image appears to move. The images shown in Figure 8.2

Go On-Line

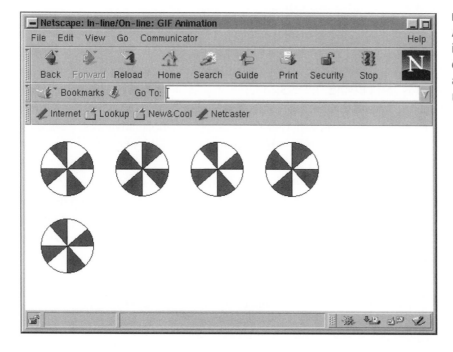

FIGURE 8.2
A series of GIF images used to create a GIF animation of a rotating disk.

illustrate a series of frames that, when displayed as a GIF animation, appear to be a disk that is rotating.

A GIF animation program puts the frames together in a single GIF file that you can include in your HTML document, using the image tag in the customary manner. The program also lets you specify various parameters, such as how much time should elapse between displaying each frame, and whether the animation should loop continuously or play a fixed number of times. The **Stop** button on the browser can be used to freeze animated GIFs.

Go On-Line

Several Web presentations and tutorials discuss how to create effective GIF animations. Also, a number of locations have software that you can download for creating animated GIFs. The list of software includes:

- *GIF Animator*, Microsoft (Microsoft Windows)

- *GIFBuilder*, Yves Piguet (Macs)

- *GIF Construction Set*, Alchemy Mindworks (Microsoft Windows)

- *GIF Converter*, Kevin Mitchell (Macs)

- *GIFMerge*, Rene Müller (UNIX)

- *WhirlGIF*, Kevin Kadow (UNIX)

8.3.2   Interlaced GIFs

Normally, an image is displayed on your browser screen (or image viewing screen) starting from top to bottom. The top half of the image is visible approximately halfway through the download, but at that point the bottom half is still missing. Interlaced GIFs appear on your screen in such a way that the "whole image" appears to load at one time, but it starts out blurry. The image comes into sharper focus as the download advances. This way, the user can get a sense of what is being displayed without having to wait for the whole image to download.

Interlaced and noninterlaced GIF files contain the same image information and are the same size. The difference is the order in which the rows of data making up the image are saved. In a *four-pass interlaced image*, four passes are used to save the image. Each succeeding pass specifies more detail. The information is divided as follows:

- *Pass one*—The first row and every eighth row after it is saved.

- *Pass two*—The fifth row and every eighth row after it is saved.

- *Pass three*—The third row and every fourth row after it is saved.

- *Pass four*—The second row and every second row after it is saved.

Table 8.1 shows the order in which the rows will appear when displayed as an interlaced GIF. Some browsers fill in the rows that have not yet been loaded, with the information already available. We have illustrated this process in the table by using the information in a given row to fill in its succeeding rows until reaching a row for which the data is available. For example, in the third column of the table "After Pass 1 Is Loaded," only information for rows 1, 9, and 17 is available. The information in row 1 is used to fill up rows 1–8, the information in row 9 is used to fill up rows

■ **TABLE 8.1**

■ The Order in Which Rows Are Displayed in an Interlaced GIF.
The boxed items are the ones loaded during a given pass. In this case, the browser has filled in the information that has not yet loaded, using the available data.

Row #	Original Image Rows	After Pass 1 Is Loaded	After Pass 2 Is Loaded	After Pass 3 Is Loaded	After Pass 4 Is Loaded
1	aaaaaa	[aaaaaa]	aaaaaa	aaaaaa	aaaaaa
2	bbbbbb	aaaaaa	aaaaaa	aaaaaa	[bbbbbb]
3	cccccc	aaaaaa	aaaaaa	[cccccc]	cccccc
4	dddddd	aaaaaa	aaaaaa	cccccc	[dddddd]
5	eeeeee	aaaaaa	[eeeeee]	eeeeee	eeeeee
6	ffffff	aaaaaa	eeeeee	eeeeee	[ffffff]
7	aaaaaa	aaaaaa	eeeeee	[aaaaaa]	aaaaaa
8	bbbbbb	aaaaaa	eeeeee	aaaaaa	[bbbbbb]
9	cccccc	[cccccc]	cccccc	cccccc	cccccc
10	dddddd	cccccc	cccccc	cccccc	[dddddd]
11	eeeeee	cccccc	cccccc	[eeeeee]	eeeeee
12	ffffff	cccccc	cccccc	eeeeee	[ffffff]
13	iiiiii	cccccc	[iiiiii]	iiiiii	iiiiii
14	bbbbbb	cccccc	iiiiii	iiiiii	[bbbbbb]
15	cccccc	cccccc	iiiiii	[cccccc]	cccccc
16	dddddd	cccccc	iiiiii	cccccc	[dddddd]
17	eeeeee	[eeeeee]	eeeeee	eeeeee	eeeeee
18	ffffff	eeeeee	eeeeee	eeeeee	[ffffff]

9–16, and the information in row 17 is used to fill up rows 17 and 18. In Pass 2, the information in rows 5 and 13 is loaded, and so on. Notice how this image loading process creates a striped effect. If you squint at a twist-handle Venetian blind and slowly open your eyes along with the blind, you can create a similar effect.

A progressive JPG format similar to interlaced GIF is also available. PNG offers a two-dimensional interlacing scheme, as well.

8.3.3   Transparent Images

Transparent images can create a visual effect in which an image appears to be sitting on the surface of a Web page. They allow the background of the page to "poke through" the image. Transparent GIFs are created by image editing programs that provide the *transparency* function. You designate that a particular color (for example, the background color of the image) be transparent. You then save the image in the GIF89a format. If the image background consists of more than one color, only the chosen color will be invisible; the other colors will still appear. (If this is the case, you may want to use the image editor to create a single-colored background first.) The color that you select will be transparent throughout the entire image. Thus, you may want to choose a background color that does not appear in the image itself. Figure 8.3 depicts how a transparent GIF and a nontransparent GIF display on a Web page.

FIGURE 8.3
Examples of transparent and nontransparent GIF images.

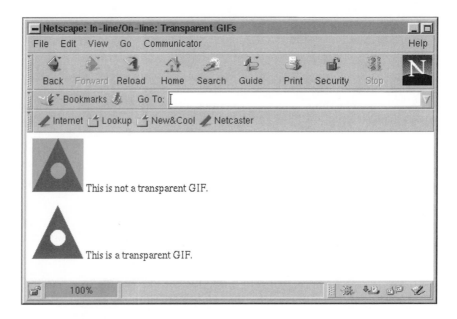

GIF designates a pixel as either completely transparent or completely visible. PNG offers a transparency feature that improves on the GIF feature in that it allows variable transparency in an image. No transparent image support is currently available in the JPG format, but a proposed *JPiG* format is being developed.

EXERCISES 8.3

GIF Features

5. Provide the URLs for two presentations that display JPG images of mountains.

6. Find Web pages that use interlaced and animated GIFs and report their URLs. Do you prefer interlaced to standard GIFs? What does the animation speed of an animated GIF depend on?

7. Will changing the default background color in your browser window cause transparent images to appear to be nontransparent? Find a transparent image and try it. Report your findings.

8.4   Image Tag Revisited

In Chapter 2, you learned how to include images in your Web pages, using the image tag and its `ALT`, `HEIGHT`, `SRC`, and `WIDTH` attributes. You also learned how to make clickable image hyperlinks. In this section, you will learn other attributes of the image tag that provide flexibility in image positioning and border creation.

8.4.1   Image and Text Alignment

When you include an image within a line of text on a Web page, the browser displays the image such that the bottom of the image is even with the bottom of the text. The imaginary line on which a line of text "rests" is called the *baseline*. The following HTML code, which is rendered in Figure 8.4, demonstrates this idea:

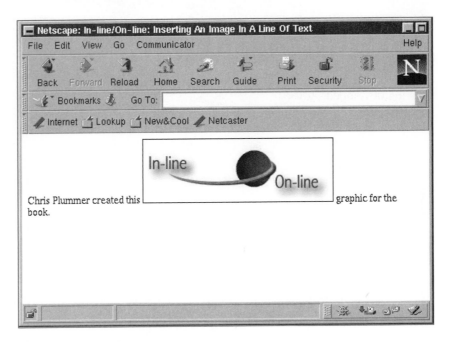

```
<P>
    Chris Plummer created this
    <IMG SRC = "../../GRAPHICS/TITLE3.JPG"
         ALT = "In-line/On-line Logo"
         BORDER = "1"
         HEIGHT = "83"
         WIDTH = "257">
    graphic for the book.
</P>
```

In some cases, this may be the look you want. If not, the ALIGN attribute
of the image tag will let you position the image vertically with respect to
the line of text. In Figure 8.5, we demonstrate the effect of having the
ALIGN attribute set to the values of top, middle, and bottom. To position
the image in the top line displayed in the figure, the image tag looks like
this:

```
<IMG SRC = "julie.jpg"
     ALIGN = "top"
     ALT = "Julie"
     HEIGHT = "168"
     WIDTH = "112">
```

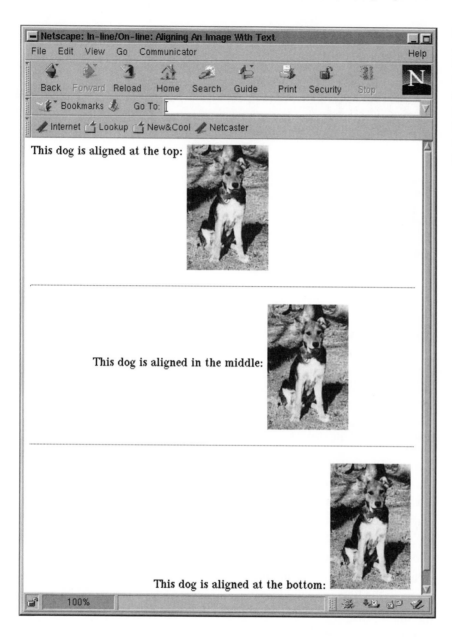

FIGURE 8.5
An example illustrating the effects of the top, middle, and bottom values of the ALIGN attribute of the image tag.

This causes the top of the image to align with the top of the text. Similarly, the second line displayed in the figure was created using a value of middle for the ALIGN attribute. The vertical center of the image lines up with the baseline. The third line used a value of bottom. This result is the same as not specifying the ALIGN attribute at all—the bottom of the image lines up with the baseline by default.

FIGURE 8.6

Aligning in-line images with other images in the line, using the `top`, `absmiddle`, and `absbottom` values of the image tag `ALIGN` attribute.

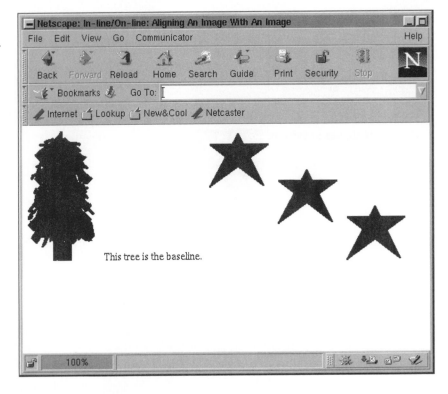

8.4.2   Additional `ALIGN` Attribute Values

The `ALIGN` attribute has several other values that allow you to fine-tune how an image is placed vertically within a line of text. Note that the values are supported on the Netscape browser, but may have unpredictable results when rendered by other browsers.

Some of the `ALIGN` attribute values take into consideration the height of other images in the same line. For instance, a value of `absbottom` will position the image such that the image bottom is aligned with the lowest object in the line, instead of with the baseline. The object could be text, or it could be another in-line image. Figure 8.6 shows the results of the values `top`, `absmiddle`, and `absbottom` for aligning the star images. Since the tree is the highest and lowest object in the line, the stars are aligned with respect to the tree image, not the text.

8.4.3   Summary: `ALIGN` Attribute Values

- To position an image in a line with respect to the text, use one of the following:

- `baseline` or `bottom`: Aligns the bottom of the image with the baseline. This is the default setting.
- `middle`: Aligns the middle of the image with the baseline.
- `top`: Aligns the top of the image with the highest point of the text in the line.

- To align an image with the highest or lowest object in the line (which can be either text or another image), use one of the following:

  - `absbottom`: Aligns the bottom of the image with the bottom of the lowest object in the line.
  - `absmiddle`: Aligns the middle of the image with the middle of the line.
  - `top`: Aligns the top of the image with the top of the highest object in the line.

8.4.4   Horizontal Image Alignment

In addition to letting you position images vertically in a line of text, the `ALIGN` attribute lets you position images in the horizontal dimension. To position an image along the left side of a page, use a value of `left`; to position an image along the right side, use a value of `right`. Note that the first `ALIGN` attribute in an `<IMG>` tag takes precedence. It is not possible to use the `ALIGN` attribute to position an image both vertically and horizontally at once.

8.4.5   Wrapped Text

In experimenting with image placement on a Web page, you will notice that only one line of text will display on either side of the image. This was not an issue in the examples presented so far, because we purposely chose text lines that did not wrap. If the text is longer than will fit on one line, the browser will display the remainder of the text below the image. Try experimenting with our on-line examples. Resize the browser window and observe how the text is displayed beneath the image when the window becomes small enough.

Go On-Line

The `ALIGN` attribute provides a way to wrap text next to an image. Using a value of either `left` or `right` positions the image next to either the left or the right margin, respectively, and permits multiple lines of text to wrap alongside an image. It is also possible to display two images, one on the left side of the page and the other on the right side of the page, with text flowing in between. An example of this is shown in Figure 8.7. The

FIGURE 8.7
Text wrapped
between two
California
redwood tree
images that were
positioned using
the `left` and
`right` values of
the image tag
`ALIGN` attribute.

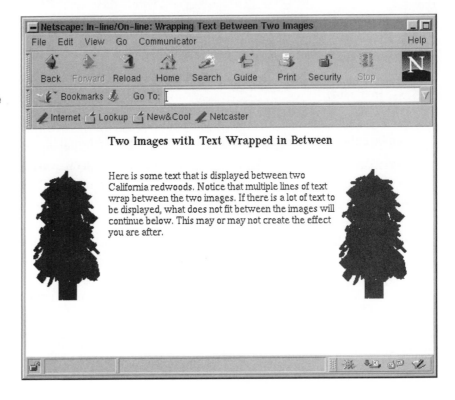

relevant portion of the HTML code used to produce this page is as follows:

```
<H3>Two Images with Text Wrapped in Between</H3>
<P>
    <IMG SRC = "tree.gif"
         ALIGN = "left"
         ALT = "redwood tree"
         HEIGHT = "173"
         WIDTH = "102">
    <IMG SRC = "tree.gif"
         ALIGN = "right"
         ALT = "redwood tree"
         HEIGHT = "173"
         WIDTH = "102">
    Here is some text that is displayed between two
    California redwoods. Notice that multiple lines of
    text wrap between the two images. If there is a lot
    of text to be displayed, what does not fit between
```

```
    the images will continue below. This may or may not
    create the effect you are after.
</P>
```

8.4.6   Text Wrap Prevention

Sometimes, you may not want all of the text to be wrapped next to an image. Using the line-break tag, `<BR>`, starts a new line of text alongside the image. Rather than guessing how many line breaks to include, you can use the tag's `CLEAR` attribute to continue the text below the image. Three values of `CLEAR` are available:

- `left`: The text breaks to a clear line to the left side of the page. This is useful with images that are aligned to the left.

- `right`: The text breaks to a clear line to the right side of the page. This is useful with images that are aligned to the right.

- `all`: The text breaks to a line that is clear to both sides of the page. This is useful when text is wrapped between two images.

The code for a break tag that causes a break to a clear line to the left side of the page is

```
<BR CLEAR = "left">
```

8.4.7   Spacing Control

By default, the text that wraps around an image is usually positioned too close to the image. The `HSPACE` and `VSPACE` attributes of the image tag can be used to avoid this crowded look. The attributes are assigned numerical values indicating the number of pixels of empty space to insert between the image and the text. In the following HTML code, the `HSPACE` attribute creates a horizontal space of 15 pixels to the left and right of the image; the `VSPACE` attribute creates a vertical space of 10 pixels above and below the image.

```
<IMG SRC = "house.jpg"
     ALT = "my house"
     HEIGHT = "245"
     WIDTH = "340"
     HSPACE = "15"
     VSPACE = "10">
```

8.4.8   Centered Images

Using the values of `left` and `right` for the image tag `ALIGN` attribute, you can align your images with the left and right edges of the browser window. There are several ways to center images, as the following examples show:

1.   Use the division tag.

```
<DIV ALIGN = "center">
     <IMG SRC = "starry.jpg"
          ALT = "Vincent's Starry Night"
          HEIGHT = "200"
          WIDTH = "250">
</DIV>
```

2.   Use the center tag.

```
<CENTER>
     <IMG SRC = "starry.jpg"
          ALT = "Vincent's Starry Night"
          HEIGHT = "200"
          WIDTH = "250">
</CENTER>
```

3.   Use the paragraph tag.

```
<P ALIGN = "center">
   <IMG SRC = "starry.jpg"
        ALT = "Vincent's Starry Night"
        HEIGHT = "200"
        WIDTH = "250">
</P>
```

4.   Use a header tag.

```
<H3 ALIGN = "center">
    <IMG SRC = "starry.jpg"
          ALT = "Vincent's Starry Night"
          HEIGHT = "200"
          WIDTH = "250">
</H3>
```

However, because the header tag is a semantic tag indicating the information it contains is a "heading," one of the other methods is preferable unless the image is actually being used in a heading. At some point in the future, header tags could be rendered as numbered sections or in some other appropriate manner for headings.

8.4.9 Image Borders

The BORDER attribute of the image tag lets you create borders around images. Figure 8.8 shows two images. The image on the left appears without a border; the image on the right is the same except that it has a border of 7 pixels. The code for displaying the second image is as follows:

```
<IMG SRC = "house.jpg"
     ALT = "82 Indian Road"
     BORDER = "7"
     HEIGHT = "122"
     WIDTH = "170">
```

Not all browsers support borders, so a border that looks good using one browser may not appear at all using another. Therefore, do not rely heavily on HTML borders; it is better to add the border to the image using an image editing tool.

Images that serve as hyperlinks are automatically rendered by the browser with a "text hyperlink" (LINK) color border that is 2 pixels wide.

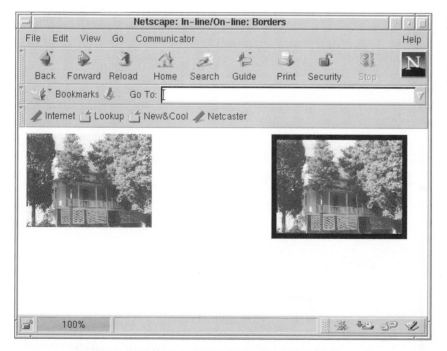

FIGURE 8.8
The image with no border and the same image with a 7-pixel border.

Useful Item

By setting the BORDER attribute to 0, it is possible to eliminate this border. However, this is usually not a good idea, because it may no longer be obvious to the reader that the image is clickable.

8.4.10   Low Source (LOWSRC) Images

The low source image (presumably a smaller, faster loading image) provides a preview of what is coming. The LOWSRC attribute of the image tag allows another image to display in place of the intended image while the remainder of the page is loading. The LOWSRC image is replaced by the image specified in the SRC attribute when this higher quality image has been transferred over. The LOWSRC attribute can be used as follows:

```
<IMG SRC = "cat.jpg"
     LOWSRC = "previewcat.jpg"
     ALT = "our cat"
     HEIGHT = "153"
     WIDTH = "182">
```

The SRC attribute should be specified first, to avoid confusing the browsers that do not support the LOWSRC attribute. The HEIGHT and WIDTH attributes apply to both the SRC and the LOWSRC images, so the two images should be the same size. If neither the HEIGHT nor WIDTH attributes are specified, the dimensions of the LOWSRC image will be used for both images. Unless you are trying to create a special effect, it is a good idea to use images having the same dimensions.

Note that the LOWSRC attribute is a Netscape extension and is ignored by some browsers.

EXERCISES 8.4

Image Tag Revisited

8.   Create a "sampler" Web page that demonstrates the various uses of the image tag ALIGN attribute. Include text to explain what you are trying to illustrate.

9.   Design an experiment to determine if there is a way to center an image on a Web page and have text wrap around both sides of it. Explain your results.

10.   Create an HTML document that contains five copies of the same image, with varying border sizes. What is the largest border size that will display? Will a negative border size display?

11.   Locate a Web presentation that has an image stored in JPG format that would likely be smaller if stored in GIF format. Report the URL of the image.

12.   Create a page containing wrapped text and an image. Illustrate how the `HSPACE` and `VSPACE` attributes of the image tag can be used to improve the appearance of the document.

8.5   Image Maps

You have already seen that an image can serve as a hyperlink and that clicking anywhere on the image will activate the link. *Image maps* take this idea one step further, making it possible to load different URLs by mousing over and clicking on various parts of an image.

Useful Item

Image maps have become quite popular as navigation aids, and some applications lend themselves especially well to their use. For example, a geographic map is an excellent candidate for an image map, since viewers can click on a specific region on the map and the link will lead them to a page describing that region. A calendar of events is another application that is well-suited to the use of an image map. Figure 8.9 depicts a screen shot of a Web page containing an image map that is used as a navigational tool. The image map is visually pleasing, and it serves to entice the viewer to explore the Web presentation further. Any item can be clicked on, and information related to that object will be provided. For example, in the presentation shown in Figure 8.9, clicking on the frisbee in the lower left corner provides information about the game "Tip It."

Two types of image maps are currently being used: *server-side image maps* and *client-side image maps*. Server-side image maps have been around longer and are supported by practically all browsers. Client-side image maps are a more recent development, and some browsers may not support them. However, client-side image maps are quickly gaining acceptance, as they are more efficient and easier to implement than server-side image maps.

8.5.1   Server-Side Image Maps

A server-side image map involves three components:

1.   An image that is used as the image map.

FIGURE 8.9

An example of an image map contributed by former In-line/On-line student Damon Gabrielle.

A user can select any item in the image. The selection results in a page being displayed that contains information about the item.

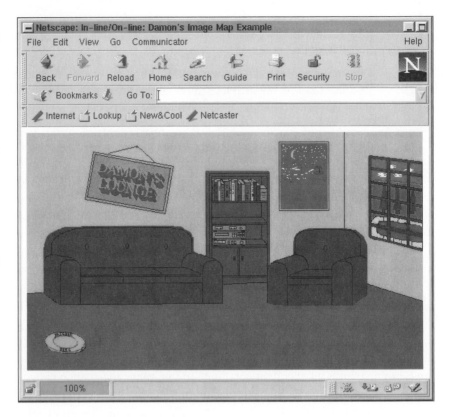

2.   A *map file* that defines the areas of the image and their corresponding URLs.

3.   An image map program.

The map file and image map program must reside on the server. The image is displayed by the browser. Each time a user clicks on an area of the image map, a connection is made to the server and the image map program handles the request. The browser sends the location of the mouse click in the form of x and y coordinates. The image map program performs some calculations and looks up the location in the map file to determine the associated URL. The corresponding document is then sent to the client to satisfy the request.

Server-side image maps place an extra burden on the server, since they require the Web server to perform calculations. This results in a delay between clicking on an image map area and seeing the resulting Web page. Client-side image maps remedy this delay by having the browser perform the calculations, as explained in the next section.

8.5.2   Client-Side Image Maps

In client-side image maps, instead of maintaining the image information files on the server, the HTML document (or possibly some other file) contains the map information and the browser performs the necessary calculations. The result is that the performance of client-side image maps is better than that of server-side image maps.

Client-side image maps are preferable for other reasons, as well. For example, another drawback to the server-side maps is that in order to test them, the map file and image map program must be installed on the server. Many users do not have permission to install programs on a Web server, so creating server-side image maps is not an option. The corresponding benefit of client-side image maps is that you can test and implement the image map locally, since the Web browser does all the processing.

A final plus of client-side image maps is that the URL of the hyperlink related to each image area map will display in the Web browser status bar without the area having to be selected. With a server-side image map, the URL is not available from the server until the user actually clicks on the area. Server-side image maps display the URL of the image map itself (and perhaps the x and y coordinates, as well) in the status bar, but not the URL of the page to be loaded.

The process of creating a client-side image map can be broken down into four steps:

1. *Select an image to be used as the image map.*

The image should have clearly defined areas. Prominent boundaries make it easier for the user to select an area. For this reason, line drawings or images consisting of distinct shapes tend to work better than photographs. If the areas are not distinct, it will be difficult for the reader to use the image map and difficult for you to decide where to have one area start and another end.

2. *Define the areas of the image map.*

You need to define the areas of the image map in terms of their shape and position. That is, you need to specify explicitly the areas that will be associated with given hyperlinks. One way to determine the coordinates of the perimeters of the areas is to use an image editing program. Such a program will display the x and y coordinates of the mouse cursor location. Tracing the mouse over the perimeter of the shape will reveal the coordinates of its boundary.

There are three ways to describe an area in an image map: a circle, a rectangle, or a polygon. If the area being defined is circular, you will need to determine the (x, y) location of the center of the circle and the radius of the circle, in pixels. A rectangular shape requires the coordinates of the upper left-hand and lower right-hand corners. A polygon involves listing the coordinates for each corner.

3.   *Include the map information in the HTML code.*

To accomplish this, you use the map, <MAP>, and area, <AREA>, tags to define the image map. The map declaration is as follows:

```
<MAP NAME = "mapname">
    . . .
</MAP>
```

The value of NAME (in this case, mapname) is used to tie the information in this tag to the image tag where you specify the filename of the image map. The connection is made through the USEMAP attribute of the image tag.

The information on the area coordinates and shapes, plus the URLs to be activated when the mouse is clicked in a given area, goes between the beginning and ending map tags. This information is included by using the area tag, <AREA>, which has no ending tag. The syntax of the area tag is as follows:

```
<AREA SHAPE = "shapename" COORDS = "cvalues" HREF = "link">
```

The value of shapename can be either circle, rect, or poly. The type of shape being defined determines how the coordinates are specified in the COORDS attribute. Table 8.2 outlines the coordinates required for each type of shape. The column labeled shapename indicates the value of the SHAPE attribute; the column labeled cvalues indicates the required values of the COORDS attribute. The HREF value is the name of the URL to be loaded when the corresponding map area is selected.

A simple image map is shown in Figure 8.10. We have chosen the value samplemap for the NAME attribute. The map tag for the figure is as follows:

```
<MAP NAME = "samplemap">
    <AREA SHAPE = "poly"
        COORDS = "139,140,204,214,101,195"
        HREF = "triangle.html">
```

■ **TABLE 8.2**
....
■ Area Tag Attributes.

Type of Area	shapename	cvalues
Circle	circle	x, y, z, where (x, y) indicates the center of the circle and z is its radius in pixels.
Rectangle	rect	x_1, y_1, x_2, y_2, where (x_1, y_1) are the coordinates of the upper left-hand corner, and (x_2, y_2) are the coordinates of the lower right-hand corner.
Polygon	poly	x_1, y_1, x_2, y_2, ..., x_n, y_n, where (x_i, y_i) are the (x, y) coordinates of the ith corner of the polygon.

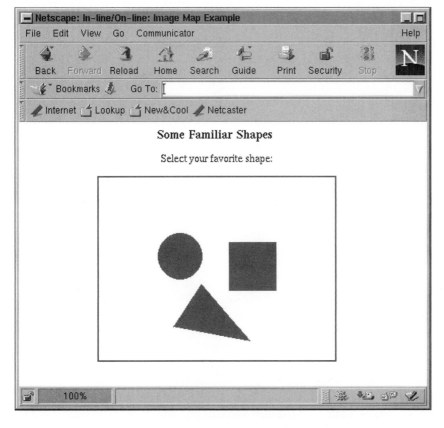

FIGURE 8.10

An example of a simple image map.

Clicking on the triangle shape will cause the document `triangle.html` to be loaded.

```
        <AREA SHAPE = "circle"
              COORDS = "110,103,27"
              HREF = "circle.html">

        <AREA SHAPE = "rect"
              COORDS = "176,84,239,148"
              HREF = "square.html">
    </MAP>
```

It is apparent from our example that the *y* coordinates are not what you might expect, because (0, 0) is located in the upper-left corner of the image, with positive *x* going right and positive *y* going down. You can observe this coordinate layout when viewing the image with an image editing program.

4.   *Connect the image with the map information.*

The final step in creating a client-side image map involves "connecting" the image with the map information in the map tag. This is done through the USEMAP attribute of the image tag. The value assigned to USEMAP is the same as the NAME attribute in the map tag, but with a preceding # symbol. The # symbol tells the browser to look within the current HTML document for the map information. The following HTML code ties everything together; it is rendered in Figure 8.10.

Go On-Line

```
<H3>Some Familiar Shapes</H3>

<P ALIGN = "center">
    Select your favorite shape: <BR>

    <IMG SRC = "shapes.gif"
         ALT = "Shapes Image Map"
         HEIGHT = "240"
         WIDTH = "320"
         USEMAP = "#samplemap">
</P>

<MAP NAME = "samplemap">
    <AREA SHAPE = "poly"
          COORDS = "139,140,204,214,101,195"
          HREF = "triangle.html">

    <AREA SHAPE = "circle"
          COORDS = "110,103,27"
          HREF = "circle.html">
```

```
    <AREA SHAPE = "rect"
          COORDS = "176,84,239,148"
          HREF = "square.html">
  </MAP>
```

In a text-based browser, such as Lynx, the code is rendered as a list of clickable hyperlinks. Since the reader will not have the advantage of seeing the corresponding image, you should use descriptive file names, so they can get an idea of the meaning of the hyperlinks. The <AREA> tag also has an ALT attribute that functions like the ALT attribute of the <IMG> tag. If the ALT attribute is used, Lynx will display the text in it as a hyperlink instead of the filename. The ALT attribute should be descriptive, so a user who does not see the image can get a sense of what the hyperlink will lead to.

In our sample image map containing the circle, square, and triangle, hyperlinks are activated only when the user clicks on one of the three areas defined in the map tag. Sometimes, it may also be desirable to activate a default hyperlink if the user clicks anywhere else in the image map. To do this, you define a new area. In our example, the area of the rectangle enclosing the entire image is appropriate. A default URL can be associated with this large rectangle. Since the order of the area tags within the map tag determines precedence, the default area tag is always placed after the other area tags, as follows:

```
  <MAP NAME = "samplemap">
    <AREA SHAPE = "poly"
          COORDS = "139,140,204,214,101,195"
          HREF = "triangle.html">

    <AREA SHAPE = "circle"
          COORDS = "110,103,27"
          HREF = "circle.html">

    <AREA SHAPE = "rect"
          COORDS = "176,84,239,148"
          HREF = "square.html">

    <AREA SHAPE = "rect"
          COORDS = "0,0,320,240"
          HREF = "default.html">
  </MAP>
```

Now, clicking on any part of the image other than the circle, square, or triangle will activate a hyperlink to the default.html page.

Useful Item

In some cases, it may be advantageous to have a separate map file containing the map tag. For example, if the image map requires a lot of area tags, or if the image map is going to be used in more than one document, you may want to keep it in a separate file, to simplify future modifications. To point to the map file, specify the filename before the # symbol in the USEMAP attribute of the image tag. This is similar to what you do when referring to a hyperlink labeled by the NAME attribute of the anchor tag.

8.5.3   Summary: Image Maps

In this section, we have covered the difference between server-side and client-side image maps, and the method for creating client-side image maps. Information outlining how to create server-side image maps is available through the references and on the Web. We urge the interested reader to explore these resources further.

Go On-Line

Image map editing programs are available to simplify the task of creating both server-side and client-side image maps. Some of the programs currently available are:

- *Client-Side Image Map Editor*, Michael Chiang (UNIX, Mac, and Microsoft Windows).

- *Imaptool*, Teemu Maijala (X Windows System).

- *Live Image*, MediaTech, Inc. (Microsoft Windows).

- *Mapedit*, Boutell.Com, Inc. (Microsoft Windows and X Windows System).

These programs will create the map file for you, including determining the area coordinates, based on your tracing the areas in the image using the mouse. A Web search for image map editing software will produce locations from which such software can be downloaded.

EXERCISES 8.5

Image Maps

13.   Locate a Web page containing an image map that you feel is effective. Report its URL and describe why you think the image map is useful for that Web page.

14. What happens to an image map when the browser window in which it is being displayed is resized?

15. If an image map is viewed using Lynx, is the information in the `ALT` attribute of the image tag displayed? Is navigation still possible in your version of Lynx?

16. Create an image map either by producing your own image, or by obtaining a legal one from the Web. Include a default area tag.

17. Describe how one could make use of an image map on an Appalachian Trail Web presentation.

18. Can you locate a weather site that has a document containing an image map? If so, how is the image map used? List two other occasions when an image map would prove useful.

19. Describe how you could define an image map area that does not fall into the `circle`, `rect`, or `poly` category.

20. Provide three URLs for presentations that contain image maps of European cities. Compare and contrast the effectiveness of the various sites.

8.6 Scanners

Scanners are devices that can convert an image to a *digital format* that is suitable for manipulation by computers. Scanners are relevant to a discussion of Web graphics because they can transform pictures into a form that can be used to enhance Web pages. In addition, scanners play a significant role in desktop publishing and the office environment. Two applications of scanners are as follows:

Hot Topic

1. Scanners can be used for text recognition. With the use of *optical character recognition* (*OCR*) software, scanned documents can be converted into a format suitable for text editing (such as Microsoft Word format). The OCR software examines each character of the scanned document and attempts to "guess" what the character is by comparing it to a database of character shapes. Although not perfect, OCR software is fairly accurate and is often included when a scanner is purchased.

2. Scanners may serve as a sort of copier by being used to make digital images of documents. A digital copy of a scanned document can be stored on disk, and can then be printed, or faxed, or utilized in another

manner. This is different from text recognition in that the document copy cannot be changed using a text editor; the image you have is just a picture of the original document.

8.6.1   Scanner Types

Three types of scanners are currently on the market: hand-held, sheet-fed, and flatbed. Each type contains a light source and a *charge-coupled device* (*CCD*). The CCD is an array of electronic sensors that are able to read light variations and convert them to digital form. An *optical resolution* of 300×600 dpi (*dots per inch*) means that there are 300 sensors per linear inch of the CCD array, and each vertical inch covered by the array is divided into 600 lines. A greater vertical resolution means that the scan head will move slower and the scanning process will take a bit longer.

Scanning color involves measuring the amount of red, green, and blue in the image. Some color scanners make three passes with the scan head (one per color) to collect the color information. A single-pass color scanner performs the collection with one pass of the scan head.

A typical scanner resolution of 300×600 dpi is much higher than the resolution of a typical monitor. A monitor's resolution is usually specified in terms of the entire screen size. For example, a 15-inch monitor[6] normally has a resolution of 800×600. This means there are 600 lines in the vertical dimension and each line is comprised of 800 pixels. A 17-inch monitor usually has a resolution of 1024×768.

The manner in which the CCD array passes over the page being scanned distinguishes the three types of scanners.

Hand-Held Scanners

With a hand-held scanner, the scanner unit is passed over a stationary page. The scanning width is small, usually no more than 4 inches, and larger images may require two or more passes that must then be "stitched" together. This means that hand-held scanners are usually not suitable for OCR scanning, or for scanning large images. Hand-held scanners are compact and portable, and are good for scanning small images and text in bound publications that will not fit into sheet-fed or flatbed scanners.

---

6   The "15-inch" refers to the length of the diagonal measured from the lower-left corner of the screen to the upper-right corner. This is the same way television screens are measured.

Sheet-Fed Scanners

Sheet-fed scanners remain stationary. The page to be scanned is drawn into the unit using rollers. The scanning width is larger than the hand-held units, but thick or bound documents present a problem. Sheet-fed scanners are smaller than flatbed scanners and larger than hand-held scanners; they are sized to fit on your desktop.

Most sheet-fed scanners do not currently support colors; however, this is not an issue when documents are scanned for text recognition, or for black and white documents. You probably will not want to use a sheet-fed scanner for creating digital images for a Web page, since the images will lack color.

Flatbed Scanners

Flatbed scanners also remain stationary, but unlike sheet-fed scanners, the document remains stationary as well. The scanner looks like a small photocopier. The CCD and light pass over the document during the scanning process. These scanners are good for creating digital images, OCR scans, and document images. Since the scanner must be at least large enough to accept an 8.5×11 inch piece of paper, the unit is quite a bit larger than a hand-held or sheet-fed scanner. This larger size restricts portability and presents a drawback for those with limited workspace.

8.6.2 Scanner Selection

Since not all scanners perform equally well in all situations, you should first consider your primary use when purchasing a scanner. If you only need to scan small images for Web pages, an inexpensive hand-held scanner may suffice. Scanning black and white documents for the purpose of text recognition might only require a sheet-fed scanner. If you need to scan larger color images, you will want to consider a flatbed scanner.

Another major consideration is cost. The hand-held units are the cheapest, followed by the sheet-fed scanners. The more versatile flatbed scanners are the most expensive, though their cost has been dropping considerably.

Once you have your selection narrowed down, you should consider a couple of other factors before making your final decision. For instance, you should compare the optical resolutions of the various scanners. Although higher resolution may seem like a good idea, if your images are intended for the Web, you will not need to scan at more than 100 dpi, since very few monitors can display at more than 85 dpi. Scanning at a higher resolution

Useful Item

only produces larger image files.[7] Similarly, selecting a color scanner that records more than 16.7 million colors is overkill for images destined for Web pages; the extra color information only serves to generate a much larger image file.

Scanners are a quick and easy way to create images for Web pages. Though not inexpensive, scanners are becoming more affordable at the same time that scanner technology is improving. For those who cannot justify purchasing a scanner to create the occasional image for a Web page, there is always the option of using a commercial copy center that does scanning. The result of using your own scanned photographs and artwork will be personal and memorable Web pages.

EXERCISES 8.6

Scanners

21. Suppose that you had $100 to spend on a scanner. Find out what kinds of scanners are available in your price range and then select one to purchase. Justify your choice by describing what you intend to use it for, what software is bundled with it, and so on.

22. Name another image acquisition device (besides a scanner) and describe how it would interface with TWAIN-compliant software.

23. If a square-shaped 15-inch monitor has a resolution of 1000 × 800, what is its resolution as expressed in dots per inch?

24. Scan one of your favorite color photographs. Save it as a JPG file at several different rates of compression. Display the results side-by-side on a Web page, along with their file sizes. What happens to the image quality as the file size gets smaller?

25. Scan a photograph and save it as a GIF file. Display it on a Web page. How does it look? Is the file size too large to be practical?

26. Research *digital cameras*. How much do they cost? What is the process involved in downloading a picture from the camera to the Web?

27. Imagine you just concluded a five-month thru-hike of the Appalachian Trail. What would be the advantage of having a digital

---

7   In extremely rare situations, when someone needs a high-resolution printout, it may be useful to scan at a higher resolution than can be displayed effectively on-line.

camera at the summit of Mount Katahdin versus having a conventional camera?

8.7   Miscellaneous Graphics Topics

8.7.1   Thumbnail Sketches

Thumbnail sketches are small images that provide a preview of what an image will look like. Some Web documents use thumbnail sketches to save time during downloading. If a user is interested in seeing a full-sized version of the thumbnail sketch, they can click on it (assuming that the Web author made the thumbnail a clickable hyperlink) and display the larger image. Since thumbnail files are typically a lot smaller, they take considerably less time to download than their full-sized counterparts. Using thumbnail sketches in a document lets the document display quicker and gives the user the flexibility to select only those images that they are interested in viewing.

Thumbnail sketches are not created using the `HEIGHT` and `WIDTH` attributes of the image tag on a full-size image. Scaling an image display size down in this fashion does not save any downloading time, since the image file remains the same size; that is, no file compression takes place. The entire file is still transferred over the network, and once it arrives, the browser scales the display size of the image.

To create a thumbnail sketch, you need to use an image editing program to scale down the original image display (and file) size. The resulting file size should be much smaller; therefore, the file should be much faster to load. In addition to creating a smaller image for display, you may also opt for a lower resolution and fewer colors, to reduce the file size further.

Another way to create a thumbnail sketch is to use an image editing program to crop a portion of the original image down to the size desired. For instance, instead of creating a scaled-down thumbnail sketch of a family portrait, which would be too small to be recognizable, you could create a thumbnail sketch containing one of the people in the portrait. This may be enough information for the user to tell what the image is about.

Useful Item

Some image editing programs use thumbnail sketches when you browse files, as a way of displaying the contents of the files. Figure 8.11

FIGURE 8.11
Thumbnail sketches created with Paint Shop Pro.

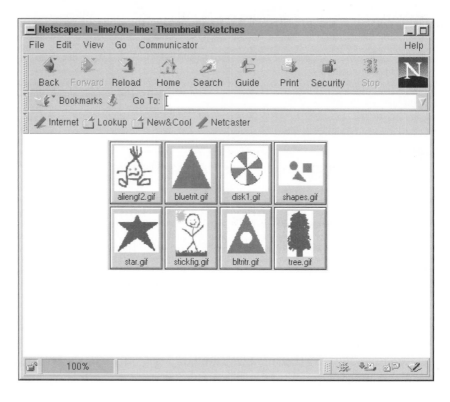

contains thumbnail sketches, created by Paint Shop Pro, of some images used in this chapter.

8.7.2   Image Height and Width

The HEIGHT and WIDTH attributes of the image tag were described previously. The benefit of using these attributes with pixel values is that the browser can lay out a Web page faster, because the browser can determine how much space to leave for an image, based on the HEIGHT and WIDTH attributes, before the image file is retrieved. Recall that retrieving each in-line image in a document requires a separate connection to the server. If the browser must determine the image sizes from the image files, the rendering of the document will be delayed. If you specify the HEIGHT and WIDTH attributes for an image, you will notice that the browser renders all of the text first when loading the page containing the image. It leaves

Useful Item

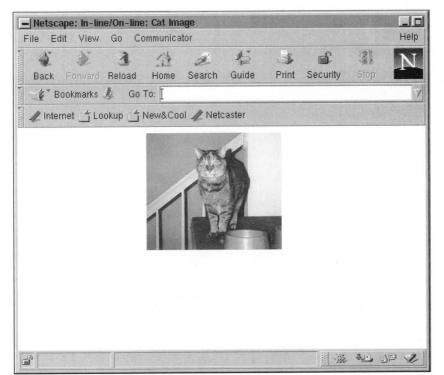

FIGURE 8.12
Killface.
She is scaled in
Figures 8.13
and 8.14.

the appropriate amount of space for the image, and when the image finally arrives, it fills in the blank space.[8]

The HEIGHT and WIDTH attributes can also be used to create some special effects, such as stretched images. The following lines of code are used to include the 182×153 pixel image cat.jpg on a Web page:

```
<IMG SRC = "cat.jpg"
     ALT = "Killface"
     HEIGHT = "153"
     WIDTH = "182">
```

The rendered code is shown in Figure 8.12.

The effect of using percentage values for the HEIGHT and WIDTH attributes is that the image is scaled in proportion to the browser window

---

8   Actually, most browsers render an icon in the "blank" space, to indicate that an image is going to load. If an ALT value has been specified for the image, it is usually displayed in the space until the image arrives.

FIGURE 8.13
A long-faced
Killface, created
using percentage
values of 75 and
40 for the HEIGHT
and WIDTH
attributes of the
image tag.

size. The following code, which is rendered in Figure 8.13, scales the image upward, because of the dimensions of the browser window.

```
<IMG SRC = "cat.jpg"
     ALT = "Stretched Killface"
     HEIGHT = "75%"
     WIDTH = "40%">
```

You can also use pixel values to scale an image. The following code, which is rendered in Figure 8.14, is used to reduce the size of the image:

```
<IMG SRC = "cat.jpg"
     ALT = "Shrunken Killface"
     HEIGHT = "76"
     WIDTH = "91">
```

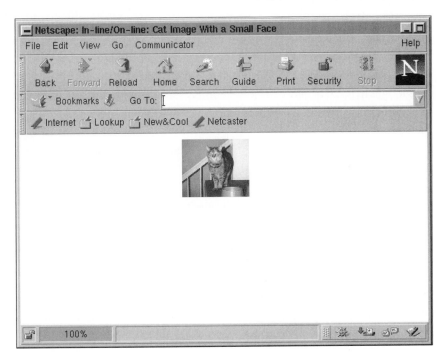

FIGURE 8.14
A small version of Killface, created using pixel values of 76 for the HEIGHT and 91 for the WIDTH attributes of the image tag.

Whether you use percentages or fixed pixel values, the final size of the image can be predetermined by the browser. Thus, the page can be quickly rendered. To control the exact size of a scaled image, use pixel values. Also, you can use a percentage value for one attribute and a pixel value for the other; the outcome is as you would expect.

Unless you are doing minor scaling, it is probably best to use an image editing tool to produce a scaled version of an image. You will obtain a better resolution, resulting in a higher-quality appearance.

8.7.3   Image Load Time

At times, it seems to take forever for Web pages to display. The number and type of images used in the Web page greatly affect the time needed to download the page. *Syntax checkers* can provide an image analysis of a page. Here we mention a couple of image-related factors that affect the load time.

The size of an image file is the major factor in the amount of time it takes to transmit the image over a network. Note that the size of the file is not the same as the size of the image. Two images that are the same dimensions may not have the same file size. Higher-quality images require larger file sizes. Achieving a good balance between file size and image quality takes practice and is the ultimate goal.

The image format is another factor that affects the amount of time it takes to load an image. A JPG file that is the same size as a GIF file will take longer to load, because the lossy compression used by JPG takes longer to decompress. In most cases, this factor is insignificant compared to image file size.

File size and type should be taken into consideration when including an image in a Web presentation. If a page takes too long to display because you have included a lot of slow-loading images, you will lose some viewers. Our suggestions for developing quick-loading images are as follows:

Useful Item

- Use the appropriate file format for the type of image you are displaying: JPG for photographs and realistic artwork; GIF or PNG for icons, line drawings, logos, and images with a limited number of colors.

- Use the HEIGHT and WIDTH attributes of the image tag to provide the browser with the dimensions of the image.

- Use thumbnail sketches when images are large and are going to load slowly. This gives users the option to skip the images, but it still gives them the opportunity to read the other information in the page after a relatively quick download. Next to your thumbnail sketches, include the actual image sizes. For example, the code

  ```
  <A HREF = "flowers.gif">Flowers</A> (50K image)
  ```

  placed adjacent to a thumbnail sketch indicates that the user can load a 50K image by clicking on the hyperlink, "Flowers." Notice that we have included the image file itself as the file to load when the hyperlink is selected. The image will be rendered alone in the browser window. If the image is large (occupying a good portion of the screen), it should look fine displayed by itself with no background or other HTML elements. The 50K provides a warning to the user that the image may take a while to load. A savvy user can predict how long an image will take to load.

- Try increasing the amount of compression for your JPG images. While this will result in a slightly poorer-quality image, such a tradeoff may be acceptable if the file size can be reduced significantly.

- Use images only when they clearly enhance a Web presentation. If the images are just "fluff," there is no point in forcing users to spend the extra time downloading them.

EXERCISES 8.7

Miscellaneous Graphics Topics

28. Create an HTML document that scales an image of a mountain by using the HEIGHT and WIDTH attributes. Vary the attributes three different ways to achieve three different special effects using the same image.

29. Are there other ways to improve the loading time of an HTML document that contains images? When might an HTML document contain many copies of the same image?

30. Suppose an HTML document contains multiple copies of the same image. Does the browser bring over multiple copies of the image, or is the browser smart enough to determine it only needs one copy of the image?

Advanced HTML

9

I hiked New York in great spirits. Entering a new state was a real psychological boost. However, it was extremely hot that summer. In fact, an all-time high temperature record for New York state was set where I was hiking one day. It was 106°F. I was now carrying close to two gallons of water (16 pounds) since it was very hard to find any drinkable water near the trail. The trail actually goes through a zoo in Bear Mountain, New York. I got to the zoo early in the morning and was not aware that the trail went through the zoo. I was not carrying any maps of the trail, having discarded them to save weight. The zoo gate was closed early in the morning, so I could not see the trail markings inside the zoo. About an hour later, I realized the trail must go through the zoo. I jumped the fence to the zoo and proceeded to tip-toe through it thinking "what if the lions are loose?" I was hiking the trail "pure" and did not want to miss any section of it no matter how small.

New York
88 miles

Chapter 9

9.1 INTRODUCTION

In this chapter, you will learn about the following topics:

Objectives

- Frames
- Forms
- Common Gateway Interface (CGI) scripts
- Dynamic documents
- HTML tools: editors, syntax checkers, and converters
- Next-generation HTML
- Cascading Style Sheets

These HTML tags will provide you with greater capabilities and extra flexibility for Web page development.

9.2 Frames

Frames are an HTML feature introduced by Netscape Communications. They allow you to divide a browser's window into several independent parts. Frames are now considered standard HTML. Here we present the basic frame tags and the type of material that is suitable for being displayed in frames. The exercises explore other attributes of these tags.

Figure 9.1 presents an example of frames. In the left-hand frame is a list of different lecture numbers. Each of these is a hyperlink. In the right-hand frame is a listing of lecture content. When you click on a specific lecture on the left, the corresponding lecture information appears at the top of the right-hand frame. Thus, the left-hand frame functions as a table of contents; the information in it is *static*. The right-hand frame is the *target* of the hyperlinks in the left-hand frame. Because the material in the

Go On-Line

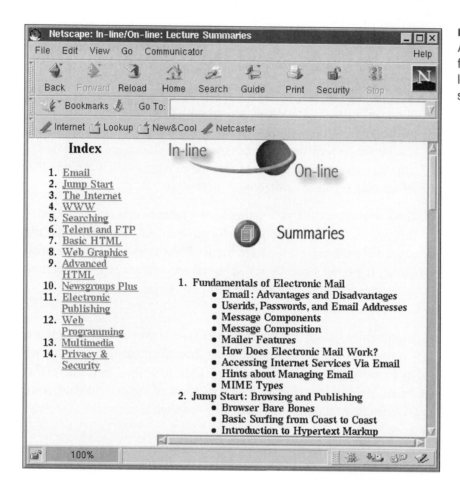

FIGURE 9.1
A sample use of frames displaying lecture summaries.

right-hand frame changes according to the hyperlink selected, the information is called *dynamic*.

9.2.1   Frame Usage

You have probably seen a number of Web pages that use frames. Some may have been impressive and facilitated your visit, while others may have been confusing and actually gotten in the way. When is it appropriate to use frames?

Useful Item

•   *Common content*—If you have a collection of documents that share information, you may want to display the common material in a frame. For example, a header or a footer could be put into a small frame. You might also display copyright information and navigational aids in a frame. In this case, all of the other information to be displayed would go in a separate frame. A company might want to display its logo in one frame, so that the logo is always visible while you are viewing their presentation.

- *Form verification*—If the user is to submit a form, you may want to have the original information displayed in one frame and the information that the server receives and sends back displayed in an adjacent frame. This way, the user can do a side-by-side comparison to make sure that all the data is entered correctly.

- *Table of contents*—If your pages have a table of contents or an index that you want to remain on-screen for navigational purposes, you could place this material in a separate frame. If the material fits into a small frame, hyperlinks can be set up to target a larger frame. Such an arrangement is another effective form of navigation.

Hot Topic

We should point out that the subject of frames evokes strong opinions; many people recommend against their use, because most of the effects created by frames can be achieved by other HTML techniques (such as *tables*) and frames present indexing problems for most of the current-generation *search engines*. In addition, only the latest-generation browsers can render frames properly.

9.2.2   Frame Tags

The name "frame" is an analogy with window frame. A group of frames in a single browser window is called a *frameset*. The frameset tag, <FRAMESET>, and corresponding ending tag, </FRAMESET>, are used for creating a set of frames, by specifying how the browser's window is to be partitioned. The frameset tag in an HTML document replaces the body tag.

Once the browser's window is partitioned, you need to tell the browser what to load into the different frames. This is done using the frame tag, <FRAME>. No ending tag is necessary for the frame tag. Consider an example of two frames, in which the browser's window is divided vertically into two equal-sized left-hand and right-hand parts.

```
<HTML>

<HEAD>
<TITLE>Two Vertical Frames of the Same Size</TITLE>
</HEAD>
```

```
<FRAMESET COLS = "50%,50%">
        <FRAME SRC = "foo1.html" NAME = "frame1">
        <FRAME SRC = "foo2.html" NAME = "frame2">

    <NOFRAMES>
            This material is best viewed with Netscape
            Navigator version 2.0 or higher.
            <A HREF = "noframes.html">View</A>
            a version of the material without frames.
    </NOFRAMES>
</FRAMESET>
</HTML>
```

Useful Item

Again, the body tag is not allowed in a frameset HTML document. If you do accidentally use both tags, the results will be unpredictable. You may not end up with frames as intended.

The code for the frameset given is rendered in Figure 9.2. The COLS attribute of the frameset tag was used to specify that we were creating two columns, each of equal width, where a column is a vertically oriented frame. The COLS attribute can take a number of different values. In the given code, we have defined each column as a percentage of the browser's window, that is, each column was allocated 50 percent of the width of the window. You can also specify the column width using a fixed pixel amount. For example, this can be useful if you want to match the frame size to that of a particular image.

Additionally, you can use the wildcard symbol ∗ (asterisk), in a couple of ways. One way is to assign leftover amounts of space. For example, in the three-column frameset code that follows, the remaining 25 percent of the width of the browser's window is allocated to the third frame.

```
<FRAMESET COLS = "40%,35%,*">
```

Another way of using the asterisk symbol is to divide the browser's window into proportions. For example, suppose you wanted the columns to be in proportions of two, six, and two. That is, columns 1 and 3 have the same size, whereas column 2 is three times as wide. This can be conveniently specified as follows:

```
<FRAMESET COLS = "2*,6*,2*">
```

Useful Item

The SRC attribute of the frame tag is the location where the file to be loaded into the frame is specified. Notice in our initial example that we loaded the files, called foo1.html and foo2.html, into the two frames. It

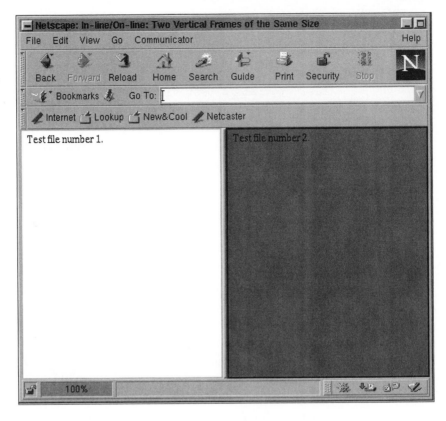

is a good idea to create test files, such as foo1.html and foo2.html, which are just simple HTML files that can be used for testing frameset designs. Such files are excellent debugging tools, since they are actually loaded into the frames. The files can also include hyperlinks to test their targets (see Section 9.2.5).

The NAME attribute of the frame tag is used for associating a name with the frame. We will explain later how the NAME attribute can be used to direct a hyperlink into a frame. In our example, we call the frames frame1 and frame2. For specific applications, more descriptive names should be used.

We have also included the noframes tag, <NOFRAMES>, and its ending tag, </NOFRAMES>, in the sample code. This tag should appear at the same level as the frame tags, in the outermost frameset declaration. The reason for this is that frames are relatively new in the HTML world, and many early browsers do not support them. Such browsers cannot display frameset declarations, and readers who have these browsers cannot view pages that include these declarations. To accommodate these users, the noframes tag was incorporated into HTML.

Browsers not capable of displaying frames render the information that appears between the noframes tag and its corresponding ending tag. This works because the frames-unaware browser ignores the HTML tags <FRAMESET> and <FRAME>, which it does not recognize. It also ignores <NOFRAMES> and </NOFRAMES>, but it sees the text within them and displays it in the normal way. In contrast, the frames-aware browser knows to ignore any material between the <NOFRAMES> and </NOFRAMES> tags.

Between the <NOFRAMES> and </NOFRAMES> tags, Web authors typically provide a note about how best to view their pages, or they provide a hyperlink that leads to a nonframes version of the material contained in the frames. Naturally, it is difficult for Web authors to maintain two separate versions of their pages: with frames and without. Fortunately, many browsers now support frames.

The browser window can be divided horizontally, as well as vertically, using the ROWS attribute of the frameset tag. The following HTML code shows how to divide the browser window into three separate rows. The rows occupy 20 percent, 48 percent, and 32 percent of the browser window height. In this case, the rows are called header, body, and footer, respectively. The HTML files with the same names are loaded into the applicable frame.

```
<HTML>

<HEAD>
<TITLE>Three Horizontal Frames</TITLE>
</HEAD>

<FRAMESET ROWS = "20%,48%,*">
        <FRAME SRC = "header.html" NAME = "header">
        <FRAME SRC = "body.html" NAME = "body">
        <FRAME SRC = "footer.html" NAME = "footer">
</FRAMESET>

</HTML>
```

Figure 9.3 shows how this code is rendered.

9.2.3   Frequently Asked Questions

Frames are more complex than the other HTML tags we have discussed thus far. We encourage you to experiment with HTML to resolve any other questions you may have about frames.

FIGURE 9.3
Three horizontally oriented frames that divide the browser window into rows of height 20%, 48%, and 32%, respectively.

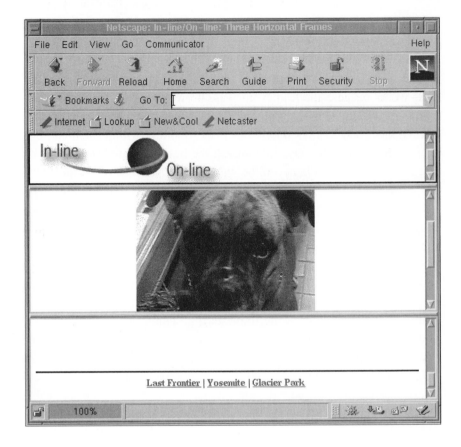

- *Can* COLS *and* ROWS *be used in conjunction with one another? If so, what is the result?*

Yes, COLS and ROWS can be used together. When combined in the same frameset declaration, they create a grid-like pattern. For example, to create a tic-tack-toe layout, you could use the following HTML code:

```
<FRAMESET COLS = "33%,33%,*" ROWS = "33%,33%,*">
```

- *The examples mentioned so far have been easy enough to follow, but in general, how are the source files loaded into the frames?*

The frames are loaded in a top-to-bottom, left-to-right manner. For example, in the tic-tack-toe board specification, the fifth frame is the one in the center. The sixth frame is the one immediately to the right of the center frame, and so on.

- *If each document in a frameset has a title, which title is displayed in the lone title bar when the group of frames is being displayed?*

The title of the most recently loaded frame is displayed. We recommend using the same title for all frames included in the same frameset tag.

- *How can the HTML source code be viewed for a document created using the frameset tag? How can the source code of individual frames be viewed?*

Most browsers contain a **View source** or **Page source** button, with which you can view the source code of the document containing the frameset tag. By clicking on a particular frame on the screen, you make that frame the "currently selected frame." To look at its source, you use the **View frame source** or **Frame source** button that most browsers now have.

- *Is it possible to load a document that is itself a document consisting of a frameset declaration into the* SRC *attribute of a frame tag?*

Yes, this is allowed (as long as you avoid infinite loops) and is often a convenient way to partition the browser window further. To view the source code for such documents, you may need to traverse several levels.

- *Can a hyperlink be targeted into a specific frame? Can a new browser be launched automatically, if you do not wish to load a large page into a small frame?*

The answer to both of these questions is yes; Section 9.2.5 goes into the details.

- *Can frames be nested?*

Yes, and Section 9.2.6 explains how to nest frames.

- *Is there an easy way to produce any frame layout?*

Yes, and we describe a method for doing so in Section 9.2.7.

9.2.4   Additional Frame Tag Attributes

We have already encountered the SRC and NAME attributes of the frame tag. These are used to load a specific file into a frame and to provide the frame with a name, respectively.

The NORESIZE attribute stops the user from resizing a frame and is used when the content of a frame only looks good in a certain size. For example, you may have an image map that is used for navigation and that you always want to be fully displayed. This attribute functions like a switch and so has no value.

The SCROLLING attribute takes a value of yes or no either to allow scrolling or not. The default for browsers is the insertion of a horizontal or a vertical scroll bar, or both if the page requires them. The value auto assigned to the SCROLLING attribute has the same effect as the default.

Other attributes of the frame tag include:

- MARGINHEIGHT

- MARGINWIDTH

- FRAMEBORDER

9.2.5   Targeted Hyperlinks

 The TARGET attribute of the anchor tag is used to direct hyperlinks into specific frames. You specify the frame by using the frame's name as the value of the TARGET attribute. If the value of TARGET does not match the name of any frame, a completely new browser window will be created. As an example, suppose the file oz.html contains the following HTML code:

```
<HTML>

<HEAD>
<TITLE>The Wizard of Oz</TITLE>
</HEAD>

<FRAMESET ROWS = "33%,33%,*">
        <FRAME SRC = "scarecrow.html" NAME = "scarecrow">
        <FRAME SRC = "tinman.html" NAME = "tinman">
        <FRAME SRC = "toto.html" NAME = "toto">
</FRAMESET>

</HTML>
```

When the browser renders oz.html, it creates three horizontal frames. The first one contains the file scarecrow.html and is named scarecrow; the second one contains the file tinman.html and is named tinman; the third one contains the file toto.html and is named toto. Suppose that you would like to include a hyperlink in the file scarecrow.html to load the file dorothy.html into the first frame, the one initially occupied by scarecrow.html. The hyperlink in the following HTML code achieves this action:

```
<HTML>
<HEAD>
<TITLE>The Wizard of Oz</TITLE>
</HEAD>
<BODY>
        . . .
I traveled to Oz with a girl named
<A HREF = "dorothy.html" TARGET = "scarecrow">Dorothy</A>
        . . .
</BODY>
</HTML>
```

Since the name of the first frame is scarecrow and this matches the TARGET attribute's value, the file dorothy.html will be loaded into the first frame. If the value assigned to the TARGET attribute were toto instead of scarecrow, the file dorothy.html would be loaded into the third frame when the hyperlink for "Dorothy" is selected.

A number of *special targets* can be used:

- _blank
  This value, read "underscore blank," when used as the value of the TARGET attribute, creates a hyperlink that causes a new, unnamed browser window to open. The content of the new browser window is specified in the HREF attribute of the anchor tag.

- _top
  This value, read "underscore top," causes the HTML document specified in the HREF attribute of the anchor tag to be loaded into the entire browser window containing the hyperlink. If the document to be loaded does not contain the frameset tag, it will occupy the

complete browser window. In this case, the browser window will not be subdivided.

Useful Item

The __top value is very useful for displaying the pages pointed to by hyperlinks that are not part of your presentation. You can thus avoid loading a Web page into a smaller space than its designer intended.

Figure 9.1 illustrates how lecture names can be displayed in one frame and summaries of the corresponding lectures are shown in another frame. In this example, several different hyperlinks all have the same target. To avoid having to specify the TARGET attribute for every single hyperlink in the left-hand frame, you can use the base tag, <BASE>.

To illustrate, suppose lectures.html is the file loaded into the left-hand frame of Figure 9.1. This file contains the hyperlinks targeting the right-hand frame. Further, suppose that the name of the right-hand frame is summary. The following code for lectures.html illustrates how to use the base tag, as well as how to specify a hyperlink directed to the frame summary:

```
<HTML>

<HEAD>
<BASE HREF = "http://www.location.edu/~wallace↩
            /public_html/"
                TARGET = "summary">
<TITLE>Lecture Summaries</TITLE>
</HEAD>

<BODY>
        . . .
<A HREF = "lecture7.html">Lecture7</A>
        . . .
</BODY>

</HTML>
```

In this code, we set a base HREF value: the file lecture7.html is contained in the directory

~wallace/public_html

at the site

www.location.edu

We also specified a base target of summary. Thus, all hyperlinks in the file lectures.html will be directed to the frame named summary, unless specifically directed somewhere else. So, if you click on the hyperlink "Lecture7," for example, the HTML file `lecture7.html` will be rendered in the `summary` frame. In this case, by using the `TARGET` attribute of the base tag, we avoid having to use the following to specify each hyperlink:

```
<A HREF = "lecture7.html" TARGET = "summary">Lecture7</A>
```

Our example shows that the base tag can be used to make a set of pages more portable. If the collection of pages moves or the name of the `summary` frame changes, only the base tag needs to be updated, not every single hyperlink appearing in the document.

Useful Item

9.2.6   Nested Frames

You learned how to nest lists in Section 7.4. The same principles apply to nesting frames. Suppose you want to create a frameset declaration that divides the browser window as shown in Figure 9.4. This division can easily be accomplished using nested frames, as shown in the following HTML code:

```
<HTML>
<HEAD>
<TITLE>Nesting Frames</TITLE>
</HEAD>
<FRAMESET ROWS = "50%,50%">
    <FRAMESET COLS = "33%,67%">
            <FRAME SRC = "left-third.html"
                    NAME = "left-third">
            <FRAME SRC = "right-twothirds.html"
                    NAME = "right-twothirds">
    </FRAMESET>
    <FRAME SRC = "bottom-row.html" NAME = "bottom-row">
</FRAMESET>
</HTML>
```

Care must be taken to match up the beginning and ending frameset tags correctly. The omission of an ending `</FRAMESET>` could result in serious problems. Also, loading an HTML file into a frame contained in that same HTML file results in a loop, which is not a good idea. If you have not yet created the "real" `left-third.html`, `right-twothirds.html`, and `bottom-row.html` files, simply load your test file `foo.html`.

FIGURE 9.4
A division of a
browser's window
to illustrate how
frames can be
nested.

FIGURE 9.4
A division of a browser's window to illustrate how frames can be nested.

9.2.7   Frameset Design Algorithm

There is a systematic procedure (i.e., an algorithm) you can use to design any frameset, regardless of how complicated it seems. This algorithm assumes that you have a *storyboard* specification of the browser window division you want to create. A storyboard is a rough sketch of how the browser window is to be partitioned. An example of a storyboard is shown in Figure 9.5. The steps of the *framing algorithm* are as follows:

1. First, decide whether to use COLS or ROWS in the outermost frameset declaration. To do so, determine whether a frame spans the entire width of the browser window.

    a. If so, use ROWS. Pick one of the frame's horizontal borders that is not also an edge of the browser window.

    b. If not, use COLS. Pick one of the frame's vertical borders that is not also an edge of the browser's window.

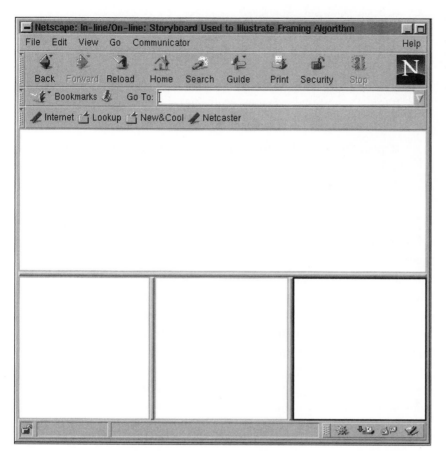

FIGURE 9.5
A storyboard
illustrating the
framing
algorithm.

2. If you use ROWS, generate a frameset declaration as follows:

    ```
    <FRAMESET ROWS = "x%,y%">
            <FRAME SRC = "foo.html" NAME = "frame1">
            <FRAME SRC = "foo.html" NAME = "frame2">
    </FRAMESET>
    ```

    Here, x and y are estimates of the heights of frame1 and frame2, respectively. That is, they are heights based on the horizontal border you picked in step 1.

3. If you use COLS, generate a frameset declaration as follows:

    ```
    <FRAMESET COLS = "x%,y%">
            <FRAME SRC = "foo.html" NAME = "frame1">
            <FRAME SRC = "foo.html" NAME = "frame2">
    </FRAMESET>
    ```

    Here, x and y are estimates of the widths of frame1 and frame2, respectively. That is, they are widths based on the vertical border you picked in step 1.

4.   Repeat the algorithm for `frame1` and continue until no further subdivisions are necessary. If another layer is required, textually replace the frame declaration for `frame1` by the next layer's frameset declaration. Also "increment" the frame names.

5.   Repeat the algorithm for `frame2` until no further subdivisions are necessary. If another layer is required, textually replace the frame declaration for `frame2` with the next layer's frameset declaration. Also "increment" the frame names.

The algorithm is a *recursive* algorithm because it uses itself in subsequent steps.

Let us now apply this algorithm to the storyboard shown in Figure 9.5. An inspection of the storyboard reveals that a frame spans the width of the browser window. According to the framing algorithm, we therefore need to use a ROWS attribute in the outermost frameset declaration. We must also pick a horizontal border that is not an edge of the browser window. There is only one such border, and that is the line going across the middle of the window. Carrying out the next step of the algorithm, we generate the following frameset declaration:

```
<FRAMESET ROWS = "50%,50%">
        <FRAME SRC = "foo.html" NAME = "frame1">
        <FRAME SRC = "foo.html" NAME = "frame2">
</FRAMESET>
```

We now recursively apply the algorithm to `frame1`. Since `frame1` has no further subdivisions, we are done processing it. We now turn to `frame2`, which is further divided. We then apply the entire algorithm to `frame2`, looking at `frame2` as though it is the entire browser window.

You can readily see that no frame spans the entire width of `frame2`. Therefore, according to the framing algorithm, we need to use a COLS attribute in this level's frameset declaration. Next we need to select a vertical border on which to focus, and we choose the first one. As specified by the algorithm, we generate the following code:

```
<FRAMESET COLS = "33%,67%">
        <FRAME SRC = "foo.html" NAME = "frame3">
        <FRAME SRC = "foo.html" NAME = "frame4">
</FRAMESET>
```

The border we selected divides frame2 into parts that are one-third and two-thirds in size. We increment the frame names and call the new frames frame3 and frame4. Putting all of the declarations together, using the textual substitutions required by the algorithm, results in:

```
<FRAMESET ROWS = "50%,50%">
      <FRAME SRC = "foo.html" NAME = "frame1">
      <FRAMESET COLS = "33%,67%">
            <FRAME SRC = "foo.html" NAME = "frame3">
            <FRAME SRC = "foo.html" NAME = "frame4">
      </FRAMESET>
</FRAMESET>
```

No further subdivisions of frame3 are necessary; however, frame4 does require partitioning. Applying the algorithm to frame4, we see that a COLS attribute is necessary for this frameset declaration. There is only one vertical border to consider, and it divides the "window" into two equal-sized parts. Putting everything together results in the following HTML code:

```
<FRAMESET ROWS = "50%,50%">
      <FRAME SRC = "foo.html" NAME = "frame1">
      <FRAMESET COLS = "33%,67%">
            <FRAME SRC = "foo.html" NAME = "frame3">
            <FRAMESET COLS = "50%,50%">
                  <FRAME SRC = "foo.html"
                        NAME = "frame5">
                  <FRAME SRC = "foo.html"
                        NAME = "frame6">
            </FRAMESET>
      </FRAMESET>
</FRAMESET>
```

Note that our numbering scheme results in only frames 1, 3, 5, and 6 being real frames. Normally, you will use more descriptive names, suggesting the content of the different frames. Also observe that the framing algorithm produces one group of frameset declarations for a given storyboard. Many other frameset declarations could also be used to generate the same storyboard. The framing algorithm does not always produce the frameset declaration with the fewest number of nestings.

9.2.8   Frames Reality Check

Useful Item

Even though we can construct complex framesets, in most cases it makes no sense to construct frames with more than two or three subdivisions. Frames reduce an already limited amount of display space on most monitors. Even the ability to open a frame in a separate window is of limited help if it largely obscures the underlying window, as is the case on most 15-inch or smaller monitors.

EXERCISES 9.2

Frames

1. Provide three URLs of Web pages that make effective use of frames. Explain why their content is appropriately suited to frames.

2. Demonstrate the following attributes of the frame tag by creating an HTML document in which they are used:

    *   FRAMESPACING

    *   MARGINHEIGHT

    *   MARGINWIDTH

    *   FRAMEBORDER

3. Can a document that contains just one frame be created? If so, can you think of a situation when this might be useful?

4. Create a Web page with a frameset declaration consisting of four columns, each of which takes up 25 percent of the width of the browser window. Write three different frameset declarations that achieve the same result.

5. Using * as a value to the COLS attribute, create a Web page whose columns have the proportions 5, 1, and 14. Load the names of three adjacent states along the Appalachian Trail into the frames.

6. What is the maximum number of COLS your browser supports?

7. Create the French flag, using frames.

8. What happens if, in a file called test.html, you include a frame that uses test.html as a value for the SRC attribute?

9. Make a checkerboard (eight by eight) using frames. Be sure the colors are correct.

10. Create a Web page that consists of three borderless frames. Display the three words "plodding to Maine" one per frame.

11. How do the **Back** and **Forward** buttons on the browser behave with frames?

12. Create a frameset declaration that creates a tiled image of the letters AT. (You may need to use a large number of frames to do this.)

13. Create a Web page that has three frames. Load each one with a different background. Include hyperlinks in each frame so that any of the background files can be loaded. Thus, any possible combination of the three backgrounds can be achieved.

14. What are the _self and _parent values of the `TARGET` attribute of the anchor tag used for? Create sample Web pages to test them.

15. Create a Web page that illustrates the use of the _blank value of the `TARGET` attribute.

16. Create a Web page that illustrates the use of the _top value of the `TARGET` attribute.

17. Write frameset declarations to create the browser window divisions shown in Figure 9.6.

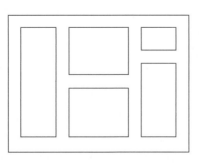

(a)

(b)

(c)

FIGURE 9.6
Browser window divisions for which you need to provide frameset declarations.

18. Explain how the same storyboard can be specified in many different ways. For example, the framing algorithm may produce one method of generating a frameset declaration, whereas another algorithm might produce an entirely different frameset declaration, and both declarations achieve the same results.

19. Describe two storyboards that no frameset declarations can produce. Our informal definition of *storyboard* is not precise enough to relate only to frameset browser partitions. Propose a more specific definition of storyboard that does the job.

20. Describe how frames might prove useful for designing a Web presentation about hiking in Virginia.

9.3   HTML Forms

Forms allow you to type information into fields on a browser screen and submit that information to a Web server. They allow you to create *interactive Web pages*. That is, you can fill out a form, submit it, and then, depending on the values you submitted, the resulting Web page can be customized for you. For example, suppose you want to obtain the current market value of your stock portfolio. You can fill out a form from a broker's Web page indicating your stock holdings. When you submit the form, the information is uploaded to the server designated to handle the form. A program on the server processes the information and then returns a new HTML document that shows how much money your stocks are worth. Figure 9.7 illustrates this example.

Figure 9.7*a* depicts the values the user entered: 100 shares of CISCO stock and 100 shares of BAY stock. The user clicks on the **SUBMIT** button, and the information is sent to the stockbroker's Web server, where the form-processing application resides. The information is then coded and transmitted by the program.

Figure 9.7*b* shows that the program

```
/cgibin/stock_process
```

is located on the Web server. This program is used to process the stock information and compute the current value of a portfolio, using the most recent stock prices available. The calculation of the portfolio's worth is also performed on the Web server. After the value of the portfolio has

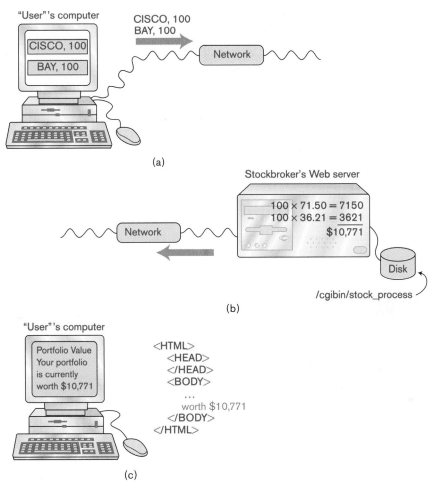

FIGURE 9.7
The process of submitting a form to a stockbroker's Web server to have the current value of a portfolio computed.

been computed, it is returned—included within an HTML document that is rendered by the browser of the person who originally submitted the form. This is shown in Figure 9.7*c*.

Forms have many functions. They can be used for gathering information about a user, conducting a survey, selecting something of interest, placing an order on-line, submitting a query to a search engine, and so on. In each case, when the user submits a form, values are uploaded to the receiving server. The server that processes the form does not have to be the server from which the form was retrieved, although it usually is. After some processing, the server usually replies by returning an HTML document to the browser of the person who submitted the form. If the user filled out the form incorrectly, the HTML document may contain a message asking the user to redo the form and resubmit it.

Note that if you retrieve a Web page containing a form, the server does not wait specifically for you to return the form. The connection by which the form was retrieved is released immediately after the form is delivered. You can decide either to submit the form or not. Submitting it requires that a new connection to the server be established.

9.3.1   Form Tags

You can include multiple forms in a single HTML document, although normally, only one form appears on a given Web page. Also, forms can have a number of different types of fields in which to enter information. Figure 9.8 depicts a sample form. This form has text input fields, radio buttons, checkboxes, a select field, a **Submit** button, and a **Reset** button.

FIGURE 9.8
A sample form illustrating several different input fields.

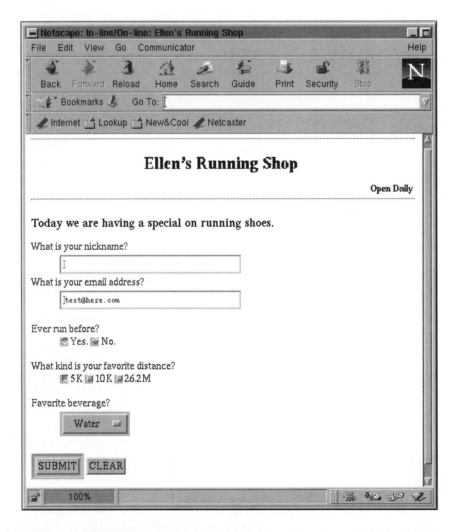

The beginning and ending tags for form creation are <FORM> and </FORM>. All of the values assigned to items between these tags are up-loaded to the server when a user submits a form. The most important attributes of the form tag are ACTION and METHOD. For example, in Figure 9.7, how did the stockbroker's Web server know to use the program

```
/cgibin/stock_process
```

to process the incoming form? The form itself must contain the name of the program that processes the information submitted. The program's location is specified using the ACTION attribute, and the value of the ACTION attribute is an absolute URL, usually that of a program. For example, the following HTML code,

```
<FORM ACTION = "http://www.stockers.com/cgibin ↵
                /stock_process"
      METHOD = "get">
      . . .
</FORM>
```

specifies that the program to process the form resides on the Web server

```
www.stockers.com
```

in the cgibin directory and is called stock_process. Most Web managers keep form processing applications in a directory called cgibin or something similar. The cgi stands for *Common Gateway Interface* and the bin stands for binary.

9.3.2 Form Methods

Introduction

There are two different ways of sending values to a Web server. They are specified by the value assigned to the METHOD attribute of the form tag. The get METHOD appends the values of the input parameters to the URL specified in the ACTION attribute. In a single communication, this information is transmitted to the server that processes the form. The ACTION URL is separated from the parameter names and values by a question mark symbol. For example, when the query

```
+"Pacific Crest Trail"
```

is submitted to Infoseek's search engine, the string

```
http://www.infoseek.com/Titles? ↵
       qt=%22Pacific+Crest+Trail%22& ↵
       col=WW&sv=IS&lk=noframes&nh=10
```

is passed to the search engine. Here, the ACTION URL is

$$\texttt{http://www.infoseek.com/Titles}$$

The input parameter names and values passed to Infoseek are included in the following string:

```
qt=%22Pacific+Crest+Trail%22&col=WW&sv=IS&lk=noframes&nh=10
```

Notice that the quote marks are coded as %22, and blank spaces are coded as plus signs. In the string, there are values for the parameters qt (which stands for "query text"), col, sv, lk, and nh (which stands for "number of hits"). The parameter name/value pairs are separated by ampersand signs (&). It is important to note that in submitting this query, we did not explicitly specify values for the col, sv, and lk parameters. This illustrates that hidden values may be included in the form itself.

The post value assigned to the METHOD attribute provides another way of submitting input values from a form to a Web server. In the post METHOD, the server specified in the ACTION attribute of the form tag is contacted. After communication has been established, the input values are sent to the server. (The encoding style of parameter names and values may differ from server to server.) Some programs, which are publicly available, echo back the values that were submitted when a form is submitted, via the post METHOD. Such programs are useful for testing forms to see if the parameter name/value pairs submitted are the ones expected. The on-line presentation of this book provides the URLs of some sites containing such programs.

Whether a form uses the get or post METHOD, the program that handles the form must be able to decode the parameters and then use them. Form processing programs are usually written in such languages as C, C++, Java, or Perl. For efficiency reasons, it is best to use a *compiled language* to process forms.

Go On-Line

Comparison: get **and** post

To determine which of the two methods you should choose, consider the following:

- For a novice programmer, the get METHOD is probably preferable, since the post METHOD may require more programming expertise.

- Recall that when the get METHOD is used, the values are sent with the ACTION URL to the server. Therefore, if you have a small number of input parameters, the get METHOD is preferable, for efficiency reasons. However, if a long list of parameters is involved, the post METHOD is preferable.

- Neither METHOD is secure, but the post METHOD is preferable to the get METHOD if security is an issue.

9.3.3   Mailto URLs

You can use a mailto URL in the ACTION attribute of the form tag. The values of the parameters are sent as a message to the email address specified. You can thus create a simple *guest book* by using a mailto (see Section 12.5.3). For example, the following form specifies an ACTION that causes its parameter name/value pairs to be emailed to the user heidi-sol when the form is submitted:

```
<FORM ACTION = "mailto:heidi-sol@electric.com"
      METHOD = "post">
      . . .
</FORM>
```

You can use a mailto ACTION in a number of ways:

Useful Item

1. As a technique for testing forms.
2. To learn more about parameter encodings.
3. To make use of forms, even if you cannot program or are not allowed to install a form processing program.
4. To set up a simple guest book, in which sign-ins are emailed to you.

9.3.4   Form Input Tags

The basic structure of a form is created using the following HTML code:

```
<FORM ACTION = "http://www.server.com/cgibin/program"
      METHOD = "get">
      . . .
</FORM>
```

In this code, the ellipsis represents the main part of the form. Also, the post METHOD could have been used instead of the get METHOD.

You may include nearly any type of HTML formatting command inside a form tag, and forms may be nested. To create most form elements, you use the input tag, <INPUT>.

It is a good idea to provide clear instructions on how to fill out a form. You should specify what data types are expected in a given field, if this is unclear from context. Remember that you have no real control over what the user types into a field. The program on the server-side must do type checking and must handle errors.

Text Boxes

A rectangular-shaped field in which a user can enter text is called a *text box*. A text box is produced using the input tag and specifying the appropriate attributes. For example, the following HTML code was used to produce the first text box of the form shown in Figure 9.8 and the question posed above it.

```
<DL>
    <DT> What is your nickname?
    <DD> <INPUT TYPE = "text"
                NAME = "nn"
                SIZE = "40"
                MAXLENGTH = "60">
    ...
</DL>
```

The first couple of input fields are formatted using a definition list. The TYPE and NAME attributes are required for the input tag. In this case, the value assigned to the TYPE attribute is text, which is used for producing a text box. In the next sections, we cover the other TYPE values. The NAME attribute specifies the name of the parameter that will be assigned the value that the user enters into the field. For example, if someone enters the nickname Fiddlehead, the parameter nn would be assigned the value Fiddlehead:

$$nn = Fiddlehead$$

A similar convention is followed with other types of inputs. The value assigned to the parameter specified in the NAME attribute gets the value the user inputs into that field.

In our example, the SIZE attribute is set to 40. This specifies that the text box is to be 40 characters wide. Notice in Figure 9.8 that the field is in fact rendered as 40 characters wide.

Useful Item

The MAXLENGTH attribute specifies that the most characters a user can enter into this field is 60, even though only 40 will be displayed in the field at any one time. It is a good idea to set maximum values on input lengths, using the MAXLENGTH attribute, so users cannot submit huge amounts of useless data.

The VALUE attribute of the input tag may be used to specify a default value for a parameter. This can be useful for presetting information that is going to be the same for a majority of users. The default value is initially displayed in the corresponding field, and the user may change the value if desired.

Checkboxes

A *checkbox* is represented by an icon that the user can select or deselect by clicking on it. A selected checkbox is usually shown in dark gray, and an unselected checkbox is usually shown in light gray. Checkboxes are often used in series, so that users can easily specify all of their preferences. For example, in Figure 9.8, three checkboxes are shown, allowing users to select their favorite running distance: 5K, 10K, or 26.2 miles. These checkboxes were produced with the following code:

```
<DL>
    <DT> What kind is your favorite distance?
    <DD> <INPUT TYPE = "checkbox"
               NAME = "distance"
               VALUE = "5"
               CHECKED> 5K
         <INPUT TYPE = "checkbox"
               NAME = "distance"
               VALUE = "10"> 10K
         <INPUT TYPE = "checkbox"
               NAME = "distance"
               VALUE = "26"> 26.2M
</DL>
```

Notice that we have used a definition list here to format the checkboxes.

By specifying the TYPE attribute of the input tag as checkbox, we can create a checkbox. The NAME and VALUE attributes behave the same as for text boxes. Notice though that depending on the distance selected, the parameter distance is assigned a different value: 5 for the 5K, 10 for the 10K, and 26 for the marathon. If the user selects multiple checkboxes, a set of values will be sent to the server. For example, suppose a user selects both the 5K and 10K; then

```
distance = 5,10
```

will be sent.

Another interesting point is that we specified the CHECKED attribute of the input tag for the entry corresponding to the 5K. This allows us to set a default value. In this case, the 5K was specified as the default, since most people prefer running this distance to either a 10K or a marathon.

Radio Buttons

In the old days, radios allowed you to preset six stations. The controls for the stations were buttons. The radios were designed such that only one button could be depressed at a given time; that is, pushing in one button forced the currently selected button to deselect. You can also use *radio buttons*, which are a group of buttons from which only one can be selected at a time. In the form shown in Figure 9.8 we included two radio buttons to determine whether or not the person filling out the form had ever run before. These buttons and the corresponding text were produced using the following code:

```
Ever run before?
<INPUT TYPE = "radio"
       NAME = "run"
       VALUE = "yes"
       CHECKED> Yes.

<INPUT TYPE = "radio"
       NAME = "run"
       VALUE = "no"> No.
```

In this case, for illustration purposes, we have coded the form so that the "Yes" button is selected. In fact, the default is the first button, unless the CHECKED attribute is included. A user can deselect the default by clicking on the "No" button. Buttons that have the same NAME are elements of the same set of radio buttons, and only one of them may be selected at any given time.

Finally, we have displayed both the checkboxes and radio buttons horizontally. If you have a short description for each box or button, this is fine. However, when the accompanying text is longer, it may be better to display the choices vertically, using lists.

Action Buttons

There are two types of *action buttons*. They are submit and reset. When the user clicks on the submit button, the values that have been entered into the form are sent to the program that processes the form. The submit button shown in Figure 9.8 was produced using the following code:

```
<INPUT TYPE = "submit"
       VALUE = "SUBMIT">
```

The argument to VALUE is displayed inside the graphic corresponding to the submit button. Naturally, the most commonly used word is SUBMIT. Some authors also use SEND.

The function of the reset button is to allow the user to clear all of the input they have thus far entered into the form. This is a quick way for users to start over from the original default values. The reset button shown in Figure 9.8 was produced by the following code:

```
<INPUT TYPE = "reset"
        VALUE = "CLEAR">
```

Here again, the argument specified for VALUE is displayed inside the reset button. In this case, we have labeled it CLEAR. The other popular word is RESET. It is common practice to display submit and reset buttons next to each other. Also, browsers usually display the two buttons differently.

Useful Item

Selects

We have seen that radio buttons can be used to select exactly one choice from a group and checkboxes can be used to select any combination of values from a group. However, for all but very small groups of items, these types of multiple-choice selections require a lot of space on the screen. Another alternative is the select tag, <SELECT>, with corresponding ending tag </SELECT>. The select tag lets you choose any subset of items from a group, and it does not take up a lot of screen space. The items in a given select tag are usually rendered in the style of a pop-up menu. In Figure 9.8, we included a select tag for which the default selection was Water. Here, we reproduce the code for the entire menu, which is shown in Figure 9.9.

```
Favorite beverage?
<SELECT NAME = "drink">
        <OPTION> Coke
        <OPTION> Cytomax
        <OPTION> Flat Coke
        <OPTION> Gatorade
        <OPTION> Metabol
        <OPTION> Powerade
        <OPTION SELECTED> Water
</SELECT>
```

The attributes of the select tag are MULTIPLE, NAME, and SIZE. When specified, the MULTIPLE attribute allows the user to select more than one item; in this case, the select tag behaves like a group of checkboxes. If the MULTIPLE attribute is omitted, the select tag behaves like a set of radio

FIGURE 9.9
A select pop-up
menu that
provides a
number of
different choices
of beverage.

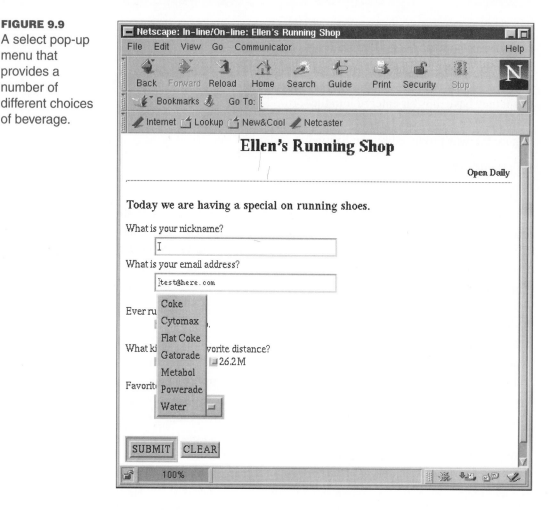

buttons—only one item may be chosen. The NAME attribute serves its usual purpose. The SIZE attribute specifies how many options are to be displayed concurrently on the screen. For example, if SIZE is 3, three different choices would be displayed. When SIZE is greater than one, the different options are usually displayed as a scrolling list.

There are two attributes to the option tag, <OPTION>: SELECTED and VALUE. The SELECTED attribute is used to preselect an item. The VALUE attribute allows you to specify the content to be returned if a given option is selected. In our select example, NAME was assigned the value drink. By default, when a given option is selected, the text following the option tag is designated as a value to the parameter specified in NAME. In our code, if Water is selected, we get

```
drink = Water
```

The `VALUE` attribute can be used to change this. So if we instead wanted `H2O` to be returned when `Water` was selected, we would use the following code:

```
<OPTION SELECTED VALUE = "H2O"> Water
```

The `</OPTION>` ending tag is nearly always omitted.

Text Areas

You may want to specify a multirow text field, rather than just a single row. This is useful when you expect to receive comments or short messages. The textarea tag, `<TEXTAREA>`, with its corresponding ending tag, `</TEXTAREA>`, is used for this purpose. For example, suppose you want to create a 20-row, 80-column area in which messages can be entered. The following code could be used:

```
<TEXTAREA NAME = "message"
          ROWS = "20"
          COLS = "80"
          MAXLENGTH = "2000"
          WRAP>

Enter your message here

</TEXTAREA>
```

When the form containing this code is submitted, the characters typed by the user are transmitted in the variable `message`. In this example we have set a `MAXLENGTH` value of `2000`, so no more than 2,000 characters will be accepted. We have also set the `WRAP` attribute of the textarea tag, so that if a user types continuously without hitting the return key, the text automatically wraps at the end of the field.

The comment "Enter your message here" is displayed initially in the text area. Usually, such initial messages provide the reader with guidelines about the information they need to enter.

Passwords

You can create a password text field using the following code:

```
<INPUT TYPE = "password"
       NAME = "nn"
       SIZE = "20"
       MAXLENGTH = "40">
```

Hot Topic

This creates a *masked field* in which a user can enter a password; the password is not shown on the screen. However, no security, other than a masking of the password, is provided in the way the password is transmitted to the server.

Form Layout

A number of Web pages describe how to create effective forms. This book's on-line Web presentation is hyperlinked to many of them. Remember that nearly all HTML tags can be used for arranging the content of a form. One useful tag we have not yet mentioned is the preformatted tag, <PRE>, with its corresponding ending tag, </PRE>. With the preformatted tag, items are left in their ASCII text format. For example, white space counts; if you leave blank spaces inside the preformatted tag, the browser will render these spaces, where it normally would ignore them. This allows you, for example, to tab over to line up columns and so on.

Syntactic- and semantic-based style types can be used inside a preformatted tag; this is not true, however, for all HTML tags. Since various tags are legal inside the preformatted tag, when the browser sees the < symbol it interprets that symbol as the beginning of a tag. To include the < symbol as part of the text, you can specify it using the expression:

```
&lt;
```

The `lt` stands for "less than." Many character entities may be specified using a similar format. That is, you can use the formula,

```
&abbreviation;
```

where `abbreviation` is replaced by the shorthand for the character. Table 9.1 lists several of the most common character entities. Note that some symbols can be specified in one of two ways.

Useful Item

The preformatted tag is useful for formatting column-based material, program code, or poetry. As an example, the following poem is coded using the preformatted tag. The result is rendered in Figure 9.10.

```
<PRE>
                    Never
                 Before Did
             I See, A Triangle Of
         A Poem Formatted With PRE
</PRE>
```

TABLE 9.1
Common Character Entities.

Character	Mnemonic Code	Numeric Code
´	&acute;	&#180;
&	&amp;	&#038;
©	&copy;	&#169;
°	&deg;	&#176;
>	&gt;	&#062;
<	&lt;	&#060;
"nonbreaking space"		

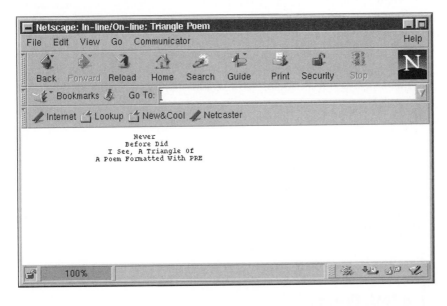

FIGURE 9.10
Poem rendered using the preformatted tag.

9.3.5 Frequently Asked Questions

- *Can a user load a new Web page or an image by pressing a "submit" button on a form?*

Yes, you can use either a relative or an absolute URL as the value of the ACTION attribute. When someone submits the form, the specified page or image is loaded.

- *I have seen some pages in which the navigation seems to be done using forms. That is, there is a button that looks like a submit button, but it says something like "BACK." Is this accomplished with forms, and if so, how?*

Yes, you can do this with a form. The submit button is labeled with a navigational indicator, such as "BACK." For example,

```
<INPUT TYPE = "submit" VALUE = "BACK">
```

In the ACTION attribute of the form, you must specify the URL for the page you want loaded when the user submits the form.

- *Is there a way to use a form to create a navigational button such that when a user submits the form, I can have another page loaded into a specific frame?*

Yes, you can use the TARGET attribute of the form tag. Along with the METHOD and ACTION attributes, you would specify the name of the frame into which the new material is to be loaded by assigning that value to TARGET.

- *Can you name a form?*

Yes, the form tag has a NAME attribute that can be used to assign a name to a form.

EXERCISES 9.3

HTML Forms

21. Submit a query about the Appalachian Trail to your favorite search engine. What string was passed to the search engine based on your query? Examine each part of the string and describe the parameters that were sent, as well as their corresponding values. What was the ACTION URL?

22. Why might the designer of a form want to include `hidden` parameters and assign them values?

23. Provide the URLs of two stock quote services that provide functionality similar to that illustrated in Figure 9.7. Compute the current worth of the portfolio described in the text, using each service. Were the results the same? Explain.

24.   Research the `get` METHOD and write a paragraph describing as many specifics as you can of the way parameters are encoded.

25.   Write a declaration for the input tag to create a set of checkboxes that allow someone to check off any number of your favorite trail foods. The values should be transmitted in the variable named `yummy`.

26.   Write a declaration for the input tag to create a group of four radio buttons that allows a user to select one of your favorite radio stations. Specify the code such that the third button is selected by default, and the value selected is returned in a variable called `rs`. The value of `rs` should be the radio station number.

27.   Write a select declaration with three options: camp here, push on, and go to town. The select tag should behave like a set of radio buttons.

28.   Write a select tag declaration to offer a selection from a group of ten CDs, from which the user can pick six. Allow six options to be displayed at a given time. The default selections should be CDs 1, 2, 5, 6, 7, and 10.

29.   What happens if you try to type in more characters than are allowed by the `MAXLENGTH` setting?

30.   Write a declaration for the input tag to create a text field 35 characters long that is masked, has a default value of `pass`, has a maximum length of 56, and is called `password`.

31.   Create a complete form for your pizza shop such that users can enter their pizza selection, drink order, payment method, and so on. Use the `post` METHOD and an `ACTION` that echoes the user's choices on-screen.

32.   What is the function of the `ALIGN` attribute of the input tag?

33.   What HTML tags cannot be used inside a preformatted tag? Experiment with these tags and see what happens if you do include them. Explain your findings.

34.   List ten character entities (and their codes) that are not already listed in Table 9.1.

9.4   CGI Scripts

The *Common Gateway Interface* (*CGI*) is a set of rules that specify how parameters are passed from programs to Web servers. We have seen that when a user submits a form, a program may be executed by the Web server, and the results are returned to the browser. The particular program that is to be executed is specified in the ACTION attribute of the form tag. In general, any program run by a Web server in response to a user's request is called a *script* or *CGI script*. Scripts do not have to be written in a *scripting language* such as Perl. While they may be written in scripting languages, they can more generally be written in any language that a server is capable of executing.

Hot Topic

Scripts are useful for interacting with databases. For example, when you submit a query to a search engine, you are actually submitting a form. The Web server corresponding to the search engine then runs a program that interacts with the search engine's index of Web pages. Once the program determines the result set of your query, it returns this information as an HTML document to your browser. The browser then renders the document on your screen.

Because of the intermediary role that scripts play, they are sometimes called *gateways*. In our example, the script serves as a passage between the Web and the search engine's database.

9.4.1   Scripts and Forms

Figure 9.7 illustrates how a form works, at a conceptual level. Here, we expand on part (b) of the process. Part (b) occurs just after the user has submitted the form. The server, mentioned in the ACTION attribute of the form tag, receives a request from the user when the user submits the form. The server must then locate the script the user has requested. The server makes calls to the operating system on which the Web server is running to determine if the script exists. If the script is located and is world executable, then the server runs it.

The inputs to the script are the values that the user transmitted with the form. The script must decode these values to use them. Once the script has run, the results it computed are passed back to the Web server. The Web server then sends the results, usually an HTML document, back to the client that submitted the form.

Go On-Line

The interested reader should consult the references for additional details about how scripts and forms interact.

9.4.2   Security

A CGI script is a program that anyone can run on a Web server. Such scripts must therefore be carefully written, and all but the most straightforward scripts should be written by very experienced programmers. It is easy to write a script with security holes, but very hard to verify that a script has no loopholes. With a flawed script, certain inputs can be passed to the script that may allow the script to gain control of the Web server's operating system. Once this happens, the program can delete files and cause other damage.

As noted earlier, scripts usually need to be placed in a special directory, called something like `cgibin` on most systems. Because of the security problems mentioned here, some installations do not allow users to install CGI scripts.

EXERCISES 9.4

CGI Scripts

35. Research some of the security problems people have had with CGI scripts. Summarize your findings.

36. Are you permitted to write and install CGI scripts at your installation? Are any local scripts available for your use? If so, what are their functions?

9.5 Dynamic Documents

When you request a Web page, your browser sends a request to a server that in turn sends back the file you requested. In the case of *dynamic documents*[1] more than just a single transaction may take place. As the name implies, a *dynamic document* is one that has the capacity to change. There are two varieties of dynamic documents, and their differences result from the way in which multiple transactions are initiated. (Note that not all browsers support dynamic documents.)

9.5.1 Client Pull

In the *client pull* model, your browser (or client) initiates the document's change. Periodically, your browser may automatically request information

---

1 Be aware that there is something different called *dynamic Web pages*.

from the server. Each time it does, a new connection to the server must be established. Using client pull, you can cause a document to "refresh" itself, or you can load a completely new document. Why would you want a document to refresh automatically every so often? Suppose, for example, that the document contains timely information, such as price updates, auction bids, or stock quotes, which change very rapidly. It would be more convenient to have it reload automatically. Other times, you may want to load a "splash screen" to create an interesting visual effect, and then load in a completely different document.

Useful Item

The meta tag, along with its `HTTP-EQUIV` and `CONTENT` attributes, are used to create client pull documents. Remember, the meta tag is included within the head tag of an HTML document. The meta tag syntax for client pull applications in which you would like to refresh the same document continually, is as follows:

```
<META HTTP-EQUIV = "refresh" CONTENT = "n">
```

The `HTTP-EQUIV` attribute takes the value `refresh` and the `CONTENT` attribute takes a number `n` indicating how many seconds to wait before automatically reloading the page. A value of `n` equal to 15 would cause the page to reload every 15 seconds; a value of 0 would cause the page to reload continuously, with little or no delay. The smaller the value of `n`, the higher the demand placed on the Internet.

The example given here shows how to refresh the same document. What if you want to reload a different document? Suppose you would like to display the file `splash.html` for 10 seconds before automatically loading the file `data.html`. The following HTML code included in the head tag of the file `splash.html` accomplishes the desired effect:

```
<META HTTP-EQUIV = "refresh"
      CONTENT = "10;
          URL=http://www.mycomputer.edu/~you/data.html">
```

When you load the file `splash.html`, it will be displayed for 10 seconds, and then the file `data.html` will automatically be loaded. The amount of time you display a splash screen will depend on how long it will take a reader to assimilate the information.

Note that the syntax required to load a new page automatically is different. As before, the `HTTP-EQUIV` attribute is assigned the value `refresh`. The `CONTENT` attribute is assigned two values in a single assignment step. In the example, the first value is `10`, which indicates how many seconds to wait before loading the next page. After the `10` is a `;` followed by a blank space. This in turn is followed by the expression:

```
URL=http://www.mycomputer.edu/~you/data.html
```

Observe three things in the following code:

```
<META HTTP-EQUIV = "refresh"
    CONTENT = "10;
        URL=http://www.mycomputer.edu/~you/data.html">
```

1.   There are no spaces around the equals sign in the URL expression.

2.   The URL is an absolute URL.

3.   The quote marks precede the `10` and follow the `html`.

You must follow these conventions. Be careful to check your syntax, because debugging this statement is not easy.

You should be aware that it is possible to make an extremely annoying Web page using client pull! Such pages force you to watch a series of graphics load in slow motion, with no recourse but to bail out. Also, the performance can be very dependent on the speed of the link (to download the information) and the speed of the desktop (to render the page).

9.5.2   Server Push

In the *server push* model, the server initiates the document's change. Periodically, the server may send the browser some new information to display; for example, current weather data, or recently changed stock prices. For server push to work, the client–server connection must remain open after the client's initial request is satisfied. This places a continuous demand on the server. Server push is not accomplished using HTML tags. Server push programs are usually written in Java or Perl. To use server push, you need to develop program code, and you must also know some technical details about your server. The interested reader can explore server push further through on-line documentation.

Go On-Line

9.5.3   New-Address Notification

The most important use of client pull is to notify readers that your presentation has moved. A typical message would be:

Useful Item

This site has moved to
`http://www.blah-blah.edu/blah.html`
please make a note of it and update your bookmarks.

If you wait 5 to 10 seconds, you are usually "pulled" over to the new presentation. Notice that we have underlined the URL to indicate that it is a hyperlink, which means you could click on the hyperlink and be immediately transferred to the new presentation, rather than waiting. Making the

URL a hyperlink is a convenience to readers, because they can transfer to the new presentation whenever they are ready.

An HTML document that incorporates this "moved" message can be coded as follows:

```
<HTML>

<HEAD>
<TITLE>The Blah Site Has Moved</TITLE>
<META HTTP-EQUIV = "refresh"
      CONTENT = "10;
           URL=http://www.blah-blah.edu/blah.html">
</HEAD>

<BODY>
   <CENTER>
   This site has moved to <BR>
   <A HREF = "http://www.blah-blah.edu/blah.html"> ↩
       http://www.blah-blah.edu/blah.html</A> <BR>
   please make a note of it and update your bookmarks.
   </CENTER>
</BODY>

</HTML>
```

Notice that the title of the document is "The Blah Site Has Moved." Also, the message has been centered so that it looks better on the screen.

The new URL is displayed for 10 seconds before the `blah.html` page is loaded. This should give the reader adequate time to jot down the new address. We have also included a hyperlink to the new presentation, so that it can be loaded more quickly.

EXERCISES 9.5

Dynamic Documents

37.   Code a Web page that reloads itself every 5 seconds. Time it. Does it actually reload every 5 seconds? Explain.

38.   Using client pull, create a set of three Web pages that continuously cycle every 15 seconds. That is, if the pages are called A, B, and C, then 5 seconds after A is loaded, B should automatically be loaded; 5 seconds later, C should automatically be loaded; 5 seconds later, A should automatically be loaded, and so on.

39.   Create a simple *animation* using client pull. The animation should cycle through consecutive states along the Appalachian Trail.

40. Suppose your Web page has moved to a new location called `new.html`. Create an HTML document that directs visitors to your new address. Be sure to create a `new.html` file to test your code.

9.6   HTML Tools

9.6.1   Editors

An *HTML editor* is a software tool that helps develop HTML code. It is a tag and text editor that is specialized to HTML. Figure 9.11 depicts a version of the Netscape HTML editor's user interface, with a page from this book's

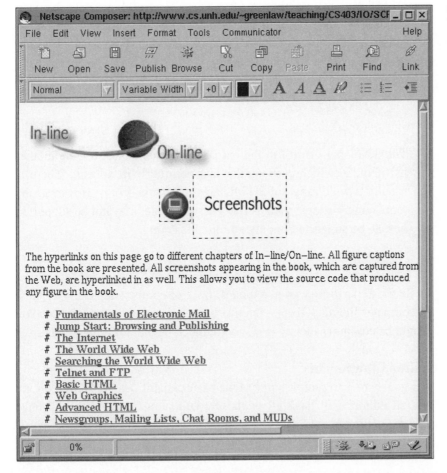

FIGURE 9.11
The user interface of Netscape's HTML editor.

Web presentation. Prior to 1996, HTML editors, for the most part, were rather limited in their capabilities. Over time, editors have become more powerful and have proliferated. The functions performed by the several dozen currently available editors vary, as does their basic philosophy.

There are essentially two different types of HTML editors:

- *WYSIWYG HTML editors*—WYSIWYG means "what you see is what you get." In this model, "programmers" are almost totally isolated from HTML. They do not become directly involved in HTML programming. The programmer selects items from menus, clicks on them, possibly fills in some text, and positions the items. The on-screen material they see is not the HTML document, but rather the rendered HTML document. In other words, during the development process, the page developer does not actually see the tags comprising the source code, unless they specifically decide to view the code.

- *Tag-oriented HTML editors*—In this model, the page developer selects HTML tags from menus and has the option to manipulate the code directly. The HTML code is not hidden. For example, a programmer might select a list tag, such as <OL>, and then be presented with a template like the following one:

```
<OL>
    <LI>
</OL>
```

The developer can fill in the list item and then select to add another list item, in which case another list item tag will appear. There is usually a wide range of HTML tags to choose from. However, the more complex tags, such as frameset and table, may not be supported or may be supported in only a limited fashion.

Even a novice page developer can use a WYSIWYG HTML editor. However, to perform at even a modest level of competency, the user must be computer literate. To be effective in the tag-oriented model, a person should be computer literate and should understand at least basic HTML.

Editor Components

Our goal here is to sample some of the basic capabilities of HTML editors. Not all editors will have all of these components, and some will have features not mentioned here.

- *Color selector*—Some editors provide a built-in color selector. You can either manipulate three measure bars that control the amounts of red, green, and blue, or you can choose a color from a palette. A small splotch displays the currently selected color. You can then apply that color to any part of the HTML document where colors can be user specified. For example, you could set the background color of a document to the color you selected. In this case, the HTML code for the body tag with the BGCOLOR attribute will automatically be generated and will include the hexadecimal number of the color you selected.

- *Documentation*—Because of their limited nature, early HTML editors were easy to figure out and required no (or extremely little) documentation. If you were computer literate, you could immediately begin using them. However, as HTML editors have become more complex, offering more features, the need for good off-line and on-line documentation has become necessary.

- *HTML converter*—Many editors allow you to input a text file and have it converted directly into an HTML document. The conversion is usually done in a quick-and-dirty, unsophisticated manner that needs to be heavily fine-tuned.

- *Hyperlink inserter*—You can "cut and paste" hyperlinks using most HTML editors. Since URLs are often cumbersome to type, making them inherently error prone, this is an important feature. You can select a URL, say from a bookmark list, and it will be formatted for you in an anchor tag.

- *Spell checker*—It is always a good idea to run your HTML documents through a spell checker. A built-in spell checker is featured in many HTML editors. This can be used as a first pass to eliminate typos; however, mixups such as "there" versus "their" need to be flushed out by hand.

  There are separate spell-checking programs that are often more comprehensive than those included with HTML editors. However, since most on-line dictionaries may not contain HTML tags, you may be frustrated when the spell checker complains all too often about "words" like SRC.

- *Tag generator*—Most HTML editors allow you to select from a wide range of tags by clicking on menu items. Others allow you to type in tags directly. Once you have selected the desired tag, a *dialog box* is usually presented, so you can enter the text to be formatted.

- *Template creator*—Some editors provide you with a variety of predefined HTML templates. For example, they may have a generic business, personal, and resume page, among others. You can customize these templates to meet your needs by removing the placeholders they have inserted and filling in your own information. Other editors allow you to create and then load your own templates.

- *Tutorial*—A number of editors provide an interactive tutorial. This is usually a very good way to learn how to use a complicated HTML editor.

- *Viewer*—Not all HTML editors are WYSIWYG. However, most provide a *viewer* (sometimes called a real-time viewer) so that you can see what the document you have created will look like on-line. That is, you can view a locally rendered copy of the document without having to put it up on the Web.

Editor Usage

Computer-literate users who are not planning to design complex Web presentations can make excellent use of HTML editors, even if they have little or no HTML knowledge. For experienced HTML programmers, editors can serve at least three useful functions:

- They allow you to generate a draft of a page quickly. That is, you can create a prototype of the page, with many of the tags inserted for you. If you decide to use an HTML editor to help you generate a page, you will definitely want to go in later and edit the code by hand. Some of the code an editor produces will probably look strange. You should therefore make its style consistent with your other pages, so that future maintenance[2] of the pages will be easier. Additionally, you will probably need to fine-tune a number of items and code more complex structures from scratch.

- They can facilitate the development of a collection of pages that is expected to be around for a while. As HTML rapidly evolves, future versions may not support all of the older tags, and bugs that rendered without problems in previous versions of HTML may cause problems in newer versions. It is therefore important to develop code that meets

Hot Topic

---

2   We note that in the realm of programming, much more time is usually spent maintaining a program than in actually developing it. This is especially true if the program is rushed to market, or is not carefully documented the first time around.

certain specifications, especially for pages that will be around longer. Some current editors strictly enforce HTML syntax. For example, they might generate code that complies with the HTML 4.0 standard and prohibit any code that does not. If a user tries to do something that is illegal in HTML 4.0, the editor will complain.

- They can help in developing a consistent set of pages. If you use the HTML editor to develop all of the basic parts of each page, the code in these sections will be consistent. This could simplify future maintenance. If you do produce a lot of code using an editor, you should comment the code to indicate which editor you used.

Editor Drawbacks

In spite of their convenience, HTML editors have a number of drawbacks.

- *Feature-itis*—With dozens of companies producing HTML editors, the competition in the marketplace is fierce. One benchmark used in evaluating HTML editors is the number of features they contain. As a result, the new HTML editors are overloaded with features. (They are *fatware*.) They are no longer straightforward to use, and the number of choices they offer can be overwhelming.

- *Incomplete support*—More sophisticated HTML elements may be missing, or may be dealt with in only a limited capacity. Unfortunately, these are the items that beginners need the most help with. The classic examples of tags that are not fully supported are frameset and table.

- *Poor error reporting*—If there is a bug in your code, the HTML editor may not be that effective in letting you know where it is and how to correct it. For novice users who cannot debug their own code, this can create a serious problem.

- *Programming style*—The programming style of the editor may be quite different from yours. By the time you are done editing the code generated for you, you may decide that it would have been easier to start from scratch. For example, not all editors allow you to choose between lowercase and uppercase tags. If you greatly prefer one style to the other and have a large set of pages using your style, you may decide not to use an editor. When you start to hand-tune editor code, you may have to spend some time figuring out how the editor's code works.

- *User interface*—Because of the increased number of features in HTML editors, the user interface has become crowded, more complex, and in some cases, awkward. It is no longer easy to figure out what all of the available features are and how to use them. Furthermore, you may end up having to mouse click many times in order to accomplish anything significant.

Editor Availability

Go On-Line

Many HTML editors are currently on the market. A few that we are familiar with are listed here. Reviews of each and information about how to obtain your own copy can be found on the Web.

- *Frontpage*, Microsoft (Microsoft Windows).

- *HotDog Pro*, Sausage Software (Microsoft Windows).

- *HoTMetaL*, SoftQuad (Microsoft Windows).

- *Navigator Gold*, Netscape (Mac, Microsoft Windows, UNIX).

- *SiteMill*, Adobe (Mac).

9.6.2   Syntax Checkers

Go On-Line

An *HTML syntax checker* is a program that processes an HTML document to see if there are any coding errors (bugs) in it. A syntax checker is a *compiler* for HTML. Figure 9.12 shows the *Doctor HTML* syntax checker's Web page. In addition to reporting syntax errors, such as "missing ending tag," "undefined tag," and so on, syntax checkers often provide a number of other useful features. Some of these features are as follows:

- *Code analysis*—Some syntax checkers provide you with statistics about your code, such as how many hyperlinks, images, and tables you used.

- *Error report*—Error reporting is the main function of a syntax checker. Although your code may look fine when rendered on your platform, there could still be bugs in it. The problems might manifest themselves when a different browser is used.

- *Feature subsetting*—You have the option to select only those tests that you want the syntax checker to perform. For example, you may only want to obtain the "code analysis," "error report," and "structure report."

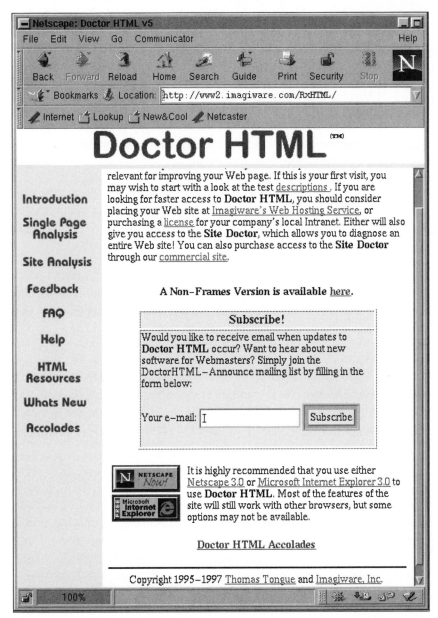

FIGURE 9.12
The doctor HTML syntax checker (www2.imagiware.com/RxHTML).

- *Image analysis*—You may be presented with statistics about each image; for example, its size and its load time over a 28.8 Kbps modem line. This information could alert you to what is causing your page to take so long to load.

- *Link verification*—Many syntax checkers will try to follow all of the hyperlinks in your document and report back those it was unable to access. This notifies you that some of your hyperlinks may be out of date. Bookmark editors have a similar feature to test for outdated bookmarks.

- *Spell checking*—The same comments we made for an HTML editor's spell checker apply here.

- *Structure report*—The syntax checker may pretty-print your program's tags by eliminating all intervening text and using indentation. This makes it easier to locate coding errors.

- *Making suggestions*—Some syntax checkers will provide you with suggestions that may help your page load faster. For example, the syntax checker may report all images that did not have the HEIGHT and WIDTH attributes specified.

- *Load timing*—An estimate of how long it will take your page and its in-line images to load over a 14.4 or 28.8 Kbps modem line is usually given. This information can then be taken into consideration if you are planning to add another image to the page.

Useful Item

From beginners to experts, nearly everyone can benefit from the use of a good syntax checker. We recommend using a syntax checker to help you with the final cleanup of an HTML document. However, do not rely on a syntax checker to debug every few lines of code during the development process. This is a very inefficient use of a syntax checker.

Syntax Checker Availability

Some syntax checkers can be used over the Internet by submitting a form containing the URL of the document you want processed. The ACTION associated with the form is the syntax checker. When you submit a URL over the Internet, the platform on which you are running does not matter. The analysis is done on another machine and the results are sent back to your browser.

Most syntax checkers will not work with *secure servers*. Also, the free syntax checkers may not include all of the features of the commercial versions; nevertheless, they can be quite useful.

Go On-Line

A limited number of good HTML syntax checkers are available. Here we mention a few with which we are familiar. Reviews of each and information about how to obtain your own copy (if available) can be found on the Web.

- *Doctor HTML*, Thomas Tongue and Imagiware, Inc.

- *Dr. Watson*, Cliff Addy of Addy & Associates.

- *Weblint*, Neil Bowers.

9.6.3   Converters

An *HTML converter* program takes one type of document as input and produces the same information in an HTML format. Figure 9.13 illustrates the idea. An HTML converter must strip out all of the document's original formatting information and replace it with the appropriate HTML tags. In Figure 9.13, we have indicated an increase in size from the plaintext file caused by the insertion of HTML tags.

There are converters for plaintext, LATEX, and Microsoft Word documents, among others. The quality of the HTML documents produced varies widely, depending on both the converter used and the format (and complexity) of the original document. In general, a large amount of fine-tuning will be necessary.

Many entities that have their information in a non-HTML format use converters to obtain a quick-and-dirty on-line presentation. The results are often less than desirable. The same remarks we made about the style of the code produced by HTML editors apply here. You will need to do extensive editing to transform the generated HTML document into your own style.

Useful Item

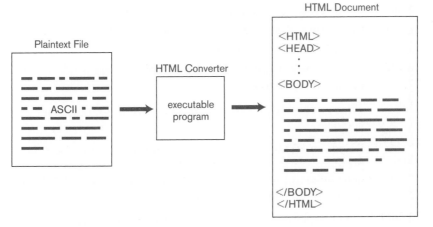

FIGURE 9.13
The process of transforming a document from one format into HTML format, using an HTML converter.

In this case, the plaintext document has increased in size because of the insertion of HTML tags.

On-line Résumé

After careful consideration, you may decide that you want to have an on-line résumé. If you currently have your résumé in an ASCII text file, you could display it that way using a MIME file extension of `.txt`. Alternatively, you can use an HTML converter to generate an on-line version from your current format. If you do this, you will need to hand-tune the HTML code that the converter produces.

You may decide, for example, that the on-line version is not going to look best if it is exactly like the off-line version. In this case, you will need to make some adjustments. Another way to put your résumé on-line would be to start from a resume template, such as one provided by an HTML editor. Using these templates, for the most part, you simply need to insert your personal information in the predefined fields.

The final option, which requires the most work but probably yields the best results, is to reformat your résumé from scratch in the manner that you think it would appear best on-line and then code it directly.

The interested reader may pursue the references to learn more about HTML tools and to find links to many of the tools that are currently available. New software is constantly being released.

EXERCISES 9.6

HTML Tools

41. Choose one HTML editor. Review it and design a Web page using it. Describe your experience.

42. Select an HTML editor that provides templates. Develop a page using one of them. Were you satisfied with the end result, or did it need a lot of hand-tuning?

43. Do you think a good HTML editor can replace a good HTML programmer? Explain.

44. Choose one HTML syntax checker. Review it and explain your findings.

45. Select an HTML syntax checker. Run one of your more complicated Web pages through it. Were any bugs detected? Did you gather any useful information about your document? Do you think you will use such a tool in the future?

46. What predictions do you have about the future of HTML converters? Review one HTML converter.

47. Try one HTML converter on a document format of your choice. Were you pleased with the resulting HTML document's appearance? Why? Was the converter's documentation easy to understand and complete?

48. Develop an on-line résumé using whatever method you feel generates the best results.

9.7 Next-Generation HTML

HTML is rapidly evolving. Companies such as Netscape and Microsoft develop and incorporate new HTML features into their browsers long before the features are standardized. In fact, this has been one of the driving forces behind the evolution of HTML. With a wider range of browsing tools available and a growing number of Web users, standards must be maintained in order for everyone to be able to view everyone else's pages, regardless of the platform being used.

Hot Topic

The W3C released a working draft of the HTML 4.0 specification in September 1997 and released a working draft of HTML 4.01 in December 1999. In these versions of HTML, a number of new tags have been added, deprecated tags have been phased out, and still others have been extended through attributes. For the most part, the succeeding versions of HTML have been backward-compatible.

A separate effort has focused on the *eXtensible Markup Language* (*XML*) that will support user-defined tags. The W3C is recommending XHTML 1.0 as the latest release of HTML. This version combines HTML version 4 with XML. A lot of effort is also being focused on *Cascading Style Sheets* (*CSS*), which afford HTML developers more flexibility in creating sets of pages. We discuss these in the next section. A great deal of on-line information is devoted to the latest breaking news about HTML. This information is best traced through W3C's Web page.

Go On-Line

EXERCISES 9.7

Next-Generation HTML

49. Research recent trends in HTML. Report on one issue of interest. What is the version number of the latest HTML release?

50. What is the *Standard Generalized Markup Language* (*SGML*)? How does it differ from HTML?

51. Research the layer, <LAYER>, and span, <SPAN>, tags. Describe them. Does your browser support them?

9.8   Cascading Style Sheets

The goal of this section is to provide you with an introduction to *Cascading Style Sheets* (*CSS*), or *styles* for short. You will learn the basics of CSS and how to use in-line, internal, and external styles. We will look at examples of all three ways to use styles. This is not a comprehensive description of CSS. Since CSS are an evolving topic, it is best to obtain the latest information about them on the Web. This additional material can be traced through the references provided with this book or by entering a query of "Cascading Style Sheets" to your favorite search engine. When including styles on a Web page, it is a good idea to test them out on both IE and Netscape browsers in order to verify that the styles are working as intended.

Go On-Line

9.8.1   Introduction

Hot Topic

The presentation style of material on the Web is evolving rapidly. It used to be that content was the only issue that mattered. Now, however, the form and style of the material is also very important. CSS allow the user to exercise greater control over how their work appears on the Web. Thus far, we have studied many different HTML tags with a focus on putting content on a Web page. We have also looked at tags and attributes of tags to improve the appearance of our content. For example, we have seen how to change the color of a text item using the COLOR attribute of the <FONT> tag. CSS allow us to do a lot more in terms of creating and manipulating the appearance and feel of a Web page. We can justify text, alter the spacing between lines of text, change the color of the background behind text, and so on. More importantly, we can essentially redefine individual tags to create a certain appearance, impose a style for an entire Web page, and even define a style that can be applied consistently to an entire collection of Web pages. These effects can be achieved using *in-line styles, internal styles,* and *external styles,* respectively. In the next three sections we visit each of these in turn. Following this, we describe the advantages and disadvantages of CSS.

9.8.2 In-line Styles

An *in-line style* allows you to change the behavior of an HTML tag to achieve a desired appearance. The change effected by the in-line style is a local one. That is, it applies only to the single tag where the in-line style is included. To make this discussion concrete, we consider a simple example in which we explain how to use in-line styles. This is followed by a more complex example.

We have already seen how to use the various heading tags. For example, the code

```
<H5>In-line/On-line: Cascading Style Sheets,
Inline Style</H5>
```

is used to include a level five heading of "In-line/On-line: Cascading Style Sheets, Inline Style" on a Web page. Graphical browsers render this code in a normal, bold font in a browser-specified font size. Using an in-line style, this heading could be rendered, for example, in italics as follows:

```
<H5 STYLE = "font-style:italic">In-line/On-line: Cascading
Style Sheets, Inline Style</H5>
```

Notice here the STYLE attribute of the heading tag is used. The attribute value font-style:italic tells the browser to render this heading in italics. Notice the font-style property is assigned a value of italic and that a colon separates the property from its value. White space around the colon is not significant, although it is common practice not to leave any extra spaces around the colon.

Various properties can be combined to create all sorts of headings. For example, the following code

```
<H5 STYLE = "background:gray;text-transform:uppercase;
text-align:center; font-style:italic">In-line/On-line:
Cascading Style Sheets, Inline Style</H5>
```

produces a heading of "In-line/On-line: Cascading Style Sheets, Inline Style" that has a gray background, is all in uppercase letters, has the text centered, and appears in italics. Notice that the various properties are separated from each other by semicolons, and again properties and their values are separated by colons. Note also that some of these effects, but not all, can be achieved using the ALIGN attribute of the <H5> tag and the <FONT> tag with appropriate attributes.

In what follows we show the code for a portion of an HTML document that uses in-line styles in conjunction with the heading tag.

```
<H5>In-line/On-line: Cascading Style Sheets,
Inline Style</H5>

<H5 STYLE = "text-align:center">In-line/On-line: Cascading
Style Sheets, Inline Style</H5>

<H5 STYLE = "font-style:italic">In-line/On-line: Cascading
Style Sheets, Inline Style</H5>

<H5 STYLE = "text-transform:uppercase">In-line/On-line:
Cascading Style Sheets, Inline Style</H5>

<H5 STYLE = "background:gray">In-line/On-line: Cascading
Style Sheets, Inline Style</H5>

<H5 STYLE = "text-align:center;font-style:italic">
In-line/On-line: Cascading Style Sheets, Inline Style</H5>

<H5 STYLE = "background:gray;text-transform:uppercase;
text-align:center; font-style:italic">In-line/On-line:
Cascading Style Sheets, Inline Style</H5>

<H5 STYLE = "color:blue">In-line/On-line: Cascading Style
Sheets, Inline Style</H5>

<H5 STYLE = "font-style:italic; color:blue">
In-line/On-line: Cascading Style Sheets, Inline Style</H5>
```

The first line of code depicts a standard use of the <H5> tag. The default use of the <H5> tag is included for comparison purposes in the figures that follow. This line of code is followed by examples where an in-line style is used to center text, put text in italics, transform text to all uppercase letters, and include a gray background behind the text. Following these four styles are several examples where various properties are combined. First the header is centered and put in italics, and then put with a gray background, in uppercase letters, centered, and in italics. The last two <H5> tags show how to include color using in-line styles. Figure 9.14 shows how Netscape renders these in-line styles and Figure 9.15 shows how IE renders them.

Notice that although the figures do not appear identical, both versions of the browsers with which we took the snapshots support all of the properties used here. The most notable difference is how the background property is handled. The Netscape browser fills in a color background just around the box of text itself, whereas IE fills in the entire line.

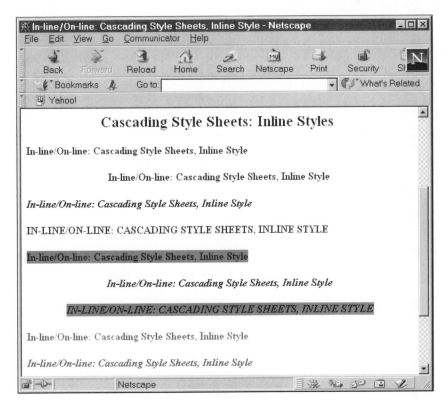

FIGURE 9.14
In-line styles
rendered by
Netscape.

It is important to remark that although the examples presented in this section all pertained to the heading tag, in fact, in-line style properties can be applied to most HTML tags. We will see examples of how the style of various other tags can be affected in the next couple of sections.

To obtain the latest information about what properties are supported by which browsers and to find a list of which properties are available, you can search on-line for "Cascading Style Sheets" or pursue the references provided with this book.

Go On-Line

9.8.3 Internal Styles

You have seen how to use in-line styles to alter the display properties of a given HTML tag. This may come in handy from time to time, but you can get more utility out of defining styles that can be applied to all of the tags in an HTML document. In other words, a style is more useful if it can be applied globally rather than locally. For example, using in-line styles, if you want each <H1> header tag to have the same appearance throughout a document, then the properties associated with the <H1> tag that are desired need to be repeated each time the <H1> tag is used. If you decide to

FIGURE 9.15
In-line styles
rendered by
Internet Explorer.

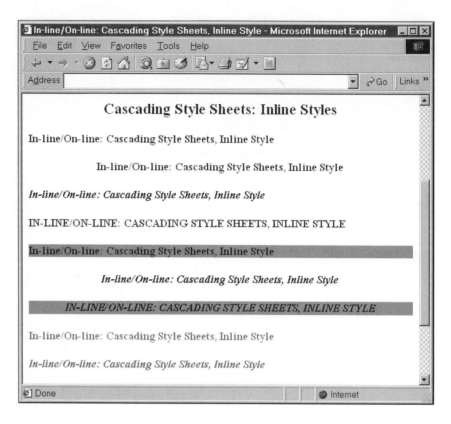

change the style of the <H1> tag, then all <H1> tags scattered throughout the document need to be found and edited. This is a cumbersome process. The concept of *internal styles* can be used to define tag properties that are applied globally throughout a document.

The following HTML code fragment illustrates how a global style for a document can be defined using internal styles.

```
<HEAD>
<TITLE>In-line/On-line: Cascading Style Sheets,
Internal Style</TITLE>
<META NAME = "keywords"
      CONTENT = "Internet, Web, World Wide Web,
                 tutorial, guide, teaching,
                 book, textbook, learning, Java,
                 Javascript, HTML">
<STYLE>
<!--
H3 {background:gray;text-align:center}
```

```
H4, H5 {text-align:center;text-transform:uppercase}
P {font-style:italic;text-align:justify}
-->
</STYLE>
</HEAD>

<BODY BGCOLOR = "#FFFFFF">

<H3>
Cascading Style Sheets: Internal Styles
</H3>

<H4>A Sample Paragraph</H4>

<P>
This text should appear in italics on browsers that
support style sheets.  It should also appear justified
along both margins.  One could also use other properties
in order to create an even fancier
paragraph.  However, don't go overboard.
Remember, content is also very important.
</P>

<H5 STYLE = "background:gray">
&copy; <A HREF = "http://www.mhhe.com/">McGraw-Hill</A>
1997. All rights reserved.
</H5>
```

The new item featured here is the <STYLE> tag. The <STYLE> tag is used to define global properties within an HTML document. It has a corresponding ending tag of </STYLE>. Notice this tag must be included within the head portion of an HTML document. In the sample code, we have included the material inside the <STYLE> tag as an HTML comment. This allows browsers that do not handle styles to render the page correctly, albeit without including any style elements.

In this HTML code fragment there are three lines that define styles. We consider the first line in order to describe the syntax used within the <STYLE> tag.

```
H3 {background:gray;text-align:center}
```

The syntax is to include on the left the HTML tag being modified, followed by an open bracket ({), followed by a list of property:value pairs separated by semicolons, and lastly a closing bracket (}). The code given here says that for all <H3> tags used in this HTML document, include a gray background and center them. Notice that to change all <H3> tags to have a blue background color, only one change needs to be made—replace the word `gray` with `blue`. This example demonstrates how internal styles can be used to create a Web page with a consistent look and feel, and how easy it is to modify the page's overall style.

The second line in the sample HTML code illustrates how to specify the same properties and values for two tags at once.

```
H4, H5 {text-align:center;text-transform:uppercase}
```

In this case, <H4> and <H5> are both set up so they center their headings in uppercase letters. In general, tags that are to have the same appearance can be specified in a comma-separated list.

The third line of code in the <STYLE> tag defines all paragraph environments throughout the document to be in italics and right justified.

```
P {font-style:italic;text-align:justify}
```

Figure 9.16 shows how Netscape renders this internal style, and Figure 9.17 shows how IE renders it.

Both browsers support all of the elements defined by the internal styles specified in the sample code given in this section. For example, notice that the text in the paragraph is right justified. Again, the primary difference is how the background property is handled.

FIGURE 9.16
Internal styles rendered by Netscape.

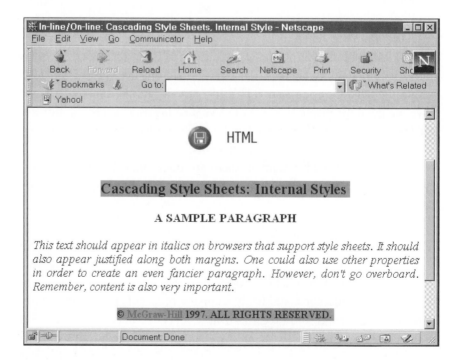

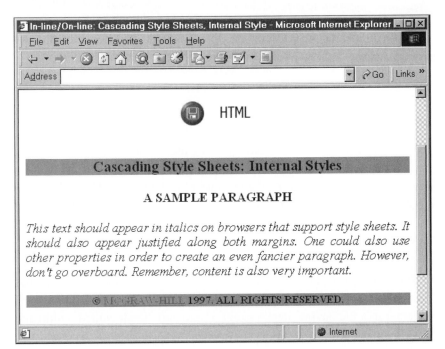

FIGURE 9.17
Internal styles
rendered by
Internet Explorer.

You have no doubt been wondering how Cascading Style Sheets got their name. It is now evident where the style sheets portion of this phrase originated. The cascading part comes from the folding together of properties at various locations in a document. For example, in the preceding code we defined `<H5>` as follows:

```
H4, H5 {text-align:center;text-transform:uppercase}
```

Later on in the document, we included the following code:

```
<H5 STYLE = "background:gray">
&copy; <A HREF = "http://www.mhhe.com/">McGraw-Hill</A>
    1997. All rights reserved.
</H5>
```

Notice in this `<H5>` specification that we have included a gray background. The effect is to cascade the various properties of `<H5>` already specified with those defined here. Thus, the latter `<H5>` is equivalent to the specification

```
H5 {text-align:center;text-transform:uppercase;
    background:gray}
```

In Figures 9.16 and 9.17, you will see that the last `<H5>` was rendered with all of these properties cascaded together. The basic rules for how items

Go On-Line

are cascaded together are as expected. For complex situations involving multiple inclusions of styles one can refer to the references accompanying this book for a detailed explanation of how items cascade together.

9.8.4   External Styles

You have seen that in-line styles are useful for changing the display of individual items and that internal styles are useful for applying a consistent style to all similar elements within a given HTML document. Usually Web presentations consist of more than just a single document. Throughout this book, we have encouraged you to use a consistent format when designing a collection of Web pages. The question is how to do that with style sheets, since neither in-line nor internal styles provide a convenient way to achieve such consistency. The answer to this question is to use *external styles*. External styles allow you to group a set of style declarations together that can be applied to any document. Such declarations can be grouped together in a file having an extension of `css` and then included within any HTML file as desired.

The following HTML code groups three separate style declarations together in a file called `headspars.css`. Any set of style declarations can be grouped similarly.

```
H3 {background:gray;text-align:center}
H4, H5 {text-align:center}
P {font-style:italic;text-align:justify}
```

These declarations can be included in any HTML file, thereby providing a new style for the `<H3>`, `<H4>`, `<H5>`, and `<P>` tags. To include a `css` style file inside any HTML document, one can use the following code:

```
<HEAD>
<TITLE>In-line/On-line: Cascading Style Sheets,
Internal Style</TITLE>

<LINK REL = "stylesheet"
      TYPE = "text/css"
      HREF = "headspars.css">
</HEAD>
```

The `<LINK>` code goes into the head portion of the file in which you want to include the style declarations. The `<LINK>` tag is used here to specify a style sheet with mime type `text/css` having the file name `headspars.css`. Note that the name specified in the `HREF` attribute of the `<LINK>` tag can be either an absolute or relative URL.

Consider the following HTML code fragment:

```
<HEAD>
<TITLE>In-line/On-line: Cascading Style Sheets,
Internal Style</TITLE>
<LINK REL = "stylesheet"
      TYPE = "text/css"
      HREF = "headspars.css">
</HEAD>
<BODY BGCOLOR = "#FFFFFF">
<H3>
Cascading Style Sheets: External Styles
</H3>
<H4>Trail Register Entry</H4>
<P>
The goal is to take a look inside oneself.  To know
oneself. To push oneself.  It is only by pushing beyond
ordinary physical and mental limits that one can achieve
true peace of mind. For if one does not know the
boundary of something, how can one be sure where one
side stops and the other begins?
</P>
<H5>
&copy; <A HREF = "http://www.mhhe.com/">McGraw-Hill</A>
      1997. All rights reserved.
</H5>
```

Assume that the file headspars.css consists of the following style declarations:

```
H3 {background:gray;text-align:center}
H4, H5 {text-align:center}
P {font-style:italic;text-align:justify}
```

Figure 9.18 shows how Netscape renders this external style, and Figure 9.19 shows how IE renders it.

Note that the various elements included in the file headspars.css are supported by both browsers as shown in Figures 9.18 and 9.19. Furthermore, to change the appearance of the document shown in these figures (namely, external.html), one does not need to edit external.html directly. Instead, one can make changes to the file headspars.css.

FIGURE 9.18
External styles
rendered by
Netscape.

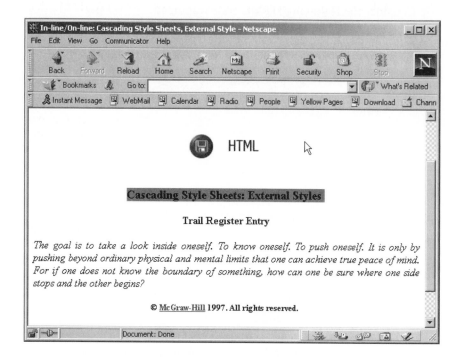

FIGURE 9.19
External styles
rendered by
Internet Explorer.

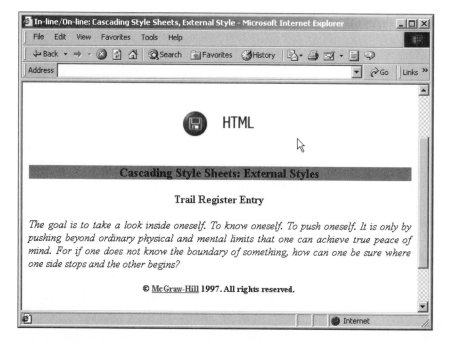

The file `headspars.css` can be included in any number of HTML documents, not just the file `external.html`. For example, if `headspars.css` is included in files `A.html`, `B.html`, and `C.html`, then all three of these files will render `<H3>`, `<H4>`, `<H5>`, and `<P>` tags similarly (assuming no other styles are embedded in any of the files).

It should be clear now that external style sheets are very powerful. They can be used to create a master layout for each document in a Web presentation. Changes to the entire presentation can be achieved by editing the master style sheet.

9.8.5   Advantages and Disadvantages of CSS

In this section, we summarize the advantages and disadvantages of CSS. The key advantages of style sheets are that they allow you to

Hot Topic

- collect all style definitions together in one place

- reduce time for maintaining a set of Web pages

- test new layouts for a collection of Web pages with only a few global edits

- create a master layout for a Web presentation

The primary disadvantages of style sheets are that

- they are not supported in a consistent manner by all browsers

- if you make a syntax error, it can be hard to debug your code

The advantages of style sheets outweigh their disadvantages. Style sheets are becoming more popular, and you can expect to see a wider use of them in the future.

EXERCISES 9.8

Cascading Style Sheets

52.   Write an in-line style for producing an `<H2>` heading tag that has a blue background, is in italics, and is centered. The content of the header should be "Appalachian Trail." Write HTML code to

generate the same effects, but do not use any style elements to produce the effects. Compare and contrast the two pieces of code.

53. Write an in-line style for the <P> tag that produces italics and double-spaced paragraphs.

54. What are the six font properties specified by the CSS standard?

55. What is the *text-decoration* property, and what values can it take? Provide an example illustrating how this property is used.

56. Write an internal style for producing an <H2> heading tag that has a blue background, is in italics, and is centered.

57. Create an HTML document that contains an internal style that formats paragraphs so that they appear double-spaced. The document should consist of three paragraphs: one that lists the state flower of each state along the Appalachian Trail, one that lists the state bird of each state along the Appalachian Trail, and a third that lists each state you have traveled in.

58. Suppose you are out hiking the Appalachian Trail and meet a thru-hiker who is keeping updates on a Web page about her hike as she goes along. Write a paragraph or two in response to her question, "How can external style sheets help me enhance my presentation?"

59. Write sample HTML code to include the external style sheet `hike.css` in the file `at.html`. Assume that the two files reside in the same directory.

60. What elements do you feel should be specified in a master external style sheet?

61. Provide the URLs of two Web pages that discuss Cascading Style Sheets.

62. Write a summary describing how Cascading Style Sheets can be used to modify hyperlinks. Give an example of some sample HTML code where the styles of the <A> tag have been modified.

Newsgroups, Mailing Lists, Chat Rooms, and MUDs

10

There are two words in combination that all English-speaking hikers fear: "deer flies." The deer flies were fierce in Connecticut. I had already dealt with waist-high poison ivy, chiggers, seven-foot-high stinging nettles, hurricane volumes of rain, spider bites, mice, black flies, and mosquitos; so now I dealt with deer flies, too. No insect was going to turn me back from my dream now. There were a lot of streams in Connecticut and the trail was very wooded. I was able to make excellent progress there. I also found a deli that had the most delicious meatballs I have ever had. Some day I will return to it.

Connecticut

52 miles

Chapter 10

10.1 INTRODUCTION

In this chapter you will learn about *newsgroups*, *mailing lists*, *chat rooms*, and *Multi-User Dimensions (MUDs)*. The topics covered include:

Objectives

- The history of newsgroups and mailing lists

- Newsgroup fundamentals

  - Newsgroup terminology
  - The basic functions of newsreaders
  - Newsgroup postings and newsgroup netiquette
  - Newsgroup functions

- Mailing list fundamentals

- Mailing list terminology

  - Mailing list subscriptions and postings
  - Mailing list inner workings

- Newsgroup and mailing list availability

- Chat room principles

- Multi-User Dungeons or Dimensions (MUDs) and their use

10.2 Newsgroups and Mailing Lists History

Newsgroups and *mailing lists* allow the exchange of electronic messages on a stated focus or purpose among numbers of readers ranging from a few dozen to tens of thousands or more. The differences, as we shall see, are primarily in the way distribution occurs and in what is meant by a subscription. There are also some style and content differences, though some discussions are distributed in both formats.

A newsgroup is an electronic forum that allows users from all over the world to participate in a discussion about a specific topic. There are currently tens of thousands of newsgroups, covering nearly every imaginable subject area.

A mailing list is an electronic list of email addresses that can be used to send email to each member on the list. Here, we use the term *mailing list* to refer to the nearly 100,000 mailing lists currently available all over the world. In most cases, individual lists deal with specific subjects. Contrast these types of mailing lists with your own personal email distribution list.

New newsgroups and mailing lists are continually being formed, and some of the older, less popular ones are occasionally phased out. Tens of millions of users participate in newsgroups and mailing lists, and each day about a gigabyte[1] of "new information" is generated. In fact, more data is generated in a single day than nearly anyone reads in a lifetime. The distribution of audio, video, and image binaries greatly increases these numbers.

Hot Topic

Newsgroups got their start in the late 1970s. The first newsgroup was set up between Duke University and the University of North Carolina at Chapel Hill. The newsgroup functioned like a *bulletin board system* (*BBS*), through which information about the events in the area could be shared by people at the two schools. Gradually, the software for implementing this "discussion group" was distributed more widely. Additional sites began exchanging information and new discussion groups were added. As the system evolved, experiencing incredible growth, the way in which the news was distributed had to be changed and new protocols had to be developed to handle the increased load.

Mailing lists were formed in the early 1980s. Many of the original mailing lists got their start on BITNET. BITNET did not originally use TCP/IP protocols. In fact, it was formed as a low-cost alternative, given the relatively high cost of supporting TCP/IP network links at the time. In the early stages of BITNET, the participants were universities. As a result, most of the original mailing lists dealt with research and technically oriented hobbies and topics. Over time, the number of mailing lists expanded greatly, and there are now mailing lists on nearly every subject imaginable.

The manner in which mailing lists handle the vastly increased traffic also evolved over time. Before the development of the Internet in its present form, there was much reliance on *packet switching* over 9600-baud lines,

---

1   Recall, a byte consists of 8 bits. A gigabyte consists of a billion bytes.

for both news and email. This was sometimes limited just to late at night, to obtain the lowest rates.

As we get further into our discussion about newsgroups and mailing lists, the differences between the two will become more apparent.

EXERCISES 10.2

Newsgroups and Mailing Lists History

1.   How many newsgroups are there now? How many mailing lists are there now?

2.   Can you locate a newsgroup about backpacking? About the Appalachian Trail? Can you locate a mailing list about backpacking? About the Appalachian Trail?

3.   Plot the number of newsgroups from their origins until the present. What kinds of relationships do you see in the data?

4.   Plot the number of mailing lists from their origins until the present. What kinds of relationships do you see in the data?

5.   What does USENET mean?

6.   Determine as many of the following items as possible. List your sources.
     (a) How many users read newsgroups?
     (b) How many new messages are generated and sent to newsgroups each day?
     (c) How many bytes of news are generated each day?

7.   Choose either newsgroups or mailing lists and develop a Web page explaining their history. Try to be as detailed as possible. List your sources on your Web page.

10.3   Newsgroup Fundamentals

Hot Topic

A newsgroup is a discussion group in which computer users throughout the world participate. Users interested in a particular topic may subscribe to the same newsgroup. Boundaries such as age, gender, and background generally do not play a role in the discussion, since users usually only see messages from each other. Someone can email a message, called an *article*, to the newsgroup at any time. The message then becomes available

```
    Subject: Welcome!
       Date: Mon, 13 Oct 1997 12:48:21 -0400
       From: "Mark L. Bochert" <mbochert@cs.unh.edu>
Organization: University of New Hampshire - Durham, NH
 Newsgroups: unh.cs.cs403-10

Welcome to the CS403-10 news group. This group is for the exclusive use
of the CS403 section 10 students at the University of New Hampshire for
the Fall 1997 semester. The group provides a forum for discussing
topics relating to the course work. Feel free to post messages with
questions,
answers, comments, or anything else (almost) that you think your
classmates might be interested in,
and perhaps it will start a discussion. In addition, feel free to use
the group to become acquainted with using newsgroups, for example to
practice posting messages (something very much frowned upon in most news
groups.)

Send questions to:
Mark Bochert  mbochert@christa.unh.edu
```

FIGURE 10.1

An example of a news article.

for others to read. They can then respond to the article, sharing their opinions or expertise. This in turn may stimulate others to respond. In this way, a question or an opinion can create a lively and lengthy discussion.

10.3.1 Newsgroup Terminology

Most of the terminology for newsgroups is borrowed from newspaper news. The meanings of most terms are straightforward.

article—A message written and sent to a newsgroup. An example is shown in Figure 10.1.

post—A synonym for article.

posting—The process of sending an article to a newsgroup.

follow-up—An article that is posted in response to a previous newsgroup article.

thread—A collection of one or more follow-up articles, together with the original posting.

subscribe—The procedure you follow to add a newsgroup to the list of those you read on a regular basis. Once subscribed, you will receive

FIGURE 10.2
A sample
newsreader's
user interface.

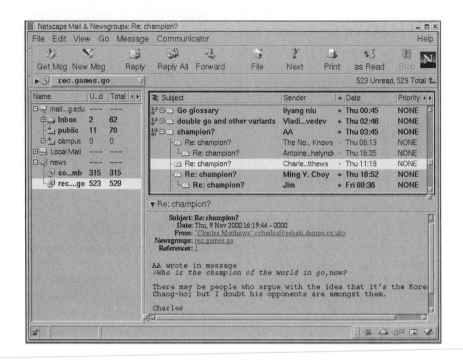

the new postings of the newsgroup. The subscription is also used to track which messages in a group you have seen. In most cases, subscriptions do not cost money.

unsubscribe—The process of removing a newsgroup from the list of those that you read. You must have been subscribed in order to unsubscribe.

newsreader—A program that serves as the user interface for newsgroups. Newsreaders allow you to read, post, subscribe, and unsubscribe from newsgroups, among other things. You should select a newsreader that also displays threads. Figure 10.2 provides a screen shot of the Netscape newsreader. The descriptive labels on the pop-up menus and buttons provide a good indication of the functions the newsreader offers.

news client—A synonym for newsreader.

expired news—News that is removed from a system, usually after a short period of time. A huge number of new articles are posted daily. It is neither possible nor desirable for many sites to store this tremendous volume of news for more than a few days, or at most a couple of weeks. Important or generally informative posts are often

Useful Item

sent to a newsgroup on a periodic basis, so that new subscribers can read them.

news server—A computer that saves, forwards, and manages news articles. Normally, each organization runs its own news server and limits access to its customers or user community.

newsfeed—A news server that provides recent articles to a news client. The term also encompasses the process of delivering the news articles themselves.

way-station—A news server that functions as a newsfeed for at least two (and usually many more) other sites.

Network News Transfer Protocol (NNTP)—The protocol used for distributing news articles.

news administrator—A person who is in charge of running a news server. The news system is distributed, and each site that receives and posts news must have a site administrator. This person is in charge of determining what news will be received by the site. Administrators can also add or delete newsgroups. The email address for this person is usually `newsmaster@domain`, where `domain` is replaced by the appropriate site name.

news moderator—A person associated with a specific newsgroup, who reads and critically evaluates all articles submitted for posting to the newsgroup, and then decides whether or not each article should be posted. Moderators serve as a (primitive) sort of quality control. They either accept an article to post or reject it. The job of news moderator is time-consuming, voluntary, and often thankless.

moderated newsgroup—A newsgroup that has a moderator.

unmoderated newsgroup—A newsgroup that has no moderator. Because a good moderator can filter out poor or irrelevant posts, moderated newsgroup posts sometime have more valuable content than unmoderated newsgroup articles. The vast majority of newsgroups are unmoderated, which is why they are so vulnerable to spam. A much higher fraction of mailing lists is moderated.

cross-post—The process of simultaneously submitting the same article to two or more newsgroups.

digest—A collection of related articles, usually edited, that is posted as a single article to a newsgroup.

kill files—A filter based on names or topics that you specify, so that you are not even shown those messages.

10.3.2   Newsreaders

As defined earlier, a newsreader is a program that serves as the user interface with newsgroups. Figure 10.2 depicts a typical newsreader's interface. The functionality of the graphical buttons make reading the news very easy. In the past, most newsreaders were keyboard-driven, typically cryptic, and unfriendly by today's expectations. Pine has a built-in newsreader, and UNIX has several newsreaders to choose from, including `rn` and `slrn`. Many Web browsers have built-in newsreaders, which makes reading news a much more enjoyable and interactive process; hyperlinks can be followed right from within a news article.

Useful Item

It is always a good idea to begin reading a newsgroup for a while before posting to it. This will give you a feel for the types of posts that are suitable for that newsgroup.

Newsreader Interface

We will examine the Netscape newsreader; other newsreaders operate in a similar manner. The screen in Figure 10.2 is divided into several panels. Netscape allows you to resize the relative proportions of the panels, as well as the columns within the panels. At the top are several pull-down menus, with the headings **File**, **Edit**, **View**, **Go**, **Message**, and **Communicator**. Here, we briefly elaborate on the functions of each menu. As is customary for menus, menu items that are not available for the current configuration of the newsreader are shown in a lighter gray color.

Useful Item

- Among other things, the **File** menu allows you to launch a new browser, compose a new email message, compose a new news article, add a newsgroup, get more messages, print a message, and exit the browser.

- The **Edit** menu allows you to undo your most recent action, select a thread, and select all messages, as well as perform basic editing functions.

- The **View** menu item lets you view the article's source, reload, refresh, sort, wrap long lines, and unscramble messages that are encoded in ROT13. ROT13, which stands for "rotation 13," is an *encryption scheme* in which letters are mapped 13 characters further down the alphabet. Table 10.1 illustrates the mapping. Capital letters are

TABLE 10.1

The Mapping Used in the Caesar Cipher Encryption Scheme.

Original Character	Mapped Value	Original Character	Mapped Value
a	n	n	a
b	o	o	b
c	p	p	c
d	q	q	d
e	r	r	e
f	s	s	f
g	t	t	g
h	u	u	h
i	v	v	i
j	w	w	j
k	x	x	k
l	y	y	l
m	z	z	m

similarly mapped. The scheme is used to encode messages that readers might find offensive. For example, a potentially offensive joke might be encoded using ROT13, so that a young child or unsuspecting adult does not accidently stumble across inappropriate language. This code dates back to the time of Julius Caesar and is known in cryptography as a *Caesar cipher*.

- The **Go** menu lets you move to the next message, the previous message, the first unread message, the previous unread message, and marked messages.

- The **Message** menu lets you manipulate a message; for example, you can forward it, reply to it, ignore the thread, and so on.

- The **Communicator** menu provides access to news, mail, your address book, bookmarks, Netscape's HTML editor, and a history mechanism.

Beneath the pull-down menus, there are a number of buttons. For the most part, these are self-explanatory. The most commonly used ones are: post a new article, send email, reply to email, or reply to a posting.

The next part of the news window is divided into two sections. On the top is the name of the newsgroup you are currently reading, and a list of the messages with their subjects. If you click on one of the articles, it will appear in the bottom part of the screen. As shown in Figure 10.2, an article can contain hyperlinks.

Reading News

Reading news is straightforward. In a text-based newsreader, this often amounts to simply entering the number or name of a newsgroup and then entering the number of the article you want to read. In a graphical news-reader, all you need to do is select a newsgroup and then select an article from within the newsgroup.

Since the number of newsgroups is so vast, many people zero in on those that focus on their specific hobbies or newsgroups that may contain answers to their questions. A lot of interesting information can be found in newsgroups, but it can sometimes be time-consuming to locate. We suggest you begin by subscribing to one or two newsgroups in your main areas of interest. You will quickly become familiar with how the newsgroup culture works and will obtain a better sense of how to find something you want. *Deja News*, which is described later in this chapter, can also help you filter the news to locate what is of interest to you. Another strategy is to read the frequently asked questions (FAQs) files of a newsgroup. This is a good way to determine what a newsgroup is about and whether you should subscribe. In addition, the FAQs for certain newsgroups can provide answers to many common technical questions. So, the FAQs serve as an excellent up-to-date on-line help facility.

Posting News

Once you have been reading a newsgroup for a while, you will obtain a sense of what types of postings are appropriate for the group. It is therefore a good idea to look back at the most recent set of articles, to avoid repeating a recent posting. Remember that when you post to a (large) newsgroup, tens of thousands of people could read your message. Therefore, take care in composing the message, and do not post unless you have something worthwhile or new to add. Some users will become highly critical of others and a full-blown *flame war* may erupt. A flame war is a series of messages in which people relentlessly trash each other. Flame wars are unproductive, other than to permit people to let off steam.

Useful Item

When generating an article, follow the netiquette rules we have discussed, as well as the rules for email message composition.

Keeping Track

Newsreaders maintain a data file, often named `newsrc`, that is processed when you activate your newsreader. When you subscribe to a newsgroup, an entry is put in this file. This is how your newsreader "knows" what to show you. Each newsgroup assigns unique `id` numbers to its postings. When you read a posting, the `id` information is updated in your subscription file; that is, the newsreader records the `id` numbers you have read. If you view your news data file, you will see that it looks pretty cryptic, as the file is meant to be read only by a newsreader, not a person. We recommend that you not edit this file; let the newsreader keep it up to date.

Useful Item

10.3.3   Newsgroups Model

Here, we present the basics of how news is propagated around the Internet. More detailed explanations can be obtained by pursuing the references. Figure 10.3 illustrates the manner in which news is distributed around the world.

The three methods by which news is distributed are: *news push*, *news pull* (sometimes also called *news suck*), and *news search*. In news push, the news is delivered without being specifically requested; it is pushed over to the client. In news pull, the client requests the news and has it delivered. The push and pull in essence indicate the party initiating the contact. Since

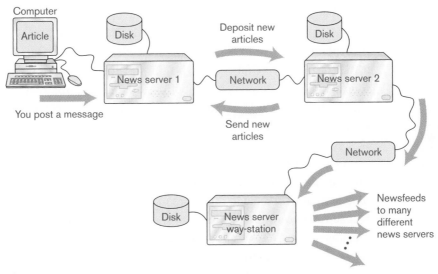

FIGURE 10.3
An illustration of how news articles are propagated throughout the world.

the volume of news is so great and since not all sites are interested in all of the available articles, sites need to filter out the articles that they do not want or have already obtained from a different newsfeed.

At a basic level, in news push, a newsfeed contacts its client and indicates that it has new articles available. The client must respond by telling the newsfeed which articles it wants. The newsfeed then sends over the appropriate articles. In news pull, a news client contacts one of its newsfeeds and asks if there are new articles. The newsfeed responds by listing the new articles available. The client must then determine which articles it needs and must make a request to retrieve those. The newsfeed then sends the articles over the network to the client. In either case, when business is complete, the connections are closed.

The third method of news distribution is called news search. The Web is changing the way a reader may approach newsgroups. This change is possible because major search engines now index newsgroups. *Deja News* is a search engine that specializes in newsgroups.

Go On-Line

Instead of subscribing to newsgroups in the traditional way, many people find it easier to search and browse Deja News. Deja News has a larger collection of newsgroups than most sites, and they often have the postings available before they would be received at an individual site. The *signal-* (good stuff you care about) *to-noise* (uninteresting stuff of no interest to you) *ratio* on many newsgroups is dreadful; the use of a search engine allows you to leapfrog over the unwanted material to find and follow the threads you care about.

In addition, Deja News offers extremely powerful search options not available anywhere else. For example, you can request a profile of all the newsgroups to which any user has posted. This visibility or transparency is revolutionary. For example, using Deja News, someone has constructed a Web page showing newsgroup postings made by public employees, state by state, from state-owned computers and during normal working hours.

Useful Item

Think about this; a prospective employer could do a search for all your postings, maybe discovering something you posted when you were younger or less informed.

Due to the incredible volume of news articles, it is not possible for one machine simply to forward new articles to another machine, have that machine forward them to one more machine, and so on, until the news has reached all news servers in the world. By the time the news reached the last machine it would be too out of date. To propagate the news more rapidly, way-stations are used. A way-station is a news server that distributes articles to a number of other news servers, instead of just one. Figure 10.4 depicts the basic model.

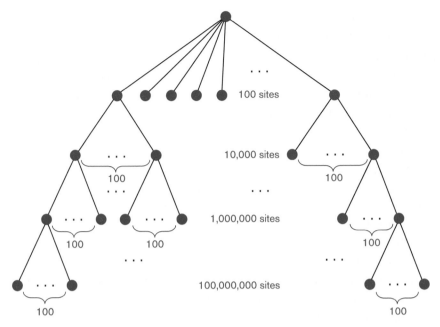

FIGURE 10.4
Fanning out news via way-stations.

If each site fans out to 100 new and different sites, in only four levels of the distribution process a total of 101,010,100 new sites can be reached.

In Figure 10.4, we assume for the sake of simplicity that each way-station connects to 100 new and different sites. After the first level, 100 new sites have acquired the news. In the second level, the 100 way-stations distribute to an additional 10,000 sites. Since the 100 way-stations can be distributing in parallel, this process only takes 100 "distribution steps." At the next level, the 10,000 way-stations can distribute to 1,000,000 new way-stations. Again, if everything is done in parallel, this process only takes 100 distribution steps. Finally, in level four, the 1,000,000 way-stations reach 100,000,000 new sites, again taking the same number of distribution steps. Therefore, in taking only 400 sequential distribution steps, we have reached more sites (101,010,100) than there currently are Internet users!

Clearly, we did not need to go this deep in the distribution tree to propagate news all over the planet. In contrast, if each news server simply connected to a single other one, the whole process would have taken over 100,000,000 steps! By the time the news was distributed using such a scheme, it would have been history. We should remark that news distribution used to be free or very low cost, but greater reliance is now placed on commercial providers such as UUNET.

Let us return to Figure 10.3 for a moment. Suppose you post an article to a newsgroup. The article will first be routed to your news server—call it news server 1. At some future time, say news server 2 asks news server 1 for new articles, in this case using news pull. Assuming your article is not filtered out, it will eventually make its way to news server 2. Similarly, it could wind up at the way-station and from there be rapidly distributed around the Internet. Keep in mind that news is only around for a short period of time before it expires. This is necessary to make room for newly propagated articles.

10.3.4   Newsgroup Hierarchies

News is partitioned into two major categories: *mainstream* and *alternative*. The mainstream category is more prevalent, conventional, and better organized than the alternative one. Table 10.2 shows the hierarchies within the mainstream category and a brief summary of the topics they cover. The alternative category, denoted `alt`, is also considered one of the hierarchies. `Alt` is more radical, more free-form, less widely distributed, and easier to create a newsgroup in. Table 10.3 shows a number of topic areas within the alternative category; most of the headings are self-explanatory.

We should note that not all newsgroups are propagated throughout the entire world. Some have regional restrictions, and the domain of others may be just a college campus. In addition, a news administrator can filter out certain newsgroups that might be inappropriate for a given audience. Thus, even if a newsgroup could be distributed to a particular site, you will not be able to read it unless the news administrator deems it worthy

◾ **TABLE 10.2**

◾ A Listing of Some Popular Mainstream Newsgroup Hierarchies.

Hierarchy Name	Unabbreviated Name	Brief Description
`biz`	business	Any business-related subject.
`comp`	computers	All subjects relevant to computers.
`misc`	miscellaneous	Topics not falling into one of the other groups.
`news`	newsgroups	All subjects relevant to newsgroups themselves.
`rec`	recreational	Yippee.
`sci`	science	Anything science related.
`soc`	social	Social gatherings and social issues.
`talk`	talk	General discussion and debate.

▓▓ **TABLE 10.3**

▓▓ A Listing of Some of the Main Subject Areas in the `alt` Hierarchy.

Topic Name		
animals	art	autos
bbs	binaries	books
building	business	christnet
comedy	comics	culture
current-events	drugs	education
family-names	fan	flame
folklore	food	games
internet	irc	japanese
journalism	med	music
pets	personals	politics
radio	recovery	religion
sci	sex	society
sport	sports	startrek
support	sys	test
tv		

of obtaining. Usually, decisions about which newsgroups to receive are influenced by storage considerations.

A site can create its own local newsgroups that are limited in distribution to the site's domain. Many sites do this.

Several countries have a large number of newsgroups. Table 10.4 summarizes these countries, their approximate number of newsgroups as of this writing, and the corresponding hierarchy names. Many of these newsgroups are not in the English language.

Newsgroup Naming Conventions

A newsgroup name is formed by the hierarchy under which it falls, the main topic area, a more specific subtopic area, and so on, with dots separating the individual elements. For example,

```
rec.animals.wildlife
```

can be split into the hierarchy

```
rec
```

■ TABLE 10.4
■ A Listing of a Few Countries Other Than the United States That Have a Large Number of Newsgroups.

Country Name	#	Hierarchy Name(s)
Australia	110	aus
England	170	uk
Finland	440	finet, sfnet
France	125	fr
Germany	1080	cl, de, z-netz
Italy	160	it
Japan	560	tnn, fj
Norway	130	no
Taiwan	290	tw

the topic

```
animals
```

and the subtopic

```
wildlife
```

Similarly,

```
soc.singles.moderated
```

is a moderated newsgroup in the soc hierarchy discussing issues related to single people. Newsgroups can have as many qualifying pieces as necessary to subdivide a topic to the appropriate level of detail. For example,

```
comp.os.ms-windows.networking.win95
```

has more divisions than usual. Also, there are some bogus or short-lived newsgroups with bizarre names ending in .die.die.die.

We summarize the different levels of organization in news as follows:

1.   Hierarchy.

2.   Specific newsgroup.

3.   Thread.

4.   Individual posting.

10.3.5 Controversy

Newsgroups exist on all topics, and most newsgroups are unmoderated. Some newsgroups deal with controversial subjects. In particular, the language used and the images displayed may be very offensive to some readers. The debate over freedom of expression on the Internet continues.

EXERCISES 10.3

Newsgroup Fundamentals

8. Familiarize yourself with a newsreader available to you. What is its name? Describe some of the features that you like and dislike, and others that you wish it had.

9. Practice subscribing to and reading news. Print out an interesting thread consisting of between three and five messages.

10. Print out a sample news article that was cross-posted. Did it make sense to cross-post this article, or was the author merely spamming?

11. Contrast and compare email and newsgroups.

12. What is one of your hobbies? Is there a newsgroup relating to it? If so, what is the name of the newsgroup? Are you subscribed to it? If not, subscribe to it and report the number of posts in one week's time. How many different threads got started during a one-week interval?

13. Encrypt the message, "Meet me at the shelter," using ROT13. Can you come up with a message at least 10 characters long that, when encrypted, results in another message that makes sense in English? For example, if "the eye of the Tiger" encrypted to "I hate Rocky movies," this would be a solution. Unfortunately, using ROT13, "the eye of the Tiger" maps to "gur rlr bs gur gvtre," which does not make sense without being decoded.

14. Suppose a site receives a single newsfeed from another news server. What happens if the news server crashes? How is this potential problem usually dealt with?

15. Which of the newsgroups shown in the box on page 448 are moderated?

16. Research five newsgroups not mentioned in this chapter. Provide a brief description of the topics they cover.

Go On-Line

ELLEN AND RAY'S CHOICES

Here are a few of our favorite newsgroups. Most of the topics they deal with are self-explanatory.

- `alt.ascii-art`
- `alt.cult-movies`
- `alt.fishing`
- `comp.parallel`
- `comp.theory`
- `k12.ed.comp.literacy`
- `misc.consumers.house`
- `misc.invest.stocks`
- `news.answers`—Frequently asked questions about newsgroups and their answers.
- `rec.art.poems`
- `rec.bicycles.off-road`
- `rec.humor.funny`
- `sci.fractals`—Discussions about *fractals*, that is, self-similar patterns.
- `soc.college.gradinfo`

10.4   Mailing List Fundamentals

A mailing list is a group of users with a shared interest whose email addresses are collected in an electronic list that can be used to send email to each member on the list. The key to a mailing list is a program called a *list server*, which receives and distributes postings and automatically manages subscriptions.

Hot Topic

Mailing lists provide a forum in which users from all over the world can ask questions and have them answered by others with similar interests. They can be a good place to get specialized, difficult-to-obtain information. Mailing lists are also a good vehicle for discussion. Finally, mailing lists are available for nearly every imaginable subject. If you have a hobby or

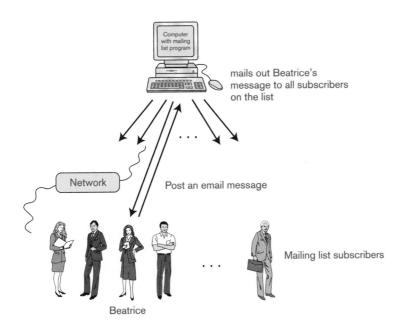

FIGURE 10.5
The basic idea of how an mailing list works.

Most lists are set to send a copy of the posting back to the author as shown, but some lists are set not to do this.

a medical condition that no one in your local area can relate to, you might find at least one mailing list of people with similar interests.

To participate in a mailing list, you only have to know how to use email; you do not have to learn any new software. Contrast this with newsgroups, for which you must learn to operate a newsreader. For a mailing list, a user posts a message to a special mailing list program called the list server, which has the email addresses of all the users subscribed to the list. The list management program then distributes the message to each member on the list via email. The message body consists of the post.

Figure 10.5 illustrates the process. In the picture, we show a computer that handles the mailing list, to which Beatrice is a subscriber. When Beatrice posts a message to the mailing list, the message goes to the computer's list management program. The program then distributes a copy of Beatrice's message to each member of the list. In essence, each member of the list receives an email message that looks like it came from Beatrice.

10.4.1   Mailing List Terminology

Much of the terminology used with newsgroups carries over to mailing lists. For example, article, cross-post, follow-up, post, posting, subscribe, thread, and unsubscribe can all be used in the mailing list setting. In addition, there are moderated and unmoderated mailing lists, as there are for newsgroups. Additional helpful terms are:

subscriber—A person whose email address is on an electronic mailing list. They will receive all posts to the list. Note that for the majority of mailing lists, subscriptions are free.

list owner—The person in charge of a mailing list. While most mailing lists have only one person who handles the administrative duties, sometimes a couple of people may split the responsibilities.

list administrator, list coordinator, and *list manager*—Synonyms for list owner.

lurker—A person who is subscribed to and reads a mailing list, but does not post messages. Such a person is said to lurk.

closed list—A mailing list for which the list owner either accepts or rejects subscriptions. List membership is filtered. It is not possible to subscribe automatically to a closed list. Only postings from subscribers are accepted.

private list—Synonym for closed list.

newbie—A person who only recently joined a mailing list.

open list—A mailing list to which anyone may subscribe. Such a list typically accepts posts even from users who are not subscribers.

edited list—A mailing list in which posts to the lists may be edited by the list owner or moderator.

digested list—A mailing list in which postings are grouped by topic and sent out as batches instead of individually. Sometimes, when you subscribe, you have a choice of getting either individual postings or digests.

10.4.2   Mailing List Subscriptions and Posts

Subscriptions

Mailing lists produce a huge volume of email. Because of this, most people find they can only be active in a few mailing lists at a time.[2]

---

2   It is important not to let your email run out of control and exceed your disk quota (on a central system). If this happens, it often leads to the rejection (return to sender as undeliverable) of subsequent email and may cause the system administrator to disable your account.

■ TABLE 10.5

■ The Platforms on Which the Three Major Mailing List Servers Run, and Their Costs.

Program	Platform(s)	Cost
LISTSERV	UNIX, Win95, WinNT	Scaled to usage; modest for limited usage
LISTPROC	UNIX	$2,000
Majordomo	UNIX	Free

Mailing list subscriptions and deletions are automated for all but the shortest mailing lists. To subscribe, you send an email message, along with subscription instructions, to the computer on which the list is kept. You will need to know the name of the mailing list, the site where the list is maintained, and the name of the program used to manage the mailing list.

A number of different list server programs are available for automating the duties of a list owner. How these programs work is not important for our purposes, but you can trace them through the references, if interested. The programs process commands for subscriptions and deletions, as well as performing other functions. The names of the big three list servers are: LISTPROC, LISTSERV, and majordomo.[3] Table 10.5 describes the platforms on which these programs are available and their costs. It is obvious that LISTPROC is an abbreviation for "list processor" and LISTSERV is an abbreviation for "list server." Some people use the term "Listserv" generically, but it actually refers to a particular mailing list software program.

Let us examine the details of the subscription process by considering an example. Suppose Julia Stone wants to subscribe to the mailing list called `cooking`. Further suppose that the list is managed using the LISTSERV software and that the site where the list is stored is named `food.cook.com`. To subscribe to `cooking`, Julia simply sends an email message to

`LISTSERV@food.cook.com`

with a message body of

`SUBSCRIBE cooking Julia Stone`

---

3   The capitalization of the first two names is unusual and is an artifact of IBM's tendency to capitalize everything. We follow the most common capitalization of these names, but ListProc is bicapitalized by its owners.

The word SUBSCRIBE is a command directed to LISTSERV. The command takes two arguments: a mailing list name, followed by a person's first and last name.[4]

Useful Item

LISTSERV and other mailing list management programs can handle many different commands. One of the most important commands is HELP. It is always a good idea to send this command to the list management software, so that it can reply with a list of the commands that are available. Since the commands you send are being processed by a computer, you must get the syntax and spelling exactly right. If you do not, the command will not be recognized by the list server.

To delete her subscription to cooking, Julia can send the message

    UNSUBSCRIBE cooking

to the address

    LISTSERV@food.cook.com

Many mailing lists assign a password to you, so that you can securely change settings related to your subscription. Otherwise, someone might forge your email address and make unwanted changes.

Although our example deals with LISTSERV, the procedures for subscribing and unsubscribing to a mailing list are similar for the other list servers. Once you have successfully subscribed to a mailing list, the list server will generally send you two messages:

1.   A brief acknowledgement that the subscription was accepted.

2.   A more detailed explanation of commands and their use for the list. At intervals of one to three months, a list owner will often repost this message as a reminder.

Useful Item

It is a good idea to save this information, and you may want to create an email folder called "lists" just for this purpose.

How does the list server know that you really want to subscribe or unsubscribe to a list and that someone else is not using your name? This is an important question that you will address in the exercises.

Posts

When posting to a mailing list, you should follow a set of guidelines similar to those we outlined for newsgroups. Everyone on the list receives the posts,

---

4   Think of the first and last name as a single argument.

and this can be thousands of people for some mailing lists. It is a good idea to consider carefully whether or not your message is appropriate for the list. You often do not know who the other subscribers on a mailing list are, except as you see them make postings. For privacy reasons, many mailing lists make this information off-limits.

When following up on a message, think about whether the reply should be sent to the entire list or to a subset of the list. That is, determine if your post will be of interest to a large number of people on this list, to just the sender, or to a small group of members. If the message is likely to be of interest to only three or so people, send it directly to them. (Of course, sometimes there is no way to gauge the interest level of others until you send the message out and get back a flurry of "Why did you send that to everybody?" messages.)

Suppose Julia[5] wants to post a question to the `cooking` list about accurately determining the interior temperature of a turkey. Each Christmas, Melvin Stone complains that the turkey is overcooked. Julia can simply send her email query to the entire mailing list; that is, her email should be sent to

```
cooking@food.cook.com
```

Notice that the message is sent to the mailing list itself, not to the LISTSERV program. Remember, `cooking` is an email alias for "folks interested in cooking."

Since many users accidently, and embarrassingly, send subscription deletion messages and other "administrivia" to the entire list, let us stress here that there are two different addresses involved with mailing lists.

Useful Item

1.   The first address has the form

```
list.server.name@site
```

and all commands to be processed by the list server should be sent here.

2.   The second address has the form

```
mailing.list.name@site
```

and all posts intended for distribution to the entire mailing list should be sent here. Do not send any commands to this address, because everyone on the mailing list will receive them. This is particularly annoying when someone is requesting a subscription deletion.

---

5   Julia did not really delete her subscription; that was only for illustration purposes.

Occasionally, you may encounter a mailing list that is not automated. Again, such lists have two important addresses: one to send posts to, and the other to send commands to the list administrator. For example, suppose a mailing list called `boots` is managed by Tex Brooks at the site named `list.texas.com`. To send a message to the list, you would post the message to the address

<code>boots@list.texas.com</code>

To send a message to the list administrator, you would post the message to the address

<code>boots-request@list.texas.com</code>

Notice that the word `request` preceded by a dash is appended to the name of the mailing list. This causes the message to be sent only to the list administrator. Be careful not to send requests meant for Tex to the entire mailing list, and vice versa. Automated lists also support this feature, so that subscribers can reach a human (owner) if they need to.

10.4.3   Helpful Hints

Here, we summarize a number of guidelines pertaining to mailing lists.

- If possible, try to obtain information about a mailing list before subscribing to it. For example, what topics are relevant to it, how many people are subscribed, how many messages are posted daily, and so on. Even if you are interested in the subject, the message volume may simply be too high for you.

- Do not let mailing list email interfere with other more important email.

- Some mailing lists have `-L` appended to the name, such as `COOK-L`, but this habit is decreasing.

- The 80–20 rule applies to many types of human interaction, including mailing lists. On many lists, 20 percent (or fewer) of the subscribers generate 80 percent (or more) of the postings. This is not necessarily wrong.

- If you are a new subscriber to a mailing list and a novice at mailing lists in general, read the list for a couple weeks before posting. This will give you a feel for what is appropriate for the list.

- If you get a message from the list server when you join a mailing list, save it for future reference.

- Send all commands to the list server, not to the list itself.

- Do share your thoughts, expertise, experience, and opinions with those on the list. Your ideas may be valuable to others.

- Do not post advertisements to mailing lists.

- Follow the basic rules of netiquette.

- If you get a post that bothers you, wait and cool down before responding. Starting a flame war is considered bad form. You may decide to send your message to just one person, rather than to the entire list.

- If you plan to be away from your email for an extended period, you may want to unsubscribe temporarily from mailing lists, and resubscribe when you return.

10.4.4   Mailing Lists and Web Pages

Mailing lists can be coupled with Web pages to make a powerful information distribution system. The primary content, including images, can be placed on Web pages. A form can also be placed on the Web page that allows people to subscribe by leaving their email address. This is also an opportunity for the Web page owner to obtain additional information for marketing or development purposes. The Web page owner can then place all the email addresses on a mailing list and can post notices at regular or irregular intervals to let people know that the content has changed and to describe the new information.

Such a model takes advantage of the best features of each medium:

- Email comes up "in your face" as an announcement that does not require any action, just the time to skim or read it.

- Web pages are good repositories for lengthy material that is not charged to your disk quota and that you can read at any time. This long-term availability can also be a drawback, if you are not conscientious about following up on the email messages to obtain potentially important material.

10.4.5   Mailing Lists Versus Newsgroups

Both mailing lists and newsgroups involve lots of people with similar interests discussing their favorite topics electronically. The two differ in several aspects, as follows:

1. In a mailing list, messages are sent directly to your mailbox, whereas in a newsgroup, you read copies of messages that are stored by your news server.

2. You manage messages from your mailing list subscriptions using your email client, whereas your newsreader helps you manipulate the articles in the newsgroups to which you are subscribed.

3. Your newsreader provides a convenient method for you to subscribe to a newsgroup, and you can subscribe directly. To subscribe to a mailing list, you must send a message to the appropriate list server.

4. News usually expires within a short period; however, messages in a mailing list are typically archived much longer.

5. To access news, you need to learn a newsreader, whereas to join a mailing list, you only need to know how to use email.

6. Messages from mailing lists arrive in your mailbox every day, and if you do not clean them out periodically, their numbers can grow alarmingly fast. With news, you can read it whenever you want, with the caveat that you must get to the news before it expires. Services such as Deja News make it increasingly easy to do retroactive searches.

EXERCISES 10.4

Mailing List Fundamentals

17. What does the word "majordomo" mean? Why do you think it was chosen for the name of a mailing list management program?

18. Find a mailing list for which the subject is one of your hobbies. What is the name of the list? What is the name of the list server used to manage the list (or is it managed by a person)? Where is the list kept?

19. Subscribe to a mailing list of your choice. What is its name? For one week, record the number of messages the mailing list receives daily. In this brief period, did a small group of users dominate the postings, or were there many different users involved in the discussions?

20. What security mechanisms are in place to prevent someone from subscribing someone else to a number of mailing lists? Can you unsubscribe someone else from a mailing list? Explain.

21.   Is there a mailing list about cooking? What is the address to which subscriptions should be posted? What is the name of the list?

22.   Locate one mailing list that you were surprised to find. Give the list name and a brief description of it.

23.   Present three more differences between mailing lists and news-groups that were not described in the text.

24.   Which of the mailing lists mentioned in Ellen and Ray's Choices are moderated lists?

ELLEN AND RAY'S CHOICES

In this section, we list a few interesting mailing lists.[6] Most of the topics they deal with are self-explanatory. Both the subscription address and the list name are provided.

Go On-Line

- Subscription address: `LISTSERV@vm3090.ege.edu.tr`
  Mailing list name: `BESTWEB`

- Subscription address: `LISTSERV@ucsbvm.ucsb.edu`
  Mailing list name: `DICKNS-L`   Charles Dickens.

- Subscription address: `LISTPROC@cornell.edu`
  Mailing list name: `FELINES-L`

- Subscription address: `LISTSERV@listserv.aol.com`
  Mailing list name: `FEM-BIBLIO`   Discussion group relating to women and spirituality.

- Subscription address: `LISTSERV@ua1vm.ua.edu`
  Mailing list name: `ADV-HTML`

- Subscription address: `majordomo@shore.net`
  Mailing list name: `lost-chords`   Moody Blues fans unite.

- Subscription address: `LISTPROC@raven.cc.ukans.edu`
  Mailing list name: `talking-heads`   Air, air can hurt you too.

- Subscription address: `ULTRA-request@listserv.dartmouth.edu`
  Mailing list name: `ULTRA`   Long may you run.

---

6   We follow the usual capitalization of the names.

ELLEN AND RAY'S CHOICES   CONTINUED:

- Subscription address: `LISTSERV@psuvm.psu.edu`
  Mailing list name: `YAWRITING`   Writing discussion group for young adults and children.

10.5   Newsgroups and Mailing Lists Availability

Go On-Line

It is no exaggeration to say that no matter what topic you are interested in, there is probably either a mailing list or a newsgroup or both that deals with it. The real question is, how do you locate the name of that mailing list or newsgroup? A number of on-line newsgroup and mailing list directories are available. These are easily located by using a search engine or consulting the references. The directories typically provide some basic facts about newsgroups and mailing lists, along with an extensive list of what is available. This book's accompanying Web presentation also links to a few.

Since the number of mailing lists and newsgroups is increasing rapidly, it is worthwhile checking back every so often to see if a new discussion forum has been created on your pet topic. In addition, you might decide to take the initiative and create your own mailing list or newsgroup. Forming a mailing list is not that hard, if someone will provide access to a server. The prime directives are:

1.   Make sure a similar list is not already in existence. Do some research.

2.   Do not underestimate the time it takes to be a list owner on an active and popular list. Despite software to automate some tasks, well-run mailing lists still take time and attention.

EXERCISES 10.5

Newsgroups and Mailing Lists Availability

25.   Give the URLs for three directory services that are useful for locating mailing lists or newsgroups. Compare their capabilities in a table you create in HTML. Compare their results when you tried to locate the phrase "Appalachian Trail."

26.   Locate a mailing list that would be of interest to vegetarians. Describe how to subscribe to it. Is it moderated?

27.   Locate a newsgroup that would be of interest to photographers. What is its name? Is it moderated?

10.6   Chat Rooms

One Internet application that has become incredibly popular since the software was developed by Jarkko Oikarinen in 1988 is the *chat room*.[7] A chat room is a forum through which you can interactively discuss your favorite subject with people located anywhere on the Internet. A chat room, in essence, is a virtual room in which two or more people with a common interest (entertainment, literature, movies, music, politics, religion, and so on) can share ideas and have a real-time "conversation."

The chat room is actually a *channel* or path that allows communication between two or more computers on the Internet. The communication occurs in real time and is similar to a conference call or meeting. However, messages are typed on the keyboard, not spoken (some voice chat software is available but is generally not common), and the conversation appears on the monitors of all the users on that channel. Figure 10.6 depicts the interface of a typical chat room.

10.6.1   Chat Room Entrance

When signing into a chat room for the first time, you are asked to select a username and password. Unless the chat room is moderated and the moderator wants you to use your real name (which they can verify by sending you a letter via s-mail, requiring a response from you), you may create any username (or nickname) you like, providing it is not already in use. Often many nicknames must be tried before you find one that is not yet taken. You also need to create a password, but remember, you should never use your computer account password.

Go On-Line

---

7   Oikarinen developed the *Internet Relay Chat* (*IRC*) protocol. The protocol is a set of rules defining how clients and servers can support conferencing mechanisms, such as chat rooms, over the Internet.

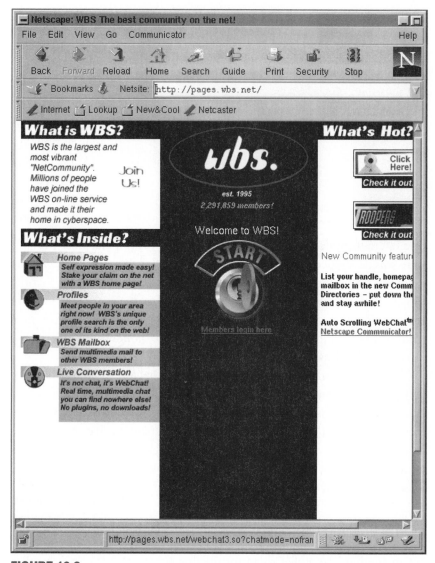

FIGURE 10.6

A sample chat room interface (`pages.wbs.net/webchat3.so?`).

Some chat services allow you to lurk; that is, you may "listen" to others communicating, but you cannot transmit messages. If you are just lurking, you usually do not need to specify any information. In other situations, you are asked to fill out a form containing such data as your name, password, birth date, occupation, and email address. This information can be used for authentication and also for advertising purposes.

Once you have signed in with a chat service, you can select a "room" to which you want to go. You will usually have an extensive choice of topics.

The number of participants in each room is displayed either via a number or a list of the room's occupants. A room with a large number of participants is likely to be more lively.

When a chat room is active (i.e., being used), a scrolling window displays the "conversation" as lines of text, and each line is preceded by the nickname of the person who "spoke." When you enter a chat room, you may discover that the text is scrolling by very quickly, indicating a very active membership. You will also be provided with a second area called a *message box*, in which you can type your own messages. Many participants display images (sometimes of themselves) and URLs. Some people provide URLs to their personal Web page. The level of privacy you want to maintain is your choice. You can remain anonymous, or you can provide any degree of personal information you desire. Remember, it is a small world, and the person with whom you are chatting may not be at all like their on-line character in real life.

Useful Item

In many chat rooms, a menu bar displays the usernames of all the people in the chat room. (We should note that you can find people chatting at all hours.) Selecting someone from this list allows you to send a private message to them. Another menu bar lets you select an emotion such as giggle, groan, scream, smile, and wink, to accompany your message. Several buttons allow you to submit your message, go to another chat room, or refresh the screen if you have been idle for a period of time.

10.6.2   Chat Room Culture

A significant chat room culture has emerged. Many abbreviations for words and phrases have been developed or adopted, so that conversation can move along more quickly. Inexperienced users often find it difficult to decipher messages in real time, especially when the room has many occupants. As with email and newsgroups, the general rules of netiquette apply, spamming is not acceptable, and typing in all caps is considered rude.

Occasionally, someone in a chat room becomes obnoxious. To deal with them, most chat rooms offer a gag or ignore option. If you choose to ignore a particular person in the chat room, none of their messages will display in your chat window. Finally, some chat services provide a set of guidelines to which users must adhere (no foul language, no harassing, no repeating the same message over and over again, and so on), and when these rules are violated, a user may be removed from the service.

Hot Topic

Go On-Line

As far as finding a chat room in which to participate, we suggest using a search engine. Searching with a query of `chat rooms` or `Web chat` should turn up a large number of options.

10.6.3   Chat Rooms and Education

Chat rooms are becoming a popular forum for educational discussions. For example, there are now on-line "universities" in which each course has an associated chat room. The students in the class can discuss homework and share their knowledge to help other students. Sometimes the course instructor participates in the discussion. Using this forum, the instructor need only answer a question once, since all students connected to the chat room can read the answer. Although on-line courses of this nature are new, the level of participation is high, and many people are enthusiastic about the possibilities of such an approach. In particular, the phrase *distance learning* is becoming very popular in academic circles. Distance learning encompasses any form of teaching in which the instructor(s) and students are not located in the same room.

EXERCISES 10.6

Chat Rooms

28.   Provide the URLs of three chat services you found on the Web. Explore a chat service. What are the different chat topics offered by each source?

29.   Research Internet Relay Chat (IRC) on the Web. Write a paragraph summarizing your findings.

30.   Research the concept of distance learning on the Web and describe its current state. Does your institution offer distance learning courses?

31.   Provide the URLs of three on-line universities. How many courses does each offer, what is the duration of each course, and what is the tuition? Are the courses all computer related, or are other subjects offered as well?

32.   Describe the advantages and disadvantages of an on-line course. Would you enroll in such a course? Elaborate.

10.7   MUDs

The acronym *MUD* stands for *Multi-User Dungeon* or *Multi-User Dimension*. MUDs are also referred to as *3D Worlds* and *Chat Worlds*. A MUD is a real-time interactive game that takes place in an imaginary environment where multiple computer users can play simultaneously. As in a chat room, all communication and activity take place via keyboard input. Descriptions of the imaginary environment's rooms and objects are provided. As you travel through these virtual surroundings, you can interact with other players who are logged in at the same time.

MUDs originated in 1979 when Richard Bartle and Roy Trubshaw wrote a game program that allowed multiple users to play and interact at the same time. MUDs have become increasingly popular, and various versions have emerged. These variations include *MOOs* (*Multi-User Dungeons, Object-Oriented*), various *MUSHes* (*Multi-User Shared Hallucinations*), and *MUCKs* (not an acronym).

The action in a MUD is "directed" by a server that is usually a complex C program. The server allows players to connect to the MUD, and it maintains the database of objects, players, and rooms. There are several types of MUDs, and they fall into one or more of the following categories:

- Role-playing and fantasy MUDs

    - MUSHes
    - LPMUDs

- Combat MUDs

    - AberMUDs
    - DikuMUDs
    - LPMUDs

- Social MUDs

    - LambdaMOO
    - TinyMUCK
    - TinyMUSH

- Educational MUDs

    - LambdaMOO

10.7.1   MUD Connections

To participate in a MUD, you will need to Telnet to a server running a MUD. Using a search engine, you can easily generate a list of the currently available MUDs. You can connect to a MUD by using the `telnet` command and specifying the MUD's network address and port number. If you receive a `login` prompt, you have connected to the computer running the MUD,

Go On-Line

but not to the MUD itself. You will need to check the address and port number and try to connect again.

Another way to connect to a MUD is to use a MUD client. A MUD client is a program that functions like Telnet, but provides a user-friendly interface for interacting in a MUD. The client takes care of text wrapping, separates your input from the MUD's output, and provides a way to create shortcuts for long commands. Clients are designed to run on specific operating systems, so if you want to install one, make sure it is compatible with your system. Some examples of MUD clients and their corresponding platforms are:

- *FooTalk* (VMS)

- *MacMOOSE* (Macintosh)

- *MUD.el* (Emacs)

- *MUSHClient* (PC Winsock)

- *TinyTalk* (UNIX)

10.7.2 MUDding

When you connect to a MUD for the first time, you should read the welcome screen. Figure 10.7 is an example of a MUD introductory screen. The welcome screen permits you either to create a character (a must in order to play) by selecting a name and password, or connect by entering your already-existing name and password. The introductory screen may also provide other useful information about the game, such as the rules and where to find help.

Many MUDs also have an accompanying Web page that supplies the background story for the game. Before starting to play, new players should try to become familiar with the commands (which may differ from MUD to MUD) and the particular MUD culture. Many MUDs are structured in levels, and the "top level" is one where beginners can practice commands before entering the "real" game. Once you have mastered the commands, the enjoyment you derive from MUDding should increase dramatically.

A MUD typically consists of four basic components: passageways, objects, players, and levels composed of different rooms. The character that you create for yourself can interact with and manipulate other things in the MUD. Also, players can talk to each other through their characters. Rooms can be entered and exited using passageways. Play involves moving your

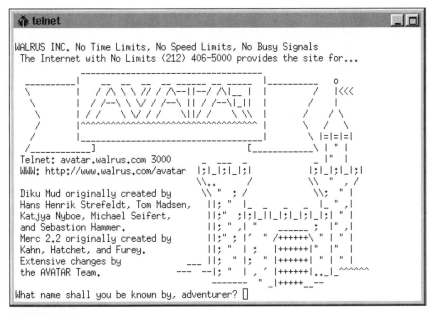

FIGURE 10.7

An example of a MUD welcome screen (www.walrus.com/~avatar).

character around, discovering your surroundings, battling monsters and other players, collecting objects and using them, and so on. The following short list of commands may give you a sense of the types of actions you can perform (although the commands used by any particular MUD may differ):

- emote Indicate an action, such as a sigh or a laugh.

- help Provide help.

- look Describe the contents of the room you are in.

- page Talk to someone in another room.

- say Speak to everyone in the room.

- whisper Talk privately to someone.

- who List who is playing.

Sophisticated MUDs can recognize natural-language commands, as well. Such a MUD interface can understand simple expressions, usually common action verbs, like "jump," "go," "move," "run," and so forth.

MUDding is similar to playing an adventure game. One advantage of playing on-line is that you can interact with users located anywhere on the Internet. Additionally, the game itself can be very complex, interesting, and intricate, especially if a number of creative people participated in its initial development and continually revise, improve, and maintain it.

10.7.3   MUD Etiquette

Useful Item

It is important to know the rules of the MUD before you begin to participate. Read the documentation before asking for help on-line. While you are still learning to play, it is a good idea to stay in the designated "novice" area. Do not ask for a character's real name, age, or gender if it is not already provided. Log out when you are not actively playing, and of course, avoid spamming and flaming. All other rules of netiquette apply in MUDs as well.

10.7.4   Additional MUD Uses

Social MUDs are similar to chat rooms. MUDs can facilitate communication by creating virtual meeting places in which people can collaborate and brainstorm. MUDs can also be used as educational tools by providing a place where, for example, students can improve and practice their foreign language skills.

The following brief transcript depicts a typical MUD communication between characters Helen, Juan, and Linda. We have added some punctuation to make the exchange more readable; however, as with chat rooms, users typically provide very little punctuation. This social MUD is used for introductory conversational Spanish.

Helen: Logged on.

Helen: "Hola."

Linda: "Hola Helen. Que pasa?"

Helen: "Nada."

Juan: "Tengo sed."

Linda: "Si."

Helen: "Yo tambien."

Juan: "Hasta pronto."

Juan: Logged off.

10.7.5 MUD Creation

It is possible to start up your own MUD by using FTP to obtain a generic
version of the MUD you are interested in developing. Lists of various
types of servers and FTP sites from which the files can be downloaded are
available on the Web. Once installed, the MUD source code can be modified
and customized. To do this, you need to be a competent programmer. As
the creator of the game, you will have the most power and control, as well
as the title of Wizard.

Go On-Line

MUDs tend to take up a lot of disk space (10 to 90 megabytes), and some
monopolize CPU time. If you cannot set up shop on your own machine,
you are probably out of luck. Most companies and universities discourage
the use of MUDs, except for educational purposes.

EXERCISES 10.7

MUDs

33. Locate three USENET newsgroups associated with MUDs and
     select one to read. Summarize the contents of the postings you
     read. Provide the names and subscription addresses of three
     mailing lists that discuss MUDs.

34. What are some of the advantages and disadvantages of using a
     MUD as a communications tool? Compare and contrast a MUD
     with other tools, such as chat rooms, email, and newsgroups.

35. What are the distinctions between a social MUD and a chat
     room?

36. Can you locate a MUD that is set in a wilderness area?

Electronic Publishing

11

I had a good routine down by this point of my hike. I would wake up around 6:30 A.M. with the sun. I would then make two one-quart shakes for breakfast. I was eating about 8,000 calories per day and it was important to get a lot of them early in the morning. My shakes consisted of 1 quart of stream water iodized to kill bacteria, 3 Carnation instant breakfasts, 6 heaping teaspoons of Nestle's Quik, and powdered milk. I haven't had (or desired!) such a shake since then but they were great on the trail. I had long ago dumped all luxuries from my pack and all cooking gear. I was eating only cold food now. This saved me having to find water at night, lighting my stove, cooking dinner, and then cleaning my dishes. All combined, my gear and pack weighed in at only about 17 pounds when devoid of food and beverages. The contents included my tent, sleeping bag, ground cloth, and clothes. I would often carry 30 pounds of food immediately after a resupply. However, this weight went down very quickly. I bumped into the infamous "Ward Leonard," who spends most of his time on the trail, while I was going up Mount Greylock.

Massachusetts
91 miles

Chapter 11

11.1 INTRODUCTION

One reason for the great success of the Web is that so many people are interested in publishing on-line. In this chapter, you will learn about the following electronic publishing topics:

Objectives

- Electronic publishing advantages and disadvantages

- Copyright and credit issues

- Project Gutenberg and on-line books

- Electronic magazines, journals, and newspapers

- Miscellaneous topics: plagiarism and electronic publishing do's and don'ts

11.2 Electronic Publishing Advantages and Disadvantages

Throughout history, humans have made continual improvements in the way we share and transmit knowledge. Oral storytelling was replaced by the handwritten word, which was eventually replaced by the printed word. With the advent of the Web, electronic publishing promises to continue the trend. In this section, we highlight some of the advantages claimed by electronic publishing and describe some of its disadvantages.

11.2.1   Advantages

Some of the current advantages of electronic publishing are listed here. Others will probably arise as Web technology continues to improve.

- *Convenient*—On-line publishing makes it possible for users to conduct text searches in an article or document quickly and easily. Electronic publishing also makes it easy to access previous issues of a magazine or journal.

- *Dynamic*—Electronic publications are very easy to modify; changes can be made almost instantaneously. Traditional publications may require errata pages, next editions, or perhaps correction announcements in subsequent issues. With on-line magazines and journals, articles can be released as they are ready for publication, instead of waiting until the end of a week, month, or in some cases, year. In addition, readers can respond to authors and editors on-line, providing timely feedback.

- *Easy*—Nearly anyone can publish material on-line. HTML is not difficult to learn, although it may be challenging to master. If necessary, you can use an HTML converter that will transform text files into HTML files. Currently, people from all walks of life—children, doctors, homemakers, lawyers, professionals, researchers, students—are publishing electronically.

- *Fast*—Electronic publishing provides a quick way to get information to your audience. Traditional publishing can take a year or longer from the time you finish writing to the time your information is actually put into print and distributed. On-line publishing is accomplished in a fraction of that time, and distribution is immediate.

- *Inexpensive*—Aside from the development cost of writing your documents in HTML, your only other expense may be keeping your HTML files on a server so that they can be accessed by others. Compare this to the cost of printing a book, magazine, or journal (including the cost of the paper), together with the expense of s-mailing hardcopies or distributing them through stores. Electronic publishing is much, much cheaper.

- *Research friendly*—There is an enormous advantage to researchers from on-line publishing. Research articles can be made available via FTP for anyone to obtain and read. This distribution is a fast and convenient way to disseminate new research results. Conference papers can be made available on the Web before the conference even occurs and long before the conference proceedings are published. On-line publishing has increased the speed with which new research is being done in some fields.

11.2.2   Disadvantages

There are some disadvantages to electronic publishing. Advances in Web technology may resolve some of these in the future.

- *Computer literacy*—To take advantage of material published electronically, readers must be computer literate and must have Internet access.

- *Credibility*—Because it is easy to publish electronically and because there is usually no separation between the writing and editing phases, some authors tend to be less concerned about details. While some electronic publications do enforce rigorous standards, other documents contain glaring spelling errors or other inaccuracies, which damage their credibility. In contrast, because of the permanent nature of printed materials (as well as the expense of producing them), more care goes into reviewing materials that are published in the traditional way.

- *Viewing difficulty*—Materials that are published on-line must be viewed using a monitor. Until larger monitor screens (21 inches or more) become standard, readers may not be comfortable reading lengthy works on-line. A good quality 21-inch monitor today is much too pricey for most users.

- *Advertising increases*—To offset the lower revenues generated by electronic publishing, advertising may continue to increase. Those who have been surfing the Web for a few years have already noticed a dramatic increase in the amount of advertising.

- *Ownership*—Some potential Web authors are leery of electronic publishing because material—images as well as text—can easily be copied from the Web simply by using the browser to view and save the source. Although electronically published material can be copyrighted, it may be difficult to track down offenders and pursue legal action. If a work has some commercial value that will be lessened by widespread distribution, authors may want to be very sure that their material is copyright protected if it is going to be available on-line.

- *Document unavailability*—Documents may be unavailable if the applicable server is down, or if too many readers are trying to access that server. However, document unavailability can also be a problem with printed materials. A magazine issue or book may be sold out, or the library's copy may be out on loan. The difference, of course, is that we have come to expect on-line information to be available, if not immediately, then at least within a very short time.

EXERCISES 11.2

Electronic Publishing Advantages and Disadvantages

1. What is your projection for the future of electronic publishing? If you feel it is viable, will it replace traditional publishing? If you do not feel that it is viable, describe why not.

2. What do you think (off-line) libraries of the future will be like, and what purpose will they serve?

3. What role do you feel off-line publishers will play in the future? Will small publishers continue to exist?

4. Locate and report on an FTP site that distributes research articles in your major subject.

5. Can you find any on-line registers from the Appalachian Trail? If so, how might these be of use to prospective thru-hikers?

6. Try to locate information about *custom books* on-line. These are books for which the reader can select the various chapters; they are customized to the individual reader's needs. Summarize your findings.

11.3   Copyright Issues

11.3.1   Definition

The early Internet provided a mechanism for industry and academia to exchange ideas and to collaborate. Today, a great deal of commercial information is available on the Internet, in the form of books, magazines, newspapers, tutorials, and so on. The purpose of much of this electronically published material is no longer merely to provide information and promote the exchange of ideas, but also to generate income for its authors. Despite the feelings of some Internet users that information on the Internet should be free, most authors would agree that financial compensation motivates them to create and publish on-line, as well as off-line.

   To encourage and promote creative expression, United States copyright law (or *copyright statute*) was established to protect an individual's creative effort and to allow them to benefit financially from it. Other countries provide copyright protection as well. A *copyright* is a set of rights extended

Useful Item

to an individual who has produced a creative work. In the United States, the creative work must meet three requirements in order to be eligible for copyright protection:

- The work must be original and not copied (or derived) from someone else's work.

- The work must be in a "tangible" form, that is, either written down, or recorded on tape, videotape, disk, CD, and so on. The spoken word is not copyrightable.

- The work must be more than just an idea; an idea is not copyrightable, although a particular expression of the idea is.

As soon as a creative work is "fixed" in some tangible form, the work can receive copyright protection. It is not necessary to register a copyright, though doing so may provide additional benefits. This implies that your email and newsgroup postings are copyrighted, as well as your Web page creations.

You may have seen copyright notices at the bottom of some Web pages. In the United States, the notice consists of three parts:

1. The copyright symbol © (created by using `&copy;` or `&#169;` in HTML), or the word `copyright`.

2. The year the work was first published.

3. The name of the owner.

In other countries, the phrase "All rights reserved" needs to appear. For example, here is a copyright notice that Ellen might place at the bottom of her Web page:

© Ellen Hepp, 2002. All rights reserved.

We suggest using a copyright notice and including the "All rights reserved" phrase on your Web presentations. Even though the copyright notice need not be displayed on works published after March 1, 1989, it is a good reminder to others that the work is copyrighted. Everything you see on the Web is automatically copyrighted unless the author explicitly gives the material away.

The copyright notice can usually be found on the bottom of the first page of a Web presentation, though it can be placed in any noticeable location on the page. It is also sometimes included as a comment inside HTML documents.

Copyright is important because it allows people to have control over their creative works and to benefit financially from them. The holders also have control over derivations of their work. The copyright holders can either prohibit copies of their works from being made, or they can profit by charging for the copies.

Unfortunately, it is also difficult to monitor who is making copies of on-line materials. Since the quality of an on-line work is not diminished if the work is copied, it is difficult to determine if the version being viewed is the original.

You may have discovered that some books are available on-line in their entirety (see Section 11.4). Is this copyright infringement? That depends. Copyrights expire a certain number of years after the death of the owner, so the Web presentation offering the complete works of Shakespeare is legitimate. If the copyright has expired, the work is said to be in the *public domain*, and anyone can make it available on-line, or can use it for whatever other purpose they would like. If the copyright has not expired, then a copyright infringement may be involved.

11.3.2   Credit Issues

Several methods are currently being developed to address the issue of controlling access to copyrighted electronic works. The *World Intellectual Property Organization (WIPO)* has decided that copyright protection needs to include electronically published material. This stand is supported by the United States government, as well. Other groups, such as the *Digital Future Coalition* and the *Electronic Frontier Foundation*, favor making all information on the Web freely available.

Two approaches are emerging to make materials freely accessible on-line and at the same time ensure the rights of the creator/owner of the work.

One approach supports using legal constraints and enacting legislation with stiffer penalties for copyright violations. A strong proponent of this method is the *Creative Incentive Coalition*. For printed materials, an "honor system" currently in place leaves it up to the user to respect both the law and the copyright of a work when photocopying documents. The *Copyright Clearance Center* is a nonprofit group that currently provides a collective licensing system as a way to make lawful photocopies from a collection of printed materials. The Copyright Clearance Center is working on extending this concept to electronic materials.

The second approach in dealing with both credit and copyright issues involves developing technology to ensure that electronic materials and information are protected and secure. Several companies have already designed some form of *digital rights management systems.*

InterTrust Technologies, Inc., has developed a way to track and control the use of digital documents by encasing them in *DigiBox containers.* Access to the information inside these secure containers requires a Web browser plug-in that will monitor and control the use of the document. For example, the browser `Copy`, `Print`, and `Save` commands can be disabled, if desired, by the document owner. Tracking how often a document is accessed makes it possible to use a pay-per-use pricing scheme.

IBM offers a secure *Cryptolope container* that can only be opened with an IBM-supplied helper application. Other companies have developed ways to identify and "stamp" images and documents with a concealed digital watermark as a means of establishing and confirming ownership (see Section 14.6).

Being able to establish ownership and determine whether or not an on-line document has been tampered with are two ways that digital rights management systems protect the owners of copyrighted works. Such systems, when combined with a micropayment system that permits pay-per-use document pricing, may provide a way to compensate copyright owners, as well as protect them.

EXERCISES 11.3

Copyright Issues

7. Write a paragraph explaining what you feel is the most effective method for preventing electronic copyright infringement.

8. Research the subject of intellectual property on-line. Write a paragraph defining the differences between *copyrights*, *trademarks*, and *patents*.

9. Determine what is meant by "fair use," and define exactly when it is permissible to use a copyrighted work. Provide two examples of fair use.

10. Search the Web to find out the current duration of a copyright in the United States. Does this time period vary for other countries?

11.4   Project Gutenberg and On-Line Books

Around the mid-1400s, Johannes Gutenberg of Germany developed the movable-type printing press.[1] Like electronic publishing today, the printing press and printed books heralded a new age. Just as the printing press made books and the knowledge they contain much more accessible, electronic publishing is making information available on an even larger scale.

At present, efforts are underway to use the Web to make previously published books available on-line as *e-texts* or *electronic texts*. Of course, only books in the public domain (that is, books for which either the copyrights have expired, or the authors have granted permission to publish on-line) can be made available. Several groups have been working to put classic literature on-line. Here, we discuss one of the most notable of such endeavors, *Project Gutenberg*.

Go On-Line

11.4.1   Project Gutenberg

In 1971, Michael Hart started Project Gutenberg when he made a copy of the Declaration of Independence and sent it out to everyone he could over the network. Since that time, volunteers have converted thousands of books into e-text, with the hope of making 10,000 books available in the *Project Gutenberg Electronic Public Library* by the end of the year 2001. Volunteers strive to convert four books per month to e-text format. The underlying goal of Project Gutenberg is summarized by their statement of philosophy:

> The Project Gutenberg Philosophy is to make information, books, and other materials available to the general public in forms a vast majority of the computers, programs and people can easily read, use, quote, and search.

In accordance with this philosophy, the project uses "plain vanilla ASCII" to encode the texts, which means that underlined text, italics, and bold print all appear as capital letters. Using this format permits nearly all hardware and software currently available (and hopefully, future hardware and software as well) to read and search the e-text. This ability is just

---

1   Although there is strong evidence that the Chinese and Koreans had their own versions of a movable-type printing press before the 1400s, Gutenberg is credited with the invention.

one of the benefits of having books on-line; it allows the reader to locate phrases and quotes easily.

The vast collection of e-texts in the Project Gutenberg collection is divided into three groups:

- **Heavy literature**   Includes the works of Shakespeare and the Bible.

- **Light literature**   Includes books such as *Alice in Wonderland* and *Peter Pan*.

- **References**   Contains an assortment of dictionaries, almanacs, fact books, and encyclopedias.

11.4.2   Other On-Line Books

Go On-Line

In addition to Project Gutenberg, other efforts with the same purpose in mind are underway—to make public domain literature and reference materials available to as many people as possible by putting them on-line. The projects include the following:

- Alex: A Catalogue of Electronic Texts on the Internet

- On-line Book Initiative

- Project Bartleby

- World Wide Web Virtual Library

There are many other indices available on-line that provide links to these and other resources containing electronic texts.

EXERCISES 11.4

Project Gutenberg and On-Line Books

11.   Find and report the URL of an index of titles from Project Gutenberg. Report the number of books currently archived by Project Gutenberg. Does it appear that their goal will be achieved by the end of 2001?

12.   Is *Tom Sawyer* available on-line? How about *Little Women*? What about your favorite book? Do you have to download an entire book at a time? Explain.

13. Find and report the URLs for two presentations containing the works of Shakespeare. Are entire plays contained in a single HTML document? If not, how are they divided?

14. Can you find any free books available on-line about hiking or backpacking?

11.5   Electronic Journals, Magazines, and Newspapers

In general, the purpose of publishing material on-line is to convey information. For electronic magazines and newspapers, the overriding goal is often to make a profit by providing news and information. A reader might have to subscribe to an on-line magazine or newspaper in order to access it. However, sometimes the on-line version is abridged, offering only a few articles. In such a case, the on-line version simply serves as advertising for the purpose of selling subscriptions to the printed version.

In contrast, for e-zines and some scholarly journals, the motivation to publish electronically may not be profit. These electronic publications exist primarily to express the opinions, creativity, and discoveries of their authors.

11.5.1   E-zines

An *e-zine* is an electronic version of a *zine*. Zines, which have been around for about 20 years, are self-published works concerning whatever the creator/writer/publisher is interested in. The topics originally focused on science fiction and comic books; today, however, zines can be found relating to nearly every imaginable topic, from collecting to music to poetry, etc.

Go On-Line

The name zine appears to derive from magazine, but zine culture claims that it is a derivative of *fanzine*, which represents "fan magazine"—a magazine produced by the fans of a particular topic, published strictly for personal expression. Topics are usually related to science fiction or fantasy literature. Similarly, zines are not published for profit; any fee charged is usually barely enough to cover printing and distribution costs. Zines are clearly a labor of love.

The Web creates a very suitable arena for publishing and distributing zines, since it is inexpensive and fast. Many e-zines are reviewed and indexed on the Web. Some presentations are "slicker" than others and may carry advertising to offset expenses. These e-zines might offer live chatting, role-playing games, and links to related sites, in addition to the traditional reviews, essays, and artwork.

11.5.2   Journals

Like zines, the goal of scholarly journals is to convey information, not to make money for the authors (although publishers can make some money from these endeavors). Despite all the benefits of electronic publishing—fast, inexpensive, dynamic—people in research and academia are still somewhat reluctant to publish their works in on-line journals. However, in fields such as computer science, many on-line journals do exist and are gaining acceptance.

Probably the biggest concern of authors about publishing in on-line journals is credibility; that is, will others accept their articles as being of the same quality as off-line journal articles? Traditional journals ensure quality by requiring peer review. However, peer review can take months or even years, since most reviewers are not paid. Such a long delay defeats the purpose of electronic publication. Thus, reviews for on-line articles are often performed more quickly, and possibly less thoroughly.

Administrators in academia, who try to evaluate the work of a professor based on the journals in which the professor has published, need to be knowledgeable about on-line journals. The time lag in this education process means that untenured faculty may be less inclined to publish on-line.

In computer science, a number of top-name researchers have taken the initiative to publish in on-line journals. This has greatly added to the credibility of on-line journals. In addition, many on-line computer science journals have a distinguished list of editors. This also adds to the credibility of these journals. Some other fields seem to be moving in this direction, though perhaps more slowly, since they are less comfortable with the technology.

Bernard Moret suggests charging for access to on-line journals that have been refereed. An on-line journal could then be made widely available at a fraction of the cost (since printing and distribution costs would have essentially been eliminated), while the credibility of the journal would remain intact.

In addition to immediate, widespread availability, another benefit of on-line journals is that all supporting data, graphs, and illustrations can be included, since there is no page limit. In contrast, in a printed journal,

ELLEN AND RAY'S CHOICES

Go On-Line

- **E-zines**

    - "Dazzlers Digital Domicile" (`www.redbay.com/dazzler`).
    - "Moondance" (`www.moondance.org`).

- **Journals**

    - "The Journal of Electronic Publishing"
      (`www.press.umich.edu/jep`).
    - "ACM's Journal of Experimental Algorithmics"
      (`www.jea.acm.org`).

- **Magazine and Newspaper Lists**

    - "Ecola Newsstand" (`www.ecola.com`).
    - "The Electronic Newsstand" (`www.enews.com`).

authors are sometimes limited in the number of pages they can submit for
review. Some authors currently provide links from their Web pages to their
research, to make this additional information available. New information
or errata discovered a year or two after the paper has been published can
also be included in such a link.

11.5.3   Magazines and Newspapers

Go On-Line

The purpose of publishing magazines and newspapers electronically is almost always to make money. One way to do this is to charge for the
on-line subscription. Another way is to use the on-line version as a form
of advertising, to increase the sale of print subscriptions. Generally, having an on-line version provides good exposure and advertising. Finally,
some publications are supported by advertising revenues and provide their
information free to users.

Magazines and newspapers may require that their readers register, providing personal information that can then be sold to advertisers for target
marketing.

Many newspapers currently available on-line are simply electronic ren-
derings of the print versions. Some are free of charge and are supported
by advertising. Others are subscription-based. Still others, such as the
on-line version of the *The New York Times*, do not charge a fee but require

readers to register. Once registered, the reader is allowed to browse freely and access back issues.

There is an occasional need by some readers to search through the archives of newspapers. The on-line papers sometimes provide convenient methods for doing this. The interested reader can find links to most major newspapers and such archive services by pursuing the references.

EXERCISES 11.5

Electronic Journals, Magazines, and Newspapers

15.   Find the URLs of three e-zines that relate to an area in which you are interested. Describe the format and theme of each e-zine.

16.   Compile a list of five on-line magazines and their associated URLs. Indicate which magazines are abridged versions that are designed to sell print subscriptions and which are "genuine" on-line magazines.

17.   Compile a list of five newspapers and their associated URLs. Indicate whether they are free, are subscription-based, or require registering in order to browse. (Make sure you have at least one of each type in your list.) For newspapers not requiring a subscription, comment on the advertising you encounter.

18.   Locate a newspaper on-line that provides an archive searching service. Is the service available freely? Report on your findings.

11.6   Miscellaneous Publishing Issues

11.6.1   Plagiarism

Plagiarism is the act of using someone else's work and calling it your own. In the United States, there is no punishment for plagiarism until it becomes copyright infringement. However, it is immoral and unethical. Many institutions impose severe disciplinary actions for plagiarism; for example, many universities suspend students who are caught plagiarizing.

11.6.2   Electronic Publishing Do's and Don'ts

Do:

Useful Item

- Ensure the quality of the material you are publishing. Verify that the information is accurate, reliable, and free of spelling and grammatical errors.

- Make it clear when you are stating your opinion, so that no one will mistake it for fact.

- Use a copyright notice on all material you publish electronically (as a friendly reminder to others).

Don't:

- Use someone else's material on your Web page unless you have received permission from the copyright owner. If permitted to use the material, be sure to acknowledge its owner and/or author.

- Assume that because an electronic document does not possess a copyright notice, it is not copyrighted; it is.

EXERCISES 11.6

Miscellaneous Publishing Issues

19.   Have you heard of any cases in which someone got caught for plagiarism or copyright infringement? Elaborate.

20.   Add two more recommendations to our list of Electronic Publishing Do's and Don'ts.

21.   Suppose you arrived at a shelter along the Appalachian Trail and were the last person to have room for an entry in the trail register. The trail tradition is that you can leave a new register there, including with it your name and address, and that you mail the existing register back to its owner. When your register came back to you, what issues would be involved if you wanted to display the entire contents of "your register" on-line? How would you display it? Would you need any disclaimers?

22.   Referring to question 21, can you find any trail registers that have been published on-line? If so, report their URLs.

Web Programming Material

12

The Appalachian Trail follows the Long Trail for about 100 miles in Vermont. The Long Trail is the oldest long-distance hiking trail in the United States, completed in 1931. This rugged trail has spectacular mountain scenery and extends to the Canadian border. I met up with my family in Vermont, and it was very hard to leave them behind and continue my hike. What I did not realize was that Fish Out of Water had skipped Massachusetts and Vermont, and jumped ahead to near the border of New Hampshire. All along the trail, hikers sign into trail registers. It turned out that Fish's move ahead had put him only about one half-day behind me. He was able to deduce this from my entries in the registers. I was hiking big miles as I was getting close to New Hampshire and he was never quite able to catch up. I had no idea he was right behind me or I would have waited for him. Once again, fate waved its mysterious hand.

Vermont
146 miles

Chapter 12

12.1 INTRODUCTION

In this chapter, you will learn more advanced Web programming. The features described here will allow you to add more sophistication to your Web pages, and make them more interactive. This chapter will not teach you how to become a *JavaScript* or *Java* programmer—that requires a separate course and two more separate books. The idea of this chapter is to give you a better sense of what is available and where you can continue your studies of Web programming if you decide to pursue them further. You will learn about the following topics here:

Objectives

- How to program the most important elements in the *JavaScript* programming language

- What an *applet* is, and how to include one in your Web pages

- What the *Java* programming language is, and some basics about object-oriented programming

- How *guest books* work, guest book styles, and how to include one in your Web presentation

- How and when to use *counters* on your Web pages

- What a *server-side include* is

12.2 The JavaScript Programming Language

JavaScript is a scripting language that was developed by Netscape Communications with the Web in mind. It is useful for adding dynamic features to Web pages. Here, we describe some basic facts about JavaScript and how to incorporate the most commonly used JavaScript elements into your pages. Comprehensive books about programming in JavaScript are as long as this book. So, many JavaScript topics cannot be covered here. There are also some very good resources available on-line, and these can be found by conducting a search for "JavaScript resources" or "JavaScript tutorials" using a search tool. We have listed several Web presentations here that provide instruction and code. Other resources can be traced through the references or on-line.

JavaScript Web presentations:

Doc JavaScript
  `www.webreference.com/js`

JavaScript World
  `www.jsworld.com`

EarthWeb.com
  `www.developer.com/directories/pages/↩`
  `dir.javascript.jsutil.html`

Go On-Line

JavaScript was originally developed by Netscape under the name Live-Script in late 1995. In early December 1995, Netscape and Sun released LiveScript under the name JavaScript. There has been a lot of confusion about the relationship between JavaScript and Java, which is a separate programming language (see Section 12.4). Many people confuse the two because of the similarity of their names. JavaScript statements are typically embedded directly within HTML code; in contrast, *Java applets* (Section 12.3) and Java programs are separate. JavaScript is a simple, interpreted programming language, whereas Java is a compiled *object-oriented programming language*.

You may already have seen lots of Web pages that contain JavaScript code. Some common uses for JavaScript are to create *alert boxes*, create color fades, include dynamic-conversion form elements, provide information in the status line when someone mouses over a hyperlink, and verify form input. In this book's accompanying Web presentation, we use JavaScript to load a new image when you mouse over one of the main menu buttons. For example, when you mouse over the blue `Assignments` button, a gold ring appears around the button. This is actually an entirely new image with a gold ring drawn around it. When you move your mouse off the button, the old image reloads using JavaScript. We describe the details of how this is accomplished in Section 12.2.2.

Go On-Line

12.2.1   JavaScript and HTML

To include JavaScript code in an HTML document, you can use the script tag, `<SCRIPT>`, and its corresponding ending tag, `</SCRIPT>`. A browser that is capable of processing JavaScript is said to be *JavaScript-enabled* and will treat everything between this pair of tags as executable JavaScript code. Browsers that do not support JavaScript will try to format the material between the two tags as they would any other HTML code. For this reason, many Web authors hide their JavaScript by including it within comments. For example, an HTML document that includes JavaScript might be coded as follows:

```
<SCRIPT LANGUAGE = "JavaScript">
        <!-- Begin hiding for browsers that
            cannot process JavaScript.
        Include JavaScript statements here.
        ...
        Last JavaScript statement goes here.
        End hiding script. -->
</SCRIPT>
```

Browsers that cannot process JavaScript ignore the JavaScript statements because they are commented out. Browsers that are JavaScript-enabled ignore the comment tag and the plaintext and execute the JavaScript statements. To put a line with a comment on it within the JavaScript code, the commented part of the line needs to start with //. If the comment spans more than one line, you may see /* at the start of the comment and */ at the end. With this style of programming, users whose browsers are not JavaScript-enabled are minimally affected. Note that we used the LANGUAGE attribute of the script tag and assigned it a value of JavaScript, since we are using JavaScript as our scripting language. Other scripting languages are available, but JavaScript is by far the most widely used.

The script tag also supports the SRC attribute, which can be used to include a JavaScript program that resides in a separate file. The file containing the JavaScript program can be specified using either a relative or an absolute URL. The MIME file extension .js is used to denote JavaScript. The SRC attribute is useful if you want to include a large number of JavaScript statements, allowing them to be bundled into one file ending in the .js extension and then neatly included in one step in an HTML document.

It is important to realize that JavaScript is not supported in the same way by all browsers. What works on one browser may produce error messages on another. Both Netscape and Internet Explorer support a wide range of JavaScript elements. However, the set of elements they support is not identical, and the supported elements change fairly quickly over time. When designing Web pages that include JavaScript, it is very important to test them on both Netscape and Internet Explorer, as well as any other popular browsers to make sure the JavaScript functions as intended. To obtain the latest information on JavaScript, and to find out which features the various browsers support, you can pursue the references provided.

The script tag can appear repeatedly in an HTML document. Additionally, it can appear within either the head or the body tags. Most beginning users do not include large JavaScript programs in their code, but instead use only smaller JavaScript codes. We will examine some of the more popular ones in the next section.

12.2.2   JavaScript Basics

JavaScript is *object-oriented,* which is a way to describe how information is organized as objects in a hierarchical structure. Other programming languages such as C++ and Java are object-oriented as well. Various browsers use a *document object model* as a sort of blueprint that defines what the browser's objects are and how they are organized in the hierarchy. Since the document object models used by earlier browser versions varied greatly, you can expect that running JavaScript on older browsers may produce unpredictable results.

Some of the objects that are used by JavaScript include the browser window, the HTML document, images in the document, forms in the document, and elements in the forms. The window object represents the browser window and is at the top of the hierarchy. The document object is contained within the window object, and as an HTML document loads, it becomes a document object. Various parts of the Web page, usually as defined by HTML tags such as the <FORM> tag, become sub-objects of the document object. The document object model is quite complex, and we do not try to describe the whole thing here. To become proficient at using JavaScript, you will have to become very familiar with the object hierarchy. In Figure 12.1 we have included the objects discussed in this section. This is a very small part of the big picture. The complete JavaScript object hierarchy can be found in books devoted to Javascript.

Once a Web page has loaded, the browser saves all information about the document in memory. In order to access any of that information, you need to know how to refer to it. For instance, to access information that a user entered in a text box, you need to know how to refer to it. Objects are named using dot syntax that is similar to newsgroup naming conventions. For example, the newsgroup

```
rec.animals.wildlife
```

identifies a newsgroup whose main group is rec, its subtopic is animals, and whose more specific subtopic is wildlife as described in the

```
                            window
                              |
                          .document
              |               |               |
          .links[]        .forms[]        .images[]
                              |
                         .elements[]

window object:                      .images[] object:
    methods - .alert()                  event handler - onLoad
            .confirm()
            .prompt()               .forms[] object:
    properties - .status                event handler - on Submit
    event handlers - onLoad
                                    .elements[] object:
                                        event handler - onChange (text)
document object:                        property - .value
    methods - .write()
    properties - .bgColor           navigator object:
              .lastModified             properties - .appName
.links[] object:                                     .appVersion
    eventhandlers - onMouseOver
          onMouseOut
```

FIGURE 12.1
Description of some JavaScript objects, methods, properties, and event handlers.

newsgroup hierarchy. In a similar way, a particular object is identified by concatenating the hierarchy of objects above it using dots. To refer to the text box, you would use

```
window.document.theForm.theText
```

in your JavaScript code. In this example, theForm is what we named the form in the HTML code and theText is what we named the text box using the NAME attributes:

```
<HTML>
...
<BODY>
<FORM NAME =  "theForm">
```

```
<INPUT TYPE = "text"
       NAME = "theText"
       VALUE = "Enter your name">
</FORM>

</BODY>

</HTML>
```

The value of the NAME attribute of the <FORM> tag, theFORM, is used to associate a name with the form. If the form is not named in this way, the form can still be accessed using the following array syntax (providing this form was the first form on the Web page):

```
window.document.forms[0].theText
```

In the same way, if the text box was not named using the NAME attribute of the <INPUT> tag, it could still be addressed using the following:

```
window.document.forms[0].elements[0]
```

JavaScript stores information about objects in the document in the order in which they appear in the HTML code. The images object is an array of the images that appear in the document, and the array starts with an index of zero. To refer to the third image on a Web page, you would address it using:

```
window.document.images[2]
```

Some information, such as the current date or the browser version that is running, is not related to the Web page at all. These are built-in objects, and they are not addressed as sub-objects of the window. The object named

```
navigator
```

contains information about the browser, including version and name.

12.2.3   Objects, Properties, and Methods

Each object has certain *properties* and *methods* associated with it. Properties are things that describe the object, and they include sub-objects. If you consider a person an object, then hair color and height are properties, as are children. In this illustration, the children are sub-objects as well.

To access the properties of an object, refer to the object and then append the property name to the end of it using the dot notation. The document object has properties of `bgColor` and `lastModified` (as well as others), and these can be addressed as follows:

```
window.document.bgColor
```

and

```
window.document.lastModified
```

To address the name and version properties of the navigator object, respectively, use

```
navigator.appVersion
```

and

```
navigator.appName
```

Methods are things that the object can do or things that can be done to the object. Any number of methods can be associated with an object, including zero. One method associated with the document object is `write()`. Notice that methods have () at the end. The parentheses at the end of the method name make it possible to send along *arguments* or *parameters* that provide additional information. For example, the `document.write()` method writes HTML to a Web page. The argument to be passed to the method is a string of text that will be written. So, if we wanted to write "Hello World!" in an HTML document, we could use the following:

```
window.document.write("Hello World!")
```

To activate a method, you need to include a reference to the object followed by the method name with a dot in between.

12.2.4   Events and Event Handlers

Another characteristic of objects is how JavaScript responds to events. The word *event* is used in many ways in computer science and usually signifies some sort of action or occurrence. In our current context, an event refers to a repositioning of the mouse cursor, a mouse click, or the pressing of the Enter key. JavaScript lets you react to these events by specifying an extra attribute in the object's HTML tag called an *event handler*. Different objects usually have different event handlers. For example, a hyperlink object has event handlers for onMouseOver[1] and onMouseOut (as well as others), a form button object has an onClick event handler, a form object has an onSubmit event handler, and the window object and image objects have onLoad event handlers.

To use an event handler, include it in the HTML tag for the object. Here are some lines of code that demonstrate how the event handler onLoad causes a new message to appear in the form text box displayed on a Web page when the page finishes loading. The text box is initialized to "Still loading. . ." but displays "Lets go!" when the page finishes loading:

```
<BODY onLoad = "document.forms[0].elements[0].value =
                'Lets go!'">

<FORM>
<INPUT TYPE = "text"
       VALUE = "Still loading...">
</FORM>

</BODY>
```

Notice that we used

```
document.forms[0].elements[0].value
```

to refer to the contents of the text box in the form. We used the array syntax because we had not named the form or the text box. Because the form was the first (and only) form in the document, and the text box was the first element within the form, we referenced each of them with an index of 0.

Quite often, a function is created to handle an event. A function is lines of JavaScript code that perform some action or actions. It is efficient to use functions when you expect that more than one event may trigger the action. In that way the code only has to be included in one place, the head of the document. The code that follows shows how to accomplish the "Lets go!" display, this time using a function called ready():

```
<HTML>

<HEAD>
<TITLE>onLoad Example with JavaScript</TITLE>
```

---

1   Note the style of capitalization.

```
<SCRIPT LANGUAGE = "JavaScript">
<!-- Begin hiding for browsers that cannot process↩
    JavaScript.
function ready() {
        document.forms[0].elements[0].value = "Lets go!"
}
//Stop hiding script. -->
</SCRIPT>

</HEAD>
<BODY onLoad = "ready()">

<FORM>
<INPUT TYPE = "text"
        VALUE = "Still loading...">
</FORM>

</BODY>

</HTML>
```

12.2.5   Dialog Boxes

One very simple response to an event is to display a dialog box. Dialog boxes are all methods of the window object and are preceded by window. (We have left out the reference to window in our examples of code.) JavaScript provides three types of dialog boxes: *alert box, confirm box,* and *prompt box.* The box pops up overlaid on the browser window and displays information. In order to clear the box, the user has to select the OK button in the dialog box.

The next sample of code demonstrates an alert box that displays a welcome message when someone enters their name in the text box of the form:

```
<HTML>

<HEAD>
<TITLE>Alert Box Example with JavaScript</TITLE>

<SCRIPT LANGUAGE = "JavaScript">
<!-- Begin hiding for browsers that cannot process
    JavaScript.
function welcome(yourname) {
        var name = yourname.value
        alert("Welcome to our Web page, " + name + "!")
}
```

```
//Stop hiding script. -->
</SCRIPT>

</HEAD>
<BODY>

<FORM>
<INPUT TYPE = "text"
       VALUE = "Enter your name here"
       onChange = "welcome(this)">
</FORM>

</BODY>

</HTML>
```

Figure 12.2 displays the alert dialog box created by this code. (Note that Figure 12.6 also shows an alert box on Killface's page that is triggered by a mouse click.)

The example using welcome() is a little different than the earlier example using the function ready(), because welcome() takes an argument. That is, it takes information passed to it that in this case is the new text entered in the form text box. When the user enters a name, the onChange event triggers the event handler, which in turn passes the new text to the function welcome() as a parameter. In the example we refer to the text as this, which is a shortcut for specifying the full name of the textbox object:

```
window.document.forms[0].elements[0]
```

When the name of the text box is passed to the welcome() function, the value of the text box is stored in the variable called name. The keyword var in the code indicates that a variable is being defined. The variable called name is then used when the alert box is displayed. The expression

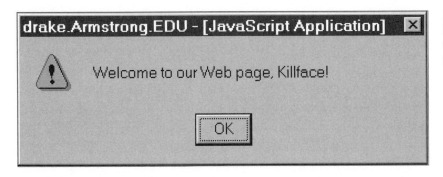

FIGURE 12.2
Enter your name welcome dialog box.

"Welcome to our Web page, name!" is displayed in the alert box, where name is replaced by whatever the user entered into the form text box.

Another type of dialog box is the confirm box. It is very similar to the alert box except that it provides yes and no buttons instead of just an OK button. Since the confirm box returns information to the user in the form of true or false, the information can be used to customize a Web page even further. Following is an example of using a confirm box instead of an alert box. Some of the message in the dialog box was changed to ask the user a yes or no question:

```
<HTML>

<HEAD>
<TITLE>Confirm Box Example with JavaScript</TITLE>

<SCRIPT LANGUAGE = "JavaScript">
<!-- Begin hiding for browsers that cannot process
     JavaScript.
function question(yourname) {
     var name = yourname.value
     var theAnswer
     theAnswer = confirm("Are you really " + name + "?")
}
//Stop hiding script. -->
</SCRIPT>
</HEAD>

<BODY>

<FORM>
<INPUT TYPE = "text"
     VALUE = "Enter your name here"
     onChange = "question(this)">
</FORM>

</BODY>

</HTML>
```

Figure 12.3 displays the confirm dialog box created by this code. The answer that the user selects, either OK or Cancel, is returned and saved in the variable we created called theAnswer as a Boolean value. A Boolean is either true or false, so if the user selects the OK button on the confirm dialog box, a value of true is stored in the variable theAnswer. If the user selects the Cancel button, a value of false is stored in theAnswer.

The third type of dialog box is the prompt dialog box. This displays a text field in which the user can type information. When the user clicks the

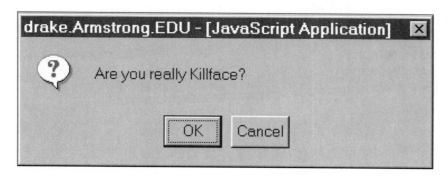

FIGURE 12.3
Enter your name confirm dialog box.

OK button, the text string they entered is returned. Following is an example of a prompt dialog box for which the returned text string is saved in the variable `reply`:

```
<HTML>
<HEAD>
<TITLE>Prompt Box Example with JavaScript</TITLE>
<SCRIPT LANGUAGE = "JavaScript">
<!-- Begin hiding for browsers that cannot process
     JavaScript.
function question() {
     var reply = prompt("What is your REAL name?", "")
}
//Stop hiding script. -->
</SCRIPT>
</HEAD>

<BODY>

<FORM>
<INPUT TYPE = "text"
       VALUE = "Enter your name here"
       onChange = "question()">
</FORM>

</BODY>

</HTML>
```

Figure 12.4 shows the prompt dialog box created by this code. In this example, the prompt dialog box is displayed as a result of the user entering a name in the form text box. Notice that the prompt method takes two parameters: the first parameter is the message that gets displayed as the

FIGURE 12.4
Enter your name
prompt dialog
box.

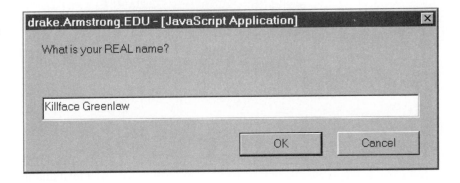

prompt, and the second parameter is a default entry for the text field. If
you do not want to include a default entry, then you can specify an empty
string " " as we did in our example. The text that the user enters in the
text field is returned in the reply variable that we created.

We can also combine event handlers. In the following code, notice that
we have added to the previous HTML example by displaying a message in
the window's status bar:

```
<HTML>
<HEAD>
<TITLE>Prompt Box Example with JavaScript</TITLE>
<SCRIPT LANGUAGE = "JavaScript">
<!-- Begin hiding for browsers that cannot process
     JavaScript.
function question() {
     var reply = prompt("What is your REAL name?", "")
}
function showWelcome() {
     var now = new Date
     var theHour = now.getHours()
     var welcomeMsg = null
     welcomeMsg = ((theHour < 12)? "Good Morning!" :
                   ((theHour < 18)? "Good Afternoon!" :
                    "Good Evening!"))
window.status = welcomeMsg
}
//STOP HIDING -->
</SCRIPT>
</HEAD>

<BODY onLoad = "showWelcome()">
```

```
<FORM>
<INPUT TYPE = "text"
       VALUE = "Enter your name here"
       onChange = "question()">
</FORM>

</BODY>

</HTML>
```

As before, when the user enters something in the form text box, the event handler onChange causes the window prompt method to generate a dialog box. Before that happens, though, the onLoad event handler causes a greeting to be displayed in the status bar of the window. A greeting is displayed when the status property of the window object is assigned some text:

```
window.status = "Good day!"
```

Rather than just display the greeting "Good day!," this HTML code calls the function showWelcome() to look at the current time and then determine if it is morning, afternoon, or evening. Using the Date() method, we were able to extract the current hour and assign it to the variable theHour. If the hour is before 12 (noon), the text message "Good Morning!" is assigned to the window.status property. If the hour is not before 12 but is before 18 (that is 6 P.M.), the text message assigned to the window.status property is "Good Afternoon!" If neither of the other two cases are met the hour must be greater than or equal to 18, and the text message assigned to the window.status property is "Good Evening!" The code

```
(theHour < 12) ? "Good Morning!" : ((theHour < 18) ?
   "Good Afternoon!" : "Good Evening!")
```

is a conditional expression that returns a value; in this case the value is the text message assigned to window.status. To evaluate the expression, start on the left and evaluate theHour < 12. This is a Boolean condition that is either true or false. The question mark can be interpreted as "then" and the colon can be interpreted as "otherwise" (or "else"). Reading the conditional expression yields:

> If theHour is less than 12 then assign the text "Good Morning!" to the variable welcomeMsg. Otherwise, evaluate the next expression: If theHour is less than 18 then assign the text "Good Afternoon!" to the variable welcomeMsg. Otherwise, assign the text "Good Evening!" to the variable welcomeMsg.

Notice that the `welcomeMsg` variable was initialized to null or empty when it was first declared.

One other thing to notice in this example is how we accessed the current time using the `Date` object. The following line of code from the previous HTML example creates a `Date` object that contains a snapshot of the current date (including the time) as of that particular moment:

```
var now = new Date()
```

The actual value of `now` is the time in milliseconds from January 1, 1970. By using the `Date` object method `getHours()`, we can determine what the current hour is (or the hour it was when the copy of the current date was made). The code

```
var theHour = now.getHours()
```

extracts the hour from the `now` instance of the `Date` object and assigns it to the variable `theHour`.

12.2.6   More Event Handlers

In addition to the events `onLoad` and `onChange`, there are many other event handlers. One of the simplest, and therefore most commonly used, JavaScript event handlers is called `onMouseOver`. As the name suggests, when you move your mouse over a particular item, an action is triggered. A corresponding `onMouseOut` event handler works in a similar fashion; when you move your mouse out of a particular area, an action is triggered. The following code shows how these two event handlers could be used in this book's Web presentation:

Go On-Line

```
<A HREF = "ASSIGNMENTS/assign.html"
    onMouseOver = "loadimage('01', 'GRAPHICS/4ON.GIF');
                  status = 'Assignments';
                  return true;"
    onMouseOut = "loadimage('01', 'GRAPHICS/4OFF.GIF');
                  status = '';
                  return true;">
                  <IMG SRC = "GRAPHICS/4OFF.GIF"
                      WIDTH = "42"
                      HEIGHT = "42"
                      NAME = "01"
                      ALT = "Assignments"
                      BORDER = "0"></A>
```

Notice that the JavaScript code is embedded directly within the HTML. The entire code fragment defines a hyperlink that is a clickable image. The image is called 4OFF.GIF and is located in the GRAPHICS directory. The file assign.html is loaded when someone clicks on the hyperlink. This file is located in the ASSIGNMENTS directory. When a user mouses over the image on their screen, the onMouseOver event handler is triggered. In our sample code, this results in three things:

1.   A function call is made to the JavaScript routine loadimage(), which we previously defined in the file containing this code. The job of loadimage() is to load a new image. In this case, it loads the image called 4ON.GIF in the place where the old image was displayed; 4ON.GIF is the Assignments button with the gold ring around it.

2.   The word Assignments is displayed in the status line of the browser as the code

```
status = 'Assignments';
```

is executed.

3.   The return true; instruction indicates that the browser can return normally from processing the JavaScript code.

Figure 12.5 shows the "Class" page for *In-line/On-line*. By viewing this page on-line in the book's Web presentation, you will notice that when you position the mouse cursor over the Assignments button, the Assignments button is highlighted and the status line contains the word Assignments.

The onMouseOut event handler works similarly. In this case, when the mouse is moved off the Assignments button, the original image (without the gold ring) is loaded and the status line is assigned an "empty" value. This results in a screen that appears as shown in Figure 12.5.

A few important points should be noted about the syntax of JavaScript and the JavaScript event handlers. The syntax for an event handler has the name of the event handler followed by an equals sign followed by a double-quoted set of JavaScript instructions. The instructions are delimited by semicolons. "Arguments" to the instructions are single-quoted. For example, to display the word Assignments in the status line of the browser, we used the instruction

```
status = 'Assignments';
```

The syntax for JavaScript is less forgiving than that of HTML, so you need to take extra care to make sure all symbols are in place properly. When a

FIGURE 12.5
The
In-line/On-line
class page used
to illustrate
JavaScript
commands.

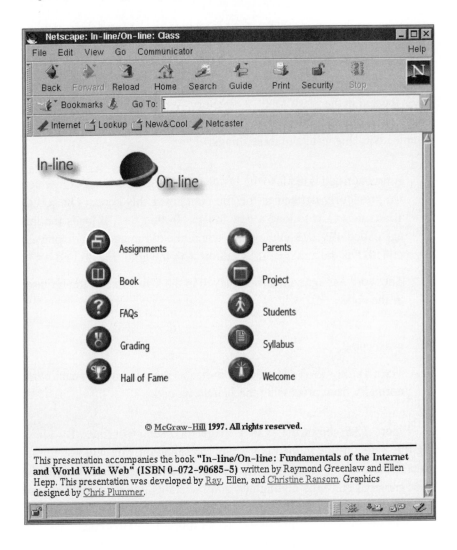

page is loaded, even a small mistake could result in a cryptic error message being displayed in a pop-up dialog box.

onClick and Alert Boxes

Another convenient and very easy-to-use JavaScript event handler is called onClick. It is commonly used to trigger some JavaScript code execution when a user selects a hyperlink. The following code is an example:

```
<A HREF = "killface.html"
        onClick = "alert('Thanks for loading my page:
            Killface.')">Killface's Page</A>
```

When the hyperlink "Killface's Page" is selected, the code assigned to the `onClick` event handler is triggered. In this case, a call is made to the routine `alert()`. This routine displays an alert box whose content is the message specified between the single-quote marks. In this example, the message is

```
Thanks for loading my page: Killface.
```

The result of selecting this hyperlink is shown in Figure 12.6. You can dismiss the alert box by clicking on the OK button.

Other JavaScript event handlers are included in the exercises.

12.2.7   Sample JavaScript Temperature Conversion Code

The goal of this section is to illustrate further how JavaScript can be used to create an interactive page, and to show how JavaScript interacts with forms. We will use temperature conversion as our example.

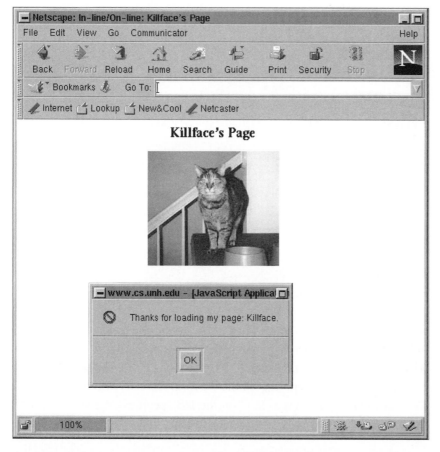

FIGURE 12.6
Killface's page is used to illustrate the JavaScript `onClick` event handler and an alert box.

Many U.S. citizens who travel abroad get confused over temperature readings. They end up either dressing too warmly (in southern Europe) or too lightly (in northern Europe). In most countries, degrees are specified in Celsius, whereas in the United States, they are given in Fahrenheit. How many people know that 30 degrees Celsius equals 86 degrees Fahrenheit?

The code presented here produces a form in which users can enter a temperature in either Celsius or Fahrenheit. They are then automatically provided with the equivalent temperature reading in the other units.

```
<FORM ACTION = "mailto:killface@inspector.tuna.com"
      METHOD = "post">

<STRONG>
Temperature Conversion Example Using JavaScript <BR>
</STRONG>

<P>
 
</P>

<INPUT TYPE = "text"
       NAME = "cels"
       VALUE = "0"
       SIZE = "3"
       MAXLENGTH = "3"
       onChange = "fahr.value = ↩
Math.round(10 * (1.8 * this.value + 32))/10;">
       &#176; <STRONG>C</STRONG>

  <STRONG>equals</STRONG>  

<INPUT TYPE = "text"
       NAME = "fahr"
       VALUE = "32"
       SIZE = "3"
       MAXLENGTH = "3"
       onChange = "cels.value = ↩
Math.round(10 * (this.value - 32)/1.8)/10;">
       &#176; <STRONG>F</STRONG>

</FORM>
```

The rendered version of the code is shown in Figure 12.7. (Note: Although the form has no SUBMIT button, we have included an ACTION and a METHOD. Most browsers will handle the form correctly without specifying these attributes.) The input field on the left specifies degrees in Celsius; the field on the right specifies degrees in Fahrenheit. The input fields are

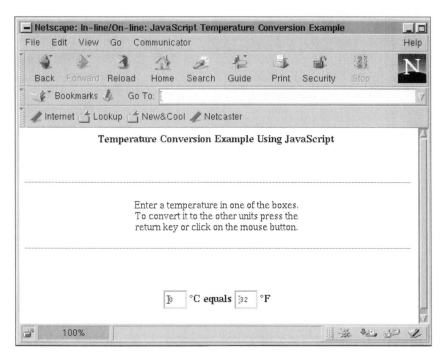

FIGURE 12.7
An example of a JavaScript form. A user can enter a value into either of the form's INPUT fields and the result will be the equivalent temperature displayed in the other units, either Celsius (°C) or Fahrenheit (°F), as appropriate.

created using the techniques described in Chapter 9, except that they use the JavaScript event handler onChange. When a user enters a number in either field and then presses the enter key or clicks the mouse, the JavaScript instruction quoted in the onChange declaration is executed. For example, if a user enters a value in the field label °C,[2] the following instruction is executed:

```
fahr.value = Math.round(10 * (1.8 * this.value + 32))/10;
```

This has the effect of displaying the equivalent Fahrenheit value in the field labeled °F. How does this work? Notice that the NAME of the second input field in the form is fahr. The variable fahr.value specifies the value of this field. Initially, the value is set to 32. The instruction listed above assigns a new value to fahr.value, and that value is automatically updated when the user presses the enter key or clicks the mouse.

The mathematical formula given in the instruction is a well-known formula for converting Celsius to Fahrenheit. The JavaScript routine Math.round() simply rounds its argument to a whole number. If a user

---

2 Recall, ° is the character entity for the degree symbol.

enters a value in the °F field first and then presses enter or clicks the mouse, an analogous sequence of events occurs and the °C field is updated.

Go On-Line

A good starting point for learning more about JavaScript is the source code of existing Web pages that include JavaScript. Some experimentation will also help you understand JavaScript better.

EXERCISES 12.2

The JavaScript Programming Language

1. Who developed JavaScript and when? Which browsers support JavaScript?

2. Locate three Web tutorials on JavaScript. Scan them and report four interesting facts about JavaScript.

3. Locate a JavaScript calculator and explain how it works.

4. Locate three books on JavaScript. Build an HTML table that lists the author, title, number of pages, and cost for each book. What was the average number of pages per book that you found?

5. Conduct several experiments to determine whether or not case is significant in JavaScript event handlers. For example, are onMouseOver and onmouseover treated the same?

6. Design a Web page that uses the onMouseOver and onMouseOut event handlers to load a new image when a user mouses over an image, and to restore the image when the user moves the mouse off the image.

7. Name three additional JavaScript event handlers and describe how they are used. Create a Web page that incorporates them.

8. What are some practical uses for alert boxes?

9. What happens with the JavaScript temperature conversion example if a user enters invalid data, such as nonnumeric data?

10. Using JavaScript, design a Web page that converts yards to meters and vice-versa.

12.3   Applets

Most of the information you retrieve from the Web is static, just like the pages in a book. Exceptions to this static mode can be created using features like animated gifs, forms, JavaScript, and plug-ins. Web pages may not feel static, because hypertext allows us to choose easily from multiple paths for a relatively unique tour through a presentation. The idea behind applets, which is short for "little application," is to provide even greater capabilities for embedding dynamic content into otherwise static Web pages.

If you use a Java-enabled browser, it supports Java applets and you may have already seen applets in action, without knowing it. For example, CNN's Web site uses a very simple applet that demonstrates the two primary applet features:

1. The information presented by the applet is dynamic, meaning it changes over time.

2. The applet can respond to user input.

The applet on CNN's homepage looks like a small banner. It is located at the top of the page and it periodically flashes a new summary headline, such as "Movie this weekend? Read our reviews & previews," or "Click here for college football scores." Each headline appears for a few seconds, so a user can comfortably read it, and then a new one is displayed. If someone viewing the applet finds an interesting topic, they can click on the headline. This action will load a new page at CNN's site, containing further details about their selection.

An applet is a small Java program, written in the Java language (not JavaScript), that the user downloads from a Web server. The applet then runs locally on their own computer within their browser. (This is different than a CGI script, which is run on the remote server.) The browser takes care of all the details of downloading and running the program, without the user having to do more than simply visit the Web page that includes the applet. CNN's applet works by cycling through a number of different headlines that were provided as input to the applet. If the user clicks on a headline, the program knows what new Web page to visit and automatically takes the user there. If important news stories break, such an applet could display this information to the user without the user explicitly having to reload the Web page. This is a fairly simple applet, but because applets are written in a programming language, they can be very complex.

12.3.1 HTML Applet Tags

Applets are easy to include on a Web page. The difficult (and technical) part is writing the corresponding Java program. A search on the Web will turn up a number of sites that offer free Java applets. The special HTML tag for including an applet is, of course, `<APPLET>`, and the ending tag is `</APPLET>`. While the applet tag supports a number of different attributes,

Go On-Line

the simplest way to include an applet is to specify the name of the *Java class file* (i.e., the executable program code), along with the applet's height and width. The HTML code for doing so is as follows:

```
<APPLET CODE = "HiMom.class"
        HEIGHT = "75"
        WIDTH = "125">
</APPLET>
```

In this case, the executable code is contained in a file called HiMom.class. The applet will be displayed in a 125-by-75 pixel area.

The applet tag supports the following attributes:

- ALIGN   The way to specify the alignment of the applet, used as in the image tag.

- ALT   Alternate text that can be displayed by text-only browsers, or by browsers that are not Java-enabled.

- CODE   The file in which the applet code is located. This file is relative to the base URL of the applet. Note that this is not a URL, but just a file name.

- CODEBASE   A URL that specifies where the applet's code is located relative to the page's URL. Omission of this attribute means the Java class files can be found in the same location as the Web page.

- HEIGHT   A required attribute that specifies the initial height of the applet, in pixels.

- HSPACE   The horizontal space around the applet, used as in the image tag.

- NAME   The symbolic name of the applet. Other applets in the same HTML document can refer to this to locate each other.

- VSPACE   The vertical space around the applet, used as in the image tag.

- WIDTH   A required attribute that specifies the initial width of the applet, in pixels.

12.3.2   Java-Enabled Browsers

For readers using a browser that is not Java-enabled, HTML developers usually include a message such as the following, between the beginning and ending applet tags:

```
You are running a browser that is not Java-enabled.
These pages are best viewed using Netscape 3.0 or higher.
```

Browsers that are text-only or are not Java-enabled will ignore the applet tags but will display the message. Browsers that are Java-enabled will run the applet without displaying the message. The message can occur anywhere between the beginning and ending applet tags. Also, in the ALT attribute of an applet tag, you should provide a brief description of the applet so that a user of a text-only browser will not lose continuity when reading your page.

We should note that some system administrators are reluctant to allow Java-enabled browsers to be run on their systems, for security reasons. A browser that is Java-enabled can, in theory, run any possible Java program on the machine running the browser. Although many security mechanisms are built into Java, it is conceivable that a clever hacker could write a Java program that could cause some problems on the local system. As the security of Java improves, this will become less of an issue.

12.3.3   Sample Applets

In addition to specifying the attributes of the applet tag, you need to be able to specify certain applet input parameters, so that it can be customized to your needs. The best way to illustrate how this is accomplished is by using a simple example.

```
<APPLET CODE = "HiMom.class"
        HEIGHT = "75"
        WIDTH = "125">
<PARAM NAME = "message"
       VALUE = "Hi Mom.  How do you like my applet?">
</APPLET>
```

The parameter tag, <PARAM>, has two attributes: NAME and VALUE. In this case, the NAME attribute is assigned a value of message. The Java program HiMom contains the word message as one of its variables and expects to receive a value for it that is a string of text. The value is conveyed to the program through the VALUE attribute. In our example,

```
"Hi Mom.  How do you like my applet?"
```

is specified as the value for message. The applet occupies a 125-by-75-pixel area on the screen, and the value of message is cycled endlessly

FIGURE 12.8
The HiMom
applet.

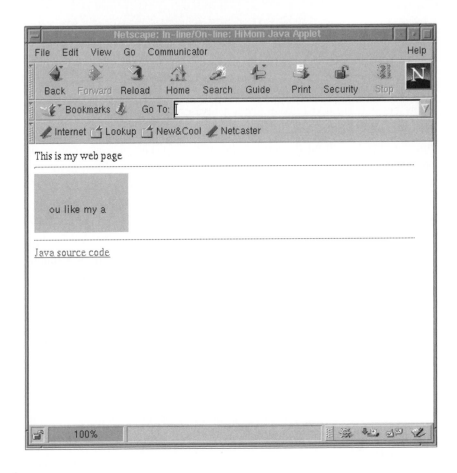

through this small area. The actual Java code for this applet is available
on-line. Figure 12.8 shows how the applet appears on a Web page. Since
the text is scrolling across the screen, it appears differently at any given
moment, until the cycle is repeated.

In general, an applet may allow many different parameters to be specified. For example, an applet that displays a *marquee* might allow you to
specify a color, font face, text size, and time limit. Each of these parameters
permits customization of the applet; each parameter is specified in its own
parameter tag, which is included within the applet beginning and ending
tags.

Go On-Line

EXERCISES 12.3

Applets

11.   Provide the URLs of three Web pages that contain applets. Ex-
       plain how the pages use the applets. Provide the URLs for two

on-line tutorials about applets. Provide the URLs for three sites where you can obtain free applets.

12.   Locate three books that describe Java applets. Design a table in HTML that lists the author, title, number of pages, and cost of each book. What was the average number of pages per book?

13.   Design a Web page and include an applet. Customize the applet for your page. Include information for users of text-only browsers and for those whose browsers are not Java-enabled.

14.   What are some of the most common uses of applets? What features do they contain?

15.   Does your computer slow down when processing an applet? Explain.

16.   Do you find pages that include dynamic elements distracting? Which do you prefer, static pages or more dynamic pages?

12.4   The Java Programming Language

Hot Topic

One of the hottest topics in software development and the Internet is the programming language called *Java*. The language was originally developed at Sun Microsystems as part of an effort to design a wide range of sophisticated consumer electronic devices with the ability to "communicate" with one another. The Sun developers soon realized, however, that most such devices, like VCRs, Nintendo, and stereos, were built around different computer chips. This meant that any program running on those devices would have to be written in separate programming languages. The engineers at Sun decided they needed to develop a new software technology that would allow them to write complex, object-oriented programs that could run on a wide range of computer CPUs.[3] The language that the Sun engineers developed was originally named *Oak*, after the tree outside the office window of James Gosling, the principal inventor of the language.

The group at Sun Microsystems developed some prototype devices and tried to win a large contract for developing TV set-top boxes. However, their efforts in the personal consumer electronics market did not go well and

---

3   CPU stands for *Central Processing Unit*. You can think of the CPU as the brains of the computer.

the project was nearly abandoned, just when interest in the Internet started to explode. Rather than promoting the language for electronic devices, Sun switched their focus to ways of delivering small applications, called applets, over the Internet. Also at about this time, Sun changed the name of the language from Oak to Java, and as interest in the Internet ballooned, so did interest in the Java programming language.

The term *Java* has come to take on many different meanings (aside from a name for coffee, or an island in Indonesia). The term *Java language* refers to the rules of syntax and semantics for writing programs in Java, as well as a set of Java libraries containing portions of programs that software developers can use when coding their own applications.

There is also the *Java Virtual Machine*, which allows you to run a Java application on any type of computer (for example, a Mac or a PC). The Java Virtual Machine was Sun's solution to having the same program run on many different kinds of computers or devices. The idea is that you only have to write your program once in the Java language. To run it on any given computer, all you need is a virtual machine that can interpret instructions in the Java language and execute them on the computer in question. This is an enormous benefit to software developers who need only write a program once and can have it run on many different computers. It also benefits consumers, who can purchase and use a program without worrying about whether or not it was written to run on their particular type of computer (try running Windows 2000 on a Mac!).

In addition to the Java language and the Virtual Machine, Sun and the Java community are trying to put together a large range of libraries and specifications for using Java for such things as telephony applications, smart cards, 3D imaging, sound, video, and database access, among many others.

12.4.1   Sample Java Source Code

In this section, we include the source code for a simple Java applet called Shapes. The display of this applet on a Web page is shown in Figure 12.9. Our purpose is to provide you with an example of what Java code looks like, not to explain its exact syntax and semantics. The interested reader can pursue Java further through the references.

Go On-Line

```
import java.awt.*; import java.applet.*;

/**
A simple applet called "Shapes" that
simply draws a circle and a square.
*/
```

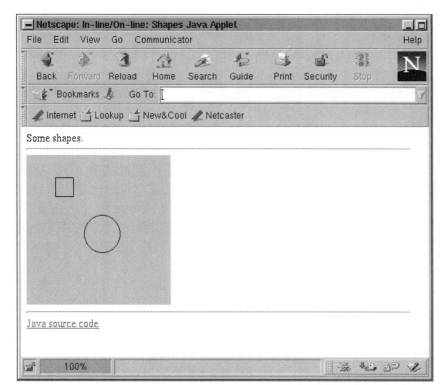

FIGURE 12.9
The Shapes applet, which draws a circle with a radius of 50 pixels and a square with a side length of 25 pixels.

```java
public class Shapes extends Applet
{
public void paint(Graphics g) {
    Circle c = new Circle(50);
    Square s = new Square(25);
    c.draw(g,80,80);
    s.draw(g,40,30);
    }
}

/**
The Shape class.  It has no member data and
supports a single method called draw.
*/
abstract class Shape {
  public abstract void draw(Graphics g, int xloc, int yloc);
}
```

```
/**
The Circle class is a subclass of Shape.
New circles are created with a given radius.
*/
class Circle extends Shape {
    private int radius;
    public Circle(int r) {
        radius = r;
    }
    public void draw(Graphics g, int xloc, int yloc) {
        g.drawOval(xloc,yloc,radius,radius);
    }
}

/**
The square class is a subclass of Shape.
A square is created with a given edge size.
*/
class Square extends Shape {
    private int size;
    public Square(int s) {
        size = s;
    }
    public void draw(Graphics g, int xloc, int yloc) {
        g.drawRect(xloc,yloc,size,size);
    }
}
```

12.4.2 Java and Object-Oriented Programming

Java supports *object-oriented programming* (*OOP*), which is a style of programming that can best be explained by a simple example. The Shapes Java applet presented in Section 12.4.1 draws a circle and a square. The object-oriented techniques are mainly used in the drawing of the geometric figures. We defined a *class* of objects called Shape that know how to draw themselves at a specified location. We also defined two subclasses of Shape called Circle and Square. The Circle class has one member variable called radius, which defines the size of the circle. The Circle's drawing method draws the circle at the specified location, using the radius that was specified when the Circle object was created. Similarly, the Square subclass has a member variable called size, for the length of one edge, and the Square knows how to draw itself at a specified location.

In the Shapes example, there is one other use of object-oriented techniques, and that is the Shapes applet itself. The Java language defines a class called `Applet`, from which all applets must descend. The `Applet` class takes care of implementing all the behavior needed to run within a browser. For example, the `Applet` class has methods to "start" and "stop" the applet when a user goes to or leaves a Web page containing the applet. In the Shapes subclass of `Applet`, we only changed one of the applet's "paint" methods to suit our needs. By overriding the paint method, we were able to make the applet function as we wanted. The paint method automatically gets called for us when the applet is first started. In the Shapes example, the paint method creates a new instance of a `Circle` with a radius of 50 pixels and a `Square` with sides 25 pixels in length. The `Applet` then asks each shape to draw itself at a different location. Figure 12.9 shows how the applet displays.

EXERCISES 12.4

The Java Programming Language

17.   What is *HotJava*? Assess its popularity.

18.   What is *ActiveX*? How widely is it used and supported?

19.   Locate three books that describe the Java programming language. Design an HTML table that lists the author, title, number of pages, and cost of each book. What was the average number of pages per book?

20.   Locate two Web presentations that provide free Java programs. What types of programs are available? Did the presentations contain advertisements for general Java program development?

21.   If you have access to a Java compiler, modify and recompile the source code of the program Shapes so that the circle and square intersect when drawn on the screen.

12.5   Guest Books

An electronic *guest book* provides a way for readers who visit your Web pages to "sign in" and perhaps leave you a note. Visitors will usually comment on your presentation, but they can leave a message about whatever topic they choose. Usually, all sign-ins are collected and displayed together

FIGURE 12.10
A sample guest
book.

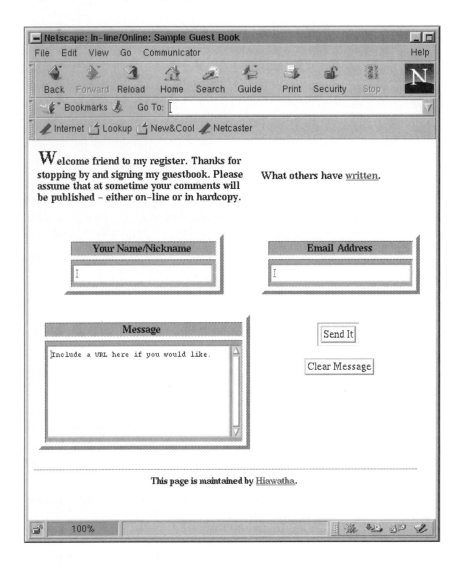

in an HTML document. In this section we describe how you can implement
a `mailto` guest book. We do not describe CGI programming, which we
touched on in Chapter 11 and which can be pursued through the references,
but we do point out where to obtain CGI scripts that process guest book
entries automatically.

Guest books are implemented using forms. Tables are useful for positioning the various form elements. A visitor signs a guest book by simply
filling out a form and submitting it. Figure 12.10 illustrates the appearance
of a typical guest book. You should be able to construct your own guest
book, using the techniques described in Section 9.3.

Hot Topic

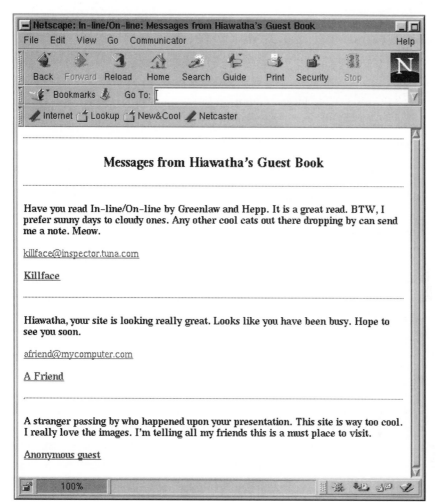

FIGURE 12.11
The sign-ins from a sample guest book.

Guest books allow you to keep an informal record of who visited your presentation. As your pages progress, the nature of the comments you receive will probably change, too. Guest books typically display a list of previous messages. Figure 12.11 displays a portion of a guest book, illustrating how sign-ins are typically formatted.

12.5.1   Standard Input Fields of a Guest Book

The most common fields included in a guest book form are:

- *Email address*—If a visitor enters an email address, you can display a `mailto` hyperlink to them so that other guest book readers can send them messages. If two people have a mutual friend who has a guest book, the `mailto` links can be useful for putting these friends in contact with each other. Reading a prior sign-in may provide the impetus for contacting the corresponding author and sharing ideas.

- *Message*—The largest input field is usually labeled `message` or `comment`, where a visitor can type in a note. The message field is typically created using the textarea tag.

- *Name*—This is the field in which visitors enter their name or nickname.

- *URL*—This is a field for visitors to specify their URL. Guest books often display hyperlinks to visitors' pages.

All fields in the form should be restricted in length. For example, most guest book owners do not want to allow space for more than several paragraphs of text. Also, the script that processes the guest book usually takes care of the HTML formatting, but some guest books allow readers to enter HTML code in the messages they submit.

12.5.2   Guest Book Dynamics

Guest books are created using a form. The `ACTION` attribute of the form tag specifies the name of a CGI script to be run when a visitor submits a sign-in. (`Mailto` guest books are described in Section 12.5.3.) The `post` `METHOD` is usually used to send the parameters to the guest book. Here, we outline the steps that take place during sign-in and updating of an on-line guest book.

Suppose a visitor brings up a guest book on screen. They will normally fill in all[4] of the fields specified on the guest book form and then submit the form by clicking on the `SUBMIT` button. The parameters entered in the form are then sent to the CGI script specified in the `ACTION` attribute of the form declaration. For example, suppose the name of the script that receives the parameters is `process-gb`. This program resides in the corresponding Web server's `cgibin` directory. (The server is named in the `where` part of the `ACTION` attribute URL.)

When the form is submitted, the Web server runs the program `process-gb`. Usually, the program first checks to make sure that the user

---

4   You can use the input tag with TYPE hidden to specify default values for each field. This way, the script that is processing the form is guaranteed to have a value for each field.

has entered valid values in each of the fields. Nothing can prevent a malicious user from typing in nonsense; however, the script can be used to filter the parameters. Once the appropriate syntax checks have been executed and the parameters decoded, the program opens the file where the messages contained in the guest book are stored. Suppose the previous sign-ins are stored in a file called `messages.html`. In order for `process-gb` to be able to open `messages.html`, the file must be world writeable. In other words, `process-gb` must have the same privileges as an anonymous FTP user.

After opening the file `messages.html`, `process-gb` inserts the recent sign-in, with the appropriate HTML formatting. Once this is done, the file is written back to disk. In the next step, the CGI script returns an HTML document to the user who just signed the guest book. The document often contains a message saying something like, "Thank you for stopping by and signing in," and a hyperlink that the reader can click on to view the `messages.html` file, which now contains their entry. The person who signed in cannot edit the entry once it has been submitted.

As we stated, the file containing the sign-ins needs to be world writeable in order for `process-gb` to add to it. From a security point of view, this means that anyone with access to the file can delete it. On a UNIX system, for example, this would be any local user. Furthermore, a malicious user can sign in and fill your guest book with foul language or other unacceptable messages. For these reasons, it is a good idea to keep a backup copy of your guest book that is not world writeable, and to check the contents of your guest book periodically, removing inappropriate entries.

What happens if two users try to sign your guest book at the same time? Unless the program `process-gb` takes care of *locking* the file, this can cause problems.

The CGI script needed to implement the guest book is usually written in a programming language such as C, Java, or Perl. Writing a program like `process-gb` requires a lot of programming expertise in order to avoid security problems. In addition, you need to be able to install such a program in a `cgibin` directory on some Web server. Since you may not have the ability to write a guest book program, nor the permission to install a CGI script, you can seek out the many sites on the Web that provide free guest books. Some ISPs provide guest book software, as well. You can then download a guest book, the corresponding CGI script, and the instructions on how to install it. Since there have been security problems with some free guest books, be sure to read the documentation before downloading and installing them. The URLs for several sites that provide guest books can be found in this book's on-line presentation.

Go On-Line

12.5.3   Mailto Guest Books

A different and simpler way to create a guest book does not involve a world writeable file, nor CGI programming. In the form that represents the guest book, you can specify an ACTION as a mailto hyperlink. You should use the post METHOD in the corresponding form. When the form is submitted, the email address specified in the mailto hyperlink is sent a message. The message contains the values entered by the visitor. Although the message is encoded, it is very easy to determine what the reader typed in. You can then edit the email message to strip out the encoding information; for example, plus signs will have to be converted to spaces, and so on. Finally, you insert the edited message, with the appropriate HTML formatting, into your messages.html file.

Although a mailto hyperlink is not a completely automated solution for developing and managing a guest book, it does provide a simple-to-use and relatively secure mechanism for creating one. The guest book example shown in Figure 12.10 uses a mailto hyperlink. As is always the case with any figure in this book containing HTML code, you may go to the book's Web presentation and examine the source code that produced the figure. This will show you exactly how a mailto guest book is programmed in HTML. We include the HTML code that produced this guest book in Figure 12.12.

In summary, a typical guest book consists of the following items:

- A form in which a user can sign in (guestbook.html).

- A collection of previous entries (messages.html).

- A CGI script that processes sign-ins (process-gb).

The names in parentheses are the filenames we have used in this section for the corresponding elements. If a mailto is used for the ACTION attribute of the form tag, the functions carried out by process-gb must be done manually.

EXERCISES 12.5

Guest Books

22.   List the URLs of three presentations that provide free guest books. Does any one seem preferable? Why?

23.   Implement a guest book using a `mailto` hyperlink. Include the standard fields and any others that you feel are important. Restrict the amount of information a visitor can enter into each field.

24.   What kind of problems could arise if the CGI script corresponding to a guest book implementation is not secure?

25.   Locate the guest books of two different thru-hikers. Report the URLs of both and an interesting entry from each one.

```
<!-- copyright (c) McGraw-Hill, 1997-as updated. ↩
     All rights reserved. -->
<!-- Guest book implemented via a mailto hyperlink. -->
<HTML>

<HEAD>
<TITLE>In-line/Online:  Sample Guest Book</TITLE>
<META NAME = "keywords"
      CONTENT = "Internet, Web, World Wide Web, tutorial,
         guide, teaching, book, textbook, learning,
         Java, Javascript, HTML">
</HEAD>

<BODY BGCOLOR = "#FFFFFF">

<TABLE>

<TR>
<TD WIDTH = "45%">
<STRONG>
<FONT SIZE = "+4">W</FONT>elcome friend to my register. Thanks for
stopping by and signing my guestbook. Please assume that at sometime
your comments will be published - either on-line or in hardcopy.
</STRONG>

<TD WIDTH = "5%">

<TD WIDTH = "45%">
<STRONG>
What others have <A HREF = "messages.html">written</A>.
</STRONG>
```

FIGURE 12.12

Source code for producing the guest book shown in Figure 12.10.

```
<TR>
<TD>  

<FORM METHOD = "post"
      ACTION = "mailto:killface@inspector.tuna.com">

<TR>
<TD ALIGN = "center">
<TABLE BORDER = "5" CELLSPACING = "5" BGCOLOR = "#00FFFF">

<TD ALIGN = "center">
<STRONG>Your Name/Nickname</STRONG>

<TR>
<TD ALIGN = "center">
<INPUT TYPE = "text" NAME = "handle"
       SIZE = "30" MAXLENGTH = "50">
</TABLE>

<TD>
 

<TD>
<TABLE BORDER = "5" CELLSPACING = "5" BGCOLOR = "#00FFFF">

<TR>
<TD ALIGN = "center">
<STRONG>Email Address</STRONG>

<TR>
<TD>
<INPUT TYPE = "text" NAME = "from"
       SIZE = "30" MAXLENGTH = "40">
</TABLE>

<TR>
<TD>  

<TR>
<TD ALIGN = "center">
<TABLE BORDER = "5" CELLSPACING = "5" BGCOLOR = "#00FFFF">

<TR>
<TD ALIGN = "center">
<STRONG>Messsage</STRONG>

<TR>
<TD>
```

FIGURE 12.12
Continued.

```
<TEXTAREA NAME = "message" ROWS = "10" COLS = "40"
         WRAP MAXLENGTH = "500">
Include a URL here if you would like.
</TEXTAREA>

</TABLE>

<TD>  

<TD ALIGN = "center" VALIGN = "top">

<TABLE>

<TR>
<TD ALIGN = "center">
<INPUT TYPE = "submit" VALUE = "Send It">

<TR>
<TD ALIGN = "center">
<INPUT TYPE = "reset" VALUE = "Clear Message">
</TABLE>
</FORM>
</TABLE>

<H5 ALIGN = "center">
<HR>
This page is maintained by
     <A href = "mailto:hiawatha@north.edu">Hiawatha</A>.
</H5>

</BODY>

</HTML>
```

FIGURE 12.12
Continued.

12.6   Web Page Counters

A *Web page counter* (counter, for short) is a program that tracks how many times a page has been loaded. Each time the page is loaded, the counter value is increased by one. Figure 12.13 shows a typical counter display. Although it is possible to initialize a counter to an arbitrary value, people usually start their counters at zero. That way, they can tell how many times the page has been visited, at least since the counter was installed. Because repeat visitors are counted each time they visit a page, the counter does not specify how many different people have loaded the page.

FIGURE 12.13
A counter on a
Web page.

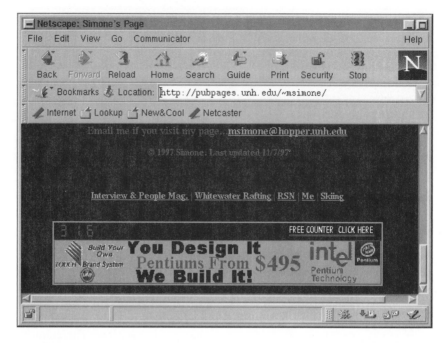

The accuracy of counters varies. For example, a counter may increment every time the page gets loaded, regardless of who loads it and how often. Thus, someone who wanted to increase their counter could simply load their own page all day long. Other counters increment only when the page gets loaded by someone other than the owner of the page, and only once per day per visitor. Some counters increment when the page is visited by a Lynx user, while others do not. If you see an unusually large counter value, do not assume it is valid.

Some people like to display a counter at the bottom of their page to imply how popular their page is. However, as you have seen, the actual meaning of a counter differs from page to page. Also, a large count does not imply that the information on the page is reliable or interesting.

12.6.1   HTML Code for a Counter

The most common approach to displaying a counter on a Web page is to use the image tag. The second most popular way is to use *server-side includes*, which you will learn about in Section 12.7. It is possible to specify an absolute URL for a CGI script as the value of the SRC attribute of the image tag. Parameters may be passed to the script using the conventions of the get METHOD. The following code illustrates how this is done:

```
<IMG SRC = "http://www.colt.com/cgibin/↩
              counter?data=ellen.dat&style=1"
```

```
ALIGN = "absmiddle"
ALT = "counter"
HEIGHT = "20"
WIDTH = "70">
```

In our example, the program named `counter` is located in the `cgibin` directory of the `www.colt.com` Web server. This CGI script receives two parameters: `data` with a value of `ellen.dat`, and `style` with a value of `1`. When the page containing this sample code is loaded, the program `counter` is run on the `www.colt.com` server. In this example, the counter is displayed in an area that is 20 pixels high and 70 pixels wide.

The program opens the file `ellen.dat` to extract the current value of Ellen's counter. It adds one to this value and rewrites the file `ellen.dat` so that the next time Ellen's counter is retrieved, it will be one larger. Like a guest book message file, this file must be world writeable.

The `style` parameter tells the script how the counter should be displayed. Using `style` type 1, the program returns an image consisting of the digits that make up the current value of Ellen's counter. The counter value is usually constructed using a subset of ten small images; an image for 0, an image for 1, . . . , and an image for 9.

Many sites offer free counters. These can be found in the references accompanying this book. That is, they allow you to have a file on their server containing your counter's value, and they let you use their CGI script. Since many users cannot install CGI scripts on their Web servers, this is the route that people usually follow for obtaining a counter. The exact parameters you need to specify in order to implement a counter vary. For example, with some counters, you may have a choice of color or digit style, and different choices with others.

Go On-Line

12.6.2   Counter Usefulness

A counter provides useful information on how many times a presentation has been visited. For businesses and Webmasters, the number of hits per page may be very important. For example, advertising rates are usually based on these statistics. Obviously, a page that receives 30,000,000 hits per day may charge significantly more for advertising than a page that gets 100 hits per week. If a page is not as successful as projected, a decision may be made to redesign it or conduct an analysis to determine why people are not visiting the page more often.

12.6.3   Counter Display Decision

While counters provide useful information to Webmasters, it is not always necessary or desirable to broadcast a counter to the world. Some users take offense at counters (especially ones displayed on personal pages). They feel counters are a way of showing off or boasting about the popularity of a presentation. Many businesses and Webmasters do not display their counters on screen. They prefer to keep an off-line record of the number of hits. If you decide to display a counter, it should probably be included at the bottom of a page. Remember, you can track the number of hits your page receives without actually displaying a counter on screen. You can also track the number of hits your page receives via the Web server's logs, if you have access to them.

EXERCISES 12.6

Web Page Counters

26.   Why does a counter place a load on a server?

27.   Design a Web page that has a counter on it. Does the counter increment each time you access the page?

28.   How many hits per day do the Microsoft, Netscape, and Yahoo! Web presentations receive?

29.   What is the largest counter value you have seen on a Web page? Report the URL for the page and whether or not you thought the counter value was valid.

12.7   Server-Side Includes

12.7.1   Common Inclusions

A *server-side include (SSI)* is a way to send a command to a Web server from inside an HTML document. If you have ever seen a Web page showing the current time and date, this is usually accomplished by a server-side include. Server-side includes are most commonly used for displaying the following:

- Another HTML document inside the current one.

- A counter.

- The current time and date.

- The last-modified date of a document.

- A random quote.

- A random page. (This is a fun way to provide a reader with a "mystery" page.)

A file extension of .shtml or .shtm is usually used to designate an HTML document that incorporates a server-side include. Because it initiates a specific action, a server-side include places an additional demand on a server.

12.7.2   Utilization

The basic syntax for a server-side include is

```
<!--#exec cgi = "/cgibin/script.cgi"-->
```

to run a program, or

```
<!--#include virtual = "insert.html"-->
```

to insert another HTML document. Notice how the commands that go to the server are embedded in comments. The first case shows how to run the CGI script called script.cgi when the corresponding page is loaded. As an example, the script might be a program that processes a counter. The second case illustrates how to include the HTML document insert.html into the HTML document containing this code. The exact syntax for server-side includes varies, depending on the server being used.

EXERCISES 12.7

Server-Side Includes

30.   Provide the URLs of three pages that have tutorials about server-side includes. Give the URL for a page that makes effective use

of a server-side include. Why do you think more people do not use server-side includes?

31. Design a page that uses a server-side include to show a time stamp.

32. What is the server-side include syntax for including the file `appalachian.html` in the HTML document `myhike.html`?

multimedia

13

The White Mountains of New Hampshire are simply known as "The Whites" to hikers. I was very familiar with The Whites because I had lived in New Hampshire for years. It was a very emotional moment when I entered New Hampshire; this is where I left from on my trip to Georgia to start the trail. I had now walked all the way back home. The Whites are very rugged by any trail standards. I was fortunate to have perfect weather in The Whites, and the views were marvelous. I was hiking extremely well and had gotten in great shape. One day I climbed over 25,000 feet of vertical. Looking back on it, I am not sure how I did it. Going over Mount Washington during my thru-hike was a great feeling; all other summits to come would be lower in altitude. Mount Washington is known for its unpredictable and sometimes deadly weather; I was blessed with ideal conditions and thoroughly enjoyed the views.

New Hampshire
160 miles

Chapter 13

13.1 INTRODUCTION

Web pages can be very exciting and dynamic with the inclusion of *multimedia*, which encompasses animation, audio (sound), graphics—both two-dimensional (2D) and three-dimensional (3D) images—text, and video[1] (silent or with sound). Any combination of these media can be specified in HTML documents. Of course, a typical Web page contains in-line images and text, but more and more Web pages are using other types of media as well. Since we have already addressed image formats, simple animations, and text, this chapter will focus on audio, 3D images, and video.

In many ways, multimedia is still in its infancy and is one of the most complex and rapidly changing areas on the Web. There are entire books devoted to this subject. A number of these can be traced through the references. The goal of this chapter is to provide you with a brief glimpse into multimedia topics so that you can have a good starting point for pursuing areas that interest you in more detail. It is important not to go overboard by displaying too much multimedia content. If you decide to include a multimedia item, it should have a value to the average reader of your Web page. We will cover the following relevant topics:

Objectives

- Important multimedia issues, such as the process of playing/displaying multimedia documents

- Audio

- Video (movies)

- Virtual reality and 3D modeling

- Multimedia and HTML documents

---

1   We use the words *movie* and *video* interchangeably throughout this chapter.

13.2   Important Multimedia Issues

There are many questions about multimedia:

- What helpers and plug-ins are available for your operating system?

- Is it safe to download a plug-in, and which plug-in should you use? How can you check to see if a plug-in is virus-free? How do you install a plug-in? How much memory does a plug-in require?

- What percentage of users can take advantage of multimedia? Should you include some on your Web page? What, if anything, should you provide for those who cannot take advantage of multimedia?

- What is the future of multimedia? Are any standards being developed?

- How do you use the *Virtual Reality Modeling Language (VRML)*?

- What is the most widely supported way of including multimedia on a Web page? What HTML tags do you use?

- How long will it take a typical user to download your multimedia file? How large a file does a 10-minute video require?

- Do you need special hardware to play multimedia? How fast a computer do you need? What is the minimum configuration required?

- What kind of quality can you expect from multimedia applications? Are movies choppy? Is sound clarity good?

Here, we will provide valuable information about multimedia, answer some of the questions, ask you to address others in the exercises, and provide references for still others.

13.2.1   Multimedia Displays

A number of different outcomes are possible when you use your graphical browser to load a Web page that contains a multimedia element. (You may want to review Section 4.3.3 about helper applications and plug-ins before proceeding.)

1. *Helper*—If your browser is properly configured to play/display the multimedia element using a helper application, the helper will

automatically be launched when you download the page. You will usually be presented with a "control panel" allowing you to play, adjust volume, start, stop, fast forward, reverse, and manipulate the multimedia element, just as you would a video cassette in a VCR, or a CD in a compact disc player. The control panel and the window in which the multimedia element is displayed are separate from the browser window. When finished, you can dismiss the control panel. Often, under this scenario, you can continue to browse the Web (in the original window) while playing the multimedia element.

2.   *Plug-in*—If your browser is properly configured to play/display the multimedia element using a plug-in, the multimedia element will automatically be included in the page. For example, if you load a page that contains an audio clip, you will hear the sound. In the status line, you may notice a message such as "loading plug-in" during the loading phase.

3.   *Neither*—If your browser has neither a helper nor a plug-in capable of processing the multimedia element, you may be provided with a hyperlink to a location from which you can download a plug-in to process the file. If you download and install the plug-in (you should first run virus detection software on it), you should then be able to play/display the multimedia element in the browser window. Sometimes you will have the option of saving the multimedia file.[2] In this case, you may be able to play/display it using a helper application that you have but have not yet configured into the browser.

13.2.2   Current Multimedia Concerns

Hot Topic

Multimedia can be very entertaining, especially if you have a fast computer, all the necessary plug-ins installed, and access to the Internet at a quiet time. We encourage you to test and use multimedia applications. However, you might run into a number of problems that can be frustrating.

One problem is the lack of standards. The field of multimedia is emerging rapidly. Because of this and because multimedia of this nature is so new, standards have not yet been developed. Many of the technologies for creating and displaying multimedia are proprietary, which means that a given plug-in may only be able to process one of the many multimedia

---

2   Record companies often provide sound bites or video clips of their artists. If a full video is provided, it is usually *buffered* in such a way that it is difficult to copy.

formats. For example, there are several common video formats, but each plug-in can usually only deal with one of these formats. This means that you need to download separate plug-ins for different movie formats.

When experimenting with plug-ins for this chapter, we found that they often caused our system to crash. Much of the technology is still unstable. Furthermore, different plug-ins are needed for different operating systems. While many plug-ins are available for Mac and PC users, the choices are much more limited on UNIX systems. Finding the appropriate plug-in can sometimes be difficult, and keeping up with the latest version also requires time.

A second problem with multimedia is that no graphical browser can handle every kind of multimedia format that it encounters. In fact, due to the wide range of formats and the size of the players, no browser in the foreseeable future will be able to handle a significant percentage of the different types of formats. As we have seen, to get around this, browsers can start a plug-in or helper application to play/display the multimedia file. However, many users are not comfortable downloading and installing plug-ins. They may also not be comfortable with the procedure itself, nor with the possibility of downloading a virus. In addition, you might sometimes have to fill out a form to obtain a plug-in, and the information you enter could end up being used for advertising purposes (resulting in lots of spam). If you decide to download a plug-in, you will often be asked to read and agree to a licensing statement.

A third problem is that multimedia elements are usually very large, much larger than typical images. Files can easily be one megabyte or more. Therefore, they take a long time to download, and they place a strain on the Internet. Downloading an application to play/display multimedia elements can take a long time as well, since the tools are large and the sites that offer them are often busy. If your computer is slow and you are working over a modem line, you can expect to experience lengthy delays. Furthermore, on a slow system, the results of displaying multimedia are not that impressive; for example, the frames in a video might not be able to update quickly.

Because multimedia files are so large, file compression plays an important role in downloads. Many multimedia formats have built-in compression and decompression algorithms. However, even with significant compression, some multimedia elements may be too large to transfer over and play in real time. Therefore, when you go to play a large audio clip or a movie, the file containing the data will usually be *buffered*. To explain: A portion of the movie will be brought over and stored before the movie actually begins playing. The data in the buffer is displayed, while more data is brought over in parallel. This process is known as *streaming*. If the buffering is done properly and if the user has a fast connection to the Internet, the movie will play without breaking up or getting choppy. In contrast, for real-time applications, such as videoconferencing, where such buffering is not possible, the quality of the display over the Internet is usually not great.

Multimedia applications are continuously and rapidly improving, and they are definitely worth checking out and learning.

EXERCISES 13.2

Important Multimedia Issues

1. Describe your experiences with multimedia. Have you ever had to download or install a plug-in to view a page you visited?

2. Download, install, and experiment with a plug-in for a form of multimedia of your choice. Describe how long the process took and what was involved.

3. List five helpers and plug-ins currently configured in your browser. Is it easy to add new ones? Explain.

13.3   Audio

The term *audio* refers to sound. A number of audio formats exist, and audio can be included in a Web page. Obviously, to hear sound from a Web page, your computer must be equipped with speakers. The process of streaming is used with large audio files.

A large number of audio file formats are in use. They include:

- AIFF (.aif, .aiff, and .aifc extensions), which stands for *Audio Interchange File Format*. This format was developed by Apple.

- AU (.au and .snd extensions). This format was developed by Sun Microsystems.

- MIDI (.midi and .mid extensions), which stands for *Musical Instrument Digital Interface*.

- RealAudio (`.ra` and `.ram` extensions). This format was developed by Progressive Networks.

- WAV (`.wav` extension). This format was developed by Microsoft.

The developers of the formats should tell you which platforms will support each format. To play any of these formats, you will need an appropriate plug-in. Some audio plug-ins are capable of playing more than one format. The MIDI format can be used to create very small, yet musically interesting, audio files.

13.3.1   Audio Installation

When you load a Web page that contains an audio file, one of the following things usually happens:

1. The file automatically plays and you hear sound; or,

2. You are given the option to download the sound file. Once the file is retrieved, you can listen to it by playing the file on an appropriate audio player; or,

3. You are given the option to download a plug-in that can play the sound file; or,

4. You get a pop-up dialog box that says something like "no audio player installed."

You should be aware that downloading even a 10-to-15-second audio clip can take a while. In addition, when you play the file, depending on the speed of your computer and the quality of the recording, you may be disappointed by what you hear. If you do decide to include audio on your Web page, try to do it in a way that users who either are not equipped for audio, do not want to spend a long time downloading a file, do not have a fast machine, or do not want to download an audio player will still enjoy your Web page.

13.3.2   Audio and Web Pages

One approach to including an audio file in a Web page involves the object[3] tag, `<OBJECT>`, and its corresponding ending tag `</OBJECT>`. (This tag

---

3   Many Web authors use the embed tag, `<EMBED>`, for including multimedia. We emphasize the object tag, since it is included in the latest HTML specification, while the embed tag is not.

is discussed more fully in Section 13.6.1.) To include the WAV audio file called `mymusic.wav` using the object tag, you could use the following code:

```
<OBJECT DATA = "mymusic.wav"
        TYPE = "audio/wav">
</OBJECT>
```

The `DATA` attribute specifies the source file, and the `TYPE` attribute specifies the object's MIME type.

Microsoft's Internet Explorer (IE) supports the background sound tag, `<BGSOUND>`. (Netscape currently does not.) To include the same audio file on a page to be loaded by IE, you could use the following code:

```
<BGSOUND SRC = "mymusic.wav">
```

In either case, when a user equipped for audio loads this document, they will hear the sounds in the file `mymusic.wav`.

The background sound tag also supports the `LOOP` attribute. `LOOP` can be assigned a natural number indicating the number of times the audio file is to be played, or it can take a value of `infinite`, indicating that the sound should be played endlessly. We do not recommend using this value, however, because hearing the same thing over and over again can get very annoying.

13.3.3   Audio Repositories

Go On-Line

An amazing amount of audio is now available on-line. You can obtain music by many popular recording artists, as well as audio clips of historical interest. There are also sites where you can listen to live concerts, news broadcasts, and other types of programs. However, like written documents and images, these audio clips may be protected by copyright.[4] The reader may pursue the references for more information on this burgeoning area.

EXERCISES 13.3

Audio

4.   Is your browser configured to play sound files? If so, what types of files can you play?

---

4   One individual, who had some Three Stooges audio clips on his Web page, found this out the hard way.

5. Have you ever heard sounds played on a computer? How would you rate the sound quality?

6. What is the size of the executable file of a typical audio player?

7. What audio formats does the RealAudio player process?

8. What is the syntax for including the audio file `song.midi` on a Web page?

9. Provide the URLs of three Web presentations from which you can download music. Were you able to find any music that was of interest to you? Was it possible to download entire compositions?

10. What is Napster? Who developed it?

11. Construct a table to illustrate the file sizes of "typical" audio files consisting of 30 seconds of playing time. Include data for as many audio formats as possible.

12. Describe several popular audio players. Include URLs from which they can be downloaded, their cost (if any), their size, and the types of audio formats they can handle.

13. Can you locate any on-line speech of John Muir? If so, provide the URL and a summary of what he said.

14. Locate a sound archive that contains a speech given by a United States president. Can you find other audio archives of historical interest?

13.4 Movies and Video

On-line video in essence is a motion picture. A video may or may not include sound. The same issues described in Section 13.3 for audio pertain to video. Because video consists of many image frames plus sound, video files are much larger than audio files. This means that downloading a 10-to-15-second movie clip can take a long time[5] (particularly over a slow modem line). When you download a movie, you place a heavy load on the Internet. However, if you can download and install the proper plugins, if you have a fast computer, and if you use the Internet during an off

---

5 You could, for example, start the download before dinner and watch it finish during dessert.

time, it can be very interesting to download movies and play them on your machine.

Just as with audio clips, many sites offer free music videos or very short blips from movies. Some organizations, states, and geographical regions also have promotional videos available on-line.

13.4.1   Formats

As with audio, a large number of video formats are currently in use. Some of the most popular ones are:

- AVI (.avi extension), which stands for *Audio Video Interleaved*. This format was developed by Microsoft.

- MPEG (.mpeg or .mpg extensions), which stands for *Motion Picture Experts Group* (but you may see it also as *Moving Pictures Expert Group*). This format was developed by the Motion Picture Experts Group.

- QuickTime (.qt or .mov extensions). This format was developed by Apple.

The process of loading a Web page containing video is similar to that for loading one containing audio, although it is usually much slower. Also, movies are always buffered. To play any movie format, you will need to download and install the appropriate plug-in.

13.4.2   Video and Web Pages

To include a video in a Web page, you can again use the object tag. For example, to include the movie reunion.avi in a 150-by-150-pixel area on the screen and have it start playing when the corresponding Web page is loaded, you can use the following HTML code:

```
<OBJECT DATA = "reunion.avi"
        TYPE = "video/msvideo"
        HEIGHT = "150"
        WIDTH = "150">

        <PARAM NAME = "autostart"  VALUE = "true">

        You are unable to play AVI movies.
        Please install a plug-in for them.

</OBJECT>
```

Assuming the reader has installed a plug-in to play AVI movies, the movie `reunion.avi` will be buffered and will then start playing automatically when this page is loaded.

Values specified in the parameter tag are passed directly to the corresponding plug-in and are not processed by the browser. For example, the browser uses the `DATA` attribute to load the appropriate file, the `TYPE` attribute to obtain the MIME type of the file, and the `HEIGHT` and `WIDTH` attributes to lay out the required amount of space on the screen for the multimedia element. However, the value `true` assigned to the parameter `autostart` is passed directly to the plug-in itself. This tells the plug-in to start playing the movie as soon as it is loaded. Other parameters may specify such items as the number of times the movie is supposed to be played, or whether it is to play continuously. The information passed is plug-in-specific.

Notice that we included the message, "You are unable to play AVI movies. Please install a plug-in for them," between the object beginning and ending tags. Browsers that are not capable of processing the object render the material between the object tags, except for the parameter tags. In our example, the descriptive message tells the user what is going on.

EXERCISES 13.4

Movies and Video

15. Have you ever viewed a movie on-line? Describe your experience in a couple of paragraphs.

16. Download and install a plug-in to play a movie format of your choice. How long did the download take? Find a site containing free movies and download and watch a couple. How would you rate the quality of the display?

17. We mentioned *Shockwave* in Section 4.3. What is it? From what site can it be downloaded? Is it free? What formats can it play? Elaborate.

18. What is the syntax for including the movie `shane.mpg` on a Web page?

19. Provide the URLs of three Web presentations that offer free movie clips. How large a file does a one-minute movie occupy? (Specify the video format for which you answered this question.)

20. Locate three movies about the Appalachian Trail. Report their titles. Can any of them be viewed on-line?

21.   Describe several popular movie players. Include URLs from which they can be downloaded, their cost (if any), their size, and the types of video formats they support.

22.   What is the *MBone*?

13.5   Virtual Reality and 3D Modeling

Virtual reality involves a three-dimensional (3D) simulation of a real or imagined environment, using computers. A lot of applications are suited to 3D displays, from engineering designs to medical research and imaging to on-line art galleries to games. If a virtual landscape is being rendered, you should be able to "walk" through it, exploring the features of the landscape. Similarly, if an object such as a cube is being displayed in a virtual reality setting, you should be able to examine the cube from various points of view (top, bottom, right side, and so on). You might rotate the cube in a continuous motion. Software for creating 3D solid figures and line drawings has been available for some time. However, the first step was the creation of static images. Initially, users were not able to interact with the object being rendered. Adding dynamic user interaction has greatly enhanced the interest in 3D modeling.

Virtual reality is becoming another exciting extension of the Web. The development of 3D worlds and objects, and 3D browsers in which to view them, is bringing us closer to Web-based virtual reality. Even while 2D graphical browsers were being introduced and accepted, 3D specifications were already in the planning stages.

Today, we are just beginning to have access to these 3D virtual worlds via the Web. Judging by the popularity of the Mars Pathfinder Mission Web presentations, which featured virtual reality models, the public seems to be embracing the new technology enthusiastically. Unfortunately, a limited color screen shot of Mars is not too impressive when displayed in a book, so we do not show it here. However, this book's on-line Web presentation includes several links to Mars presentations and other 3D sites. The material you will find there is very impressive.

Go On-Line

As with the other forms of multimedia, the processes of downloading files, installing and configuring plug-ins, and obtaining a special browser are time-consuming. You also need a fast and powerful computer system to achieve the full effect of a virtual world. With such capabilities, the results are very impressive.

Currently, several different implementations of virtual reality are available on the Web. Two of the more popular approaches are VRML and QTVR. Although the underlying methodology is very different, the navigation techniques experienced by the user are similar.

13.5.1   Virtual Reality Modeling Language (VRML)

Initially called *Virtual Reality MarkUp Language*, the VRML 1.0 specification was originally established by Silicon Graphics to use simple text-based files to create virtual reality environments. The first release of VRML produced environments that were static and noninteractive. The current version is VRML97 and the specification that defines it is VRML 2.0. This collaborative effort extends the capabilities of VRML 1.0 by supporting interaction, motion, and sound. A VRML world does not have to model something geographic—any object can be modeled as a VRML world.

A VRML file is a plaintext or compressed text file. Such files are identified by a file extension of `.wrl`, `.wrl.gz`, or `.wrz`, and they have a MIME type of `model/vrml`. Where HTML files are rendered as "pages" by a browser, VRML files are rendered as "worlds." (The letters `wrl` can be interpreted as "world.") The `z` at the end of the file extensions `.gz` and `.wrz` denotes a `zip` or compressed file.

Viewing a VRML world requires a special VRML viewer or a plug-in. If you do not have the necessary viewer, and you try to open a VRML file, your browser will complain and ask you to install the appropriate plug-in. The latest versions of Internet Explorer and Netscape come bundled with viewers that support VRML. Other browsers require downloading an appropriate plug-in. We have tried a number of such plug-ins, and the downloading and installation processes did not always go smoothly. In addition, the virtual reality plug-ins quite often caused our systems to hang. Over time, the technology will become more stable.

Virtual World Creation Tools

As with an HTML file, a text editor is all that is required to create a VRML file, since it just consists of plaintext. The technical details of writing VRML code are available in VRML reference books, on-line tutorials, and the VRML 2.0 specification. Since VRML files contain information that describes cameras, colors, event handlers, lighting, 3D objects, and textures, these files are quite complex. Because of this, many VRML authors use modeling software to help them create their VRML files. Modeling software is analogous to an HTML editor for creating HTML documents, and they offer WYSIWYG tools for authoring VRML worlds.

Go On-Line

Converters that permit you to convert 3D and CAD[6] file formats (such as 3D Studio, AOFF, and Wavefront) to the VRML file format are also available. Other converters can convert VRML 1.0 to VRML 2.0, which is important because VRML viewers currently only support one form or the other.

Virtual Reality and Web Pages

Most users are probably not equipped to view 3D Web presentations, and those that are either have special browsers or the appropriate plug-ins. Once you have a VRML file, there are several ways to include it in a 2D Web presentation. One approach involves providing a hyperlink to the VRML file from your HTML document, using the anchor tag. As an example, the following code shows how to create a hyperlink labeled "3D World" that will display the `artgallery.wrl` file:

```
<A HREF = "artgallery.wrl">3D World</A>
```

You can also include the VRML world file right in your HTML document. This causes the 3D world to display automatically. In the following example, the object tag is used to create a 200-by-200-pixel area in which the virtual world `artgallery.wrl` is displayed:

```
<OBJECT DATA = "artgallery.wrl"
        TYPE = "model/vrml"
        HEIGHT = "200"
        WIDTH = "200">

    <PARAM NAME = "color" VALUE = "brown">

    You are missing a great 3D gallery.

</OBJECT>
```

A VRML world (or for that matter a movie) can also be included in a frame. For example,

```
<FRAME SRC = "artgallery.wrl" NAME = "3DPictures">
```

displays the virtual world called `artgallery.wrl` in its own frame named `3DPictures`.

---

6   CAD stands for *Computer-Aided Design*.

13.5.2 QuickTime Virtual Reality (QTVR)

Another virtual reality implementation found on the Web uses *QuickTime Virtual Reality (QTVR)*, also called *QuickTime VR*. This technology was designed by Apple and was first introduced in mid-1995. While a Mac is necessary to create the virtual-reality-style 3D panoramas and objects, any Mac or PC can be used to view them.

A 3D panorama (or scene) created by QTVR is actually a QuickTime movie (file extension .mov) that represents a 360-degree image. A Quick-Time VR movie can be included in a Web page in the same way as a VRML file. Navigating through the movie gives users the impression that they are in a 3D world. Creating a panorama involves working from photographs or 3D-computer-generated images. It requires a great deal of technical skill. Details may be found on-line.

Go On-Line

To view QTVR, you need a QTVR plug-in. The QTVR plug-in interprets and responds to your movements as you navigate through a scene or manipulate an object.

13.5.3 Virtual Reality Summary

Virtual reality on the Web is still in its infancy. The ability to interact with scenes and manipulate objects is just now becoming available, and users are very intrigued. The ability to use *hotspots* to link to 2D documents, 2D images, and other 3D applications is being developed and should be available soon (if it is not already by the time you read this). We expect that the next several years will see great advances in virtual reality technology on the Web, accompanied by an increasing interest in 3D Web presentations. Some people, in fact, have referred to the realization of virtual reality on the Web as the "Second Web."

Hot Topic

EXERCISES 13.5

Virtual Reality and 3D Modeling

23. What advantages can you see to including a VRML world in its own frame?

24. Explain how virtual reality technology (VRML, QTVR, and so on) might enhance each of the following: MUDs, educational models, medical research, and on-line shopping malls.

25. Find three Web presentations offering information on VRML authoring tools and cite the URLs. Is the documentation complete enough for someone to construct their own VR worlds?

26. What is the syntax for including the virtual reality content of `spinning.wrl` on a Web page?

27. Use your favorite search engine to find out more about "Moving Worlds," and then write a paragraph describing it. Cite the URL(s) from which you gathered your information.

28. Of the two methods described in this section for creating 3D Web presentations (VRML and QTVR), do you feel that one is better than the other? Are there certain situations when one might better represent a certain type of 3D environment? Elaborate as fully as possible and provide references for your comments.

13.6   Multimedia and HTML Documents

You have already learned the basics of including multimedia in HTML documents using the object tag. In previous sections, you learned about the `DATA`, `HEIGHT`, `TYPE`, and `WIDTH` attributes. In this section, we will discuss other attributes of the object tag and will address the use of the embed tag for including multimedia in an HTML document.

13.6.1   Object Tag

The object tag is used to let a graphical browser know that a plug-in or helper application is needed to display a file. The browser retrieves the file specified in the `DATA` attribute. If the `TYPE` attribute is specified, the browser can use it as the MIME type. Otherwise, the server that sends the file over can specify the MIME type for the file. The browser uses the MIME type to determine which plug-in or helper to use to display the file. If the `TYPE` attribute is left unspecified and the server cannot notify the browser of the MIME type, the browser can determine it from the suffix of the URL. For example, a URL ending in `.wrl` indicates a VRML file that might require a special VRML viewer to display.

Many of the other attributes available for the object tag are used in the same way as with the image and applet tags. The attributes include `BORDER`, `CLASSID`, `CODEBASE`, `CODETYPE`, `DECLARE`, `HSPACE`, `NAME`, `SHAPES`, `STANDBY`, `TABINDEX`, `USEMAP`, and `VSPACE`.[7] The information provided by these attributes is used by the browser to display the multimedia object.

---

7   These are the object tag attributes specified in the HTML 4.0 specification.

Additional information to be passed to the plug-in or helper handling the multimedia file is specified using the parameter tag. As with the applet tag, multiple parameter tags can be included inside the object tag. This extra information is plug-in and helper specific. If you want users to view your material using a specific program, you can customize the inputs that the program receives. You will need to read the documentation corresponding to these applications to determine what options you need to set.

Go On-Line

13.6.2   Embed Tag

The embed tag is similar to the object tag in that it allows you to include multimedia in an HTML document. In Appendix E, we list its most important attributes, most of which are self-explanatory. It is not completely clear which tags for multimedia elements and objects will be supported in the future. For example, the HTML 4.0 specification describes the applet and object tags, but not the embed tag. The best approach is simply to be consistent in your use of these tags. This will make it easier to maintain and update your HTML files when a tag(s) is no longer supported.

Hot Topic

EXERCISES 13.6

Multimedia and HTML Documents

29. Write a sample object tag specification to include the video `lassie.mpeg`. Include as many object tag attributes as make sense. Write a similar specification using the embed tag.

30. Is there a noobject tag, `<NOOBJECT>`? If so, describe its purpose and how it is used.

31. What is the intended use of the `STANDBY` feature of the object tag?

32. At this point in time, which of the tags for including multimedia in an HTML document are being supported, and by which browsers?

33. Write a sample object tag specification to include the audio file `songs.aiff`. Include as many object tag attributes as make sense. Write a similar specification using the embed tag.

Privacy and Security Topics

I had entered the last state of my journey—Maine, with its motto "The Way Life Should Be." Even though I still had close to 300 miles to go, my dream was now within my grasp. I had left Gorham, New Hampshire, near the NH/ME border, with the intention of not resupplying for 150 miles. The section of trail just north of the New Hampshire border leads into the Mahoosuc Mountains. This is probably the most difficult section of the AT. The ground is very rocky and rooty. Unfortunately, the perfect weather that I had encountered in the Whites did not hold up in the Mahoosucs. It rained for about four straight days. I was going up and down the mountains, grabbing trees to pull myself up and lower myself down the same way Batman and Robin scale buildings. I was also eating a lot and moving slower than I had anticipated. This meant I was out of food about 40 miles from my resupply point. Since I had no excess fat to burn, I had really hit a wall. I was looking for insects and berries to eat. Eventually, I came out to a logging road where trail angel "Missouri Man" saved me. He provided me with sandwiches, candy, trail mix, sodas, powerbars, and other assorted goodies. I am forever indebted to this man. Family and friends hiked with me to the summit of Mount Katahdin in Maine, where we celebrated the conclusion of my hike. I had fulfilled my dream by completing the trail pure in 97 days. I deposited a pebble on top of one of the cairns on the summit of Mount Katahdin; I had carried the pebble with me from Springer Mountain, Georgia. It was a special moment. I was glad to reduce my pack weight for the final time. Fish finished up the trail a few weeks later, and completed Massachusetts and Vermont during the next season. I think about the trail every day, and am thankful for the lifetime of memories that the journey has provided me.

Maine
281 miles

Chapter 14

14.1 INTRODUCTION

In this chapter, we cover a number of important privacy and security issues. Although this area is highly technical, our goal is simply to acquaint you with the basic concepts, such as *cryptographic algorithm*, *digital signature*, and *firewall*. The reader interested in pursuing the intricacies of privacy and security should consult the references. Here, we will cover the following topics:

Objectives

- The information already known about you

- The complexity of large software systems

- Encryption schemes, including *private key*, *public key*, and *hashing algorithms*

- Secure documents

- Digital signatures

- Firewalls

14.2 Known Information

In Section 3.7.4, you learned about cookies and about how items of personal information could be recorded. This information is used for advertising, allowing Web pages to be customized to individual users. In essence, if information exists in a public database, that information may be available to others on the Web. Three scenarios illustrate the types of information that might be available:

Useful Item

1. *Telephone listings*—The data contained in a telephone book is sometimes available on the Web. In Section 5.2.8, we saw a number of white pages tools that can be used to look up personal information, including email address, telephone number, and s-mail address. Some

of this information probably comes from an existing database, such as a telephone directory.

2.   *Public events*—If you participate in a public event, such as a race, the results may be posted on-line. If you run in the Boston Marathon,[1] for example, information about your time will be posted on-line by the Boston Athletic Association (BAA). A runner from Seattle, who took that Monday off as a "sick day," might get caught if someone happens to stumble across the race results on-line. (Seattle newspapers do not carry a complete listing of finishers from the Boston Marathon, but someone in Seattle can easily obtain this information over the Web.) Unofficial race results are often posted on-line within less than 24 hours of the completion of the event.[2]

   If you are involved in a number of public events, someone may be able to track down information about you on the Web and perhaps put together a limited dossier.

3.   *Company profile*—If the company you work for has a Web presentation, they may have some information about you on-line. Usually, such information is very limited—maybe only a job title and perhaps contact information. In fact, many companies run a private Web over their own intranet, so that company information is not publicly available. Other businesses use a security measure called a firewall, so that outsiders cannot view private information. You will learn more about firewalls in Section 14.7.

14.2.1   Volunteered Information

The manner in which most on-line information about you is obtained is probably directly through you. You may not even be aware that you are providing such information. For example, if you go to a Web site and fill out a form, the information you submit will likely end up in a database. At some point, such information could be displayed on the Web or retrieved by a search engine query. In general, do not give out any unnecessary personal information when filling out on-line (or off-line) forms.

Hot Topic

---

1   1996 was the 100th running of the Boston Marathon. The yearly event is traditionally held on the third Monday in April.

2   In 1997, several runners ingested special "computer chips," and their vital signs were displayed in real time on the Web.

Computers are great at processing and collecting information. Once information is entered into a database, it is easy to automate the manipulation of that information. It is certainly conceivable that some information could be used in a manner not originally intended. This is another reason to avoid giving out personal information.

14.2.2   Information Collection

A simple example will illustrate how the Internet simplifies information collection. Without using the Internet, if someone in Seattle wanted to construct a list of the names of the five runners who finished in 2,000th place at the last five Boston Marathons, they would have to call or write someone in Boston. However, it would be just as challenging to find out who to contact and how to do so. If you contacted the Boston Globe, for example, you might need to pay to have the newspapers s-mailed to Seattle. You would not want to send cash, so you would need a name and an amount to send a check. Also, mailing five sports sections[3] is going to be awkward, even if you find someone to collect them, and four of the five will be back issues, which will have to be located in storage.

Another approach would be to use your public library. If they do not have the relevant newspapers, you could use interlibrary loan, but that could take several weeks. You could try to obtain the information by telephone, but who would you call? If you have to hold, or make repeated calls, using the telephone could get expensive.

Go On-Line

In contrast, typing in a query of `Boston Marathon` to any search engine on the Web will start you well on your way to obtaining the desired information. Within 10 to 15 minutes, you will probably compile the list of names you wanted. Just imagine how easy it is for a professional information collector to gather data over the Internet.

EXERCISES 14.2

Known Information

1. Do you consider the manipulation and collection of information from "public" databases an invasion of personal privacy?

2. How much information about yourself can you track down on-line?

---

3 A listing of close to 10,000 finishers takes up several pages. To simplify matters you would probably just ask that the entire sections be mailed—copying a full page from a newspaper requires special copiers.

3. How much information can you find about Myron Avery on the Web? Was he a thru-hiker of the Appalachian Trail?

4. Locate a Web presentation that asks you to submit a form containing personal information. What do they ask for, and do they really need this information?

14.3   Software Complexity

14.3.1   Contributing Factors

Due to the inherent complexity of large software systems, such as those used for the Internet, it is difficult to make them completely secure. By their very nature, they could have a number of susceptible points. They are also very difficult to make error-free.

- *Program size*—A browser may consist of as many as 75,000 lines of source code. For comparison, consider that all the text files used to produce this book contain just over 35,000 lines.[4] The latest browsers contain even more features, resulting in even larger programs. The executable file for a browser is usually on the order of 5 to 7 megabytes. It is very difficult to eliminate all errors in such an immense program.

- *Software interfaces*—The need for browsers to interface with other software creates an even larger code base and more potential problem areas. For example, the other software may not be performing exactly as documented. Debugging large programs that interact is more complicated because it is not always clear which piece of software contains the error.

- *Market forces*—Products must often be hurried to market in order to maintain a competitive edge. It is often challenging to test all parts of them thoroughly before release. One reason why new versions of large software systems come out so frequently is that bugs (including security problems) are addressed in the newer releases.

---

4   We did not count them directly; instead, we used the UNIX wc command, which stands for "word count." The command also prints the number of lines in a file.

- *Team development*—Large teams of programmers are often used to develop complicated programs such as browsers. Very few individuals can handle such a task alone. Inconsistent styles, or even just carelessness on the part of a single programmer, can result in bugs that are very difficult to find and correct. There is something to be said for having another set of eyes studying the code. However, as in many facets of life, a development team is only as good as its weakest member. It is more difficult to assemble a large team of top-notch programmers than to gather a small team of equal competency.

14.3.2   Browsers, Networks, Operating Systems, and Servers

The browser is a very complex piece of software. However, it is only one part of the overall system that must be considered when assessing the security of the Web. Other software areas of concern include: networks (your LAN, the server's LAN, the Internet), your server, and operating systems (yours and the server's). Each of these components is complex, and a breach in any one part of these can cause major security problems.

Go On-Line

One solution is *patches*, which are frequently installed to fix known security holes. Other solutions are also used, and they are sometimes as complex as the original programs. The interested reader may learn more about security risks, common security problems, approaches for dealing with security problems, and other security-related issues by pursuing the references provided in the Bibliography.

EXERCISES 14.3

Software Complexity

5. Search the Web for information about any legendary computer criminal, that is, someone who was infamous for breaking into systems. Write a small on-line biography about them.

6. Can you find out how many lines of source code the two most popular browsers contain?

7. Do some research on the Web about current security issues. Create an HTML document describing several interesting things you learned.

8. What does it mean to "crack" a password? What are some common techniques people use to try to crack passwords?

9.   Locate a Web page that describes an interesting security breach. Summarize the results of your findings.

14.4   Encryption Schemes

14.4.1   Basic Concepts

An *encryption scheme* is a method of encoding information. In Section 10.3, you learned about the ROT13 encryption scheme. With ROT13, a plaintext message can be converted into an encrypted version of the same message. The encrypted version is called *ciphertext* and the encryption scheme is referred to as a *cipher*. (As we noted in Chapter 10, ROT13 is a Caesar cipher.) Figure 14.1 illustrates these ideas. If the plaintext

```
"Buy 1,000 shares of IGCO now."
```

is encrypted using a cipher, the resulting ciphertext might be, for example,

```
"zabxyabc egtum pa wclfp"
```

We cannot make sense of the ciphertext without knowing both the cipher and the *encryption key*.

Because ROT13 is so simple, the plaintext is easy to figure out, given the ciphertext. That is, practically anyone could *decrypt* (or *decipher*) an encrypted ROT13 message. We therefore say that ROT13 is not a secure

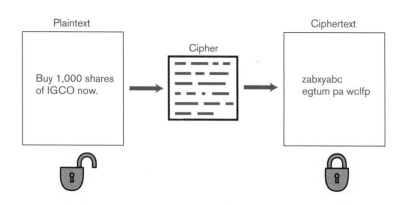

FIGURE 14.1
The concepts of plaintext, cipher, and ciphertext.

encryption scheme. ROT13 is best used for encrypting information that does not require security, such as potentially offensive jokes.

Computer scientists have studied encryption schemes for many years. The goal in most cases is to develop a scheme that allows information to be exchanged securely between two parties. In computer science examples, the two parties are usually referred to as Alice and Bob. Even if a third party intercepts the messages (in the form of ciphertext), they should not be able to decipher what the messages really say.

Figure 14.2 illustrates the basic idea. We have shortened the messages to simplify the discussion, and we show the ciphertext as a garbled sequence of characters (rather than displaying it as a binary string), to indicate that it is encrypted. Alice encrypts her plaintext message of

```
"My bank account # is 47"
```

to a ciphertext of

```
"paqmcx rtuw foolrg mu"
```

She sends the ciphertext over the network to Bob. While the message is being transmitted, a spy[5] intercepts it. In this context, intercept means obtains a copy of the message; the message is still transmitted to Bob. If the cipher Alice used is secure, the spy will have a difficult time understanding the message. When Bob receives the message, he decrypts it, using the scheme he and Alice had previously agreed to. Bob determines that the plaintext of the ciphertext is "My bank account # is 47."

Because of the great interest in conducting business and other types of transactions over the Web, a number of the technologies developed by computer scientists have been adopted (or adapted) for use on the Web. New technologies have also emerged. However, computer spies have also become more sophisticated in their decryption abilities. Therefore, complex encryption schemes are necessary to ensure security.

In the next sections, you will learn about several different types of encryption mechanisms. Our goal is to give you a basic understanding of the techniques used in developing secure systems. The interested reader can

---

5   The word "hacker" is sometimes used to describe computer thieves or computer criminals. However, it is also used to describe clever programmers, or people who program a great deal. Therefore, we prefer to use the word "spy" to indicate illegal activity.

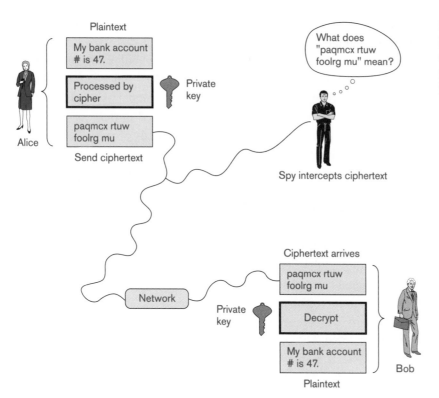

FIGURE 14.2
Illustration of an encrypted message sent from Alice to Bob.

find more detailed information in any computer science text on *cryptography*, the field dealing with the study of encryption schemes and secure systems. Before getting into the specific encryption schemes, we must first discuss *prime numbers*, which are used in many encryption schemes.

14.4.2 Prime Numbers

Some encryption schemes rely on prime numbers. A number is prime if its only whole-number factors are 1 and itself. For example, the numbers 2, 13, 17, 29, and 101 are all prime. A number such as 12 is not prime because it has several other factors: 2, 3, 4, and 6. Numbers that are not prime are called *composite*.

Mathematicians have studied prime numbers for hundreds of years. One result that is not difficult to prove is that there are an infinite number of prime numbers. This means there are extremely large prime numbers. (Why?) What is so special about prime numbers? We answer this question with another one: Is the following number prime?

1182233332324084750276863408750745720874020745864784874020204071

How can you resolve this question? You could try to divide this number by every smaller number.[6] The difficulty is that there are lots and lots of smaller numbers. In fact, there are so many smaller numbers that for all practical purposes, determining whether a 200-digit number is prime is impossible. Even using the most powerful computers available today (or even those that will conceivably be developed in the foreseeable future), the process we outlined would take hundreds of years to determine whether such a number is prime. Furthermore, there is no known computational method that is significantly better at determining whether a number is prime.

What does all this have to do with encryption schemes? Suppose you have two 100-digit prime numbers. Using a computer, it would be a "simple" task to multiply them together.[7] The resulting number will contain about 200 digits. Furthermore, it will have only two factors other than 1 and itself, namely, the original two primes that were multiplied together to obtain the number. The designers of encryption schemes use the fact that it is very hard to factor such a number. The idea is that in order to decipher a given ciphertext, you either have to be able to factor very large numbers that are "almost" prime (which is a computationally infeasible task), or you must be given one of the factors as a *key*. Here by "almost prime," we mean the only factors of the number are 1, two primes, and itself.

14.4.3   Private Key Cryptography

Hot Topic

In *private key cryptography*, both the sender and the receiver share the same private key. The key is used to encrypt the plaintext and also to decrypt the ciphertext. The key must be kept private (secret) to ensure system security. A spy who obtains the key will likely be able to decrypt encoded messages. In the encryption schemes currently in use, keys are often either very large prime numbers or the product of large primes.

A simple example, using a cipher that is not secure, should clarify the idea behind private key cryptography. Suppose Alice wants to send the message

```
"meet me at the roadhouse at noon urgent"
```

---

6   You would only need to test numbers up to the square root of this number.

7   The multiplication is not as simple as you might imagine, because the numbers are so large.

to Bob. One cipher based on a shared private key, which in this case is a small number, simply "wraps" the words based on the key's value. That is, you write the characters in lines, based on the key's value. The ciphertext is then constructed by listing the characters in the order in which they appear in the columns. For example, if Alice and Bob agree on a key of 5, the ciphertext of Alice's message will be

```
"meehannearotutetounrttasogmhdeoe"
```

When Bob receives the ciphertext, he decrypts it using the private key, 5. First, Bob counts the number of characters in the ciphertext, which in this case is 32. Since there are 5 characters per row, based on the agreed-upon cipher and key, Bob realizes that the message is seven rows long—six full rows and one row containing two characters. Bob writes out the message in row-format as follows:

```
meetm
eatth
eroad
house
atnoo
nurge
nt
```

Writing the text horizontally row-by-row, Bob obtains

```
meetm eatth eroad house atnoo nurge nt
```

Reading from left to right, Bob can determine the original message. If a spy knew the cipher and the private key, he or she could also decrypt the intercepted message.

In practice, both the cipher and private keys are much more complex than this simple example. Many other issues need to be dealt with as well, such as changing private keys periodically and distributing private keys securely.

14.4.4   Public Key Cryptography

Another security issue is the problem of *authentication*. When Bob receives a message, how can he be sure that Alice sent it? That is, how can he be sure that the message is authentic? Private key cryptography allows two parties to exchange messages and maintain confidentiality but not authenticity. If the ciphertext is intercepted, it will be difficult to decrypt without access to the private key and without knowing the encrypting cipher. *Public key cryptography* is useful for this purpose.

In public key cryptographic systems, every person who intends to send a message has a private key. In addition, every person has a *public key* that matches up with their private key. The private key is used to encrypt messages, and those messages can only be decrypted using the matching public key, and vice versa.[8] As the name implies, public keys are not kept secret. Suppose Alice sends Bob a message that she has encrypted using her private key. When Bob receives the ciphertext, he tries to decrypt it using Alice's public key, which is available to everyone. If Bob can decrypt the message, he knows that it must have come from Alice, because Alice's public key can only decrypt messages encrypted by her private key, and only Alice knows her private key.

Notice that if Alice's message had been intercepted, anyone could have decrypted it using her public key. Privacy is not provided by public key cryptography, only authentication. Many other issues must also be dealt with when using public key cryptographic schemes, including creating secure keys, distributing public keys, and so on.

14.4.5   Hashing Algorithms

Suppose Alice sent Bob a message and it was intercepted. The person who intercepted the message might be able to alter its contents before passing it along. A way to verify that the message received is the same as the message sent involves the use of *hashing algorithms*.

A hashing algorithm takes a plaintext message as input and then computes a value based on that message. The length of the computed value is usually much shorter than the length of the original message. While it is possible that several plaintext messages could generate the same value, hashing algorithms are designed such that this is very unlikely.

For illustration purposes, we will define a very simple hashing algorithm. The algorithms used in practice are much more sophisticated. Our hashing algorithm will multiply the number of a's, e's, and h's in the message and will then add the number of o's to this value. For example, suppose the message is

---

8   The computer science theorists Rivest, Shamir, and Adleman developed the public key encryption scheme that is most commonly used. It is called the *RSA encryption scheme*.

`"the combination to the safe is two, seven, thirty-five"`

The *hash* or *message digest* of this message, using our simple hashing algorithm, is as follows:

$$(2 \times 6 \times 3) + 4 = 40$$

The message digest of the plaintext is sent to Bob along with the ciphertext. After Bob decrypts the message, he computes its hash using the agreed-upon hashing algorithm. If the hash value sent by Alice does not match the hash value of the decrypted message, Bob will know that the message has been altered. For example, if Bob received a hash value of 17 and decrypted a message Alice had sent as

`"you are being followed, use backroads, hurry"`

he could conclude the message had been altered. This is because the hash of the message he received is

$$(3 \times 4 \times 1) + 4 = 16$$

which is different from the value 17 that Alice sent.

These simple examples illustrate the most common encryption schemes. Private key cryptography is useful for sending confidential messages; public key cryptography is useful for authenticating that the message came from the sender; and hashing algorithms are useful for verifying *message integrity*. In practice, some combination of these schemes is usually used.

Useful Item

EXERCISES 14.4

Encryption Schemes

10. Explain how cable television companies use private key cryptography. Make sure to include your sources.

11. Why might the United States government be concerned about exporting encryption schemes?

12. Encode the message, "The credit card is in the bottom zippered part of my backpack," using the private key cryptography scheme described in Section 14.4.3. Assume a private key of 7 and ignore punctuation marks.

13. How might private keys be securely exchanged?

14. In a public key cryptographic scheme, how might public keys be distributed?

15. Using the hashing algorithm described in Section 14.4.5, compute the message digests of the following messages:
     (a) The far end is the deep end.
     (b) You will find the money buried twenty paces north of the large oak.
     (c) Victoria is a spy. Keep under cover.

16. Come up with two messages that make sense in English, are at least 30 characters long, have the same length, and have the same message digests as computed by the hashing algorithm described in Section 14.4.5.

17. Define your own hashing function that meets the following property: on no two alphabetic strings of length exactly five should the function return the same value.

14.5   Secure Web Documents

Go On-Line

If you notice a broken skeleton key or an unlocked padlock displayed in the lower-left corner of the browser window, you are looking at icons that indicate that a document is not secure. Most documents on the Web are not secure. When the skeleton key is whole or the padlock is locked, you are looking at a *secure document*. Secure documents require a *secure server*, which is a server that uses encryption schemes. The URL for a secure document usually begins with `https`, rather than `http`, where the s means secure.

When a client requests a secure document, the server must first determine if they have the permission required to retrieve the document. The authentication process may require the user to submit a password. The server and the client must agree on an encryption scheme, so that all messages (including passwords) can be transmitted securely. Users may have to obtain a private key via some other mechanism (such as s-mail) before they can authenticate themselves to a secure server and decrypt messages. A high level of security can thus be achieved on the Web, using the encryption schemes currently available. Researchers are continuously working on even more secure systems.

As an example, if you are using a server that is not secure, and you enter a credit card number, it is possible that it could be intercepted. But this is not very likely. If the credit card number were not encrypted and the number were intercepted, someone could steal and use the number. However, for the credit card number to be intercepted in the first place, someone would have to be *sniffing* the network; that is, they would have to be intercepting packets transmitted over the network. The likelihood of this is roughly the same as that of someone tapping your telephone line and obtaining your credit card number while you place a phone order. Nevertheless, it could happen and you should be aware of it. If you use a secure server, however, it is unlikely that the message could be decrypted, even if it is intercepted.

We should point out that submitting information from a form to a CGI script is really no more secure than submitting the information in a `mailto` hyperlink. In particular, the `get` METHOD provides no security. To obtain a greater level of security, you must use a secure server.

EXERCISES 14.5

Secure Web Documents

18. Provide the URLs for three secure Web documents.

19. The Internet was originally an *open system*, and most informa-tion was available to everyone. Why is it more difficult to add security to an existing system than it is to incorporate it from the start? How has this affected Internet security?

20. Describe S-HTTP (*Secure-HyperText Transfer Protocol*).

21. If someone had a list of 20,000 valid credit card numbers, how might these numbers be used in a scam to obtain money?

22. What is a *network sniffer*? Can anyone buy one? If so, what is the cost?

23. Is your browser capable of encrypting and decrypting messag-es? Explain.

14.6   Digital Signatures

In Roman times, an important message was sealed by dripping wax on the outside envelope and then stamping the wax with a special insignia. The insignias used were intricate and difficult to copy. Thus, if someone received a letter that was properly sealed and they were familiar with the insignia of the sender, they could be reasonably sure that the letter came from the correct source. Even today, college recommendation letters are often sent in envelopes on which professors are required to sign their names over the back flap of the envelope. This provides little or no security, since a student could write and sign a letter and then sign the back of the envelope, as well. In today's electronic world, many confidential and important messages are sent via computer. A signature mechanism has been developed to authenticate signatures for electronic communications.

Useful Item

A *digital signature* is a mechanism that can be used to sign an electronic document officially. Because digital signatures are difficult to forge, documents that contain such signatures can be considered authentic. The details concerning how digital signatures are actually implemented are complex. They usually involve a combination of the encryption schemes discussed in Section 14.4. Digital signatures provide a way of verifying both the sender of the information and the content of the message, ensuring that it has not been modified. In essence, a digital signature is like an official seal on both a document and the envelope that protects the document from being altered.

14.6.1   Digital Signature Example

Figure 14.3 represents one possible digital signature scheme. Suppose Alice wants to send Bob a confidential message, "Buy gold," and Bob needs to know for sure that Alice sent the message and that it arrived unaltered. A combination of the three cryptographic schemes we have discussed can be used. Alice computes the hash of her plaintext message, using a hashing algorithm she and Bob have chosen. In this example, Alice obtains a value of 12. She then uses her private key (key1) to her matching public key and an agreed-upon public key cryptography scheme to encrypt the hash of the plaintext, getting "wr." Alice then uses a different private key (key2) and an agreed-upon private key cryptography scheme to encrypt the plaintext. In this case, she obtains "axzmqtu." She sends Bob the following two items:

- The private-key-encrypted ciphertext of the plaintext (in our example, "axzmqtu").

- The public-key-encrypted hash of the plaintext (in our example, "wr").

When Bob receives the message, he essentially needs to reverse the steps that Alice took. He first splits the message into "axzmqtu" (the ciphertext of the original plaintext "Buy gold") and "wr" (the ciphertext of the hash of 12). Bob processes "axzmqtu" using the private key (key1)

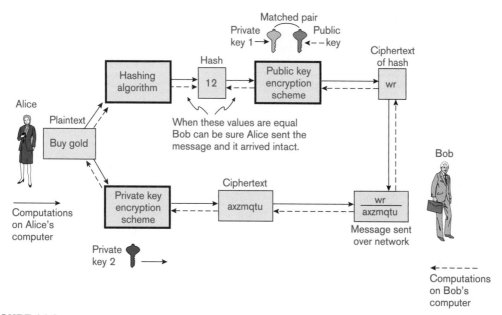

FIGURE 14.3

An example of a digital signature.

Alice sends a digitally signed confidential message to Bob over the network. The solid arrows indicate Alice's computations on her computer, and the dashed arrows show Bob's computations on his computer. The computations performed by the encryption schemes are not the same in both directions. To simplify the figure, we have shown the computations going through the same boxes.

that he and Alice chose, and he comes up with the original plaintext "Buy gold." Next, he uses the hashing algorithm on "Buy gold" and obtains a value of 12. Bob then uses Alice's public key to decrypt the ciphertext of the hash "wr." He again obtains a value of 12. Since the two hash values match $(12 = 12)$, Bob can be sure that Alice sent the message and that it arrived intact. In the exercises, you are asked to explain how Bob was able to reach this conclusion.

If Alice's message had not been confidential, she could have sent it as plaintext. The public key encryption scheme could be used as before to sign the message digitally. In this case, a spy who intercepts the message sees the plaintext of the message directly, as well as its corresponding hash value (since Alice's public key is widely available). If enough messages are intercepted, the spy may be able to deduce the hashing function and then successfully change future messages. For this reason, you can achieve greater security by using the digital signature scheme and a private key encryption scheme.

14.6.2   Pretty Good Privacy

Hot Topic

In 1995, Phil Zimmermann developed an email security package called *Pretty Good Privacy* (*PGP*). The software includes authentication, compression, digital signature, and privacy capabilities. It uses the RSA algorithm, as well as *MD5* and *IDEA*, where MD5 stands for *Message Digest 5*, a hash function developed by Ronald Rivest, and IDEA stands for *International Data Encryption Algorithm*.

Rather than trying to explain the complex details of PGP, we will describe an important use of the system. The *Computer Emergency Response Team* (*CERT*) is an organization that sends out information about known security holes in software. For example, if there is a widely used guest book through which people can break into computer systems, CERT might post a message about it. When systems administrators receive information about a security problem, they need to verify that the message is from CERT and that it is unaltered. Otherwise, they might receive a forged message that actually creates a security problem, rather than solving one.

Using PGP, CERT can send out email messages that include its digital signature. A system administrator can verify that the message is from CERT by decoding its digital signature, using CERT's public key. The content of the message can be verified by comparing the hash encrypted in the digital signature with the hash of the message received. If the two are equal, the systems administrator can feel confident about installing the security fix. If the two hashes are different, the systems administrator knows that the message has been altered. The user interface of PGP makes the encrypting and decrypting process easy.

EXERCISES 14.6

Digital Signatures

24.   Contrast an in-person signature and a digital signature. Why does a digital signature need to be more complex?

25.   Give three examples of situations in which digital signatures are needed.

26.   When you read a register entry in an Appalachian Trail register, how do you know the person who signed the entry is really the hiker with that name? Or do you?

27.   Carefully explain how Bob was able to conclude that Alice sent him the message "Buy gold." How did he know Alice was definitely the sender, and how did he know that the message arrived unaltered?

28.   In practice, how widely available are public encryption keys that are part of matched-key pairs?

29.   Why is there some controversy over PGP?

30.   Describe how to obtain your own digital signature with PGP.

14.7   Firewalls

A *firewall* is a security mechanism used by organizations to protect their LANs from the Internet. A firewall keeps private resources confidential and minimizes security risks. The idea is simply to restrict LAN access to trusted users. Basically, a firewall controls network traffic, in both directions.

Figure 14.4 depicts a sample firewall between a LAN and the Internet. The connection between the two is the point of vulnerability. Both hardware

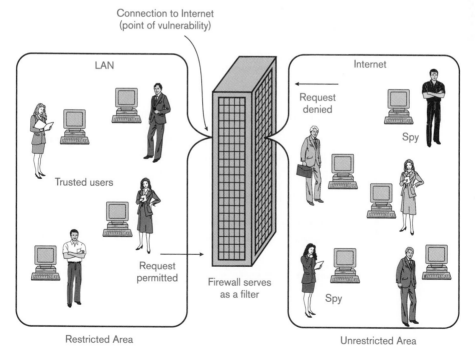

FIGURE 14.4
A sample firewall.

and software may be used at this point to filter network traffic. The users shown in the "restricted area" are trusted users, whereas the users in the "unrestricted area" are people who are not to be allowed into the LAN.

There are two types of firewall systems. One works by using filters at the *network layer*. The other works by using *proxy servers* at the user, application, or network layer.

Problems regarding firewalls can arise between network managers and system managers. Network managers typically like to leave the operating system out of their network configuration, and system managers do not like to get involved with network management. However, firewalls encompass both entities and so must be addressed by both. Because of this natural barrier, few people understand firewalls well.

The amount of filtering a firewall provides varies. In addition, for the same firewall, the amount of filtering may be different in different directions. For example, in one scenario, users in the restricted area may be able to send email to anyone on the Internet, surf the Web, use remote login, and transfer files, while users in the unrestricted area may not be allowed to do anything except send email to people inside the firewall. In another situation, using the same firewall, only email might be permitted in either direction.

Go On-Line

Details on security risk assessments, available technology, firewall installation, and so on can be pursued through the Bibliography.

| EXERCISES 14.7

Firewalls

31. Can you find any information about a "Firewall Challenge"?

32. Do you have any friends who work for companies that use firewalls? What restrictions are placed on outside users? For example, can you view internal Web pages?

33. What is a proxy server?

34. Can you locate any books that cover the topic of firewalls? If so, report on the titles, page lengths, authors, and costs of two of them.

Internet Service Providers

A.1   Introduction

An *Internet Service Provider* (*ISP*) is a business that sells computer access to the Internet. If a connection to the Internet is not available through an account at work or school (or if these connections do not permit you to roam freely, due to *firewalls* or *filters*), you may want to consider an ISP.

An option that we will mention only briefly is that of subscribing to a commercial on-line service provider, such as *America Online* (*AOL*). These commercial providers are designed to be user-friendly and are intended for people with little or no computer experience. They usually provide their own interfaces and proprietary services, such as *bulletin/message boards*, *chat rooms*, and *news hosts*. Content may be monitored,[1] which is something an Internet veteran may resent. However, those with children who are planning to use the service to access the Internet may appreciate this feature. In the past, the major drawback to using a commercial on-line service was the expense, but the current rates are fairly competitive with ISPs.

A persistent problem of the large commerical providers is that their service is oversubscribed. Sometimes, too many users are trying to get on-line at one time; this can often result in frustrating busy signals and email delays.

ISPs typically offer a no-frills, cheaper alternative to commercial providers. People who are wise in the ways of the Internet find such a service appealing. Also, a good ISP will make newcomers to the Internet feel comfortable by providing on-line support and initial guidance.

Once you have decided that an ISP is the way to get on-line, the question becomes how to choose from the thousands that are available. A plethora of information on selecting an ISP is available on the Web, but if you do not currently have access to the Internet, this is not a viable solution. In the next sections, we offer several suggestions on how to shop for an ISP.

---

1   A recent *Prodigy* case showed that monitoring can legally backfire with increased liability if something slips through.

A.2   Questions to Ask

When searching for an ISP, try to obtain answers to the following questions:

- Does the ISP provide a local-access telephone number for your area? This is probably the most important question, since you will otherwise wind up paying the telephone company long-distance charges for every minute on-line. You can verify that the access number is local by checking the phone book or asking the operator. Also find out if the ISP has more than one local access number, in case the line is busy during high-volume times (usually between 5:00 P.M. and 9:00 P.M.).

- What rate plans are available? Some ISPs offer a flat-rate fee for unlimited access. They may also offer an option for a lower monthly fee that includes "free" usage for a limited number of hours, after which you are charged for each additional hour. If both options are available, find out if you can switch between rate plans without a penalty. Also inquire about any other fees, such as a start-up fee, or surcharges for being on-line at certain times during the day.

- Does the ISP offer a free trial period? This is a good way to find out if the ISP is right for you. Test the connection during the same times that you anticipate using the service.

- What is the ISP's "user-to-modem" ratio? In general, a ratio higher than twelve to one (twelve users for one modem) means you may get a lot of busy signals when you dial in.

- What is the modem connection speed for each of the ISP's local access numbers? The connection speed should be at least 14.4 Kbps (hopefully, 28.8). What is the connection speed between the ISP and the Internet? A *T1* or *T3* connection is desirable. A T1 link supports a data transmission rate of 1.5 Mbps; a T3 link supports a rate of 44.7 Mbps. Thus, a T3 link is a much higher-volume connection.

- What types of accounts does the ISP offer? They may have *SLIP*, *PPP*, and/or shell accounts. SLIP (*Serial Line Internet Protocol*) and PPP (*Point-to-Point Protocol*) accounts permit TCP/IP traffic over telephone lines using a modem, and they allow the use of graphical browsers. Shell accounts provide only text browsing capabilities. A knowledge of UNIX, *VMS* (*Virtual Monitoring System*), or other appropriate operating system is also necessary to use a shell account.

Some ISPs throw in a shell account gratis. A novice would be very happy with a personal PPP account, though a SLIP account is not very different. (PPP is gradually replacing SLIP.) If possible, you should obtain a PPP account.

- What software (such as Web browser, mail client, newsreader, and so on) does the ISP provide for Internet access? Is their documentation adequate? Do they s-mail you the software on disk, or do they provide a place from which you can download it? Does the ISP provide technical support for this process? If you do not care for their choice of software, will they allow you to obtain and use your own software? If possible, try the software the ISP supplies before making any subscription decisions.

- How much disk space is provided for email? Does the ISP provide any disk space for customers to create and publish Web pages? If they do, how much storage is available and is there a fee involved? What if you need more space? These questions might not seem relevant now, but they will be once you start accumulating HTML files and images. You will probably need a minimum of 2 megabytes (2 megs) of space to work comfortably.

- Does the ISP have a toll-free technical support number? When are they available? Technical support 7 days a week, 24 hours a day (called 24–7) is wonderful, but smaller ISPs often do not have the staff to supply it. Technical support via email works well if the technical support personnel respond in a timely manner and if the problem you are having does not involve the login process. Ask current users about their experiences with the ISP you are considering.

- Does the ISP offer an access number that you can use when you are traveling out of town and want to get on-line? If so, what is the charge per minute? Again, this may not seem important now, but it could be in the future.

- How many newsgroups does the ISP carry? How long do they keep the postings? Do they carry the newsgroups you like, and will you have an adequate chance to read them?

- If you are interested in registering your own domain name, does the ISP offer domain name services? In order for you to do this, the ISP must provide static IP addresses.

- If you plan to run a business via your Web access, compare the ISP's business rate schedule versus their nonbusiness rates.

A.3   Desirable Features

Some of the desirable features provided by good ISPs are outlined here. The weight you place on each item will depend on your needs. This short list was culled from the questions in the previous section. You may wish to add or delete features, depending on how you are planning to use your Internet connection.

- Local-access phone numbers for dialing in (a necessity).

- Local-access phone numbers that are not busy, even during the most congested times of the day (5:00 P.M. to 9:00 P.M.).

- Toll-free telephone number for customer support, plus the flexibility to email questions to technical support staff.

- A 28.8 Kbps or faster modem connection between you and the ISP; a T1 or T3 connection between the ISP and the Internet.

- Five to ten megabytes of space for your personal Web pages.

- A rate plan that suits your needs. For example, if you only plan to be on-line for a couple of hours each month, you may save money by not opting for a flat-rate plan.

- Newsgroup access that includes the newsgroups in which you are interested. Postings should be retained for at least two weeks. (Some ISPs keep postings for months.)

- Positive recommendations from other ISP customers.

A.4   Connection Setup

To connect to the Internet via an ISP, the following equipment is necessary: modem, telephone line, and computer with TCP/IP networking software installed. A connection is obtained by the modem dialing up the access number provided by the ISP. Assuming you have a SLIP or PPP account, you supply a login userid (which was assigned to you or which you had previously selected) and a password (again, selected by you), and you are then connected directly to the Internet. SLIP and PPP permit the TCP/IP data to be transferred over the telephone lines. Certain Internet software tools must also be installed on your computer, including a Web browser, mail program, newsreader, and so on. You actually run these clients on your computer. For shell accounts, these clients are run on the *remote host*. As noted earlier, the ISP may make these clients available to you or allow you to select and install your own. Getting all of these components installed and configured may not be trivial, but it can be made much easier by both good basic information from the ISP and help from someone with experience.

A.5   Typical Problems

Despite your asking all the right questions and doing your ISP homework, problems may arise. Some problems are common among ISPs, and they can motivate people to switch ISPs.

One of the most frustrating problems associated with ISPs (and commercial on-line services) is the busy signal when you are trying to connect. This may occur only at certain times of the day, but if you need to get on-line, this situation presents a problem. Also, the problem may develop over time, as the ISP grows and cannot keep up with user demand. While evaluating the ISP, we recommend dialing the access numbers and trying to connect, to determine how often the line is busy (if at all) at various times of the day. Talking to others who use the ISP can also provide insight into how difficult it is to connect. In addition, remember that your own telephone line will be busy when you are on-line, so you might have to consider getting a second phone line.

Another problem sometimes encountered is slow download times, even though your modem connection is fast. If your modem is 28.8 Kbps and the ISP's modem connection is 14.4 Kbps, data is transferred at the slower rate. You will also feel this effect if the ISP's connection to the Internet is slow, or if they have a lot of customers placing high demands on the system. Even if you have a 56 Kbps modem, consider that the quality of your local telephone lines may limit you to 28 Kbps or lower. Talk to others in your area and to your ISP to find out their experiences.

ISPs to which you cannot connect create an annoying problem, especially since this may not become apparent until after you have subscribed. Similar problems can arise with an *email only service*. Email messages may be lost, or may not be delivered in a timely manner. If your ISP addresses your problems right away, these issues may not be a concern. The best way to ascertain the ISP's reliability is talk to their customers.

Many users have difficulty configuring TCP/IP software for their systems. Sometimes, the setup documentation provided is not clear or is hard to follow. The installation process is usually not intuitive and is system-specific. If you encounter any technical difficulties, the best way for you to proceed is to contact the ISP's technical support staff immediately. When describing your problem, try to provide the technical support personnel with as much detail as possible.

A.6   Internet Service Provider Selection

Go On-Line

To select an ISP, you need to find out which ISPs are in your area (remembering that you do not want to make a toll call to connect). If you currently have access to the Internet, you can check the Web for lists (and critiques, too) of providers in a specific area. There are also newsgroups that address ISP selection. Other alternatives include looking up ISPs in the off-line Yellow Pages or talking to your friends.

Go On-Line

Once you have compiled your list of ISPs, contact them by phone or email to get answers to the questions posed here. Some ISPs have Web presentations, and visiting them would provide you with additional information. In fact, the appearance of their Web presentation might provide some insight into how thorough and professional they are. Whether the ISP's staff answers your email inquiries quickly might provide clues about how promptly they will respond to your questions once you are a customer.

Using the answers to the list of questions as a guide, eliminate the ISPs that are not suitable. For example, one of them may not carry a newsgroup you always read, or another may not provide an access number for you to use when you travel. Next, if possible, test the ISP's access lines by using your modem to connect to theirs. Connect at different times of the day, to establish when and if busy signals are going to be a problem. Also, try calling their toll-free technical support number, if they have one. Note how long you have to wait until you speak with someone. Was the person who answered knowledgeable and friendly?

Hot Topic

Once you have narrowed down your list, try to talk to other users about the candidate ISPs. Their comments may be the most useful pieces of information. If the ISPs offer a free trial period (or a money-back guarantee for a period of time), try them out. Keep a record of the research you have done up to this point, since it may come in handy later.

Once you have selected your ISP, unexpected problems may arise after you have used the service for a while. If a problem becomes acute, you may have to switch to your second choice.

Our last piece of advice is to pay for the service by the month, not by the cheaper yearly rate (if offered). Then, if you want to change to another ISP, you do not have to wait a year, or get penalized by leaving earlier.

Text Editing

B

B.1   Introduction

This appendix contains basic information about *text editing*. It is intended for those who have little or no editing experience. A text editor is a program that is used to create and modify ASCII files. To introduce you to basic text editing commands and editing principles, we will use the *Pico* (pronounced PEE-ko) editor, but any simple text editor will suffice. Details about other editing software are readily available on-line.

Go On-Line

Many different varieties of text editors are available. Many word processing programs also come with built-in text editors. Some text editors have graphical user interfaces, and many commands are mouse driven. Other editors are more keyboard-based. The decision as to which style of editor to use will depend in part on what is available to you. Hopefully, you will be able to experiment with a number of different editors and then select the one you prefer. Here, we focus on keyboard-based editors, as opposed to graphical editors. Graphical editors usually provide extensive on-line help and pull-down menus, with icons to indicate how to perform the various commands.

B.2   Keyboard-Driven Editors

Two popular and powerful text editors are `vi` and `emacs`, which are a little too complex to be used in an introduction to text editing. You may however decide to pursue these editors on your own by following the references. Another, simpler text editor is called Pico, which is supplied with the *Pine mail program* developed at the University of Washington. Pico stands for *Pine composer*, and during message composition, the Pine mailer defaults to the Pico editor. The basic principles and editing features of Pico apply to other keyboard-driven editors.

B.3   Pico

This short tutorial will provide a new user with the minimum editing skills needed for file composition. Editing commands can be split into several groups: cursor movement, cut and paste, save and insert files, and miscellaneous. Most editors, including Pico, let you insert text at the current cursor position simply by typing it in.

Figure B.1 shows a screen shot of the Pico interface. Many of the commands are executed by depressing the *Control* key and another key simultaneously. On any system, the command for obtaining help is very important. Pico help allows you to obtain documentation about all of the editor's commands on-line. To get help from inside Pico you type (2 keys)

```
CONTROL-G
```

The G does not need to be uppercase. In the figure, the control key is shown as a caret ($\wedge$). In our examples, we prefer to use the word CONTROL. We

FIGURE B.1
The Pico text editor interface.

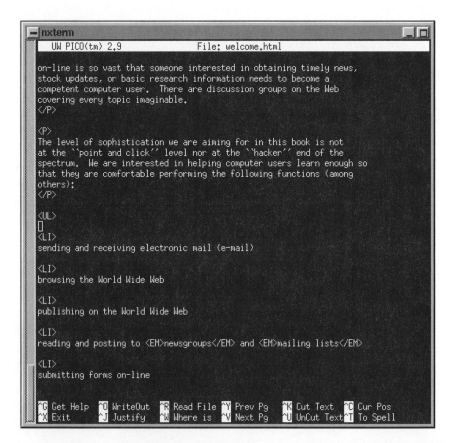

will describe each of the other commands listed at the bottom of the Pico screen and will follow the Pico convention of using all capital letters.

B.3.1   Cursor Movement

The basic cursor movement commands are:

- CONTROL-F—Forward one space.

- CONTROL-B—Backward one space.

- CONTROL-N—Next line.

- CONTROL-P—Previous line.

- CONTROL-A—Beginning of line.

- CONTROL-E—End of line.

More specialized movement commands, such as CONTROL-Y to return to the previous screen and CONTROL-V to move forward a page, are also available. The command CONTROL-C reports the current cursor position on the screen. The arrow keys can also be used to reposition the cursor.

B.3.2   Cut and Paste

One of the most important editing operations is the ability to *cut* and then *paste* a piece of text. If done properly, this move can save considerable time. In Pico, the cutting is done using the CONTROL-K command, and the pasting is done using the CONTROL-U command. By repeatedly using CONTROL-K, you can "select" a number of lines to be cut. For example, five CONTROL-K's will cut five lines. Moving the cursor and then using a single CONTROL-U will paste the cut text into the place where the cursor is positioned.

B.3.3   Save and Insert Files

How do you insert a file into the file you are currently editing? This is done using CONTROL-R. When you execute this command, you will be prompted for the name of the file to insert.

How do you save a file? To save a file, use the CONTROL-O command. To exit the editor without saving a file, use the CONTROL-X command.

How do you create a new file? Enter the command Pico at the operating system prompt, and then edit and save the new file using the CONTROL-O command. Another way of doing this is to type

```
%pico new.file
```

where `new.file` is the name of the file you want to create. When you save the file, it will be written to `new.file`.

B.3.4   Miscellaneous

There are four important miscellaneous features. They are spell-checking, searching within a file, justifying text, and suspending the editor.

Spell-Check

Pico has a built-in spell-checker, which is invoked by the command `CONTROL-T`. If the spell-checker finds a word that it thinks is misspelled, it offers you the opportunity to correct the word. On most systems, other spell-checkers are available. It is a good idea to run your files through the spell-checking phase, but do not assume that all spelling errors have been corrected. The spell-checker will not catch words that are spelled correctly but are the wrong words. For example, if "there books" should be "their books," the spell-checker will not catch it.

Search

To search for text (or a string of text) within a file, use the `CONTROL-W` command. This command is very useful when you are entering edits from a hardcopy. The command allows you to search the file to get close to where you need to enter a change. Simple cursor movements can then bring you to the exact spot to edit.

Justify Text

The `CONTROL-J` command is used to justify the text of the current paragraph. (It does not allow you to set the margins within which justification takes place.) When composing email, this is very useful for pretty printing a paragraph. That is, `CONTROL-J` makes the lines appear near equal in length.

Suspend Pico

If you invoke Pico with the -z flag,

```
%pico -z new.file
```

you will be able to suspend editing by typing `CONTROL-Z`; that is, using `CONTROL-Z` exits Pico to the shell prompt. This lets you look up or obtain

information with other commands and then resume your editing session by
issuing the command:

%fg

<hr>

B.4 Commands Summary

- CONTROL-A—Move cursor to beginning of line.

- CONTROL-B—Move cursor backward one space.

- CONTROL-C—Report current cursor position on the screen.

- CONTROL-E—Move cursor to end of line.

- CONTROL-F—Move cursor forward one space.

- CONTROL-G—Display Pico help.

- CONTROL-J—Justify text in current paragraph.

- CONTROL-K—Cut text.

- CONTROL-N—Move cursor to next line.

- CONTROL-O—Save file.

- CONTROL-P—Move cursor to previous line.

- CONTROL-R—Insert file.

- CONTROL-T—Invoke spell-checker.

- CONTROL-U—Paste text.

- CONTROL-V—Move forward a screen.

- CONTROL-W—Search for a pattern of text.

- CONTROL-X—Exit Pico without saving the file.

- CONTROL-Y—Move backward a screen.

- CONTROL-Z—Suspend Pico.

Pine Mail Program

C.1   Introduction

This appendix explains some of the features of the *Pine mail program*, a popular email program developed at the University of Washington in 1989. The name "Pine" stands for *Program for Internet News and Email*. Pine provides an easy-to-use, keyboard-driven interface for composing, sending, reading, and managing email and newsgroup messages.

We will explain some of the basic features of Pine. Other mailers have similar functionality, but their user interfaces may differ. For example, *Eudora* is a popular mouse-driven email program. Nearly all features found in Pine exist in Eudora and vice versa. However, in Pine, one or two keystrokes are needed to execute a command, whereas in Eudora, several mouse clicks are necessary. (Both Pine and Eudora have extensive on-line documentation.) As with any software, the best way to learn about it is to get on-line and experiment.

Go On-Line

C.2   Getting Started

Pine is text-driven; that is, all commands are entered as keystrokes. The mouse is not used, as there is no graphical interface. Menus, located at the bottom of the screen, guide the user by displaying the various commands and options. On-line help is easily accessible, making Pine particularly user-friendly.

Pine software must be installed on your computer (or on the system of which your computer is part). Typing `pine` at the UNIX prompt, or selecting `Pine` from a menu of options, are two ways to start the program.

When Pine starts, the menu shown in Figure C.1 is displayed. This is the *Pine Main Menu*, which lists Pine's features/options. The top line of the screen indicates the version of Pine that is running (in this case, 3.96). The title of the screen, MAIN MENU, appears next to the version, and to the

Go On-Line

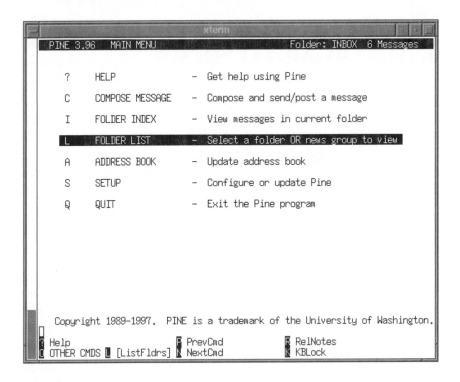

right is a message indicating how many messages are there. In Figure C.1, we see that there are six messages in the folder named INBOX.

The features available, as listed on the screen, along with their associated commands, are as follows:

- Getting on-line help about Pine—?

- Composing a message—C

- Viewing messages—I

- Selecting a folder of messages to view—L

- Updating the address book—A

- Customizing Pine—S

- Exiting Pine—Q

Notice in Figure C.1 that in addition to listing the options with their descriptions, the screen also offers a summary of commands along the bottom. Since all of the available options cannot fit at the bottom, pressing the O key will display "other commands" that are available. Some of the commands displayed include P (or PrevCmd) for "previous command" and N (or NextCmd) for "next command." Using the P (or N) key highlights the previous (or next) option in the features list. A highlighted option can then be selected by pressing the Return key.

Another way to select an option is to press the associated key, either uppercase or lowercase, without pressing the Return key. Case is not significant. Pine itself displays commands in uppercase letters, and we have adopted that convention. For example, pressing the C[1] or c key allows you to compose a message, and pressing the Q key allows you to quit Pine. (When using a conventional mouse, only one hand remains on the keyboard. However, one advantage of Pine is that both hands may remain on the keyboard, so you are always in a position to type. Not having to reposition the mouse cursor and the other hand on the keyboard can let a skilled typist operate more efficiently.)

The R at the bottom of the Main Menu screen stands for "Release Notes." The Release Notes describe any changes from the previous version of Pine, bugs, and so on. The K command permits you to lock your keyboard, for those times when you want to step away from your computer for a few minutes, but do not want to log out and do not want anyone else to use your computer.

In addition to the summary of commands and the list of options, the Main Menu screen provides an area for messages and prompts. They will be displayed in brackets just below the copyright/trademark declaration. For instance, entering D on the Main Menu screen results in the following message being displayed in the message/prompt line:

```
[Command "D" not defined for this screen. Use ? for help]
```

C.3   Composing and Sending Mail

To compose an email message, press the C key (or select the COMPOSE MESSAGE option by highlighting it and pressing the return key) from the Main Menu. A new screen titled COMPOSE MESSAGE will appear, containing a *template* for constructing the message. Figure C.2 depicts that template.

Like the Main Menu, the bottom of the Compose Message screen contains a menu of pertinent commands. These commands show a ∧ character

Go On-Line

---

1   Pressing the C key is shorthand for typing SHIFT-c.

FIGURE C.2
Pine's template
for message
composition.

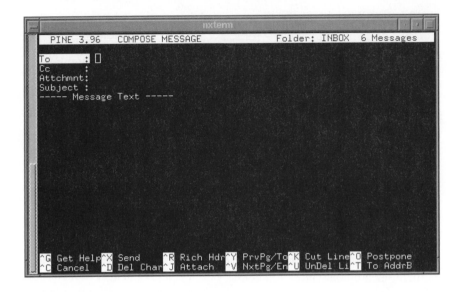

before a letter, such as ∧G. The commands are executed by pressing the
Control key (Ctrl) at the same time as the letter key, either uppercase or
lowercase. In our discussion, we use the word CONTROL to refer to these
commands; that is, we use CONTROL-G, although what you will see on the
screen and in our figures will be ∧G.

The CONTROL-G (Get Help) command found on the bottom of the
screen provides help information about whichever template field is highlighted. The basic template includes a To: field, Cc: field, Attchmnt:
field, Subject: field, and Message Text area. Use the arrow keys (←,
→, ↑, or ↓) or CONTROL-P (previous line) and CONTROL-N (next line) to
move from field to field.

You will notice that as different fields in the template are highlighted,
the commands at the bottom may change. For instance, when the To:
field is highlighted, selecting the CONTROL-T option provides access to a
list of addresses in the *address book*. When the Message Text field is
highlighted, CONTROL-T invokes the spell-checker. Pine provides the help
menus at the bottom of each screen.

Text is entered in the various fields using the Pico text editor. More
information about Pico can be found either in Appendix B or on-line while
using Pine. When you highlight the To: field and enter the CONTROL-G command, the help screen provides a short summary of Pico cursor movement
and editing commands.

C.3.1 The To: Field

When composing an email message, you enter the address of the recipient in the To: field. Position the cursor at the To: field, which is then highlighted, and type in the email address. More than one recipient can be specified by separating them with commas. (This is called *comma delimiting*.)

A nickname or alias can be specified in the To: field. Pine will check your address book to determine the full email address(es) and will expand the nickname for you. (Recall that an alias can specify a list of email addresses, as well as a single address.) Nicknames can be specified, along with regular email addresses, when more than one recipient is listed. For example,

```
To: dickens@aol.com, marty, club
```

The nickname "marty" is an alias for mphillips@biology.uchio.edu, and "club" is an alias for a list of email addresses belonging to the members of the "Breakfast Club."

C.3.2 The Carbon Copy Field

The Cc: field allows you to send copies of a message to other people. Email addresses, as well as nicknames, can be entered in the field. This field is optional and can be left blank either by skipping over it (CONTROL-N) or by pressing the Return key when the cursor is positioned at it.

C.3.3 The Attachment Field

The Attchmnt: field lets you specify the name of files to append (or "attach") to a message. Attachments are appended separately and are not part of the message text. Only files residing on the same machine as the mailer can be appended to the message, and only recipients with MIME-capable mail programs (such as Pine) will be immediately able to view attachments that are other than just plaintext. When the cursor is positioned at the Attchmnt: field, the CONTROL-T command displays files from which to select. After entering the name of the file, or using CONTROL-T to select a file, you simply press the Return key to attach the file.

C.3.4 The Subject Field

The Subject: field provides a place for you to tell the recipient what your message is about. Enter a short, clear description of your message.

C.3.5   Other Header Fields

Entering the CONTROL-R (Rich Hdr) command while in the Compose Message screen causes your template to display other optional fields. To use one of these fields, simply fill in the appropriate information. The Bcc: field permits you to send "blind carbon copies," that is, the addresses of the copied recipients are not displayed. The Fcc: field lets you specify a folder in which to keep a copy of the outgoing message. Other fields, including Newsgrps: and Lcc:, can be explored by using the CONTROL-G command.

C.3.6   Message Text Field

To enter the body of your message, position the cursor over the Message Text field. Using Pico text editing and cursor movement commands, type your message. When you are done, invoke the spell-checker by pressing CONTROL-T. The CONTROL-R command lets you insert a file into the message.

Once your message is complete, you can either send the message using the CONTROL-X command, cancel the message with the CONTROL-C command, or postpone sending the message until a later time, using the CONTROL-O command. Each of these commands causes Pine to ask you if that is what you really want to do. You respond by pressing either the Y key for "yes" or the N key for "no." Pressing the Return key will invoke the default selection, which is shown with brackets around it. Figure C.3 illustrates a Pine Compose Message screen that is ready to be sent.

C.4   Reading Mail

Go On-Line

When you receive email messages, Pine places them in a folder called INBOX. To view the messages in your INBOX folder, press I (Folder Index) from the Main Menu, which brings up a screen called Folder Index. This screen displays information about each message in your INBOX folder. Figure C.4 shows a sample INBOX folder screen.

The Folder Index screen does not display the full text of the messages you have received; instead, it displays specific information about each message, so that you can decide which (if any) messages you want to read. In Figure C.4, four messages are shown on the screen. This is also indicated on the top line of the screen, where it identifies the folder as INBOX and the highlighted message as 4 of 4.

For each message displayed on the Folder Index screen, seven pieces of information are provided:

FIGURE C.3
A sample Pine
Compose
Message screen.

Column 1—Either a blank or a "+" symbol, where a + indicates that this message was sent directly to you (as opposed to being carbon copied, for instance).

Column 2—Message status; either A, D, or N. An A means that the message was answered using the Reply command, a D signifies that you have read the message and have marked it for deletion, and an N indicates that the message is new.

Column 3—Message number.

Column 4—Date the message was sent.

Column 5—Sender of the message.

Column 6—Size of the message, in bytes.

Column 7—Subject of the message, as specified by the sender.

To read a particular message, select it by using the arrow keys or by pressing the P (PrevMsg for Previous Message) key or the N (NextMsg for Next Message) key. The selected message is highlighted in reverse video

FIGURE C.4

A Pine Folder
Index screen.

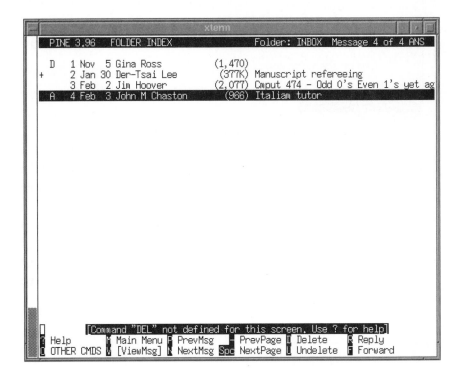

and indicated on the top line: Message 4 of 4, for instance. Pressing the
V key displays the entire message on another screen (perhaps replacing
the original screen) called the Message Text screen. Simply pressing the
Return key does the same thing, since V is the default. The commands
to continue reading messages are listed on the bottom of the screen: N
(NextMsg) to view the next message, or P (PrevMsg) to view the previous
message in this folder. To return to the index of messages, press I.

After reading a particular message, you might decide to respond to it.
One way to do this is to go to the Compose Message screen, fill in the
header information, write the message, and send your response. Another
way is to use the Reply command, R, from the Message Text screen. From
the message/prompt line, Pine will ask if you want to include the original
message in the reply. Responding "no" (the default) causes the Compose
Message Reply screen to appear with the header information already filled
in. The Subject: field will contain Re:, followed by the subject line of
the original message.

Responding "yes" causes the entire text of the message sent to you
to be copied into the message text area, with header information filled in
as well. The copied message text is preceded by a line identifying who
wrote the original text and when. For example, if Enrico were using the
R command to respond to a message sent by Laura (verona@books.com),

Pine would put the following into the Message Text area:

```
On Sun, 18 Jan 1998, verona wrote:
```

Laura's original message would appear after that, with each line from her original message marked by a > symbol along the left margin. Lines can be added, deleted, and modified using the Pico text editing commands.

   After completing your reply, you would use the same commands that appear on the Compose Message screen to finish: CONTROL-X to send the message, CONTROL-C to cancel the message, or CONTROL-O to postpone sending the message.

   The Forward command (F) is similar to the Reply command. It allows you to forward the message you are currently reading to another email address. A screen appears containing a copy of the message, and you must fill in the To: field. Like the Reply command, the original message can be modified and added to.

C.5   Managing Mail

Managing email involves deleting unwanted messages and organizing those messages you want to save. The saved messages can include copies of e-mail that you have sent, as well as mail you have received. Messages are organized and kept in *folders*. Pine provides the following three default folders for each account:

* INBOX The folder where new incoming messages are stored.

* saved-messages The default folder for saving copies of messages.

* sent-mail The folder where copies of messages that you have sent are saved.

   Pine allows you to create your own folders, in addition to these three.
   To move around between folders, press L (FOLDER LIST) from the Main Menu. A Folder List screen appears, showing the *collections of folders*. To select a collection, highlight the phrase

```
"[ Select Here to See Expanded List ]"
```

below the desired collection and press the Return key. The folders within that collection will be displayed on a new Folder List screen (possibly replacing the original screen), and you can highlight a specific folder to view.

A menu of commands is shown at the bottom of the screen. These let you: view what is in the selected folder (V—ViewFldr), delete (D—Delete) folders, add (A—Add) folders, and rename (R—Rename) folders. Another way to access the index of another folder is to use the G (GotoFldr) command, which prompts you to enter the name of the folder you want to view.

C.5.1   Deleting Messages

It is important to delete unwanted messages, since they clutter up folders and make it difficult to keep track of more important correspondence. Also, most email accounts only have a limited amount of memory allocated to them, so cleaning out folders is necessary to conserve disk space.

Deleting a message requires two steps. First, the message is marked for deletion by selecting the message from the Folder Index screen. Using the D command marks the message for deletion. A message can also be marked for deletion from the Message Text screen, when you are viewing the message. If you decide later that you do not want to delete the message, unmark the message using the undelete command, U, from either the Folder Index screen or the Message Text screen.

Second, *expunge* the messages that have been marked for deletion. You can deliberately expunge a message from the Folder Index screen by using the X command. Otherwise, when you terminate Pine or when you leave a folder (other than the INBOX folder), Pine asks if you want to expunge messages marked for deletion. Note that a message marked for deletion can be undeleted. However, once a message is expunged, it is gone for good and Pine cannot restore it.

C.5.2   Saving Messages

Incoming messages are automatically put in your INBOX folder. After reading a message (and possibly responding to it), you may decide to save it. If you are in the Message Text screen, pressing S saves a copy of the message and marks the INBOX copy for deletion. The saved-messages folder is the default folder in which messages are saved, but you can specify another folder. After you press S, Pine prompts you with:

```
SAVE to folder in <mail/[]> [saved-messages]:
```

Pressing the Return key selects the default folder (saved-messages), or you can enter another folder name. If the folder name you specify does not exist, Pine asks if you want it created. Pine then saves the message to the file specified.

Messages can also be saved from the Folder Index screen by selecting the message (i.e., highlighting it) and then using the S command, in the same way as messages are saved from the Message Text screen.

C.5.3   Additional Features

While we have covered the most important features of Pine, the software includes many other features. To explore these features, we encourage you to experiment with Pine, especially the S (SETUP) command from the Main Menu, which will, among other things, allow you to create a signature file. Exploring the various commands and trying them out—sending mail to yourself, if necessary—is the best way to become proficient at using Pine.

Go On-Line

Basic UNIX

D.1 Introduction

UNIX is a widely used operating system, particularly in academic and research settings. In addition, many operating systems have adopted UNIX-like commands and features.

In Section 2.5, we explained how to install a Web page on a UNIX-based Web server. (Installation of Web pages on Windows-based servers or other types of servers requires a different procedure.) In this appendix, we describe basic UNIX commands and the UNIX file structure. Our aim is to provide an overview, so that you will feel comfortable creating and manipulating files for your Web page.

D.2 Sundry Facts

When using a UNIX account, you will be greeted by a *prompt* character. The default prompt is usually the % symbol, indicating that the system is ready for you to enter a *command*. The default is also called the *shell* prompt, because you are interacting with the outer layer (interface, or shell) of the operating system. The prompt symbol % may be changed, and many users change it to something like

```
computername>
```

where `computername` is the name of their machine.

Commands are instructions you give to the computer. While there are hundreds of UNIX commands, about a dozen will suffice for our purposes. Fortunately, UNIX also provides an on-line manual that can be accessed using the `man` command. As long as you can recall a command name, the on-line manual can tell you how that command is used, as well as the *options* and *arguments* associated with it. For example, typing

Go On-Line

```
%man man
```

provides you with on-line help about the `man` command.

Options to commands are typically specified by single-character *flags* prefaced by a dash (–) symbol. For example,

```
%man -k time
```

requests manual information about commands that have something to do with the keyword `time`. Notice the single blank spaces between the individual items in this command line. The `k` is a flag to the `man` command. The word `time`, as used here, is an argument to the command. Arguments are values that are passed to the command.

Normally, you will type in a command at the prompt, along with associated options and arguments. As an example, the command to list a *directory*'s contents is `ls`. (Think of a directory as a *folder*, if the folder terminology is more familiar to you.) When you type the command

```
%ls
```

the resulting output might look as follows:

```
calendar      classes      finances      letters
misc
```

By adding flags to the `ls` command, you can request additional information about the directory's contents, or format the output in a particular way. To list a directory's contents in the "long form," which provides associated properties of the files and subdirectories contained within it, use the `ls -l` command.

So far, we have seen that `man` stands for manual, and `ls` represents list. Many UNIX commands are *mnemonic*. Since most commands are only two characters, some of the mnemonics are not terribly helpful for new users.

Hopefully, the basic style of UNIX commands is now clear. Their general form is

```
%"mnemonic command name" -flag(s) argument(s)
```

Multiple flags are written adjacent to each other with no intervening white space, whereas multiple arguments are separated by blank spaces. (Note, there are exceptions to these rules.)

We will now look at the UNIX file structure.

D.3   File Structure

It is important to understand how files and directories are organized under UNIX, so that you will be able to access them. The purpose of this section is to describe this structure.

Among other things, UNIX commands are used to create, manipulate, and change permissions on files. Many commands take a file name as an argument. The exceptions include the `date` command, which is used to report the current date and time.

Directories and files are organized in a tree-like hierarchy. The directory at the top of the hierarchy is known as the *root directory* and is represented by a forward-slash character, `/`. On a large UNIX system, some standard subdirectories under the root directory are `etc`, `usr`, and `tmp`.

Under normal circumstances, if you have an account on a UNIX system, you will begin your login sessions in your assigned *home directory*. You can use the tilde symbol (∼) to refer to your home directory. Starting from the root directory and proceeding through the hierarchy until you reach your home directory results in a *path* to your home directory.

When the directory names you traverse through are concatenated together, the result is a *pathname*. Like URLs, pathnames can be absolute, called *full* in UNIX jargon, or relative, which is the same term used in HTML. The first forward slash in a pathname represents the root directory. Additional forward slashes in a pathname separate the names of the subdirectories. As an example, Figure D.1 shows Mary McCarthy's directory and file structure.

The UNIX file system has some special files (and directories) that are called *hidden files* (respectively, *hidden directories*) or *dot files*. The names of these files begin with a period symbol (`.`), such as `.cshrc`, `.login`, `.newsrc`, and `.pinesrc`. The `rc` stands for "run command" and is a historical artifact of some old operating systems. These hidden files usually contain configuration or initialization information, and you should not edit these files unless you are absolutely sure of what you are doing. Even then, you should make a backup copy of any such files you intend to edit. Some of these files are not intended to be edited by hand, but only by other programs. To list the hidden files and directories, you can use the `-a` flag (which stands for "all") to the `ls` command. Since you would rarely want to see or edit these files, the default for the `ls` command is not to list them.

Hot Topic

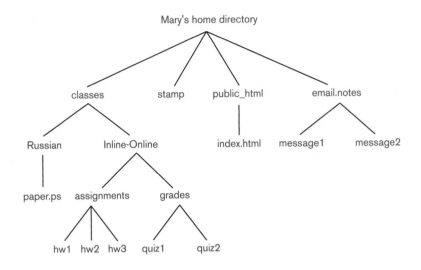

Mary's home directory

classes   stamp   public_html   email.notes

Russian   Inline-Online   index.html   message1   message2

paper.ps   assignments   grades

hw1   hw2   hw3   quiz1   quiz2

D.4   File and Directory Organization

You have total control in creating and maintaining both files and directories in your home directory. One reason for using subdirectories is to organize files. In Figure D.1, for example, we see that Mary has subdirectories for classes, email correspondence, and Web material. She also has a file called `stamp` in her home directory.

To create a subdirectory in any directory, use the `mkdir` command and provide the subdirectory name as an argument to this command. For example, to create a subdirectory called `job.apps` in the *current directory*, you would enter

```
%mkdir job.apps
```

The phrase "current directory," also called the *working directory*, refers to the directory in which you are working.

To move to another directory, you use the *change directory* command, `cd`. The command by itself, with no arguments, will place you in your home directory. To verify a change of directory, you can use the *print working directory* command, `pwd`. The output of the `pwd` command is the full pathname of the directory in which you are working. Suppose Mary just logged into her account named `marymc` and executed the command

```
%pwd
```

For output, she might see something like `/export/home/marymc`.

By specifying a pathname as the argument to the cd command, you can change directories. For example, to go into her Web directory, Mary can enter

```
%cd /export/home/marymc/public_html
```

Notice that a full pathname is specified in the command. Typing in a full pathname every time you want to change directories is time consuming; it is often more efficient to use a *relative pathname*. Using relative pathnames when navigating through the file structure can save a lot of typing time, not to mention potential typing errors. To move up one level in a directory hierarchy, follow the cd command with two dots

```
%cd ..
```

The two dots represent the *parent directory* for the directory in which you are currently located. To move from within her public-html directory to her grades directory, Mary can enter

```
%cd ../classes/Inline-Online/grades
```

Note that UNIX is case sensitive. In particular, some commands have both lowercase and uppercase flags that involve the same letter yet have totally different meanings.

D.5   File Manipulation

Once you know how to move around in the file structure, you are ready to create and edit files. Appendix B provides a short introduction to text editing for file creation. Here we concentrate on file manipulation. At some point, you will want to move a file to another directory, delete a file or directory, make a copy of a file, or just view a file. Numerous commands are used for manipulating files. One is the mv command, which is used to rename or move a file. To rename a file, follow the mv command by two arguments; the first is the name of the file you wish to rename, and the second is the new name for that file. For example,

```
%mv index.html index.old
```

renames the file index.html to index.old. After the command is executed, the file named index.html will no longer exist.

Another useful command is rm, which is used to delete or remove a file. The rm command should be used with care, because once the file is deleted, it is really gone—there is no undo. Using the -i option with the rm command will cause the system to ask for verification before deleting the file. We encourage you to use this flag. For example, entering the command

```
%rm -i mystuff.txt
```

will generate a query about whether or not you really want to delete the file mystuff.txt. The rmdir for deleting an empty directory is analogous to the rm command for deleting a file.

The more command can be used to look at the contents of a file. For example,

```
%more index.html
```

displays one screenful of the file index.html. Hitting the space bar brings up the next screenful of text, and typing q "quits" the command and brings you back to the prompt. The more command only allows you to view the file; you need a text editor to alter the file's contents.

The cp command is used to copy a file. This is different from the mv command in that you end up with another exact copy of the file; the original file and its name remain intact. As an example,

```
%cp index.html mypage.html
```

copies the file index.html to the file mypage.html. By using copies of HTML files that have similar tags, you can save considerable keyboarding and editing time. These copies become *templates* of the common HTML file formats on your Web presentation.

D.6   File Permissions

Permissions provide a measure of security by establishing who is able to access what files and directories, and how they can access them.

Three identifiers can be used to specify who can access an item. They are:

- The user who owns a file, designated u.

- The various users who are members of the same group as the file owner, designated g.

- All other users, designated o.

Coincidentally, UNIX provides three different levels of file permissions as well. The permissions, which are as follows, indicate how items can be accessed:

- Read, designated r.

- Write, designated w.

- Execute, designated x.

Their meanings are self-explanatory. To permit the use of its contents on Web pages, a subdirectory must allow both x and r access. With UNIX, write permission also means deletion ability. That is, if someone has write permission to a file (or directory), they can also delete the file (or directory).

Hot Topic

File and directory permissions can be conveniently displayed using the ls -l command. This command results in a listing of all files and subdirectories, along with their permissions, as given by a string of ten characters. Suppose the current working directory has just one file, called README. The command

```
%ls -l
```

might generate a response such as

```
-r--r--r-- 1 marymc Spanish 167 Jul 27 08:15 README
```

The first character identifies the type of item. In this case, a dash is displayed, which means an ordinary file. The other important type is directory, which is represented by a d.

Let us explain the other nine characters in the coding. The following graphic is helpful in visualizing these characters:

The graphic shows that the remaining nine characters are split into three sets of three characters each. The first three characters are associated with user, the second set with group, and the last set with other.

For each set of three characters, an r in the first position indicates that the item can be read by members of the corresponding category. Similarly, a w in the second position indicates write permission, and an x in the third slot indicates execute permission. If any of the permissions are denied, the corresponding symbol is replaced by a dash. In this way, it is possible to have any combination of read, write, and execute permissions for each category.

For example,

```
-r--r--r-- 1 marymc Spanish 167 Jul 27 08:15 README
```

means the user, group members, and others can read the file named README; that is, everyone can read this file. In contrast, the permissions

```
-r-------- 1 marymc Spanish 167 Jul 27 08:15 README
```

indicate that only the user can read the file. Finally, the permissions

```
-rw-r----- 1 marymc Spanish 167 Jul 27 08:15 README
```

mean the user can read and write the file, group members can read the file, and everyone else is denied access.

In each of the examples presented here, the 1 in the second column indicates the number of *hard links* to the file. The user of the file is identified in the third column as marymc. The group is identified in the fourth column as Spanish. Finally, the 167 in the fifth column tells us that the size of the file README is 167 bytes; that is, it contains 167 characters.

As explained in Chapter 2, certain file and directory permissions are required so that others can read your Web pages. To set the permissions, UNIX provides the chmod command, which stands for change mode. There are two ways to use the command; numerically and symbolically. We will only describe the symbolic method here.

The chmod command takes as arguments a permissions setting and the category to be altered. Let us look at a couple of examples to clarify the use of this command. Suppose you execute an ls -l command and receive the following listing:

```
-rw-r----- 1 marymc Spanish 167 Jul 27 08:15 README
```

To add read permission for others, you would use the following:

```
%chmod o+r README
```

In other words, to add read permission for others, we specify others using o and use the plus (+) sign followed by an r flag. Similarly, to remove permission, we use the minus[1] (–) sign. For example, to remove the write permission on README, we enter the following command:

```
%chmod u-w README
```

An ls -l now results in the following:

```
-r--r--r-- 1 marymc Spanish 167 Jul 27 08:15 README
```

For illustration purposes, suppose we need to add write permission for the user and group, and execute permission for the user, group, and other. We can do this in two steps:

```
%chmod uog+wx README
```

followed by

```
%chmod o-w README
```

Notice that the first command temporarily gives write permission to everyone.

To change permissions on all items in a directory to world readable, we could do the following:

```
%chmod uog+r *
```

Hot Topic

The star (∗) is a wild card that equates to every item in the directory.

It is always good practice to check the file protections after using the chmod command, just to make sure they are really set the way you intend.

D.7   UNIX Command Summary

Hot Topic

We have now provided sufficient background for you to install your Web pages on a UNIX server. For easy reference, we list the commands presented in this appendix, along with their functions:

---

1   This is the same symbol as dash, but we call it minus to indicate the removal of permission.

- `cd`   Change directory.

- `chmod`   Change file permissions.

- `cp`   Copy a file.

- `ls`   List the contents of a directory.

- `man`   Display an on-line manual page.

- `mkdir`   Make a directory.

- `more`   Display a file one screenful at a time.

- `mv`   Rename a file.

- `pwd`   Print the working directory.

- `rm`   Delete a file.

- `rmdir`   Delete an empty directory.

HTML Tags

This appendix contains a convenient reference list of the HTML tags discussed in this book, along with a brief description of the function of each tag. The tags are listed in alphabetical order. The ellipsis symbol ($\cdots$) represents the material to be included between the beginning and ending tags. This appendix can be used in conjunction with the index to locate sample uses of the tags and additional information.

Useful Item

- `<A>` $\cdots$ `</A>`

    - Anchor tag, used for setting a hyperlink.
    - Attributes: `HREF`, `NAME`, and `TARGET`.

- `<ADDRESS>` $\cdots$ `</ADDRESS>`

    - Semantic-based style type.
    - Used to indicate an address.

- `<APPLET>` $\cdots$ `</APPLET>`

    - Used to include an (Java) applet.
    - Parameters are passed to the applet using the parameter tag.
    - Attributes: `ALIGN`, `ALT`, `CODE`, `CODEBASE`, `HEIGHT`, `HSPACE`, `NAME`, `VSPACE`, and `WIDTH`.

- `<AREA>`

    - No associated ending tag.
    - Used to define the clickable areas of an image map.
    - Used within the map tag.
    - Attributes: `COORDS`, `HREF`, and `SHAPE`.

- `<B>` $\cdots$ `</B>`

    - Syntactic-based style type.
    - Used to place text in boldface.

- `<BASE>` $\cdots$ `</BASE>`

    - Used for setting global parameters.
    - Attributes: `HREF` and `TARGET`.

- `<BASEFONT>` ⋯ `</BASEFONT>`

  - Used for specifying a document's font size.
  - Attribute: `SIZE`.

- `<BIG>` ⋯ `</BIG>`

  - Semantic-based style type.
  - Used to increase the relative font size of the text.
  - Produces the opposite effect of the small tag.

- `<BGSOUND>`

  - No associated ending tag.
  - Used to include an audio file.
  - Attributes: `LOOP` and `SRC`.

- `<BLINK>` ⋯ `</BLINK>`

  - Syntactic-based style type.
  - Used to create blinking text.
  - Use sparingly, since some users find the effect annoying.

- `<BODY>` ⋯ `</BODY>`

  - Indicates the start of the main part of an HTML document.
  - Attributes: `ALINK`, `BACKGROUND`, `BGCOLOR`, `LINK`, `TEXT`, and `VLINK`.

- `<BR>`

  - No associated ending tag.
  - Used to force a line break.
  - Attribute: `CLEAR`.

- `<CAPTION>` ⋯ `</CAPTION>`

  - Used to annotate a table.
  - Attribute: `ALIGN`.

- `<CENTER>` ⋯ `</CENTER>`

  - Syntactic-based style type.
  - Centers whatever is enclosed between the beginning and ending tags.

- `<CITE>` ⋯ `</CITE>`

  - Semantic-based style type.
  - Used to specify a reference.

- `<CODE> ··· </CODE>`

    - Semantic-based style type.
    - Used to specify program code in the text.

- `<!-- ... -->`

    - Comment tag, used for including notes to yourself in an HTML document.
    - Useful for including copyright notices in files.
    - Comments are not rendered by the browser.

- `<DD> ··· </DD>`

    - Used to identify the definition portion of an item in a "Definition List."
    - DD stands for "Data Definition."
    - Ending tag is usually omitted.

- `<DIV> ··· </DIV>`

    - Used to surround a group of HTML tags to control their alignment.
    - Attribute: `ALIGN`.

- `<DL> ··· </DL>`

    - Used to specify a "Definition List," where each item in the list consists of a term and its corresponding definition.

- `<DT> ··· </DT>`

    - Used instead of the list item tag to identify the terms in a definition list.
    - DT stands for "Definition Term."
    - Ending tag is usually omitted.

- `<EMBED>`

    - No associated ending tag.
    - Used to include multimedia elements in an HTML document.
    - Similar to the object tag.
    - In the HTML 4.0 specification, embed is listed as a deprecated tag.
    - Attributes: `ALIGN`, `BORDER`, `HEIGHT`, `HIDDEN`, `HSPACE`, `NAME`, `SRC`, `TYPE`, `VSPACE`, and `WIDTH`.

- `<EM> ··· </EM>`

    - Semantic-based style type.
    - Used to emphasize a portion of text.

- `<FONT> ··· </FONT>`

  - Used for changing the font specifications for any piece of text.
  - Attributes: `COLOR`, `FACE`, and `SIZE`.

- `<FORM> ··· </FORM>`

  - Used to create a form.
  - The location of the program that processes the form is specified using the `ACTION` attribute.
  - The two ways to send values to a Web server are `get` or `post`, which are specified using the `METHOD` attribute.
  - Nearly any type of HTML formatting may be included inside a form tag.
  - Can be nested.
  - Attributes: `ACTION`, `METHOD`, `NAME`, and `TARGET`.

- `<FRAME> ··· </FRAME>`

  - Used to specify what to load into existing frames.
  - Ending tag is usually omitted.
  - Attributes: `FRAMEBORDER`, `MARGINHEIGHT`, `MARGINWIDTH`, `NAME`, `NORESIZE`, `SCROLLING`, and `SRC`.

- `<FRAMESET> ··· </FRAMESET>`

  - Used to specify how the browser's window is to be partitioned.
  - Used in place of the body tag.
  - Attributes: `COLS`, `FRAMESPACING`, and `ROWS`.

- `<HEAD> ··· </HEAD>`

  - The first part of every HTML document.
  - Includes such items as the title of a page.

- `<Hi> ··· </Hi>`

  - Used to specify a heading.
  - i can be any value from 1 to 6.
  - Attribute: `ALIGN`.

- `<HR>`

  - No associated ending tag.
  - Produces a horizontal line or "rule."
  - Attributes: `ALIGN`, `NOSHADE`, `SIZE`, and `WIDTH`.

- `<HTML> ··· </HTML>`

  - Surrounds all text in an HTML document.

- `<I>` ··· `</I>`

  - Syntactic-based style type.
  - Used to italicize a portion of text.

- `<IMG>`

  - No associated ending tag.
  - Used for including in-line images in HTML documents.
  - Attributes: `ALIGN`, `ALT`, `BORDER`, `HEIGHT`, `HSPACE`, `LOWSRC`, `SRC`, `USEMAP`, `VSPACE`, and `WIDTH`.

- `<INPUT>`

  - No associated ending tag.
  - Used to produce a text box for use with forms.
  - `TYPE` and `NAME` attributes are required.
  - Attributes: `ALIGN`, `CHECKED`, `MAXLENGTH`, `NAME`, `SIZE`, `TYPE`, and `VALUE`.

- `<KBD>` ··· `</KBD>`

  - Semantic-based style type.
  - Used for describing keyboard input.

- `<LI>` ··· `</LI>`

  - Used to identify each item in an ordered or unordered list.
  - Ending tag is usually omitted.
  - Attributes: `TYPE` and `VALUE`.

- `<LINK>`

  - No associated ending tag.
  - Used to include another file in an HTML document.
  - Used in `HEAD` part of an HTML document.
  - Attributes: `HREF`, `REL`, and `TYPE`.

- `<MAP>` ··· `</MAP>`

  - Used to define a client-side image map.
  - Attribute: `NAME`.

- `<META>`

  - No associated ending tag.
  - Used to create client pull documents.
  - Attributes: `CONTENT`, `HTTP-EQUIV`, `NAME`, and `URL`.

- `<NOFRAMES>` ··· `</NOFRAMES>`

  - Provides a way to display information when a browser does not support frames.

- `<OBJECT>` ··· `</OBJECT>`

  - Used to include applets and multimedia elements in an HTML document.
  - Similar to but more general than the embed tag.
  - Attributes: `BORDER`, `CLASSID`, `CODEBASE`, `CODETYPE`, `DATA`, `DECLARE`, `HEIGHT`, `HSPACE`, `NAME`, `SHAPES`, `STANDBY`, `TABINDEX`, `USEMAP`, `VSPACE`, and `WIDTH`.

- `<OL>` ··· `</OL>`

  - Used to specify an "Ordered List."
  - Attributes: `START` and `TYPE`.

- `<OPTION>` ··· `</OPTION>`

  - Used to indicate individual options within a selection element on a form.
  - Must be used within a select tag.
  - Attributes: `SELECTED` and `VALUE`.

- `<P>` ··· `</P>`

  - Used to split text into paragraphs.
  - Attribute: `ALIGN`.

- `<PARAM>`

  - No associated ending tag.
  - Used within the applet and object tags.
  - Inside the applet tag, it is used to pass parameters to the corresponding applet.
  - Inside the object tag, it is used to pass parameters to the corresponding helper or plug-in.
  - Attributes: `NAME` and `VALUE`.

- `<PRE>` ··· `</PRE>`

  - Used to enclose text that is to be left formatted as it appears in the ASCII text file.
  - Not all HTML tags can be used inside these tags.

- `<SCRIPT>` ··· `</SCRIPT>`

  - Used to include code from a scripting language such as JavaScript.
  - Attributes: `LANGUAGE` and `SRC`.

- `<SELECT>` ··· `</SELECT>`

  - Used to indicate a selection in a form that is displayed as either a pull-down menu or a scrolling list.

- Must be used within a form tag.
- Attributes: `MULTIPLE`, `NAME`, and `SIZE`.

- `<SMALL> ⋯ </SMALL>`

  - Semantic-based style type.
  - Used to reduce the relative font size of text.
  - Produces the opposite effect of the big tag.

- `<STRIKE> ⋯ </STRIKE>`

  - Syntactic-based style type.
  - Used to produce a line through the text to achieve a cross-out effect.

- `<STRONG> ⋯ </STRONG>`

  - Semantic-based style type.
  - Used to indicate an even higher degree of emphasis than the emphasis tag.

- `<STYLE> ⋯ </STYLE>`

  - Used to define internal styles as part of cascading styles.
  - Used in `HEAD` part of an HTML document.

- `<SUB> ⋯ </SUB>`

  - Syntactic-based style type.
  - Used to generate a subscript.

- `<SUP> ⋯ </SUP>`

  - Syntactic-based style type.
  - Used to generate a superscript.

- `<TABLE> ⋯ </TABLE>`

  - Used to define a table.
  - Useful for controlling the layout of information.
  - Attributes: `ALIGN`, `BGCOLOR`, `BORDER`, `CELLPADDING`, `CELLSPACING`, `HSPACE`, `VALIGN`, `VSPACE`, and `WIDTH`.

- `<TD> ⋯ </TD>`

  - Used to specify entries in the row of a table.
  - TD stands for "Table Data."
  - Ending tag is usually omitted.
  - Used within the table row tag of the table tag.
  - Attributes: `ALIGN`, `BGCOLOR`, `COLSPAN`, `NOWRAP`, `ROWSPAN`, and `WIDTH`.

- `<TEXTAREA>` ··· `</TEXTAREA>`

  - Used to specify a multirow text field on a form.
  - Must be used within a form tag.
  - Attributes: `COLS`, `MAXLENGTH`, `NAME`, `ROWS`, and `WRAP`.

- `<TH>` ··· `</TH>`

  - Used to specify table headings.
  - `TH` stands for "Table Header."
  - Ending tag is usually omitted.
  - Used within the table tag.
  - Attributes: `ALIGN`, `BGCOLOR`, `COLSPAN`, `NOWRAP`, `ROWSPAN`, and `WIDTH`.

- `<TITLE>` ··· `</TITLE>`

  - Used to specify the title of an HTML document.

- `<TR>` ··· `</TR>`

  - Used to position all items in the row of a table.
  - Used within the table tag.
  - `TR` stands for "Table Row."
  - Ending tag is usually omitted.
  - Attributes: `ALIGN`, `BGCOLOR`, and `VALIGN`.

- `<TT>` ··· `</TT>`

  - Syntactic-based style type.
  - Used for displaying a portion of text in typewriter font.

- `<U>` ··· `</U>`

  - Syntactic-based style type.
  - Used to underline text.
  - Use sparingly, since some confusion can result as to whether or not the underlined item is a hyperlink.

- `<UL>` ··· `</UL>`

  - Used to specify an "Unordered List."
  - Attribute: `TYPE`.

- `<VAR>` ··· `</VAR>`

  - Semantic-based style type.
  - Used to indicate a variable.

Acronyms

This appendix lists the acronyms used in the text. Each acronym and its meaning are presented. The list is sorted based on the acronym itself. Page numbers on which the acronym is used can be traced via the index.

Useful Item

AFAIK—As Far As I Know.

AIFF—Audio Interchange File Format.

AOL—America Online.

ARPA—Advanced Research Projects Agency.

ARPANET—Advanced Research Projects Agency Network.

ASCII—American Standard Code for Information Interchange.

AVI—Audio Video Interleaved.

BAA—Boston Athletic Association.

BBN—Bolt, Beranek, and Newman, Inc.

BBS—Bulletin Board System.

BITNET—Because It's Time Network.

BRB—Be Right Back.

BTW—By The Way.

CAD—Computer-Aided Design.

CCC—Copyright Clearance Center.

CCD—Charge-Coupled Device.

CD—Compact Disk.

CDA—Communications Decency Act.

CERN—French acronym for the European Laboratory for Particle Physics.

CERT—Computer Emergency Response Team.

CGI—Common Gateway Interface.

CIC—Creative Incentive Coalition.

CNET—Consumer Network.

CPU—Central Processing Unit.

CSNET—Computer Science Network.

CSS—Cascading Style Sheets.

DARPA—Defense Advanced Research Projects Agency.

DNS—Domain Name System.

DPI—Dots Per Inch.

DTVC—Desktop Videoconferencing.

EDT—Eastern Daylight Time.

FNC—Federal Networking Council.

FOAF—Friend Of A Friend.

FTP—File Transfer Protocol.

FWIW—For What It's Worth.

GIF—Graphics Interchange Format.

GII—Global Information Infrastructure.

GMT—Greenwich Mean Time.

GUI—Graphical User Interface.

HTML—HyperText Markup Language.

HTTP—HyperText Transfer Protocol.

HTTPS—HyperText Transfer Protocol Secure.

IBM—International Business Machines.

IDEA—International Data Encryption Algorithm.

IE—Internet Explorer.

IETF—Internet Engineering Task Force.

IMAP—Interactive Mail Access Protocol.

IMHO—In My Humble Opinion.

IP—Internet Protocol.

IPv6—Internet Protocol Version 6.

IRC—Internet Relay Chat.

ISDN—Integrated Services Digital Network.

ISP—Internet Service Provider.

JPEG or **JPG**—Joint Photographic Experts Group.

LAN—Local Area Network.

LOL—Laughing Out Loud.

LZW—Lempel, Ziv, and Welch.

MAN—Metropolitan Area Network.

MD5—Message Digest 5.

MIDI—Musical Instrument Digital Interface.

MIME—Multipurpose Internet Mail Extensions.

MOO—Multi-User Dungeon, Object-Oriented.

MPEG—Motion Picture Experts Group.

MUD—Multi-User Dungeon, or Multi-User Dimension.

MUSH—Multi-User Shared Hallucination.

NCSA—National Center for Supercomputing Applications.

NIC—Network Information Center.

NNTP—Network News Transfer Protocol.

NSF—National Science Foundation.

NSFNET—National Science Foundation Network.

NSP—Network Service Providers.

OC—Optical Carrier.

OCR —Optical Character Recognition.

OOP—Object-Oriented Programming.

PC—Personal Computer.

PDT—Pacific Daylight Time.

PGP—Pretty Good Privacy.

PICS—Platform for Internet Content Selection.

PNG—Portable Network Graphics.

POP—Post Office Protocol.

PPP—Point-to-Point Protocol.

QTVR—QuickTime Virtual Reality.

RFC—Request for Comments.

RGB—Red Green Blue.

ROTFL—Rolling On The Floor Laughing.

RSA—Rivest, Shamir, and Adleman.

RTFM—Read The Fine Manual.

SET—Secure Electronic Transactions.

SGI—Silicon Graphics, Inc.

SGML—Standard Generalized Markup Language.

S-HTTP—Secure-HyperText Transfer Protocol.

SLIP—Serial Line Internet Protocol.

SMTP—Simple Mail Transfer Protocol.

SSI—Server-Side Include.

TCP—Transmission Control Protocol.

TCP/IP—Transmission Control Protocol/Internet Protocol.

3D—Three-Dimensional.

TIFF—Tagged Image File Format.

TTYL—Talk To You Later.

2D—Two-Dimensional.

TY—Thank You.

URC—Uniform Resource Characteristic.

URL—Uniform Resource Locator.

USENET—User Network.

UUCP—UNIX to UNIX CoPy.

UW—University of Washington.

VC—Videoconferencing.

VMS—Virtual Monitoring System.

VRML—Virtual Reality Modeling Language.

WAIS—Wide Area Information Service.

WAN—Wide Area Network.

WIPO—World Intellectual Property Organization.

WWW, W^3, or W3—World Wide Web.

W3C—World Wide Web Consortium.

WYSIWYG—What You See Is What You Get.

XML—eXtensible Markup Language.

YMMV—Your Mileage May Vary.

My URLs

For each chapter, we provide space for you to record your own URLs, as well as URLs associated with your Internet class. Many up-to-date references can be found in this book's accompanying Web presentations.

Go On-Line

MISCELLANEOUS NOTES

My ISP's help information telephone number is:

_____

_____

_____

_____

_____

_____

_____

_____

_____

_____

_____

_____

http://www.webfoot.com/advice/email.top.html

SEARCHING THE WORLD WIDE WEB

NEWSGROUPS, MAILING LISTS, CHAT ROOMS, AND MUDS

PRIVACY AND SECURITY TOPICS

Glossary

This glossary contains a list of important terms used in the text. Both the terms and their meanings are presented. Page numbers on which each concept is used can usually be traced through the index. This list is not intended to be exhaustive. For example, many of the HTML concepts are not included, but can easily be traced through the index.

A

account name   A name that identifies you to a computer; also called a userid.

alert box   A pop-up dialog box that contains an important message.

algorithm   A well-defined set of rules for carrying out a procedure.

alias   An easy-to-remember name associated with an email address. The alias is saved by your email software. Aliases can also be used in some operating systems to rename commands.

all-in-one search engine   See **metasearch engine**.

animated GIF   A series of GIF images that are displayed in rapid succession, thereby creating a simple animation.

anonymous file transfer   A mechanism that allows any user to transfer a file from a system.

applet   A small Java program. Applet means "little application."

Archie   A program that is useful for searching file archives.

article   A message that is sent to a newsgroup. Posting is a synonym for article.

attribute   A property associated with an HTML tag. For example, the anchor tag has an HREF attribute that is used to specify a hyperlink reference.

audio   Sound.

authenticate   A term meaning to verify that you are who you say you are.

𝔅

baud rate or **bit rate**   A measure of the rate at which data is transferred over telecommunications lines. Many modems have a data transfer rate of 56 Kbps, that is, 56,000 bits per second, or 56,000 baud.

binary transfer mode   A file transfer mode setting that allows binary files, such as executable programs and images, to be transferred.

bit rate   See **baud rate**.

blind carbon copy   A copy of an email message that is sent to another user, but without the address for that user being displayed in the email message's header.

bookmark   A way to identify a URL and make it easy to recall. The browser saves the URL and its title. The saved URL is also referred to as a bookmark.

Boolean query   Queries that involve the Boolean operations AND, OR, and NOT.

browser   A software application that provides an interface between users and the Internet. Netscape's Navigator and Microsoft's Internet Explorer are two popular browsers. Browsers are also called Web clients.

buffer   A location where data can be temporarily stored.

byte   A computer measurement equal to eight bits and used to indicate file size. It is also used in conjunction with time to indicate transfer rates.

C

cache   Local memory where copies of frequently used or recently requested Web pages are saved.

Caesar ciphers   A class of simple encryption schemes in which letters of the alphabet are rotated in a circular fashion. ROT13 is an example of a Caesar cipher.

Cascading Style Sheets   A method of specifying content that is common to a series of Web pages.

CGI script   See **script**.

chat room   An on-line forum where you can discuss your favorite subject interactively with other people located anywhere on the Internet.

ciphertext   An encrypted message.

circuit switching   A method of data transmission that was popular before the advent of packet switching.

clickable text   A hyperlink that consists solely of text.

client pull   A model of a dynamic document in which the browser (or client) initiates the document's change. This can be used to cause a document to "refresh" itself or to load a completely new document, among other things.

client-server model   The scheme in which many clients make requests to a small number of servers. The servers respond to clients' requests.

clip art   A collection of images that have been developed using image editing tools.

closed list   A mailing list for which the list owner either accepts or rejects subscriptions. It is not possible to subscribe automatically to a closed list. List membership is filtered, and only postings from subscribers are accepted. Private list is a synonym for closed list.

collaborative computing   A computing platform that allows the sharing of information and resources among two or more users. Lotus Notes,

Novell's Groupwise, and Microsoft Exchange are some applications that support collaborative computing.

color palette   See **palette**.

comment   A note, placed in an HTML file, that is not interpreted (or displayed) when the file is processed.

Common Gateway Interface (CGI)   A set of rules that specify how parameters are passed from programs to Web servers.

composite number   A number containing factors other than 1 and itself.

compression algorithm   Any computer algorithm that is used to reduce the size of files. On rare occasions, compression algorithms may increase the size of a file.

Computer Emergency Response Team (CERT)   An organization that sends out information about known security holes in software.

computer literacy   A basic knowledge of computer usage.

cookie   A piece of information saved by your Web browser to a file on your disk. The information can be retrieved by a Web server that your browser accesses.

copyright   A set of legal rights extended to an individual or company that has produced a creative work.

cross-post   The process of simultaneously submitting the same article to two or more newsgroups.

cryptographic algorithm   An algorithm that is used for either encoding or decoding information.

cryptography   The science of encoding and decoding information.

cyberspace   A popular term for the Internet.

D

default password   The initial password you are assigned to grant you access to an on-line item (for example, your computer account). Default passwords should be changed during your first access. The word *default* applies in other settings, usually with similar meaning.

deprecated tag   An HTML tag that should no longer be used because it is being phased out of the language.

digest   A collection of related articles, usually edited, that is posted as a single article to a newsgroup.

digested list   A mailing list in which postings are grouped by topic and sent out as batches instead of individually.

digital signature   A mechanism that can be used to sign an electronic document officially.

distance learning   Any form of teaching in which the instructor(s) and students are not located in the same room.

dithering   A process that approximates the color of each pixel in an image by using a combination of colors in a limited color palette.

Doctor HTML   A popular HTML syntax checker.

document area   The part of the browser window that is used to display the currently loaded document.

domain name system (DNS)   A distributed naming scheme in which unique names are assigned to computers on the Internet.

double key cryptography   See **public key cryptography**.

dynamic document   A document that has the capacity to change, either by client pull, server push, or some other mechanism.

dynamic IP address   The address assigned by your ISP when you connect to the Internet; this address usually changes each time you log on. This is in contrast to a static IP address.

edited list   A mailing list in which items posted may be edited by the list owner or moderator.

email   Messages that are sent electronically over a network. The term *email* stands for "electronic mail."

email address   An address that identifies a specific user's electronic mailbox, and has the form:

```
username@hostname.subdomain.domain
```

emoticons   Symbols made up of keyboard characters designed to express emotion; most commonly used in text-only communication, such as email.

encryption scheme   A method of encoding information to make it private and secure.

event   An action or occurrence, usually initiated by a user.

event handler   A computer program that is executed in response to an event.

expired news   Old news that has been removed from a system.

eXtensible Markup Language (XML)   A Web page design language that will support user-defined tags.

e-zine   An electronic magazine.

file compression   A means of reducing a file's size by encoding the contents so that the file takes up less space.

file transfer   A way of transferring files from one computer to another computer, using a network.

firewall   A security mechanism that organizations use to protect their intranets from the Internet.

flame   A nasty, electronic response from an offended party.

flame war   A series of nasty, electronic responses that are part of the same newsgroup thread.

follow-up   A newsgroup article posted in response to a previous newsgroup article.

footer   The content displayed at the bottom of a Web page.

frame   An HTML feature that allows you to divide a browser's window into several independent parts.

freeware   Software that you can use at no charge. The author usually retains any copyright on it, and freeware frequently is unregistered. The source code is usually not provided.

frequently asked questions (FAQs)   Questions that many computer users ask. Because the answers to such questions are important to many people, they are usually collected and posted to either a mailing list or a newsgroup, or displayed on a Web page.

G

gigabyte   A billion bytes.

gopher   A menu-based Internet browsing tool that was very popular in the early 1990s.

graphical user interface (GUI)   A mouse-driven, rather than a keyboard-driven, graphically oriented computer interface.

groupware   The body of software that comprises a collaborative computing platform.

guest book   A mechanism that provides a way for readers visiting your Web pages to "sign in" and leave you a note.

H

hash or **message digest**   The value computed by a hashing algorithm.

hashing algorithm   An algorithm that takes a plaintext message as input and then computes a value based on the message.

header   The content displayed at the top of a Web page.

helper or **helper application**   A stand-alone program that is used to process or display data that a Web browser cannot handle.

hit   A URL that a search engine returns in response to a query. Match is a synonym.

homepage   The Web page that is loaded when a browser is first activated; also, the first page in a set of related Web pages.

hot buttons   Single-click buttons in a browser that provide a number of convenient features.

HTML   HyperText Markup Language; the programming language in which most Web pages are written.

HTML converter   A program that takes one type of document as input and produces the same information in an HTML format.

HTML editor   A software editing tool that helps in developing HTML code.

HTML syntax checker   A program that processes an HTML document to see if there are any coding errors in it.

hyperlink   Text and/or graphics on a Web page that, when selected, will cause the browser to retrieve and render another Web page or graphic.

hypermedia   A Web document that contains any combination of audio, graphics, movies, or video (versus a document containing only text), as well as links, and navigational tools.

hypertext   Web pages that have hyperlinks to other pages or to other places on the same page.

hypertext transfer protocol (HTTP)   The rules that govern how hypertext is exchanged over the Internet.

J

image map   An image used in an HTML document with clickable areas that cause the loading of other documents.

Information Superhighway   A popular name for the Internet.

in-line image   An image that is displayed as an HTML document loads.

interlaced GIF   A form of GIF image in which the "whole image" starts to load initially, but appears blurry, and then comes into sharper focus as the download advances, until the image is finally complete.

Internet   A global system of networked computers, including their users and data.

Internet addresses   Numerical computer names that uniquely identify each computer on the Internet. Each address consists of four bytes, and each byte represents a decimal number from 0 to 255. The address is often represented by four decimal numbers separated by dots.

Internet Engineering Task Force (IETF)   A group that provides an open forum to facilitate communication between individuals dealing with matters related to the Internet.

Internet Explorer   The name of Microsoft's Web browser.

Internet Protocol (IP)   One of the primary protocols in the TCP/IP suite; IP specifies how data is routed from computer to computer on the Internet.

Internet Protocol Version 6 (IPv6)   The latest version of the Internet Protocol (IP).

intranet   A private network in which access is limited to authorized users and a security measure known as a firewall is employed to prevent unauthorized users from gaining access.

IP address   See **Internet addresses**.

J

Java   An object-oriented programming language that was developed by Sun Microsystems and is widely used to create dynamic Web pages.

Java-enabled   A browser that can run Java code.

JavaScript   A scripting language that is embedded in HTML and is useful for adding dynamic features to Web pages.

JavaScript-enabled   A browser that can run JavaScript code.

Java Virtual Machine   A computer program that allows you to run a Java application on a particular type of computer (for example, a Mac or a PC).

K

kill files   A filter based on names or topics you specify, for the purpose of blocking those newsgroup messages matching your criteria.

kilobit   1,000 bits; a unit of measurement often associated with modem transfer rates. Example: 56 Kbps (kilobits per second).

kilobyte   1,000 bytes; a unit of measurement often associated with file size or transfer rates (when combined with time).

L

list owner   A person in charge of a mailing list. Synonyms are list administrator, list coordinator, and list manager.

LISTPROC   A popular mailing list server program.

LISTSERV   A popular mailing list server program.

Local Area Network (LAN)   A privately owned computer network that is usually confined to a single building.

location area   The place in a browser window where URLs are entered and displayed.

lossless compression   A form of image compression in which no information is lost.

lossy compression   A form of image compression in which information is removed. The key is to delete information that has little or no impact on the appearance of the image.

lurker   A person who has subscribed to and reads a mailing list, but does not post messages. Such a person is said to lurk.

Lynx   The most popular text-based Web browser.

M

mailbox   A file that holds a user's email messages.

mailer   A program that is used to compose, manipulate, and send email. Synonyms are mail application, mail client, and mail program.

mailing list   A group of users with a shared interest, whose email addresses are kept in an electronic list that can be used to send email to each member on the list.

Majordomo   A popular mailing list server program.

megabyte   A million bytes; a unit of measurement often associated with file size or transfer rates (when combined with time).

menu bar   The place in a browser window where the headings of the main pull-down command menus are displayed.

message digest   See **hash**.

metasearch engine or **all-in-one search engine**   A search tool that calls on more than one other search engine to do the actual searching.

Metropolitan Area Network (MAN)   A computer network that spans an area about the size of a city. Such a network is larger than a LAN but smaller than a WAN.

mirror site   A site that contains a duplicate copy of a Web presentation from another site in order to reduce server traffic.

moderated newsgroup   A newsgroup that has a moderator.

Mosaic   The first widely popular graphical Web browser. It was developed by Marc Andreessen and several other graduate students at the University of Illinois in 1993.

multimedia   More than one type of media; any combination of two or more of animation, audio, graphics, text, and video.

Multipurpose Internet Mail Extensions (MIME)   A system that is used by mailers and Web browsers to identify file contents by use of file extensions.

Multi-User Dungeon or **Dimension (MUD)**   A real-time interactive game that takes place in an imaginary environment where multiple computer users can play simultaneously.

N

navigational tools   The buttons, hyperlinks, and images that allow a user to navigate a Web presentation.

netiquette   Informal rules of network etiquette.

Netscape   The Netscape Communications Company's Web browser.

Network News Transfer Protocol (NNTP)   The protocol that is used for distributing news articles.

newbie   A person who only recently joined a mailing list.

news administrator   A person who is in charge of running a news server.

newsfeed   A news server that provides recent articles to a news client. The term also encompasses the process of delivering the news articles.

newsgroup   An on-line forum that allows users from all over the world to participate in a discussion about a specific topic.

news moderator   A person associated with a specific newsgroup who reads and critically evaluates all articles submitted for posting to the newsgroup and then decides which articles should be posted.

newsreader   A program that serves as the user interface for newsgroups and allows a user to read, post, subscribe, and unsubscribe from the newsgroup. News client is a synonym.

news server   A computer that saves, forwards, and manages news articles. Normally each organization runs its own news server and limits access to just its customers or user community.

object-oriented programming (OOP)   A computer programming style that uses classes and methods.

open list   A mailing list to which anyone may subscribe. Such a list typically accepts posts even from users who are not subscribers.

packet   A small piece of a message that is transported over the Internet.

packet switching   The technology employed to route messages over the Internet.

page   See **Web page**.

pages   See **Web pages**.

palette or **color palette**   A defined group of distinct colors available for a particular purpose or use.

password   A secret code you provide when you log in that is used to authenticate you to a computer.

pattern matching query   A query formulated using a keyword or a group of keywords.

plaintext   A message in its original form; that is, not encoded.

plug-in   A software application designed to extend the functionality of a Web browser. Plug-ins are launched from within the browser and are capable of playing audio, showing movies, and running animations, among other things.

Point-to-Point Protocol (PPP)   A protocol that is widely used for transferring packets over telephone lines.

post   The process of sending an article to a newsgroup; also, an article that is sent to a newsgroup.

Pretty Good Privacy (PGP)   An email security package developed by Phil Zimmermann. It includes authentication, compression, digital signature, and privacy capabilities, and uses the RSA encryption algorithm.

prime number   A number whose only factors are 1 and itself.

private key cryptography   An encryption scheme in which both the sender and the receiver share the same private key.

Project Gutenberg   An on-line book project whose goal is to put 10,000 books on the Web by the end of the year 2001.

protocol   A set of precisely specified rules for carrying out a procedure.

prototyping   The process of designing a system to work out the design deficiencies before building the final product.

public domain software   Free software available over the Internet; the source code is seldom available, but there may be guidelines as to how you are "allowed" to modify the original source code.

public key cryptography   An encryption scheme in which a message encrypted using a private key can only be decrypted using its matching public key.

query   Information entered into a form on a Web page, describing the topic on which information is sought. A query is usually not phrased as a question.

query semantics   A set of rules that defines the meaning of a query.

query syntax   A set of rules describing what constitutes a legal query. On some search engines, special symbols may be used in a query.

R

recursive algorithm   An algorithm that calls itself.

register a Web page   The process of submitting the URL of a Web page to a search engine or directory.

relevancy score   A value that indicates the closeness with which a URL matches a query. It is usually expressed as a value from 1 to 100, with the higher score meaning more relevant.

remote login   A method of logging into another (distant) computer from the one to which you are currently connected. Once logged in, you can execute commands on the remote computer.

render   The browser process displaying a Web page on the screen.

Request for Comments (RFC)   The official documents provided and distributed by the Internet Engineering Task Force.

resolver   A computer program that translates between domain names and IP addresses.

result set   The list of hits returned by a search or metasearch engine.

revolving advertisements   Advertisements, displayed on Web pages, that change every time you visit the page, or while you are viewing the page.

RGB color model   A way to represent colors as combinations of red, green, and blue.

Rotation 13 (ROT13)   A simple encryption scheme in which letters are rotated 13 positions further down the alphabet.

router   A special-purpose computer that directs packets of data along a network.

RSA encryption scheme   The most widely used public key encryption scheme. It is named for its developers, Rivest, Shamir, and Adleman.

S

scanner   A device that converts images to a digital format.

script or **CGI script**   Any program that is run by a Web server in response to a user's request.

scroll bar   Arrows along the side or bottom of a window that allow the user to display a different part of a document that is larger than the screen size.

search engine   A search tool that allows a user to enter queries. The program responds with a list of matches from its database. A relevancy score for each match and a clickable URL are usually returned.

search tool   Any mechanism for locating information on the Web; usually refers to a search or metasearch engine, or to a directory.

secure document   An electronic file that has been encoded so only those who know how to decode the file can read the information it contains.

secure server   A server that sends and receives encrypted (private and secure) messages.

semantics   The meaning associated with commands or statements in a given computer language; the interpretation of the syntax of a computer language.

semantic-based style type   An HTML style that pertains to meaning; for example, emphasis and citation.

Serial Line Internet Protocol (SLIP)   A protocol that is used for transferring packets over telephone lines.

server   A computer that satisfies user (client) requests.

server push   A model of a dynamic document in which the server initiates the document's change. Server push is not accomplished using HTML tags.

server-side include (SSI)   A way to send a command to a Web server from inside an HTML document.

7 by 24 machine   A machine that runs 7 days a week, 24 hours a day.

shareware   Software that you can download and test for a brief trial period. If you decide to use the software, you pay a small fee. Many times, the fee is collected on an honor system basis.

signature file   A file that contains an email signature. A person's signature file is usually appended to all email messages they send.

s-mail   See **snail mail**.

smiley   A happy face, written as :-); an example of an emoticon.

snail mail   Regular postal mail; also referred to as **s-mail**.

sniffing   The process of tapping into a network and reading the packets that are being transmitted.

spam   Inappropriate or junk email.

static IP address   A permanently assigned IP address.

status bar   A field the browser uses to convey helpful (and current) information to the user.

stemming   The process a search tool uses to add variations to the endings of words you query on, to turn up more hits.

storyboard   A sketch of how a browser's window is to be partitioned when a document that uses frames is being designed.

streaming   The process of buffering data and using it to achieve a continuous-play effect, while the next part of the data is being transported in parallel over the Internet; widely used in the context of multimedia.

subscribe   The procedure you follow to join a newsgroup. Once subscribed, you will receive the new postings of the newsgroup. The subscription is also used to track which messages in a group you have seen. In most cases, subscriptions do not cost money.

surfer   A person who spends time exploring the Web.

syntactic-based style type   An HTML style that pertains to form, not meaning; for example, boldface and italics.

syntax   The rules or structure that describe the form of statements in a computer language.

tag   The name given to HTML commands. For example, the image tag, `<IMG>`, is used to include an image in an HTML document. Tags usually come in matched pairs, such as `<FORM>` and `</FORM>`.

target   The location (frame or window) to which a hyperlink is directed.

Telnet   A program that allows you to log into a remote computer.

thread   A collection of one or more follow-up articles, together with the original posting in a newsgroup.

thumbnail sketch   A reduced-size image that is used to give a reader a preview of an image, so they can decide whether or not they would like to spend the time loading the full image.

tiling or **tiling algorithm**   A method used to fill in a background on a Web page by taking a small image and laying out repeated copies of that image until it covers the browser's entire window.

title bar   The location in a browser window where the HTML document title is displayed.

toolbar   The area in a browser window for accessing a number of single-mouse-click commands.

tooltip   Usually a light-colored dialog box that displays helpful information when you mouse over an item in the browser window.

Transmission Control Protocol (TCP)   One of the primary protocols in the TCP/IP suite. TCP defines a set of rules for allowing computers on the Internet to communicate.

Transmission Control Protocol/Internet Protocol (TCP/IP)   The protocol suite that determines how computers connect, send, and receive information on the Internet.

transparent GIF   A GIF image that creates a visual effect in which the image appears to be "floating" on a Web page.

triage   A strategy designed to process the most important items first, such as dealing with priority email messages first and less important messages second.

Trojan horse   A program within which code is hidden. When the hidden code is triggered, it might release a virus, permit unauthorized access to the computer, or destroy files and data.

U

under construction   A phrase used to describe unfinished Web pages.

Uniform Resource Locator (URL)   A Web page address, such as

```
http://www.playground.com/~killface/cats.html
```

universal service   Any service that is available worldwide. For example, many people consider the telephone to be a universal service.

UNIX   A widely used computer operating system, particularly in academic and research environments.

unmoderated newsgroup   A newsgroup that has no moderator.

unsubscribe   The process of removing your name from a newsgroup to which you have previously subscribed.

userid   A name that identifies you to a computer; also called a "user name" or "account name."

vacation program   A program that can be set up to reply automatically to each email message you receive. Such a program is usually installed when you are going to be away for a week or more.

videoconferencing   A system designed to permit real-time interaction between multiple parties. It can involve one or more of the following: real-time talk or chat, whiteboard graphics, audio, black and white video, or color video.

virtual reality   A three-dimensional simulation of a real or imagined environment, using computers.

virus   A program that, when run, can replicate and embed itself within another program, usually with the intent of doing damage.

way-station   A news server that functions as a newsfeed for at least two (and usually many more) other sites.

Web   See **World Wide Web**.

Web directory   A hierarchical representation of hyperlinks to Web presentations that are organized into categories.

Webmaster   A person who maintains, creates, and manages a Web presentation, and is responsible for responding to questions and comments. The term *Webmaster* usually implies a certain minimal level of knowledge. Web manager is a synonym.

Web page or **page**   A file that can be read over the World Wide Web.

Web pages or **pages**   The global collection of documents associated with and accessible via the World Wide Web.

Web presentation   A collection of associated and hyperlinked Web pages that usually has some underlying theme.

Web server   A computer that satisfies requests for Web pages.

Web site   An Internet entity that publishes Web pages. A Web site typically has a computer serving Web pages, whereas a Web presentation is the actual Web pages themselves.

white pages   A database that serves as an on-line telephone book.

Wide Area Information Service (WAIS)   A database search system that employs sophisticated feedback mechanisms. Its popularity has been waning in recent years.

Wide Area Network (WAN)   A computer network that spans a large geographical area, such as a country or a number of cities.

World Wide Wait Problem   The delay experienced on the Internet, caused by the tremendous popularity of the Web.

World Wide Web or **Web**   An application that uses the Internet to transport hypertext/multimedia documents. Synonyms are WWW, W^3, and W3.

World Wide Web Consortium (W3C)   A group that provides an open forum to facilitate communication between individuals dealing with matters related to the World Wide Web.

worm   A stand-alone program that tries to gain access to computer systems via networks.

XYZ

Yahoo!   A popular search engine and directory developed by former Stanford graduate students David Filo and Jerry Yang.

Bibliography

Notes

This book deals with a rapidly emerging area. Most of our research was conducted on-line. As a result, many of our references are Web presentations. Each citation for a Web presentation provides its title (as capitalized by the author), date, and URL. For the sake of readability, we have omitted the leading `http://` and also any trailing `/` on URLs. Sometimes we just include the URL for the main page of a presentation, although we may have read through many of its subpages. In this bibliography, URLs are sorted by title, and other references are sorted by the author's last name.

Most presentations do not provide dates indicating when the document was written, nor are the original document creation dates available on-line (or anywhere, for that matter). Some documents written in 1996 may have been completely overhauled in 1997, meriting a 1997 date, whereas others may have only been modified slightly, meriting a 1996 designation. Some authors include "last update" messages in headers, while others do not. Due to the inherent inconsistencies in dating Web presentations, the date we used in most cases indicates when we successfully accessed the site. Most of the Web presentations in the following list were written in 1997. We would appreciate any corrections to the dates from the authors of the presentations and also notices of changed URLs.

The Web presentation that accompanies this book contains a number of useful URLs, sorted by chapter, plus many other additional hyperlinks. Some URLs are from these references, while others are new.

Hot Topic

Go On-Line

1   AmericaNet.Com Since July 4, 1995, 1997.   `www.americanet.com`

2   Apple QuickTime VR Home, 1997.   `qtvr.quicktime.apple.com`

3   AprilFools.com, 1997.   `www.aprilfools.com/home.htm`

4   Assessing Your Scanner Options in a Buyer's Market, 1997.
     `www.zdnet.com/cshopper/content/9611`

5   Atlantic Records, 1997.   `www.atlanticrecords.com`

6   10 Big Myths About Copyright Explained, 1997.
     `www.clari.net/brad/copymyths.html`

7   Bridging the Gap Between Theory and Practice—the Journal of Electronic Publishing, 1997.
     `www.press.umich.edu/jep/03-01/JEA.html`

8   A Brief History of the Internet, 1997.
     `www.isoc.org/internet-history/#Introduction`

9   A Brief History of Type, 1997.
     `tug.cs.umb.edu/tetex/html/fontfaq/cf_28.html`

10   A brief intro to copyright, 1997.
     `www.clari.net/brad/copyright.html`

11   BUILDER.COM—Web Authoring—20 questions about HTML 4.0, 1997.
     `www.cnet.com/Content/Builder/Authoring/Html40/?bl.auth.5`

12   Castro, Elizabeth. *HTML for the World Wide Web*. 4th ed. Peachpit Press, 2000.

13   Choosing an ISP, 1997.
     `www.currents.net/resources/netprov/intquest.html`

14   CNET reviews—comparative reviews—11 HTML editors, 1997.
     `www.cnet.com/Content/Reviews/Compare/11htmleds`

15   Collaborative Networked Communication: MUDs as Systems Tools, 1997.   `www.ccs.neu.edu/home/remy/documents/cncmast.html`

16   Comer, Douglas. *The Internet Book*. 2nd ed. Upper Saddle River, NJ: Prentice-Hall, 1997.

17   Computers and Copyrights: Bibliography, 1997.
     `www.iat.unc.edu/guides/irg-04.html`

18   Cookie Central, 1997.   `www.cookiecentral.com`

19   cookie—PC Webopaedia Definition and Links, 1997.
     `www.sandybay.com/pc-web/cookie.htm`

20   Copyright and Fair Use in the Digital Age: Q&A with Peter Lyman, 1997.
     `www.educom.edu/web/pubs/review/reviewArticles/30132.html`

21   Copyright Clearance Center Online, 1997.   `www.copyright.com`

22   Copyright in a digital age, 1997.
     `www.onlineinc.com/articles/onlinemag/weiner975.html`

23   Copyright in the New World of Electronic Publishing, 1997.
     `www.press.umich.edu/jep/works/strong.copyright.html`

24   The Copyright Question—Internet World January 1997, 1997.
     `www.internet.com/search`

25   Cornell University's CU-SeeMe Page, 1997.
     `cu-seeme.cornell.edu`

26   Cunningham, Sally Jo. Teaching students to critically evaluate the quality of Internet research resources. *SIGCSE Bulletin*, 29(2), June 1997, pp. 31–34.

27   Debunking Myths About Internet Commerce, 1997.
     `commerce.ssb.rochester.edu/papers/comment.htm`

28   Deja News, 1997.   `www.dejanews.com`

29   The Digital Press, 1997.   `www.iw.com/1995/09/feat58.htm`

30   The Economist: Internet, too cheap to meter & the World Wide Wait 19 Oct 96, 1997.
     `www-uvi.eunet.fr/hacking/nov13=17nov96-6.html`

31   Electronic Publishing, 1997.   `www.parkcce.org/index.html`

32   Emerging Technologies, 1997.
     `commerce.ssb.rochester.edu/emerging.html`

33   Fakemail, pranks, & gags: Rubberchicken.com, 1997.
     `www.rubberchicken.com`

34   Federal-Express Sets New Strategic Direction With On-line Ordering, 1997.   `www.informedusa.com/t/fedexautoorder10.11.html`

35   FedEx: Electronic Commerce Connections, 1997.
     `www0.fedex.com/connections`

36   Finding An ISP That You'll Really Enjoy Using, 1997.
     `www.accesss.digex.net/~mccork/isp.html#intro`

37   FNC Resolution: Definition of Internet, 1997.
     `www.fnc.gov/Internet_res.html`

38   food-online.com—Corporate Background, 1997.
     `www.food-online.com/pr/corp_bg.htm`

39   About a Framework for Global Electronic Commerce, 1997.
     `www.whitehouse.gov/WH/New/Commerce/about-plain.html`

40   A Framework for Global Electronic Commerce Executive Summary, 1997.   `www.whitehouse.gov/WH/New/Commerce/summary-plain.html`

41   Frequently Asked Questions: Basic Information about MUDs and MUDding, 1997.   `www.cs.okstate.edu/~jds/mudfaq-p1.html`

42   Frequently Asked Questions: MUD Clients and Servers, 1997.
      `www.cs.okstate.edu/~jds/mudfaq-p2.html`

43   The Future of Electronic Journals—Neurotrophism, 1997.
      `www.physiol.washington.edu/ngf/editorial.HTM`

44   GIF Animations, 1997.   `www.babylon6.demon.co.uk/gif.html`

45   DiP Pixel Explorations—A GIF Transparency FAQ, 1997.
      `www.bruin.ucla.edu/TaskForce/transparent↩`
      `/gif_faq.htm#PSPandGIFcon`

46   Gilster, Paul. *The New Internet Navigator*. New York: Wiley, 1997.

47   Graphics FAQ, 1997.   `www.aldridge.com/faq_gra.html`

48   Early Adopters: Groceries To Go, 1997.
      `www.food-online.com/pr/gtg.htm`

49   Groceries To Go—FAQ, 1997.
      `www.food-online.com/gtg/gtgfaq1.htm#1`

50   Groupware Grows Up, 1997.
      `techweb.cmp.com/iw/569/69iugrp.htm`

51   Hafner, Katie, and Matthew Lyon. *Where Wizards Stay Up Late: The Origins of the Internet*. New York: Simon & Schuster, 1996.

52   Hahn, Harley. *The Internet: Complete Reference*. 2nd ed. Berkeley, CA: Osborne McGraw-Hill, 1996.

53   The History and Characteristics of Zines, 1997.
      `www.thetransom.com/chip/zines/resource.html`

54   The History of the Internet, 1997.
      `www.davesite.com/webstation/net-history.shtml`

55   How An ISP Really Works, 1997.
      `www.mindspring.com/~mcgatney/ispwork.html`

56   How the Internet Works, 1997.   `www.iw.com/1996/howitworks.html`

57   How to Buy Flatbed Scanners, 1997.
      `www1.zdnet.com/complife/rev/9707/scanner1.html`

58   How To Select An Internet Service Provider, 1997.
      `web.cnam.fr/Network/Internet-access/how_to_select.html`

59   IBM Cryptolope Home, 1997.
      `www.cryptolope.ibm.com/cryptolp.htm`

60   Imagemap Help Page—Instruction, 1997.   `www.ihip.com`

61 Inclusions in HTML documents, 1997.
www.w3.org/TR/WD-html40-970708/struct/includes.html#h-7.7.1

62 Inline Images Frequently Asked Questions, 1997.
galway.informatik.uni-kl.de/./comp/Mosaic/inline-images.html

63 Intelligent Manufacturing—December 96: Collaborative Computing, 1997. www.lionhrtpub.com/IM/IM-12-96/autofact.html

64 The Internet Index Home Page, 1997.
www.openmarket.com/intindex

65 Internetter: SSI—The WebMasters Secret Weapon, 1997.
www.internetter.com/papers/ssi.html

66 InterTrust Industry Applications, 1997.
www.intertrust.com/products/applications.html

67 Introducing MUDs!, 1997. andes.ip.ucsb.edu/~krend/muds.html

68 An Introduction to Electronic Data Interchange, 1997.
www.nlc-bnc.ca/publications/netnotes/notes6.htm

69 IRC INTRO—Introduction to IRC for People using Windows, 1997.
www.mirc.co.uk/ircintro.html

70 JPEG image compression FAQ, part 1/2, 1997.
www.cis.ohio-state.edu/hypertext/faq/usenet/jpeg-faq ↩
/part1/faq.html

71 DiP presents the JPiG Project, 1997.
www.algonet.se/~dip/JPiG/jpig_1a.html

72 Lemay, Laura. *Teach Yourself Web Publishing with HTML 3.2 in a Week*. Indianapolis, IN: Sams.net, 1996.

73 Life on the Internet: Net Timeline, 1997.
www.pbs.org/internet/timeline

74 Linux IPv6 FAQ/HOWTO, 1997. www.terra.net/ipv6

75 Liszt, the mailing list directory, 1997. www.liszt.com

76 Lynx Users Guide Version 2.5, 1997.
tincan.tincan.org/help/lynx/lynx_help/Lynx_users_guide.html

77 Mars Pathfinder in VRML!, 1997.
www.ncsa.uiuc.edu/mars/vrml/vrml.html

78 Messaging Magazine—Collaborative Computing: Empowering People to Accelerate the Decision Making Process, 1997.
www.ema.org/html/pubs/mmv1n5/collabco.htm

79   Messaging Magazine—The New Business Paradigm, 1997.
`www.ema.org/html/pubs/mmv1n5/paradigm.htm`

80   Messaging Magazine—Three Trends in Collaborative Computing, 1997.   `www.ema.org/html/pubs/mmv1n5/3trends.htm`

81   Messaging Magazine—Security in Collaborative Computing Environments, 1997.   `www.ema.org/html/pubs/mmv1n5/securcc.htm`

82   Musciano, Chuck, and Bill Kennedy. *HTML: The Definitive Guide.* 2nd ed. Sebastopol, CA: O'Reilly and Associates, 1997.

83   The Net and Netizens: The Impact the Net has on People's Lives, 1997.   `www.columbia.edu/~rh120/ch106.x01`

84   NetscapeWorld—Cookies offload server overhead and can reduce some client overhead issues, 1997.
`www.netscapeworld.com/netscapeworld/nw-07-1996 ↩`
`/nw-07-cookies.html`

85   NetscapeWorld—Use Cookies to Analyze User Activity & Create Custom Web Pages—February, 1997.
`www.netscapeworld.com/netscapeworld/nw-02-1997 ↩`
`/nw-02-cookiehowto.html`

86   *The New York Times* on the Web, 1997.   `www.nytimes.com`

87   ONSALE, Inc., 1997.   `www.onsale.com`

88   Paulallen.com, 1997.   `www.paulallen.com`

89   *PC Magazine*: VRML Brings 3-D Worlds to the Web, 1997.
`www8.zdnet.com/pcmag/issues/1614/pcmg0060.htm#top`

90   Platform for Internet Content Selection (PICS), 1997.
`www.w3.org/PICS`

91   Portable Network Graphics Home Page, 1997.   `www.wco.com/~png`

92   Professional Software Engineering MUD Description and Links Page, 1997.   `www.professional.org/pse/mud.html`

93   Project Gutenberg—History and Philosophy, 1997.
`promo.net/pg/history.html`

94   QTVR FAQ, 1997.   `www.convrgence.com/smallsite/QTVRFAQ2.html`

95   The Role of Publishers in the Digital Age—Educom Review, 1997.
`www.educom.edu/web/pubs/review/reviewArticles/30344.html`

96   Royalties, Fair Use & Copyright in the Electronic Age—Educom Review, 1997.
`www.educom.edu/web/pubs/review/reviewArticles/30630.html`

97   Scanning For the Rest of Us, 1997.
`www.macworld.com/pages/march.97/Feature.3297.html`

98   A few scanning tips, 1997.
`www.cyberramp.net/~fulton/scans.html`

99   Scanning Tips, 1997.   `www.jasc.com/scantip.html`

100 Seltzer, Richard, Eric Ray, and Deborah Ray. *The AltaVista Search Revolution.* Berkeley, CA: Osborne McGraw-Hill, 1997.

101 The Short Little Guide To Selecting An ISP That You'll Enjoy, 1997.   `www.mindspring.com/~mcgatney/ispfast.html`

102 SLIP/PPP Homepage, 1997.   `sunsite.nus.sg/pub/slip-ppp`

103 The slow evolution of electronic publishing, 1997.
`www.research.att.com/~amo`

104 The Spider's Web: News Feature—How the HTTP Cookies Crumble, 1997.   `www.incontext.ca/spidweb/may15_96/news/cookie8.htm`

105 Tanenbaum, Andrew. *Computer Networks.* Upper Saddle River, NJ: Prentice-Hall, 1996.

106 TechTools—ISP, 1997.   `techweb2.web.cerf.net/tools/isp`

107 TechWeb, 1997.
`www.techweb.com/se/directling.cgi?WIN1997090150120`

108 the truth about cookies—Christopher Barr, 1997.
`www.cnet.com/Content/Voices/Barr/042996`

109 Transcopyright: Dealing with the Dilemma of Digital Copyright—Educom Review, 1997.
`www.educom.edu/web/pubs/review/reviewArticles/32132.html`

110 TWAIN White Paper, 1997.   `www.twain.org`

111 Videoconferencing FAQ, 1997.   `www.bitscout.com/faqtoc.htm`

112 Vint Cerf On the Past, Present & Future of All Things Internet, 1997.
`www.wiredguru.com/cd2.html`

113 The Virtual Reality Modeling Language, 1997.
`tom.di.uminho.pt/vrmlut/frmstrct.htm`

114 VRML Authoring & 3D Modeling Software, 1997.
`www.webdeveloper.com/categories/vrml/vrml_editors.html`

115   comp.lang.vrml Frequently Asked Questions, 1997.
      `hiwaay.net/~crispen/vrml/faq.html#q1`

116   A VRML Primer, 1997.
      `www.ncsa.uiuc.edu/mars/vrml/primer/primer.html`

117   The VRML Repository, 1997.   `www.sdsc.edu/vrml`

118   VRML Update, 1997.   `www.meshmart.org/vrmlup.htm`

119   W3C Electronic Commerce Area, 1997.   `www.w3.org/Payments`

120   W3C Recommendations Reduce World Wide Wait, 1997.
      `www.w3.org/pub/WWW/Protocols/NL-PerfNote.html`

121   The Wall Street Journal Interactive Edition, 1997.
      `interactive6.wsj.com/home.html`

122   Web Graphics Format Page, 1997.   `www.jasc.com/filetip.html`

123   Weblynx—Step By Step Guide to VRML, 1997.
      `weblynx.com.au/guide.htm`

124   The Web Multimedia Tour—Virtual Reality, 1997.
      `ftp.digital.com/webmm/vr.html`

125   Web Review: VRML — History, 1997.
      `webreview.com/sept29/features/vrml/history.html`

126   Welcome to Internet Travel Agency, Inc., 1997.
      `www.internettravelagency.com`

127   Welcome to the Ultimate Band List, 1997.   `ubl.com`

128   What is a MUD, actually?, 1997.
      `www.cwrl.utexas.edu/moo/mudhandouts/beginning.html`

129   What Is Project Gutenberg?—rec.art.books FAQ, 1997.
      `www.cis.ohio-state.edu/hypertext/faq/usenet/books/faq↩`
      `/faq-doc-6.html`

130   Whither the electronic journal?—SLS UK User Group, 1997.
      `www.lib.ic.ac.uk:8081/leah.htm`

131   Wilson, Lee. *The Copyright Guide.* New York: Allworth Press, 1996.

132   With mars under its belt, VRML good to go, 1997.   `www.listz.com`

133   Yeager, Nancy, and Robert McGrath. *Web Server Technology.* San Francisco, CA: Morgan Kaufmann Publishers, Inc., 1996.

Additional On-line References

For each chapter of the book, we provide a set of on-line references. These are for Web presentations that we have visited and found helpful in providing additional useful information about topics covered in the book. As of this writing, all of the references are active. However, like most Web material, this content is dynamic. These references are easy to access through the text's corresponding "Book site." There the hyperlinks are arranged chapter-by-chapter.

Chapter 1: Fundamentals of Electronic Mail

1   `www.webfoot.com/advice/email.top.html`
     Beginners' Guide. Beginners' guide to email by Kaitlin Duck Sherwood.

2   `www.surfplaza.com/`
     Surfplaza. Some ASCII art and figlets for your email signature.

3   `www.qucis.queensu.ca/FAQs/email/finding.html`
     How to Find People's Email Addresses. FAQs and links from Queen's University in Canada (maintained by David Alex Lamb).

4   `w3.one.net/~alward/etable.html`
     Troubleshooting. A chart with hints about troubleshooting email problems.

5   `www.montypython.net/scripts/spam.php3`
     Monty Python's Spam. The script and sound clips from the infamous Monty Python "Spam" sketch.

6   `www.thrall.org/domains.htm`
     Top Level Domain Names. A list of top level domain names.

7   `www.washington.edu/pine/overview/project-history.html`
     Pine History. A history of the Pine mailer.

8   `www.washington.edu/pine/tutorial.4/`
     Pine Tutorial. A how-to introduction to the Pine mailer.

9   `www.eudora.com/`
     Eudora Place. Lots of information about the Eudora mail client.

10   `www.imap.org`
     The IMAP Connection. Information about IMAP from the University of Washington.

11   `www.Sendmail.org`
      Sendmail. A discussion of sendmail and email.

12   `www.oac.uci.edu/indiv/ehood/MIME/MIME.html`
      MIME RFCs. An index of RFCs for MIME.

13   `www.hunnysoft.com/mime/`
      MIME Info. Lots of information about MIME.

14   `www.northernwebs.com/senate/`
      U.S. Senators. Contains a list of email addresses for all U.S. Senators and a tutorial on how to send email to them.

Chapter 2: Jump Start: Browsing and Publishing

1   `www.boutell.com/openfaq/browsers/`
      Browser FAQs. Contains answers to many commonly asked questions about Web browsers.

2   `www.zdnet.com/yil/filters/channels/netezuser.html`
      Surf School. Covers all of the important topics for beginning Web surfers.

3   `www.imagitek.com/bcs.html`
      Backgrounds. Good for choosing and previewing background colors and text combinations.

4   `www.netscapeworld.com/common/nw.color.html`
      Consistent Color. A document describing how to obtain consistent colors on all Web browsers.

5   `www.ncsa.uiuc.edu/General/Internet/WWW/HTMLPrimer.html`
      HTML Primer. The NCSA (at UIUC) beginners' guide to HTML.

6   `scholar.lib.vt.edu/reports/soasis-slides/HTML-Intro.html`
      Introduction to HTML 3.2. An introduction to HTML Version 3.2.

7   `werbach.com/barebones/`
      Bare Bones HTML. The essentials of HTML 4.0 explained by Kevin Werbach.

8   `www.w3-tech.com/crash/HTMLMenu.html`
      HTML Crash Course. An HTML tutorial for beginners.

9   `www.hotwired.com/webmonkey/teachingtool/`
      Web Monkey. An HTML tutorial for beginners.

10   `www.earth.com/bad-style/`
      Don'ts in HTML. A collection of links to bad style HTML pages.

11   `www.mcli.dist.maricopa.edu/tl/`
Teaching and Learning. A presentation dedicated to issues about teaching and learning on the Web.

12   `www.microsoft.com/insider/internet`
Web Tutorial. An Internet Guide and Web Tutorial from Microsoft.

13   `mindit.netmind.com`
Mind-it. A service that notifies you if the URL for a Web page has changed.

Chapter 3: The Internet

1   `www.fnc.gov/Internet_res.html`
Internet Definition. The Federal Networking Council (FNC) Resolution: Definition of "Internet" from 10/24/95.

2   `www.isoc.org/internet-history/brief.html`
History. A Brief History of the Internet.

3   `www.isoc.org/guest/zakon/Internet/History/HIT.html`
Internet Timeline. An extensive timeline of the Internet by Hobbes.

4   `www.ietf.org/`
Internet Engineering Task Force. Organization that is responsible for defining and managing all aspects of Internet technology.

5   `www.aldea.com/bluepages/stat.html`
Statistics. Internet statistics compiled by Matthew Gray of net.Genesis Corporation.

6   `www.glreach.com/globstats/index.php3`
Global Stats. Global Internet statistics and a breakdown by language usage.

7   `www.isc.org/ds`
Network Wizards. This is a comprehensive Internet Domain Survey site.

8   `www.cookiecentral.com`
Cookie Central. Lots of interesting information about cookies.

9   `www.netscape.com/newsref/std/cookie_spec.html`
Cookie Specification. Here is Netscape's persistent client state HTTP Cookies specification.

10   `www.epic.org/privacy/internet/cookies/`
Cookies and Privacy. The electronic privacy information center's

page about cookies and privacy contains valuable information about cookies and you.

11   `sagan.earthspace.net/jargon/`
Jargon File. The list of cyberspace jargon.

12   `www.w3.org/PICS`
W3C—PICS. The Platform for Internet Content Selection.

13   `www.smartparent.com`
Smart Parent. "... a resource dedicated to educating parents on the best ways to safeguard their children from the dangers presented by cyberspace."

14   `www.netparents.org`
America Links Up. "A Kids On-Line Teach-In that is a public awareness and education campaign ... concerned with providing children with a safe and rewarding experience on-line."

15   `www.altavista.digital.com`
Altavista. A sample advertising business.

16   `www.america.net/`
AmericaNet. A sample marketing business.

17   `www.llbean.com/`
L. L. Bean. A sample retail business.

18   `www.InternetTravelAgency.com/`
Internet Travel Agency. A sample service business.

19   `home.netscape.com/`
Netscape. A sample software company.

20   `www.eventures.ups.com`
UPS e-Ventures. A sample partnership.

21   `www.fedex.com/us/ebusiness/`
FedEx. A sample partnership.

22   `www.wsj.com/`
Wall Street Journal. A sample subscription business.

23   `www.agromarches.fr/uk/frameset.html`
Food On-line. You will find an e-commerce expert in food products.

24   `www.onsale.com/`
Onsale Auction. A popular auction supersite.

25   `www.ebay.com/`
Ebay Auction. Another popular auction supersite.

26   `www.cuseeme.com/`
CuSeeMe. Some of the leaders in videoconferencing and information about their products are available at this presentation.

Chapter 4: The World Wide Web

1   `www.w3.org`
W3C. A consortium that among other things seeks to promote standards for the evolution of the Web.

2   `www.ietf.org/`
IETF. The Internet Engineering Task Force homepage.

3   `www.isoc.org/`
ISOC. The Internet Society Web site.

4   `www.dsiegel.com/tips/index.html`
Design Tips. Web Wonk's tips for Web page designers.

5   `www.killersites.com/`
Creating Killer Web Sites. Information about David Siegel's book, including a few design tips.

6   `www.hotwired.com/webmonkey/`
Webmonkey. Cutting-edge Web design material.

7   `info.med.yale.edu/caim/manual/contents.html`
Web Guide. The Yale Web style guide.

8   `www.webpagesthatsuck.com`
WebPagesThatSuck site. Vince Flanders' site where you "learn good Web design by looking at bad Web design."

9   `ecommerce.ncsu.edu/business_models.html`
Business Models on the Web. An on-line course offered by Professor Michael Rappa at North Carolina State University.

10   `www.paulallen.com`
Paul Allen's Homepage. A sample biography.

11   `www.rubberchicken.com`
RubberChicken. A sample Web business.

12   `ubl.com`
Ultimate Band List. A sample Web guide.

13   `www.cookiecentral.com`
Cookie Central. A sample Web tutorial.

14   `www.123registerme.com/`
Page Registration. A company that can and will register your Web pages—for a small fee.

15   `www.cc.ukans.edu/lynx_help/Lynx_users_guide.html`
Lynx Guide. A comprehensive users' guide from the University of Kansas.

16   `www.mentovai.com/lynx.shtml`
Lynx. "Lynx: The Browser of the Future, Not the Past"—some thoughts by Mark Mentovai.

Chapter 5: Searching the World Wide Web

1   `www.kcpl.lib.mo.us/search/srchengines.htm`
Review. Kansas City Public Library's introduction to search engines with detailed reviews of several search engines.

2   `searchenginewatch.com/`
Search Engine Watch. Lots of excellent information about search engines.

3   `searchengineshowdown.com`
Search Engine Showdown. "The Users' Guide to Web Searching" features comparisons of and statistics about many search engines.

4   `www.yahoo.com`
Yahoo! The first search engine and directory service.

5   `www.metacrawler.com`
Metacrawler. Great metasearch engine developed at the University of Washington.

6   `altavista.digital.com`
Altavista. One of our favorite search engines.

7   `www.go.com`
Go. Another of our favorite search engines.

8   `www.northernlight.com`
Northern Light. One of the newer search engines.

9   `www.google.com`
Google. A search engine that ranks sites by hyperlink popularity.

10   `bigfoot.com/`
Bigfoot. Great for locating lost friends.

11   `info.webcrawler.com/mak/projects/robots/robots.html`
Web Robots. A great introduction to Web Robots, Wanderers, and Spiders.

12   `www.northernwebs.com/set/`
Hits Tutorial. Search engine tutorial for Web designers.

13   `www.sofer.com/research/search_engine_submission.html`
Search Engine Submission. Provides information about "how to improve the ranking of your site on the major search engines."

14   `www.globalserve.net/~iwb/search/`
Search Engine Secrets. Information about search engines that will enable you to "increase visibility and traffic to your site."

15   `www.go.com/Titles?qt=%22Pacific+Crest+Trail%22&col=WW&sv=` ↵
`IS&lk=noframes&nh=10`
Pacific Crest Trail. The longest continuous foot path in the world.

Chapter 6: Internet Applications

1   `www.ncl.ox.ac.uk/it/telnet.html`
Telnet Tutorial. Basic information about Telnet.

2   `www.compuserve.com/internethelp/telnet.asp`
Telnet FAQ. Some questions and answers about telnet from Compuserve's Internet Help Center.

3   `www.freesoft.org/CIE/RFC/854/index.htm`
Telnet Protocol. The specification for the Telnet Protocol from RFC 854.

4   `telnet://locis.loc.gov`
Library of Congress. Telnet to the Library of Congress.

5   `www.vandyke.com/vandyke/products/index.html`
Products. Telnet and FTP products that can be downloaded from Van Dyke Technologies, Inc.

6   `www.pubserv.washington.edu/copy/ftptutorial.html`
FTP Tutorial. An introduction to file transfer from the University of Washington.

7   `www.islandnet.com/~tmc/html/articles/ftp.htm`
The Internet and FTP. A comprehensive article written by Tim McLellan about FTP.

8   `hoohoo.ncsa.uiuc.edu/ftp/index.shtml`
Monster List. NCSA's monster list of FTP sites and information about FTP.

9   `www.ipswitch.com/Products/WS_FTP/index.html`
WS_FTP. Ipswitch, Inc.'s WS_FTP client.

10   `www.dartmouth.edu/pages/softdev/fetch.html`
Fetch. All about the Mac FTP client Fetch.

11   `www.inetnebr.com/help/tutorials/archie.html`
Archie Tutorial. A page devoted to explaining Archie—a program that is useful for searching FTP archives.

12   `www.symantec.com/pys95nt.html`
Virus Center. Symantec's antivirus research center.

13   `www.geocities.com/SiliconValley/1710/`
Viruses. Geocities' introduction to computer viruses.

Chapter 7: Basic HTML

1   `drake.armstrong.edu/~greenlaw/teaching/CS403/IO/HTML/` ↩
`EXAMPLES/index.html`
Examples. Some examples from *In-line/On-line* covering all the basics.

2   `werbach.com/barebones/`
Bare Bones. The basics and lots of interesting links.

3   `www.jmarshall.com/easy/html/`
Tutorial. James Marshall's "HTML Made Really Easy."

4   `www.hwg.org/`
HTML Writers Guild. The largest international organization of Web authors.

5   `www.webreference.com/html`
HTML with Style. Includes a number of HTML resources and a tutorial.

6   `www.ncsa.uiuc.edu/General/Internet/WWW/HTMLPrimer.html`
Primer. NCSA's HTML primer.

7   `www.quadzilla.com/`
Ultimate HTML Site. "Your one-stop HTML resource site, period."

8   `www.willcam.com/cmat/html/crossref.html`
Tags. Willcam's compact index of HTML tags.

9   `wally2.rit.edu/instruction/web/tablesframes/tablesframes.html`
Tables/Frames. Great examples of how tables and frames are used and how to create them from the Rochester Institute of Technology Web site.

10   `www.w3.org/TR/REC-html40/struct/tables.html`
W3C Tables Descriptions. Examples of tables provided by the World Wide Web Consortium.

11   `www.w3.org/TR/WD-html40-970708/`
HTML 4.0. The HTML 4.0 specification from the World Wide Web Consortium.

Chapter 8: Web Graphics

1   `www.unplug.com/great/`
Tips. Lots of ideas for preparing graphics from the beginner to the expert.

2   `www.ist.net/clipart/index.html`
Clip Art. A huge collection of clip art.

3   `www.ender-design.com/rg/`
Realm Graphics. Great place to download graphics.

4   `www.iconbazaar.com/`
Icon Bazaar. Great place to download icons and graphics.

5   `www.pixelsight.com/`
PixelSight. A site containing many nice images.

6   `www.widearea.co.uk/designer/`
Creating Graphics. Introduction to and some important points about creating Web graphics.

7   `desktoppublishing.com/webgraphics.html`
Web Graphics. Pointers to many excellent resources.

8   `www.angelswebgraphics.com/`
Angel's Web Graphics. Professional graphics presentation.

9   `www.pambytes.com/default.html`
Pambytes. Lots of free graphics.

10   `www.abcgiant.com`
Clip Art Collection. Lots of free graphics.

11   `www.mit.edu:8001/transweb.html`
TransWeb. A way to create transparent gifs.

Chapter 9: Advanced HTML

1   `www.newbie.net/sharky/frames/menu.html`
Frames Tutorial. Learn frames in five easy lessons.

2   `www.webcom.com/html/tutor/forms/intro.shtml`
Forms Tutorial. A comprehensive introduction to forms.

3   `www.freeandclear.ws`
Forms Processing. You can get your forms processed here and have the results echoed back to you.

4   `www.cc.ukans.edu/~acs/docs/other/cgi-with-perl.shtml`
Perl Scripts. Tutorial for building CGI (Common Gateway Interface) scripts in Perl.

5   `www.zdnet.com/anchordesk/story/story_1098.html`
XML. Anchor desk discussion on Extensible Markup Language.

6   `www.itm.com/cgicollection/`
CGI Collection. Many links and scripts can be found here.

7   `www.anchordesk.com/story/story_1066.html`
HTML 4.0. Anchor desk discussion and other links to HTML 4.0.

8   `www.w3.org/TR/WD-html40-970708/`
HTML 4.0 Spec. Working draft release from the W3C.

9   `www.anchordesk.com/story/story_1080.html`
Dynamic HTML. Anchor desk discussion and other links to Dynamic HTML.

10   `www.zdnet.com/pcmag/features/htmlauthor/rev5.htm`
HotDog. PC Magazine review of the HotDog Pro HTML editor.

11   `www2.imagiware.com/RxHTML`
Doctor HTML. This syntax checker will diagnose your Web page.

12   `www.websitegarage.com/`
Web Site Garage. A great site for a free Web site tuneup.

13   `www.w3.org/Style/CSS`
Cascading Style Sheets. Lots of links and material about cascading style sheets from the World Wide Web Consortium.

14   builder.cnet.com/Authoring/CSS/index.html
Get Started with Cascading Style Sheets. A beginner's guide from CNET on using CSS.

15   www.htmlhelp.com/reference/css/quick-tutorial.html
CSS Quick Tutorial. A tutorial from WDG for learning CSS.

Chapter 10: Newsgroups, Mailing Lists, Chat Rooms, and MUDs

1   www.dejanews.com/
Deja News. A powerful newsgroup search tool, plus lots of information about newsgroups.

2   www.magmacom.com/~leisen/master_list.html
Newsgroup Hierarchies. The Master List of Newsgroup Hierarchies Home Page.

3   www.geocities.com/ResearchTriangle/Lab/6882/
news.newusers.questions. Official Homepage. Important information for new newsgroup users, including a list of helpful links.

4   www.liszt.com/
Liszt. A huge directory of mailing lists and newsgroups.

5   www.lsoft.com/lists/listref.html
CataList. A large catalog of mailing lists from the LISTSERV's LISTS database that can be searched by subject, host site, host country, or number of subscribers.

6   www.webcom.com/impulse/list.html
Email Discussion Groups/Lists. This page supplies the basics about mailing lists, including an introduction to list server commands.

7   db.tidbits.com/getbits.acgi?tbart=05386
Mailing List Manners 101. Some tips and information about mailing lists from TidBITS.

8   www.fred.net/kathy/at/atlist.html
Appalachian Trail Mailing List. Information about how to subscribe to the A.T. Mailing List as well as info about other mailing lists and chat pages related to the A.T. and hiking.

9   www.the-park.com/
The PARK. "A popular, member-supported international online community" with over 100 chat rooms.

10   `dir.yahoo.com/Computers_and_Internet/Internet/World_Wide_Web/`
`Chat/Chat_Rooms/`
Chat Rooms. A collection of chat room links from Yahoo!

11   `www.outland.org/cgi-bin/main.pl`
Avatar MUD. The Web page for the "Advanced Virtual Adventuring Through Alternate Realities System"—a MUD with a medieval/fantasy theme.

12   `dir.yahoo.com/Recreation/Games/Computer_Games/` ↩
`Internet_Games/MUDs__MUSHes__MOOs__etc_/Talkers/`
MUDS. A collection of MUD links from Yahoo!

13   `www.godlike.com/muds/`
MUD Resource Collection. An extensive collection of MUD-related links.

14   `tecfa.unige.ch/edu-comp/WWW-VL/eduVR-page.html`
Educational Technology. Information and links to education and research-related MUDs.

Chapter 11: Electronic Publishing

1   `www.clari.net/brad/copymyths.html`
Copyright Myths. Brad Templeton explains ten big copyright myths.

2   `lcweb.loc.gov/copyright/`
U.S. Library of Congress. Their copyright page provides lots of information about copyright law.

3   `www.benedict.com/`
Copyright Website. An interesting Web presentation providing the basics of copyright, current news and discussion pertaining to copyright issues, as well as some entertaining examples of copyright infringement.

4   `digital.library.upenn.edu/books/`
On-Line Books Page. A directory of on-line books and links to other directories and archives of on-line books.

5   `www.pathfinder.com`
Pathfinder. A site loaded with links to magazines such as *Time* and *Life* (and Lifetime?).

6   `www.promo.net/pg/`
Gutenberg. Project Gutenberg information. This is the ambitious project to put a tremendous number of classics on the Web by the year 2001.

7   `www.4mesa.com/4mesa/weblist/ejournal.html`
Electronic Journals. The World Wide Web Virtual Library: Electronic Journals. A site with a huge number of electronic journals indexed, a convenient search engine, and many related topics.

8   `www.utexas.edu/computer/vcl/`
Virtual Library. The University of Texas's virtual computer library.

9   `www.ssrn.com/update/lsn/cyberspace/csl_menu.html`
CyberSpace Law. CyberSpace Law for Non-Lawyers.

10   `www.wired.com/wired`
WiReD. WiReD magazine site. A site with lots of interesting articles about networking, including many articles about social issues.

11   `www.tbtf.com/index.html`
Tasty Bits. News from the technology front.

12   `www.cc.emory.edu/WHSCL/electronic.publishing.html`
Electronic Publishing. "A Field Guide to Sources On, About, and On the Internet" provides an extensive bibliography for information relating to electronic publishing.

13   `www.cc.emory.edu/WHSCL/resource.ejs.html`
Internet Resource Discovery Tools. A list of links to electronic journal collections.

14   `www.meer.net/~johnl/e-zine-list/about.html`
E-Zine-List. John Labovitz's directory of e-zines, containing over 2,000 zines.

Chapter 12: Web Programming Material

1   `www.webreference.com/js/`
Doc JavaScript. A great presentation for anything related to JavaScript.

2   `www.bloke.com/javascript/RandomURL/`
Random URL. JavaScript code that returns a random URL.

3   `www.jsworld.com/`
JavaScript World. Lots of useful information about JavaScript.

4   `javascript.internet.com/`
JavaScript Source. JavaScript reference with lots of examples.

5   `echoecho.com/javascript.htm`
JavaScript Tutorial. A tutorial from EchoEcho.Com that teaches everything you need to know to create your own scripts.

6   www.developer.com/
Developer Resources. A large collection of useful Web development resources.

7   www.webreference.com/programming/
Web Programming. A large collection of useful Web programming resources.

8   www.python.org/topics/web/
CGI Programming. Resources for CGI programming with Python.

9   java.sun.com/
Java Home Page. "The Source for Java Technology" from Sun Microsystems contains current news about Java technology.

10   www.geom.umn.edu/~daeron/docs/javaguide/index.html
Java Tutorial. A step-by-step on-line guide to creating Java programs and applets.

11   java.sun.com/docs/faqindex.html
Java FAQs. Sun's Java FAQs list.

12   echoecho.com/freejamenus02.htm
Java Archive. A list of free Java applets from EchoEcho.Com with instructions on how to add them to your pages.

13   java.sun.com/sfaq/index.html
Java Security. A list of FAQs about security in Java.

14   www.internetter.com/papers/ssi.html
Server Side Includes. Jim Walker's SSI: The Webmaster's Secret Weapon.

Chapter 13: Multimedia

1   www.babylon-6.demon.co.uk/raframes.htm
Audio Guide. A thorough introduction to Real Audio.

2   www.advances.com/sa/
Sound Archive. Billed as the ultimate sound repository.

3   www.mpeg.org/MPEG/links.html
MPEG. An index of MPEG information and resources.

4   www.mcli.dist.maricopa.edu/authoring/
Multimedia Authoring. Resource collections pointing to many multimedia development sites.

5   www.posturepro.com/digit.htm
D.I.G.-IT!. Digital Image Gallery of 3D anatomy.

6   www.eyewire.com
    EyeWire. Lots of information about images.

7   hotwired.lycos.com/webmonkey/multimedia
    Multimedia tutorials. Tutorials on Audio/MP3, Shockwave/Flash,
    Video, and Animation.

8   idm.internet.com/articles/200002/dream_index.html
    IDM's Macromedia Dreamweaver Tutorial. A tutorial from Intranet
    Design Magazine on using Dreamweaver, a WYSIWYG HTML
    editor that works well with Macromedia Flash and Shockwave.

9   www.web3d.org/vrml/vrml.htm
    VRML Repository. Links to information about the Virtual Reality
    Modeling Language including documentation and specifications,
    software, mailing lists, and a selection of tutorials.

10 www.virtpark.com/theme/proteinman/
    VRML 2.0 Worlds. Proteinman's top ten VRML worlds, as well as
    a list of past winners.

11 home.hiwaay.net/~crispen/vrmlworks/
    VRMLworks Site. This site from VRMLworks enables you to do
    everything from selecting a VRML browser to building your own
    VRML world.

12 www.yahoo.com/Computers/Multimedia/
    Multimedia. Yahoo's multimedia link.

13 www.mbone.com/
    MBONE. Great site for learning all about the MBONE. Click on the
    search button.

14 www.cs.columbia.edu/~hgs/internet/mbone-faq.html
    MBONE FAQ. A list of frequently asked questions about the Mul-
    ticast Backbone.

Chapter 14: Privacy and Security Topics

1   www.cnet.com/Content/Features/Dlife/Law/?dd
    Law and Internet. A discussion of some privacy issues.

2   www.2020tech.com/maildrop/privacy.html
    Privacy Pages. An excellent source of information about privacy
    issues, including links to current daily news articles, privacy orga-
    nization links, privacy software links, and a list of UseNet links
    dealing with privacy.

3   `www0.delphi.com/navnet/securitymenu.html`
Security and Privacy Guides. This page provides a good explanation of what information is made available about you while you are surfing the WWW as well as access to public databases that permits you to see what information is currently available about you.

4   `www.epic.org/`
Privacy Center. Lots of the latest information about electronic privacy.

5   `www.jjtc.com/Security/cryptanalysis.htm`
The Codebreakers. Lots of references to cryptography resources and articles.

6   `www.cert.org`
CERT. Computer Emergency Response Team site.

7   `www.gocsi.com`
Computer Security Institute. Lots of information about computer security.

8   `www.rsa.com/rsalabs/`
RSA Homepage. Lots of news about encryption, challenges, and standards can be found here.

9   `www.eff.org/`
Electronic Frontier Foundation. Resources and current news about privacy issues and free expression.

10   `www.isoc.org`
Internet Society. Lots of material relating to the Internet, including various standards and protocols.

11   `www.cpsr.org/program/privacy/privacy.html`
CPSR Computer Professionals for Social Responsibility. Information and links about privacy and civil liberties, plus an informative collection of links about cryptography.

12   `www.eff.org/blueribbon.html`
Blue Ribbon. The Web page for "on-line freedom of speech, press and association" and the Blue Ribbon graphic, as well.

13   `web.mit.edu/network/pgp.html`
PGP Freeware. MIT's distribution site for Pretty Good Privacy for noncommercial use.

14   `scratch.abanet.org/scitech/ec/isc/dsg-toc.html`
Digital Signatures. Reference to a handy guide book.

15   `news:alt.security.pgp`
alt.security.pgp. A USENET newsgroup pertaining to PGP.

16   `news:alt.privacy`
alt.privacy. A newsgroup for discussing issues relating to privacy
and security.

Credits

Figure 4.3, 154
From `http://www.paulallen.com/`. Copyright © 1997–2001 by Vulcan Northwest, Inc. Reprinted by permission of Paul Allen.

Figure 4.4, 156
From `http://www.rubberchicken.com/`. Copyright © 2001 InfoSpace, Inc. All rights reserved. INFOSPACE, RUBBERCHICKEN.COM and their designs and related marks are the intellectual property of InfoSpace, Inc.

Figure 4.5, 158
From `http://ubl.com/`. Copyright © 1997–2001 by ARTISTdirect, Inc. Reprinted by permission of ARTISTdirect, Inc.

Figure 4.6, 159
From `http://www.cookiecentral.com/`. Copyright © 1997–2000 by Cookie Central. Reprinted by permission of Cookie Central.

Figure 4.14, 180
From Adrian Geoffery Brown's Web site. Reprinted by permission of Adrian Geoffery Brown.

Figure 5.1, 189
Reprinted with permission from
`www.internet.com` <`http://www.internet.com`>. Copyright 2001 internet.com Corporation. All rights reserved, internet.com is the exclusive Trademark of internet.com Corporation.
From `http://www.searchenginewatch.com/`. Copyright 2001 internet.com Corp. All rights reserved. Reprinted by permission of internet.com Corp.

Figure 5.2, 192
From `http://www.yahoo.com/`. Reproduced with permission of Yahoo! Inc. © 2000 by Yahoo! Inc. YAHOO! and the YAHOO! Logo are trademarks of Yahoo! Inc.

Figure 5.13, 211
From `http://www.google.com/help/index.html`. Copyright © 2001 Google. All rights reserved. Reprinted by permission of Google.

Figure 5.14, 217
From `http://www.metaspy.com`. Copyright © 2001 InfoSpace, Inc. All rights reserved. INFOSPACE, METASPY, and their designs and related marks are the intellectual property of InfoSpace, Inc.

Figure 5.15, 218
From `http://www.metaspy.com/spy/filtered_b.html?` ↩
`shadow=98165902.845`. Copyright © 2001 InfoSpace, Inc. All rights reserved. INFOSPACE, METASPY, and their designs and related marks are the intellectual property of InfoSpace, Inc.

Figure 5.16, 222
From `http://www.google.com/search?q=mileage+` ↩
`%22appalachian+trail%22+%22new+hampshire%22&hl=en&l` ↩
`r=&safe=off&btnG=Google+Search`. Copyright © 2001 Google. All rights reserved. Reprinted by permission of Google.

Figure 8.9, 348
From files of Damon Gabrielle. Reprinted by permission of Damon Gabrielle.

Figure 9.12, 413
From `http://www2.imagiware.com/RxHTML/`. Reprinted by permission of Imagiware, Inc. Copyright © 1995–2001 Imagiware, Inc.

Figure 10.6, 460
From `http://pages.wbs.net/`. Reprinted by permission. Infoseek, Ultrasmart, Ultraseek, Ultraseek Server, Infoseek Desktop, Infoseek Ultra, iSeek, Quickseek, Imageseek, the Infoseek logos, and the tagline "Once you know, you know," are trademarks of Infoseek Corporation, which may be registered in certain jurisdictions. Other trademarks shown are trademarks of their respective owners. Copyright © 1994–1998 Infoseek Corporation. All rights reserved.

Figure 10.7, 465
From `http://www.walrus.com/~avatar`. Reprinted by permission of Sean Freyholtz.

Figure 12.8, 510
From files of Meghan Simone. Reprinted by permission of Meghan Simone.

Index

A

\<A\> tag, 87–92, 601
    HREF attribute, 377–379
    NAME attribute, 90–92
    TARGET attribute, 376–379
About.com, 194
account name, 7, 631
ACM's Journal of Experimental Algorithmics, 481
ACTION attribute, form tag, 389–391, 399–400, 402, 518, 520
action buttons, 394–395
address book, 582
\<ADDRESS\> tag, 267, 271–272, 601
Addy, Cliff, 415
Adobe
    Acrobat, 149
    SiteMill, 412
Advanced Research Projects Agency Network (ARPANET), 102–104, 609
advertising, 127, 130, 455, 472, 533, 548
ADV-HTML, 457
AFAIK, 126, 609
.aif extension, 42, 534
.aifc extension, 42, 534
.aiff extension, 42, 534
AIFF file format, 534, 609
Alchemy Mindworks, 334
alert boxes, 487, 494–496, 503, 631
algorithm, 15, 60, 631
    compression, 634
    cryptographic, 634
    frameset design, 380–383
    hashing, 558–559, 563, 637
    line breaking, 60
    recursive, 382, 644
    tiling, 648
alias, 13–14, 631
ALIGN attribute
    applet tag, 508
    caption tag, 307–308
    heading tag, 87, 283
    horizontal rule tag, 280–281
    image tag, 338–344
    table data tag, 305–306
    table header tag, 305
    table row tag, 305–306
    table tag, 298–300
ALINK attribute, BODY tag, 78
Allen, Paul, 153–155
alt, 444–445

ALT attribute
    applet tag, 508
    area tag, 353
    image tag, 95, 179
alt.ascii-art, 448
AltaVista, 130, 194, 202
alt.cult-movie, 448
Alternative Medicine Home Page, The, 200
alt.fishing, 448
America Online, 36, 567, 609
AmericaNet, 130
analog, 112
anchor tag, 87–92, 601
    HREF attribute, 377–379
    NAME attribute, 90–92
    TARGET attribute, 376–379
Andreessen, Marc, 105
animated GIFs, 333–334, 631
animation, 332
anonymous file transfer, 258–260, 631
antivirus software, 262–263
AOL. *See* America Online
Apache, 62
Apple, 534, 538
applet, 100, 506–511, 631
\<APPLET\> tag, 507–508, 601
    ALIGN attribute, 508
    ALT attribute, 508
    CODE attribute, 508
    CODEBASE attribute, 508
    HEIGHT attribute, 508
    HSPACE attribute, 508
    NAME attribute, 508
    VSPACE attribute, 508
    WIDTH attribute, 508
Archie, 260, 631
\<AREA\> tag, 350–351, 353, 601
    ALT attribute, 353
    COORDS attribute, 350
    SHAPE attribute, 350
areo domain name, 10
arguments, 492, 591–592
Argus Clearinghouse, 194
ARPANET. *See* Advanced Research Projects Agency Network (ARPANET)
art, clip, 326, 633
article, newsgroup, 434–435, 631
    cross-post, 437
    digest, 437
    follow-up, 435
    posting, 435
    thread, 435

ASCII, 24, 609
AskJeeves, 202
AskJeevesPeekThroughthe Keyhole, 217
at (@) sign, 9
AT&T, 103, 112
Attachment field, email, 20
attachments, email, 18, 20, 24
Attchmnt: field, 583
attribute, 57, 632
.au extension, 42, 534
AU file format, 534
auction, 132
audio, 534–537, 632
    file formats, 534–535
        AIFF, 534
        AU, 534
        MIDI, 534
        RealAudio, 535
        WAV, 535
    file installation, 535
    repositories, 536
    Web pages and, 535–536
Audio Interchange File Format, 534, 609
Audio Video Interleaved, 538, 609
authenticate, 632
authentication, 8, 557–558
.avi extension, 42, 538
AVI file format, 538, 609

B

\<B\> tag, 274–275, 601
BAA, 609
Back button, 48
BACKGROUND attribute, BODY tag, 76–77
background sound tab (\<BGSOUND\>), 536, 602
bandwidth, 139
Bartle, Richard, 463
\<BASE\> tag, 67–71, 601
\<BASEFONT\> tag, 66, 602
baseline, 337, 339, 341
baud rate, 111, 632
BBN (Bolt, Beranek, and Newman, Inc.), 102, 609
BBS (bulletin board system), 433, 567, 609
Bcc field, 18, 584
Because It's Time Network (BITNET), 104, 433, 609
Bell Labs, 103
Berners-Lee, Tim, 105

BESTWEB, 457
beta test, 150
BGCOLOR attribute, 76–79, 310
<BGSOUND> tag, 536, 602
<BIG> tag, 273, 602
Bigfoot, 206, 207
binary files, 40, 258, 389
binary numbers, 72–74
binary transfer mode, 248, 632
biography, 153–155
bit, 72
bit rate, 111, 632
BITNET, 104, 433, 609
biz domain name, 10
blind carbon copy, 18, 584, 632
<BLINK> tag, 276, 602
<BODY> tag, 58–60, 75–79, 602
    ALINK attribute, 78
    BACKGROUND attribute, 76–77
    BGCOLOR attribute, 76–79
    LINK attribute, 78
    TEXT attribute, 75–76
    VLINK attribute, 78
Boeing, 112
bold tag, 274–275, 601
Bolt, Beranek, and Newman, Inc. (BBN),
    102, 609
bomb, email, 6
bookmark, 47, 59, 145–148, 632
    folders, 146–148
    list, 145–146
    in Lynx Web browser, 182
Bookmarks menu, Web browser, 47
Boole, George, 214–216
Boolean query, 214, 220, 632
Boolean value, 496, 499
BORDER attribute
    object tag, 544
    table tag, 300
borders
    frame, 382–383
    image, 345–346
bot, 227
bounce, email, 35–36
Boutell.Com, Inc., 354
Bowers, Neil, 415

 tag, 270, 343, 602
bracketed text, 27–28
brackets, 423
BRB, 126, 609
breadth-first search, 227–228
BrightPlanet, 196, 198
browser. *See* Web, browser
BTW, 126, 609
buffer, 632
buffering, 533–534
bulletin board system (BBS), 433, 567, 609
bullets, 287, 288, 290
business exposition, 155–157
business, on-line
    advertising, 130
    legal environment, 134–135
    marketing, 130
    partnership, 130
    problems and concerns, 132–133
    retail, 130
    sample companies, 131–132
    security, 134

    service, 130–131
    software, 131
    subscription, 131
    U. S. government commitment to,
        135–136
button
    action buttons, 394–395
    Back, 48
    Compose, 26
    Destinations, 50
    directory, 49
    Edit, 47
    File, 26
    Find, 49
    Forward, 48
    Frame source, 375
    Guide, 49
    Home, 48
    hot buttons, 45, 49–50, 638
    Images, 49
    Internet, 50
    Lookup, 50
    Net Search, 50
    Netcaster, 50
    New&Cool, 50
    Open, 49
    Page source, 375
    Print, 49
    radio buttons, 394
    Reload, 48
    Reply, 26
    Search, 49
    Security, 49
    Software, 50
    Stop, 49
    View frame source, 375
    View source, 375
bye command, 253
byte, 114, 632

C

C++, 489
cache, 47, 48, 144, 633
CAD, 609
Caesar cipher, 439, 633
<CAPTION> tag, 307–308, 602
captions, table, 307–308
carbon copy (cc), 17, 19, 583
Cascading Style Sheets (CSS), 120, 417,
    610, 633
    advantages of, 429
    disadvantages of, 429
    external styles, 426–429
    in-line styles, 419–421
    internal styles, 421–426
case
    HTML, 57
    password, 8
Cc field, 17, 19, 583
CCC (Copyright Clearance Center), 475,
    609
CCD (charge-couple device), 356, 609
cd command, 64, 253, 594, 595, 600
CDA, 609

CELLPADDING attribute, table tag,
    301–303
CELLSPACING attribute, table tag,
    301–302
censorship, 125
<CENTER> tag, 275, 602
central mail spool system, 33
CERN, 105, 609
CERT (Computer Emergency Response
    Team), 564, 610, 634
CGI (Common Gateway Interface), 389,
    401–403, 516, 518–520, 610, 634
change directory command (cd), 64, 253,
    594, 595, 600
channel, 459
character. *See also specific characters*
    recognition, 355, 611
charge-couple device (CCD), 356, 609
chat room, 459–462, 567, 633
    channel, 459
    culture, 461
    in education, 462
    entrance, 459
    lurking, 460
    password, 459
chat worlds, 462
checkbox, 393–394
CHECKED attribute, input tag, 393, 394
Chiang, Michael, 354
chmod command, 64, 598–599, 600
CIAC Internet Hoaxes Page, 263
CIC (Creative Incentive Coalition), 475,
    610
cipher, 553–554
ciphertext, 553–558, 562–563, 633
circuit switching, 101, 633
circular arrangement of Web pages,
    169–170
citation tag, 269–271, 601
<CITE> tag, 269–271, 601
Clark, Jim, 105
class of objects, 514
CLASSID attribute, object tag, 544
CLEAR attribute, line-break tag, 343
clearinghouses, 194
clickable image, 89–90
clickable text, 633
client pull model, 403–405, 633
client-server model, 113–114, 633
Client-Side Image Map Editor, 354
client-side image maps, 349–354
Clinton, Bill, 135
clip art, 326, 633
closed list, 450, 633
CNET, 610
CODE attribute, applet tag, 508
<CODE> tag, 272, 273, 603
CODEBASE attribute
    applet tag, 508
    object tag, 544
CODETYPE attribute, object tag, 544
collaborative computing, 47, 136–140, 633
    applications, 137–139
    defined, 136–137
    future prospects, 139–140
    impact of, 139
color, 409
    background, 76–79
    font, 79

GIF support, 329
in HTML documents, 72–79
hyperlink, 77–78
JPG support, 330
RGB color model, 74
scanners, 356, 358
in tables, 310–311
text, 75–76
COLOR attribute, FONT tag, 79
color picker utility, 75
color selector, HTML editor, 409
COLS attribute, frameset tag, 371, 374,
380–383
COLSPAN attribute, table header tag,
304–305
columns
in frames, 371
table, 298–300
com domain name, 10
comma delimiting, 583
comment, 634
<COMMENT> tag, 81, 603
Common Gateway Interface (CGI), 389,
401–403, 516, 518–520, 610, 634
Communicator, 46
Communicator menu, Web browser, 47
compiled language, 390
compiler, 412
Complete Planet, 197
composite number, 634
comp.parallel, 448
compress, 258
compression
algorithm, 634
file, 258, 533
graphics, 325, 328–329, 330–331, 332
lossless, 328–329, 332, 640
lossy, 330–331, 640
multimedia files, 533
comp.theory, 448
CompuServe, 328
Computer Emergency Response Team
(CERT), 564, 610, 634
computer literacy, 472, 634
Computer Science Network (CSNET), 103,
610
confirm box, 496
Connect pull-down menu, 235, 240
Connect window, Telnet, 235, 237
CONTENT attribute, meta tag, 72, 404–405
content-based style types, 266
control panel, 532
converter, HTML, 415–416
cookie, 47, 133–134, 144, 634
persistent, 133
Cookie Central, 158–160
coop domain name, 10
COORDS attribute, area tag, 350
Copernic, 204
Copy Image Location option, 328
copying a Web graphic, 327–328
copyright, 473–476, 536, 634
defined, 473–474
digital rights management systems, 476
eligibility requirements, 474
infringement, 475, 482
notices, 474, 483

Copyright Clearance Center (CCC), 475,
609
Copyright Resources on the Internet, 200
Cornell University, 139
counter, Web page, 523–526
display, decision on, 526
HTML code for, 524–525
usefulness of, 525
country codes, 10, 11
cp command, 600
CPU, 610
crawler, 227
Creative Incentive Coalition (CIC), 475,
610
credit card, security of, 134, 561
cross-post, 437, 634
cryptographic algorithm, 634
cryptography, 439, 555, 634. *See also*
encryption
private key, 556–557, 562–563
public key, 557–558, 562–563
Cryptolope container, 476
CSNET (Computer Science Network), 103,
610
CSS. *See* Cascading Style Sheets (CSS)
culture, Internet, 122–128
current directory, 594
CUSeeMe, 139
Cyber Patrol, 125
Cyber Sentry, 125
cyberspace, 125, 634. *See also* Internet

D

DARPA (Defense Advanced Research
Projects Agency), 102, 610
dash (-) symbol, 592
DATA attribute, object tag, 536, 539, 544
data definition tag (DD), 288–289, 603
Date field, email, 16–17
Dazzlers Digital Domicile, 481
<DD> tag, 288–289, 603
debugging HTML, 317–321
DECLARE attribute, object tag, 544
decryption, 553–554, 557, 558, 559
deep Web, 196
default password, 634
Defense Advanced Research Projects
Agency (DARPA), 102, 610
definition lists, 288–290
definition term tag, 288–289
Deja News, 440, 442
DELETE command, 272–273
deleting email messages, 588
deprecated tag, 277, 635
depth-first search, 228–229
Desktop Videoconferencing (DTVC), 138,
610
Destinations button, 50
dialog boxes, 494–500
DICKNS-L, 457
digest, 437, 635
digested list, 450, 635
DigiBox containers, 476
Digital Future Coalition, 475
digital rights management systems, 476

digital signature, 561–565, 635
digitizer, 139
Direct Search, 197, 199
DirectHit, 226
directory, 63–64, 190, 191–200
buttons, 49
current, 594
general, 191–194, 199–200
hidden, 593
home, 593
Looksmart, 191, 193, 194, 199
Lycos, 199
navigating, 191–192
Open Directory Project (ODP), 191
organization, 594–595
parent, 595
permissions, 63, 597
root, 593
services, 177
specialized, 191, 194–198, 200
working, 594
Yahoo!, 191, 192, 194, 199
Directory menu, Web browser, 47
distance learning, 462, 635
distributed naming scheme, 10
distribution list, 13
dithering, 329, 635
<DIV> tag, 603
dividers, table, 296, 300
<DL> tag, 288–289, 603
DNS (Domain Name System), 103, 610
Doctor HTML, 412, 413, 415, 635
document
area, Web browser, 45, 635
dynamic, 403–407, 635
HTML
background, 78–79
color, 72–79
creating, 58–60
design and coding, 173
font, 66–67, 79–80
global parameters, setting, 67
images, 93–95
outlining, 165–168
tiling, 76–77
URLs, relative *versus* absolute,
67–71
intradocument linking, 90–92
object model, 489
printing Web, 182
security, 560–561, 646
DogPile, 204, 206
domain name, 10–12
country codes, 10, 11
server, 36, 115, 635
space, 10–12
top-level, generic, 9, 10
Domain Name System (DNS), 103, 610
dot file, 593
dots per inch (DPI), 356, 610
downloading, 244
DPI (dots per inch), 356, 610
Dr. Watson, 415
<DT> tag, 288–289, 603
DTVC (Desktop Videoconferencing), 138,
610
Duke University, 433
dynamic document, 403–407, 635
client pull model, 403–405
server push model, 405

dynamic information, 368
dynamic IP address, 116, 635

ℰ

eBusiness Tools, 130, 131
Ecola Newsstand, 481
Edit button, Web browser, 47
edited list, 450, 635
editor. *See* HTML, editor
EDT, 610
edu domain name, 10
education
    chat rooms, 462
    distance learning, 462
Electronic Frontier Foundation, 475
electronic mail. *See* email
electronic money, 134
electronic newspaper, 131
Electronic Newsstand, The, 481
electronic publishing, 470–483
    advantages, 470–471
    copyright issues, 473–476
    disadvantages, 472
    do's and don'ts, 483
    e-zines, 479–480, 481
    journals, 480–481
    magazines, 481
    newspapers, 481–482
    on-line books, 477–478
    plagiarism, 482
    Project Gutenberg, 477–478
    public domain, 475
electronic texts, 477
Elm, 3
<EM> tag, 267, 603
emacs, 577
email, 2–42, 569, 571, 636. *See also*
    mailing list
    address, 8–9, 636
        aliases, 13–14
        determining, 12–13
        domain names and, 12
        in guest book, 517–518
    advantages, 4, 6
    bomb, 6
    bounce, 35–36
    client, 27–28
    as collaborative computing application,
        137
    composition, 19–25
    disadvantages, 5–6
    emoticon use, 22
    encryption, 35
    files, transferring, 244
    forwarding, 5, 29, 587
    header, 16, 17
    help, on-line, 22
    inbox, 31–32
    inserting files into messages, 24
    invention of, 103
    junk, 5
    mailer features, 25–30
    management, 36–40
        arrival of messages, signaling, 37

    filters, 40
        index of messages, 37
        vacation program, 39
    message components, 16–19
        attachments, 18, 20, 24
        Bcc field, 18
        body, 18
        Cc field, 17, 19
        Date field, 16–17
        From field, 16
        To field, 17, 19
        greeting, 18, 22
        header, 16, 17
        message id, 16
        signature, 18, 23–24
        Subject field, 17, 20
        text, 18
    MIME and, 18, 40–42
    netiquette, 22
    obtaining, 31–35
    passwords, 8
    pine mail program, 579–589
    programs, 2–3
    reply, 21, 26, 27–28, 587
    retrieving with Telnet, 241
    security, 35
    sending, 24
    spam, 5
    spell check, 23
    structure, 19–22
    userids, 7
    viruses, 41, 263
embed tag, 545
<EMBED> tag, 603
emote command, 465
emoticon, 22, 125–126, 636
emphasis tag (<EM>), 267, 603
encryption, 35, 133, 553–560
    basics of, 553–555
    hashing algorithm, 558–559, 563, 637
    key, 553
    prime numbers use of, 555–556
    private key cryptography, 556–557,
        562–563
    public key cryptography, 557–558,
        562–563
    ROT13 scheme, 553–554
    scheme, 438, 636
.eps extension, 42
equal (=) command, 183
equal (=) key, 182
error checking, packet, 110
e-texts, 477
Eudora, 3, 579
European Laboratory for Particle Physics,
    105, 609
evaluator, 224, 225–227
event, 492, 636
event handlers, 493, 498–499, 500–503,
    636
Excite, 202
Excite Search Voyeur, 217
expired news, 436–437, 636
exploratory arrangement of Web pages,
    170–171
expression, freedom of, 123–125
eXtensible Markup Language (XML), 203,
    417, 613, 636

extension
    aif, 42, 534
    aifc, 42, 534
    aiff, 42, 534
    au, 42, 534
    avi, 42, 538
    eps, 42
    gif, 42, 93, 325
    gz, 258
    gzip, 258
    htm, 42, 58
    html, 42, 58
    jpe, 42
    jpeg, 42
    jpg, 42, 93, 325
    js, 488
    mid, 42, 534
    midi, 42, 534
    mov, 42, 538, 543
    movie, 42
    mpeg, 42, 538
    mpg, 42, 538
    png, 93, 325–337
    ps, 42
    qt, 42, 538
    ra, 42, 535
    ram, 42, 535
    roff, 42
    sgml, 42
    snd, 42, 534
    t, 42
    tex, 42
    tif, 42
    tiff, 42
    tr, 42
    txt, 42, 416
    wav, 42, 535
    wrl, 42, 541
    wrl.gz, 541
    wrz, 541
    z, 258
    zip, 258
external styles, 426–429
e-zines, 479–480, 636

ℱ

FACE attribute, FONT tag, 80
fanzine, 479
FAQs (frequently asked questions), 637
FAST Search, 202
fatware, 411
favorite, 145. *See also* bookmark
Fcc: field, 584
Federal Networking Council (FNC), 98
FedEx eBusiness Tools, 130, 131
FedEx Express Saver, 132
FELINES-L, 457
FEM-BIBLIO, 457
file
    compression, 258, 636
    extension (*See* extension)
    manipulation, UNIX, 595–596
    name, 54, 173
    organization, UNIX, 594–595
    permissions, 58, 62–64, 596–599

structure, UNIX, 593
transfer, 4, 100, 243–261, 631, 636 (*See also* FTP)
File button, 26
File menu, 47, 327
file transfer protocol. *See* FTP
Filo, David, 105, 188
filter, 40, 125, 567
Financial Aid Resource Center, 200
Find button, 49
Find command, 235, 236
finger, 12
firewall, 139, 565–566, 567, 636
flags, 592
flame, 636
flame war, 440, 455, 636
flaming, 22, 127
flashing text, 276
FNC, 610
FOAF, 126, 610
follow-up, 435, 637
font
    color, 79
    size, 66–67, 79–80
        increasing relative font size, 273
        reducing relative font size, 273
    type, 80
    Web browser, 144
<FONT> tag, 79–80, 604
    COLOR attribute, 79
    FACE attribute, 80
    SIZE attribute, 79–80
FooTalk, 464
footer, 174, 175, 281–284, 637
forgery, email, 5
form, 386–401
    action buttons, 394–395
    check boxes, 393–394
    functions of, 387
    input tags, 391–397
    intelligent, 137
    interactive Web pages, 386
    layout format, 398–399
    mail to URLs, 391
    masked fields, 398
    methods, 389–391
    option tag, 396–397
    passwords, 397–398
    radio buttons, 394
    scripts and, 402
    select tag, 395–396
    tags, 388–389
    text areas, 397
    text boxes, 392–393
    verification, 370
<FORM> tag, 489, 491, 604
    ACTION attribute, 389–391, 399–400, 402
    METHOD attribute, 389–391
    NAME attribute, 400, 491
    TARGET attribute, 400
Forward button, 48
forward slash (/), 57, 593
forwarding email, 5, 29, 587
Four11, 207
frame, 637
Frame source button, 375
<FRAME> tag, 370–373, 604

FRAMEBORDER attribute, 376
MARGINHEIGHT attribute, 376
MARGINWIDTH attribute, 376
NAME attribute, 371
NORESIZE attribute, 376
SCROLLING attribute, 376
SRC attribute, 371
FRAMEBORDER attribute, frame tag, 376
frames, 368–386
    frameset design algorithm, 380–383
    nested, 379–380
    tags, 370–376
    targeted hyperlinks, 376–379
    usage, 369–370
<FRAMESET> tag, 370–373, 604
    COLS attribute, 371, 374, 380–383
    design algorithm, 380–383
    ROWS attribute, 373, 374, 380–383
freedom of expression, 123–125
freeware, 258–260, 327, 637
frequently asked questions (FAQs), 637
From field, email, 16
Frontpage, 412
FTP, 55, 467, 610
    closing a session, 248
    get command, 255–256
    graphical file transfer clients, 245–252
    procedure for file transfer, example, 249–252
    put command, 256
    text-based file transfer clients, 252–258
    transfer setting mode, 248
FTP Search, 260
full text indexing, 230
function, 493
FWIW, 126, 610

G

Gates, Bill, 112
gateway pages, 194
gateways, 194, 197–198, 402
gatherer, 224, 227–230
    breadth-first search, 227–228
    depth-first search, 228–230
get command, 253, 255, 259
get METHOD, 389–391, 524, 561
GIF, 120, 324, 328–329, 610
    animation, 333–334
    interlaced, 325, 334–336
    size, file, 364
    transparent, 325, 336–337
GIF Animator, 334
GIF Construction Set, 334
GIF Converter, 334
.gif extension, 42, 93, 325
GIFBuilder, 334
GIFMerge, 334
gigabyte, 637
GII (Global Information Infrastructure), 135, 610
Global Information Infrastructure (GII), 135, 610
GMT (Greenwich Mean Time), 16, 610
Go menu, Web browser, 47

Good Times hoax, 263
Google, 106, 191, 194, 202, 206, 208–215, 226
gopher, 4, 55, 105, 637
Gosling, James, 511
GoTo, 204, 226
gov domain name, 10
graphical file transfer clients, 245–252
graphical user interface (GUI), 25, 610, 637
graphics, 162, 163, 175, 324–365. *See also* image
    alignment, 337–344
    borders, 345–346
    clip art, 326, 633
    compression, 325, 328–329, 330–331, 332
    copying from Web, 327–328
    copyright issues, 326
    editing software, 327
    file size, 363–364
    formats, 324
        GIF, 328–329, 333–337
        JPG, 330–331
        PNG, 331–332
        TIFF, 331
    image maps, 347–355
    thumbnail sketches, 359–360
Graphics Interchange Format (GIF). *See* GIF
Greenwich Mean Time (GMT), 16, 610
grocery shopping, online, 131–132
groupware, 139, 140, 637
guest book, 515–523, 637
    dynamics, 518–519
    input fields, standard, 517–518
    mailto, 520
    sample code for, 521–523
GUI (graphical user interface), 25, 610, 637
Guide button, 49
gunzip, 258
Gutenberg, Johannes, 477
.gz extension, 258
.gzip extension, 258

H

handshaking, 35
Hart, Michael, 477
hash, 559, 564, 637
hashing algorithms, 558–559, 563, 637
<HEAD> tag, 58, 66, 604
header, 174, 175, 278–279, 637
    email, 16, 17
    table, 303–305
heading tags, 86–87, 419–420
HEIGHT attribute
    applet tag, 508
    image tag, 94–95, 360–363
    object tag, 539
help
    command, 253, 465
    menu, Web browser, 47
    Telnet feature, 238, 240
helper applications, 44, 145, 148–150, 531–532, 638
hexadecimal numbers, 73–75

<Hi> tag, 86–87, 604
hidden directory, 593
hidden Web, 196
hierarchical arrangement of Web pages,
    171–172
hits, 177, 212, 226, 638
hoax, Good Times, 263
home directory, 593
homepage, 48, 145, 638
horizontal image alignment, 341
horizontal rule tag, 279–281, 604
hot buttons, 45, 49–50, 638
HotDog Pro, 412
hotlist, 145
HoTMetal, 412
hotspots, 543
<HR> tag, 279–281, 604
HREF attribute, anchor tag, 377–379
HSPACE attribute
    applet tag, 508
    image tag, 343
    object tag, 544
    table tag, 300
.htm extension, 42, 58
HTML, 41, 610, 638
    comments, 80–82
    converter, 415–416, 638
    copying code, 58
    debugging, 317–321
    document
        background, 78–79
        color, 72–79
        creation, 58–60
        design and coding, 173
        font, 66–67, 79–80
        global parameters, setting, 67
        images, 93–95
        outlining, 165–168
        tiling, 76–77
        URLs, relative *versus* absolute,
            67–71
    editor, 407–412, 638
        components, 408–410
        drawbacks of, 411–412
        Frontpage, 412
        HotDog Pro, 412
        HoTMetaL, 412
        Navigator Gold, 412
        Page Composer, 47
        SiteMill, 412
        tag-oriented, 408
        usage, 410–411
        WYSIWYG, 408
    footers, 281–284
    formatting, 84–96
    forms, 386–401
    frames, 368–386
    headers, 278–279
    horizontal lines, 279–281
    hyperlink creation, 87–93
    lists, 284–286
        definition, 288–290
        nested, 291–294
        ordered, 284–286
        unordered, 287–288
    style type
        semantic-based, 266–273, 276
        syntactic-based, 273–276, 277
        usage, choice of, 276–277

syntax checker, 638
table, 296–317
    borders, 300
    captions, 307–308
    colors, 310–311
    columns, 298–300, 309–310, 311
    dividers, 296, 300
    element spacing, 301–302
    headers, 303–305
    HTML editor use to produce, 315
    hyperlinks in, 313–315
    images in, 313–315
    item positioning, 305–306
    nesting, 312–313
    positioning, 299–300
    production with, 315
    rows, 298–300
    tags, 298–311
    usage, 296–297
    vertical alignment, 310
    width, 308–309
tags (*See also* tag; *specific tags*)
    attribute, 57
    case, 57
    overview, 56–57
    syntax, 57–58
tool
    converters, 415–416
    editor, 407–412
    syntax checkers, 412–415
    versions, 417
.html extension, 42, 58
<HTML> tag, 58–59, 604
HTTP, 54, 55, 109, 129, 610, 638
HTTP-EQUIV attribute, META TAG,
    404–405
HTTPS, 55, 610
hyperlink, 45, 50–51, 163, 638
    anchor tag and, 87–92
    clickable image, 89–90
    clickable text, 88–89
    color, 77–78
    creation guidelines, 92
    definition, 52
    HTML editor manipulation of, 409
    images as, 345–346
    intradocument linking, 90–92
    mailto, 90
    mouse over, 50
    as navigation tools, 168–172
    in tables, 313–315
    testing, 175
    thumbnail as, 359
    underlining, 276
    verification of links by syntax checkers,
        413–414
hypermedia, 52, 638
hypertext, 52, 638
HyperText Transfer Protocol (HTTP), 54,
    55, 109, 129, 610, 638
HyperText Transfer Protocol Secure
    (HTTPS), 55, 610

I Love You virus, 106
<I> tag, 275, 605

IBM, 102, 476, 610
ICANN (International Corporation for
    Assigned Names and Numbers), 10
icons, 364
IDEA, 610
IE. *See* Internet Explorer
IETF (Internet Engineering Task Force),
    610, 639
image, 145, 182–184
    alignment, 337–344
    borders, 345–346
    centered, 344
    compression, 325
    copying from Web, 327–328
    copyright issues, 326
    decompression, 331
    dithering, 329
    editing, 331
    editing software, 327, 359–360
    embedded into text, 337–338
    height and width, 360–363
    as hyperlinks, 345–346
    load time, 363–364
    maps, 171, 638
        client-side, 349–354
        server-side, 347–348
    scanners for, 355–359
    in tables, 313–315
    thumbnail sketches, 359–360
    transparent, 336
image tag. *See* <IMG> tag
ImageMagick, 329
Images button, 49
Imagiware, Inc., 415
IMAP (Interactive Mail Access Protocol),
    34–35, 610
Imaptool, 354
<IMG> tag, 93–95, 179, 605
    ALIGN, 338–344
    BORDER attribute, 345–346
    HEIGHT attribute, 360–363
    HSPACE attribute, 343
    LOWSRC attribute, 346
    SRC attribute, 524
    USEMAP attribute, 350, 352, 354
    VSPACE attribute, 343
    WIDTH attribute, 360–363
IMHO, 126, 611
inbox, 31–32
INBOX folder, Pine, 584, 587, 588
includes, server-side, 524, 526–528
indexer, 230
indexing
    full text, 230, 370
    Web pages, 191
Indurain, Miguel, 123
InFind, 206
info domain name, 10
Infomine, 195, 198
information, personal
    collection of, 550
    from company profile, 549
    from public events, 549
    from telephone lists, 548–549
    volunteered, 549–550
Information Superhighway, 98, 99–100,
    639. *See also* Internet
Infoseek, 127, 389–390
in-line image, 45, 639
in-line styles, 419–421

<INPUT> tag, 391–397, 605
  CHECKED attribute, 393, 394
  MAXLENGTH attribute, 392
  NAME attribute, 392, 393, 491
  SIZE attribute, 392
  TYPE attribute, 392, 393
  VALUE attribute, 393, 395
instant messaging, 125
int domain name, 10
Integrated Services Digital Network
  (ISDN), 112, 611
intelligent form, 137
IntelliSeek's BullsEye, 198
Interactive Mail Access Protocol (IMAP),
  34–35, 610
interlaced GIFs, 334–336, 639
internal styles, 421–426
International Corporation for Assigned
  Names and Numbers (ICANN), 10
Internet, 98–140, 639
  addresses, 639
  advertising on, 127
  benefits provided by, 124
  business and, 128–136
  censorship, 125
  collaborative computing and, 136–140
  congestion, 118–122
  cost, 121
  culture, 122–128
  defined, 98–99
  history, 101–108
    1960s, 101–102
    1970s, 102–103
    1980s, 103–104
    1990s, 104–106
    growth of the Internet, 106–107
    timeline, 102
  how it works, 108–118
    client server model, 113–114
    data transmission, 109–111
    IP addresses, 114
    network connections, 111–113
    physical components, 111
    TCP/IP protocol, 109
    Web page retrieval, 116–117
  Information Superhighway metaphor,
    98, 99–100
  as open system, 104
  societal impact of, 127–128
  statistics, 100
Internet button, 50
Internet Engineering Task Force (IETF),
  610, 639
Internet Explorer, 45, 106, 125, 149,
  150–151, 536, 610, 639
  JavaScript support, 488
  semantic-based style types, rendering
    of, 270
Internet Protocol (IP), 99, 109, 611, 639
Internet Protocol Version 6 (IPv6), 116,
  611, 639
Internet Relay Chat (IRC), 104, 125, 459,
  611
Internet Service Provider (ISP), 3,
  111–112, 121, 567–572, 610
  connection setup, 570–571
  features, desirable, 570
  problems, 571
  questions to ask, 568–569

searching for, 568–569
  selection, 572
  software, 569
Internet Worm, 104, 262
InterTrust Technologies, Inc., 476
intranet, 121, 639
Invisible Web, 195–198, 204
IP. *See* Internet Protocol (IP)
IP addresses, 114–116, 639
  dynamic, 116
  static, 115
Ipswitch, 245
IPv6. *See* Internet Protocol Version 6
  (IPv6)
IRC. *See* Internet Relay Chat (IRC)
ISDN (Integrated Services Digital
  Network), 112, 611
ISP. *See* Internet Service Provider (ISP)
italics tag, 275, 605

J

Java, 106, 145, 487, 507–515, 639
  applets, 506–511
  class file, 508
  history of, 511–512
  JavaScript compared, 487
  object-oriented programming, 514–515
  server push, 405
  source code, sample, 512–514
  Virtual Machine, 512, 640
Java-enabled Web browser, 507, 508–509,
  639
JavaScript, 145, 486–506, 640
  basics, 489–491
  dialog boxes, 494–500
    alert box, 494–496, 503
    confirm box, 496
    prompt box, 496–498
  event handler, 493, 498–499, 500–503
  events, 492
  function, 493
  Java compared, 487
  methods, 491–492
  objects, 491–492
  properties, 491–492
  sample, Temperature Conversion Code,
    503–506
  script tag, 487–489
JavaScript-enabled Web browser, 488, 640
Joint Photographic Experts Group,
  330–331. *See also* JPEG; JPG
Journal of Electronic Publishing, The, 481
journals, on-line, 480–481
.jpe extension, 42
JPEG, 324, 611
.jpeg extension, 42
JPG, 324, 330–331, 611
  progressive format, 336
  size, file, 364
.jpg extension, 42, 93, 325
.js extension, 488
junk mail, 5
justification of text, 576

K

k12.ed.comp.literacy, 448
Kadow, Kevin, 334
<KBD> tag, 272, 605
keyboard tag, 272
keywords, 212
kill files, 438, 640
kilobits, 111, 640
kilobyte, 256, 640

L

L. L. Bean, 130
LAN. *See* Local Area Network (LAN)
language
  C++, 489
  compiled, 390
  Java, 507–515
  JavaScript, 486–506
  Oak, 511–512
  object-oriented, 487, 489, 514
  Perl, 402, 405
  scripting, 402
LANGUAGE attribute, script tag, 488
LATEX, 415
Lcc: field, 584
lcd command, 257
LexiBot, 198
<LI> tag, 285–288, 604
licensing statement, 533
line break tag (<BR>), 270, 343, 602
line breaking algorithm, 60
lines, horizontal, 279–281
LINK attribute, BODY tag, 78
<LINK> tag, 426–427, 605
list, 284–286. *See also* mailing list
  administrator, 450
  bookmark, 145–146
  closed, 450
  coordinator, 450
  definition, 288–290
  digested, 450, 635
  distribution, 13
  edited, 450, 635
  manager, 450
  nested, 291–294
  open, 450, 643
  ordered, 284–286
  owner, 450, 640
  private, 13, 450
  server, 448
  telephone, 548–549
  unordered, 287–288
list item tag, 284–288
<LISTING> tag, 277
LISTPROC, 451, 640
LISTSERV, 451–453, 640
Live Image, 354
LiveScript, 487
load time, 162
Local Area Network (LAN), 103, 552, 611,
  640
location area, 640
LOL, 126, 611
look command, 465

Looksmart, 191, 193, 194, 199
Lookup button, 50
LOOP attribute, background sound tag, 536
lossless compression, 328–329, 332, 640
lossy compression, 330–331, 640
lost-chords, 457
Lotus Notes, 137, 140
low source (LOWSRC) images, 346
LOWSRC attribute, image tab, 346
ls command, 65, 253, 592, 593, 598, 600
lurker, 450, 641
lurking, 460
LViewPro, 182, 329
Lycos, 199, 260
Lynx, 45, 353, 641
    bookmarks, 182
    commands, 184
    commands, summary of, 184
    exiting, 181
    features, 181–182
    images, 182–184
    images, ALT attribute for, 179, 183
    navigation, 181
    printing, 182
    semantic-based style type, rendering of,
        268, 271
    starting, 180
LZW, 328, 332, 611

M

MacCaw, Craig, 112
Macintosh, 239
MacMOOSE, 464
macro viruses, 41
Macromedia's Shockwave, 149
magazines, on-line, 481–482
Maijala, Teemul, 354
mail. *See also* email
    applications, 2, 30
    client, 2, 3, 13, 30
        header information, display of, 16
        help, 22
    program, 30 (*See also* Pine mail
        program)
    server, 31
        mail spool, 33
        store-and-forward feature, 31–33
    spool, 33
mailbox, 31, 641
mailer, 2, 13, 19–22, 30–31, 641. *See also*
    email; Pine mail program
    index of messages, 37
    interface, 25
mailing list, 2, 4, 104, 125, 641
    advertisements on, 455
    availability, 458
    email volume and, 38
    examples
        ADV-HTML, 457
        BESTWEB, 457
        DICKNS-L, 457
        FELINES-L, 457
        FEM-BIBLIO, 457
        lost-chords, 457

        talking-heads, 457
        ULTRA, 457
        YAWRITING, 458
    flaming, 22
    guidelines for, 454–455
    history, 432–434
    newsgroups compared, 455–456
    overview of, 448–449
    posts, 452–454
    subscriptions, 450–452
    terminology, 449–450
    Web pages, coupling with, 455
mailto, 55, 90, 160, 561
    guest book, 516, 520
    hyperlink, 517–518, 520
    URL, 391
mail-tool, 3
mailx, 3
Majordomo, 641
Mamma, 206
MAN (Metropolitan Area Network), 611,
    641
man command, 591, 592, 600
map file, 348, 349
<MAP> tag, 350, 352–353, 605
Mapedit, 354
maps, image, 347–355
MARGINHEIGHT attribute, frame tag, 376
MARGINWIDTH attribute, frame tag, 376
Mars Pathfinder Mission, 540
masked field, 398
MasterCard, 134
MAXLENGTH attribute, input tag, 392
McGraw-Hill, 180
MCI, 112
MD5, 611
MediaTech, Inc., 354
megabits, 112
megabyte, 641
Menu bar, 45, 46–48, 641
    Bookmarks, 47
    Communicator, 47
    Directory, 47
    Edit, 47
    File, 47
    Go, 47
    Help, 47
    Options, 47
    View, 47
    Window, 48
message. *See also* email
    board, 567
    box, 461
    digest, 559, 641
    integrity, 559
Message Text field, 584
<META> tag, 72, 605
    CONTENT attribute, 404–405
    HTTP-EQUIV attribute, 404–405
MetaCrawler, 204, 206, 216–218
Metasearch, 206
metasearch engines, 204–206, 641
Metaspy, 216–218
METHOD attribute, form tag, 389–391
methods, object, 491–492
Metropolitan Area Network (MAN), 611,
    641
mget command, 256–257

Microsoft, 334, 412, 417, 535, 536, 538
    Exchange, 3, 137
    Internet Explorer, 45, 106, 125, 149,
        150–151, 270, 488, 536, 610, 639
    Word, 42, 415
Microsystems Software, 125
.mid extension, 42, 534
.midi extension, 42, 534
MIDI file format, 534, 611
mil domain name, 10
MIME, 40–42, 611, 642
    email attachment, 18
    types, table of, 42
mirror site, 53, 641
misc.consumers.house, 448
misc.invest.stocks, 448
Mitchell, Kevin, 334
mkdir command, 63, 594, 600
modem, 111–112, 568
moderated newsgroup, 437, 641
monitor resolution, 356
monospaced typewriter text tag, 275
Moondance, 481
MOOs (Multi-User Dungeons,
    Object-Oriented), 463, 611
more command, 596, 600
Moreover, 203, 204
Moret, Bernard, 480
Morris, Robert, 104, 262
Mosaic, 45, 105, 641
Motion Picture Experts Group, 538, 611
mouse over, 50
.mov extension, 42, 538, 543
.movie, 42
MP3 Search, 204
.mpeg extension, 42, 538
MPEG file format, 538, 611
.mpg extension, 42, 538
mput command, 256–257
MUCKs, 463
MUD, 462–467, 611, 642
    client, 464
        FooTalk, 464
        MacMOOSE, 464
        MUD.el, 464
        MUSHClient, 464
        TinyTalk, 464
    connecting to, 463–464
    creation, 467
    etiquette, 466
    overview of, 462–463
    play, 464–466
    social, 466–467
    types of, 463
MUD.el, 464
Müller, Rene, 334
multimedia, 153, 530–545, 642
    audio, 534–537
        file formats, 534–535
        file installation, 535
        repositories, 536
        Web pages and, 535–536
    buffering, 533–534
    concerns, current, 532
    definition, 52
    display, 531–532
    movies, 537–540
    question, important, 531
    standards, lack of, 532–533

streaming, 534
video, 537–540
virtual reality, 540–544
    QTVR (QuickTime Virtual
        Reality), 543
    VRML (Virtual Reality Markup
        Language), 541–542
MULTIPLE attribute, select tag, 395
Multipurpose Internet Mail Extensions. *See*
    MIME
Multi-User Dimension, 462, 611, 642. *See
    also* MUD
Multi-User Dungeon, 462, 611, 642. *See
    also* MUD
museum domain name, 10
MUSHClient, 464
MUSHes (Multi-User Shared
    Hallucinations), 463, 611
Musical Instrument Digital Interface
    (MIDI), 534, 611
mv command, 595, 600
MySimon, 203, 204

N

NAME attribute
    anchor tag, 90–92
    applet tag, 508
    form tag, 400, 491
    frame tag, 371
    input tag, 392
    map tag, 350
    object tag, 544
    parameter tag, 509
    select tab, 395–396
name domain name, 10
National Center for Supercomputing
    Applications (NCSA), 105, 611
National Science Foundation Network
    (NSFNET), 104, 611
navigation
    of Lynx Web browser, 181
    tools, 642
    Web presentation, 168–173
        circular arrangement, 169–170
        exploratory arrangement, 170–171
        hierarchical arrangement, 171–172
Navigator Gold, 412
NCSA (National Center for
    Supercomputing Applications), 105,
    611
nested
    frames, 379–380
    lists, 291–294
    tables, 312–313
net domain name, 10
Net Search button, 50
Net Shepherd, 125
Netcaster button, 50
NetGrocer, 131–132
netiquette, 22, 642
Netscape, 412, 417, 642
    Communications, 105, 106, 127
    Communicator, 46, 150
    downloading software, 131

icon, 45
JavaScript development, 486–487
Messenger, 27–28
Navigator, 12, 45–49, 105, 150–151,
    168
    searching from, 201–202
newsreader, 438–439
plug-ins, support, 149
semantic-based style type, rendering of,
    267, 268, 269
network. *See also* Internet
    benefits of, 108–109
    corrections, 111–112
    interface cards, 112
    intranets, 121
    layer, 566
    load distribution, 110
    physical components, 111
    sniffer, 561
Network Information Center (NIC), 114,
    611
Network News Transfer Protocol (NNTP),
    437, 611, 642
Network Service Provider (NSP), 112, 611
New York Times, 481
newbie, 450, 642
New&Cool button, 50
news
    administrator, 437, 642
    client, 436, 442
    expired, 436–437
    host, 567
    moderator, 437, 642
    pull, 441, 442, 444
    push, 441
    reading, 440
    search, 441, 442
    server, 437, 442–444, 643
    suck, 441
news.answers, 448
newsfeed, 437, 642
newsgroup, 2, 55, 103, 125, 432–448, 570,
    642
    article, 434–435
    availability, 458
    distribution of news, methods of,
        441–444
    examples
        alt.ascii-art, 448
        alt.cult-movies, 448
        alt.fishing, 448
        comp. theory, 448
        comp.parallel, 448
        k12.ed.comp.literacy, 448
        misc.consumers.house, 448
        misc.invest.stocks, 448
        news.answers, 448
        rec.art.poems, 448
        rec.bicycles.off-road, 448
        rec.humor.funny, 448
        sci.fractals, 448
        soc.college.gradinfo, 448
    hierarchies, 444–446
    history, 432–434
    mailing lists compared, 455–456
    model, 441–444
    moderated, 437
    naming conventions, 445–446

newsreaders, 438–441
    subscribing to, 435–436
    terminology, 435–438
    thread, 435
    unmoderated, 437
    unsubscribing to, 436
Newsgrps: field, 584
newspaper
    format, 296, 311
    online, 131, 481–482
newsrc, 441
newsreader, 436, 438–441, 642
    data file, 441
    interface, 438–440
NextMsg (Next Message), 585, 586
NIC (Network Information Center), 114,
    611
NNTP (Network News Transfer Protocol),
    437, 611, 642
<NOFRAMES> tag, 372–373, 605
nonbreaking space, 300
NORESIZE attribute, frame tag, 376
NorthernLight, 202
NOSHADE attribute, 280
Novell's Groupwise, 137
NSFNET (National Science Foundation
    Network), 104, 611
nslookup, 115
NSP (Network Service Provider), 112, 611

O

Oak, 511–512
<OBJECT> tag, 535–536, 538, 606
    BORDER attribute, 544
    CLASSID attribute, 544
    CODEBASE attribute, 544
    CODETYPE attribute, 544
    DATA attribute, 536, 539, 544
    DECLARE attribute, 544
    HEIGHT attribute, 539
    HSPACE attribute, 544
    NAME attribute, 544
    SHAPES attribute, 544
    STANDBY attribute, 544
    TABINDEX attribute, 544
    TYPE attribute, 536, 539, 544
    USEMAP attribute, 544
    VSPACE attribute, 544
    WIDTH attribute, 539
object-oriented programming (OOP), 487,
    489, 512, 611, 643
obscene material on the Internet, 124
OC, 119, 611
OCR (optical character recognition), 355,
    611
Oikarinen, Jarkko, 104, 459
<OL> tag, 284–286, 606
onChange event handler, 495, 499, 505
onClick event handler, 502–503
on-line books, 477–478
on-line businesses, 129–133
onLoad event handler, 493, 499
onMouseOut event handler, 500, 501
onMouseOver event handler, 493, 500–501
ONSALE, Inc., 132

onSubmit event handler, 493
OOP. *See* object-oriented programming (OOP)
Open button, 49
open command, 253–255
Open Directory Project (ODP), 199
open list, 450, 643
open system, 104
optical carrier, 119, 611
optical character recognition (OCR), 355, 611
optical resolution, 356
<OPTION> tag, 396, 606
    SELECTED attribute, 396
    VALUE attribute, 396
Options menu, Web browser, 47
options, UNIX command, 591
ordered list, 284–286
org domain name, 10
outlining, Web presentation, 164–168

P

<P> tag, 85–86, 606
packet, 35, 109–111, 112–113, 120, 643
    advantages of, 109–110
    splitting messages into, 110
    switching, 101, 110, 433, 643
page command, 465
Page Composer, 47
Page source button, 375
Paint Shop Pro, 329, 360
palette, 643
paragraph tag, 85–86, 606
parameter tag (<PARAM>), 509, 606
parameters, 492
parent directory, 595
password, 8, 643
    anonymous file transfer, 258–259
    case, 8
    chat room, 459
    default, 15
    email, encrypted, 35
    history file of, 8
    text field, 397–398
patches, 552
pathname, 593, 595
pattern matching query, 212–214, 220, 643
PC, 611
PDT, 612
period (.) symbol, 593
Perl, 402, 405
permissions, 58, 62–64, 596–599
persistent cookie, 133
PGP (Pretty Good Privacy), 564, 612, 644
physical-based style types, 273
Pico text editor, 22
    commands, summary of, 577
    cursor movement, 575
    cutting and pasting, 575
    interface, 574
    invoking, 576
    justifying text, 576
    saving and inserting files, 575–576
    searching for text, 576
    spell checking, 576
    suspending, 576

PICS (Platform for Internet Content Selection), 125, 612
Piguet, Yves, 334
Pinakes, 195
Pine mail program, 2, 3, 22, 438, 579–589
    Attchmnt: field, 583
    Bcc: field, 584
    Cc: field, 583
    composing and sending mail, 581–584
    deleting mail, 588
    Fcc: field, 584
    forwarding mail, 587
    Lcc: field, 584
    main menu, 579–580
    managing mail, 587–589
    Message Text field, 584
    Newsgrps: field, 584
    options, 580–581
    Pico text editor, 573–577
    quitting, 581
    reading mail, 584–587
    saving messages, 588–589
    starting, 579
    Subject: field, 583
    To: field, 583
pixels, 94
PKUNZIP, 258
PKZIP, 258
plagiarism, 482
plaintext, 40, 415, 643
Platform for Internet Content Selection (PICS), 125, 612
plug-ins, 44, 148–150, 532, 533, 643
PNG, 120, 324, 331–332, 336, 611
.png extension, 42, 93, 325
Point-to-Point Protocol (PPP), 115, 568–569, 570, 612, 643
polling, 33
POP (Post Office Protocol), 32–33, 612
pornographic materials on the Internet, 124
Portable Network Graphics (PNG), 120, 324, 326, 331–332, 611
post, 435, 452–454, 644
post METHOD, 390–391, 518, 520
Post Office Protocol (POP), 32–33, 612
posting, 435, 440
PPP. *See* Point-to-Point Protocol (PPP)
<PRE> tag, 398, 606
Pretty Good Privacy (PGP), 564, 612, 644
PrevMsg (Previous Message), 585, 586
prime numbers, 555–556, 644
printing Web documents, 182
privacy. *See also* security
    information collection, 550
    known information, 548–549
    Pretty Good Privacy (PGP), 564
    volunteered information, 549–550
private key cryptography, 556–557, 562–563, 644
private list, 13, 450
pro domain name, 10
production software, 150
Program for Internet News and Email. *See* Pine mail program
programming language
    C++, 489
    compiled, 390
    Java, 507–515
    JavaScript, 486–506

Oak, 511–512
    object-oriented, 487, 489, 514
    Perl, 402, 405
    scripting, 402
Progressive Networks, 535
Project Gutenberg, 477–478, 644
prompt character, 591
prompt dialog box, 496–498
properties, object, 491–492
protocol, 32, 54, 644
prototyping, 174, 644
proxy servers, 566
.ps extension, 42
public alias, 13
public domain, 327, 475, 644
public key cryptography, 557–558, 562–563, 644
publishing on-line. *See* electronic publishing
put command, 253, 256
pwd command, 253, 594, 600

Q

.qt extension, 42, 538
QTVR, 543, 612
query, 212–216, 644
    Boolean, 214–216, 220
    defined, 212
    generalization, 220
    pattern matching, 212–214, 220
    search engine, 200–202
    semantics, 212, 644
    specialization, 220–221
    stemming, 214
    stop word, 213
    syntax, 212, 220, 644
QuickTime file format, 538
QuickTime Virtual Reality (QTVR), 543, 612

R

.ra extension, 42, 535
radio buttons, 394
.ram extension, 42, 535
rc command, 593
RealAudio file format, 535
rec.art.poems, 448
rec.bicycles.off-road, 448
rec.humor.funny, 448
recursive algorithm, 382, 644
registering a Web page, 176–178, 645
relative pathname, 595
Release Notes, Pine, 581
relevancy score, 212, 226–227, 645
Reload button, 48
remote host, 571
remote login, 100, 234, 241–243, 645
RemoteSystem option, 235
render, 645
Reply button, 26
replying to email messages, 21, 26, 27–28, 587
Request for Comments (RFC), 612, 645

resolution
    monitor, 356, 357
    scanner, 356, 357
resolver, 115, 645
result set, 645
resume, on-line, 416
revolving advertisements, 645
RFC, 612, 645
RGB color model, 74, 329, 612, 645
rlogin command, 241–243
rm command, 596, 600
rmdir command, 600
rn, 438
robot, 227
.roff extension, 42
root directory, 593
ROT13 encryption scheme, 553–554
Rotation 13 (ROT13), 645
ROTFL, 126, 612
router, 111, 114, 120, 645
ROWS attribute, frameset tag, 373, 374,
    380–383
rows, table, 298–300
ROWSPAN attribute, table header tag,
    304–305
RSA encryption scheme, 612, 645
RTFM, 126, 612
RubberChicken.com, 155–156

S

Sausage Software, 412
Save As option, 327, 328
Save Image As option, 328
saved-messages folder, 587, 588, 589
say command, 465
scaling, 107, 109
scanner, 325, 355–359, 645
    color, 356, 358
    flatbed, 357
    hand-held, 356
    selection, 357–358
    sheet-fed, 357
    types, 356–357
sci.fractals, 448
script, 645
<SCRIPT> tag, 487–488, 606
scripting language, 402
scroll bar, 20, 646
    Web browser, 45
SCROLLING attribute, frame tag, 376
search engine, 200–206, 461, 646
    AltaVista, 130, 202
    AskJeeves, 202
    choosing, criteria for, 219–220
    components, 224
        evaluator, 224, 225–227
        gatherer, 224, 227–230
        indexer, 224, 230
        searcher, 224, 225
        user interface, 224, 225
    DogPile, 204, 206
    Excite, 202
    FAST search, 202
    foe email address determination, 12–13
    frames, problems with, 370

Google, 106, 202, 208–215
hits, 177
HTML document title, effect of, 59
Infind, 206
Infoseek, 389–390
invisible Web, 196
lists of popular, 202, 204
Lycos, 260
Mamma, 206
MetaCrawler, 204, 206
Metasearch, 206
metasearch engines, 204–206
Moreover, 203, 204
MP3 Search, 204
MySimon, 203, 204
    for newsgroups, 442
NorthernLight, 202
overview of, 200–202
query language, 201
registering Web pages, 176–178
Specialty, 202–204
stemming, 214
Travelocity.com, 204
Yahoo!, development of, 105
Search Engine Guide, 189
Search Engine Watch, 188–189
search tool, 646
searcher, 224, 225
searching for text, 576
searching the Web, 188–231
    directories, 190, 191–200
        general, 191–194, 199–200
        navigating, 191–192
        specialized, 191, 194–198, 200
    fundamentals, 208–219
    queries, 212–216
        Boolean, 214–216
        pattern matching, 212–214
        stemming, 214
        stop word, 213
    relevancy, 212
    relevancy scores, 226–227
    resources for, 189
    sample searches, 221–223
    strategies, 219–224
        breadth-first search, 227–228
        depth-first search, 228–230
        generalization, 220
        specialization, 220–221
    terminology, 212
    white pages, 206–207
secure document, 561, 646
Secure Electronic Transactions (SET), 134,
    612
secure server, 560, 646
security. *See also* password; virus
    authentication, 557–558
    CGI scripts, 402–403
    credit card, 134
    digital signatures, 561–565
    document, 560–561, 646
    encryption, 35, 553–560
        basics of, 553–555
        hashing algorithm, 558–559, 563,
            637
        prime numbers use of, 555–556
        private key cryptography, 556–557,
            562–563

        public key cryptography, 557–558,
            562–563
        ROT13 scheme, 553–554
    firewall, 139, 565–566, 567, 636
    MIME, 41
    patches, 552
    Pretty Good Privacy (PGP), 564
    Secure Electronic Transaction (SET),
        134
    server, 560–561
    software complexity and, 551–553
    Telnet *versus* remote login, 243
    viruses, 41
Security button, 49
select menu, 159
<SELECT> tag, 395–396, 606–607
    MULTIPLE attribute, 395
    NAME attribute, 395–396
    SIZE attribute, 395–396
SELECTED attribute, option tag, 396
semantic-based style type, 266–273, 276,
    646
semantics, 646
Send Link option, 47
sendmail, 30
sequence number, 35, 110
Serial Line Internet Protocol (SLIP),
    568–569, 570, 612, 646
server, 111, 646
    client-server model, 113–114
    domain name, 36, 115, 635
    news, 437, 442–444, 643
    proxy, 566
    push model, 405, 646
    secure server, 560, 646
    Web server, 13, 61, 62–64, 133, 650
server-side image maps, 347–348
server-side include (SSI), 524, 526–528,
    612, 646
SET (Secure Electronic Transactions), 134,
    612
7 by 24 machine, 646
SGI, 541, 612
SGML, 612
.sgml extension, 42
SHAPE attribute, area tag, 350
SHAPES attribute, object tag, 544
shareware, 327, 646
shell prompt, 591
S-HTTP. *See* HTTPS
signal-to-noise ratio, 442
signature
    digital, 561–565
    email, 18
    files, 23–24, 145, 647
Silicon Graphics, 541, 612
Simple Mail Transfer Protocol (SMTP),
    32–33, 109, 612
SiteMill, 412
SIZE attribute
    FONT tag, 79–80
    horizontal rule tag (<HR>), 280
    input tag, 392
    select tab, 395–396
SLIP. *See* Serial Line Internet Protocol
    (SLIP)
s-mail, 3, 30, 459, 560, 647
<SMALL> tag, 273, 607
smiley **: −**), 22, 647
SMTP. *See* Simple Mail Transfer Protocol
    (SMTP)

snail mail, 3, 647
.snd extension, 42, 534
sneakernet, 244
sniffing, 561, 647
soc.college.gradinfo, 448
SoftQuad, 412
software
    complexity, 551–553
    ISP-provided, 569
    patches, 552
    team development, 552
Software button, 50
space, nonbreaking, 300
spam, 5, 647
spamdexers, 72
spell check, 23, 175
    in HTML editor, 409
    Pico, 576
    in syntax checkers, 414
spider, 227
Spider's Apprentice, 189
splash screen, 77
Sprint, 112
spy, 554
Spyglass, 125
SRC attribute
    frame tag, 371
    image tag, 93, 524
    script tag, 488
s/rn, 438
SSI. *See* server-side include (SSI)
STANDBY attribute, object tag, 544
star (*), 599
START attribute, ordered list tag, 286
static information, 368
static IP address, 115, 647
status bar, 45, 647
status command, 257
stemming, 214, 647
Stop button, 49
stop word, 213
storyboard, 647
streaming, 534, 647
<STRIKE> tag, 275, 607
<STRONG> tag, 269, 607
STYLE attribute, heading tag, 419–420
<STYLE> tag, 423–425, 607
style types
    semantic-based, 273–276, 277
    syntactic-based, 266–273, 276
    usage, choice of, 276–277
styles, 418. *See also* Cascading Style
    Sheets (CSS)
<SUB> tag, 276, 607
subject directory, 191
Subject field, 17, 20, 583
subject guides, 194–195, 200
subscribe, 435–436, 647
subscriber, 450
subscript tag, 276
subscription
    mailing list, 450–452
    online, 131
Sun Microsystems, 106, 487, 534
    Java development, 511–512
<SUP> tag, 276, 607
superscript tag, 276
surface Web, 196

surfer, 647
surfing the Web, 52
Surfwatch, 125
switches, command names as, 257
syntactic-based style types, 273–276, 277,
    647
syntax, 647
syntax checkers, 363, 412–415
    availability, 414–415
    Doctor HTML, 412, 413, 415
    Dr. Watson, 415
    Weblint, 415

T

.t extension, 42
T1, 568
T3, 568
TABINDEX attribute, object tag, 544
table cells, 298
table data tag (<TD>), 298–300, 305–306,
    310, 607
table header tag (<TH>), 304, 608
table of contents, 370
table row tag (<TR>), 298–300, 305–306,
    310, 608
<TABLE> tag, 298–300, 607
    ALIGN attribute, 298–300
    BGCOLOR attribute, 310
    BORDER attribute, 300
    CELLPADDING attribute, 301–302
    CELLSPACING attribute, 301–302
    HSPACE attribute, 300
    VSPACE attribute, 300
    WIDTH attribute, 308–309
tables, 296–317
    borders, 300
    captions, 307–308
    colors, 310–311
    columns, 298–300, 309–310, 311
    dividers, 296, 300
    element spacing, 301–302
    headers, 303–305
    HTML editor use to produce, 315
    hyperlinks in, 313–315
    images in, 313–315
    item positioning, 305–306
    nesting, 312–313
    newspaper format, 296, 311
    positioning, 299–300
    rows, 298–300
    tags, 298–311
    usage, 296–297
    vertical alignment, 310
    width, 308–309
tag, 648
    A, 87–92, 376–379, 601
    ADDRESS, 267, 271–272, 601
    APPLET, 507–509, 601
    AREA, 350–351, 353, 601
    B, 274–275, 601
    BASE, 67–71, 601
    BASEFONT, 66, 602
    BGSOUND, 536, 602
    BIG, 273, 602
    BLINK, 276, 602

    BODY, 58–60, 75–79, 602
    BR, 270, 343, 602
    CAPTION, 602
    CENTER, 275, 602
    CITE, 269–271, 602
    CODE, 272, 273, 603
    COMMENT, 81, 603
    DD, 288–289, 603
    deprecated, 277
    DIV, 603
    DL, 288–289, 603
    DT, 288–289, 603
    EM, 267, 603
    EMBED, 545, 603
    FONT, 79–80, 604
    FORM, 604
    FRAME, 370–373, 376, 604
    FRAMESET, 370–373, 380–383, 604
    HEAD, 58, 66, 604
    Hi, 86–87, 604
    HR, 279–281, 604
    HTML, 58–59, 604
    I, 275, 605
    IMG, 93–95, 338–344, 360–363, 524,
        605
    INPUT, 391–397, 605
    KBD, 272, 605
    LI, 285–288, 605
    LINK, 426–427, 605
    LISTING, 277
    MAP, 350, 352–353, 605
    META, 72, 404–405, 605
    NOFRAMES, 372–373, 605
    OBJECT, 535–536, 538, 544, 606
    OL, 284–286, 606
    OPTION, 396–397, 606
    P, 85–86, 606
    PARAM, 509, 606
    PRE, 398, 606
    SCRIPT, 487–488, 606
    SELECT, 395–396, 606–607
    SMALL, 273, 607
    STRIKE, 275, 607
    STRONG, 269, 607
    STYLE, 423–425, 607
    SUB, 276, 607
    SUP, 276, 607
    TABLE, 298–300, 607
    TD, 607
    TEXTAREA, 397, 608
    TH, 304, 608
    TITLE, 608
    TR, 608
    TT, 275, 608
    U, 276, 608
    UL, 287–288, 608
    VAR, 272–273, 608
    XMP, 277
tag generator, HTML editor, 409
talking-heads, 457
target, 648
TARGET attribute
    anchor tag, 376
    form tag, 400
TCP, 612, 648
TCP/IP, 99, 103, 104, 109, 115, 568, 570,
    571, 612, 648
<TD> tag, 298–300, 607
    ALIGN attribute, 305–306

BGCOLOR attribute, 310
VALIGN attribute, 310
teamware, 139
technical support, ISP, 569
telecommunications
    1960s, 101–102
    1970s, 102–103
    1980s, 103–104
    1990s, 104–106
Teledesic, 112
telephone listings, 548–549
Telnet, 55, 463, 648
    clients, 235
    connecting to remote computer with,
        235–241
    email retrieval, 241
    escape sequence, 239–240
    help feature, 238, 240
    icon, 235, 236
    invoking, methods of, 235, 239
    protocol, 234
temperature conversion, JavaScript code
    for, 503–506
templates, 596
    HTML editor creation of, 410
.tex extension, 42
text
    box, 392–393
    editor, 19, 21, 573–577
        emacs, 577
        HTML, 58
        keyboard-based, 577
        Pico, 22, 573–577
        vi, 577
    recognition, 355
    style tags
        semantic-based, 266–273
        syntactic-based, 273–276
    transfer mode, 248
    wrapping, 60, 341–343
        preventing, 343
    TEXT attribute, BODY tag, 75–76
<TEXTAREA> tag, 608
text-based file transfer clients, 252–258
<TH> tag, 304, 608
    ALIGN attribute, 305
    BGCOLOR attribute, 310
    COLSPAN attribute, 304
    ROWSPAN attribute, 304
TheTrip.com, 196, 198
thread, 435, 648
3D, 612
    modeling, 540
    Website presentations, 540, 542, 543
    worlds, 462, 540–544
thumbnail sketch, 95, 359–360, 648
TIFF (Tagged Image Format File), 331, 612
.tiff extension, 42
tilde (~) symbol, 593
tiling, 76–77, 648
tiling algorithm, 648
time zone, 16–17
TinyTalk, 464
Title bar, 45, 648
To field, 17, 19, 583
Tomlinson, Ray, 103
Tongue, Thomas, 415
toolbar, 45, 648

buttons, 48–49
tooltip, 95, 648
top-level domain name
    country codes, 10, 11
    generic, 9, 11
.tr extension, 42
<TR> tag, 298–300, 608
    ALIGN attribute, 305–306
    BGCOLOR attribute, 310
    VALIGN attribute, 310, 311
traffic, 177
transfer setting mode, 248
TransGIF, 329
Transmission Control Protocol (TCP), 612,
    648
Transmission Control Protocol/Internet
    Protocol (TCP/IP), 99, 103, 104, 109,
    115, 568, 570, 571, 612, 648
transparent GIF, 648
transparent images, 336
Travelocity.com, 130–131, 204
triage, 649
trigger, 262
Trojan horse, 262, 263, 649
Trubshaw, Roy, 463
<TT> tag, 275, 608
TTYL, 126, 612
Tufts University Nutrition Navigator, 194,
    195, 196, 200
tutorial, 158–160
.txt extension, 42, 416
TY, 126, 612
TYPE attribute
    input tag, 392, 393
    object tag, 536, 539, 544
    ordered list tag, 286, 292
    unordered list tag, 294
typewriter text tag, 275

𝒰

<U> tag, 276, 608
<UL> tag, 287–288, 608
Ultimate Band List, 157–158
ULTRA, 457
uncompress, 258
under construction, 649
underline tag, 276
Uniform Resource Locator. *See* URL
Unisys, 332
United States Department of Defense, 102
universal service, 649
University of Illinois, 105
University of Minnesota, 105
University of North Carolina, 433
University of Washington, 579, 613
UNIX, 591–600, 649
    arguments, 591–592
    command
        cd, 64, 253, 594, 595, 600
        chmod, 64, 598–599, 600
        cp, 600
        FTP, 252–258
        ls, 65, 592, 593, 598, 600
        man, 591, 592, 600

mkdir, 63, 64, 594, 600
more, 596, 600
mv, 595, 600
pwd, 594, 600
rc, 593
rlogin, 241–243
rm, 596, 600
rmdir, 600
summary of, 600
Telnet, 238
file and directory organization, 594–595
file manipulation, 595–596
file structure, 593
flags, 592
overview, 62
pathnames, 593, 595
permissions, file, 596–599
prompt, 64, 591
viruses, 262
Web servers, 62–64
UNIX to UNIX CoPy (UUCP), 103, 613
unmoderated newsgroup, 437, 649
unordered list, 287–288
    bullets, 287–288
    definition lists, 288
unsubscribe, 436, 649
uploading, 244
URC, 612
URL, 116–117, 143, 649
    absolute and relative, 67–71
    bookmark, 47
    in bookmark list, 145
    components of, 54
    definition, 52
    hyperlink, 50–51
    protocols occurring in, 23
    sending links, 47
URl, 45, 53–55, 612
USEMAP attribute
    image tag, 350, 352, 354
    object tag, 544
USENET (User Network), 103, 613
user interface
    HTML editor, 412
    search engine, 224, 225
user name, 7
User Network (USENET), 103, 613
userids, 7, 649
username, chat room, 459
UUCP (UNIX to UNIX CoPy), 103, 613
UUNET, 443

𝒱

vacation program, 39, 649
VALIGN attribute
    table data tag, 310
    table row tag, 310
VALUE attribute
    input tag, 393, 395
    option tag, 396–397
    ordered list tag, 286
    parameter tag, 509
<VAR> tag, 272–273, 608
VC. *See* videoconferencing (VC)
version control, 137–138

vi, 577
video teleconferencing, 138–139
videoconferencing (VC), 126, 138–139,
    613, 649
    CUSeeMe, 138
View frame source button, 375
View Image, 328
View menu, 47, 327
View source button, 375
View Source command, 181
Virtual Monitoring System (VMS), 568,
    613
virtual reality, 650
Virtual Reality Modeling Language
    (VRML), 541–542, 613
virus, 41, 261–264
    avoidance and precautions, 262–263
    definition, 262
    detection software, 262–263, 650
    I Love You, 106
    Internet Worm, 104
Visa, 134
VLINK attribute, BODY tag, 78
VMS (Virtual Monitoring System), 568,
    613
VRML (Virtual Reality Modeling
    Language), 541–542, 613
VSPACE attribute
    applet tag, 508
    image tag, 343
    object tag, 544
    table tag, 300

W3C. *See* World Wide Web Consortium
    (W3C)
WAIS (Wide Area Information Service),
    613, 650
walknet, 244
Wall Street Journal Interactive Edition,
    The, 131
WAN (Wide Area Network), 613, 651
.wav extension, 42, 535
WAV file format, 535
way-station, 437, 650
Web, 650
    bookmarks, 145–148
    browser, 3, 632 (*See also* Internet
        Explorer; Netscape, Navigator)
    bookmarks, 145–148
    comparison of, 150–151
    definition, 44, 52
    document object model, 489
    graphical-based *versus* text-only, 45
    helper applications, 44, 148–150
    hot buttons, 49–50
    HTML code display, 56
    Java-enabled, 507, 508–509, 639
    JavaScript-enabled, 488, 640
    Lynx, 178–185
    menu bar, 46–48
    multimedia display, 531–532
    options, 144–145
    plug-ins, 148–150
    security, 552
    text wrapping, 60

toolbar, 48–49
    UNIX Web page setup, 62–64
    "What's New" feature, 148
    window terminology, 45–46
creation of, 105
defined, 142–144
directory, 191, 650
guide, 191
invisible, 195–198
manager, 53
page, 52, 650
    address (*See* URL)
    background, 76–78
    bogus, 123
    color, 72–79
    cookies, 133–134
    copyright issues, 474
    counter, 523–526
    hyperlinks, 87–93
    installation, 61–65
    interactive, 386
    load time, 162, 363–364
    mailing lists, coupling with, 455
    registering, 176–178
    reloading, 48
    retrieval, 116–117
    setup, 66–84 (*See also* HTML)
    traffic, 177
    writing styles, 152–161
presentation, 53, 161–176, 650
    3D, 542, 543
    designing and coding, 173–174
    elements of, 162–163
    goal setting, 163–164
    navigation, 168–173
    outlining, 164–168
    revising, 174–175
secure documents, 560–561
server, 13, 61, 62–64, 133, 650
site, 650
    definition, 53
    mirror site, 53
surfing, 52
terminology, 52–53
WebFerret, 204
Weblint, 415
Webmaster, 53, 173, 650
WhirlGIF, 334
whisper command, 465
white pages, 12, 206–207, 650
who command, 465
WhoWhere, 207
Wide Area Information Service (WAIS),
    613, 650
Wide Area Network (WAN), 613, 651
WIDTH attribute
    applet tag, 508
    horizontal rule tag (<HR>), 280
    image tag, 94–95, 360–363
    object tag, 539
    table data tag, 309–310
    table header tag, 309–310
    table tag, 308–309
wildcard symbol * (asterisk), 371
Window menu, Web browser, 48
Windows
    Find command, 235, 236
    Telnet interface, 235, 237, 240

wink ; −), 22
WIPO (World Intellectual Property
    Organization), 475, 613
wireless devices, 106
working directory, 594
world executable permissions, 63
World Intellectual Property Organization
    (WIPO), 475, 613
world readable permissions, 62–63
World Wide Wait, 119, 651
World Wide Web, 613, 651. *See also* Web
World Wide Web Consortium (W3C),
    119–121, 417, 613, 651
World Wide Web Virtual Library, 194, 195,
    197
worm, 227, 651
worms, 262, 263
wrapping text, 60, 341–343
writing style
    genre
        biography, 153–155
        business exposition, 155–157
        guide, 157–158
        summary of, 160–161
        tutorial, 158–160
    on-line vs off-line style, 152–153
.wrl extension, 42, 541
.wrl.gz extension, 541
.wrz extension, 541
WS_FTP Pro client, 245, 246, 248, 250,
    251
WWW. *See* Web; World Wide Web
WYSIWYG HTML editors, 408, 613

X

XML (eXtensible Markup Language), 203,
    417, 613, 636
<XMP> tag, 277

Y

Yahoo!, 12, 105, 127, 188, 191, 192, 194,
    199, 206, 651
    Buzz Index, 218
    Reference, 195
    user interface, 225
Yang, Jerry, 105, 188
YAWRITING, 458
Yellow pages, 207
YMMV, 126, 613

Z

.z extension, 258
zines, 479–480
.zip extension, 258